The Architecture of the Italian Renaissance

THE ARCHITECTURE OF THE ITALIAN RENAISSANCE

Jacob Burckhardt

Translated by James Palmes
Revised and edited by Peter Murray

THE UNIVERSITY OF CHICAGO PRESS

The University of Chicago Press, Chicago 60637

 Published 1985
Paperback edition 1987
Printed in the United States of America

10 09 08 07 06 05 04 03 02 2 3 4 5 6
ISBN 0-226-08049-8 (paperback)

LIBRARY OF CONGRESS CATALOGING IN PUBLICATION DATA

Burckhardt, Jacob 1818–1897
The architecture of the Italian Renaissance.
Translation of: Die Geschichte der Renaissance
Bibliography: p.
Includes index.
1. Architecture, Renaissance—Italy. 2. Architecture–Italy.
I. Murray, Peter, 1920– II. Palmes, James
III. Title.
NA1115.B8 1984 720'.945 83-18113
⊗ The paper used in this publication meets the minimum requirements of the American National Standard for Information Sciences—Permanence of Paper for Printed Library Materials, ANSI Z39.48-1992.

In Memoriam
Rudolf Wittkower
1901–1971

Contents

Introduction by Peter Murray xv
Bibliography xix
List of Illustrations xxxi
Credits xxxv

BOOK ONE

Architecture

CHAPTER ONE

The Monumental Temper of Italian Architecture

1 *The Cult of Fame and Pious Foundations* 3
2 *The Florentine Concept of Architecture* 3
3 *The Sienese Concept of Architecture* 5
4 *Attitude to Architecture in Other Towns* 5
5 *The Attitude of the Despots* 6
6 *Romagna, the Marches, Umbria* 6
7 *The Monumental Temper of Pope Nicholas V* 7
8 *Later Popes, up to Julius II* 8
9 *Attitudes in Private Building* 9
10 *The Counter-Reformation* 10

CHAPTER TWO

Patrons, Dilettanti and Master Builders

11 *Connoisseur-Patrons of the Fifteenth Century* 11
12 *Architectural Dilettanti of the Sixteenth Century* 12
13 *Consultations and Committees* 12
14 *The Versatility of Architects* 12
15 *Life of Architects* 13

CHAPTER THREE

Proto-Renaissance and Gothic

16 *The Proto-Renaissance in Tuscany and Rome* 16
17 *San Miniato and the Baptistry* 17
18 *The Penetration of Gothic and Extent of Its Influence* 17
19 *The Character of Italian Gothic* 19
20 *Relationship with the Other Arts* 20
21 *Gothic Secular Building in Italy* 21
22 *Later Hatred of Gothic* 23
23 *Gothic at the Time of the Renaissance* 24

CHAPTER FOUR

The Study of Antique Buildings and of Vitruvius

24 *General Character of the Innovations* 26
25 *Neglect of Greek Architectural Remains* 27
26 *Fifteenth-Century Studies of Roman Remains* 27
27 *Sixteenth-Century Studies of Roman Remains* 28
28 *The Influence of Vitruvius* 29
29 *The Later Vitruvians* 30

CHAPTER FIVE

The Theorists

30 *Leon Battista Alberti* 31
31 *Alberti's Successors, up to Serlio* 32
32 *Poliphilus* 32
32a *Buildings in Pictures* 33

CHAPTER SIX

Treatment of Form in the Early Renaissance

33 *Inevitability of Roman Detail* 34
34 *Attitude to Decorative Forms* 34
35 *The Column, Arch and Entablature* 35
36 *The Antique Orders in the Fifteenth Century* 38
37 *Half-Columns and Free-Standing Columns* 39
38 *The Pilaster and the Cornice* 40
39 *The Rusticated Façade in Florence and Siena* 41
40 *Rustication with Pilasters* 45
41 *Rustication Outside Tuscany* 45
42 *Venice and Incrustation* 46
43 *Relationship of Incrustation to Form* 49
44 *Northern Italy and Brick and Terracotta Architecture* 50
45 *Brick Façades* 51
46 *Brick and Terracotta Cortili and Church Façades* 53
46a *Windows and Doors of the Early Renaissance* 54
47 *Interior Forms* 57
48 *Vaults in the Early Renaissance* 58

CHAPTER SEVEN

Treatment of Form in the Sixteenth Century

49 *Simplification of Detail* 59
50 *Experiments with Details and Influence of Festivals on Ornament* 59
51 *Strengthening of Forms* 60
52 *The Doric and the False Etruscan Order* 61
53 *The Doric Interpreted by Bramante and Sansovino* 61
54 *Increased Contrasts* 64
55 *The High Renaissance Vault* 64
56 *Forms of the Late Flowering* 66
57 *Proportion* 70

CHAPTER EIGHT

The Architectural Model

58 *Models of the Gothic Period* 77
59 *Models of the Early Renaissance* 77
60 *Models of the High Renaissance* 79

CHAPTER NINE

The Design of Churches

61 *The Lack of a Specific Church Architecture* 80
62 *Character of the Centralised Building* 80
63 *The Earliest Centralised Buildings of the Renaissance* 81
64 *Later Centralised Buildings of the Fifteenth Century* 83
65 *Bramante and His First Centrally Planned Buildings* 87
66 *Bramante and S. Peter's in Rome* 88
67 *Other Centralised Buildings of the Sixteenth Century* 91
68 *Triumph of the Long-Nave Type in the Interests of Façades* 95
69 *L. B. Alberti's Façades* 95
70 *Other Façades of the Early Renaissance* 97
71 *The Façade of the Certosa at Pavia* 100
72 *Façades of the High Renaissance* 100
73 *Façades of the Later Flowering* 101
74 *Internal Arrangement of Long-Nave Churches: Basilicas* 104
75 *Flat-Ceilinged Single-Nave Churches* 107
76 *Single-Nave Vaulted Churches* 109
77 *Three-Aisled Vaulted Churches* 111
78 *The Campanile in the Early Renaissance* 113
79 *The Campanile in the Sixteenth Century* 119
80 *Individual Chapels and Sacristies* 121
81 *The Exterior of Long-Nave Churches* 123
82 *General View of Church Architecture* 124
83 *The Symmetry of the View* 125

CHAPTER TEN

Monasteries and Buildings of Religious Orders

84 *Monasteries in the North and South* 126
85 *A Summary View of Monastic Architecture* 126
86 *Bishops' Palaces and Universities* 130
87 *Buildings of Religious Confraternities* 132

CHAPTER ELEVEN

The Architectural Character of the Palazzo

88 *A Retrospective Glance at Earlier Italian Palace Architecture* 133
89 *Emergence of Rules for Three-Dimensional Proportions* 133
90 *Nature and Beginnings of the Renaissance Palace* 134
91 *The Tuscan Type* 135
92 *The Influence of Tuscan Palace Architecture* 139
93 *The Palace of Urbino and the Buildings of the Romagna* 139
94 *The Venetian Type* 139
95 *Rome and Roman Patrons* 141
96 *Roman Types of Façade* 143
97 *Cortili of Roman Palazzi* 144
98 *Irregular Ground-Plans: Mezzanines* 145
99 *Roman Staircases* 147
100 *Palaces in Serlio* 148
101 *Public Palaces: the Great Halls* 149
102 *Colonnaded Architecture of Public Buildings* 150
103 *Sansovino and Palladio: Arcades* 152
104 *The Family Loggie* 154
105 *Palace Architecture of the Aftermath: Exteriors* 156
106 *Palace Architecture of the Aftermath: Interiors* 159

CHAPTER TWELVE

Hospitals, Fortresses and Bridges

107 *Hospitals, Inns and Pleasure Buildings* 162
108 *Fortified Buildings* 165
109 *Renaissance Gateways* 165
110 *Bridges* 167

CHAPTER THIRTEEN

Improvements and Town-Planning

111 *Levelling and Paving* 168
112 *Street Improvements* 169
113 *The Fate of Street Arcades* 169
114 *The Piazza as a Monumental Concept* 170
115 *New Towns and Quarters* 170

CHAPTER FOURTEEN

Villas

116 *Types of Villas* 172
117 *Further Theories of Villa Architecture* 173
118 *Villas of the Early Renaissance* 174
119 *Villas of the High Renaissance* 175
120 *Villas of the Aftermath* 182
121 *Villas of the Baroque Period* 183
122 *Baths* 184

CHAPTER FIFTEEN

Gardens

123 *Gardens Principally of Botanic Interest* 185
124 *Infiltration of Architectonic Elements* 185
125 *Antique Sculptures and Ruins* 186
126 *Complete Dominance of Architecture* 187
127 *The Part Played by Large Trees* 187
128 *Gardens of Venice* 188
129 *Gardens of the Baroque Period* 188

BOOK TWO
Decoration

CHAPTER ONE

The Nature of Renaissance Decoration

130 *Relationship to Antiquity and to Gothic Decoration* 191
131 *The Architectonic Element and Surface Ornament* 191
132 *Summary of Modes of Expression* 192

CHAPTER TWO

Decorative Sculpture in Stone

133 *Importance of White Marble* 193
134 *Arabesques* 193
135 *Siena and Florence* 194
136 *The Rest of Italy* 197
137 *The Decorative Spirit of the Sixteenth Century* 201
138 *The Tomb and the Cult of Fame* 203
139 *Tombs of the Rich and Prominent* 204
140 *The Most Important Types of Tomb* 205
141 *Secondary Types of Tomb* 207
142 *Sepulchral Monuments of the Sixteenth Century* 209
143 *The Free-Standing Altar and the Aedicule Against a Wall* 210

144 *The Wall-Altar* 210
145 *The Sixteenth-Century Altar* 211
146 *Screens, Pulpits, Holy Water Basins, Chimney-Pieces etc.* 212
146a *Decoration of Fountains* 214

CHAPTER THREE

Decoration in Bronze

147 *The Technique and Large Castings* 219
148 *Doors, Screens and Altar-Rails* 219
149 *Candlesticks and Miscellaneous Objects* 221

CHAPTER FOUR

Works in Wood

150 *Decline of Decorative Painting* 224
151 *Status of Intarsia* 224
152 *Intarsie According to Subject* 226
153 *Carved Wooden Choir-Stalls* 228
154 *Wooden Doors and Wall-Panelling* 229
155 *Altarpieces and Frames* 229
156 *Furniture* 231
157 *The State Bed and the Chest* (Cassone) 231
158 *The Carved Flat Ceiling* 233
159 *The Painted Flat Ceiling* 234

CHAPTER FIVE

Pavements, Calligraphy

160 *Pavements of Hard Stones, Marble and Tiles* 236
161 *Inscriptions and Calligraphers* 238

CHAPTER SIX

Painting of Façades

162 *Origin and Extent* 239
163 *The Patrons* 239
164 *Methods of Façade Painting* 242
165 *The Testimony of the Writers* 243
166 *Themes Used in Façade-Painting* 244
167 *The Passing of Façade-Painting* 244
168 *Coats of Arms: Painted and Carved* 245

CHAPTER SEVEN

Interior Painting and Stucco-Work

169 *Friezes and Wall-Decorations* 246
170 *Decorative Painting of Architectural Elements* 247
171 *The Painting of Vaulted Ceilings in the Early Renaissance* 247
172 *Vaulted-Ceiling Paintings of the School of Perugino* 249
173 *The Beginnings of Stucco-Work* 251
174 *Influence of Antique Grotesques* 251
175 *Raphael and Giovanni da Udine* 252
176 *Giulio Romano and Perino del Vaga* 254
177 *White Stucco* 255
178 *Later Decorative Painting and Works in Stucco* 256
179 *Decadence of the Type* 257

CHAPTER EIGHT

Goldsmiths' Work, Ceramics and Related Crafts

180 *General Status of this Art* 259
181 *Ecclesiastical Works of the Early Renaissance* 259
182 *Secular Works of the Early Renaissance* 260
183 *The Art of the Goldsmith in the High Renaissance* 262
184 *Vessels of Semi-Precious Stones and Crystal* 262
185 *Adornment, Weapons and Seals* 263
186 *Majolica and Other Pottery* 264

CHAPTER NINE

Temporary Decorations

187 *Festivals and Festival Artists* 266
188 *Festival Decorations of the Early Renaissance* 266
189 *Sixteenth-Century* Feste 267
190 *Triumphal Arches* 268
191 *Festival Sculpture* 268
192 *Theatre Architecture* 269
193 *The* Scena 271
194 *Artistic Purpose of the* Scena 273
195 *Fireworks and Table-Centres* 273

Index of Personal Names 277
Index of Place Names 280

Introduction

A seven-year-old friend of mine, more concisely than Bacon, divides books into two classes only: reading-books and looking-books. The first thing to be said about this book is that it is certainly not a reading-book – that is, it is not to be read at a sitting, as a continuous narrative expounding the history of architecture in Italy during the fifteenth and sixteenth centuries, as a glance at the first few pages will rapidly convince anyone. Equally, it is not a looking-book, by which I understand a book based on pictures, with an accompanying text which does no more than expound and amplify the pictures themselves: this, it might be thought, is merely another word for a "coffee-table book", undeserving of further notice; but that would be a mistake. The first such book, in terms of architectural history, was Serlio's treatise, based on the idea that illustrations can tell more about a building than words can, and words are needed only as a supplement to the pictures. Many and famous books on architecture have followed this principle in the last four and a half centuries; but, obviously, this is not one of them.

In fact, it is perhaps not a book at all, but rather a set of reading-notes, as the terse, even telegraphic, style will quickly confirm. It is certainly not a book for the general reader, seeking an introduction to Italian Renaissance architecture; but it is a mine for the specialist, although perhaps even specialists may now need some help with the very bare bones of a text here presented in English for the first time. Considering that all the other works of Jacob Burckhardt have been translated into many languages, and that the *Civilisation of the Italian Renaissance*, which was first published in 1860 (and translated into English in 1878), is one of the most famous of all historical works, in the same class as Gibbon's *Decline and Fall*, this may seem strange and in need of explanation. Such is the purpose of this Introduction.

To begin with, it is important to remember that Burckhardt's *Civilisation* was published in 1860, and on the first page he says: "It was formerly our intention to fill up the gaps in this book by a special work on *The Art of the Renaissance* – an intention, however, which we have been able to fulfil only in part." We know that, in fact, much of the vast reading he had done for that book (and its predecessor, the *Cicerone*) could also be used for the new book on the arts of the Italian Renaissance, given that the arts were perhaps the greater part of that phenomenon. Burckhardt had read virtually every primary source, and most of the secondary ones, on Italy in the period between Dante and Michelangelo, in so far as they were available in the mid-nineteenth century, and this is one of the reasons why the book is worth translating after the lapse of well over a century: the number of contemporary books on Italian art, and especially on Italian Renaissance architecture, was so small that he was virtually compelled to read the original sources with close attention; a situation the reverse of that which applies now, when we are all too busy "keeping up with the literature" to be able to find time to read anything published long ago, particularly if it happens to be in Latin. It is interesting to recall that in 1870, three years after this book was published, *The Universal Catalogue of Books on Art* was circulated in proof-sheets, by order of the Science and Art Department, on the proposal of Henry Cole. It was thought then that it was possible – and more sensible – to compile a complete catalogue of every book ever published on the fine and decorative arts, so that the National Art Library (now the Library of the Victoria and Albert Museum) would be able to know what to acquire, rather than merely list the books they happened already to possess. This feeling, that it was actually possible to read everything on a specific area of art history (even one as large as the Italian Renaissance), is what most sharply distinguishes Burckhardt's world from ours. It is also responsible for one of the main difficulties which the modern reader experiences with this book, and one to which I shall return, namely, the off-hand way in which Burckhardt cites his references. One can only wonder at an audience to whom Pliny, Platina, Martène, Eccardus and the *Allgemeine Bauzeitung* were all such everyday names that no more precise references were needed. Yet these quotations are in fact the greatest merit of the book, for it must be confessed that Burckhardt's aesthetic judgements seem tiresomely simplistic, especially when one considers that the laconic style often makes for difficulty in understanding, so that jejune remarks about "noble and exquisite beauty" or "Baroque decline" seem no more than wasted words, and the statement that the façade of the Villa Giulia is "worthless" remains – to me at least – incomprehensible. Nevertheless, the novelty of his method should not be overlooked, for he rejected the history of architecture as a chronological sequence of works by successive architects in favour of a more typological approach. This has been of great consequence in recent architectural history; but in Burckhardt it is subject to one severe limitation which also had a malign Hegelian effect on much nineteenth- and twentieth-century German art-historical writing. This can be summed up as the Pathetic Fallacy: take, for example, "Venice wanted a masterpiece", or the constantly recurring refrain "the fifteenth century" did this, while "the sixteenth century" did that; as though at one moment there was a single Will-to-Form which applied equally all over Italy, or that each town had clearly defined stylistic goals, regardless of the complex web of social, liturgical, economic and personal factors that condition every building at all times and in every place. To impose order on the crude mass of facts involves simplification of this kind; and this is a pioneer attempt, which still has much to teach us.

It is notorious that Burckhardt hardly bothered with his books once they were written, and, indeed, preferred to leave the boring business of proof-reading and final correction to others. When later editions were called for, he seems to have been quite content to get others to add new material, with little supervision on his part. It is therefore necessary to say something about the origin of this book and the text which has been used for this translation.

Jacob Burckhardt (1818–97) was born in Basle and trained in Berlin during the great period of that University, Ranke being one of his teachers. He soon abandoned the idea of becoming a Protestant pastor and devoted himself to history. Almost all his life was spent in teaching, as Professor of Art History (and later of History) in his native Basle, with a short interlude in Zürich. His first book, on the Emperor Constantine, was published in 1853 as part of a grand design which would have covered much of European history, but it was followed by an entirely different work, the *Cicerone*, described on the title-page as a guide to the enjoyment of the works of art – painting, sculpture and architecture – in Italy. It was published in 1855 and is (to the best of my knowledge) still in print: the references in this book are usually to the tenth edition. Five years later he published one of the most important historical works since Ranke and Gibbon – *Die Kultur der Renaissance in Italien* – which met with discouragingly little success at first, but has long been established as one of the great books of the nineteenth century, and a leading example of the new cultural history. This is not the place to discuss it further, but clearly his interest in the art of the Renaissance in Italy, manifested in the *Cicerone*, was now combined with the enormous breadth of reading he had undertaken for the *Civilisation*, and the two could be combined for a general history of all the arts in Italy during the Renaissance. That is how the present book began; and there are headings, if no more, for the sections on painting and sculpture (three essays on aspects of painting in the Renaissance have survived as fragments and have been published). The sections on sculpture never got beyond a series of brief headings, which Burckhardt himself specifically said were not to be published. The present book is, therefore, Burckhardt's expansion of the headings on architecture, with references added. There seems never to have been any attempt to work them up into a more polished literary form: we are told that this was a book always "close to Burckhardt's heart"; but it seems strange that he was content to allow it to appear in 1867, and in a second edition in 1878, in so different a form from the *Kultur*, if not the *Cicerone*. The most likely reason is that he was addressing a specialist audience in this book; but that still fails to explain why, in such a case, he so frequently uses unnecessary adjectives of praise or blame – it is well known that professionals never make that mistake.

The following quotations cast some light on the genesis of the book.* On 5 January, 1862, he wrote to his friend Otto Mündler, the art expert, about the poor sales of his *Cicerone*; "with that experience behind me, I have decided only to work out a skeleton for the *Art of the Renaissance* [i.e. he was still thinking in terms of a book on all three arts], about twenty sheets, and simply to use the occasion to communicate results that seem to me new. Of course that will not make a readable book, but however readable one is one can't break the ice in Germany. And even so short a work will have to wait a good while . . ." To another friend, Paul Heyse, he wrote on 3 April, 1864: "I worked out seven-eighths of my *Art of the Renaissance* in the winter of 1862/3, but then found it inadequate both in principle and in execution, and put it back in my desk, probably for ever, as I can't hope to make good the lacunae with only six months in Italy . . . My consolation is that at least I was not afraid of a great work." Later in that year he wrote to the same correspondent, on 6 December, 1864: "The best demonstration I can offer you of the sort of author I am was given last Friday when I gave Lübke, who was here, the MS. of my *Art of the Renaissance*, which is seven-eighths finished, for him to do as he pleased with, and so that he could at least use part of the material for a fourth volume to Kugler's *History of Architecture*. I was not satisfied with the work, and cannot pursue my studies, so gave it away on condition my name only occupied second place on the title-page – although I should prefer it not to appear at all . . ."

Most of the rest of the story is told in successive Prefaces to the numerous reprints and new editions up to 1932, when it appeared with a Preface by Heinrich Wölfflin, Burckhardt's pupil and successor in the Chair at Basle, as Vol. VI of the *Gesamtausgabe*, the collected edition of all Burckhardt's writings. In fact, the *Gesamtausgabe* text has not been used for this edition (which has been based on the sixth edition, of 1920), because the *Gesamtausgabe*, correctly but pedantically, is a reprint of the 1878 edition, the last one incontestably by Burckhardt alone. For a similar reason, the *Gesamtausgabe* has no illustrations at all, since it is known that the woodcuts in the earlier editions were chosen by Lübke rather than by Burckhardt himself (according to Wölfflin, Burckhardt wanted to have a separate Atlas of illustrations arranged upon systematic principles, but his publisher feared the expense). Yet the *Gesamtausgabe* contains § 57, which is by A. Thiersch, because it is known that it was added at Burckhardt's express desire. This is confirmed by the Preface, by Heinrich Holtzinger, to the third edition, of 1891. In the Prefaces to the third, fourth and fifth editions Holtzinger makes several points clear. In 1891 he claims that many of the additions were by Burckhardt himself (and there is no reason to doubt this); that § 57 was added by Burckhardt's desire; and that there were many new illustrations (the implication being that Burckhardt concurred in the choice, but had not actually made it). In the fourth edition, of 1904 – after Burckhardt's death, in 1897 – Holtzinger says that the book had always been close to its author's heart and that he had continued to add to it: he specifies § 32a and § 146a – on buildings represented in paintings, and on fountains – as being entirely his (*rühren ganz vom Autor selber her*). This is one good reason for following the text of the later editions rather than that of 1878 as the *Gesamtausgabe* does. In 1912 Holtzinger specifies some new bibliographical references as well as new illustrations, substituting some photographs for the original engravings. (The opportunity has been taken in the present edition to make some further substitutions and additions, while preserving the original woodcuts where they continue to give the information needed to complement the text.) After 1912 the later editions reprint the text and illustrations of that edition.

This is perhaps the place to point out that references to books and articles which appeared after 1897 – e.g. Schlosser's *Ghiberti* – cannot have been known to Burckhardt, but it would not really be helpful to a modern reader to remove them. Similarly, all Burckhardt's numerous references to Vasari are to the

* These quotations are from the *Letters of J. Burckhardt*, selected, edited and translated by A. Dru, London (Routledge & Kegan Paul), 1955.

edition, partly by Milanesi, published by Le Monnier in Florence in 1846–70. This edition was almost immediately superseded by the famous nine-volume edition by Gaetano Milanesi, published in Florence (by Sansoni) in 1878–85, which is still the standard text for scholarly purposes. Holtzinger helpfully provided his editions of Burckhardt with references to Milanesi in brackets, following the Le Monnier citations given by Burckhardt himself. The *Gesamtausgabe*, on the grounds that these were not original, cited only Le Monnier. This seems sheer pedantry, since every major library has the Milanesi edition, and it has been universally cited in the literature since its appearance. For this reason, I have deleted all the Le Monnier references. It was hoped, when this translation was first mooted, to be able to add references to the great new edition in progress, under the editorship of Rosanna Bettarini and with a commentary by Paola Barocchi (Florence, 1966–), but their progress has not been fast enough for this to be feasible, so the Milanesi citations are alone retained. A word of caution is necessary here: Burckhardt does not properly distinguish between the actual text of Vasari and the very extensive annotations and appendixes added by Milanesi from his archival researches, so that what appears to be a reference to Vasari may well be a reference to Milanesi – though it is fair to add that that probably means any such statement has archival authority, which cannot be often said of Vasari himself. Still, there can be a confusion between sixteenth and nineteenth centuries here, and the reader should be warned. It may also be mentioned here that, for the convenience of the reader, misprints and slips have been silently corrected, and proper names are given in the form likely to be most familiar to the English-speaking reader (the spelling Brunellesco has been retained, as having good authority). Footnotes are Burckhardt's own, except when followed by the initials PM – this indicates an alteration or a new note, for which I am responsible. Such notes in the text have been added when, for example, a work has been moved from one museum to another (or even destroyed): notes at the end of a section have been added, sparingly, when there seems good reason – e.g. when later research has altered or modified Burckhardt's statements. These have been kept to a minimum, and are, of course, factual only.

To revert to the question asked at the beginning: is it worth publishing a translation of a book that first appeared in 1867? Do we not know everything in it, and more? There are two answers to this question. In the first place, I will wager that no living architectural historian could open this book at random and read for a quarter of an hour without coming across at least one reference to an author – Leandro Alberti, Corio, Eccardus, even Milanesi and Müntz, with whom his familiarity is less than complete and who may well be able to offer a new insight into what seemed known territory. Secondly, Burckhardt's approach through such things as diaries (Infessura, Landucci) and chronicles (Scardeonius, Malipiero), or even guide-books (Sansovino, Albertini), is no longer as new as it was in 1867, because we have learned from him and, in particular, from men like Wittkower, who learned from him. But there is still much more to be done in the way of a social history of architecture – how did the pattern of Italian family life actually determine the shape of palaces, did the Italian desire *fare una bella figura* actually influence decoration more than the desire not to spend too much money? How did Confraternities decide to build, what did they require of their architects, and how did they finance the work? These, and many other, questions will be raised by an attentive reading of this book.

Peter Murray
January, 1983

Bibliography

Burckhardt's references are extremely exiguous and, after the lapse of more than a century, often very difficult to understand. Each of the abbreviated references to books and periodicals is therefore given here in a form which should be adequate to identify it: no attempt has been made at strict bibliographical exactitude, partly because Burckhardt himself rarely gave enough information for anyone to be sure which edition he was quoting, especially in the case of books published in the fifteenth and sixteenth centuries. However, it is hoped that enough detail has now been given for the present-day reader to be able to identify any of the sources which he may wish to investigate in greater detail. The citations from periodicals or series should be easily recognisable – thus, Malipiero, *Ann. Veneti* in Arch. Stor., will not be found under Malipiero, but is an abbreviated reference to *Archivio storico italiano*, which will be found under the Periodicals at the beginning of the Bibliography; similarly, references to Murat. mean Muratori, *Rerum Italicarum Scriptores*, but the details will be found under Muratori.

English editions cited are usually those published in London, but American editions are often the same; and, in the few cases where there seems to have been an American but not a British edition, the American edition is specifically cited. So far as is known to the present editor, English translations are given where they exist. Where quotations in the text are given in sufficient detail for identification no further details have been given.

I should like to thank Mrs Roberta Taylor for her help in tracing several difficult items.

PERIODICALS CITED BY BURCKHARDT

ALLGEM. BAUZEITUNG
Allgemeine Bauzeitung, Vienna, 1836–1918

ANNALI DELL' ISTITUTO ARCHAEOL.
Annali dell' Istituto di Correspondenza Archeologica, Rome, 1829– published by the Deutsches Arch. Inst.; after 1885 united with

ARCHÄOLOGISCHE ZEITUNG
Archäologische Zeitung, Berlin, 1843–

ARCHIVIO DELLA R. SOCIETÀ ROMANA DI STORIA PATRIA
Archivio della R. Società Romana di Storia Patria, Rome, 1878–85 (8 vols. only)

ARCH. STOR.
Archivio storico italiano, Florence, 1842–

ARCHIVIO STORICO DELL' ARTE
Archivio Storico dell' Arte, Rome, 1888–97 (from 1898, *L'Arte*)

ATTI E MEMORIE
Atti e Memorie della (R.) Deputazione di Storia patria per le provincie di Romagna, Bologna, 1862–

DEUTSCHE BAUZEITUNG
Deutsche Bauzeitung, Berlin, 1867–

ERBKAMS ZEITSCHRIFT . . . see *Zeitschrift für Bauwesen*

GAZETTE DES BEAUX-ARTS
Gazette des Beaux-Arts, Paris, 1859–68 (2e période, 1869–88, and onwards)
GIORNALE DI ERUDIZ. ARTIST.
Giornale di Erudizione Artistica, Perugia, 1872–77 (6 vols. only)
JAHRBUCH D. ARCHÄOLOG. INSTITUTS
Jahrbuch des [kaiserlichen] deutschen archäologischen Instituts, Berlin, 1886– (after 1918 the word *kaiserlich* was dropped)
JAHRBUCH DES KAISERL. DEUTSCH. ARCHÄOLOG. INST.
Jahrbuch des kaiserlichen deutschen archäologischen Instituts.
JAHRBÜCHER FÜR KUNSTWISSENSCHAFT
(Zahns) Jahrbücher für Kunstwissenschaft, Leipzig, 1868–73
JAHRBUCH DER PREUSSISCHEN KUNSTSAMMLUNGEN
Jahrbuch der königlich preussischen Kunstsammlungen, Berlin, 1880–
JANITSCHEKS REPERTORIUM see *Repertorium für Kunstwissenschaft*
LÜTZOWS ZEITSCHRIFT see *Zeitschrift für bildende Kunst*
MÉMOIRES DE LA SOC. NAT.
Mémoires de la société nationale des antiquaires de France, Paris, 1817–
MISCELLANEA D' ARTE
Miscellanea d' Arte, Florence, 1903 only (afterwards *Rivista* . . .)
MITTEILUNGEN DES KAISERLICHEN DEUTSCHEN ARCH. INST.
Mitteilungen des Kaiserlichen deutschen archäologischen Instituts (Athenische Abteilung), Stuttgart, 1876–
MITTEILUNGEN DER ZENTR-KOMM.
Mittheilungen der Kaiserlichen-königlichen Zentral-Kommission für Denkmalpflege, Vienna, 1856–
POLITECNICO
Il Politecnico, repertorio mensile di studj . . . Milan, 1839–65 and then as *Il Politecnico, Giornale dell' Ingegnere Architetto* . . . 1869–1937
RASSEGNA D' ARTE
Rassegna d' Arte, Milan, 1901–22
REPERTORIUM FÜR KUNSTWISSENSCHAFT
Repertorium für Kunstwissenschaft, Stuttgart, 1876–. Also called *Janitscheks Repertorium* . . . Facsimile reprint, Berlin, 1968
REVUE ARCHÉOLOGIQUE
Revue archéologique, Paris, 1844–60 (2e série, 1860–82, etc.)
WIENER ALLGEM. BAUZEITUNG see *Allgemeine Bauzeitung*
ZAHNS JAHRBÜCHER see *Jahrbücher für Kunstwissenschaft*
ZEITSCHRIFT FÜR BAUWESEN
Zeitschrift für Bauwesen, Berlin, 1851–1931
ZEITSCHRIFT FÜR BILDENDE KUNST
Zeitschrift für bildende Kunst, Leipzig, 1866–. Also called *von Lützows Zeitschrift* in early years

BOOKS CITED BY BURCKHARDT

A

d'AGINCOURT, *Archit.*
J. B. Séroux d'Agincourt, *Histoire de l'Art par les Monuments* . . . 6 vols., Paris, 1811–23. Eng. ed. 3 vols., London, 1847
ALBERTI, *Descrizione di tutta l' Italia*
Leandro Alberti, *Descrittione di tutta l' Italia*, Bologna, 1550 (Burckhardt quotes from the 1557 Venice ed.)
ALBERTI, *Arte edificatoria/De re aedific.*
L. B. Alberti, *De re aedificatoria libri X* (first printed Florence, 1485), quoted by Burckhardt partly from the Italian translation printed in Alberti's *Opere volgari* (ed. Bonucci, 5 vols., Florence, 1843–49) and from the ed. by S. Ticozzi, Milan, 1833. For quotations from the Latin ed., see now the ed. by G. Orlandi and P. Portoghesi in Latin/Italian, 2 vols., Milan, 1966
ALBERTI, *Della Pittura*
L. B. Alberti, *Della Pittura*, written *c* 1435, quoted from Bonucci's ed. of the *Opere volgari* quoted above. See now: C. Grayson, *L. B. Alberti on Painting and On Sculpture*, London, 1972, and id. *Opere volgari*, vol. 3, Bari, 1973
ALBERTINI, *De mirabilibus Romae*
F. Albertini, *De mirabilibus Romae*, Rome, 1510 and later: see P. Murray (ed.), *Five Early Guides to*

Rome and Florence, London, 1972. Burckhardt's quotations are from the edition (*Nova Urbs* only) by A. Schmarsow, Heilbronn, 1886

ANECDOTA LITERARIA (*sic*)
Anecdota Litteraria ex mss. codicibus eruta . . ., 4 vols., Rome, 1773–83, ed. G. Amaduzzi and G. Bianconi

ANONIMO MORELLIANO see MICHIEL

ARGNANI, *Le ceramiche . . . faentine . . .*
F. Argnani, *Le ceramiche e majoliche faentine dalla loro origine fino al principio del secolo XVI; appunti storici*, Faenza, 1889

ARIOSTO, *Orl. Fur.*
L. Ariosto, *Orlando Furioso.* First ed. Ferrara, 1516; 3rd, definitive, ed. Ferrara, 1532 (and many later). First Eng. trans. by Sir J. Harington, London, 1591

ARMENINI, *De' veri precetti . . .*
G. B. Armenini, *De' veri precetti della Pittura*, Ravenna, 1587 (Eng. trans. ed. by L. Olszewski, *On the True Precepts* . . ., New York, 1977)

ARNOLD, *Der herzogl. Palast von Urbino*
F. Arnold, *Der herzogliche Palast von Urbino*, Leipzig, 1856–7 (measured drawings, with text in German and French)

B

BAGLIONE, *Vite de' Pittori*
G. Baglione, *Le vite de' Pittori, Scultori ed Architetti* . . . Rome, 1642 (facsimile reprint, Rome, 1935)

BANDELLO
M. Bandello, *Novelle.* For Bandello (*d* 1561) see now *Tutte le Opere* di B., 2 vols., Milan, 1934–5 and later eds. Eng. trans., London, 1825 and 1890

BASAN
P. Basan, *Son oeuvre, ou recueil de 650 estampes . . . d'après les tableaux des meilleurs maîtres* . . . 6 vols., Paris, 1762–79 and 6 later vols.

BELTRAMI, *Il Castello di Milano*
L. Beltrami, *Il Castello di Milano*, Milan, 1894

BEROALDUS, *Orationes*
P. Beroaldus, *Orationes et Carmina*, Brixiae, 1497 (Bologna, 1500 and later eds.)

(BIANCONI), *Guida per . . . Bologna*, 1845
G. Bianconi, *Guida del Forestiere per la città di Bologna* . . . Bologna, 1820 and later

BIONDO, *Roma Instaurata*
F. Biondo (Flavius Biondus), *Roma Instaurata*, probably Rome, 1470, and many later eds. Cf. B. Nogara, *Scritti inediti di B. F.* in Studi e Testi, Rome, 1927, and partial reprint in R. Valentini and G. Zucchetti, *Codice Topografico della Città di Roma*, Rome, 1953

BIRINGUCCI, *Pirotechnica*
V. Biringuccio, *De la pirotechnica*, Venice, 1540 and later (Burckhardt says that he had never seen the 1540 ed., but the British Library has a copy)

BLASIO, OTTO DE S. (*d* 1223)
O. de Sancto Blasio, *Chronicle*, see MURATORI, VI. (later ed. by A. Hofmeister, Hannover & Leipzig, 1912), and WURSTISEN

BOËCE, *Scotorum Historia* . . . 1526
H. Boëce, *Scotorum historiae a prima gentis origine* . . ., Paris, 1526 and many later eds. Also several Eng. trans., e.g. Edinburgh, 1946

BOSSI see ROSCOE

BOTTARI-TICOZZI
G. Bottari, *Raccolta* . . . see LETTERE PITTORICHE

BRACCIOLINI see POGGIUS

BÜHLMANN, *Die Architektur des klass. Altertums u. d. Ren* . . .
J. Bühlmann, *Die Architektur des klassischen Altertums und der Renaissance*, 4th ed., Esslingen, 1913–19. Eng. trans., Berlin, 1892 and New York, 1916 (?)

BULLARUM AMPLISSIMA COLLECTIO
C. Cocquelines, *Bullarum Privilegiorum ac Diplomatum Romanorum Pontificum amplissima collectio* . . ., 6 vols., Rome, 1739–62

BURCKHARDT, *Der Cicerone*
J. Burckhardt, *Der Cicerone; eine Anleitung zum Genuss der Kunstwerke Italiens*, 1st ed., Basle, 1855; quoted here from the 10th ed., Leipzig, 1909. The English trans. London, 1873 and later, contains only the section on Painting

BURCKHARDT, *Kultur d. Renaiss.*
J. Burckhardt, *Die Kultur der Renaissance in Italien*, Basle, 1860, and many later editions: Burckhardt here mostly gives references to the 4th. The standard English translation is by S. Middlemore, London, 1878, and many later reprints (e.g. two illustrated eds., *c* 1939 and 1944)

BURCKHARDT, *Zeit Konstantins* . . .
J. Burckhardt, *Die Zeit Konstantins des Grosses*, Basle, 1853, (3rd ed. 1898) and Eng. trans. as *The Age of Constantine the Great*, London, 1949

and Palaces in Italy, during the 15th and 16th centuries . . ., London, 1844 (2nd enlarged ed. 1854)

GUALANDI see ATTI E MEMORIE (Periodicals)

GUASTI, *SM del Fiore*
C. Guasti, *Santa Maria del Fiore, La Costruzione della Chiesa e del Campanile* . . ., Florence, 1887

H

HIRTH, *Kulturgesch. Bilderbuch*, see HOGHENBERG

HOFFMAN, *Studien zu . . . Alberti*
P. Hoffmann, *Studien zu L. B. Albertis zehn Büchern* De re aedificatoria, Frankenberg, 1883

HOFFMANN, *Die Bauten des Herzogs F. v. Montefeltro*
T. Hoffmann, *Die Bauten des Herzogs F. da Montefeltro als erste Werke der Hochrenaissance*, Leipzig, 1905

HOFFMANN, *Raffael als Architekt*
T. Hoffmann, *Raffael in seiner Bedeutung als Architekt*, 4 vols., Zittau, 1904–14

HOGHENBERG (*sic*)
J. Hogenberg and E. Bruining, *Représentation de la Cavalcade et des Réjouissances . . . à Bologne . . . 1530 à l'occasion du couronnement de Charles V* . . ., Antwerp, n.d. (*c* 1530)

I

ILG, *Über den kunsthistor . . . Hyp. Pol.*
A. Ilg, *Über den kunsthistorischen Wert der Hypnerotomachia Poliphili*, Vienna, 1872

J

JANITSCHEK, *Albertis kleine Schriften*
H. Janitschek, *Albertis kleinerer Kunsttheoretische Schriften*, Vienna, 1877

JOVANOVITS, *Forschungen über St Peter*
C. Jovanovits, *Forschungen über den Bau der Peterskirche zu Rom*, Vienna, 1877

JOVIAN. PONTAN. see PONTAN

PAUL. JOVII *Elogia*
P. Jovius (P. Giovio), *Elogia veris clarorum virorum* . . ., Venice, 1546 (Basle ed. in 3 vols., *Vitae illustrium virorum*, 1576–8)

K

KINKEL, *Mosaik zur Kunstgeschichte*
G. Kinkel, *Mosaik zur Kunstgeschichte*, Berlin, 1876

KUGLER, *Gesch. d. Baukunst*
F. Kugler, *Geschichte der Baukunst*, 3 vols., Stuttgart, 1856–59

KULTUR DER RENAISSANCE see BURCKHARDT

L

LABORDE, *Ducs de Bourgogne*
L. de Laborde, *Les Ducs de Bourgogne*, 3 vols., Paris, 1849–52

LANCIANI, *Ruins and Excavations*
R. Lanciani, *The Ruins and Excavations of Ancient Rome*, London, 1897 (modern reprint, New York, 1967)

LANDUCCI, *Diario Fiorentino*
L. Landucci, *Diario Fiorentino*, ed. I. del Badia, Florence, 1883 (reprinted Florence, 1969). Eng. trans., London, 1927, reprinted New York, 1971

LASPEYRES, *Die Kirchen der Renaissance in Mittelitalien*
P. Laspeyres, *Die Kirchen der Renaissance in Mittelitalien*, Berlin, 1882

LEODIUS, *De vita Friderici II*
H. Leodius, *Annalium de vita et rebus gestis illustriss. Princ. Friderici II*, Frankfurt, 1624

LETAROUILLY, *Edifices*
P. Letarouilly, *Edifices de Rome moderne* . . ., 3 vols., Paris, 1840–57. Abridged Eng. trans., London, 1928–30 (and later reprints)

LETAROUILLY et SIMIL
P. Letarouilly and A. Simil, *Le Vatican et la Basilique de St Pierre de Rome*, 2 vols., Paris, 1882. Eng. trans., London, 1963

LETTERE PITTORICHE
G. Bottari, *Raccolta di Lettere* . . ., 7 vols., Rome, 1754–83, and continued by S. Ticozzi, 8 vols., Milan, 1822–25

LETTERE DI PRINCIPI
(G. Ruscelli), *Lettere di principi*, Venice, 1562 (and many later eds., e.g. 3 vols., Venice, 1570–77)

LETTERE SANESI see VALLE, G. Della

LOMAZZO, *Trattato dell' arte*
G. Lomazzo, *Trattato dell' Arte della Pittura*, Milan, 1584 (not 1585). Reprinted as Vol. II of *Scritti sulle Arti*, ed. R. Ciardi, Florence, 1974

LÜBKE, *Gesch. d. Architektur*
W. Lübke, *Geschichte der Architektur*, Leipzig, 1855 (and later eds.)

FABRONI, *Laurent. Med.*
A. Fabroni, *Laurentii Medicis Magnifici Vita*, 2 vols., Pisa, 1784 (Vol. II contains the *Adnotationes et monumenta*)

FAZIO
B. Facius, *De viris illustribus*, ed. L. Mehus, Florence, 1745 (see now new Ms. and trans. in M. Baxendall, *B. Facius on Painting*, in Journal of the Warburg & Courtauld Institutes, XXVII, 1964)

FEA, *Miscellanea*
C. Fea, *Miscellanea filologica, critica e antiquaria . . .*, 2 vols., Rome, 1790–1836

FILARETE, *Trattato dell' architettura*
quoted by Burckhardt from Ms. Cod. Pal. 372; but see now the transcription, facsimiles and translation in J. Spencer, *Filarete's Treatise on Architecture*, 2 vols., Yale and London, 1965 and *Trattato* ed. A. Finoli and L. Grassi, 2 vols., Milan, 1972: see also OETTINGEN

FORESTIERE ISTRUITO . . . DI VICENZA
O. Bertotti-Scamozzi, *Il forestiere istruito delle cose più rare di architettura . . . di Vicenza*, Vicenza, 1761 (the 2nd ed., 1780, was issued anonymously, and a 3rd ed., 1804, has additions)

FRANCESCO DI GIORGIO, *Trattato d' architettura . . .*
C. Promis, *F. di G.: Trattato d' architettura civile e militare*, 3 vols., Turin, 1841: see now new ed. by C. Maltese and Maltese-Degrassi, 2 vols., Milan, 1967

FULVIUS, *Antiquitates urbis . . .* 1527
A. Fulvio, *Antiquitates urbis*, Rome, 1527 (an Italian trans., Venice, 1543)

G

GAR, *Relazioni*
T. Gar, *Relazioni della Corte di Roma nel secolo XVI*, 2 vols., Florence, 1846–57 (the 3rd vol. in the Second Series of *Relazioni degli Ambasciatori Veneti*, ed. E. Alberì)

GAURICUS, *De sculptura*
Pomponius Gauricus, *De sculptura*, quoted by Burckhardt from Gronovius (see below, Graevius): see now the ed. by A. Chastel and R. Klein, Geneva and Paris, 1969, with French trans.

GAUTHIER, *Edifices de Gênes*
P. Gauthier, *Les plus beaux Edifices de la Ville de Gênes . . .* 2 vols., Paris, 1818–25 (2nd ed. 1830–32)

GAYE, *Carteggio*
G. Gaye, *Carteggio inedito d' artisti dei secoli XIV, XV, XVI . . .* 3 vols., Florence, 1839–40 (facsimile reprint, Turin, 1961)

GERMANICUS see SILVANUS

GEYMÜLLER, *Die ursprünglichen Entwürfe . . . St Peter*
H. von Geymüller, *Die ursprünglichen Entwürfe fur St Peter/Les projets primitifs pour S. Pierre*, 2 vols., Vienna, 1875–80

GEYMÜLLER, *Raffaello studiato come architetto*
H. von Geymüller, *Raffaello Sanzio studiato come architetto*, Milan, 1884

GHIBERTI, *Comment.*
L. Ghiberti, *Commentarii*, ed. J. von Schlosser, 2 vols., Berlin, 1912

GIOVIO, *Elogium Raphaelis*
P. Giovio, *Elogium Raphaelis* quoted by Burckhardt from Tiraboschi (q.v.). See now the text in V. Golzio, *Raffaello nei documenti . . .* Vatican City, 1936

GIOVIO see also JOV., Paul.

GRAEVIUS, *Thesaurus Ital.*
J. Graevius and P. Burmannus, *Thesaurus antiquitatum et historiarum Italiae*, 30 vols., Leiden, 1704–23

GRAEVIUS and GRONOVIUS
J. Graevius and J. Gronovius, *Thesaurus antiquitatum Graecarum et Romanorum . . .*, 39 vols., Lugduni Batavorum, Venice, etc., 1694–1737

GRANDJEAN and FAMIN, *Archit. Toscane*
A. Grandjean and A. Famin, *Architecture Toscane, ou palais, maisons et autres édifices . . .* Paris, 1806, amplified ed. 1837

GRAPALDUS, *De partibus aedium*
F. Grapaldi, *De partibus aedium*, Parma, 1494? (and later eds.)

GREGOROVIUS, *Geschichte Roms im Mittelalter*
F. Gregorovius, *Geschichte der Stadt Rom im Mittelalter von V. bis XVI. Jahrhundert*, 8 vols., Stuttgart, 1859–72 (latest ed., Darmstadt, 1953–57: Eng. trans., 13 vols., London, 1894–1902)

GRIMALDI, *Cod. Barberin.*
G. Grimaldi (*d* 1623): his history of Old S. Peter's (Vatican Library, Cod. Barb. Lat. 2733) has now been published by R. Niggl, *Descrizione della Basilica antica di S. Pietro*, Città del Vaticano, 1972

GRONOV. see GRAEVIUS

GRUNER'S *Decorations*
L. Gruner, *Fresco Decorations and Stuccoes of Churches*

C

CALCAGNINI, *Opera*
C. Calcagnini, *Opera*, Basle, 1544
CALVI, *Simulacrum antiquae urbis Romae cum regionibus*
M. F. Calvus, *Antiquae urbis Romae cum regionibus simulachrum*, Rome, 1532
CALVI, *Notizia de' professori . . . in Milano*
G. Calvi, *Notizie sulla vita e sulle opere dei principali architetti, scultori . . . in Milano . . . governo dei Visconti e degli Sforza*, 3 vols., Milan, 1859–69
CALVI, *Notizie*, II, see above
CANINA
L. Canina, *L'architettura antica descritta e dimostrata coi Monumenti . . .*, 6 vols., Rome, 1830–44 (and 2nd ed., 12 vols., Rome, 1839–46)
CAROTTO, woodcuts of Verona, 1540
G. Caroto (*sic*), *De origine et amplitudine civitatis Veronae* (as quoted by Milanesi: but the British Library has only Verona, 1560)
CAUMONT, *Abécédaire*
A. de Caumont, *Abécédaire ou Rudiments d' Archéologie . . .*, 2 vols., Paris, 1851–53 (and many later eds.). Burckhardt is probably referring to the 5th ed. *Architecture religieuse*, Caen, 1867
CELLINI, *Autobiography*
B. Cellini, *Vita di Benvenuto Cellini*, first ed., Naples, 1728 (with false imprint 'Colonia'): many later eds. Eng. trans. by G. Bull, London, 1956, and earlier trans., ed. and illustrated by J. Pope-Hennessy, London, 1949
CELLINI, *Trattato secondo*
B. Cellini, *Due Trattati. Uno intorno . . . Oreficeria. L' altro . . . Scultura*, Florence, 1568 and later eds., including one by Milanesi, Florence, 1857
CENNI STORICO-ARTISTICI DI S. MINIATO AL MONTE, 1850
G. Berti, *Cenni storico-artistici per servire di guida . . . alla Basilica di S. Miniato al Monte*, Florence, 1850
CICERONE see BURCKHARDT
CODRUS see URCEUS
COLONNA see POLIPHILUS
COMINES
P. de Comines, *Mémoires*. These memoirs were written before *c* 1511 (and trans. into English in 1596): modern ed., 3 vols., Paris, 1924–25
CONTI, *Il Pal. Pitti*
C. Conti, *Il Palazzo Pitti, la sua primitiva costruzione . . .* Florence, 1887
CORIO, *Storia di Milano*
B. Corio, *L' Historia di Milano*, Padua, 1646 (and ed. Magni, 3 vols., Milan, 1855)
CROWE-CAVALCASELLE, *Tizian*
J. Crowe and G. Cavalcaselle, *Life and Times of Titian*, 2 vols., London, 1877 (Burckhardt quotes from the German trans. of 1877)

D

D'AGINCOURT see AGINCOURT
DEHIO and VON BEZOLD, *Kirchliche Baukunst des Abendlandes*
G. Dehio and G. von Bezold, *Die kirchliche Baukunst des Abendlandes*, 7 vols., Stuttgart, 1884–1901
DE LABORDE see LABORDE
DELLA VALLE see VALLE
DOHMES KUNST u. KÜNSTLER see REDTENBACHER
DOLCE, *Dialogo della Pittura*
L. Dolce, *Dialogo della Pittura, intitolato l' Aretino*, Venice, 1557 (and Florence, 1735, and ed. Battelli, Florence, 1910, and in *Trattati d' Arte del Cinquecento*, Bari, 1960). Modern ed. and Eng. trans. by M. Roskill, New York, 1968
DONI, *Disegno*
A. Doni, *Disegno partito in più ragionamenti*, Venice, 1549. Modern ed. by M. Pepe, Milan, 1970
DURM, *Die Baukunst der Etrusker und Römer*
J. Durm, *Die Baukunst der Etrusker und Römer*, (Handbuch der Architektur), 2nd ed., Stuttgart, 1905
DURM, *Die Domkuppel von Florenz*
J. Durm, *Die Domkuppel von Florenz*, separate offprint from *Zeitschrift für Bauwesen*, 1887

E

ECCARDUS, *Scriptores*
J. G. von Eckhart, *Corpus historicum medii aevii, sive Scriptores res in orbe universo . . .*, 2 vols., Leipzig, 1723 (the references to Infessura can be more easily found in MURATORI, III, 2)

F

FABRICZY, *Filippo Brunelleschi*
C. von Fabriczy, *F. Brunelleschi, sein Leben und seine Werke*, Stuttgart, 1892

M

MABILLON, *Mus. ital.*
J. Mabillon, *Museum italicum, seu collectio veterum scriptorum* . . . 2 vols., Paris, 1687
MACCHIAVELLI, *Storie fiorent.*
N. Macchiavelli, *Historie fiorentine*, Florence and Rome, 1532 (and later eds.). English trans. London and New York, 1901, and reprinted New York, 1960
MAI, *Spicileg. Romanum*
A. Mai, *Spicilegium Romanum*, 9 vols., Rome, 1839–44
MALAGOLA, *Memorie storiche . . . Faenza*
C. Malagola, *Memorie storiche sulle majoliche di Faenza* . . ., Bologna, 1880
MANCINI, *Vita di L. B. Alberti*
G. Mancini, *Vita di L. B. Alberti*, 2nd ed., Florence, 1911 (reprint Rome, 1971)
MANETTI, *Vita di Brunellesco*
A. Manetti, *Vita di Brunellesco*, ed. H. Holzinger, Stuttgart, 1887; but see now the new Italian text, ed. D. De Robertis and G. Tanturli, Milan, 1976, and the English trans. (with Italian text), by H. Saalman and C. Enggass, Penn. State Univ. Press and London, 1970
MARIOTTI, *Lettere Pittoriche Perugine*
A. Mariotti, *Lettere Pittoriche Perugine, ossia Ragguaglio di memorie* . . ., Perugia, 1788
MARTÈNE, *Coll. Ampliss.*
E. Martène and U. Durand, *Veterum scriptorum et monumentorum, historicum . . . amplissima collectio*, 9 vols., Paris, 1724–33
MARTINI, Francesco di Giorgio, see FRANCESCO
MEMORIE TREVIGIANE
D. Federici, *Memorie Trevigiane sulle opere di disegno*, 2 vols., Venice, 1803
MICHIEL, *Notizie d' opere di disegno* ('The Anonimo Morelliano')
M. A. Michiel, *Notizie d' opere di disegno*, ed. T. von Frimmel, Vienna, 1888. Frimmel's ed. is defective. There is an ed. by G. Frizzoni, Bologna, 1884, and an English trans. by G. C. Williamson, London, 1903
MILANESI, *Documenti per la Storia* . . .
G. Milanesi, *Documenti per la Storia dell' Arte Senese*, 3 vols., Siena, 1854–56 (facsimile reprint, Utrecht, 1969)
MILIZIA, *Memorie degli Architetti*
F. Milizia, *Memorie degli Architetti antichi e moderni* (this is the title of the 3rd ed.), 2 vols., Parma, 1781. Eng. trans. by E. Cresy, London, 1826
MOLINIER, *La céramique italienne au XVe siècle*
E. Molinier, *La céramique italienne au XVe siècle*, Paris, 1888
MONGERI, Bramantino sketch-book
G. Mongeri, *Bramantino. Le Rovine di Roma* . . ., Milan, 1875, 2nd ed., Pisa, 1880. Preface and notes by Mongeri
MORUS, *Utopia*
T. More, *Utopia*, Louvain, 1516 (in Latin), and many later eds.: Burckhardt quotes from the Latin ed., Basle, 1563; see now the English version in the Yale edition of the Works of S. Thomas More, Yale, 1964
MÜLLER, *Archäologie*
C. O. Müller, *Handbuch der Archäologie der Kunst*, Breslau, 1830, and later eds.: Eng. trans., London, 1847 and 1850
MÜLLER, *Memoria sul compimento del duomo di Firenze*, 1847
No copy of a book with this title can be traced, but Müller (1822–49) was a young Swiss architect who took part in the competition for the completion of the façade of Florence Cathedral, and Paatz (*Kirchen v. Florenz*) quotes his *Del Duomo di Firenze e della sua facciata*, Florence, 1852 (there is a copy in the V. & A. Museum Library)
MÜLLER-WALDE, *Leonardo*
P. Müller-Walde, *Leonardo da Vinci*, Munich, 1889
MÜNTZ, *Les arts à la cour des papes*
E. Müntz, *Les arts à la cour des Papes pendant le XVe et le XVIe siècle*, 4 vols., Paris, 1878–82 and 1898
MÜNTZ, *Nouvelles recherches*
E. Müntz, *Les arts à la cour des Papes, nouvelles recherches* . . ., Rome, 1884, 1889 (published in *Mélanges . . . Ecole française de Rome*)
MÜNTZ, *La Renaissance en Italie*
E. Müntz, *La Renaissance en Italie, et en France à l'époque de Charles VIII*, Paris, 1883
MÜNTZ, *Raphael*
E. Müntz, *Raphael*, Paris, 1881 (Eng. trans., London, 1882)
MURATORI (quoted as Muratori/Murat./*Rer. ital. script.*)
L. A. Muratori, *Rerum Italicarum Scriptores ab Anno . . . 500 ad 1500*, 25 vols., Milan, 1723–51 (new ed. in progress, Città di Castello, 1900–)

O

OCHINI, *Apologen*
B. Ochino, *Des hoch gelehrten . . . Ochinus . . . Apologen*, Augsburg (?), 1559

OETTINGEN, *Filarete*
W. von Oettingen, *Über das Leben und die Werke des Antonio Averlino genannt Filarete*, Leipzig, 1888

OETTINGEN, *Filarete's Treatise*
W. von Oettingen, *Filaretes Tractat über die Baukunst*, Vienna, 1896 (in the series *Quellenschriften für Kunstgeschichte* – but see under FILARETE)

P

PACIOLI, *Divina Proportione*
L. Pacioli, ed. C. Winterberg, *De divina proportione* (Venice, 1509), Vienna, 1889 (see now the ed. by A. Bruschi in *Scritti Rinascimentali di Architettura*, ed. A. Bruschi, C. Maltese, M. Tafuri and R. Bonelli, Milan, 1978)

PALLADIO, *Quattro Libri dell' Architettura*
A. Palladio, *I quattro Libri dell' Architettura*, Venice, 1570 and many later eds., including a facsimile of the 1570 ed. (Milan, 1945) and a new ed. by L. Magagnato and P. Marini, Milan, announced for 1980. English trans. by G. Leoni, 1715, and I. Ware, 1738 (facsimile of Ware, New York, 1965)

PALLADIUS, *Suburbanum Ag. Chisii*
B. Palladius, *Suburbanum Agustini Chisii*, Rome, 1512 (Burckhardt quotes from *Anecdota Literaria*, q.v.)

PANORMITA, *Dicta et Facta Alphonsi*
A. Panormita (i.e. A. Beccadelli), *Alfonsi regis Neapolitani dicta et facta memoratu digna*, Pisa, 1485 (a later ed. by A. Cinquini and R. Valentini, Aosta, 1907)

PANTANELLI, *Di Fr. di Giorgio*
A. Pantanelli, *Di Francesco di Giorgio Martini pittore, scultore e architetto senese*, Siena, 1870. Burckhardt also quotes his *Francesco di Giorgio e l' arte in Siena*, 1874

PANVINIUS (Platinae continuator)
O. Panvinius, continuation of Platina's *Vitae Paparum*, printed in Muratori, III, II. Panvinius's *De Vaticana Basilica* is printed in Mai, *Spicilegium*, IX (q.v.)

PARAVICINI
T. Paravicini, *Die Renaissance-Architektur der Lombardei*, Dresden, 1877/78

M. PARIS ad ann. 1243
Matthew Paris, *Chronica maiora*, ed. H. Luard, 7 vols., London, 1872–83

PASSAVANT, *Rafael*
J. Passavant, *Rafael von Urbino und sein Vater G. Santi*, 3 vols., Leipzig, 1839–58

PASSERI, *Vite de' Pittori*
G. Passeri, *Vite de' Pittori, Scultori ed Architetti . . . in Roma, morti dal 1641 fino al 1673*, Rome, 1772 (modern ed., by J. Hess, Leipzig and Vienna, 1934)

PAUSANIAS
Pausanias, *Description of Greece*, written about AD 150. Several eds. published in Italy in the sixteenth century, e.g. Venice, 1516; Mantua, 1593. English trans. in the Loeb Greek/English ed. and by P. Levi in Penguin Classics, London, 1971

PERTZ, *Monum.*
Monumenta Germaniae Historia, ed. G. Pertz, T. Mommsen et al., Hannover and Berlin, 1826 onwards (index vol., 1890)

PII II *Comment.*
Pope Pius II Piccolomini, *Commentarii rerum memorabilium . . .* Rome, 1584 and 1589, and Frankfurt, 1614: this was probably the ed. used by Burckhardt, rather than the *Opera Omnia*, Basle, 1551. The textual history of the *Commentarii* is very muddled. There is a partial Eng. trans. in F. Gragg and L. Gabel, *Memoirs of a Renaissance Pope*, New York, 1959, which contains the main description of Pienza (in Bk IX)

PIUS II (A. Sylvius)
Pius II, *Opera Omnia* (including *Europa*), Basel, 1551

PLATINA, *De vitis Pontiff.*
B. Platina, *De vitis summorum pontificum opus*, Venice, 1479, and later eds. (also in Muratori, new ed., Vol. III)

PLATINA, *Vita Nichol. V.* see above

PLATINAE CONTINUATOR see PANVINIUS

PLINY, *H.N.*
Pliny the Elder, *Historia Naturalis*. See K. Jex-Blake and E. Sellers, *The Elder Pliny's Chapters on the History of Art*, London, 1896

PLINY, *Letters*
C. Plinius Caecilius Secundus (Pliny the Younger), *Epistolae*
Many fifteenth- and sixteenth-century Italian eds., e.g. Naples, 1476. Many English trans., e.g. by B. Radice in Penguin Classics, London, 1963

POGGIO, *Dialogus de Nobilitate*
Poggio, *Opera*, Argentorati (i.e. Strasbourg), 1513

POGGIUS, *Hist. flor. populi*
Poggio, *Opera* as above, or *Opera*, Basle, 1538 (reprint, Turin, 1963–) and Italian ed. as *Historia Fiorentina*, Venice, 1476, and later eds.

POLIPHILUS
Hypnerotomachia Poliphili, Venice, 1499, ascribed to Fra F. Colonna. Several modern facsimile eds., including London, 1963

POLITIANI, *Carmina*
A. Poliziano, *Omnia Opera*, Venice, 1498. The *Carmina* are also printed in the Florence, 1867 ed.

[JOVIAN.] PONTAN. *De magnificentia*
G. Pontano (Jov. Pontanus), *Opera*, Venice, 1512 and later. Burckhardt also quotes from his *De splendore* and *De conviventia*

PONTAN. *Charon*
G. Pontano, *Dialogus qui Charon inscribitur*, Naples, 1491 (and see above)

PROMIS, *Trattato . . . F. di Giorgio*
C. Promis, *Vita di Francesco di Giorgio Martini, aggiuntovi il catalogo de' Codici*, Turin, 1841: see FRANCESCO

Q

QUATREMÈRE, ed. Longhena
A. Quatremère de Quincy, *Histoire de la vie . . . de Raphaël*, Paris, 1824; quoted from the Italian trans. by F. Longhena, Milan, 1829

R

RABELAIS, *Pantagruel*
F. Rabelais, *Pantagruel*, Paris, 1533. Modern ed., Paris, 1922, and many others including trans.

RACZYNSKI, *Les arts en Portugal*
A. Raczyński, *Les arts en Portugal*, Paris, 1846, but the quotation from F. de Hollanda, *Tractato de pintura antigua*, Lisbon, 1548, may be found in English in the trans. of Hollanda by A. Bell, London, 1928

RANKE, *Päpste*
L. von Ranke, *Die römischen Päpste*, 3 vols., Berlin, 1834–36, and many later eds.; English trans., London, 1840, and later versions

RAUMER, *Hohenstaufen*
F. L. Raumer, *Geschichte der Hohenstaufen und ihrer Zeit*, 6 vols., Leipzig, 1823–25 and later: English trans., Cambridge, 1897

V. REBER, *Kurfürst Max I v. B. als Gemäldesammler*
F. von Reber, *Kurfürst Maximilian I von Bayern als Gemäldesammler*, Munich, 1892 (offprint from Akademie der Wissenschaften zu München (Festrede))

REDTENBACHER, *B. Peruzzi und seine Werke*
R. Redtenbacher, *B. Peruzzi und seine Werke*, Leipzig, 1878–79 in the series Dohmes Kunst und Künstler, I, pt II

Rer. ital. script. see MURATORI

REUMONT, *Geschichte der Stadt Rom*
A. von Reumont, *Geschichte der Stadt Rom*, 3 vols., Berlin, 1867–70

RICCIO, *Gli artisti ed artefici*
M. Riccio, *Gli artisti ed artefici che lavorarono in Castelnuovo a tempo di Alfonso I e Ferrante I*, Naples, 1876

RICHTER, *Literary Works of Leonardo*
J. P. Richter, *The Literary Works of Leonardo da Vinci*, 2 vols., Oxford, 1880. See now the 3rd ed., with Commentary by C. Pedretti, 2 vols., London, 1969 and 2 vols., Comment., Oxford, 1977

ROSCOE, *Leone X*, ed. Bossi
W. Roscoe, *Life and Pontificate of Leo X*, 1st ed., 4 vols., Liverpool, 1805 and many later eds.: Burckhardt quotes from the enlarged Italian trans. by L. Bossi, 12 vols., Milan, 1816–17

ROSCOE, *Vita di Lorenzo de' Medici*
W. Roscoe, *The Life of Lorenzo de' Medici . . .*, 2 vols., Liverpool, 1795 (10th ed., London, 1895). Burckhardt quotes from the Italian trans., probably the 2nd, revised and enlarged, 4 vols., Pisa, 1816

DE ROSSI, *Inscriptiones christianae*
G. B. de' Rossi, *Inscriptiones Christianae urbis Romae . . .*, 2 vols., Rome, 1861–88 and Supplement, ed. J. Gatti, Rome, 1915

ROSSI, *Palazzi diversi nell' alma città di Roma*
G. B. de' Rossi, *Palazzi diversi nell' alma città di Roma et altre*, Rome, 1655(?). Another copy is dated 1665, so it is probable that it was one of the books of plates made up specially to customers' requirements: the copy cited by Burckhardt (§71) contained a plate of the Certosa at Pavia.

ROUAIX, *Les styles . . .*
P. Rouaix, *Les styles: 700 gravures classées par époques* . . . Paris (1885)

S

SABELLICUS, *De situ venetae urbis*
M. A. Coccius Sabellicus, *De situ urbis venetae*, Venice, 1495(?). Burckhardt quotes from the Venice, 1502, ed.

SACCHETTI, *Nov.*
F. Sacchetti, *Novelle*, written before 1400. Many modern eds.

SANNAZARO, *Eleg.* (or *Epigrammata*)
J. Sannazaro, *Opera omnia latine scripta*, Venice, 1535

SANSOVINO, *Venezia*
F. Sansovino, *Venetia città nobilissima et singolare descritta*, Venice, 1581 and many later eds.; reprinted in facsimile Farnborough, 1968, from the 1663 ed.

SANTI, *Federigo da Montefeltro*
G. Santi, *Cronaca rimata delle imprese del duca Federigo d' Urbino*, ed. H. Holtzinger, Stuttgart, 1897 (see also R. Papini, *Francesco di Giorgio*, Florence, 1946, for additional material)

SCAMOZZI, *Architettura*
V. Scamozzi, *Dell' idea dell' architettura universale*, Venice 1615 (facsimile reprint, 2 vols., Ridgewood, N.J., and London, 1964)

SCARDEONIUS, *De urbis Patav.* see GRAEVIUS, *Thesaurus*

SCHMARSOW, *Melozzo da Forlì*
A. Schmarsow, *Melozzo da Forlì*, Berlin, 1886

SCHÜTZ
A. Schütz, *Die Renaissance in Italien*, 4 vols., Hamburg, 1892–93 and later eds.

SERLIO, *Architettura*
S. Serlio, *Tutte l' opere d' architettura*, ed. D. Scamozzi, Venice, 1584. The various Books came out at intervals from 1537; a facsimile reprint of the 1619 ed. was published in London in 1964

SERLIO, *Extra Ordinem Liber*
S. Serlio, *Extra Ordinem Liber*, Lyons, 1551. This was an extra Book, first published in French, and then in Latin (Venice, 1568). For the bibliographical details of Serlio's treatise see W. Dinsmoor in *Art Bulletin*, XXIV, 1942. The unpublished original Book VI was published in 2 vols., Milan, 1966, and the Avery Ms. in New York has also been published (1978) but these were, of course, not known to Burckhardt

SILVANUS GERMANICUS, *In statuam Leonis X*
Caius Silvanus Germanicus, *In statuam Leonis X*, Rome, 1524

SPECULUM ROMANAE MAGNIFICENTIAE
A. Lafreri (Lafréry), *Speculum Romanae Magnificentiae* . . . Rome, 1575(?). About 118 engravings, variously made up, and issued 1548–61 and later

SPRINGER, *Bilder aus der neueren Kunstgeschichte*
A. Springer, *Bilder aus der neueren Kunstgeschichte*, 2 vols., 2nd ed., Bonn, 1886

SPRINGER, *Rafael und Michelangelo*
A. Springer, *Rafael und Michelangelo*, 2 vols., 2nd revised ed., Leipzig, 1883

STRACK, *Zentral- u. Kuppelkirchen*
H. Strack, *Zentral- und Kuppelkirchen der Renaissance in Italien*, Berlin, 1882

STROZZA, *Aeolosticha*
T. V. Strozzi (Strozzi poetae pater et filius), *Carmina*, Venice, 1513

A. SYLVIUS (*Aeneae Sylvii opera*) see PIUS II

T

TEMANZA, *Vite de' più celebri architetti*
T. Temanza, *Vite de' più celebri Architetti . . . Veneziani*, 2 vols., Venice, 1778

THEINER, *Cod. diplomat.*
A. Theiner, *Codex Diplomaticus Dominii Temporalis S. Sedis: Recueil de documents . . . des archives du Vatican*, 3 vols., Rome, 1861–62

TICOZZI, *Vite de' Pittori Vecellii*
S. Ticozzi, *Vite de' Pittori Vecellj di Cadore*, Milan, 1817

TICOZZI see also ALBERTI

TIRABOSCHI, *Storia*
G. Tiraboschi, *Storia della Letteratura Italiana*, 11 vols., Modena, 1772–95 and many other eds.

TOLOMEI, *Lettere* . . . 1589
C. Tolomei, *Delle Lettere Libri VII* . . . *Lettere, ove di cose Architettoniche, e Vitruviane si tratta*, Venice, 1547. (Burckhardt quotes from a later ed.)

U

UBERTI, *Il Dittamondo*
Fazio degli Uberti, *El libro* . . . *Dita mundi*, Vicenza, 1474, or *Ditta mundi*, Venice, 1501. Written 1350/67

URCEUS, *De renovatione Bonon.*
A. Urceus, called Codrus, *Orationes* . . ., Bologna, 1502. Burckhardt also quotes his *ad Lucam Ripam* and *Opera*, but they all seem to be the same

URLICHS, *Codex Topograph.*
C. Urlichs, *Codex urbis Romae topographicus*, Wirceburgi (i.e. Würzburg), 1871
URSTISIUS see WURSTISEN

V

della VALLE, *Lettere sanesi*
G. Della Valle, *Lettere sanesi*, 3 vols., Rome, 1782–86
della VALLE, *Storia . . . Orvieto*
G. Della Valle, *Storia del Duomo di Orvieto*, Rome, 1791
VARCHI, *Stor. fiorent.*
B. Varchi, *Storia fiorentina*. Burckhardt quotes from the 5-vol. ed., Milan, 1803; the book, written in the mid-sixteenth century, seems to have been published first at Cologne in 1721. Many later editions, e.g. by G. Milanesi, Florence, 1857
VASARI
G. Vasari, *Le Vite de' più Eccellenti Pittori Scultori ed Architettori*, Florence, 1568. Burckhardt does not quote from the first (1550) edition, and all quotations from the 2nd ed. are from the edition by G. Milanesi, 9 vols., Florence, 1878–85 (also available in a recent photographic reprint). The best modern ed. is that, still incomplete, by P. Barocchi and R. Bettarini (Florence, 1966–), but a useful modern ed., including much of the information in Milanesi's notes, was published by the Club del Libro, Milan, 1962–66, in 9 vols. ed. by P. Della Pergola, L. Grassi and G. Previtali. The usual English trans. is that by G. de Vere, 10 vols., London, 1912–15
VENUTI, *Numismata romanorum pontificum*
R. Venuti, *Numismata romanorum pontificum praestantiora a Martino V. ad Benedictum XIV.*, Rome, 1744
VERRI, *Storia di Milano*
P. Verri, *Storia di Milano*, 2 vols., Milan, 1783–98, and later eds.
VESPASIANO FIORENTINO
Vespasiano da Bisticci, *Vite di uomini illustri del Secolo XV*, written at the end of the fifteenth century, first printed in Mai (q.v.), 1839; modern ed. by P. D'Ancona and E. Aeschlimann, Milan, 1951: English trans. by W. and E. Waters, London, 1926 (and later)
VILLANI, F. *Le Vite*
F. Villani, *De origine civitatis Florentiae et eiusdem famosis civibus* (*c* 1400); in Italian, *Le vite d' uomini illustri fiorentini*, Florence, 1747 and 1826; in Latin, Florence, 1847 and 1887
VILLANI, G. (*d* 1348)
G. Villani, *Chroniche*, Venice, 1537; 8 vols., Florence, 1823, and other nineteenth-cent. eds. Partial English trans. from the first nine books, by R. Selfe and P. Wicksteed, London, 1896
VILLANI, M. (*d* 1363)
M. Villani, *Croniche di Giovanni, Matteo e Filippo Villani*, 2 vols., Trieste, 1857–58, and other eds.
VITAE PAPARUM see PLATINA
VITRUVIUS (VITRUV.)
M. Vitruvius Pollio, *De architectura libri X*
Where Burckhardt specifies the Barbaro ed. he quotes from *I Dieci Libri Dell' Architettura . . . Tradutti et Commentati da Monsignor Barbaro . . .*, Venice, 1556 (and later), with illustrations by Palladio. The editions usually cited by writers in English are: W. Morgan, Cambridge (Mass.), 1914 (in English only), or the Latin/English Loeb ed., by F. Granger, 2 vols., London, 1931–34

W

WINCKELMANN, *Anmerkungen über d. Baukunst . . .*
J. Winckelmann, *Anmerkungen über die Baukunst der Alten*, Leipzig, 1761
WURSTISEN
C. Wurstisen (Wursteisen, Urstisius), *Epitome Historiae Basiliensis*, Basle, 1577, or *Basler-Chronik*, Basel, 1580, or *Germaniae Historicorum Illustrium*, Frankfurt, 1585 (including O. de S. BLASIO)

Z

ZEISING, *Neue Lehre v. d. Proportionen*
A. Zeising, *Neue Lehre von den Proportionen des menschlichen Körpers . . .*, Leipzig, 1854

List of Illustrations

1 *Pisa, Cathedral and Leaning Tower*
2 *Civita Castellana, Cathedral*
3 *Rome, S. Paolo fuori le Mura, cloister*
4 *Florence, S. Miniato al Monte*
5 *Florence, Baptistry*
6 *Florence, Baptistry, interior*
7 *Florence, Cathedral, interior*
8 *Orvieto, Cathedral*
9 *Bologna, S. Petronio, plan*
10 *B. Peruzzi, design for the façade of S. Petronio, Bologna*
11 *Florence, Palazzo Vecchio*
12 *Milan, Cathedral roof and* tiburio
13 *Imaginary building from the* Hypnerotomachia Poliphili
14 *Arezzo, Sta Maria, loggia*
15 *Florence, Sta Croce, detail of cloister*
16 *Florence, Sta Croce, Pazzi Chapel*
17 *Vicenza, the Basilica, elevation and section*
18 *Genoa, Palazzo Sauli, detail*
19 *Siena, Chiesa dei Servi, details*
20 *Fiesole, Badia, details*
21 *Florence, Palazzo Pazzi-Quaratesi, detail of capital*
22 *Mantua, Sant' Andrea, tomb of Piero Strozzi*
23 *Rome, Palazzo Venezia, court*
24 *Florence, Palazzo Medici-Riccardi, angle*
25 *Florence, Palazzo Pitti*
26 *Florence, Palazzo Strozzi, elevation*
27 *Siena, Palazzo Spannocchi, elevation*
28 *Florence, Palazzo Pazzi-Quaratesi*
29 *Florence, Palazzo Guadagni*
30 *Rome, Palazzo Venezia*
31 *Florence, Palazzo di Parte Guelfa (before reconstruction)*
32 *Florence, Palazzo Rucellai, elevation*
33 *Pienza, Palazzo Piccolomini, elevation*
34 *Rome, Palazzo della Cancelleria, detail of elevation*
35 *Rome, Palazzo Giraud-Torlonia*
36 *Naples, Palazzo Cuomo*
37 *Bologna, Palazzo Bevilacqua*
38 *Ferrara, Palazzo dei Diamanti*
39 *Perugino,* Miracle of S. Bernardino of Siena, *dated 1473, Perugia, Pinacoteca*
40 *Venice, S. Zaccaria*
41 *Venice, Sta Maria de' Miracoli*
42 *Venice, Palazzo Corner-Spinelli*
43 *Venice, Palazzo Vendramin-Calergi, elevation*
44 *Venice, Scuola di S. Marco*
45 *Bologna, Palazzo Fava, elevation*
46 *Bologna, details of a palace*
47 *Pavia, Certosa, court*
48 *Pavia, Certosa, court, detail*
49 *Bologna, Palazzo Fava, court*
50 *Bologna, Palazzo Bevilacqua, court elevation*
51 *Ferrara, Palazzo Scrofa, court*
52 *Milan, Sta Maria delle Grazie*
53 *Crema, Madonna della Croce, elevation*
54 *Urbino, S. Domenico, portal*
55 *Florence, Sta Croce, door*
56 *Florence, Cathedral*
57 *Florence, Sta Croce, Pazzi Chapel, detail of the loggia*
58 *Perugia, S. Bernardino*
59 *Florence, Palazzo Bartolini, elevation*

60 *Rome, S. Pietro in Montorio, the Tempietto, elevation*
61 *Venice, Biblioteca Marciana*
62 *Florence, Palazzo Uguccioni, elevation*
63 *Venice, La Zecca (The Mint), elevation*
64 *Florence, Biblioteca Laurenziana, vestibule*
65 *Rome, Benediction Loggia of the Lateran*
66 *Florence, original project for the Uffizi (Gurlitt)*
67 *Florence, Palazzo Pitti, garden façade*
68 *Milan, Palazzo Arcivescovile, court*
69 *Genoa, Sta Maria delle Vigne, interior*
70 *Bramante's plan for St Peter's*
71 *Rome, S. Pietro in Montorio, the Tempietto*
72 *Rome, St Peter's, based on Michelangelo's design*
73 *Vicenza, Villa Rotonda*
74 *Florence, Palazzo Strozzi, detail*
75 *Rome, Palazzo Massimi, detail*
76 *Florence, Palazzo Bartolini, detail*
77 *Florence, Palazzo Pandolfini, detail*
78 *Diagram of door-frame*
79 *Diagram of window proportions*
80 *Diagram of window proportions*
81 *Florence, Palazzo Pitti, detail*
82 *Florence, Palazzo Strozzi, detail*
83 *Florence, Palazzo Guadagni, detail*
84 *Rome, Villa Farnesina, detail*
85 *Diagram of arch, from Palladio*
86 *Vicenza, the Basilica*
87 *Rome, Palazzo Massimi, detail of Salone*
88 *Diagram of mouldings*
89 *Model of S. Petronio, Bologna*
90 *Model of Pavia Cathedral*
91 *Florence, Sta Maria degli Angeli, plan*
92 *Florence, Sta Croce, Pazzi Chapel, plan*
93 *Florence, Sta Croce, Pazzi Chapel, transverse section*
94 *Florence, Sta Croce, Pazzi Chapel, longitudinal section*
95 *Florence, SS. Annunziata, interior*
96 *Prato, Madonna delle Carceri, section*
97 *Montepulciano, Madonna di S. Biagio, plan*
98 *Montepulciano, Madonna di S. Biagio, elevation*
99 *Pistoia, Madonna dell' Umiltà, section*
100 *Pistoia, Madonna dell' Umiltà, plan*
101 *Venice, S. Giovanni Crisostomo, section*
102 *Venice, S. Giovanni Crisostomo, plan*
103 *Brescia, Sta Maria de' Miracoli, section*
104 *Brescia, Sta Maria de' Miracoli, plan*
105 *Brescia, Sta Maria de' Miracoli, section*
106 *Pavia, Sta Maria di Canepanova, plan*
107 *Pavia, Sta Maria di Canepanova, elevation detail*
108 *Rome, S. Pietro in Montorio, plan of the Tempietto*
109 *Rome, St Peter's, Bramante's first project*
110 *Rome, St Peter's, Peruzzi's plan*
111 *Rome, St Peter's, Raphael's plan, from Serlio*
112 *Rome, St Peter's, Michelangelo's plan*
113 *Rome, St Peter's, drawing by Dupérac based on Michelangelo's design for the façade*
114 *Rome, St Peter's, elevation and section of the dome*
115 *Todi, Sta Maria della Consolazione, plan*
116 *Todi, Sta Maria della Consolazione, section*
117 *Piacenza, Madonna di Campagna*
118 *Verona, S. Bernardino, Cappella Pellegrini, section*
119 *Verona, S. Bernardino, Cappella Pellegrini, plan*
120 *Verona, Madonna di Campagna, plan*
121 *Verona, Madonna di Campagna, section detail*
122 *Milan, Sta Maria della Passione, plan*
123 *Riva, Sta Croce, plan*
124 *Riva, Sta Croce, section*
125 *Genoa, Madonna di Carignano, plan*
126 *Genoa, Madonna di Carignano, section*
127 *Rimini, S. Francesco ('Tempio Malatestiano')*
128 *Mantua, Sant' Andrea*
129 *Florence, Sta Maria Novella*
130 *Pienza, Cathedral, elevation*
131 *Bologna, Madonna di Galliera, elevation*
132 *Rome, Sta Maria dell' Anima*
133 *Siena, Sta Caterina, elevation*
134 *Siena, Sta Maria delle Nevi, elevation*
135 *Rome, S. Marco (Palazzo Venezia)*
136 *Spoleto, Cathedral loggia, plan and elevation*
137 *Rome, Sta Maria in Navicella (in Domnica), elevation*
138 *Pavia, Certosa*
139 *Lugano, Cathedral*
140 *Venice, S. Giorgio Maggiore*
141 *Venice, Il Redentore*
142 *Rome, Sta Maria de' Monti, elevation*
143 *Florence, S. Lorenzo, section*
144 *Florence, S. Lorenzo, plan*
145 *Florence, S. Lorenzo, interior*
146 *Florence, Sto Spirito, plan*
147 *Venice, S. Zaccaria, interior*
148 *Siena, Sta Maria de' Servi, plan*
149 *Siena, Sta Maria de' Servi, section*
150 *Florence, S. Francesco al Monte, interior*
151 *Mantua, Sant' Andrea, interior*
152 *Mantua, Sant' Andrea, plan*
153 *Cortona, Sta Maria del Calcinaio, section*

154 *Cortona, Sta Maria del Calcinaio, plan*
155 *Cortona, Sta Maria del Calcinaio, elevation*
156 *Milan, S. Maurizio (Monastero Maggiore), arcade*
157 *Padua, Il Carmine, detail*
158 *Padua, Il Carmine, plan*
159 *Rome, Il Gesù, plan*
160 *Rome, Sta Maria de' Monti, section*
161 *Rome, Sta Maria de' Monti, plan*
162 *Pavia, Cathedral, plan*
163 *Pavia, Cathedral, octagon*
164 *Parma, S. Giovanni, plan*
165 *Parma, S. Giovanni, transverse section*
166 *Parma, S. Giovanni, longitudinal section*
167 *Arezzo, SS. Annunziata, plan*
168 *Arezzo, SS. Annunziata, interior*
169 *Rome, S. Lorenzo in Damaso, section*
170 *Padua, Sta Giustina, section*
171 *Padua, Sta Giustina, plan*
172 *Venice, S. Salvatore, section*
173 *Venice, S. Salvatore, plan*
174 *Mantua, Cathedral, interior*
175 *Venice, S. Giorgio Maggiore, interior*
176 *Ferrara, Cathedral campanile*
177 *Rome, Sto Spirito, campanile*
178 *Florence, S. Lorenzo, Old Sacristy, section*
179 *Milan, S. Eustorgio, chapel elevation*
180 *Venice, Sta Maria de' Miracoli, interior*
181 *Florence, Sto Spirito, Sacristy, section*
182 *Florence, Sto Spirito, Sacristy, plan*
183 *Milan, S. Satiro, Sacristy: detail*
184 *Florence, S. Lorenzo, Medici Chapel, section*
185 *Rome, Sta Maria del Popolo, Chigi Chapel*
186 *Siena, Cathedral, Cappella di S. Giovanni*
187 *Florence, S. Lorenzo, detail of side elevation*
188 *Rome, Sta Maria della Pace, section and elevation of cloister*
189 *Rome, Sta Maria della Pace, plan of church and cloister*
190 *B. Peruzzi, design for a cloister*
191 *Rome, Sant' Ivo della Sapienza, court*
192 *Rome, Sant' Ivo della Sapienza, plan*
193 *Milan, Palazzo di Brera, court*
194 *Genoa, the University, court*
195 *Siena, Sta Caterina, court*
196 *Venice, Scuola di S. Rocco, elevation*
197 *Venice, Scuola di S. Rocco, plan*
198 *Florence, Palazzo Medici-Riccardi, section*
199 *Florence, Palazzo Medici-Riccardi, plan*
200 *Pienza, plan of Cathedral and palaces in centre*
201 *Florence, Palazzo Gondi, court*
202 *Florence, Palazzo Serristori, elevation*
203 *Urbino, Palazzo Ducale, court*
204 *Urbino, Palazzo Ducale, plan*
205 *Bologna, Palazzo Pizzardi, plan*
206 *Bologna, plan of house near Palazzo Pepoli*
207 *Bologna, Palazzo Fantuzzi, plan*
208 *Ferrara, Palazzo Scrofa, plan*
209 *Verona, Palazzo Bevilacqua*
210 *Verona, Palazzo Pompei, elevation*
211 *Florence, Palazzo Pandolfini, elevation*
212 *Rome, Palazzo Farnese, elevation detail*
213 *Rome, Palazzo Sciarra, elevation detail*
214 *Rome, Palazzo Caprini (House of Raphael), elevation detail*
215 *Rome, Palazzo Vidoni-Caffarelli, elevation*
216 *Rome, former Palazzo Branconio d' Aquila (after Geymüller)*
217 *Rome, Palazzo Spada*
218 *Rome, Palazzo Farnese, detail of court elevation*
219 *Rome, Palazzo della Cancelleria, court detail*
220 *Rome, former small Palazzo di Venezia, court detail*
221 *Rome, Palazzo Linotte*
222 *Rome, Vatican, transverse section of the great court in its original state*
223 *Rome, Palazzo Massimi, court*
224 *Design for a façade (I), from Serlio*
225 *Design for a façade (II), from Serlio*
226 *Design for a façade (III), from Serlio*
227 *Design for a façade (IV), from Serlio*
228 *Rome, Vatican, Sala Regia*
229 *Brescia, Palazzo Comunale, elevation*
230 *Verona, Loggia del Consiglio, elevation*
231 *Padua, Loggia del Consiglio, elevation*
232 *Lucca, Palazzo del Pretorio*
233 *Pienza, Palazzo del Pretorio*
234 *Vicenza, the Basilica*
235 *Florence, Loggia de' Lanzi*
236 *Siena, Loggia degli Uniti*
237 *Piacenza, Palazzo Farnese, elevation detail*
238 *Vicenza, Palazzo Valmarana*
239 *Vicenza, Palazzo Porto-Barbaran*
240 *Vicenza, Palazzo Chiericati*
241 *Bologna, Palazzo Malvezzi-Medici, elevation detail*
242 *Bologna, Palazzo Fantuzzi, elevation detail*
243 *Vicenza, Palazzo Thiene-Bonin-Longara, court*
244 *Milan, Palazzo Marino, court*
245 *Genoa, Palazzo Sauli, former court*

246 *Florence, Loggia degli Innocenti and Piazza di SS. Annunziata*
247 *Pistoia, Ospedale del Ceppo*
248 *Naples, Porta Capuana*
249 *Perugia, Porta S. Pietro*
250 *Naples, triumphal arch of Alfonso of Aragon*
251 *Verona, Porta S. Zeno, elevation*
252 *Rome, Porta Pia*
253 *Florence, Ponte Sta Trinità*
254 *Plan of Pienza*
255 *Rome, Vatican gardens, Casino di Pio IV*
256 *Rome, Villa Madama, section through the Villa and court*
257 *Rome, Villa Madama, section through the garden*
258 *Villa near Florence (I)*
259 *Villa near Florence (II)*
260 *Castello, Villa Cavacchia, near Florence*
261 *Mantua, Palazzo del Te, loggia*
262 *Pesaro, Villa Imperiale, plan*
263 *Pesaro, Villa Imperiale, plan*
264 *Pesaro, Villa Imperiale, elevation*
265 *Pesaro, Villa Imperiale, section*
266 *Caprarola, near Viterbo, Villa Farnese, plan and section*
267 *Rome, Villa Giulia*
268 *Rome, Villa Giulia, garden*
269 *Tivoli, Villa d'Este*
270 *Vicenza, Villa Rotonda, elevation and section*
271 *Rome, Villa Medici*
272 *Lugano Cathedral, marble decoration*
273 *Rome, Sta Maria del Popolo, marble frieze*
274 *Lucca Cathedral, tomb of Ilaria del Carretto*
275 *Siena, Casino de' Nobili, balustrade*
276 *Florence, Sta Croce, detail of Marsuppini Tomb*
277 *Florence, Sta Croce, pulpit*
278 *Florence, Bargello, relief by the Della Robbia School*
279 *Urbino, Ducal Palace, chimneypiece*
280 *Genoa, Palazzo Pallavicino, doorway (1503) by Michele and Antonio Carleone, now in Victoria and Albert Museum, London*
281 *Milan, Ospedale Maggiore, detail of façade*
282 *Pavia, the Certosa, window*
283 *Como Cathedral, portal*
284 *Brescia, Palazzo Comunale, a capital*
285 *Milan, S. Satiro, detail of pilaster*
286 *Milan, S. Satiro, sacristy*
287 *Rome, Sta Maria del Popolo, tomb of Cardinal de Castro*
288 *Florence, S. Miniato al Monte, tomb of the Cardinal of Portugal*
289 *Rome, Sta Maria della Pace, Ponzetti Tomb*
290 *Venice, SS. Giovanni e Paolo, tomb of Doge A. Vendramin*
291 *Venice, SS. Giovanni e Paolo, Mocenigo Tomb*
292 *Rome, Sta Maria del Popolo, tomb of Cardinal Ascanio Sforza*
293 *Venice, S. Marco, the Zeno Altar*
294 *Siena, Fontegiusta, the High Altar*
295 *Rome, Vatican, Sistine Chapel, gallery*
296 *Bologna, S. Petronio, chapel screen*
297 *Perugia Cathedral, pulpit*
298 *Siena Cathedral, holy water basin*
299 *Orvieto Cathedral, holy water basin*
300 *Venice, Doge's Palace, chimneypiece*
301 *Florence, Baptistry, detail from Ghiberti's second door*
302 *Florence, Palazzo Strozzi, lantern*
303 *Florence, Palazzo Strozzi, torch-holder*
304 *Venice, Sta Maria della Salute, Easter candlestick*
305 *Venice, Piazza S. Marco, socket for banners*
306 *Padua, bronze voting-urn*
307 *Siena Cathedral, ciborium*
308 *Siena Cathedral, bronze ring for torches or banners*
309 *Bologna, door-knocker*
310 *Orvieto Cathedral, choir-stall*
311 *Verona, Sta Maria in Organo, choir-stall*
312 *Parma, S. Giovanni, choir-stall*
313 *Pisa Cathedral, choir-stall*
314 *Bergamo, Sta Maria Maggiore, choir-stall*
315 *Palermo, S. Martino, choir-stall*
316 *Siena, Sta Maria della Scala, organ loft*
317 *Rome, Sta Maria sopra Minerva, organ*
318 *Giovanni Bellini, altarpiece in Sta Maria dei Frari, Venice*
319 *Berlin, Kunstgewerbemuseum, a chest*
320 *Florence, Uffizi, design for a harp*
321 *Rome, Palazzo Massimi, ceiling*
322 *Ceiling design (I), from Serlio*
323 *Ceiling design (II), from Serlio*
324 *Siena Cathedral, detail of floor*
325 *Florence, Laurenziana Library, floor*
326 *Florence,* sgraffiti *on a façade*
327 *Florence,* sgraffiti *on a façade*
328 *Rome, façade in via Sta Lucia*
329 *Rome, painted façade in via Giulia*
330 *Rome, Palazzo della Cancelleria, papal arms*
331 *Milan, Monastero Maggiore, detail of pilaster*
332 *Rome, Vatican, Stanza della Segnatura*

333 *Rome, Vatican, Sistine Chapel, diagram of decoration*
334 *Rome, Vatican, the Loggie*
335 *Rome, Vatican, the Loggie, detail*
336 *Rome, Villa Farnesina, loggia*
337 *Genoa, Palazzo Doria, detail*
338 *Rome, Palazzo della Cancelleria, chapel, detail*
339 *Rome, Palazzo della Cancelleria, chapel, mouldings*
340 *Venice, S. Marco, hanging lamp*
341 *Naples, onyx vase*
342 *Naples, maiolica plate*
343 *Naples, maiolica plate*
344 *Vicenza, Teatro Olimpico, plan*
345 *Serlio, design for a theatre, plan and perspective*
346 *Serlio, design for a theatre, section*
347 *Serlio, comic scene*
348 *Serlio, tragic scene*
349 *Peruzzi, drawing for a stage scene, Florence, Uffizi*
350 *Serlio, satyric scene*
351 *Vicenza, Teatro Olimpico,* scena

Credits

The publishers would like to thank the following sources of illustration: Archivi Alinari: Figs. 21, 22, 65, 68, 69, 232, 235, 236, 239, 248, 268, 302, 325, 340, 349; British Museum: 10; Conway Librarian, Courtauld Institute of Art: 95, 176, 287, 292; Electa editrice: 243; Mansell/Alinari: 1, 7, 23, 31, 38, 47, 140, 141, 151, 174, 175, 180, 193, 201, 238, 240, 242, 244, 247, 274, 279, 303, 318, 351; Mansell/Anderson: 2, 4, 8, 12, 30, 35, 36, 40, 42, 44, 127, 128, 129, 132, 203, 249, 252, 271; Mansell Collection: 3, 11, 29, 58, 138, 228, 286; Crown copyright, Victoria and Albert Museum: 51, 89, 280.

BOOK ONE

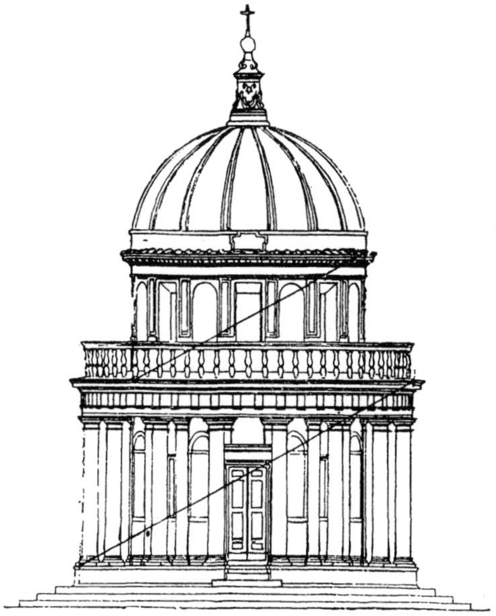

Architecture

CHAPTER ONE

The Monumental Temper of Italian Architecture

§ 1 *The Cult of Fame and Pious Foundations*

From the dawn of a higher culture in Italy, architecture was essentially dependent upon the sense of individuality among both patrons and artists, which developed here much earlier than anywhere else. Linked to this there grew up a strong and modern sense of personal fame, which sought not only to compete with rivals, but also to be markedly different from them. This is testified to by a number of early records, which are lacking in the North.

In the North there are only a few building accounts and some Indulgences, whereas in Italy there are inscriptions, chronicles and documents, some with partisan details that provide evidence about attitudes as well as facts. This monumental feeling for architecture, sometimes inclining towards the imposing, sometimes towards the handsome or elegant, remained one of the first, mostly firmly entrenched, and vital influences on the whole period from the eleventh to the sixteenth centuries, and accompanied the attempt to revive the architecture of Antiquity in the twelfth, the adoption of Gothic from the thirteenth, and the Renaissance from the fifteenth centuries, as a constant, overriding force.

In the building of churches the demands of piety had naturally to be met; its visible expression – indulgences, alms and offerings – was essential even for cathedrals, while it was the most important source of money for the churches of the monastic Orders. In Italy, however, indulgences had political boundaries; although the northern cathedrals had allowed collections for their building funds to be made outside their own jurisdiction, the people of Pisa, Bologna, Siena, Florence, or Venice would have thought it very strange if any one of these cities had tried anything similar. When a Bishop of Fiesole tried to raise money from his clergy for the building of Florence Cathedral the dissident priests at once appealed to the Pope; Guasti, *Sta Maria del Fiore*, p. 18, document of 1299. Indulgence of Boniface IX for the building of Milan Cathedral (1391), equating the visiting of the five principal churches of the city with that of the Roman patriarchal basilicas – highly remunerative; Corio, *Storia di Milano*, fol. 269. Similarly, the yearly offering for Corpus Christi; Petri Candidi Decembrii, *Vita Phil. Mariae Vicecom.*, in Muratori, *Rer. ital. script.*, vol. XX, col. 998.

The Festa del Perdono in Milan, first celebrated in 1460, allocated the proceeds in alternate years to the great Hospital and to the Cathedral fabric; W. von Oettingen, *Über das Leben . . . des Antonio Averlino, genannt Filarete*, p. 31.

Huge collections at individual pilgrimage centres, gifts from mixed companies of pilgrims, the annual pilgrimage to the tomb of S. Anthony at Padua (which often realised up to 400 gold florins); M. Savonarola, *De laudibus Patavii* in Muratori, XXIV, col. 1148 (written after 1445).

In Venice, Sta Maria de' Miracoli was built in 1480 from a purely local and rapid collection of 30,000 ducats; S. Giovanni Crisostomo in 1497, largely from the proceeds of indulgences; Malipiero, *Ann. Veneti*, Archivio storico., VII, II, p. 705.

In times of crisis there were especially numerous pious foundations and rebuildings of churches and monasteries – e.g. at the end of the fifteenth century in Perugia; Matarazzo, *Cronaca*.. Arch. stor., XVI, II, p. 6. Oblations were sometimes only apparently voluntary – *Diario Ferrarese* in Muratori, XXIV, col. 197, prescribing them from 1451 for the campanile of Ferrara Cathedral.

§ 2 *The Florentine Concept of Architecture*

In the independent cities municipal pride was, above all, to find satisfaction in an imposing cathedral and in outdoing the neighbouring cities. Simple devotion, subject to ups and downs, gave way to state decisions and taxes.

This approach was unknown in the eleventh century in Venice and Pisa, but in 1153 the costs of the Baptistry at Pisa were covered by a municipal levy and, according to tradition, columns, pillars and arches were erected in the space of fifteen days; Vasari, I, p. 239, Proemio cap. XIV.* Arezzo resolved, having spent on wars the legacy left by Gregory X (*d* 1276) for the building of the cathedral, that all future revenue from specified fines should be spent on this project; Vasari, I, p. 364, n. 3, *Vita di Margaritone.*

In particular, the Florentine state and all its official bodies seized the opportunity of proclaiming its sense of monumental glory, in writing, by praise of the artists, and in every other way.

In March, 1294, the city decided, after months of vociferous discussions, that the old cathedral of Sta Reparata should not simply be restored, but must be replaced by a new building, expenditure for this being "in honour and praise of God and of the Blessed Virgin Mary, and to the honour of the community and people of Florence and the adornment of this city". These words became a standard form in documents authorising expenditure; Guasti, *Sta Maria del Fiore*, p. 2 ff. for examples.

Arnolfo, to whose plan work was begun in 1296, was commended in a document of 1 April, 1300, which ensured his exemption from taxes, as a master who was more famous and skilled in church-building than any other in the region; by his industry, artistry and genius Florence hoped, after the already visible splendid start to the work, to possess a more worthy and glorious temple than any other in Tuscany. A commercial duty, an annual poll-tax, and other burdens were agreed to; Guasti, op. cit., p. XL ff. When building restarted after a long interruption, in the auspicious year of 1331, a quota of the customs duties and taxes was added to the existing taxes and in every booth a little collecting-box was placed for "God's money", G. Villani, X, cap. 194.

Because the cathedral was regarded as supreme for many generations the tremendous pressure for its completion could and had to be concentrated in a Florentine – Brunellesco. "Two great things he took upon himself from the start: the re-awakening of good architecture and the construction of the dome of Sta Maria del Fiore" Vasari, II, p. 337.

Giotto's appointment as architect to the cathedral and the city in 1334, fervently acclaimed as the foremost artist in the world; Gaye, *Carteggio*, I, p. 481; Guasti, op. cit., p. 43.

By its ugliness an old building may be a disgrace to the town, while a new one should redound to its honour and ornament. This was claimed, among other things, as a reason for the new building of Orsanmichele in 1336; Gaye, *Carteggio*, I, p. 46. G. Villani, XI, cap. 67 and 93. The niches in the various piers were handed over to the Guilds for decoration. The gold and silver medals placed under the foundation stone bore the inscription: *ut magnificentia populi florent. artium et artificum ostendatur.*

The building of a new monastic church was furthered by a particularly revered Lenten preacher appealing to the conscience of the eminent and rich citizens of the district. Antonio Manetti, *Vita di Brunellesco*, ed. Holzinger, p. 57, on the incentive for building Sto Spirito, 1428.†

In whatever hands the state might find itself, the highest ambitions were always centred in public works, but less came to be said about it, simply because it was self-evident.

The Florentine theorist Leon Battista Alberti, about 1450, ascribed the greatness of power of ancient Rome in large measure to its buildings, citing Thucydides, who rightly praised the Athenians for seeming, on account of their fortifications, mightier than they were. *Arte edificatoria*, Introd. (*Opere volgari*, IV, p. 198).

Antonio Manetti, who, after 1471, wrote the life of his compatriot Brunellesco, considered that in ancient times men turned to the erection of magnificent buildings to acquire fame, demonstrate splendour, and arouse admiration; but also to live in comfort and security, guarding their treasures. The latter practical objectives are characteristically placed after the first ones; Manetti, op. cit., p. 20.

The great Medici, when they subordinated the power of the state to themselves, knew that in doing so they assumed a public obligation to build. Cosimo (*d* 1464) wanted to give employment to many, paid generously and promptly, rejoiced that the money remained in the city, and regretted only that he had not started building ten years earlier. His entire outlay on building, alms, and taxes amounted to 400,000 gold florins, according to the authentic account in Fabroni, *Laurent. Med. magnif. vita*, Adnot. 2 and 25. Higher, but exaggerated, estimates in Campani, *Vita Pii II* in Murat. III, II, col. 976, and in Vespasiano Fiorentino, pp. 332–38; apposite here also Cosimo's prediction: in fifty years the sole surviving part of the possessions and splendour of the House of Medici would be what he had built. Cf. also Jovian. Pontan. *De magnificentia*. The comment of Cosimo's son Piero on the Badia at Fiesole – whatever money we spend on this building is covered *extra petulantiam ludumque fortunae*; cf. Matteo Bossi in Roscoe, *Vita di Lorenzo de' Medici*, IV, appendix 5. The overall costs of the Badia

* Burckhardt originally quoted Vasari from the Le Monnier edition, Florence, 1846 ff. In later editions references to the great nine-volume edition by Gaetano Milanesi were added (Florence, 1878–85) and these have been given here, as the standard modern edition: the splendid Edizione Nazionale, by P. Barocchi and R. Bettarini (Florence, 1966–), has, unfortunately, not yet been completed. For an English translation see the Bibliography, s.v. Vasari. (PM).

† Burckhardt quoted the *Vita di Brunellesco* as by Manetti "even if the authorship . . . has recently become subject to doubt". It now seems clear that Manetti was, in fact, the author of the *Anonymous Life* – see the recent Italian ed. by D. De Robertis and G. Tanturli, Milan, 1976, and the English translation, with Introduction by H. Saalman, Pennsylvania State Univ. Press, 1970 (the passage in question occurs on p. 122 of this ed.) (PM).

rose to 70,000 gold florins; Fabriczy, *Filippo Brunelleschi*, p. 274. Lorenzo il Magnifico, Piero's son, faced with the prodigious cost, was pleased that the money would be so well spent; cf. *Kultur der Renaissance*, 3rd ed., I, p. 78 and p. 139; 4th ed. p. 79 f. That these three men regarded the building of churches and monasteries as perhaps a politically safer investment than money, was suggested by Alessandro de' Pazzi, see Archiv. stor., I, p. 422. The renown of the Medici buildings under Lorenzo – M. Bossi, op. cit.

The Venetians were well aware of this, and for this reason forbade Cosimo during his exile (1433) there to build the façade of S. Giorgio Maggiore. Sansovino, *Venezia*, fol. 81.

In what terms the Florentine state used its influence outside on behalf of other Florentine artists, e.g. for a sculptor in 1461 see Gaye, *Carteggio*, I, p. 196.

(NOTE: For the buildings of Cosimo de' Medici, see also A. D. Fraser Jenkins, *Cosimo de' Medici's Patronage of Architecture and the Theory of Magnificence*, in Journal of the Warburg and Courtauld Institutes, XXXIII, 1970.) (PM).

§ 3 *The Sienese Concept of Architecture*

The architectural ambition of Siena often assumed an impassioned character in official utterances and looked uneasily outwards. A separate "beautifying" authority watched over street improvements. Petitions from citizens concerning architectural and artistic matters were far from rare. Cf. Milanesi, *Documenti per la Storia dell' Arte Senese*, especially I, pp. 161–4, 180 f., 188, 193; II, pp. 39, 183, 301, 337, 339, 345, 353; III, pp. 100 f., 139, 273, 275, 280, 310 and elsewhere. Allegretto, *Diarii Sanesi* in Murat., XXIII, col. 770 ff.

The stoppage of work on the cathedral was called a disgrace; in 1298 work recommenced with municipal support; the so-called new cathedral was declared in 1321 to be *ecclesia pulcra, magna et magnifica*. The former cathedral sacristy, fitting "for a village church", was described in 1407 as an insult to the town. A citizens' petition of 1389 for the completion of the cathedral and the addition of a Campo Santo of the type at Pisa, which would be one of the noblest sacred structures in all Christendom.

Already in 1286 the Franciscans were demanding, almost defiantly, the city's aid for a façade, because it did Siena no honour when eminent foreign ecclesiastical and secular deputations came and saw the temporary one, "the thing of brick and mortar". In 1329 a state grant to the Carmelites for a panel by Lorenzetti, who thus received documentary renown.

In 1288 the state ordered the cathedral building authorities to give the sculptor Ramo di Paganello a large and handsome commission, so that he might *suum magisterium ostendere et industrium suum opus*. After 1527 a petition of eager citizens regarding the engagement of Baldassare Peruzzi, a refugee from the Sack of Rome, saying that the honour and name of the city would consequently rise in other towns; and it was also hoped that Siena would become, through him, a school for the arts.

The Ufficiali dell' Ornato approved in 1469 an expropriation for the formation of a piazza, bearing in mind that piazza and city would acquire such dignity therefrom that every citizen would daily become more cultivated.

For a country town of the Sienese region, Grosseto, a particular architect and an approved plan are prescribed in 1540 for the building of the cathedral.

Citizens' complaints about an unsatisfactory Madonna fresco on the Porta Nuova; about lighting fires in the recently and beautifully painted great hall in the Palazzo del Podestà, partly out of regard for foreign visitors (1316).

The delayed completion of the Fonte Gaia was officially denounced as an insult to the town; Gaye, *Carteggio*, I, p. 96. In applying for funds to complete the Oratory of S. Catherine, the patron saint, the state refers in 1469 to the honour of the town, to the opinion of pious visitors, to the merits of the Patroness, the fame of Siena through her, to the present period of peace, and finally "because we are one of the few cities in the world which still enjoy the heavenly gift of sweet freedom".

A true idea of Sienese feeling can be gained from the beautiful description of the ceremonial with which Duccio's altarpiece was conducted to the cathedral in 1310; Milanesi, I. p. 168.

(NOTE: See also W. Braunfels, *Mittelalterliche Stadtbaukunst in der Toskana*, 3rd ed., Berlin, 1966.) (PM).

§ 4 *Attitude to Architecture in Other Towns*

In towns which were semi-independent or principalities a similar sentiment was expressed in clear terms, as soon as they were able to make their own decisions. Venice said almost nothing; when she spoke her tones were of the proudest.

In 1420 Orvieto called her cathedral a splendid church, without its like in the world. In 1380 they had the ambition to build the biggest organ in the world; Della Valle, *Storia del Duomo di Orvieto*, p. 118 and docs. 50 and 53.

In Perugia in 1426 it was the Papal governor who persuaded the citizens that such a prominent town needed a far larger and finer cathedral than the one they had had up till then; the costs were shared between the Pope, the citizenry, and the cathedral chapter. For the rebuilding of S. Domenico a trade-tax was imposed; Graziani, *Cronaca* in Arch. Stor., XVI, I, p. 318, 418, 575, 620.

On Piacenza, which had come down in the world, there lay the onus of a two-hundred-year-old promise from better times to build a church to the Madonna; the extraordinary debate of 1467, with the alarming insinuation that Duke Galeazzo Sforza might harass the town if it was seen to have resources; realisation largely achieved by collections helped by a great preacher,

Fra Giovanni da Lugo, attended by signs and portents; *Annales Placentini* in Murat., XX, col. 921 ff.

In Venice Sanmicheli (*c* 1540) obtained the commission to build the maritime fortress of Sant' Andrea on the Lido, with the comment that, since he had recently been far away building the fortifications of the Republic in Corfu, Candia and Cyprus, he might now like to consider what his heavy new responsibilities implied in a building permanently before the eyes of the Senate and so many of the nobility. Vasari, VI, p. 347, *Vita di Sanmicheli*.

§5 *The Attitude of the Despots*

The despots, almost all of them usurpers and violent men, were mostly under a psychological necessity to be as architecturally ambitious as their means permitted. Buildings were a permanent symbol of power and could be of great value for the continuation of a dynasty, or help in its return when ousted. On the relationship of the usurped princedom to fame and learning cf. *Kultur der Renaissance*, 3rd ed., I, pp. 8, 161 f.; 4th ed., I, pp. 8, 143 f.: both cover the relationship to art, and especially architecture. Cf. also the author's *Zeit Konstantins d. Gr.*, p. 464, 2nd ed., p. 413. For the building policy of the Medici see above, §2.

The beginning of Italian tyranny is marked by the building mania of the fearsome Ezzelino da Romano (*d* 1259), who built palace after palace and never lived in them, as well as mountain castles and town strongholds, as though he daily expected a siege; all to instil fear and admiration and so to imprint the fame of his name on everyone's mind that it would be impossible to forget him; Monachus Paduanus, at the end of Book II, e.g. in the collection made by Urstisius.

Both the Visconti and Sforza despots of Milan soon deliberately took first place among the princely builders.

Giangaleazzo Visconti (*d* 1402), with his special feeling for the grandiose, founded the "wonder of all monasteries", the Certosa of Pavia, and "the largest and finest church in Christendom", Milan Cathedral, "which can vie with all antiquity" (documents of 1490, in Milanesi, II, p. 438), and added to the Castello at Pavia, begun by his uncle Bernabò, the most splendid residence in the world at that time (see §21). Filippo Maria Visconti (*d* 1447) built country houses and converted the Castello of Milan into a magnificent dwelling.

Among the Sforza family, mention must be made of Francesco, who gave proof of both his initiative and his artistic sensibility by beginning and energetically carrying through the gigantic undertaking of combining all the hospitals of Milan into one huge new building, which was to represent the finest conceivable hospital. After him Lodovico il Moro was particularly important (he fell from power in 1500), who was advised by Bramante and Leonardo. Great improvements to Milan and Pavia; reconstruction of Vigevano with gardens, aqueducts, and an elegant piazza. Cagnola in Archiv. Stor., III, p. 188; for Vigevano also Decembrio (see §1) in Murat., XX, col. 998. Il Moro appointed in 1490 (Milanesi, II, p. 431 f.) the master-masons to erect a dome for the Cathedral "which should be beautiful, dignified, and everlasting – if anything everlasting can be produced in this world".

The Gonzaga of Mantua also proclaimed their taste for building, as well as something of the purse-pride of a condottiere.

Especially important for Mantua was the reign of Duke Federigo; redevelopment of entire quarters, 1526–46, building of the Palazzo del Te etc., Vasari, V, pp. 535 ff., *Vita di Giulio Romano*.

In Gaye, *Carteggio*, II, pp. 326 ff. the remarkable documents relating to the building of the new cathedral at Mantua (1545), which was treated by the ruling family as essentially a matter of worldly honour, to which their subjects were gently invited to contribute a measure of help.

The general Colleoni (*d* 1475), knowing that the Republic of Venice would be his heir, built three churches as well as his splendid funerary chapel in Bergamo (see §80) and the fine country seat at Malpaga; Paul. Jovii *Elogia* s.v. Bartol. Colleonio. Cf. *Kultur der Renaissance*, 3rd ed., I, p. 126; 4th ed., I, p. 23.

§6 *Romagna, the Marches, Umbria*

Southwards from the Po in the Romagna and the Marches of Ancona and onwards into Umbria there developed, in the relatively long period of peace from 1465 to 1480, an extremely strong interest among princes and cities in building, clearly stimulated by rivalry.

About this time the timber-frame wall tended to disappear in northern Italy, of which Lomazzo (*Trattato dell' arte*, Milan, 1585, p. 649) speaks as hitherto a common local building method.

In Faenza the prince Carlo Manfreddi built energetically, as did the Venetian government in Ravenna, and the prince Pino Ordelaffo in Forlì, who also provided private builders with help, advice, and favour; inaugurating his new palace in 1472 with a ceremonial investiture; *Ann. Foroliviens.* in Murat. XXII, col. 227, 230.

In Bologna (*Annals* of the monk Burselli, in Murat. XXIII), especially after 1460, the clergy, the Papal legate, the quasi-princely house of the Bentivogli, the city authorities, the guilds, private persons and, in particular, the rich professors were all building in mutual emulation; private palaces "worthy of a prince"; the "regal" palace of the Bentivogli; the large and expensive street improvements, see §112.

In Pesaro Costanzo Sforza, cousin of "Il Moro", did all he could to improve and embellish the town and created there the exquisite Veste "*per sua fantasia*".

The cult of glory was linked to a terrible cast of mind in Sigismondo Malatesta, lord of Rimini (*d* 1467), who destroyed what others built in order to use the materials afresh and leave no memorial to survive him except his own. For his S. Francesco (1447), which he built in honour of himself and the beautiful Isotta, he destroyed the port and many other structures, monuments, a religious foundation and a campanile at Rimini, and at Ravenna he took marble from three old churches (S. Severo, Sant' Apollinare in Classe, and Galla Placidia); Vasari, II, p. 540, note 4, *Vita di Alberti*. Cf. *Kultur der Renaiss.* 3rd ed., I, p. 271; 4th ed., I, p. 255, and see below §63.

Even the smallest joined in. Simonetto Baglione, the lord of the little town of Deruta, had the piazza paved and wanted to carry water to the town on daring arches springing from rock to rock, simply as "an ever-lasting memorial", when fate caught up with him in 1500. Matarazzo, *Cronaca*, in Arch. Stor., XVI, II, p. 107 and cf. *Kultur der Renaiss.*, 3rd ed., I, p. 30; 4th ed., I, p. 30.

For the Dukes of the house of Este in Ferrara, Borso (*d* 1471) and Ercole I (*d* 1505), their own buildings were many, modest and practical, the ultimate object being less monumental than political; to create a rich, stable, populous city. They built so much themselves and so contrived matters that others, even immigrant strangers, were induced (and indeed compelled) to build similarly according to the rules laid down; *Diario Ferrarese* in Murat., XXIV, and *Annales Estenses* in Murat., XX passim. At one time a Babylonian attitude was revealed in Borso, when he had the great artificial mound of Monte Santo raised in the plain of the Po by forced labour. Improvements and layout of urban quarters §112. Around the ducal palace of Schifanoia there grew up a palace quarter, largely due to Florentine exiles living in the city. For particular purposes building sometimes proceeded at a headlong rate, and expropriation cost a great deal.

The great Federigo da Montefeltro, Duke of Urbino (*d* 1482), a connoisseur of architecture, built in addition to many fortresses his celebrated palace, reckoned one of the finest of its time. Vespasiano Fiorentino, p. 121 f., 146; further contemporary evidence in Schmarsow, *Melozzo da Forlì*, p. 350 ff. Cf. *Kultur der Renaiss.*, 3rd ed., I, p. 45; 4th ed. I, p. 46, 253. He could easily have played the largest part in designing the palace himself (§93).

(NOTE: For the Palace at Urbino see now P. Rotondi, *Il Palazzo ducale di Urbino*, 2 vols., Urbino, 1950, and abridged English translation, 1 vol., London, 1969.) (PM).

§7 *The Monumental Temper of Pope Nicholas V*

In the unsettled state of Rome the first Popes after the Schism aimed no higher than repair-work. With Nicholas V (1447–55), however, building and book collecting amounted to an overwhelming passion, and to these interests the Pope contributed in a valid way, both intellectually and practically. In the universality of his artistic interests no other occupant of Peter's throne has been his equal; in the grandeur of his architectural aims he comes close to Julius II.

A successor of similarly lofty artistic discernment, Pius II, said of him: "He has adorned Rome wonderfully with imposing buildings in great numbers; had he been able to carry out all his schemes, he would have been surpassed by none of the Emperors of Antiquity". – Pius II, *Europa*, cap. 58.

For the activity of Martin V (1417–31), directed chiefly towards the restoration of law and order, see E. Müntz, *Les arts à la Cour des Papes*, I, p. 1 ff.; Infessura in Muratori, *Scriptores*, III, 2, p. 1122; for Martin's Bull of 1425 see *Bullarum amplissima collectio*, III, 2, p. 452; in Theiner, *Codex Diplomaticus*, III, p. 290; in Müntz, op. cit., p. 335 ff. Not for nothing did Martin invite his prelates to active participation (Muratori, III, 2, p. 867, 858; see Müntz, op. cit., p. 2). The Pope thought well enough of his own activity to have a medal struck in commemoration (Venuti, *Numismata romanorum pontificum*, p. 1; Müntz, op. cit., p. 3). Eugenius IV (1431–47) trod the same path of restoration (Müntz, *Nouvelles recherches*, 1884, p. 33 ff.); Nicholas V found the ground prepared for him. On his work and projects, see *Vitae Paparum* in Muratori, III, 2, Col. 925 ff., especially 949 (his will) – both sources also in Müntz, op. cit., I. p. 337 ff.; Platina, in *Vita Nichol. V*; Müntz, op. cit., p. 68 ff.; on the conjectural part played by Alberti in the Pope's plans, see Dehio in *Repertorium f. Kunstwissenschaft*, III, p. 241 ff. Apart from many buildings in small towns near Rome there were five major Roman projects (realised to only the smallest degree): the restoration of the City walls and the forty Station Churches, the transformation of the Borgo as a residence for the entire Curia, the rebuilding of the Vatican and of S. Peter's, and improvements to streets and piazze and linking of the latter by covered colonnades, as the Ancient and Early Christian world, following the model of Hellenistic cities, had liked to do. (Cf. also Müntz, *Nouvelles recherches*, 1889, p. 49 ff.).

According to the biographers the motives were: the honour and glory of the Apostolic Throne, promotion of Christian piety, and a concern for personal fame, expressed in imperishable buildings.

According to the Pope's own discourse to the cardinals gathered round his death-bed: the Church's need of monumentality, not for the sake of the educated, who would understand her evolution and needs without buildings, but rather for the sake of the *turbae populorum*, who would be strengthened in their frail and vulnerable faith by the grandeur of what they saw. Lasting monuments, which seemed to have been built by God himself, were of special service in this. The fortresses throughout the state, he said, he had erected against enemies from without and dangerous innovators from within (cf. *Kultur der Renaiss.*, I, pp. 99, 227, 234; 4th ed., I, pp. 105, 204, 213). "Had We been able to complete everything, churches and other buildings, then truly Our successors would be more truly venerated by all Christian peoples and would live in Rome more securely from foes without and within. Therefore not from ambition, love of splendour, empty thirst for glory or desire to perpetuate Our name, have We begun this great complex of buildings, but to enhance the reputation of the Apostolic

Throne in all Christendom, and so that, in future, the Popes may no longer be dispossessed, held prisoner, besieged and otherwise oppressed." The last, vain, plea to the Cardinals was to carry on and complete the work – *prosequi, perficere, absolvere!*

Only his tireless striving after imposing new buildings explains this Pope's otherwise incomprehensible disregard for the ancient ruins, which he unscrupulously sacrificed, if it suited him, to obtain building materials for his new works. The Forum, Colosseum, and Circus Maximus above all were plundered during his Pontificate. How little this vandalism reflected the attitude of discerning contemporaries is attested by the statements of Manuel Chrysoloras, Alberto Averardi (who, indeed, described the *cose moderne* as *molto tristi*) and Flavio Biondo *inter alia*. Cf. Biondo's *Roma instaurata*, I, cap. 104; III, cap. 8 and elsewhere, some references given in Müntz, *Les arts à la Cour des Papes*, I, p. 106; Urlichs, *Codex Topograph.*, pp. 234 ff. Cf. also §26.

§8 *Later Popes, up to Julius II*

Of the immediately succeeding Popes, Calixtus III (to 1458), Pius II (to 1464), Paul II (to 1471), Sixtus IV (to 1484), Innocent VIII (to 1492) and Alexander VI (to 1503), none revealed this degree of enthusiasm for the general weal. Rather, there emerged the sense of splendour of a temporal Prince with his eyes fixed on Rome as a residence. From the time of Pius II the richer cardinals were beginning to build palaces in emulation of each other, and they were encouraged in this by Sixtus IV; the adornment of their titular churches became a matter of honour.

Pius II had a desire to build, and a refined taste; but not so much for Rome as for his birth-place, Corsignano, which he raised to the status of a city, the seat of a bishop, and an administrative and festal centre, renaming it Pientia (Pienza) after himself, in the way that Alexander, the Diadochi, and the Emperors had called so many towns after themselves.

Paul II, who as Cardinal Barbo had already distinguished himself by building the first Renaissance palace in Rome – Palazzo di Venezia, begun before 1455 – undertook the continuation of the rebuilding of S. Peter's and extended the Vatican palace; see the documents in Müntz, op. cit., II, and Grimaldi, *Cod. Barberin.*, XXXIV, 50. Paul, while still a cardinal, had spent 15,000 gold ducats on this palace near S. Marco and had so hastened its construction that he was able to live in it for a time at the start of his pontificate; Murat., III, 2, p. 1140. The restoration of the basilica of S. Marco went hand in hand with the building of the new palace.

Sixtus IV was mainly interested in civil works and erected the long-needed central bridge over the Tiber, the Ponte Sisto with its naive inscription, and restored the Aqua Virgo (Acqua di Trevi) to Rome. Nevertheless, he also provided several churches, mainly in connection with the Jubilee Year of 1475.

On the buildings of the popes and cardinals: Müntz, *Les arts..*, I–III; of Pius II, *Comment.* Lib. VIII, p. 366, cf. Lib. VI, p. 308. *Vitae Papar.* in Murat. III, II, Col. 1018, 1031, 1034 ff., 1046, 1064, 1098. Also "Platinae continuator" (Onuphrius Panvinius), passim. Albertini, *De mirabilibus Romae*, Bk III, fol. 83–85, on restoration and new building of churches from Sixtus IV to Julius II; and fol. 99, on the buildings of Julius, from the time when he was a cardinal and including those outside Rome. Fols. 88–91, the palaces, houses, gardens and vineyards of cardinals, prelates and laymen, but this is no more than a mere list. The cardinals and prelates certainly built (cf. §95) because they knew that the Curia would distrain upon their personal estate on their death. Most of it went on their splendid tombs in any case (§139).

The forceful Julius II (1503–13), already as a cardinal architecturally ambitious to the fullest extent of his resources, undertook the rebuilding of S. Peter's (§66) and the Vatican in a generous and grandiose spirit which had hardly been shown by any earlier patron. Onuphrius Panvinius, *De Vaticana basilica*, in Mai, *Spicileg. Romanum*, Tom. IX, p. 365 ff. (Cf. Ranke, *Päpste*, I, p. 69.) The passage is to this effect: Of high courage, stubborn and unshakeable in confronting and fighting the enemies of the Church, Julius prosecuted everything that roused his interest to such a point of enthusiasm that he expected what had scarcely been planned to be completed instantaneously. Among other great gifts he had a wonderful zeal for building, even though he was responsible for more than one abortive foundation. (A reference to the law courts begun in via Giulia, the Palazzo dei Tribunali.) Moreover, he had men about him like Bramante, Raphael, Baldassare Peruzzi, Antonio da Sangallo, Michelangelo and others. Bramante, regarded at the time as the greatest of them all, had at last found in Julius the Pope he wanted; persuasive as he was, he won Julius over to a new building for S. Peter's, which would be worthy of the Pope and of the majesty of the Apostle; he arranged for the Pope to see sketches, then other drawings of the new church, constantly returning to the matter and assuring the Pope that the building would ensure him lasting glory. Julius II, with his lofty and wide-ranging outlook, which had no place for petty things and was always drawn to magnificence – *magnarum semper molium avidus* – allowed himself to be convinced by the master and decided upon the destruction of the old building and the erection of a new and imposing S. Peter's. In this desire there were ranged against him people of all classes, especially the cardinals, who would have liked to have a new and splendid church, but deplored the demolition of the old Basilica, honoured by the whole world, with its multitude of saints' tombs and countless memories. The Pope, however, remained adamant, razed half the old church and laid the foundations of the new (18 April 1506).

With this building, however precarious its fate for a time, the Papacy stood at the head of the whole concept of monumental architecture in the West. At the time of the Counter-Reformation this had not merely formal but international historical consequences. On the other hand, it is arguable that under Leo X the building contributed in some measure to the coming of the Reformation.

In 1450 Old S. Peter's had shifted almost six feet out of true and was held together only by the anchoring of the roof-timbers; Alberti *Arte edificatoria*, Bk I [cap. 10]. (*Opere volgari*, vol. IV, p. 242.) The next earthquake would have brought the church down; ibid., Bk X, cap. 17, p. 391 f. of Ticozzi's ed. (also in Müntz, *Nouv. recherches*, III, p. 52), and this was a stimulus to rebuilding.

(NOTE: For the problem of the Palazzo Venezia see V. Golzio and G. Zander, *L' Arte in Roma nel secolo XV*, Bologna, 1968, and F. Hermanin, *Il Palazzo di Venezia*, Rome, 1948.

It is an extraordinary fact that Burckhardt omits Sixtus IV's major architectural commission, the Sistine Chapel in the Vatican: see E. Steinmann, *Die Sixtinische Kapelle*, vol. I, Munich, 1901, and L. D. Ettlinger, *The Sistine Chapel before Michelangelo*, Oxford, 1965.) (PM).

§9 *Attitudes in Private Building*

Among private people as well there soon emerged in Italy an intense zeal for building. Fine, large, buildings are a natural expression of privileged living in Italy, and, for a few property owners, the first step to princely power. Venice is once again uncommunicative, Florence almost garrulous.

A Venetian who did not hide his ambition was the Doge Francesco Foscari, whose life ended in tragedy (1457). On the palace, which henceforth bore his name, he built an upper storey so that it would no longer be called, as hitherto, the Casa Giustiniana; Sansovino, *Venezia*, fol. 149.

For Florence an early, frank, admission in the letters of Niccolò Acciajuoli, who rose from merchant to High Seneschal of Naples, and from a distance charged his brother with the building of the great Certosa near Florence in 1356; Gaye, *Carteggio*, I, pp. 61, 64. Cf. Matteo Villani, III, cap. 9: "What God has also given me goes to my descendants, whoever they may be; but this monastery, with its decoration, belongs to me for ever and will make my memory evergreen and enduring in my native land. And if the soul is immortal, as Monsignor il Cancelliere says, so will my soul, wherever it is commanded to go, delight in this building."

The name of Filippo Scolari – or Pippo Spano – much esteemed in the service of the Emperor Sigismund as counsellor and general against the Turks, who, in Hungary and elsewhere, was said to have built 180 chapels, and who was regarded as the founder of the polygonal church of Sta Maria degli Angeli in Florence, must be deleted from this context, since it is clear from documentary evidence that Scolari had only briefly administered the estate of a brother and a cousin, which was not until later applied to the building of the oratory designed by Brunellesco but never completed.

The most ambitious realisation for which a private person had ever been responsible: Palazzo Pitti, built by Luca Pitti.

Of the Palazzo Strozzi, begun in 1489 by Filippo Strozzi, one of the brilliant creations in Florence at that time, there is a partly apocryphal but very revealing account; Gaye, *Carteggio*, I, p. 354 f. Strozzi, architecturally discerning and more interested in fame than possessions, after making lavish provision for his family, wanted to make a name by a building for his family which would redound beyond Italy. The actual head of the State, Lorenzo il Magnifico, who did not want the great patrician to make too dazzling an impression, yet wanted to have a splendid Florence, had the plans submitted to him and is said to have demurred at "a far too lordly" rusticated façade, and forbade him to put shops on the ground floor. (Strozzi could never have convinced Lorenzo that he was afraid of rustication *per non essere civile*, while so many other Florentines used it, and certainly not because he wanted to build shops at street level.) The building was to be paid for without breaking into capital and solely out of income, and this would have been achieved, despite other building works and overcharging for the site, had not Strozzi's death in 1491 caused an interruption. His will committed his sons to finish it, under the threat that otherwise the palace would fall into the hands of Lorenzo il Magnifico and possibly the Guild of Merchants or the Hospital of Sta Maria Nuova. They took heed, and the celebrated Filippo Strozzi the Younger (Varchi, *Stor. Fiorent.*, L. IV, p. 321) completed the building in 1533.

On an elegant private building in Milan (Casa Frigerio near San Sepolcro) is written: *elegantiae publicae, commoditati privatae*.

The character of aristocratic private building was discussed in theoretical terms about 1500, and its basic aims identified.

The Neapolitan Jovianus Pontanus in his *De Magnificentia* defines the splendour-loving man – *magnificus* – with special reference to architecture, with examples from Naples and Sicily. Four things condition the superior worth of a building: decoration, which should be somewhat overdone; size, in which there should be a measure of restraint; excellence of materials as proof that no cost has been spared; and permanence, which alone ensures the coveted imperishable fame. There is a story of a Catanese who was reduced to penury by building enormous foundations, but who found comfort in the knowledge that posterity would at least conclude that he had been a great lord. Money must not be merely spent in fact; it must be seen to have been spent willingly and with proper disdain. Admiration goes only to the builders of consummate structures, and then men will come from distant lands to admire them, and poets and historians will be constrained to spread their fame.

(NOTE: For the building history of Sta Maria degli Angeli – as for that of all Florentine churches – see W. and E. Paatz, *Die Kirchen von Florenz*, 6 vols., Frankfurt a.M., 1940–54.) (PM).

§ 10 *The Counter-Reformation*

About the middle of the sixteenth century church architecture profited by a new stimulus, the Counter-Reformation, which said little about it but brought important buildings. Only shortly earlier Serlio (*c* 1540) had been deploring the extinction of architectural fervour in the Church (Bk V).

There was a particularly striking increase in fervour from 1563, i.e. after the publication of the decrees of the Council of Trent; Armenini, *De' veri Precetti della Pittura*, Ravenna, 1587, p. 19; throughout Christendom there was from that time keen competition in the building of beautiful and costly temples, chapels and monasteries, and nothing was more to be desired than equally significant and vital painting and sculpture; that is to say, the sister arts under the domination of Mannerism did not appear to match architecture.

CHAPTER TWO

Patrons, Dilettanti and Master Builders

§ 11 *Connoisseur-Patrons of the Fifteenth Century*

In the completely personal relationship of many patrons to their own buildings, which at times were treated as the main objects of life and guarantees of fame after it, a special kind of connoisseurship or dilettantism was to develop, that now and then obscures the real authorship. The patron partly becomes the architect.

Nicholas V (§ 7) was himself almost the titular architect for the projected rebuilding of S. Peter's and therefore not to be compared with Solomon so much as Hīram, while Bernardo Rossellino would have been merely the executant; *Vitae Papar.* in Murat., III, II, col. 938.

Pius II revealed in the arrangements for his buildings at Pienza (§ 8) such detailed knowledge that it is to be supposed that much was specified by the Pope himself, and not by the architect Bernardus (Rossellino); Pii II, *Comment.*, especially Lib. X, p. 425 ff.; on Bernardo, p. 432.

Federigo of Urbino (§ 6), to hear him talk, seemed to be an architect in his own right, and not only was no other prince, but also no private person his equal in this respect. Not only for fortresses, but even for his palace "he specified the proportions and everything else"; Vespasiano Fiorent., p. 121. On the other hand he speaks in a document of 1468 (Gaye, *Carteggio*, I, p. 214) as an admirer and connoisseur of architecture, but appointed as his *alter ego* for the building of the palace Luciano da Laurana, an Illyrian, since in Tuscany, the fountainhead of architects, he found no one suitable.

How big a part did Canon Timoteo Maffei play in the Badia at Fiesole, which Cosimo had built through Brunellesco? According to Vespasiano Fiorent., p. 265, the main role may have been Timoteo's. The statement there, "l'ordine dell' architettura e della composizione fu tutta sua", Fabriczy (*Brunelleschi*, p. 268) seems to have taken to mean that only for the layout and style had the wishes of Timoteo been decisive, for nothing is known about him as a practising architect.

Lorenzo il Magnifico (*d* 1492) was involved in all the building affairs of Florence (§ 9), was as critical of the Tuscan architects as Federigo (his letter to the Crown Prince Alfonso of Naples, Gaye, *Carteggio*, I, p. 300), yet he obtained commissions for them in distant places (ibid., p. 301), and presided over and decided the deliberations regarding a new cathedral façade in 1491 (Vasari, IV, p. 299 ff. in the Comment. on the *Vita di G. da Sangallo*). Indeed, he is reputed to have designed for Giuliano da Maiano the *modello* (i.e. probably the drawing) for the Villa Poggio Reale, which Duke Alfonso was proposing to build near Naples; Luca Pacioli, *Divina Proportione*, ed. C. Winterberg, p. 48: cf. § 118. (But it is arguable whether the remarks in Vasari, V, p. 25, *Vita di A. del Sarto*, with reference to the false façade of the cathedral for the entry of Leo X in 1515, can be related to a drawing left by Lorenzo.) That he was delighted and encouraging when young patricians became artists or connoisseurs is hardly explicable by a belief on his part in greater ability among the nobles (Vasari, IV, p. 257, *Vita di Torrigiano*); rather, he may have wished that they would forget their power in the state, embellish the city, and bleed themselves white in the process.

In Siena several strikingly precise contracts for the building of palaces, relating to an earlier period, reveal a meticulous connoisseurship among the parties concerned; Milanesi, I, p. 232 (for Pal. Sansedoni, as early as 1339); II, p. 303 ff. (for Pal. Marsigli, 1459).

For Arezzo ibid., I, p. 200 (the contract for building the Pieve in 1332). For Pistoia ibid., I, p. 229 (the contract for building the Baptistry in 1339).

Francesco Sforza applied himself most zealously to the great hospital in Milan founded by him in 1456. He sent Filarete with a recommendation to Giovanni de' Medici so that he might prepare drawings of a Florentine hospital, which, perhaps, could not be improved on, but might serve to obtain the best possible design for Milan;

cf. Sforza's letter in Corio in *Politecnico*, anno XXI, and in v. Oettingen, *Antonio Averlino*, p. 59.

§ 12 *Architectural Dilettanti of the Sixteenth Century*

In the sixteenth century architecture was constantly pursued with fervour by many eminent dilettanti. The publication of illustrated books soon made participation easier for non-professionals. Among the secular princes Cosimo I (1537–74), Duke (later Grand-Duke) of Tuscany, showed most purpose and discernment, even if rather one-sided. Among the Popes was a great urge to build, but only Julius III was a genuine dilettante.

Luigi Cornaro, the author of the *Vita sobria* (*Kultur der Renaiss.*, 1st ed., p. 335, cf. 319; 4th ed., I, p. 272, II, p. 55 ff.), busied himself with architectural studies and had the famous Falconetto in his house for thirteen – some say seventeen – years, until Falconetto's death, and he also took him to Rome. The fruits of this were the two ornamental structures in the court of the present Palazzo Giustiniani, near the Santo in Padua, dated 1524; Vasari, V, p. 321, 325, *Vita di Fra Giocondo*; Marcantonio Michiel (the 'Anonimo Morelliano'), *Notizie d'opere di disegno*, ed. Frimmel, p. 10. See also the dedication of Serlio's Fourth Book (1544), in which Cornaro's share in his own town-house and villas is vindicated.

Giovanni Grimani, the Patriarch of Venice, had his palace near Sta Maria Formosa built by Sanmicheli, but helped as "an excellent architect" with "guidance" – Anonimo Morelliano.

Francesco Zeno himself made the *modello* for his family palace; Anon. Morelliano, and Sansovino, *Venezia*, fol. 143.

The poet Trissino, author of *Italia liberata dai Goti* (*Kultur d. Renaiss.*, 1st ed., p. 323 and 306 note; 4th ed., II, p. 43) built his villa at Cricoli (§ 119) himself. His student days in Milan must have coincided with the period of Bramante and Leonardo; Roscoe, *Leone X*, ed. Bossi, VII, p. 341. Like Cornaro, he wrote about architecture.

Serlio's work (from 1540): *veramente ha fatto più mazzacani architetti che non haveva egli peli in barba*, said Lomazzo, *Trattato*, p. 407; cf. p. 410. The rapid succession of editions of Vitruvius must also have affected dilettantism (see below, especially § 28, 29). A victim of this seems to have been a Ferrarese shop-keeper who became absorbed in books on building, began dabbling in the subject and regarded himself as third only to Bramante and Antonio da Sangallo, hence he was known as "Messer Terzo" – cf. Benvenuto Cellini, *Trattato secondo*, final chapter.

For Michelangelo's scorn for a grand Roman dilettante, see Vasari, VII, p. 280, *Vita di Michelangelo*.

Further discussion of the Vitruvians and of the artistic sensibility of Duke Cosimo I below.

The architectural caprices of Julius III, who changed his mind daily about the planning of his villa; Vasari, VII, p. 694, in his Autobiography and also in the *Vita di T. Zucchero*.

Palladio, who certainly expected an architect to pay particular attention to the client's needs and to build to suit him, rather than what he could afford, nevertheless complains that often the architect has to follow his client's desires rather than the rules of his own art; *I Quattro Libri*, II, cap. 1.

(NOTE: For Trissino and his villa see R. Wittkower, *Architectural Principles in the Age of Humanism*, 3rd ed., London, 1962.) (PM).

§ 13 *Consultations and Committees*

Our knowledge of the thinking behind the architecture of that time is further extended by the records of debates and decisions of official bodies and of the practitioners themselves, of which a more or less complete account has come down to us: no such records have survived from Northern Europe.

The congress of foreign architects in connection with the dome of Florence Cathedral was, according to Vasari – who based himself upon the imprecise account given by Manetti – no more than an allegory of the triumph of Genius over the Knowalls (*Vita di Brunellesco*, II, p. 343 ff.).

Consultations giving no details of the participants are recorded by Vasari (*Vita di Bramante*, IV, p. 155): *resoluzione*, *consiglio*, *deliberazione*, in his account of the Cancelleria in Rome and some churches.

Resolutions by professionals on matters of building practice, decided by majority votes *inter alia* in Florence in 1486 (Gaye, *Carteggio*, II, p. 450) to determine the number of doors for Sto Spirito, which had already been the subject of four years' deliberation. Milanesi gives other *acta* of committees and resolutions of various kinds. A particularly instructive reference to a competition for a new façade for Florence Cathedral in 1490 (Vasari, IV, p. 299 ff., commentary to *Vita di G. da Sangallo*); among the forty-six competitors, almost all Florentines, were painters, goldsmiths, wood-carvers, smiths, a herald and a town-piper.

(NOTE: For what is known of North European debates see, e.g., P. Frankl, *The Gothic*, Princeton, 1960.) (PM).

§ 14 *The Versatility of Architects*

The versatility of most artists of the time, so puzzling to our age of specialists, was of great consequence to architecture. Ghiberti (*Comment.*, p. xviii) said of Giotto: "Quando la natura vuole concedere alcuna cosa, la concede senza veruna avarizia." The beautifully fresh appearance of Renaissance buildings derives from the fact that the designer was not merely the draughtsman, but, as sculptor, painter, or woodworker, was aware of the nature of all the materials and the whole formal vocabulary, so that he was able to visualise and evaluate an entire building and all its decorative features.

In the Middle Ages such versatility was easier to achieve, in that the tasks in all the arts were simpler, and similar in kind; and, especially in sculpture and painting, conventional modes of expression predominated. An exceptional situation occurred when a master's competence embraced several arts in the process of making prodigious advances and encountering completely fresh problems, as was the case with the celebrated Tuscans of the fourteenth century, who united in their persons a new world of pictorial representation, a sculpture of consummate sensibility, an entirely individual style of large-scale church architecture, and, in addition, hitherto unprecedented developments in building practice, hydraulics and mechanics. This was more or less true of Giotto, Agostino and Agnolo (Vasari, I, p. 437 f.), Taddeo Gaddi (Vasari, I, p. 577) and Maestro Lando (Milanesi, I, pp. 228–32). Then with the fifteenth century came Brunellesco, first as goldsmith, next as mechanical engineer, sculptor, architect, perspectivist, master-builder of vast fortifications, and interpreter of Dante (he calculated geometrically the extent of the next world). Beside him Leon Battista Alberti (cf. *Kultur d. Renaiss.*, 3rd ed., I, p. 168; 4th ed., I, p. 151) and, soon after him, Bartolommeo Ridolfo Fioravante, known as Aristoteles, who came from Bologna and was active under Nicholas V in Rome (cf. Gualandi in Atti e Memorie della R. Deputazione di Storia Patria per le Provincie di Romagna, 1870).

It remains remarkable that as late as this nobody devoted himself to architecture from the beginning of his career. Vasari says of his own time (V, p. 349, *Vita di Baccio d'Agnolo*) that most architects nowadays graduate from sculpture, painting or woodcarving, and indeed are more praiseworthy than certain earlier artists, who became architects from being decorators or perspectivists. (This is the general sense of the passage.)

Giulio Romano made himself into an architect by executing the architectural backgrounds for Raphael's Vatican frescoes: Vasari, V, p. 525, *Vita di Giulio*. Regarding the yawning gap in the artistic life of Mantua, which arose from Giulio's death in 1546, see the fine letter of Cardinal Ercole Gonzaga in Gaye, *Carteggio*, II, p. 501. A particularly dazzling instance of versatility is offered by Vasari, VI, p. 315 ff., *Vita di Genga*, who, starting with painting, mastered every important branch of the arts.

Sculptors, "weary of the difficulties of their art", often became architects, says Doni, *Disegno*, fol. 14 and cf. fol. 34, probably not without irony. Perhaps the sculptors, as they grew older, simply preferred the steadier occupation – like, for example, Tribolo.

The relationship of the architect was especially close with the *legnaiuolo* in both senses of the term: master-carpenter, and woodcarver and master of *intarsia* (the latter two might be one man). The two da Majano, for example, started as woodworkers: Vasari, II, p. 468, and III, p. 333. Similarly Cronaca: Vasari, IV, p. 442, *Vita di Cronaca*; and Giovanni de' Dolci from Florence, employed under Nicholas V in Rome as *maestro di legname*, and later builder of the Sistine Chapel. Baccio Pontelli signed himself, in his letter of 1481 to Lorenzo de' Medici, as *lignaiolo* and pupil of Francione: Gaye, *Carteggio*, I, p. 275.

An admirable Doric cloister at S. Pietro in Cremona built by the intarsiator Filippo dal Sacco: Marcant. Michiel, *Notizie d'opere di disegno* (Anon. Morelliano), ed. Frimmel, p. 42. There were also, however, non-professionals of this kind.

Quite a number of well-known masters of every craft (cf. § 180) began as goldsmiths, e.g. Brunellesco.

In Venice, where the varieties of stone were often costly and difficult to work, the name *tagiapiera* (*tagliapietra*) or stonemason remained throughout the entire fifteenth century distinction enough for architects: Malipiero, *Annali Veneti*, Arch. Stor., VII, II, pp. 674, 689.

Finally, architects often recommended themselves to influential patrons as master-builders of fortifications or as engineers (§ 108 ff.), rather than as artists.

To Raphael and Michelangelo architecture came late; Leonardo (§ 198), however, was from the beginning master of every art, and his destiny may well have been an enigma even to himself. In striking contrast, Titian and Correggio were exclusively painters.

While the power of the individual artistic personality had demolished all barriers between the arts since the time of Nicola Pisano, and even before him, the institution of the Guilds re-erected them in their own fashion, but not without compromises.

In Milanesi, I, p. 122, the remarkable agreement between the Sienese architects and woodworkers in 1447, by which a measure of mutual encroachment was permitted.

§ 15 *Life of Architects*

There had never been territorial barriers for architecture; Lombard masons, especially the Comacini, made their way from time immemorial throughout Italy and later often became famous as architects; the great Florentines of the fifteenth century, the undisputed bearers of the new style, worked all over Italy and even sent designs to distant places.

Antonio Manetti (*Vita di Brunellesco*, ed. Holtzinger, p. 22) says that architects travel and allow themselves to be sent for wherever there is wealth and power and the chance of a commission.

His luck in finding generous patrons is eloquently described by Palladio (*Quattro Libri dell' Architettura*, II, cap. 3): "I am called a fortunate man, for I have found people of rank, noble and generous in mind, and of excellent judgement, who vouchsafe their belief in my ideas . . ."; he could not thank God enough for the favour of being able now to turn to practical account what he had worked at with the greatest pains on far journeys and learned with much diligence.

Michelozzo worked *inter alia* in Milan and sent drawings of church windows to Rome (Vasari, II, p. 443);

Filarete in Milan; Alberti in Rimini; Agostino di Duccio in Perugia; the three Sangallo in Rome; Giuliano da Majano in Naples; Mormandi* in the same place, to pick out only a few of the best-known examples.

The Comacini and Ticinesi came to the forefront in the sixteenth century and were completely dominant during the Baroque period.

With the warmest expressions of approbation and admiration governments and building committees recommended individual architects to each other; Milanesi, II, 430, 431, 439, 443, with reference to Francesco di Giorgio.

On the remuneration of architects at the Papal Court in the fifteenth century, cf. the numerous records of accounts in Müntz, *Les Arts à la Cour des Papes*, I–III. Often daily payments of salary were made, either direct from the client's treasury or the entire job was handed over to a contractor. The Comacino Beltramo di Martino from Varese, a leading contractor under Nicholas V, commanded a whole army of workmen and owned large-scale brickworks and limekilns in Rome; his annual claim on the Papal purse amounted to some 30,000 gold ducats; Müntz, op. cit., I, p. 104 f.

For many very busy masters it was impossible to supervise personally the execution of every job; but many also were dismayed by the independent attitude and would-be improvements of their deputies. Thus, for Brunellesco, Antonio Manetti (not to be confused with his biographer of the same name) ruined the façade of the Loggia degli Innocenti among other things; cf. Manetti, *Vita di Brunellesco*, passim.

Filarete, in his Treatise, calculated one overseer (*soprastante*) to every eighty-five masons, and in the ideal plan for building the city of Sforzinda he proposed to engage 103,200 workmen; *Trattato dell' Architettura*, Cod. Palat. 372 of the Bibl. Magl., Florence; Müntz, op. cit., I, p. 84, n. 3.

A delightful completion to the cosmopolitan lives led by such architects was often afforded by the houses they built for themselves in their later years in their homeland. It would be well worthwhile to collect all that remains or has been recorded of artists' houses in Italy. Vasari, III, p. 407, *Vita di Mantegna*, on the house which he built and decorated with frescoes for himself in Mantua, and on his chapel. (The house, now Istituto Technico in the via G. Acerbi, still exists: the façade rebuilt, the court preserved.)

Vasari, IV, p. 521, *Vita di Andrea Sansovino*, who, in his old age, built his own house at Monte Sansovino and gave pleasure to his fellow-townsmen.

Vasari, VII, p. 685 in his autobiography: his fairly well-preserved house at Arezzo, now Casa Montauti;† the salone with an elaborate fireplace includes mythological and allegorical paintings; in other rooms *inter alia* portraits of artists of his acquaintance, also female genre figures, which are better than any of the ideal concepts painted by him. Also II, p. 558, *Vita di Lazzaro Vasari*: the family chapel and family tomb.

The extant house of Giulio Romano at Mantua; Vasari, V, p. 549, *Vita di Giulio*. Outside and inside stuccoed and painted, and once filled with antiquities.

The house of the sculptor Leone Leoni in Milan, built by him, exterior with herms (the so-called *Omenoni*), the interior then had beautifully arranged plaster casts from antique models; Vasari, VII, p. 540 f.; cf. § 105.

Antonio da Sangallo's house, built by himself, in Rome, later the Palazzo Sacchetti; Vasari, V, p. 466, *Vita di A. Sangallo il Giovane*. Sketches for it among the drawings in the Uffizi (nos. 920, 928, 981 *inter alia*); Vasari, V, p. 489.

* Giovanni Donadio Mormanno, *c* 1450–*c* 1526, a pupil of Giuliano da Majano in Naples. (PM).

† Now a Vasari museum. (PM).

CHAPTER THREE

Proto-Renaissance and Gothic

§ 16 *The Proto-Renaissance in Tuscany and Rome*

The Italian towns, which in the twelfth century considered themselves almost republics, were from early times over-shadowed by the image of ancient Rome. Their acutely awakened local patriotism sought monumental expression. But in most regions of Italy barbarism, if now overcome, was still too recent a factor and the urge towards local forms too strong for an immediate re-introduction of the formal vocabulary of Rome.

North Italy was a major centre of the central European Romanesque style, and to it we perhaps owe the creation of the composite pier. Venice and South Italy were still basically loyal to the Byzantine style.

Isolated copies of antique buildings appeared here and there; S. Fedele in Como, for example, would have been unthinkable without S. Lorenzo in Milan (§ 62).

On the other hand, Rome and Tuscany show remarkably early attempts to revive the architectural forms of ancient Rome, but always with the independence which has remained peculiar to the modern Italian spirit in its relationship to Antiquity.

The word *rinascita* occurs perhaps for the first time in Vasari, I, p. 243, in the Proemio to the Second* Part, in a sense which is difficult to determine chronologically and, incidentally, only in relation to sculpture; but undoubtedly the great seminal movement from the twelfth century is broadly implied by it.

Subsequently the term was extended to every domain of life, but it remains one-sided because it stresses only half the facts. The freedom and originality with which the rediscovery of Classical Antiquity was received and assimilated, the sheer extent of the modern spirit revealed in the great movement is not fully expressed by it.

Rome and Tuscany at first stayed loyal to the Early Christian flat-roofed columnar church, the basilica; they used for the greater part antique building elements, or copied them exactly when they were lacking. Thus, enthusiasm for the column never died out; the façades of Tuscan churches are bedecked with several rows of superimposed columns or with imitations of them in the form of blind arcading of half-columns. The Leaning Tower of Pisa was the supreme expression of which its cylindrical form was capable – six open-arcaded galleries one upon another (Fig. 1).

The Roman basilicas of the twelfth century once more adopted the straight entablature instead of the arch; other buildings and smaller ornamental works reveal a true renaissance down to the smallest detail. The churches of Sta Maria in Trastevere, S. Crisogono, the new nave of S. Lorenzo fuori.

On the buildings of the Cosmati about 1200: the cloisters at the Lateran and S. Paolo, and the colonnaded portico of the cathedral at Cività Castellana (Fig. 2) the detail is in part entirely true to Antiquity, in other respects sharply divergent. The cortile of S. Paolo the most harmonious combination of discipline and fantasy (Fig. 3).

The fluted Corinthian pilaster already used as an end feature of a wall-face in the portico of the cathedral at Cività Castellana. The rosette as the centre of a coffer in many of the soffits of the arches of the cloister at S. Paolo.

§ 17 *San Miniato and the Baptistry*

For the Florentines, who might otherwise have conformed to the widely accepted Romanesque formal vocabulary, it was a matter of deliberate decision supported by historical prejudice that they turned to the ancient Roman forms.

They believed themselves to be indebted to ancient Rome, as a former and ever-loyal colony. Cf. *Kultur der Renaiss.*, 3rd ed., I, p. 327; 4th ed., I, p. 207. The relevant monuments are: the disposition of columns and arches of

* Actually the Proemio delle Vite, not that to the Second Part. (PM).

Fig. 1 *Pisa, Cathedral and Leaning Tower*

SS. Apostoli, probably of the eleventh century (the attic bases and profiles of the archivolts illustrated in Lübke's *Reisebericht* in the Mitteilungen der Zentr.-Komm., 1860, p. 170). The façade of the Badia at Fiesole. The church of S. Miniato (Fig. 4), in which the form of the basilica achieves an ultimate and supreme solemnity by harmonious spatial distribution and proportions; the individual antique forms employed in due relationship share, as if consciously, in the presentation of this beautiful building. The rebuilding of the church is mentioned in a document of Bishop Hildebrand of 1013; in 1062 the interior was apparently completed, in 1207 the pavement, and only in 1357 (both according to inscriptions) was the roof-truss executed. For the date of origin of the façade it is relevant that the lower part has a relationship to the cathedral of Empoli, with an inscription of 1093. Cf. also *Cenni storico-artistici di S. Miniato al Monte*, Firenze, 1850.

The Baptistry of S. Giovanni, facing the cathedral, is formally but not structurally derived from the Pantheon in Rome. It must here be observed that the architectural history of hardly any other monument in Florence is so subject to hypotheses as that of S. Giovanni. In the evolution of the large double-shell dome, which reached its structural zenith in the cathedral of Florence and its formal culmination in S. Peter's in Rome, S. Giovanni marks, so far as our present knowledge of the monuments discloses, the first significant step.

The building, an octagon like certain medieval baptistries, with an internal diameter of 25·5 m. (84 ft) far exceeds all domed structures of the immediately preceding centuries. Eight angle-piers absorb the lateral thrust of the vault, while "sixteen spurs or ribs, which with their arched elements (rising barrel-vaults) at the same time form the outer roof and carry the marble covering uniting the vault to the supporting wall in a rigid whole" – Durm, *Die Domkuppel von Florenz.*, p. 9 (separate off-print from the Zeitschrift für Bauwesen, 1887). The curve of the vaulting is steep, its pointed arch amounting to fully a fifth of the circumference; cf. the similar construction of the dome of the Baptistry of Cremona (1167). The mass of the walls below the dome could easily be reduced by the use of upper and lower galleries; essentially, these were to please the eye, a concession to appearance, as only the late Antique and the modern style understood it – the triforia of northern Gothic churches had a practical significance (Figs. 5, 6). On the exterior one notices how, in the attic, the frieze is supported on Corinthian pilasters and bends downwards round the angles, like a framing moulding; cf. also, on the upper part of the façade of S. Miniato, the handling of the frieze above the pilasters.

The decorative treatment of the interior belongs to the last years of the twelfth century and the early thirteenth, from which the adornment of the exterior also dates.

Fig. 2 *Civita Castellana, Cathedral*

Later, when the real date of the building had been forgotten, and yet the survival of the forms of Antiquity had been noticed, the view gained credence that the Baptistry was an ancient temple (Vasari, I, p. 236, *Proemio*; ibid., p. 332, *Vita di Tafi*); and, indeed, had once been open to the sky like the Pantheon (Gio. Villani, I, 60); and that Charlemagne, the mythical refounder of Florence, had built SS. Apostoli; Manetti, *Vita di Brunellesco*, ed. Holzinger, p. 23, suggests that when Charlemagne purged Italy of the Lombards and the Colleges (i.e. probably the Guilds of the Lombard masons) and entered into an understanding with the Papacy and the remnant of the Roman Republic, he brought with him architects from Rome – who were no great masters – but had been trained in the forms of antiquity, and hence one saw a reflection of ancient Rome in SS. Apostoli and the since destroyed S. Piero Scheraggio. The contrary was the case: Pope Hadrian I, being in no position to find builders in Rome, turned to Charlemagne with the request for Magistri (i.e. probably Comacini).

§ 18 *The Penetration of Gothic and Extent of Its Influence*

With the thirteenth century, even in Italy, there came a new style, originating in France and called Gothic. Its success did not depend in Italy or elsewhere on the qualities of its decorative aspects; it triumphed as an efficient structural system for high vaulting with minimal expenditure of materials.

The decorative side, even in France, was less developed to begin with, and the earliest emissaries did not introduce this minor aspect abroad. (Cf. the cathedral of Chartres and the oldest Gothic parts of Freiburg Minster, with almost no Gothic (or still Romanesque) detail.) In any case, Italy would have used mosaics and marble for ornamental purposes.

The supremacy of Gothic in Italy coincided with an extreme enthusiasm for monumentality, when not only cathedrals, but even the churches of the Mendicant Orders were in a mood to assume vast proportions; but since every town and every architect wanted something original and special, and nobody felt bound in principle to the new style, so the latter took to itself many different forms, which lost all connection with the vocabulary of details handed down from the North. It was a turbulent and nowhere entirely harmonious period of transition.

S. Francis and S. Dominic had seen how, despite their protests, their Orders had fallen into line with the general attitude to building. Note here the almost envious complaint of a Benedictine, Matthew Paris ad ann. 1243.

There now began in Italy the era of the great experimental buildings – the new constructional principles of

Fig. 3 *(above) Rome, S. Paolo fuori le Mura, cloister*

Fig. 4 *(below) Florence, S. Miniato al Monte*

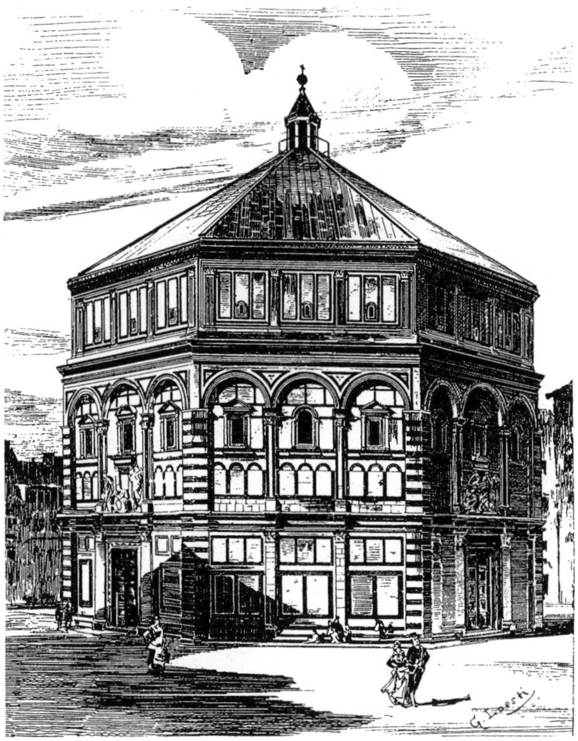

Fig. 5 *Florence, Baptistry*

Fig. 6 *Florence, Baptistry, interior*

S. Francesco at Assisi (from 1228) and other such buildings were taken over from the masters who built them and were adapted to make something quite different.

Gothic detail was misapplied without regard for its intrinsic meaning or was omitted; it had to accord with its mortal enemy, inlay. (The entertaining story of the citizens of Perugia in a feud of 1335 robbing the Aretines of encrusted slabs stacked ready for use on the Cathedral and taking them home on gaily decorated wagons, apparently to use them for the incrustation of their own Cathedral; Archiv. Stor., XVI, I, p. 618; Mariotti, *Lettere Pittoriche Perugine*, p. 107 n.) Whatever is fine in Gothic detail in Italy (work of Giotto or Orcagna) is so for other reasons than in the North. Even the expressions used are Italian or Latin, with the notable exception of *gargolle*, i.e. gargoyles (*gargouilles*), in Milanesi, I, p. 209 – document of 1336. The remaining terminology, for example, ibid., pp. 223, 227, 232, 263; II, p. 235.

Nicola Pisano and Arnolfo built, as occasion served, in the earlier and the newer style. If architects behaved in this way clients were totally uncertain in their judgements; the chapel of the Palazzo Pubblico at Siena was pulled down four times, until, in 1376, it turned out satisfactorily; Milanesi, I, p. 268. In the onrush of the Renaissance truly comical disputes arose, even in connection with unimportant buildings; Milanesi, II, p. 105, in the year 1421:

> *una die initiatur et fit una opera, et alio die destruitur, et quolibet die datur nova forma . . . quod quis eorum vellet sequi uno modo, alter alia forma, et nullam concordiam habent . . . et etiam cives variis modis loquantur . . .*

Finally, a citizens' commission of fifteen men was proposed *ad hoc*.

§ 19 *The Character of Italian Gothic*

Without seeking to distinguish sharply between what was introduced to art through Gothic and what appeared in spite of it, the new triumph of the longitudinal type of church may surely be ascribed to Gothic.

It revived the pact with the centralised plan already concluded in the cathedral of Pisa – the dome over the crossing.

In the longitudinal building, however, the Gothic structural programme just adopted was immediately and in every respect altered, indeed completely overturned; and wide spans, a minimal number of supports, oblong subdivision of the lateral aisles, and low upper walls in the nave, came in place of towering height, a multiplicity of supports, a lofty nave and lateral aisles square on plan (Fig. 7). Instead of the upward development of form, the beauty of space, surface and mass became the aim of Italian Gothic, and indeed of Italian architecture.

The exposed skeleton of northern Gothic, of buttresses and flying buttresses etc., is scarcely suggested; indeed it is hidden, and a prime occasion for elaborating detail removed. Over the wide expanses of wall the pointed gable would have had no meaning, and over the barely projecting buttresses pinnacles made no sense; instead of the former, prominent horizontal cornices; in

Fig. 7 *Florence, Cathedral, interior*

Fig. 8 *Orvieto, Cathedral*

place of the latter, statues, even including animals. Gigantic saints were to stand on the cathedral of Florence (documents in Gaye, *Carteggio*, II, pp. 454, 456, and the representation of the cathedral in the fresco on the right wall of the Cappella degli Spagnuoli), and gilded lions on the corners of the Palazzo della Signoria (Vasari, I, p. 610; *Vita di Orcagna*). Admittedly, on the pinnacles of existing northern Gothic buildings – e.g. on Milan Cathedral – it had been customary to put statues rather than finials. In the interior, the northern type of clustered column and the entire character of ribbed vaulting were completely transformed.

The dome as the supreme expression of politico-monumental dignity was tackled on a huge scale and entailed much preliminary study, now of course in its relationship with the long nave and not entirely on its own account. The highest achievement possible to architecture, it brooked no competition from towers, so that the façade remained free and at the disposition of every type of adornment.

For the realisation of the dome of the new cathedral of Florence Arnolfo would have made accurate calculations with the aid of a model; for the later work, following the enlargement of the plan designed in 1367 by Benci di Cione and Neri di Fioravante, Brunellesco (in 1420) made the structural model, and with its help solved the enormous problem: cf. §47 and 58.

The tower remained separate from, or merely placed against, the church. Such serious competition as at the cathedral of Florence was not allowed anywhere else.

The façade, because of high pretensions – Siena, Orvieto (Fig. 8) – only too often left unfinished, had, as in the preceding epoch, the character of a set-piece of decorative splendour.

§20 *Relationship with the Other Arts*

Italian Gothic, unlike northern, needed from the beginning to permit much freer and greater cooperation with the two sister arts, less on account of the higher stylistic value of Italian painting and sculpture, than because its subject-content had to be clearly and fittingly expressed. Cf. the sculptures and mosaics of the façades.

That the interior should from now on be the proper place for historical and symbolic mural painting was perhaps decided in principle in connection with S. Francesco at Assisi (after 1228); the new Florence cathedral was doubtless also designed for frescoes from the start. There was no desire at all to rely on far from explicit glass-painting. The addition of rows of chapels along the nave, incompatible with the strict northern Gothic system, attained true architectural beauty, e.g. at S. Petronio, Bologna (Fig. 9), and at the same time they became an occasion for sculpture and painting.

Also in smaller ornamental constructions, monuments, altars, pulpits, the architectonic side was not permitted in Italy to assume so assertive, and the pictorial side so minor, a role as in the North.

Fig. 9 *(above)* *Bologna, S. Petronio, plan*

Fig. 10 *(opposite)* *B. Peruzzi, design for the façade of S. Petronio, Bologna*

§21 *Gothic Secular Building in Italy*

Italian Gothic secular architecture lacks the delightful formal exuberance of some northern examples. To the roof-ornamentation, oriels, and spiral staircases of German and Dutch Town Halls and French châteaux there can only rarely be contrasted something like the Porta della Carta of the Doge's Palace in Venice (1438–52) by Giovanni and Bartolommeo Buon, where a style on the verge of dissolution displays a total freedom and worldly gaiety.

It is thus free from the partial introduction of ecclesiastical forms and is in complete contrast to the north by reason of its rational layout. Beauty and convenience evolved very early and harmoniously in the Italian palace. Cf. §88.

The thirteenth and fourteenth centuries were already a time of magnificent town palaces – Piacenza 1281 – in the midst of factional feuds, and also of very handsome princely and private palazzi. The castles of Frederick II in southern Italy, the palace at Orvieto.

Arnolfo was dismayed by his inability to plan the Palazzo della Signoria (Fig. 11) as symmetrically as the castle of Count Poppi built by his father (more accurately, colleague), Lapo: Vasari, I, p. 289, *Vita di Arnolfo.*

In Florence the external character was aggressive and fortress-like; the height of the rooms became the guiding principle, and Acciajuoli (§9) says with regard to his own residence in the Certosa: "the vaults cannot be high and spacious enough, for one of the grandest things in the art of building is the height of the storeys".

In Venice, secure from invasion and insurrection, there appeared the first house façades in the higher sense, with agreeably disposed storeys and fine grouping of the large rosette-windows; in the centre as a wide loggia, at the side singly or in pairs. (That in the loggias a column comes in the middle instead of a space was castigated late in the Renaissance period by Daniele Barbaro; note to Vitruvius, IV, 2, as *vulgaris error.*) Cf. §42, 43, 94.

The Castello of the Visconti at Pavia, begun 1360 (§5), never completed and badly disfigured, a completely symmetrical scheme, not excessively splendid; *domus cui nulla in Italia par est*, said Decembrio (cf. §1) in Murat.,

Fig. 11 *Florence, Palazzo Vecchio*

XX, col. 1006; *il primo dell' universo*, says Corio, fol. 237. And yet Francesco Sforza was to prefer the castle of Ezzelino in Padua (cf. §5); Savonarola in Murat., XXIV, col. 1176; ibid., col. 1174: a lengthy description of the residence of the princely family of Carrara at Padua.

The Visconti residence in Milan, near S. Giovanni in Conca, with spacious indoor courts for tournaments, no longer exists. Corio, fol. 235. The columns partly consisted of black and white layers of marble; Decembrio (cf. §1), col. 998.

Pius II praises the palace of the Avignonese Popes at Montefiascone (*Comment.*, Lib. IV, p. 204).

Public offices, too, early acquired in Italy a rational layout.

The first barracks built in Florence in 1394, until then troops had been quartered in churches; Gaye, *Carteggio*, I, p. 537.

Among hospitals the one at Siena was considered incomparable; travelling princes visited it, and the Emperor Sigismund requested an exact drawing of it; Uberti, *Il Dittamondo*, Lib. III, c. 8; – Gaye, I, p. 92; Milanesi, II, p. 63; – *Diarii sanesi* in Murat., XXIII, col. 798. The hospital of Fabriano in d'Agincourt, *Archit.*, pl. 72.

Was it for the sake of symmetry that false windows and doors appeared in Italian Gothic secular buildings? The earliest instance known to me was not until the Renaissance period, about 1460. Cf. Pii II, *Comment.*, Lib. IX, p. 426.

§22 *Later Hatred of Gothic*

The subsequent feelings of Italians about their Gothic period were in every respect tangled and confused, and to an imperfect historical appreciation of the real circumstances was added the most extreme prejudice. Yet Aeneas Sylvius in 1444 speaks admiringly of the architecture in Germany (*Aeneae Sylvii opera*, Basel ed., 1551, p. 740, cf. p. 718; a letter from Fra Ambrogio regarding the palace of Buda, p. 830), and praises the clean and fresh appearance of German towns (*Apol. ad Martinum Mayer*, p. 696). The German element in the church at Pienza, §77.

Otherwise, for the Renaissance it was a tiresome thought that this style should have come from Germany, and hence attention was always drawn to those aspects of the Gothic buildings of compatriots which would have seemed closest to "good" (i.e. Ancient) architecture. Cf. Vasari, I, p. 448, *Vita di Stefano* and elsewhere.

On the building and decoration of the cathedral of Orvieto (Della Valle, *Storia del Duomo di Orvieto*, p. 118 ff., Docs. 54, 55, 59, 61) some Germans were still employed at the beginning of the fifteenth century, and letters were still circulating through the entire Western world, stating that first-rate artists could apply for work there. After the triumph of the new style, however, the appointment of a Frenchman drew the comment in 1446 (Doc. 70, 71) "there was no lack of native talent"; and a glass-painter, Gasparre da Volterra, appeals *ad quemcunque magistrum ytalicum expertum in dicta arte*. A second-generation German like Vito di Marco Tedesco, Milanesi, II, pp. 271, 429, might already be regarded as Italian.

In 1460, in Filarete's architectural treatise, the solemn malediction: "Cursed be he that fabricated this botch [*praticuccia*]! I believe only a race of barbarians could bring it to Italy." Gaye, *Carteggio*, I, p. 204 – see, however, §44 below.

Involved discussions, founded upon the most extraordinary premisses, but always with the preconceived idea that one was dealing with a German style, are to be found in Manetti's *Vita di Brunellesco* (ed. Holtzinger, p. 23) and in the well-known letter (supposedly and probably) by Raphael to Leo X (reprinted *inter alia* in Quatremère de Quincy, *Storia di Raffaello*, trans. Longhena, p. 531 ff.; cf. §27). In Milan, where since 1386 a considerable influx of German master-craftsmen took place in connection with the building of the Cathedral, there came the Anonimo Morelliano – Marcantonio Michiel – mentioned in §23; a connoisseur, who *inter alia* distinguished Nordic and Italian pointed-arch styles and called the former *ponentino*. (In relation to the background of a little Flemish *Madonna*.) His overall judgement of the style of Milan Cathedral: "It was begun *alla tedesca*, thus it includes many mistakes" (some of which are then specified).

The confusion was worse confounded, when the term "Gothic" was applied to a wider sphere, that of civilisation in general, and from there passed into architectural history.

Already Biondo had suggested that the destruction of monuments, in Rome at least, was the result of age and of the savagery of the Goths; and Lorenzo Valla poured scorn upon the day which brought *Codices gothice scriptos*, by which he meant Gothic script (cf. P. Hoffmann, *Studien zu L.B. Alberti*, p. 33).

Hector Boëce (Boëthius) expressed himself more circumstantially; in *Scotorum Historia* (the dedication dated 1526), f. 382: . . . *meliores literae quae Gothorum immanitate simul cum romano imperio perierant, per totum paene terrarum orbem (scil. saeculo XV) revixerunt.*

The Goths as destroyers of noble literature and their times as centuries of misfortune: Rabelais, *Pantagruel*, II, c. 8, and in the Prologue of the Vth Book: the same view vastly expanded in 1550 by Scardeonius, *De urbis Patav. antiquitate*, in Graevii, *Thesaur.*, VI, III, pp. 259, 295 – inexcusable, when one considers that Cassiodor's collection of letters was printed in 1533, from which one can gain quite a different impression of the great Ostrogoth, Theodoric.

Vasari took the decisive step in transferring the term to the field of art in the impassioned passages of I, p. 136 ff., pp. 229, 232 ff., *Proemio* and *Introduzione*, and II, p. 328, *Vita di Brunellesco*. After a long and contemptuous description of the style of the fourteenth century he says: "This manner was invented by the Goths . . ."

His hatred was great. The nastiest thing he can say of buildings by certain of his contemporaries is "worse

Fig. 12 *Milan, Cathedral roof and* tiburio

than the German" (cf. with V, p. 467, *Vita di Sangallo*, in which his model for S. Peter's is criticised).

How Vasari somewhat earlier (1544) dealt with a pointed-arch monastery refectory, see VII, p. 674 (in his *Autobiography*).

According to Francesco Sansovino (*Venezia*, esp. f. 140; cf. f. 17, 144) he talked to him, and Sansovino deplored and rather feebly excused the invasion of Venice by the so-called Goths' style.

With the passing of time one strengthened the other in resenting the decline from greatness.

§23 *Gothic at the Time of the Renaissance*

The Gothic style continued in some places for a while, alongside the Renaissance, although drained of inspiration and on the whole without the decorative expressiveness which marked the later Northern Gothic (cf. §130).

In Venice (1457) the choir of S. Zaccaria; – in Loreto the Cathedral begun in 1468, continued 1471–79 by the Dalmatian Marino di Marco Cedrino, and 1479–86 by Giuliano da Maiano and Giuliano da Sangallo, a tripartite hall-church with a tripartite transept and a dome over the crossing; the latter completed (1500) by Giuliano da Sangallo; – in Bologna (1440) S. Giovanni in Monte newly built "according to the model of S. Petronio", cf. Bursellis, *Ann. Bonon.* in Murat., XXIII, col. 894; – the Annunziata there, after 1480, one of the last spontaneously Gothic buildings in Italy; – in Milan, Sta Maria delle Grazie (nave), built by the Dominicans 1465–82; and also the Incoronata, 1451–87, built under Francesco Sforza; – in Siena (1459) among the splendid early Renaissance palaces a Gothic one contracted for, perhaps because of the caprice of the client, Nanni Marsigli, who wanted to have a façade with details as on a specified older building; Milanesi, II, p. 303 ff.; at Città di Castello (1483–1513) Sta Maria Maggiore, three-aisled, with Renaissance details.

In addition, Gothic was reluctantly continued in the case of unfinished churches, and architects of the first rank turned back as objectively as they could to a style which they found uncongenial.

In France, which possessed an impressive stock of Gothic prototypes, it was easier to build Orléans cathedral (1601–1790) in Gothic (Kugler, *Gesch. d. Baukunst*, III, p. 114 ff.), since the Gothic idiom had not been subjected to such anarchic disruptions as in Italy.

For S. Petronio at Bologna, indeed, the vast layout of transept, dome and choir (Fig. 9) was abandoned, but the façade, begun in the Gothic manner, was the subject of daily dispute. The fiercely attacked architect Ariguzzi complained in 1514: "People of all sorts, priests, monks, artisans, farmers, schoolmasters, bailiffs, harness-makers, spindle-makers, porters, and even water-carriers behave like architects and voice their opinions . . . But nobody enters the lists with models or drawings, which I am eager to do" (Gaye, *Carteggio*, II, p. 140 f., cf. §18, on Siena).

In the event, the façade remained unfinished, perhaps less on account of scanty resources than because amid the growing number of projects (amounting to some thirty, now in the church archives), no decision could be reached. Among them were two Gothic designs by Baldassare Peruzzi (who also submitted designs for completing the dome) and Giulio Romano. Cf. Gaye, *Carteggio*, II, p. 152; Milanesi, III, p. 311; Vasari, IV, p. 597, *Vita di Peruzzi*. Peruzzi's project (still preserved in the Sacristy, see J. G. Müller, *Memoria sul compimento del duomo di Firenze*, 1847), according to the judgement of the cathedral architect, Seccadinari, in 1530, brilliantly drawn, handsome and grand, but in conflict with the basic forms of the building; cf. Springer, *Bilder aus der neueren Kunstgeschichte*, p. 156. According to Vasari, IV, p. 597, Peruzzi did two designs in different styles, *uno alla moderna ed un altro alla tedesca* (Fig. 10).

The most important achievement of this type is the dome (*tiburio*) of Milan cathedral, a votive tribute in the spirit of the Renaissance laid on the grave of faded Gothic, which would scarcely have been capable of such a solution on its own (Fig. 12).

After many abortive schemes and false starts which had to be pulled down it was built at the beginning of the sixteenth century by Amadeo and Dolcebuono, perhaps according to plans drawn up in 1490 by Francesco di Giorgio, who had been summoned to Milan (Gaye, *Carteggio*, I, p. 289; *Lettere sanesi*, III, p. 85; Milanesi, II, pp. 429–39; Girol. Calvi, *Notizie de' professori di belle arti che fiorivano in Milano sotto il governo de' Visconti e degli Sforza*, parte II, p. 159). Perhaps also the spirited and splendid crowning feature of the dome was executed later according to Francesco's design. Marcantonio Michiel (the 'Anonimo Morelliano', §22) saw it still incomplete in 1525, when indeed it was threatened with a transformation in the modern style; the "German", however, to whom surprisingly the model prepared for this purpose had been entrusted, "lost" it (luckily). On the upper parts lively detail, e.g. cupids which clamber about the Gothic tracery, as on the Porta della Carta (§21).

If, as is most likely, the expert opinion given about 1488, published by Mongeri, originated from Bramante, there is interesting evidence of how deeply the latter had penetrated into Gothic ideas; see Archiv. stor. Lombardo, V, 1877, and H. von Geymüller, *Die ursprünglichen Entwürfe für St. Peter*, p. 116 ff.; cf. ibid., p. 34 f. regarding the nine first-storey façade windows of Filarete's Ospedale Maggiore executed by him after 1485, between the Richini building and the triple-arched central loggia.

On the façade of the Cathedral the Renaissance elements by Pellegrino Tibaldi (Pellegrini) are the oldest, and everything Gothic newer, as is proved by a picture in the Palazzo Litta, in which the façade is shown as unfinished with the beginnings of Pellegrino's splendid cladding.

Gothic tracery of *c* 1500 in a strange, but inspired, confusion, painted in dark blue and gilt, on the vaulting of the Monastero Maggiore in Milan (by Dolcebuono, cf. § 48, 76).

(NOTE: For S. Petronio, Bologna, and Milan Cathedral see now R. Wittkower, *Gothic versus Classic*, London, 1974; for Bramante's memorandum see A. Bruschi, *Bramante*, Bari and Rome, 1969, and his *Bramante*, London, 1977 (not the same book).) (PM).

CHAPTER FOUR

The Study of Antique Buildings and of Vitruvius

§24 *General Character of the Innovations*

In Italy culture progressed more quickly in fields other than the fine arts. The latter would ponder carefully and at length before expressing what scholarship and poetry had already revealed. Thus, Classical Antiquity had long presented an ideal existence before it made any deep and far-reaching impression upon architecture and bore tangible fruit in buildings.

Cf. *Kultur d. Renaiss.*, 3rd ed., I, p. 224 ff.; 4th ed., I, p. 200 ff. In face of mere admiration of ancient buildings (of which there had never been any lack), and before simple aesthetic opposition because of this, the Gothic style would not have given ground: for this is needed an extraordinary city and a powerful personality to make the new thinking a fact.

In Florence, at a time of high prosperity, the feeling first gained ground that the great art of the thirteenth and fourteenth centuries had expended its vital force and that something new must come. For Florence at the beginning of the fifteenth century – Macchiavelli, *Storie Fiorent.*, beginning of the 4th Book; Poggius, *Hist. Flor. Populi*, Lib. V, ad a. 1422.

That feeling was very clearly expressed in 1435 by Leon Battista Alberti (born 1404) in his *Della Pittura* (*Opere Volgari*, ed. Bonucci, vol. IV); it seemed to him "as if Nature had become old and tired and no longer disposed to create great minds any more than giants"; now, returned to Florence after a long exile, he is astonished and delighted to find a new strength in Brunellesco, to whom the work is dedicated, in Donatello, Ghiberti, Luca della Robbia, and Masaccio, who yield nothing to the most illustrious masters of old. About 1460, when the Renaissance style was ousting Gothic from its last strongholds, Filarete commented: "if our style were not more beautiful and more practical, there would be no use for it in Florence (*a Firenze non s'usaria*)."

The new art equally brought with it a realisation that it was breaking with tradition and that, besides freedom, its destiny lay in deploying to the full every resource, and also in the attainment of the highest renown.

Alberti continues: "I now see also that everything great is not simply a gift of nature and of the ages, but depends upon our endeavours and our indefatigability. The ancients found it easier to achieve great things, for a scholastic tradition educated them in those highest arts, which today cost us so much toil; but all the greater will our name become, since we are discovering – without teachers or previous example – arts and sciences which have never been seen or heard of before." Regarding versatility, see §14.

The decision in favour of new thinking could only come through a great feat by an exceptional man, who by so doing opened the way to other aspirations for himself and his contemporaries.

Filippo Brunellesco of Florence (1377–1446) and the Cathedral dome, his recognised task from youth onwards (§2). With this essentially constructional achievement and his other skills in all the mechanic arts there triumphed the great formal and stylistic innovation for which his studies, begun in Rome in 1403, had fitted him. In addition was his fame as a sculptor and a decorative artist. Already one of his earliest works, the Old Sacristy of S. Lorenzo (between 1419 and 1428), "amazed everybody in the city and from outside by its novel and beautiful artistry" (Manetti, *Vita di Brun.*, ed. Holtzinger, p. 48). Here the master was at once to astonish by the "music of the proportions", new motives and new details. Then followed quickly the Cappella Pazzi and other works.

§25 *Neglect of Greek Architectural Remains*

Greece in the fifteenth century existed only for collectors, not for architects. More strikingly, it seems that even the Greek temples on Italian soil, at Paestum, Selinunte, Agrigento and elsewhere, were ignored.

Outstanding among the collectors was Cyriacus of Ancona (Ciriaco d'Ancona) (1390–1457), from whose travel-diaries at least one architect made accurate copies; see Giuliano da Sangallo's drawings of Greek buildings and of Sta Sophia in his sketchbook in the Biblioteca Barberini (Cod. XLIX, 33) in Rome;* the sketch of the "Temple of Apollo in Athens" is imaginary; cf. E. Reisch in Mitteilungen des Kaiserl . . . deutsch. archäolog. Instituts, athen. Abteilung, vol. 14 (1889), p. 217 ff. Original drawings by Cyriacus are to be found in the *Excerpta Varia* of Petrus Donatus in the Hamilton collection now in the Berlin Kupferstichkabinett; cf. in this connection Mommsen in the Jahrbücher der preuss. Kunstsammlungen, IV, p. 73 ff., and Michaelis in the Archäol. Zeitung, vol. 40 (1882), p. 368 ff. Regarding Cyriacus, of particular importance is De Rossi, *Inscriptiones christianae.*, Tom. II, 356 ff., and in the Archivio della R. Società Romana di Storia Patria, X, p. 16.

The Paduan painter Squarcione brought back much that was remarkable *tum mente tum chartis* from his Greek journey, but probably only in connection with sculpture; Scardeonius, apud Graev. *Thes.* VI, III, p. 442. Did Poliphilus (§ 32) make drawings in Greece?

Later on, Raphael, according to Vasari, IV, p. 361, *Vita di Raffaello*, sent draughtsmen to Greece – with what success is not stated.

The hundred-column building "from Greece" in Serlio's Third Book (fol. 96) is doubtless pure fantasy. An Egyptian pyramid and a Palestinian grotto, according to sketches by the Patriarch Grimani, ibid., fol. 93 f.

Would the Renaissance have been able to start with the authentic Doric forms of Greece, where the vault does not occur? Greek buildings, even if they did not teach vaulting, would after all have been as worthy of study as Vitruvius – who did not teach it either. Their neglect, however, was certainly not the result of aesthetic scruples.

A much stronger prejudice operated in favour of Rome, as the historic ruler, as the mother of Italian cities, and as an abiding memory of the nation, which must be revived through art. Even North of the Alps the true relationship of Greek art and culture to Roman has only been recognised since Winckelmann.

The more remarkable, therefore, was Serlio's acceptance (*Architettura*, ed. Venez., 1584, p. 69), reached on purely historical grounds, that Greek buildings must greatly have excelled Roman. On the other hand, Manetti judged (*Vita di Brunellesco*, ed. Holtzinger, p. 22), somewhat naïvely, that ancient Rome, because it had surpassed Greece in power and wealth, must have promoted architecture to a higher level of development.

Rome, which itself produced hardly one major artist, was visited from the beginning of the fifteenth century for study purposes by all well-known architects; under the Popes from Nicholas V onwards (§ 7) it became a principal centre for the practice of architecture.

That Rome in all intellectual activities has almost no native celebrities to show is due in part to the malarial climate and also to the enormous variations in population during the decisive periods in art history, but even more to the changing patronage of *parvenus* who came and went: Florence had a healthy, bracing climate and great stability among those families which patronised the arts: in addition, from childhood upwards, people were accustomed to seeing genius and determination succeed. Besides all this, to be fair, it must be remembered that the mighty fourteenth century, which in the rest of Italy laid the foundations of the entire subsequent civilisation, did not exist in Rome. Had it not been for the Avignonese Exile of the Popes, Rome would have then assumed a different and lasting position in the intellectual life of the country. From Urban IV to Boniface VIII there had been much important artistic activity in Rome; remarkably, too, the Avignon Popes, although French, sent for Italian artists and works of art: Vasari, I, p. 604, *Vita di Orcagna*, and elsewhere.

§ 26 *Fifteenth-Century Studies of Roman Remains*

Contemporary with the learned antiquaries Poggio, Blondus, Aeneas Sylvius and others, and probably not without contact with them, architects began to make surveys in Rome and the neighbourhood. The widespread cult of ruins; cf. *Kultur d. Renaiss.*, 3rd ed., I, p. 224 ff.; 4th ed., I, p. 200 ff.

Brunellesco's measurements, at first in the company of Donatello, perhaps from 1403 onwards, in which they were regarded as treasure-hunters and supported themselves by working as goldsmiths. His study of Roman building technique, the structural organisation, especially of the vault, as well as "the musical proportions" of antique buildings, and, as the result shows, the entire vocabulary of forms, which he comprehensively and freely interpreted.

L. B. Alberti's stay in Rome, before 1434 and particularly in the 40s. He also dug down to the foundations: *De re aedificatoria*, Lib. VI, c. I; apart from Rome he studied, among other places, Antium (Anzio), and Etruscan ruins; ibid., Lib. IV, c. 3.

Filarete in Rome under Eugenius IV (1431–47); his architectural illustrations (cf. Gaye, *Carteggio*, I, pp. 200–206) included actual records as well as his own fantasies.

Nicholas V employed for preference Bernardo Rossellino, whose activities would be unthinkable without drawings.

Francesco di Giorgio claimed to have explored and compared with Vitruvius most of the antique remains in the whole of Italy (Della Valle, *Lettere Sanesi*, II, p. 108).

Domenico Ghirlandaio (*b* 1449) made free-hand drawings in Rome, so accurate that subsequent measurements confirmed them; Vasari, III, p. 271. Admirable architectural backgrounds in his paintings.

Cronaca (*b* 1457) took exact measurements and returned home to Florence as a living "chronicle" of the wonders of Rome; Vasari, IV, p. 442.

In 1465 Giuliano da Sangallo began his sketch-book

* Now in the Vatican Library, Cod. Lat. Barb. 4424 (rep. in facsimile by C. Huelsen, 1910). (PM).

(now in the Bib. Barberini [Vatican], §25) *con molti disegni misurati e tratti dallo anticho* as the title in his own hand says. It contains his own records of antique buildings in Italy and the South of France (the latter in part capriciously restored – cf. Müntz and Laurière in the Mémoires de la société nat. des antiqu. de France, t. XLV), also medieval monuments (Cathedral and Baptistry of Florence, Torre Asinelli at Bologna), copies after Cyriacus of Ancona's Greek drawings (see §25), and finally sketches of contemporary works (Brunellesco's polygonal design for the Angeli, Bramante's Tempietto), but of his own work only a design for a royal palace in Naples and a plan for S. Peter's. Another codex by Giuliano, in Siena, includes sketches for projects of his own as well as other people's (enumerated by Jahn in v. Zahns Jahrbücher für Kunstwissenschaft, V, p. 172 ff.) and drawings after the antique (listed by Müntz in the Mémoires cit.).

Bramantino (Bartolommeo Suardi of Milan) measured and drew the ruins of Rome, as well as Romanesque buildings in Milan and Pavia. His sketch-book, mentioned by Vasari, was published by Mongeri (Milan, 1875).

Venetian miniaturists made attractive drawings in silverpoint from such early records, which came into hands adept in such matters. Collections of such drawings in Venetian cabinets, see Marcantonio Michiel (the *Anonimo Morelliano*), with reference to the Vendramin Cabinet (*Notizie d'opere di disegno*, ed. Frimmel, p. 108).

For the rest of Italy the ruins of Verona, in particular, were treated as an academy. The remains of Verona – theatre, amphitheatre, city gates – were in fact published by Giovanni Carotto in woodcuts of 1540, with text by Saraina (cf. Vasari, V, p. 290, *Vita di Giocondo*), but from drawings by the famous Gio. Maria Falconetto (1458–1534); cf. Vasari, ibid. 319, 323. Falconetto also recorded the remains of Pola and, more particularly, investigated the principle of Roman theatres; he had spent twelve years in Rome studying antiquities, working for half of every week for painters in order to live; he had also explored the Campagna, the Naples region, and Umbria. He was the first to make convincing restorations. Later he was often to visit Rome, also in the company of Cornaro (§12). His practice was concerned only with smaller buildings, but he indulged a fancy for the design of vast imaginary schemes, based on his recollections of Roman work.

Fra Giocondo of Verona (*b* 1435) similarly transferred his interest in the local remains to those of Rome. His distress over the ever continuing destruction, merely for the purpose of lime-burning, in a letter to Lorenzo il Magnifico (Fabroni, *Laur. Med. Vita*, adnot. 146).[1]

(NOTE: The drawings by Ghirlandaio are presumably those in the Codex Escurialensis (in the Escorial), which are now attributed to a draughtsman from the circle of Ghirlandaio, rather than Domenico himself. See J. Shearman in *Master Drawings*, XV, 2, 1977. Giuliano da Sangallo's drawings: Codex Barberini was published in facsimile by C. Huelsen, Leipzig, 1910, and the Taccuino Senese by R. Falb, Siena, 1902.) (PM).

§27 *Sixteenth-Century Studies of Roman Remains*

With the sixteenth century enthusiasm rose to a climax; there was an attempt at a comprehensive ideal restoration of Ancient Rome, using every kind of evidence. The decline of this endeavour coincided with the new, active, building movement of the Counter-Reformation (§10). No architect was spared the task of making his own measured drawings, which had the greatest influence on his artistic formation; the illustrated works appeared belatedly and incomplete.

Bramante in Rome (cf. §49) under Alexander VI (from the end of 1499), already ageing, "lonely and cogitative"; Vasari, IV, p. 155, *V. di Bramante*; at Florence drawings by him, some with accurate measurements. According to Lomazzo, *Tratt. dell' arte*, p. 410, he ascertained by exact measurement different ways of handling Roman buildings, i.e. the real freedom within the norm, and Peruzzi, his contemporary, had the same object in view. Cf. in particular the fundamental study of Bramante by H. von Geymüller in his *Ursprüngl. Entwürfen f. St. Peter*, Vienna, 1875.

Raphael also proved himself a true man of the Renaissance by devoting part of his priceless time in his last years to Ancient Rome. Unfortunately, we have little reliably dated evidence on this point. In Leo X's Brief of 27 August 1515 (Bottari, VI, 25; Passavant, *Raphael*, I, p. 537) no significant policy is yet directed towards a systematic restoration of the ancient city, but only the antique marble ruins were placed under Raphael's supervision, in order to use them either for the building of S. Peter's, or, should they include inscriptions and *monumenta* (i.e. reliefs), to preserve them *ad cultum literarum romanique sermonis elegantiam excolendam*. Celio Calcagnini was first to speak, in 1519, in a letter to Jakob Ziegler (*Coelii Calcagnini Opera*, Basil., 1544, p. 101: trans. in Passavant, *Raphael*, I, p. 244 ff.); concerning the date of composition, see Passavant, p. 246, and Tiraboschi, *Storia della Letteratura italiana*, VI, p. 67; a time of ex-

1 The vandalism seems almost incomprehensible, which Popes Martin V to Leo X, sympathetic as they were to the arts and to classical antiquity, revealed in the willingness with which they allowed ancient buildings to be robbed of their marble and travertine in order to obtain building-stone and lime. L. B. Alberti's complaint about this: *De re aedificat.*, Lib. VI, c. I; Lib. X, c. I. Cf. *Kultur der Renaiss.*, 3rd ed., I, p. 224 ff.; 4th ed., I, p. 200 ff. Gregorovius, *Geschichte Roms im Mittelalter*, VII, p. 557; E. Müntz, *Les monuments antiques de Rome au 15ième siècle* in the Revue archéolog., 1876 ff. and 1884 ff. Martin V also allowed churches to be plundered, which had decayed during the period of exile, so that material for a new pavement in the Lateran could be obtained; see the Brief of 1425 in Reumont, *Geschichte der Stadt Rom*, III, 1, p. 515. Cf. §7. Even Papal decrees, which prescribed the inviolability of ancient buildings, like that of Pius II of 1462 (Müntz, *Les arts*, I, p. 352 f.; Theiner, *Cod. diplomat.*, III, p. 422 f.), were ineffectual. Pius II complained: *Impia ter centum si sic gens egeris annos nullum indicium nobilitatis erit* (Mabillon, *Mus. ital.*, I, 1, p. 97). Even more unconscionable was the later behaviour of Sixtus V, who allowed the Septizonium to be demolished, and Paul V, who destroyed the Forum of Nerva.

tensive excavations and a restored representation of Ancient Rome, as carried out by Raphael using the ancient authors and assisted by Fabio Calvi of Ravenna. On the close relationship of the artist to this true Humanist the letter throws valuable light; cf. also *Kultur d. Renaiss.*, 3rd ed., I, p. 318; 4th ed., I, p. 308. In any case, Calvi, who translated Vitruvius for Raphael, has stronger claims to be considered his adviser on archaeological questions than Andreas Fulvius, even though the latter claims in the preface to his *Antiquitates urbis* (which appeared in 1527) to have guided Raphael's pencil; see the passage in Passavant, p. 306 n. That Raphael died (1520) in the midst of measuring and restoration work is reported by Paolo Giovio (*Elogium Raphaelis* in Tiraboschi, *Stor. della Lett. ital.*, ed. Venice, 1796, Tom. VII, parte iv, p. 1643; also in Passavant, I, p. 553, and in Springer, *Rafael und Michelangelo*, 2nd ed., I, p. 302) and by Marcantonio Michiel in his letter of 11 April 1520 (in the *Anonimo Morelliano*, ed. Frimmel, p. 210). Cf. in this connection Caius Silvanus Germanicus *In statuam Leonis X*, Romae 1524; from the task of laying bare Ancient Rome to its foundations and recording it, Raphael *in limine primo* was to be called away by death. Was the projected publication of 1532 of a prospect of Ancient Rome by Raphael (probably completed by his pupils), of which the envoy Peregrino speaks to the Duke of Mantua as a *bellissima cosa e molto copiosa* really carried out? The same informant mentions another plan of Rome *secondo che antichamente era edificata a tempo de l' antichi romani* in a letter composed shortly before the former; Archivio storico dell' arte, II, p. 251. Was the latter plan identical with the *Simulacrum antiquae urbis Romae cum regionibus* of Fabio Calvi, published in 1532? Cf., regarding the latter, Müntz, *Raphael*, p. 614.

The celebrated Report to the Pope, attributed sometimes to Castiglione, sometimes to Raphael, even if Raphael had no hand in it, is of significance in understanding the archaeological methods and tendencies of the time. It deplores the destruction, censures not merely the vandals, but even the Popes, entreating Leo to protect what still survived, reminding him of particular buildings worthy of Rome, and sets the target as restoration "in accordance with the remains still visible today, and with buildings of which enough is yet preserved that they can be reconstituted infallibly to what they must have been once". There follows a hint about an author, one Publius Victor, allegedly important in this field; finally the method of recording is laid down, and, for the first time, plan, elevation and section are specifically stipulated. On the question of authorship, only this can be said: that, if the document perhaps edited in this form by Castiglione belongs in content to Raphael, the latter can only have compiled it shortly before his death, since he refers to having spent twelve years so far (eleven, according to the Vatican Ms.) in Rome. Müntz (*Raphael*, p. 603 ff.) pleads with convincing warmth for Raphael's authorship.

Raphael sent draughtsmen throughout Italy; Winckelmann (*Anmerkungen üb. d. Baukunst. d. Alten*, p. 35) knew drawings of the Temple at Cora, which he attributed to Raphael, and he also knew of a volume of similar drawings in the collection of Lord Leicester. Probably also the drawings of Rome, Naples, Pozzuoli and the Campagna, which Giulio Romano showed in 1544 to Vasari (V, p. 552, *Vita di Giulio*) at Mantua, had been made on Raphael's behalf "by Giulio and others"; the draughtsmen divided the job between them and then exchanged copies among themselves.

With Serlio's work, about 1540, publications of lasting importance began to appear; in the Dedication of the Third Book he reserves to himself the publication of remains in Southern France still unfamiliar to him.

Among drawings by Antonio da Sangallo the younger, which are still to be found in the Florentine [Uffizi] collection, may already be noted projects for correcting individual mistakes in antique buildings – e.g. the arch of the end niche of the Pantheon (Vasari, V, p. 492, comm. on the *Vita di A. da Sangallo*). The search for general principles becomes a criticism of the monuments themselves.

Towards the middle of the century well-known architects were continuing to spend a number of years in Rome studying the ruins, like Bartol. Genga (Vasari, VI, p. 326, *Vita di Genga*) and Andrea Palladio.

(NOTE: The only drawing which is certainly by Bramante (whether in Florence or anywhere else) is UA 1, the half-plan of S. Peter's. The reference to P. Victor occurs in one of the Mss. of the Letter to Leo X, but no such classical writer seems to be known.) (PM).

§28 *The Influence of Vitruvius*

With the sixteenth century the influence of the architectural teacher from the Golden Age of Augustus, M. Vitruvius Pollio, reached its zenith. Henceforth, it was believed that Antiquity could be judged according to its own rules; Vitruvius soon assumed in architecture a position similar to Cicero's in Latinity, and eager enthusiasts formed a party in his name.

Vitruvius had never been entirely forgotten, but at the time of the early Renaissance the bad state of the text, the complicated exposition, and the inherent shortcomings – e.g. there is no explanation of vault construction (or only an incorrect one: VII, 3) – did him harm. Alberti, in his *De re aedificatoria*, makes use of him without treating him respectfully, and surpasses him in variety of treatment.

Francesco di Giorgio, who first compared ruins with Vitruvius (§26), and in his treatise dealt with the Orders by Vitruvian precedent, added none the less something which held good for the whole Renaissance: his precepts may have been laboriously drawn from the ancient world, but the designs which he presents are his own. The Renaissance treated Antiquity simply as a vehicle for its own architectural ideas.

Antonio Manetti (*Vita di Brunellesco*, ed. Holtzinger, p. 18) expresses the view that if "alcuno autore" of the olden time laid down rules for architecture, as Alberti was to do in his own day, such rules would only be applicable in a general sense; only by examining the ruins of Antiquity do we appreciate the "invenzioni" which are the prerogative of every artist, a gift of Nature or the reward of industry.

Francesco di Giorgio and his patron at the time, Federigo of Urbino, conferred with all the scholars over the interpretation of Vitruvius.

The first edition (1511) was that of Fra Giocondo, who had waited until his old age; Vasari, V, p. 265, note 1, *Vita di Giocondo*, also recording Giocondo's other archaeological work.

Raphael wrote in 1514 or 1515, in an authentic letter: "I should much like to rediscover the beautiful forms of ancient buildings, but do not know whether my flight will not prove an Icarus venture; Vitruvius gives me much light, but not so much as to be enough." *Lettere Pittoriche*, I, 52; II, 5.

In his latter days he acquired a broader outlook, defending or refuting Vitruvius, giving his reasons, with admirable zeal: Coel. Calcagnini *Opera*, ed. Basil., 1544, p. 101.

Baldassare Peruzzi designed the Cathedral at Carpi "according to Vitruvius's rules" and from 1527 made a series of drawings illustrating the Roman author. Vasari, IV, p. 598, cf. 604, *Vita di Peruzzi.*

Serlio speaks fanatically in his *Architettura* (ed. Venez. in 4°, 1584, f. 69, 99, 112, 159*v*, to which must be added the passage on f. 155 of the folio ed., Venez., 1544). The sacrosanct and unimpeachable book is always right, even as against Roman buildings; these are to be judged according to Vitruvius; those against him are heretics, etc. At the end of the Third Book is a list of ardent Vitruvians.

The gradually accumulating Vitruvian literature had to use the Italian language, because Latin interpretations would only have made the subject more difficult.

Translations of Vitruvius with explanatory notes, and generally also illustrated:

A Ms. translation in the Biblioteca Magliabecchiana [Biblioteca Nazionale], Florence, according to Milanesi (notes to Vasari, III, p. 72) is "undoubtedly" in the hand of Francesco di Giorgio and was perhaps also prepared by him.

Fabio Calvi, Ms. in Munich, Vasari, IV, p. 379, n. 2; prepared for Raphael, cf. §27.

Cesariano, 1521, Vasari, IV, p. 150, *Vita di Bramante*, with correcting note.

Caporali, 1536, Vasari, III, p. 598 n., *Vita di Perugino*; ibid., p. 694 n., *Vita di Signorelli.*

Daniele Barbaro (1567), the best known among the later ones; many correct and ingenious ideas found here for the first time, cf. ad Vitr. III, 2 and IV, 2, in which entasis of columns and consoles to pediments are discussed.

Regarding particular difficulties Gio. Batt. Bertano wrote in 1588, and also concerned himself, for example, with the theory of Ionic volutes: Vasari, VI, p. 488, n. 3, *Vita di Garofalo.*

Battista da Sangallo, brother of the Antonio mentioned in §27, left commentaries, unpublished; Ms. in the Bib. Corsini in Rome; Vasari, V, p. 472 n. 1, *Vita di Antonio da Sangallo.* With regard to the endeavours of the Florentine Canon Gio. Norchiati, see Vasari, VII, p. 227 n. 2, *Vita di Michelangelo.*

(NOTE: The first printed edition of Vitruvius was published in Rome, *c* 1484: the edition of 1511, by Fra Giocondo, was the first to be illustrated. Daniele Barbaro's translation and commentary was first published in 1556, not 1567.) (PM).

§29 *The Later Vitruvians*

In 1542 the Vitruvian Academy met in Rome, but did not get much further than a grandiose programme. The patrons most ardent in the cause were at that time rich Venetians. The works, and also the words, of Michelangelo contributed not a little to the decline of this fanaticism.

The society and the programme: *Lettere di Claudio Tolomei*, ed. Venez., 1589, f. 103 ff.; *Lettere pittoriche*, II, 1, including Bottari's annotation. Regarding Cardinal Marcello Cervini, later Pope Marcellus II, a leading member, cf. Ranke, *Päpste*, I, p. 281, 502; Vasari, VII, p. 106, *Vita di T. Zucchero* and V, p. 518, in the commentary to *V. di Ant. Sangallo*, who designed a bath in the antique style for the Cardinal (see below).

The greatest gain may have been Vignola's, who, while still a young man, once again measured the ruins of Rome in the service of the Academy.

In Venice, Jacopo Sansovino brought to an end the early Renaissance, as the representative of the stricter Vitruvian movement; this was acclaimed both in his private palaces and in his Library. On the question of the angle treatment of the entablature (cf. §53) of the Doric Order of the Library the whole of antiquarian Italy went into action; Cardinal Bembo sent in the solutions of various architectural experts, and even Tolomei, the Secretary of the Vitruvian Academy, expressed a view on its behalf; Sansovino had already produced an answer, which proved fully satisfactory. Vasari, VII, p. 502, *V. di Jac. Sansovino*; Francesco Sansovino (the master's son), *Venez.* f. 44, 113, where the story is somewhat exaggerated in the telling.

Michelangelo's efforts to "burst the bonds and chains" which architecture laid upon itself; it was apparent that he by no means "considered himself bound by any ancient or modern architectural law". In reference to the finest of his five designs for S. Giovanni de' Fiorentini in Rome, he said: "Neither the Romans nor the Greeks achieved anything like it in their temples." Vasari, VII, p. 193, 233, 263, *V. di Michelangelo*; his scorn for a prominent Vitruvian, p. 280.

He liberated art more than was beneficial. Yet perhaps no single truly great conception had been lost out of regard for a book which did not teach the vaulted arch and contained no prescription for the everyday needs of the sixteenth century, but cautioned against the misapplication of particular details.

A belated regret that no such ancient rule-book survived for painting: Armenini, *De' veri Precetti della Pittura*, p. 22.

CHAPTER FIVE

The Theorists

§30 *Leon Battista Alberti*

Since it was general at that time for scholarship to precede the arts (§24), it is not surprising that literature, the representative of culture, was present at the cradle of newborn architecture. The great Leon Battista Alberti, in his theory and rules of architecture, makes this plain. Cf. §24 and *Kultur der Renaiss.*, 3rd ed., I, p. 168; 4th ed., I, p. 151.

His youthful essay on painting was succeeded by his great work on building. The extant Italian version, written in his own hand, *arte edificatoria* (in the *Opere Volgari di L.B.A.*, ed. Bonucci, Tom. IV), extends as far as the Third Book, and this text we have felt bound to follow; from there on, however, there is a Latin text, also his, *De re aedificatoria*. All evidence points to a date of composition between 1450 and 1452, during Alberti's lifetime (*d* 1472), but shown only to a small circle of Humanist friends and not widely circulated in copies. Mattia Palmieri's note (*Opus de temporibus suis*, in Rer. Ital. Script. ed. Tartinio, I, p. 241), that Alberti had shown (*ostendit*) his book to Pope Nicholas V is not to be understood as a specific presentation or dedication; cf. Paul Hoffmann, *Studien zu L. B. Albertis zehn Büchern de re aedif.* After Alberti's death, a cousin of Angelo Poliziano, Bernardo, copied the manuscript, and this copy, together with Poliziano's dedicatory letter (dated 1480 by Tiraboschi), was presented to Lorenzo de' Medici. This Ms. is probably identical with the one in the Biblioteca Laurenziana (LXXXIX, cod. 113). Another copy, of 1483, is in the Vatican Library, to which it went from Urbino; cf. Mancini, *Vita di L. B. Alberti*, p. 392 n. 4. The first printed edition appeared in Florence in 1485. The Italian editions since the sixteenth century are later translations.

The principal relevant passages: *arte edificatoria*, pp. 229, 238, 240 (in Book I), and *De re aedif.*, Lib. VI, c. 2 and 5; Lib. IX, c. 3 and 5.

Gothic architecture was merely a dynamic rhythm, that of the Renaissance is rhythm of masses; in the one the artistic content is expressed in the organism, in the other it lies essentially in the geometrical and cubic relationships. Alberti thus makes no reference to structural forces, which had inevitably to be given individual expression, but refers to the image which the building creates, and to the eye, which contemplates and enjoys this image.

In the above-mentioned youthful essay *Della Pittura* (*Op. Volgari*, IV, p. 41) he derives architecture from pre-existent painting; the architect first learned his columns and entablatures from the painter – the strongest evidence of the painter's attitude in the early Renaissance towards architectural forms.

In the main work: the law of variety, of pleasing contrast (cf. §286)* in association with symmetry (*varietà* and *parilità delle cose*); in considering variety he goes very far, perhaps thinking of the thermae, palaces etc. of Imperial Rome. For example, no one line should dominate the whole, since certain elements appear more beautiful if they are large, others if they are made small; some when they run in straight, others in curved, lines. For the beauty of the column, Alberti, like the later theorists (e.g. Serlio, p. 98), was loud in his praise.

The important description of an admirable composition in Book VI, for the most part rather negative; at the end, *omnia ad certos angulos paribus lineis adaequanda* – which admits of various interpretations. His aesthetic assessment of the cubic proportions of interiors is highly significant: cf. §89.

His attempt at a general architectural aesthetic in the IXth Book is confused by an admixture of older definitions, but not without weight: his most expressive term is *concinnitas* – the fully harmonious. The basic response to a building, which determines the ultimate judgement upon it, he makes no attempt to analyse,

* This reference to §286 is given by Burckhardt, but refers to the unpublished section, on painting, of his book (see Introduction, p. xvi). (PM).

calling it an unfathomable something: "*Quippiam*", *quod quale ipsum sit, non requiro*. But he protests (VI, 4) against the ignorant, who considered that the verdict on architectural beauty rested upon a *soluta et vaga opinio*, and that architectural forms were inconstant and obeyed no laws, but were merely a matter of choice.

(NOTE: Bonucci's identification of Alberti's holograph Ms. is not now accepted. For the text of his *De re aedificatoria* see the Italian/Latin ed. by G. Orlandi and P. Portoghesi, 2 vols., Milan, 1966.) (PM).

§31 *Alberti's Successors, up to Serlio*

The theorists immediately following Alberti appear, so far as can be judged, to have made use of his work. Schemes relating to mechanics and construction, waterworks and the mathematical side of the art notably increased towards the end of the fifteenth century. Later, for a time, attention to Vitruvius (§28) absorbed such activity, and in due course large syntheses and architectural encyclopaedias appeared.

The richly illustrated Ms. of the treatise by Antonio Averlino, called Filarete, begun in 1460 and finished early in 1464, in the Bib. Magliabecchiana [Bib. Naz.], Florence (XVII, cod. 130); a copy, intended for Matthias Corvinus, in the Library of S. Marco, Venice; excerpts in Gaye, *Carteggio*, I, pp. 200–206, contain, besides a curse on Gothic (§22), a blessing upon the Renaissance, and a remarkable list of well-known contemporary artists belonging to the new movement. Cf. §91: detailed description and summary of contents of the treatise in Dohme, *Filaretes Traktat*... in Jahrb. der Kgl. preuss. Kunstsammlungen, I, p. 225 ff. and in W. von Oettingen, *Antonio Averlino, gennant Filarete*, Leipzig, 1888: cf. also Oettingen's publication of the treatise in the *Quellenschriften für Kunstgeschichte*, Vienna, 1896.

The *Trattato d' architettura civile e militare* by Francesco di Giorgio (§28), written about 1480, was published from the Turin Ms. by Carlo Promis, Turin, 1841: other Mss. in the Bib. Magliabecchiana in Florence and in Siena; excerpts in Della Valle, *Lettere Sanesi*, III, p. 108. The somewhat old-fashioned approach is shown by the author's lack of approval of newer tendencies. He finds "manifest errors, bad proportions, and mistakes in symmetry". Another Ms. with drawings of military architecture and war-machines is to be found in the Bibl. Magl.; another in Siena: cf. also Ant. Pantanelli, *Di Franc. di Giorgio Martini pittore, scultore e architetto senese*, Siena, Gati, 1870.

Among Leonardo's papers there is much on mechanics; his treatise on watermills, etc. Cf. the publication by J. P. Richter, *The Literary Works of L. da Vinci*.

Regarding Fra Giocondo, his waterworks, bridge-building and his theoretical and all-round learning, cf. Vasari, V. pp. 262, 266 ff., 273; *Vita di Giocondo*, text and notes.

In architecture fastidious minds paid far more heed to the mathematical than to the artistic side. Federigo of Urbino (§11) wrote in 1468: "Architecture is founded upon arithmetic and geometry, which are numbered among the most important of the seven Liberal Arts, because they possess in the highest degree the quality of certitude" (Gaye, *Carteggio*, I, p. 214: cf. 276).

Sebastiano Serlio of Bologna and his *Dell' Architettura* (with different titles for the different Books); the first edition in folio, Venice, from 1540; we cite the expanded quarto ed., Venice, 1584. Not in a theoretical, but rather in a random arrangement, illustrations from antiquity and a large number of buildings and designs of the Renaissance, some of the author's own invention, some from drawings by Baldassare Peruzzi, whom he mentions several times with gratitude. For an unfavourable comment on the influence of the book, cf. §12.

(NOTE: For further details of these treatises, especially Filarete, see the Bibliography.) (PM).

§32 *Poliphilus*

In addition to theory and mathematical principles, their direct opposite, architectural fantasy, has left its memorial in the literature.

The architectural-allegorical romance *Hypnerotomachia Poliphili*, by the Dominican traveller in the East, Fra Francesco Colonna of Venice (born *c* 1433, died as late as 1527). This work was written after 1485, first printed in 1499; thereafter several editions with the original woodcuts, unpaginated: extracts in Temanza, *Vita de' più celebri architetti e scultori veneziani*. Cf. *Kultur d. Renaiss.*, 3rd ed., I, p. 233; 4th ed., I, p. 211, and A. Ilg, *Über den kunsthistor. Wert der Hypner. Polifili*, Vienna, 1872. It is a love-story in mythological and fairy-tale disguise, which provides the essential occasion for describing and illustrating ideal buildings and interiors. Cf. §25, 64 (Fig. 13).

Meanwhile, neither theorists nor poets talk as clearly as we should like about the great transition which was taking place before their eyes and was partly brought about by them. Sometimes they are unaware of the state of events, sometimes these seem self-evident to them. Only later could the Renaissance be identified, in contrast to all earlier styles, as one of spatial and surface relationships.

The spatial style which the new era brought to architecture is in complete contrast to the organic styles; which does not prevent it from exploiting in its own way the forms produced by the latter.

The organic styles have always only one principal type: the Greek one the rectangular peripteral temple, the Gothic the many-aisled cathedral with Western towers. As soon as they are diverted to a different use, particularly one involving complex ground-plans, they are ready to be transformed into spatial styles. The Imperial Roman style is already close to this transition, developing a notable spatial beauty, which survives in differing degrees in the Byzantine, Romanesque, and Italian Gothic styles (§19), but reaches its zenith in the Renaissance.

§ 32a★ *Buildings in Pictures*

Another facet of the architectural spirit of the Renaissance in the actual process of transition is revealed in architecture represented in paintings, the uninhibited visual expression of ideas to which three-dimensional realisation has been denied.

Ideal perspective views since Brunellesco, who, according to Vasari (II, p. 332: *Vita di Brunellesco*), made linear perspective renderings of existing buildings, e.g. the neighbourhood of the Baptistry and the Palazzo della Signoria, and also taught the *intarsiatori* (§ 151, 152) to depict buildings which were and remained perspectively correct, but ideal constructions. (List up to the sixteenth century, loc. cit.; cf. Fig. 311 and §152.)

At Urbino (Gall. Nazionale) the panel-painting of an almost symmetrical deserted piazza with splendid buildings, attributed to Piero della Francesca; according to Budinich by Luciano da Laurana, probably intended to have figures added to illustrate a history.

Throughout the entire fifteenth century lavish use of often very magnificent and ingenious buildings in frescoes and panels, sometimes as seen from outside, sometimes as the location of an incident represented; for us a very important addition to what was actually executed. (Summary in the *Cicerone*, 10th impression, II, p. 117.)

Early in the sixteenth century, by Raphael, the celebrated interior of the *School of Athens*, after a sketch by Bramante; by Raphael's pupils, the *Baptism of Constantine* and the *Donation of Constantine*.

Also, on internal walls, colonnaded perspectives painted to simulate an extension of the interior space, as a calculated *trompe l'oeil* (Baldassare Peruzzi in the first-floor *salone* of the Farnesina; previously, similar work by him in connection with theatrical scene-painting, § 193); a genre which must have succeeded the custom of hanging tapestries on wall-surfaces, and one which occasionally fell into inferior hands (§ 169), yet held its place until the late Baroque period, sometimes merely displaying architectural and decorative forms, at others enlivened by figures and even perhaps with histories. By its continuing association with theatrical painting, which was gradually becoming very important, perspective in fresco maintained a certain level of distinction and is complementary to the whole historical consideration of the Baroque.

Fig. 13 *Imaginary building from the* Hypnerotomachia Poliphili

★ To avoid confusing the reader, who may be familiar with the numbering of the sections in earlier editions of this book, the author has numbered this new section 32a, instead of 33, and the same applies to § 46a and § 146a.

CHAPTER SIX

Treatment of Form in the Early Renaissance

§33 *Inevitability of Roman Detail*

Design in terms of proportion and for visual effect, which was central to the Renaissance (§30, 32), had already been stirring in the twelfth century and in the Gothic period. At this time it became particularly affected by Gothic detail, which derived from a contrary philosophy; on the other hand it would inevitably have found itself half attracted by the formal vocabulary of the Romans, because they had handled detail as a free decorative cladding. Every effort was now made to get rid of this sharp formal contradiction.

But added to this there was a very strong and widespread prejudice in favour of Ancient Rome. It is quite pointless to ask whether the Italians would or could have been able to create a new idiom of their own. Their whole education, the harbinger of their art, had long been directed to the universal triumph of Antiquity; the matter was in large part decided, before any question of defining the course of architecture arose.

For central Italy it was equally a matter of the triumph of form over material; a colourful incrustation of marble of all hues and of mosaics on the most important church façades had to yield to the austere modelling of Roman detail, even if the latter was in fact only applied externally to a structural core of another material – as had been the case with the ancient Romans.

In addition, the laws of Roman construction were adopted to a great extent. By this was understood nothing more than that the layout, principal forms, and proportions had to be contrived according to their respective purposes and also to be beautiful.

The Renaissance was responsible for hardly any copies of actual Roman buildings; for instance, despite all the admiration, it reproduced not a single temple and made use of the Antique only in the sense of very free adaptation. Cf. §28, the view of Francesco di Giorgio. Proportions are without exception freely chosen, and the influence of the Antique Orders upon them is merely superficial. In actual fact, the treatment of the Orders themselves depends upon the proportions.

§34 *Attitude to Decorative Forms*

To begin with, there was no distinction between what belonged to the good or to the debased Roman era, to buildings of the highest quality or purely utilitarian structures; also what had been created to a particular scale was reduced or enlarged at will.

A superb Ionic capital found at Fiesole (a similar example also in the crypt of the Cathedral there) was taken by Giuliano da Sangallo as the model for his colonnade of the cortile of Sta Maria Maddalena de' Pazzi in Florence; Vasari, IV, p. 270; *Vita di G. da Sangallo.* Similar occurrences, notably in cornices; see below. Forms of Roman decorative style, from altars, sarcophagi, candelabra etc. were early transferred to architecture.

A greater danger lay in the sudden, and very great, appreciation of classical decorative forms. That these did not overwhelm architecture was due entirely to the splendid architectural aims and admirable restraint of the Florentines.

Consider the passion for ornament and display of the fifteenth century, the rapidly increasing number of skilful decorators and the tendency of the great Florentines themselves towards decorative work, as far as the strict canons of art allowed them.

Michelozzo carved capitals himself, if the mood took him; for example, for a door in the Palazzo della Signoria in Florence; Vasari, II, p. 437; *Vita di Michelozzo.* Finely carved capitals sometimes led to bigger commissions – Andrea Sansovino obtained on the strength of this the job of building the vault of the vestibule linking the sacristy and church of Sto Spirito; Vasari, IV, p. 448; *V. di Cronaca*, and p. 511; *V. di A. Sansovino.*

With regard to theory the Neapolitan Gioviano Pontano (§9), for example, *c.* 1500 assigns the first place to ornament and even permits its exaggeration: *et in ornato*

Fig. 14 *Arezzo, Sta Maria, loggia*

Fig. 15 *Florence, Sta Croce, detail of cloister*

quidem, cum hic maxime opus commendet, modum excessisse etiam laudabile est. On the other hand, the Florentine Alberti, who liked it in his buildings, fifty years earlier allots it in his textbook only a secondary role: Lib. VI., c. 2: he says that beauty lies in a harmony of every part, which would be lost by any addition or subtraction; but because in practice it constantly seems as if something must be added or subtracted, and therefore the greater perfection may be hard to attain, decorative forms have been introduced as a *subsidiaria lux*, as a *complementum* of beauty. The latter must be innate in, and permeate the whole, while ornament has the nature of something tacked on externally: L. IX, c. 8, a further warning to use restraint in decoration and to apportion it prudently.

§35 *The Column, Arch and Entablature*

In Italy the column had never been seriously threatened by the composite pier; it was now restored to its true stature and again used in association with its ancient appurtenances of base and entablature.

Enthusiasm for the column as such, §30. Concerning the laws of its optical effect Alberti, *inter alia*, points out that free-standing columns appear slimmer than those in front of a wall, and, therefore, the angle column must either be made thicker or fluted, which has visually the same effect. (From Vitruvius, IV, 4, but in a fresh interpretation.)

The Early Renaissance showed itself opposed to fluting (§134). Outstanding example: the four plain columns of the portal on the splendid façade of the Certosa of Pavia (§71, and Fig. 138). Fluting first appeared in Venice (upper part of the Procuratie Vecchie; the Orders of the Pal. Vendramin-Calergi) (Fig. 43, §44). The delicate portico of S. Giacomo Maggiore at Bologna (1477–81) is also fluted: it is by a master who may well have been responsible for the similar cortile of the Pal. Bevilacqua. In Florence perhaps the earliest instance is the Capp. Strozzi in SS. Trinita: cf. M. Reymond in Miscellanea d' Arte, 1903, p. 4 ff. (The Northern Renaissance, on the other hand, liked to apply fluting to columns and pilasters.)

Brunellesco, whenever he made pilasters responding to columns (interior of S. Lorenzo; portico of the Pazzi Chapel), fluted the former to give greater animation to the wall, but left the latter plain, so that as bearers of the masonry above, they would stress their purely structural importance in contrast to the decorative function of the pilasters, and so appear more powerful.

Alluding to a motto of Lodovico Sforza, Bramante (1492) gave the shaft of some of the columns in the Canonica of S. Ambrogio in Milan the forms of tree-trunks with branches cut back to the stem; cf. H. v. Geymüller, *Ursprüngliche Entwürfe für S. Peter*, p. 45 f.

Fortunately, in Italy arches over columns continued, although there was no lack of objections to this usage. In the interiors of churches, as well as in cloisters and piazze in cities, the arch was used far more often than the straight entablature.

As is well known, Brunellesco restored the ancient archivolt to the arch, but on ceremonial buildings, such as S. Lorenzo or Sto Spirito in Florence, he felt obliged to add a sort of dosseret between the capital and the springing of the arch. This was to counter the impression that, where two arches converge on a single capital, members of differing strength might become dislocated and exert differing degrees of force; it was necessary "to give the various elements a firm common support before they are absorbed by the load-bearing columns" (Bühlmann, *Die Architektur des klass. Altertums u. der Renaiss.*, p. 30). At the same time, something else was achieved: a more slender appearance of the arch. For the same pur-

Fig. 16 *Florence, Sta Croce, Pazzi Chapel*

pose Alberti recommended a heightening of the arch by up to one-third of the radius, and also because, seen from below, something was lost on account of the impost. Compare the entablature over columns which Late Roman architects set in front of the piers supporting the vault (Basilica of Constantine, Thermae of Diocletian, etc.), the dosserets of Early Christian architecture (Rome, Ravenna etc.), and even in the Gothic period, for the purpose of heightening the arches, the superstructure above the pier capitals, e.g. in the Loggia dei Lanzi, Florence; similarly, in the fifteenth century, in the Gothic interior of the Cathedral at Pienza. In Florence indeed a Proto-Renaissance precursor of the heightened capital was apparent in the blind arcades on the face of the Baptistry (Fig. 5), and on the façade of the Badia at Fiesole.

Brunellesco's use of a dosseret made from a section of entablature found only rare imitators; on the portico of Sta Maria at Arezzo (Fig. 14), according to Vasari by Benedetto da Majano; in the Servi at Siena (Fig. 19), in the Cathedral of Cortona, on the colonnade of the Annunziata in Florence (the central arch by Ant. da Sangallo, those at the sides – as late as 1601 – by Caccini, correctly appreciating that in this way the arches of the colonnade could most easily be given approximately the same height at the crown as the adjoining Loggia degli Innocenti by Brunellesco, sited at right angles and at the top of a flight of steps, see Fig. 246, §107); as well as Giuliano da Majano's Faenza Cathedral, 1474 (see illustration in Lützows Zeitschrift f. bild. Kunst, XXIV, p. 167); Sta Maria Annunziata at Camerino, and elsewhere.

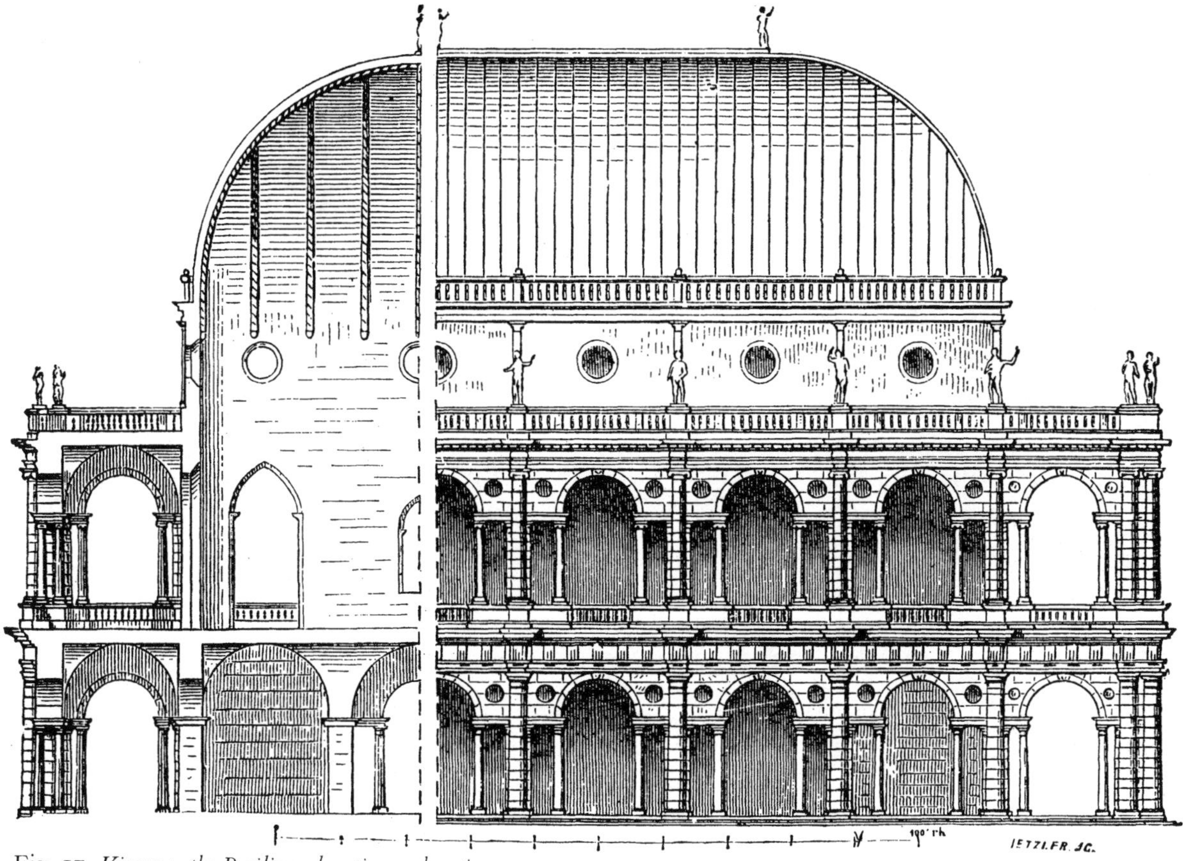

Fig. 17 *Vicenza, the Basilica, elevation and section*

Nevertheless, Alberti (Lib. VI, c. 15) requires a straight entablature over a column, the arch fitting only on a pier. The insertion of a dosseret had no appeal to a man capable of constructing hexameters and pentameters in Italian. Among his own buildings the Chapel of the Holy Sepulchre in S. Pancrazio has the straight entablature. (The portico of the Pal. Stiozzi-Ridolfi, via della Scala 75, dates only from 1500.) His ironical insinuation, L. IX, c. 4; for loggias the straight entablature is appropriate for prominent citizens (§ 104), arches will do for middling families.

It availed little: arches on columns, when correctly handled, were completely vindicated and were to predominate to the end. As soon as the colonnade was vaulted (as Alberti, loc. cit., also required), the straight entablature was no longer of value; it made the vaulting dark and did not help to carry the load. The width of the interval could not be ignored, and the straight entablature was confined to the top storeys of loggias, where it was generally constructed of wood and carried a flat timber ceiling (Fig. 15).

The interruption of a portico by an arch in the middle, corresponding to a main entrance, was already known in Antiquity (colonnade in front of S. Lorenzo, Milan; Spalato, etc.) and in Early Christian and medieval architecture, but now becomes more often an embellishment. A notable early example: the portico of the Cathedral of Cività Castellana, a work in the Cosmatesque style, from the beginning of the thirteenth century (Fig. 2).

Brunellesco most effectively interrupted the straight entablature by a large central arch in the portico of the Cappella de' Pazzi, adjoining Sta Croce in Florence (Fig. 16), as did Giuliano da Sangallo in the cloister of Sta Maria Maddalena de' Pazzi.

This feature is repeated decoratively on a blind façade with pilasters, entablature, and archivolts at the Madonna di Piazza in Pescia, probably *c* 1450, by Brunellesco's disciple, adopted son and heir, Andrea di Lazzaro Cavalcanti, called Buggiano (see illus. in Laspeyres, *Die Kirchen der Renaissance in Mittelitalien*, Fig. 62).

In scale and majesty most effective: in Vasari's Uffizi the placing of the arch over the passage at the end (see Fig. 66, § 56).

Bramante's (unexecuted) third storey in the great cortile of the Vatican, an open colonnade with a straight entablature and rectangular wall-panels above, conceived as a contrast to the arches and massive piers of the two lower floors: D'Agincourt, *Archit.* T. 57.

In small dimensions, where the antique spacing was easy to preserve, one sometimes finds an agreeable and disciplined use of the straight entablature; Cortile of the Pal. Massimi in Rome by Peruzzi; the barrel-vault lit by openings cut through the masonry on the side towards the light – see Fig. 223, § 98.

That the semicircular colonnades were better served

Fig. 18 *(left) Genoa, Palazzo Sauli, detail*

Fig. 19 *(above) Siena, Chiesa dei Servi, details*

Fig. 20 *(below) Fiesole, Badia, details*

by a straight entablature is self-evident, cf. the cortile of the Vigna di Papa Giulio [Villa Giulia], see Fig. 268, § 120.

Michelangelo's Palazzo dei Conservatori on the Capitol: the loggie with straight entablatures on piers, which, to enhance the impression, have columns next to them; a wonderful compromise between disparate elements.

A new dominance of the straight entablature with the school of Palladio. It should not be forgotten that in Rome the Septizonium of Severus, three superimposed open colonnades, all Corinthian and with straight entablatures, survived until after 1585. Palladio's Palazzo Chiericati at Vicenza was obviously inspired by it (see Fig. 240, § 105). Among the works of his followers the two vast courts of the Collegio Elvetico (now Pal. del Senato) in Milan, by Fabio Mangone after 1600.

A beautiful new feature of the sixteenth century: two short entablatures on columns with an arch in the middle* (already seen in Late Roman buildings – Spalato etc.) and then used by Bramante in his designs for S. Peter's, by Raphael at Sant' Eligio degli Orefici in Rome, and as early as 1503 by Dolcebuono in the upper colonnade of the interior of the Monastero Maggiore in Milan (see Fig. 156, § 76); later as a principal feature in Palladio's Basilica at Vicenza (Fig. 17). Alternatively, straight entablatures on two columns alternate with arches; a favourite motive of Galeazzo Alessi and his followers, with ornamental round or oval recesses containing busts above the entablature (Fig. 18).

§ 36 *The Antique Orders in the Fifteenth Century*

Among the Roman Orders the commonest, freest and richest of its type, the Corinthian, now occupied first place; but only exceptionally was it copied from the grander examples. The Ionic and Composite appeared less frequently (Figs. 19 and 20); not until the sixteenth century was the Doric seriously applied, and with constant competition from the so-called Tuscan.

Alberti, in his major work, the *De re aedificatoria* (L. VII, c. 6–10, 15), recognised the Doric, Ionic, Corinthian and "Italic" – i.e. Composite – capitals. Concerning the publication, first discovered in the nineteenth century, and, according to recent opinion, not attributable to Alberti, *I cinque ordini architettonici* (unique Ms. in the Biblioteca Chigi, Rome, VII, 149; published by Bonucci in *Opere volgari di Alberti*, Tom. IV, and by Janitschek in *Albertis kleinere Schriften*, p. 207 ff.); cf. P. Hoffmann, *Studien zu Alberti*, p. 52, in which an author from the time of Serlio is conjectured.

Alberti gives, independently of Vitruvius, the results of his own measurements and reflections. The Doric echinus was to him a *lanx* (i.e. a shallow dish); the Ionic volute a roll of fibrous bark, hanging down from such a dish (certainly more relevant to its real origin than Vitruvius's comparison with a woman's curls). The stylobate or pedestal meant to him (e.g. Lib. IX, c. 4) an *arula*, a small altar; a false image, which might well retaliate by a wrong portrayal of the element concerned, and yet any other derivation would perhaps have gone still further astray.

* i.e. what is usually referred to in English as a Palladian motive, or – in Italian – a *serliana*. (PM).

Fig. 21 *Florence, Palazzo Pazzi-Quaratesi, detail of capital*

Fig. 22 *Mantua, Sant' Andrea, tomb of Piero Strozzi*

On the Ionic capital with fluted hypotrachelion a leaf often dropped from the volutes, clinging to the neck. Thus as early as Brunellesco's buildings we find it in the Pal. Pazzi-Quaratesi on the colonettes of the windows; in the cortile of Sta Croce (Fig. 15); the cortile and garden loggia of the Badia at Fiesole (Fig. 20) by Bruosco and Benedetto dei Benedetti of the school of Desiderio da Settignano. Later examples: Cathedral of Pienza, Cathedral of Faenza, Sta Maria Maddalena de' Pazzi at Florence, the Certosa of Florence, the Servi at Siena (Fig. 18), S. Pietro at Ascoli etc.

The Composite first used by Michelozzo in the court of the Pal. Medici in Florence, and somewhat earlier (after 1427) on the Brancacci Tomb in Sant' Angelo a Nilo, Naples (§141) executed by Michelozzo in Pisa, then in the Pal. Gondi. Alberti called it the Italic Order, "so that we do not regard everything as borrowed from elsewhere".

The finest Corinthian capitals are, as a rule, the Florentine unifoliate examples, with dolphins and other fantastic forms (Fig. 21, from the cortile of the Pal. Pazzi).

In colonnaded courts the Orders are not usually varied, but the same one is retained for two or three storeys.

I do not know of any caryatids until the sixteenth century, on the tomb of Pietro Strozzi (*d* 1529), designed by Giulio Romano, in Sant' Andrea at Mantua. There are four carrying the entablature upon which the sarcophagus with the statue rests; they support the architrave with one hand, disposed in a curious oblique pattern (Fig. 22). (Atlantes leaning against an associated architectural feature are not uncommon from the sixteenth century on tombs; Michelangelo's *ignudi* on the Julius Tomb do not belong to this category, because they do not help to carry an entablature.)

§37 *Half-Columns and Free-Standing Columns*

Engaged-column Orders on stylobates, as a framing for piers with arches, principally in larger palace-cortili, and also in church interiors, had prototypes in the lower storeys of Roman "show" buildings, notably the Colosseum and the Theatre of Marcellus. Salient columns with projecting entablatures, as found on Triumphal Arches, were now used as portals.

One of the earliest engaged-column Orders, on Alberti's façade of S. Francesco at Rimini (1447) (Fig. 127, §69); the motive of the triple-arched Triumphal Arch was the model here; but as there are no secondary entrances at the sides of the portal, the arches merely frame wall-niches, so the half-columns could be placed upon a continuous raised base instead of separate pedestals; as, for example, on the Arch of Titus in Rome, where the engaged columns rest on a stylobate. Next, the rather slender columns in the court of the Palazzo di Venezia, Rome (from 1455: Fig. 23); in misunderstood imitation of the projections of the upper storey of the Colosseum the engaged half-columns of the lower colonnade are given pedestals; in contrast, these are missing

Fig. 23 *Rome, Palazzo Venezia, court*

Fig. 24 *Florence, Palazzo Medici-Riccardi, angle*

from the contemporary portico of S. Marco (see Fig. 135, §70) and in the destroyed Benediction Loggia of St. Peter's (1463). The best-known example is the Pal. Farnese (see below).

Among Roman churches: Sta Maria del Popolo, interior (1472–77) and Sant' Agostino (1479–83) by Giacomo da Pietrasanta.

The engaged column was also rarely used for palace façades, first by Bramante and Raphael and then, especially towards 1550, more frequent examples with Alessi and Palladio. Cf. §54.

The first church façade with salient columns would have been that of S. Lorenzo in Florence in Michelangelo's projects: the thorough preparatory work for it, Vasari, I, p. 119; *Introduzione*. The salient columns used in N. Italian church portals are not relevant, because they are simply re-using a medieval motive and do not constitute an Order.

§38 *The Pilaster and the Cornice*

Just as the lower storeys of Roman "show" buildings provided influential models for the piers in cortili, so for the façades the top storeys set the standard. Pilaster Orders were mainly derived from the uppermost storey of the Colosseum.

The Roman pilaster was a flattened column (unlike the Greek anta) and it played a secondary role in association with the salient column as a wall termination or at angles, while also completely replacing the engaged or free-standing column, e.g. in ceremonial gateways. The Romans had used it in rows on "show" buildings, in order – after providing the lower arcaded storeys with engaged columns – to guide the eye upwards past the closed wall-mass of the top storey and to dispel its heaviness.

Amphitheatres in the Provinces (Pola, Nîmes) also probably had pilasters from the bottom up.

Apart from the Colosseum, the Amphitheatrum Castrense must be considered, its upper disposition then being, according to old illustrations, much better preserved.

Lastly, the Middle Ages (and not merely in Italy) had kept alive the practice of giving a vertical emphasis to walls by pilaster-strips (or *lesene*).

The Renaissance now applied the pilaster inside and outside buildings without scruple or restraint; it was prized as representing the favoured column. If Palladio at times translated the swelling and tapering of the column to the pilaster there were precedents for this – the Propylea at Baalbec, etc.

The pilaster is an expression of support and transition. Its influence on the height of the storey is much less than the latter's influence upon it. On church and palace façades it is disposed singly or in pairs, and the latter may be closely or widely spaced. Alberti mentions the

Fig. 25 *Florence, Palazzo Pitti*

pilaster (Lib. VI, c. 12), but not the pilaster Order, which he nevertheless used.

The pilaster occurs in various relationships with Tuscan rustication, Venetian incrustation, and the brick building of North Italy, both on church and palace façades. In each of the three contexts the question of mouldings, especially of the topmost cornice, demands a particular solution.

It is a matter of the nicest judgement how mouldings, which cannot be adapted to low relief, as the column can be transformed into the pilaster, can be harmonised with the pilaster and also with the total effect.

For the cornice the question arises whether it is primarily related to the top storey or to the entire building. Moreover, there was a common assumption, prevalent throughout the whole period of "good" architecture, that the cornice must be completely unified and unbroken. The principal statement on this in Serlio, L. IV, fol. 178, with specific reference to Bramante.

Needing also to be blended into the harmony of the whole were: the weight of the podium, the massiveness of the ground floor, the handling of the fenestration in relation to the storeys and other matters; in particular, windows and pilasters were crucial factors. From these and other elements there grew an apparent organism, which in its details derived from Antiquity, but in combination is completely new and which should probably be considered the best possible expression of the rhythm of masses, of the architecture of proportions. In accordance with the character of the time, which developed individuality to the ultimate, there emerged a formal freedom and variety, yet one that was ordered and far from fantasy.

Regarding the forms of windows and doors cf. below §46a.

(NOTE: A Dupérac engraving of 1575 of the Amphitheatrum Castrense, reproduced in E. Nash, *Pictorial Dictionary of Ancient Rome*, London, 1961, shows it in an extremely ruinous state.) (PM).

§39 *The Rusticated Façade in Florence and Siena*

Florentine fortress construction of squared stone blocks had, by tradition, left the outer face of the block rough; accurate and fine work was confined to the angles. When the fortresses became palaces, this so-called "rustication" was retained, and the building was in this way distinguished as public or patrician (Fig. 24). With the passage of time this characteristic evolved into a matter of deliberate artistic intention. Thus, the Florentine palazzo became a massive stone structure, relying for its effect upon the paucity and monumentality of the individual elements.

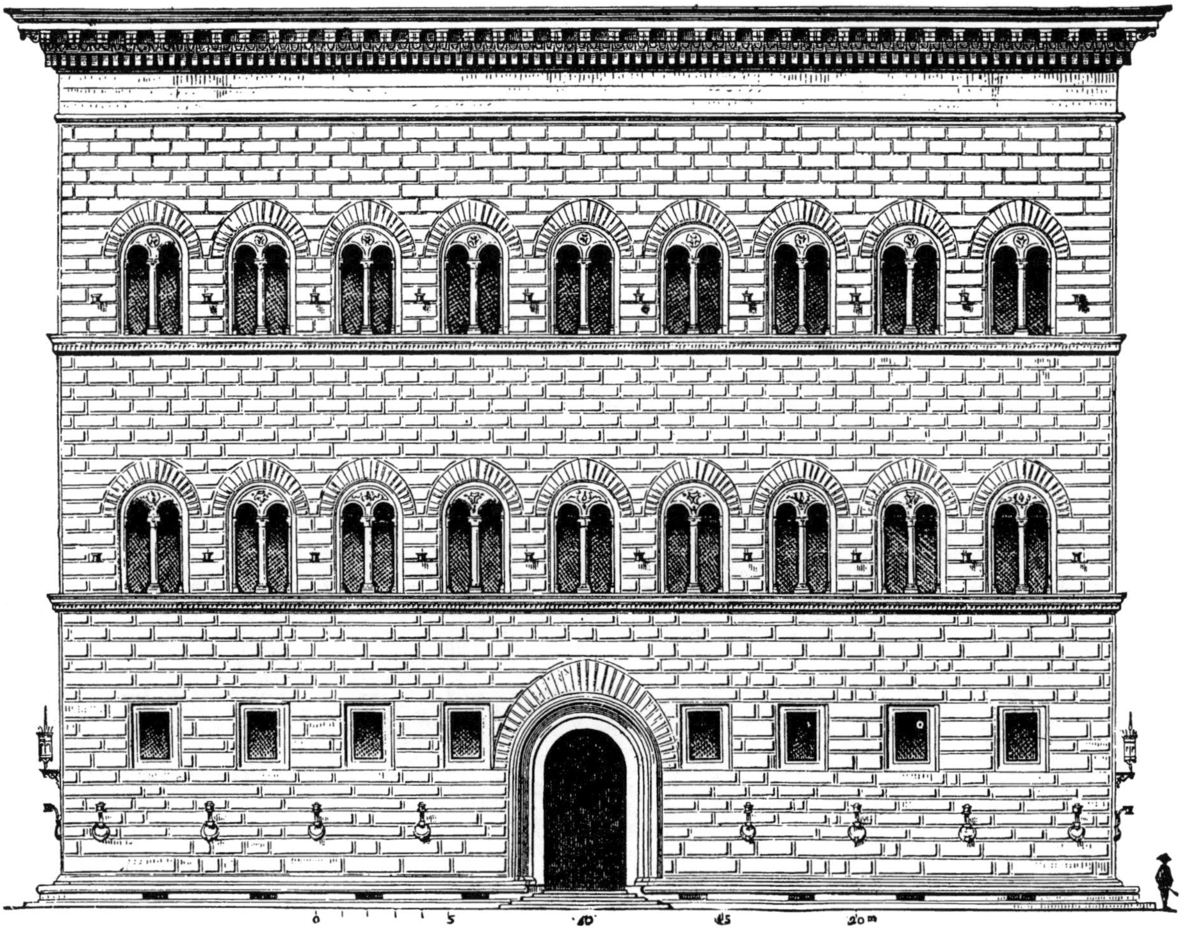

The proud impregnability of these façades and their effect on the imagination. Their aristocratic character: *non esser cosa civile*, cf. §9 in relation to the Pal. Strozzi.

The sixteenth century looked for vindication to unfinished – wrongly thought to be completed – Roman buildings (Porta Maggiore in Rome, the Amphitheatres of Pola, Verona, etc.); the early Renaissance treated rustication, without any artistic reference to Rome, as a principal means of expressing the tremendous urge towards monumentality, and, in so doing, achieved a truly Roman impression.

Roman buildings none the less afforded instances of genuine rustication, and not only as socles of buildings, as city walls, or similar structures; on the Tomb of Caecilia Metella here and there two or three ostensibly rusticated squared stones are made from a single block, so the aesthetic intention is evident: cf. Durm, *Die Baukunst der Etrusker und Römer*, p. 128 ff.

The most important Florentine and Sienese palaces have rustication without pilasters. Rustication in its various gradations, depending upon the particular storey and other considerations, became an artistic element freely exploitable according to preference. The cornice formed the only major contrasting feature, although a strongly projecting eaves-roof long held sway beside it: cf. §91.

A list of thirty palazzi built between 1450 and 1478 in Varchi, III, p. 107, to which a supplement was added, proves the widespread enthusiasm for building.

By Brunellesco: Pal. Pitti, the original façade of only seven bays (according to a view of Florence, *c* 1490, the only known example – a woodcut – in the Berlin Kupferstichkabinett, and other evidence, see Conti, *Il Pal. Pitti*, 1887); but also after its extension a completely symmetrical design, its only special attribute being the reduced width of the top storey; most majestic in its effect; a graphic instance of supreme strength of purpose in rejecting all decoration (Fig. 25).

By Michelozzo: the present Pal. Riccardi [Medici-Riccardi], (1444–52 or '59), with graduated rustication, as Brunellesco had already applied it on the Pal. Pitti, if somewhat less strikingly, and fine, if heavy, cornice.

Benedetto da Majano and Cronaca: Pal. Strozzi (begun 1489), lighter and more animated with beautifully proportioned storeys and a smooth frieze beneath the celebrated cornice (Fig. 26). Benedetto da Majano is named as the author of the building only by Vasari; in documents the submission of a model by Giuliano da Sangallo is mentioned; the cornice is documented as by Cronaca, who also did the cortile.

Giuliano da Sangallo: Pal. Gondi, 1490 onwards; Pal. Antinori scarcely by him, and other buildings.

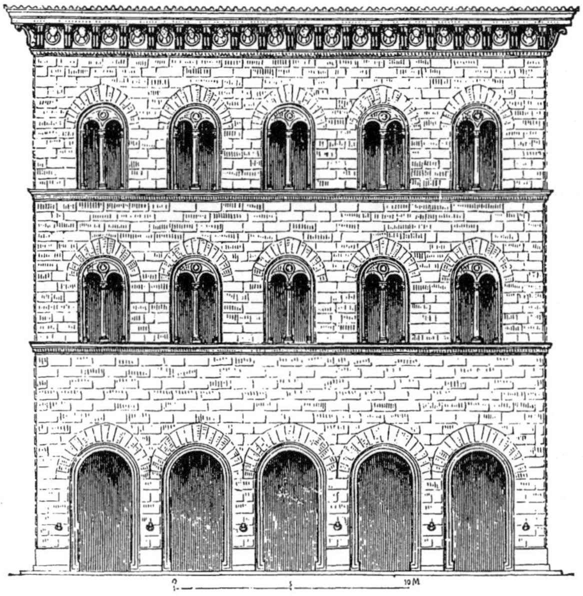

Fig. 26 *(opposite) Florence, Palazzo Strozzi, elevation*

Fig. 27 *(above) Siena, Palazzo Spannocchi, elevation*

Fig. 28 *(right) Florence, Palazzo Pazzi-Quaratesi*

In Siena: Pal. Nerucci, designed by Bern. Rossellino, built by Ant. Federighi; perhaps to a plan of Rossellino, the Pal. Piccolomini, from 1469; Pal. Spannocchi (Fig. 27), to a design by Giuliano da Majano, 1473 onwards.

Siena had up till then depended very much upon brick; these buildings were the first large stone palaces. Others, e.g. the elegant Pal. Bandini-Piccolomini and the small churches of the period, use stone as an articulating element in brick architecture.

The stone courses at first were uneven throughout and the stones of arbitrary length, so that the joints are not one above the other; they are regularly spaced, for example, on the Pal. Piccolomini at Pienza, 1462 (see below).

Differences in rustication: the omission of vertical joints; the face of the top storey left smooth or rustication restricted to the ground floor (already seen in Brunellesco's Pal. Pazzi-Quaratesi, Florence: Fig. 28); Cronaca liked to use heavy rustication only at the corners, the rusticated treatment of wall-surfaces being subdued, or rustication only at quoins (so-called *chaînes*, e.g. on the Pal. Guadagni, Florence, Fig. 29).

The Florentine cornice had a predecessor in the embattled parapet carried on strongly projecting consoles (see Fig. 11; also in the fifteenth century on the Pal. di Venezia, Rome (Fig. 30)); thus the eye was already accustomed to a massive feature and a strong shadow effect. Consummate and unequalled is the one on the Pal. Strozzi; Cronaca copied an example which he found in Rome, enlarging it to correct proportions: Vasari, IV, p. 444, *V. di Cronaca*, giving him the highest acclaim; but Baccio d'Agnolo was bitterly criticised for his cornice on the Pal. Bartolini – it was also borrowed from Rome, but incorrectly proportioned (Fig. 59 in § 51: cf. § 57).

Along with these mainly Corinthian, very costly, stone mouldings, the overhanging roof on wooden rafters, often richly and beautifully fashioned, retained its hold. These lie directly over the top of the wall, perhaps above an ovolo moulding (Pal. Quaratesi, Antinori, etc.). A striking by-product in stone: the portico of Sta Maria delle Grazie at Arezzo, with suspended decorative stone panels, which project three *braccie*: Vasari, III, p. 343, *V. di Ben. da Majano*, see Fig. 14.

This dichotomy in the form of the cornice led to marked inconsistencies. The nobly elegant Porta S. Pietro at Perugia (§ 109) lacks dentils and ovoli above, probably because the authorities suddenly stipulated other details than those which the master, Agostino da Firenze, wanted; (Mariotti) *Lettere pittoriche perugine*, p. 98.

(NOTE: The Pitti Palace was not begun until after Brunelleschi's death, but the problem of its authorship is still unsolved: there are those who are returning to the attribution to Brunelleschi, e.g. P. Sanpaolesi, *Brunelleschi*, Milan, 1962.

The wooden model of the Pal. Strozzi by G. da Sangallo is known from photographs, but I have never been able to see the original, said to be preserved in the palace itself.) (PM).

Fig. 29 *Florence, Palazzo Guadagni*

Fig. 31 *Florence, Palazzo di Parte Guelfa (before reconstruction)*

Fig. 30 *Rome, Palazzo Venezia*

Fig. 32 *(left) Florence, Palazzo Rucellai, elevation*

Fig. 33 *(above) Pienza, Palazzo Piccolomini, elevation*

§40 *Rustication with Pilasters*

From Florence also came the first attempt to enliven in a novel manner the rusticated façade with pilasters – several such, indeed, superimposed, together with their entablatures and bases. The motive only attained its full expression towards the end of the century.

Are these really the first pilaster Orders, or were there earlier instances on palaces with smooth walls?

Brunellesco was a pioneer here, too; in the twenties he provided the main storey of the Pal. di Parte Guelfa in Florence (of regular ashlar stonework) with broad, unfluted pilasters, which stand on Attic bases over a complete entablature, instead of mere string-courses (Fig. 31).

L. B. Alberti: Pal. Rucellai in Florence (Fig. 32), allegedly executed under Bernardo Rossellino's direction until 1451; the rustication very restrained, so as not to overpower the pilasters.

Bernardo Rossellino (in the documents, e.g. *Pii II Commentar.*, generally called Bern. Florentinus): Palace of Pius II Piccolomini at Pienza, about 1462 (Fig. 33): cf. the publication by K. Mayreder and K. Bender, with text by H. Holtzinger, in the Wiener Allgem. Bauzeitung, 1882.

In both the palaces mentioned the pilasters of the upper storey stand directly upon the entablature of the lower order, which at the same time serves as window-sills; the case is similar in the top storey of the Pal. Vendramin-Calergi (§43), while at the Cancelleria in Rome this defect is avoided.

This last building (Fig. 34) and the Palazzo Giraud-Torlonia (Fig. 35) are the most accomplished: the ground-floor in each case is simply rusticated; on the upper storeys the pilasters are grouped in pairs and accord perfectly with the rustication and windows; the cornice of the whole building, yet harmonising completely with the pilasters of the top floor. With reference to the advance shown by the Pal. Giraud (*c* 1504) compared with the Cancelleria in respect of finer and more mature detailing and better proportions, see the detailed interpretation of the building in Bühlmann, *Die Architektur des klass. Altertums u. der Renaissance*, p. 39. The architect of these two buildings is unknown; the façade of the Cancelleria was begun in 1486 and finished in 1489, the part next S. Damaso being completed in 1495. Cf. the author's *Cicerone*, 10th ed., II, 1, p. 273. Bernich conjectures (Rassegna d' Arte, II, p. 69) that Alberti could have designed the Cancelleria, if it was begun as early as *c* 1455.

(NOTE: For the problem of the Cancelleria – which is more likely to date from *c* 1485 than *c* 1455 – see V. Golzio and G. Zander, *L' Arte in Roma nel secolo XV*, Bologna, 1968, or L. Heydenreich and W. Lotz, *Architecture in Italy, 1400–1500* (Pelican History of Art), London, 1974.) (PM).

§41 *Rustication Outside Tuscany*

In the fifteenth century rustication outside Tuscany was an uncertain affair, which came in as a Florentine fashion and was cheerfully mingled with extraneous elements.

Naples: Pal. Colobrano (now Santangelo), 1466, with discreetly elegant entablature and portal; Pal. Cuomo (now Museo Filangieri), 1464–88, on the main storey restrained rustication and windows like those in the Pal. di Venezia in Rome – see Fig. 36, and in the Archivio storico dell' Arte, II, p. 294; Pal. Gravina (the present Post Office), begun 1513, by the Neapolitan Gabriele d' Agnolo, rustication at ground level only.

Bologna: ground floor of the Pal. del Podestà, 1492–94, with florid rustication *in modum rosarum* and (of the following century) engaged columns between; Bursellis in Murat., XXIII, col. 906: Pal. Bevilacqua, with diamond-facet rustication (Fig. 37).

Ferrara: the still more mannered Pal. de' Diamanti (now Ateneo), 1493, by Biagio Rossetti, the individual blocks sharply pointed; at the angles of the façade pilasters, with a bewildering wealth of arabesque decoration (Fig. 38).

Imola: Pal. Sforza (Paterlini), built for Caterina Riario probably by Giorgio Marchissi da Settignano (see L. Marinelli in Rassegna d' Arte, 1903, p. 154), starting

Fig. 34 *Rome, Palazzo della Cancelleria, detail of elevation*

from the bottom strictly Florentine in its squared stones, above in brick and ending in graceful Bolognese forms.

Cremona: Pal. Trecchi, most capricious in its rusticated treatment, 1496, by Bernardo di Lera.

Rome: individual good buildings, some with pilasters, from the time before Bramante, e.g. in the Via del Governo Vecchio.

Venice: the infelicitous façade of S. Michele, from 1469; the ground floor of the noble Palazzo Corner-Spinelli (Fig. 42), both by Mauro Coducci.

§42 *Venice and Incrustation*

Just as Florence was the city of rustication, so Venice, secure and serene, committed to an uncompromising splendour, and hence to costly materials, and particularly accustomed to mosaic, was the city of incrustation.

After church architecture had long made sparing use of the latter, and civil building (with the exception of the marble tapestry-like cladding of the Doge's Palace) very little, but had exposed the brickwork, all the floodgates of material prodigality broke open in a supreme climax of luxury.

Pii II *Comment.*, L. III, p. 148, *c* 1460: *Urbs tota latericia pulcherrimis aedificiis exornata; verum si stabit imperium, brevi marmorea fiet; etiam nobilium patriciorum aedes marmorae undique incrustatae plurimo fulgent aureo.* The gilding of the spire of the campanile of S. Marco had already cost many thousand ducats.

Sabellico's visit to the site office of the Certosa Sant' Andrea, where stone, probably for the façade, lay ready cut, *c* 1490: a wealth of local varieties from various quarries at the foot of the Alps, competing with Laconian, Synnadensian, Thasian, Numidian, Augustan stones and also with ophite; Sabellicus, *De situ venetae urbis*, L. III, fol. 92 (ed. Venez., 1502). Regarding these names – for their accuracy the author must be responsible – cf. Ottfr. Müller, *Archäologie*, §268. In addition, however, much marble was still obtained from Paros, and stone of various types from other Greek islands; Sabellicus, op. cit., fol. 86, 87; Sansovino, *Venezia*, fol. 141.

Shipments of stone for incrustation for other towns also passed through Venice; thus (Gaye, *Carteggio*, I, p. 166) for S. Petronio, Bologna, in 1456.

A connoisseurship of stone grew up among prominent Venetians. The Venetian envoys to Hadrian VI (1523), who were expert in the arts, fell into raptures at the sight of porphyry, serpentine, and other fine Roman stones; Tommaso Gar, *Relazioni* . . ., I, p. 104.

Serlio was perhaps thinking of connoisseurs of this kind in his design for a loggia ornamented with coloured fragments of incrustation; L. VII, p. 106.

In Rome at this time incrustation, at least on secular buildings, was an almost unheard-of exception and only possible for close connections of the Pope: *Lettere pittoriche*, I, 33, with reference to incrustation in the cortile of the palace of Lorenzo de' Medici. Pieces of porphyry, serpentine, giallo, paonazetto, breccia etc., found in ruins were customarily removed for the adornment of altars and similar structures. Peruzzi in 1532 needed a special permit to bring only four pack-horse loads of such stones to Siena, for the Cathedral high altar; Milanesi, III, p. 114.

Florence had experienced incrustation and outgrown it: Alberti (who describes the technique in L. VI, c. 10 – cf. c. 5), had applied it on the façade of Sta Maria Novella, simply because the thirteenth century had begun to use the technique at the bottom of the façade.

In Venice gilding, much used in the interiors of palaces, threatened to overwhelm the façades; only a state prohibition prevented this: Sabellicus, op. cit., L. II, fol. 90. Commines in 1494 found in the Doge's Palace that the edges of stone had an inch-width of gilding (L. VII, c. 15, or new ed., *Charles VIII*, c. 21), cf. §162. Temporary gilding of particular elements of a building for festivals is also found, e.g. windows, consoles and architraves on the occasion of a princely marriage at Bologna at the end of the fifteenth century: Beroaldi

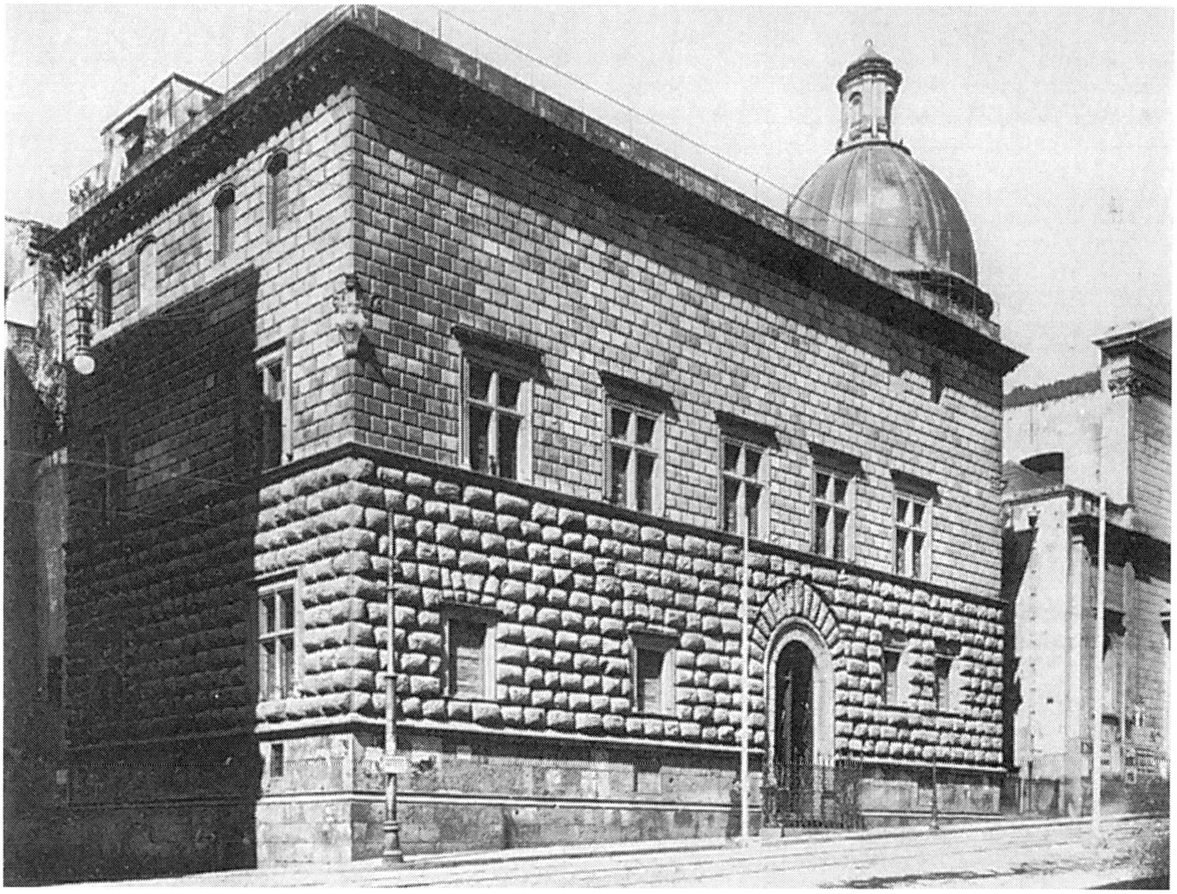

Fig. 35 *(above) Rome, Palazzo Giraud-Torlonia* Fig. 36 *(below) Naples, Palazzo Cuomo*

Fig. 37 *(above left) Bologna, Palazzo Bevilacqua*

Fig. 38 *(above) Ferrara, Palazzo dei Diamanti*

Fig. 39 *(above right) Perugino,* Miracle of S. Bernardino of Siena, *dated 1473, Perugia, Pinacoteca*

Fig. 40 *(right) Venice, S. Zaccaria*

Fig. 41 *Venice, Sta Maria de' Miracoli*

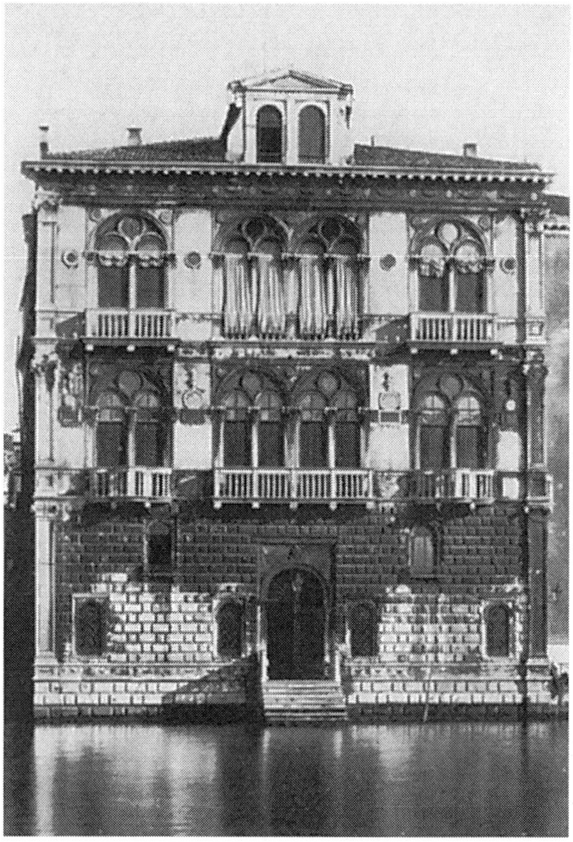

Fig. 42 *Venice, Palazzo Corner-Spinelli*

Orationes, fol. 27, Nuptiae Bentivolorum; on columns, mouldings, doors, of the Pal. Medici in Florence in 1536 for the reception of Charles V: *Lettere pittoriche*, III, 12. (The finest private house at Ferrara in 1452 was *tutta mettuda*, i.e. *messa ad oro di ducato*, but probably only inside. *Diario ferrar.*, in Murat., XXIV, col. 199.)

Just by itself much incrustation was as expensive as solid gold foil, and the prohibition of the latter was probably to prevent increase of envy against Venice.

§43 *Relationship of Incrustation to Form*

Incrustation inevitably favours the decorative at the expense of the architectonic. The early Renaissance in Venice indeed scarcely deserves the name of an architectural style.

There was an absence of real architects, or, if they existed, they failed to attract notice. Even the supreme splendour of the materials might have been matched by a higher and stronger sense of design. The architecture depicted by Mantegna and his School; the small panels of legendary scenes attributed to Benedetto Bonfigli in the Pinacoteca at Perugia;* and here and there in miniatures, more often presenting buildings with incrustation in a form unknown in Venice. The correct use of incrustation on the Certosa at Pavia, §71.

Everything starts from the beautiful polished appearance of the individual slab of marble, of no matter what colour, porphyry, serpentine etc. These slabs are symmetrically grouped and surrounded with bands of contrasting colours. The pilaster as an Order found no favour; it served simply as a border to conclude a decorated wall-surface, or as a corner feature, and, if one includes the horizontal mouldings and bases, as framing. The splendid arabesques, which often cover the pilaster, are therefore frequently identical with those of the frieze, the vertical decorative motive with the horizontal. The pilaster always has a framed outline, and often a disc of coloured stone at the centre, sometimes carrying a relief.

The fame of a building depended more on these arabesques than on architectural merit; their creators were freely named – e.g. Sansovino, *Venezia*, fol. 86, with reference to the entrance of S. Michele, its embellishment being by Ambrogio da Urbino.

When Tullio Lombardo completed his friezes in Treviso (for which building is not stated), they were conducted in triumph through the town: Pompon.

* These are presumably the *Miracles of S. Bernardino*, now attributed to Perugino, with some participation by Bonfigli. One (Fig. 39) is dated 1473. (PM).

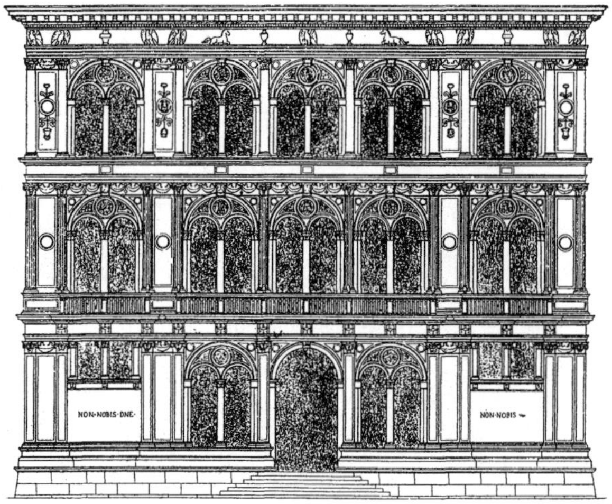

Fig. 43 *Venice, Palazzo Vendramin-Calergi, elevation*

Fig. 44 *Venice, Scuola di S. Marco*

Gauricus, *De sculptura*, in Jac. Gronov., *Thesaur. graecc. antiqq.*, Tom. IX, col. 773.

The style of these arabesques was taken from decoration of the highest class. Often a second band, also decorated, goes beneath the frieze.

The actual form of the moulding was neglected, as was everything unamenable to display. There is no distinction between pilasters of the upper and lower storeys.

A few of the buildings: S. Zaccaria (Fig. 40), Sta Maria de' Miracoli (Fig. 41), S. Giovanni Crisostomo and other churches of the same type; the Trevisan, Malipiero, Manzoni-Angarini, Dario, Corner-Spinelli (Fig. 42), Grimani a San Polo, and other palaces; the older Scuole. The palaces are saved by the beauty of features inherited from the Gothic period (§21, 94). When these are absent, e.g. in the court of the Doge's Palace, the ostentation is revealed in its full irrationality. The only palazzo with a more scrupulous approach to the antique Orders, partly in the form of half-columns – for all its tasteful luxury – simply makes one long for the Florentine School; this is the Palazzo Vendramin-Calergi, 1481, by Pietro Lombardo (Fig. 43).

On the fronts of churches (S. Zaccaria) and Scuole (especially the Scuola di S. Marco, Fig. 44) the whole gamut of incrustation, pilasters and other ornamental forms is unhesitatingly exhausted in the service of a naïve confusion of designs; semi-circular or other curvilinear wall-terminations, sometimes sumptuously interrupted by open arches. On the Scuola di S. Rocco (1517) the new motive of free-standing columns was taken up: these were sometimes twined about with floral decoration (cf. Figs. 196, 197).

Where would modern architecture have ended up, if it had fallen for any length of time into the hands of the Venetian exponents of a fretwork and jewellery aesthetic? How greatly even in Venice would the buildings of the Florentine Jacopo Sansovino and his School have been missed, through whom the discipline of the High Renaissance was pioneered there.

§44 *Northern Italy and Brick and Terracotta Architecture*

From the birth of the arts brick has probably never created its own independent forms. From the time that Egypt evolved a specific mode of expression, of stone beams laid upon stone pillars, stone architecture on the whole called the tune. Brick, bound by age-old precedents, used for thousands of years as a mere substitute for stone and perforce hidden, mimics the forms of stone also in the few Roman buildings where it comes to light.

Rome uses brick in its largest buildings and in its private houses (Pompeii), but in the one case with a marble, and in the other with a stucco, revetment. Monumentally handled and used openly in its own right it is almost only found on the Amphitheatrum Castrense (§38), on the monument at Tavolato, on the so-called "Tempio del Dio redicolo" and "Sedia del diavolo" and other tombs in the Campagna. Here the richer classical forms are produced in such an extravagant manner that one may assume that brick was preferred simply to keep away future vandals by the worthlessness of the material. The brick buildings mentioned by Vitruvius and Pausanias were sometimes certainly, and in other instances probably, faced with mortar or incrustation. On the Philippeion at Olympia, which Pausanias (V. 20) describes as brick-built, the engaged columns inside – as excavations have established – were fashioned directly from the wall-masonry, but the substructure and cyma from marble.

Perhaps brick-building attained the highest degree of relative independence in the Gothic period in Upper Italy, and also south of the Po (Via Aemilia, from Piacenza to Ancona), as well as in the Milanese and the Veneto, although here with a larger amount of stone articulation.

A start was probably made with brick because stone was dear, and then continued for its own sake and because of greater technical skill. Largely exempt from the need for pinnacles, gables, and flying buttresses;

Fig. 45 *Bologna, Palazzo Fava, elevation* Fig. 46 *Bologna, details of a palace*

windows, cornices and portals were remodelled most splendidly according to the nature of the material. Stone architecture, indeed, borrowed forms from brick-building or terracotta (some details of the marble front of Monza Cathedral).

A strong prejudice in favour of these forms was enough to delay the oncoming of the Renaissance and even to coerce Filarete (§22, 31), despite his maledictions upon Gothic, into pointed-arch windows for the Ospedale Maggiore in Milan; filling in the detail none the less with his tasteful Renaissance ornament. He, or an unknown disciple, did the same to a highly elegant private palazzo (Marliani), which was demolished in the eighteenth century, but survives in an illustration in Verri, *Storia di Milano* (also in Müntz, *La Renaissance en Italie*, p. 239).

§45 *Brick Façades*

Even the Renaissance in these districts and in these materials – brick and terracotta – is freely interpreted in a highly idiosyncratic manner, so that the eye does not miss what is lacking. The great wealth of architectural ideas was matched by a finer and livelier sense of beauty in details.

It must be stated once again that, without the great Florentines, the Bolognese and Lombards would not have emerged from their admittedly rich, but already dubious, Gothic.

On palace façades a restriction on the forms of Antiquity was dictated by the delicacy of mouldings composed of small elements. Pilasters were willingly renounced, for their size would inevitably have been prescribed by the height of the storeys (Fig. 45). In general, stricter antiquarian attitudes would have been detrimental.

In the palaces of Bologna the ground floors form part of the continuous street-arcades; to expect anything like correct Doric or Corinthian proportions for their brick columns with rich and lively sandstone capitals would have been foolish, for the eye would be disturbed by a construction too slender for the size of the intercolumniations.

(Such brick columns had, however, often to be reinforced later by conversion into piers: Serlio, L. VII, p. 156, describes the process. Where resources permitted, they were no doubt also replaced in course of time by marble columns, e.g. in a cloister at Ferrara in 1495: *Diario Ferrar.* in Murat., XXIV, col. 314.)

The archivolts of the arches are richly profiled, but not in a particularly Antique manner (Fig. 46); over a string-course splendid round-arched windows (very conspicuous in terracotta) have palmette ornamentation at the top and sides; over a second string-course there is generally a frieze with small windows and then a cornice composed entirely of small, closely spaced consoles.

Thus over a mainly felicitously disposed façade is spread at relevant points and with a judicious economy a homogeneous wealth of decorative forms, all in a lovingly manipulated material of monumental character.

Pilaster Orders would have provoked an intolerable conflict between the arcades below and the cornice. Where, in particular cases, they were to be found, the city chronicler (1496) supposed them to be built *more romano* (Murat. XXIII, col. 913).

Rich and charming, but very inharmonious in its pilasters and other decoration: Pal. Roverella in Ferrara, 1508 (the prominent bay-window a later addition).*

* The bay-window has now been removed. (PM).

Fig. 47 (*above*) *Pavia, Certosa, court* Fig. 48 (*below*) *Pavia, Certosa, court, detail*

Fig. 49 *Bologna, Palazzo Fava, court*

Fig. 50 *Bologna, Palazzo Bevilacqua, court elevation*

§46 *Brick and Terracotta Cortili and Church Façades*

In the cortili of palaces and monasteries the forms are usually architecturally richer, and combined with decoration proper to them, the columns almost always of stone.

The two celebrated terracotta cortili of the Certosa at Pavia (Figs. 47, 48) with medallions and projecting statues in the round and an extraordinary richness of ornamentation.

These cortili are older than the marble façade, so that the Certosa represents the early Renaissance in two kinds of material and stylistic character, in both cases by work of the highest class.

In Milan not only are the courts of public buildings (Broletto, older cortili of the Ospedale Maggiore) and of the fifteenth century monasteries important, but much more those of certain private palaces, e.g. Casa Frigerio at S. Sepolcro; over the colonnade the terracotta arches with medallions between; the windows, although terracotta, are sometimes rectilinear; string-courses and cornices of beautiful, unified, design.

In addition, in the Castello of Milan, the remains of two arcaded cortili of the period of Francesco Sforza. (Beltrami, *Il Castello di Milano.*)

In Pavia: a lovely, only partly preserved, palace courtyard opposite the Carmine.

In Bologna: above the colonnade of the cortile, instead of a built-up storey a second open gallery, with double the number of columns. (Figs. 49, 50.)

The noblest and most graceful example: the cortile of the Pal. Bevilacqua, after 1484 (Fig. 50), by the master of the colonnade at S. Giacomo (1477–81), in which the motive of the ground floor is almost exactly repeated. Among monastic courts: the one at S. Martino Maggiore.

At Ferrara: fragment of the cortile of the Pal. della Scrofa, 1502, by Biagio Rossetti (Fig. 51).

Pilaster Orders were fairly rare on churches, but, when used, often made of stone. Regarding the composition of church façades, see §70. Bramante's practice varied in the Milanese buildings attributed to him: on the outside of the choir of S. Satiro the fine and fairly correct Corinthian pilaster Orders entirely in terracotta; on the choir of Sta Maria delle Grazie (Fig. 52) are pilasters, wall-candelabra, mouldings and roundels executed in stone. The forecourt of Sta Maria presso S. Celso has a classically pure terracotta arcade with engaged columns in stone with capitals in bronze (1514: by an unknown master).

Fig. 51 *Ferrara, Palazzo Scrofa, court*

Church buildings carried out in richer brick and terracotta forms: the Certosa di S. Cristoforo at Ferrara, 1498–1553 (interior of marble), the decoratively fantastic round church of Sta Maria della Croce at Crema (Fig. 53) by Giovanni Battagio, 1493, the façade of S. Pietro in Modena, etc.

§46a *Windows and Doors of the Early Renaissance*

In the shaping of windows and doors the fifteenth century hesitated, in both ecclesiastical and secular buildings, between the rectangular and round-arched forms, while for certain windows in churches the complete circle was employed.

On the proportions of windows, according to Alberti's teaching, see §89.

Brunellesco always gave his churches a tall round-arched window. By itself, this form remained in vogue until towards the end of the century.

The reveals were ornamented with guilloches and festoons (especially rich in the Pazzi Chapel); on the outer side the window often carried profiled mouldings to which, in terracotta, palmettes were often added.

In palace architecture the windows were similarly treated in smooth façades; while with rustication a simple, massive surround was the custom. The medieval mullion-column was almost without exception retained (it was intended on the Pal. Pitti); on the jambs, pilasters or engaged columns generally corresponded to it. Under the two semi-circular arches, linking these vertical supports, Alberti (Pal. Rucellai) and Bernardo Rossellino (Palazzi Piccolomini at Pienza and Siena) introduced an additional cross-member, as Brunellesco had obviously intended in the Pal. Pitti, since there the pilasters in the window-jambs reach only as far as the course below the imposts (cf. Fabriczy, *Brunellesco*, p. 320).

The rectangular window is sometimes squat and provided with a solid stone mullion and transom; as in the Pal. Venezia (Fig. 30) and a house near S. Cesareo, Rome; the Pal. Vescovile, Pal. Newton,* among others at Pienza; the Pal. dei Tribunali at Perugia, etc.

This form of window only appeared sporadically without the dividing mullion towards the end of the period; thus, about 1480, in the cortile of the Palace at Urbino, similarly in that of the Pal. Strozzi, etc.

More often, there was agreement to adopt the undivided oblong window of church architecture. The Proto-Renaissance had successfully prepared the way for this (façade of S. Miniato, Baptistry of Florence, etc.), and indeed for precedent was the whole Antique form of columns or pilasters with a pediment, and even the rather frivolous consoles under the sills.

Such aediculae on windows are amply attested, as a feature of fourteenth-century practice, by being repre-

* Now Pal. Ammannati (opposite Pal. Piccolomini). (PM).

Fig. 52 *Milan, Sta Maria delle Grazie*

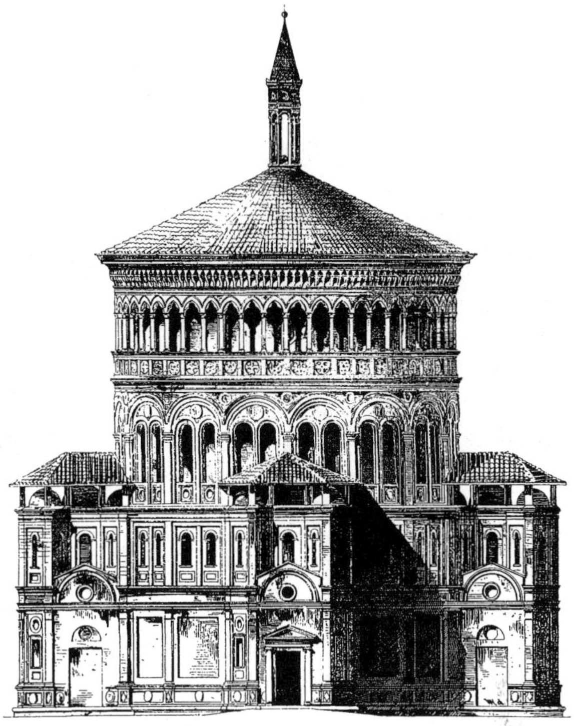

Fig. 53 *Crema, Madonna della Croce, elevation*

sented in paintings – e.g. by Taddeo Gaddi in the Cappella Baroncelli, Sta Croce (between 1352 and 1356), and elsewhere. On the Cathedral of Pienza (*c* 1460: Fig. 130) aediculae are used to frame niches, as also on the Confraternità at Arezzo.

The pediment above the lintel appears on the windows of the Spedale degli Innocenti and the sanctuary of the Capp. Pazzi by Brunellesco, and of the Madonna delle Carceri at Prato (1485–91: by Giuliano da Sangallo); the sacristy of Sto Spirito in Florence, apparently designed by Giuliano da Sangallo and executed by Cronaca, *c* 1496 (Fig. 181), and on Cronaca's S. Francesco al Monte, in this case with alternating triangular and segmental pediments (see Fig. 150). The latter, resting on columns, also in Filarete's treatise, shown on a palace (see illus. in Müntz, *La Renaissance*, I, p. 485) and in Mantegna's *Triumph of Caesar*.

A Lombardic, widely diffused speciality of the Comacini (§15) was the double round-arch window with a common rectangular surround; already seen in the fourteenth century (with round and pointed arches) in the Pal. Vitelleschi at Corneto, then in the Pal. Capranica in Rome, Pal. Possoni in Verona etc.

Foremost among them stand the four superb windows of the façade of the Certosa of Pavia; really conceived as portals; copied without posts and lintel from Antique door-cases; above the rich frieze and cornice a pediment in the shape of volutes with figures and other decoration; on the inside of the mullions, inserted as supports for every two arches, the celebrated marble candelabra (see Fig. 282).

Somewhat earlier, and in detail less ambitious, the four windows in Fra Giocondo's Pal. del Consiglio at Verona; above the entablatures, segmental pediments with relief infill (Fig. 230).

Similar Lombardic windows, e.g. in Sta Maria presso S. Celso in Milan, in Bergamo, on Biagio Rossetti's Loggia del Consiglio at Padua (see Fig. 231); further south, e.g. in Perugia (house next to Pal. dei Tribunali), at Sulmona (Pal. della Nunziata) and elsewhere.

Lastly, the round window prevailed in the drums of domes (already in Florence Cathedral, according to the model of 1367), in the upper parts of church façades (Sta Maria Novella in Florence, Cathedral of Pienza, S. Pietro in Montorio in Rome etc.), as well as in the lateral aisles above chapel entrances (e.g. S. Lorenzo in Florence, Cathedral of Cortona, etc.). In isolated instances it was also used on the top floors of palaces, e.g. in Brunellesco's Pal. di Parte Guelfa (Fig. 31) and Pal. Pazzi-Quaratesi (Fig. 28).

Regarding doors, the following is generally applicable: portals in rusticated façades are usually encased in a plain rugged framework, with wedge-shaped blocks which progressively lengthen towards the keystone, forming a semi-circular intrados (Pal. Pazzi-Quaratesi, Spannochi etc.). At the Pal. Gondi these voussoirs are fitted into the rusticated masonry with vertical butt-joints and horizontal bed-joints.

With ashlar walls, and inside buildings, the entrances are at the very least framed by a moulding, the profile of which usually turns inwards at the bottom, so that a kind of base is formed; as also often occurs with windows:

Fig. 54 *Urbino, S. Domenico, portal*

Fig. 55 *Florence, Sta Croce, door*

the decorations of the jambs are imitated from the latter as well – particularly rich, *inter alia*, on the Cappella Pazzi. On the door-lintel here the founder's coat of arms held by winged putti, probably in imitation of medallion portraits with genii on Roman sarcophagi, as – for example – on the one admired by Brunellesco at S. Domenico, Cortona.

Soon the more important doorways of churches and secular buildings had their jambs regularly faced, both inside and out, with pilasters, which were given a generous decoration of arabesques, meticulous fluting, and were occasionally made of precious materials (paonazetto or the like).

Regarding the Orders of such pilasters: Alberti, *De arte aedif.*, L. IX, c. 3: *fenestras ornabis opere corinthio, primarium ostium ionico, fores tricliniorum et cellarum et eiusmodi dorico*, which in the fifteenth century can only be interpreted as pilasters. (Hardly anybody conformed to the instructions.)

The finest contemporary portals in Rome; those of the basilica of S. Marco in the Pal. Venezia, and above all of the hospital of Sto Spirito, with fluted pilasters.

(The rather prominent free-standing columns by the main door of the Certosa, by the portal of Sta Maria delle Grazie in Milan, at S. Domenico in Urbino (Fig. 54) etc., represent a medieval tradition of Upper Italy, § 37.)

Above the lintel is the time-honoured lunette, developed from the relieving arch of Roman times with a *sopraporte* of sculpture or painting; not always a complete semi-circle, but segmental with palmettes at the ends and over the centre.

The Lombards liked to frame this lunette with a second, upper, pilaster arrangement with its own entablature and pediment; thus everywhere, even in the South, where Lombards or Comacini were engaged; under their influence, the portal of S. Domenico at Urbino; here the ornamental work is by Maso di Bartolommeo of Florence, the lunette relief by Luca della Robbia, 1449 (Fig. 54).

With the speedy departure of the Gothic pointed gable, the shallower Antique pediment appeared in place of the lunette on churches and other religious buildings of the fifteenth century. The earliest door-pediment of the Renaissance seems to have been that of the entrance to the noviciate of Sta Croce in Florence (right transept); Vasari, II, p. 442: *Vita di Michelozzo* (Fig. 55).

Fig. 56 *Florence, Cathedral*

§47 *Interior Forms*

Of the interiors of Antique buildings there had survived, when the Florentines began their studies, certainly very much more than now, but – the Pantheon apart – hardly one intact example, and in any case the interior architecture of the ancients was essentially an exterior architecture turned inwards. The only really basic influence must now have been exercised by Classical vaulting. Cf. *Kultur der Renaissance*, 3rd ed., I, pp. 225 and 236; 4th ed., I, p. 201, regarding the preservation of the Thermae.

For internal cornice- and pilaster-design, wall articulation and such matters, the Pantheon (in its then state) was by far the main source of knowledge. For the barrel-vault the better preservation of the Temple of Venus and Rome came into its own.

The greatest constructional task was undertaken by Brunellesco with his dome for Florence Cathedral; compared with that everything else appears simple, and only to be regarded as matters dearer or cheaper, of greater or less durability (Fig. 56).

After Brunellesco's advice had been sought on various occasions from 1405 onwards, and the young master had for some time received a regular salary as *consiliarius operis*, his principal employment began in 1420, after the completion of the drum according to the model of 1367 designed by Benci di Cione and Neri di Fioravante. With his skeleton construction of the dome, which he explained in a detailed Memorandum (still extant), Brunellesco carried the day over all his rivals and completed his task in sixteen years, with the co-operation of Ghiberti and Nanni di Banco at the beginning. For the structural details and the progress of the work, which diverged at times from the initial design, cf. the exhaustive appraisal by Durm in Erbkams Zeitschrift für Bauwesen, 1887, and the documents since published by Guasti, *Sta Maria del Fiore*; also H. Semper in Archivio storico ital., 1887, and in Repert. für Kunstw., 1889, p. 56 ff., and Doren in Repert. XXI and XXII. – Vasari (*Vita di Brunellesco*) draws mainly upon Antonio Manetti (cf. §2).

The earliest exposition of the theory of vaulting in Alberti, *De re aedificatoria*, L. III, c. 14, cf. V, c. 18, and VII, c. 11, according to type: *fornix* (barrel-vault), *camera* (cross-vault), and *recta sphaerica, scil. testudo* (dome); he stipulates the vault for churches because of *dignitas* and durability, and also for the ground floors of palaces.

Fig. 57 *Florence, Sta Croce, Pazzi Chapel, detail of the loggia*

§48 *Vaults in the Early Renaissance*

The first and most significant point is the opposition of the Renaissance to the cross-vault, its sovereign advantage now being lost, as oblong rooms, for which it is by nature such a harmonious covering, were either no longer built or were vaulted differently.

Northern Gothic had developed its characteristic beauty in oblong spatial forms. Perhaps the oblong cross-vault is more beautiful in itself than the square.

The cross-vault continued to be used, but was hidden. Where it is openly used, as in certain Roman churches (§76, 77), there is a disadvantage in comparison with Gothic, because the robustly expressive ribs are dispensed with.

The last to achieve a light and noble effect with diagonal ribs and oblong cross-vaults running across and above a church nave was Dolcebuono, in the Monastero Maggiore in Milan, 1503, cf. §23, 76.

True cross-vaults of the same period (?) also in the Appartamento Borgia of the Vatican.

The characteristic expressiveness of the Gothic vault arose from the system of ribs springing from the pillars and acting as a framework for the light infilling of the web. For the Renaissance on the other hand, which placed an Antique entablature over the supports and in general separated all the dynamic parts from their load-bearing elements by strong horizontals, the vault is a covering mass. A more detailed expression of this is the Roman coffer; a rapidly and highly developed decorative art (§171) thus assumed a richer expression.

Coffering is a particularly deadly enemy of the cross-vault in its stricter form; it can, however, be accommodated very well in a concave surface transformed into a spherical shape at the centre.

The earliest coffers of the modern period known to me are in the soffits of the arches of the cloister of S. Paolo fuori in Rome (between *c* 1220 and 1241, by Petrus de Capua: Fig. 3); then on a Gothic building, Sta Maria Maggiore at Bergamo, intrados of the portal on the north side; these are oblong rhomboids with rosettes alternately white, brownish red, and black.

Coffers of every kind, including those concentrically diminishing, were worked out by Alberti (op. cit., L. VII, c. 11) on paper, including those for hexagonal and octagonal spaces, and how to execute them in brick and stucco. Cf. §173.

His elegant coffering on the intrados of the portal of Sta Maria Novella. Bramante, in particular, seems to have perfected their execution in stucco; Vasari, IV, pp. 162, 165, *Vita di Bramante*. Instead of ribs there was now to be an arris, but often blunted and painted with festoons.

The early Renaissance, except for the cross-vault continued to allow the constructive form of vaults to be exposed.

Predominant forms: the barrel-vault, of semi-circular or elliptical section, sometimes with intersecting vaults on either side.

The domical, so-called "Bohemian" vault,* also often with intersecting vaults.

The sequence of shallow or loftier saucer-domes or domical vaults.

The barrel-vault interrupted at the centre by a dome; uncommonly fine on a small scale, e.g. Fig. 57 over the portico of the Cappella Pazzi in Florence (Brunellesco) or of the Umiltà in Pistoia (Vitoni); on a larger scale over the naves of some North Italian churches (§74). (The barrel-vault was already established in Upper Italy by the Romanesque period: S. Babila, S. Celso (i.e. the old church), S. Sepolcro, all in Milan, others elsewhere.)

Cupolas of different types, also oven-shaped so-called cloister vaults.* Exceptionally, a number of smaller domes of the fifteenth century fashioned like open umbrellas, or recalling the shell vault of Gothic choirs, with small circular windows round them, described as "domes with ribs and sails" (Manetti, *Vita di Brunellesco*, p. 29), used by Brunellesco in a (later rebuilt) chapel in S. Jacopo in Florence, in the Old Sacristy of S. Lorenzo and in the Cappella Pazzi; often later imitated; see Figs. 93, 94, in §63 and Fig. 178 in §80. Antique prototypes: a ruin near the Pal. Capranica in Rome (Templum Matidiae?) shown in a print by Giovannoli, 1619 (see Lanciani, *Ruins and Excavations of Ancient Rome*, p. 503); Tor de' Schiavi (Canina, VI, tav. 107); Kutschuk Aja Sophia (i.e. SS. Sergius and Bacchus) in Constantinople etc.

The basic detail forms of modern dome architecture (pier mouldings, sections of main arches, pendentives, cornices over main arches, plan and organisation of the drum, its upper moulding, articulation of the dome) were by now developed by the Tuscans, cf. Madonna delle Carceri in Prato (Fig. 96 in §64); for the lantern the pattern was already fixed in the fifteenth century by that of the dome of Florence Cathedral. The other external forms of the dome, however, were still far from established, cf. §63–65.

* The German term, *Böhmische Kappe*, is usually translated as domical vault, sometimes as sail vault, since it consists of a spherical shape fixed at four points: the term cloister vault, used in the US, is not common in English usage, where domical is again preferred. (PM).

CHAPTER SEVEN

Treatment of Form in the Sixteenth Century

§ 49 *Simplification of Detail*

With the coming of the sixteenth century architectural detail was simplified and strengthened. This was a fresh victory for the Florentine artistic spirit over the rest of Italy.

The Italy of the early Renaissance outside Tuscany had been more affected by the ornamental works of the Florentines than by the simple grandeur of their buildings; now for the first time it was not the detailing which triumphed, but the spirit of a Pal. Pitti, Pal. Gondi, Pal. Strozzi (§ 39). Bramante (1444–1514), on whom now most depended, was however from Urbino; and the great change which occurred in him about 1500 is attributed by Vasari to his measurements in Rome (§ 27) and elsewhere; yet this does not exclude the inevitable effect of the buildings of Florence upon him.

The increased study of Vitruvius (§ 28) is partly the result, partly the cause, of this new turn of events, depending on the individual case.

The simplification of form found its justification in some degree in specific Roman buildings, in part in common attitudes. With it was indissolubly linked a stronger sculptural emphasis, to make this simplicity apparent on the new and sometimes massive buildings by virtue of the more dramatic effect of cast shadow.

Serlio, *Architettura*, L. III, fol. 104, cf. L. VII, fol. 120, 126. He refers to the Colosseum, the Arch at Ancona and even to the Pantheon, where the Corinthian Order has only very little, but well distributed, detail, and he protested against the "taste of the mass of servile architects", who derived their ornamental elements entirely from the richer examples. The façades were merely rendered confused and pretentious by the many "chisellings" (*intagli*).

In fact the vegetable motives, which the richer architecture of Antiquity bestowed upon its mouldings, and which the early Renaissance had applied sparingly (and perhaps totally only on the Triumphal Arch of Alfonso in the Castello Nuovo in Naples: § 103), were now completely abandoned and the forms of capitals confined to essentials. (For the fluting, cf. § 35.) Indeed the richness, even when it was expressly sought (particularly in interiors), was not found in the more elaborate Roman forms, but in painted panels, stucco pilasters, and externally in festoons, masks, interlacing bands and so on, on windows and doors. Even for smaller decorative work (tombs, altars), there was no longer any inclination to go back to the corresponding Roman examples. The Baroque style did not find this road back either, preferring to multiply its elements rather than enriching them in this quite permissible way.

§ 50 *Experiments with Details and Influence of Festivals on Ornament*

To ensure truly effective results every method was explored. Besides experimental models of individual elements, full size or only slightly smaller, architectural decoration for festivals now became a very important source of instruction.

Michelangelo's six-braccia-high model of the angle of the cornice for the Pal. Farnese; Vasari, VII, p. 223, *Vita di Michelangelo*. He also liked to model windows, columns, arches etc. for his foremen and masons out of clay, no doubt full scale: *Lettere pittoriche*, I, 15: Benv. Cellini to Varchi, 1546. By this procedure his buildings appear to present an individual formal expression.

The most important aspect of festival decoration was that wood, plaster, and pasteboard offered an easy method of calculating what could be done in stone on the same scale. Cf. § 189.

An obvious transference from the latter to architecture was, among other things, the cartouche (*cartoccio*), a band or sheet of pasteboard turned into stone and scrolled or interlaced: cf. Serlio, L. VII, p. 78, and Lomazzo, *Trattato dell' arte*, L. VI, p. 421, in which

Fig. 58 *Perugia, S. Bernardino*

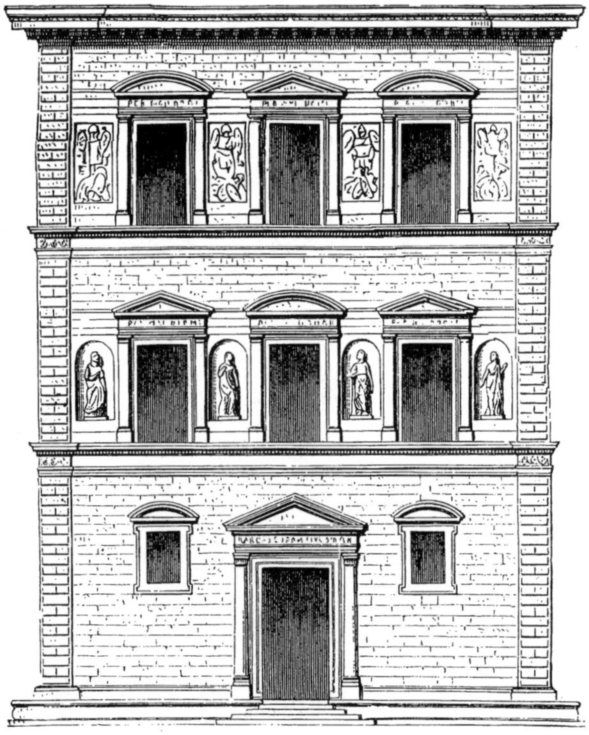

Fig. 59 *Florence, Palazzo Bartolini, elevation*

the leading sixteenth-century craftsmen for cartouches, festoons, masks etc. are enumerated.

With the value of festival decoration as an architectural testing-ground was connected the fact that its translation into architecture was effected with something more than appropriate strictness, and its freedom was not properly regarded, cf. § 56, 190.

§ 51 *Strengthening of Forms*

To the new effects of the sixteenth century belong niches in façades, as well as in piers and interior walls, and a more impressive setting for windows and doors with pilasters, engaged and free-standing columns, and shallow triangular or segmental pediments.

There is no question here of the niche as a basic element of a ground-plan, and therefore not of apses or of those series of recesses or chapels, into which sometimes the entire long wall of a church is subdivided (§ 74, 76), but only of the niche to attract the eye. From now on it was to alternate with windows on the façades of palaces, whether or not with a statue in it. Like the greater plasticity of the salient parts, the effect lies in its depth; its shadow, like that of all rounded surfaces, is most beautiful.

Already Gothic had produced here and there in Italy a genuine, deep niche (the tabernacles for the celebrated statues of Orsanmichele in Florence); but on the church façades of the early Renaissance, wherever these had sculptural ornament, the statues stand on consoles in front of very shallow niches (Certosa of Pavia, §71), or indeed inside niches covered by baldacchini, which are still very far from semi-circular (S. Bernardino at Perugia, Fig. 58; the two niches on the upper floor of the Misericordia at Arezzo are somewhat deeper). Not until the sixteenth century was the perfected half-cylindrical niche created.

In the interior of churches, on flat as well as the curved wall-surfaces, the construction of niches was the inevitable result of the desire for an extension of space, to economise in materials and to accommodate statues and altars.

Where the piers of the nave are faced with two pilasters, one niche – or two superimposed – occur between them. The earliest extensive application of the niche-system by Bramante (Tempietto of S. Pietro in Montorio, designs for S. Peter's) and by Raphael (Villa Madama). In addition, the competing designs by Giuliano da Sangallo and Michelangelo for the façade of S. Lorenzo in Florence and in the same city the only example executed there; the façade of the Pal. Bartolini by Baccio d'Agnolo (Fig. 59).

In relation to the statements in §46a about windows and doors, the following are innovations of the High Renaissance:

The round-arch window gives way in the main to the rectangular, and where it is retained it acquires a rectangular surround (Cancelleria, see Fig. 34, in imitation of the Porta de' Borsari, Verona).

The stone mullion and transom disappear from the rectangular window; under the obvious influence of the altar-tabernacles in the Pantheon the window adopts an austere, imposing appearance; the jambs generally

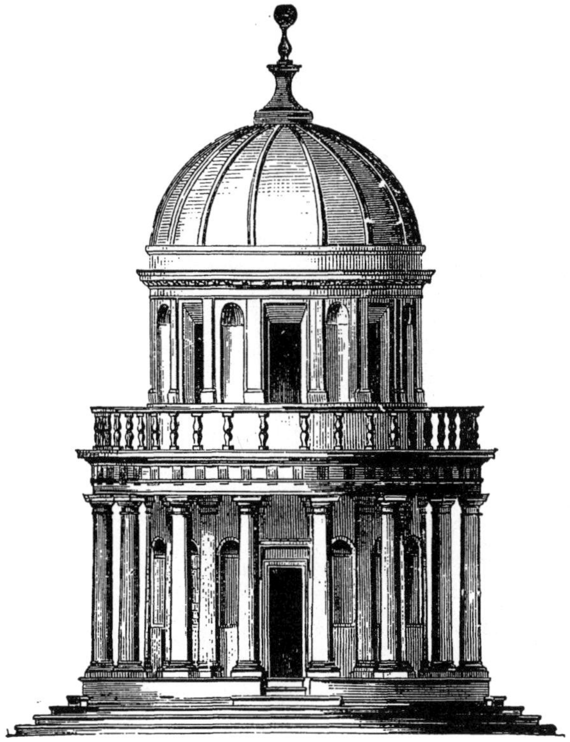

Fig. 60 *Rome, S. Pietro in Montorio, the Tempietto, elevation*

carry pilasters, engaged, or even free-standing columns; the window-sill is now used for the first time; on the window friezes inscriptions (which had been present before) continued in fashion.

On the jambs of church and palace doorways rich decoration is abandoned in favour of a mode of expression tending towards strength and simplicity; instead of the ornamentation the telling features are the profiles, often projecting or engaged columns, particularly of the Doric Order; examples rated as classical: Vasari, IV, p. 521, *Vita di A. Sansovino*; ibid., p. 596, *Vita di Peruzzi*; V, p. 322, *V. di Fra Giocondo.* The alleged Bramante design for the entrance to the Cancelleria, in Letarouilly, III, Pl. 351, is a reproduction of a drawing by Antonio da Sangallo in the Uffizi (see H. v. Geymüller, *Ursprüngliche Entwürfe für S. Peter*, p. 72).

The pediment is no longer reserved for religious buildings, but is now applied to the windows and doors of palaces. When Baccio d' Agnolo introduced this into Florence on the Pal. Bartolini (Fig. 59) – according to Milanesi, in the Prosp. Cronol. to Vasari, *Vita di B. d' A.*, V, p. 365, allegedly in 1520 – it was the occasion for satirical verses and the hanging of garlands upon it as on church doors on feast days; Vasari, V, p. 351, *Vita di B. d' A.* Soon, however, it was the common practice to alternate smaller triangular and segmental pediments, as shown in a drawing by Bramante (in H. v. Geymüller, *Raffaello studiato come architetto*, p. 56). On the middle window of three or five, sometimes the triangular, sometimes the segmental pediment is placed – the authorities for either were of equal weight.

The aediculae of the windows are linked at the same time, as for example on Raphael's Pal. Pandolfini and previously on his Pal. Branconio d' Aquila (§96), to each other and with the pilaster strips at the corners by shallow bands. "By this means repose and unity result from the aediculae appearing to have grown as parts of the wall-surface and not to have been placed upon it" (Bühlmann, *Architektur des klassischen Altertums und der Renaissance*, p. 38). So, too, in the Antique prototype – the aediculae in the Pantheon.

§52 *The Doric and the False Etruscan Order*

With the now dominant tendency towards the simplification of forms the Doric Order finally came into its own, but in an unhappy confusion and competition with the so-called Tuscan.

The true Greek Doric was not known and its use would hardly have been understood, §25.

The Romans had not been able to resist remodelling it, particularly when using Doric to face their great arches. Principal example: the ground floor of the Theatre of Marcellus.

The remains then still surviving in the Forum, probably of the Basilica Aemilia, must be specially considered: in the treatment of attached columns, pilasters, and entablature they demonstrably influenced both of the elder Sangallo and Bramante (published and reconstructed from old drawings by C. Hülsen, *Annali dell' Istituto archaeol.*, 1884).

Moreover, to the Romans the existence of an Etruscan Order had been displeasing; an Order once, no doubt, originating under the influence of the Grecian Doric, and which now infected, so to speak, the Roman Doric with its unlovely entablature and capital, unfluted shaft and separate base, while itself continuing to be used for religious buildings.

The sixteenth century not only re-adopted the Roman Doric, but also restored (e.g. Serlio) according to the precepts of Vitruvius (IV, 7) the Etruscan as the *Ordine Toscano*, which had a pleasing sound in Florentine ears. The wooden entablature with its painfully primitive forms was omitted; the *Ordine Toscano* looked more like the Roman Doric, but heavier and without triglyphs, metopes, and mutuli; favoured for rusticated ground floors and basements, fortifications and the like; in spirit indeed the artist never completely separated it from the Doric.

§53 *The Doric Interpreted by Bramante and Sansovino*

Apart from earlier isolated instances, Bramante made special and preferential use of the Doric Order as an instrument of the strict discipline of his last years and attracted to his side the greatest of his contemporaries.

The Doric pilasters on the ground floor of the Pal. Rucellai in Florence, 1451, and the Pal. Piccolomini in Pienza, *c* 1460; §40. The two lower Orders of columns

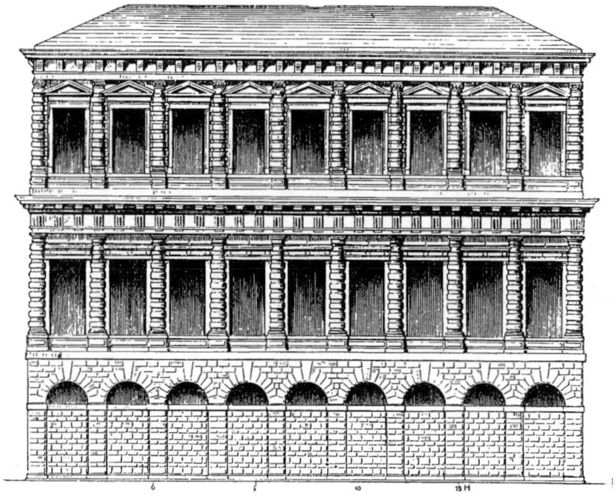

Fig. 61 *(opposite) Venice, Biblioteca Marciana*

Fig. 62 *(left) Florence, Palazzo Uguccioni, elevation*

Fig. 63 *(above) Venice, La Zecca (The Mint), elevation*

round the cortile of the Cancelleria (§97); above, a closed upper storey with Corinthian pilasters.

Giuliano and Antonio I da Sangallo, to whom Vasari (IV, p. 290) attributes particular credit for the Doric Order, may have developed a liking for it in their fortifications. Antonio's church at Montepulciano, however, with its very personal handling of Doric, was begun only in 1518; ibid., p. 288 n. 3 (Fig. 98 in §64).

Bramante: the Doric pilasters on the ground floor of the great Vatican cortile (from 1503). The round Tempietto of S. Pietro in Montorio (§66), the most elegant of ornamental buildings, without a leaf of vegetation except for the rosettes in the coffers of the peristyle (Fig. 60); part of the lower arcade of the Pal. Apostolico in the Cathedral Square at Loreto (eight arcades).

In the Consolazione at Todi (cf. for Bramante's possible participation §66) the four massive piers beneath the dome were designed in Doric as an expression of strength, but probably even more because Bramante felt the inappropriateness of Ionic and Corinthian pilaster-capitals on such a large scale. (Cf. Sta Giustina in Padua, Sta Maria di Carignano in Genoa, even indeed the Pantheon; the great foliated scrolls break up each composition.) Or did he suspect that at a certain size the original purpose of the pilaster in particular Orders evaporates? Was he on the way to a true anta, one specially suited to vaulted architecture? At all events, it was due to him that the Doric for a long time became the pre-eminent pilaster Order.

Raphael's (according to other opinions, Peruzzi's) Doric pilasters of 1509 on both storeys of the Farnesina (cf. §119).

Giulio Romano placed above a principal storey with Doric pilasters an upper storey, which is divided into simply framed square surfaces.

In the handling of portals, as mentioned in §51, the Doric Order was now preferred.

From 1536 Jacopo Sansovino was engaged in building the Library in Venice, the most splendid secular work of modern Europe (Fig. 61), as a correct demonstration of the Ionic, and, especially, the Doric Order.

As is well known, the dominant features are the two superimposed arcades with engaged columns; in the upper range the arch rests upon a rather small fluted Ionic Order. For the Venetians satisfaction lay in the true Roman formal idiom, the Renaissance being for them until then a matter of hearsay.

The effect is so beautiful that Sansovino is justified in certain liberties, e.g. the enlargement of the metopes at the expense of the size of triglyphs and architrave.

The famous dispute over the corner, §29. Sansovino hit upon the only true solution. The subtler freedoms of the true Grecian Doric – no matter whether their origins were visual or structural – including the advancement of the final triglyph on the corner, by no means apply to a mere ornamental facing-order which has to conform to its arcade; here the triglyph occurs over the centre of its column, whether it is the last or not, and whether or not Vitruvius said something about half-metopes. Sansovino needed at least the space of half a metope, because of the unavoidable solidity of his pilaster-faced corner-pier, and thus bent his metope round the angle. Vitruvius indeed probably intended no more than a segment of a metope by his *semimetopia*, but the fanatical Vitruvians who surrounded Sansovino cheerfully acquiesced in his literal interpretation.

§ 54 *Increased Contrasts*

At this time it often happened that, instead of pilasters, engaged columns, boldly prominent and sometimes coupled, were used even over a rusticated ground floor.

In Rome: Bramante's Pal. Caprini (the House of Raphael from 1517), much altered about 1580, now Pal. de' Convertendi in Piazza Scossacavalli;* Raphael's Pal. Vidoni-Cafarelli (Fig. 215 in § 96); in Florence, Pal. Uguccioni, by Mariotto di Zanobi Folfi (Fig. 62). (Cf. Michelangelo's design for the façade of S. Lorenzo, § 37.)

There were already some palace façades with numerous contrasting elements for the sake of charm. The flat surfaces between these elements began to be covered with simple stucco (§ 56).

See below § 96 with reference to palaces. Already Bramante was adding to powerful window-forms (§ 51) and coupled engaged columns the coarsely rusticated ground floor just mentioned, while Raphael was then to alternate windows with niches and idiosyncratically framed square panels (§ 51).

Rustication was now used with a very acute awareness of its effect, often mixed with the forms of the Doric and Tuscan Orders.

In Rome especially, where the ground floors contained shops which needed no decoration of their own, more than one variety of rustication was sought; square windows, flat arches with keystones, various gradations of rustication etc., all made of travertine blocks (sometimes imitation travertine made from stucco).

Elsewhere: restriction of rustication to corners, omission of vertical joints.

From a misunderstanding arising from its name it was used in garden architecture (§ 125), where the richest and most delicate ornament would have been more appropriate. Serlio, L. IV.

The rustication of the Palazzo del Te at Mantua (§ 119), which was originally begun as the stud-farm of Duke Federigo Gonzaga; crucial for the spread of rustication, for its use on rural buildings and for its counterfeit representation (it is made of stucco over a brick rubble core).

Its appropriate use on fortress architecture (§ 108) and on buildings of a generally austere character, e.g. Sansovino's Zecca (Mint) in Venice (Fig. 63), where the rustication was almost a novelty; Vasari, VII, p. 504 f., *V. di Jacopo Sansovino*; Franc. Sansovino, *Venezia*, fol. 115. The antithesis of *rustica* is *gentile* (F. Sansovino).

Vignola as a rule handled rustication very circumspectly; Serlio, on the other hand, in a later, separately published, Book employs the whole gamut of caprice and fantasy, priding himself upon his innovations: *Seb. Serlii Extra Ordinem Liber: Portarum triginta quae rusticae appellantur descriptio*, Latin translation, Venice, 1568. There are doorways for palaces, gardens (?), fortresses, some also to be interpreted as triumphal arches, in the most varied combinations of rustication with columns, pilasters, herms, ornamental panels and features above them. The beginning of those later collections of so-called Portoni, which lasted throughout the whole Baroque period.

In general, stucco only appeared on major fifteenth-century buildings in conjunction with painting. In the sixteenth century, however, it was applied to any flat surface (§ 96) and left unpainted.

§ 55 *The High Renaissance Vault*

The lovely motive created by Brunellesco for the portico of the Pazzi Chapel (§ 48), in which the barrel-vault is interrupted by a cupola, was not taken up and developed until Bramante.

Two barrel-vaults with a shallow dome between them: S. Lorenzo in Damaso, Rome (formerly: see Fig. 169 in § 77), or a cross-vault: choir of Sta Maria del Popolo; cf. some sketches for S. Peter's (Geymüller, Plates 20, 22).

Perhaps the greatest change which the detailing of the interior undergoes lies in the handsome simulated forms of the vault introduced with the help of stucco-work, or, with the same end, painting. The Renaissance now offers the vault purely in the service of beauty.

For particulars see below with reference to decoration.

Not until stucco was perfected (§ 174) were the great, richly coffered vaults with all the Ancient Roman splendour of profiling feasible.

The barrel-vault of full, or even increased, radius (§ 48) was admitted and decorated as such, especially in the naves of long churches (§ 76, 77).

The shallower, half-elliptical, type, especially as it appears in *saloni* and galleries, was now often the subject of an illusionistic form; it was given a flatter curve (*specchio*) in the centre, or a succession of flats, with the ends of the vault intersecting on all four sides and touching the edges of the flatter coving.

In the Sistine Chapel, a building of the fifteenth century, the constructional form of the barrel-vault is still fully visible, and the illusionistic *specchi*, like all the rest of the scheme, are the creation of Michelangelo.

The same applies to the famous loggia on the ground floor of the Farnesina (1509), with paintings by Raphael and his school (Fig. 336 in § 175).

In time, however, the *specchio* was smoothed out to a really flat section, while its edges and those of the vaulting were given a stucco frame in (often high) relief.

The *specchio* of course appears at its finest at the centre of the vault of rooms of cubic design, in which it forms at the same time the culmination of a painted or stuccoed decoration (Raphael's *Loggie*).

Regarding the forms of the dome interior see § 65 ff.

In addition, however, timber vaults were already beginning, their construction in general being merely simulated and having a joisted ceiling above them. They appear either in wide rooms, in which the footings of a

* Destroyed in 1936 by Mussolini; see Fig. 214. (PM).

Fig. 64 *Florence, Biblioteca Laurenziana, vestibule*

true vault would have had to be placed too far back, or when economy or convenience prescribed it, or if a large central surface was required, around which the springing of the vault is treated merely as ornament.

These springings are made of wood with reeds nailed on to hold the stucco. Serlio (L. VII, p. 98) extolled them; Vasari VII, p. 695, in his own *Vita*, defends them. Something similar as early as Vitruvius (VII, 3).

Many of these vaults are difficult to distinguish from the real thing, see the ceilings in Pal. Doria at Genoa, by Perino del Vaga and his school, mostly of wood.

The system of pilasters and cornices was now for the first time consistently applied in palace interiors.

The fifteenth century had been satisfied with simple wall-brackets, on which the vaulting rests. Now corridors and stairs especially acquired a more disciplined formality with pilasters. A fine example: Raphael's *Loggie* (Fig. 335 in § 175).

Fig. 65 *Rome, Benediction Loggia of the Lateran*

§56 *Forms of the Late Flowering*

The detailing of the period 1540–80 is, on the whole, noticeably coarse, no longer created for love, but essentially and solely for its overall effect.

Michelangelo's portentous 'liberties', among them the thrusting forward of the wall-mass between the columns in the vestibule of the Laurenziana in Florence, so that the columns, grouped in pairs, appear to be standing in boxes; an open rebuff to formal orthodoxy (Fig. 64). Vasari's view of Michelangelo's newly discovered forms was none the less that they were not merely beautiful, but *maravigliose*; I, p. 136, *Introd.* Cf. §29.

The well-known work of Vignola spread everywhere a particular interpretation of the Classical Orders, which henceforth was to become conventional; after him Palladio, and later Scamozzi among others.

Fig. 66 *Florence, original project for the Uffizi (Gurlitt)*

Late individual enthusiasts for the true forms of the Ionic: Gio. Battista Bertano; Vasari, VI, p. 488, *Vita di Garofalo*; and Giuseppe Porta, Vasari, VII, p. 47, n. 1, *Vita di Salviati*. The later Vitruvians, §28.

The universality and sameness of forms were connected with the need to build quickly, monumentally, and in quantity, with limited resources.

Simple forms with good proportions could still achieve a very noble effect. Ammanati's colonnaded cortile at the Collegio Romano; also the fine older Benediction Loggia at the Lateran (facing the obelisk), with Doric below and Corinthian pilasters above, dating from the time of Sixtus V (1586), whose chief architect, Domenico Fontana, however, is much heavier-handed in the adjoining palace and the front of the near-by Scala Santa.

Brick, on the Cancelleria (side front), and still in Bramante's later buildings very effective, also when emphasised with stone divisions (original form of the

Fig. 67 *(above) Florence, Palazzo Pitti, garden façade* Fig. 68 *(below) Milan, Palazzo Arcivescovile, court*

Fig. 69 *Genoa, Sta Maria delle Vigne, interior*

upper storey around the Vatican Giardino della Pigna), as well as in Baldassare Peruzzi's smaller buildings in Siena, was generally stuccoed over as a supposedly ignoble material. Palladio even stooped to facing brick columns with stucco. (But elsewhere in N. Italy brick could still be seen exposed on a few excellent buildings until into the seventeeth century.)

In his Introduction, in which he discusses building materials, Vasari was completely silent about brick.

The character of cheerless grandeur, peculiar to this architectural period compared with the earlier phase, was partly due also to the intellectual attitude of certain princes.

The Duke (later Grand Duke) Cosimo I (1537–74) preferred the Doric Order, "because it was more certain and sturdier than the others", hence Vasari's inevitable use of it on the Uffizi (1560: Fig. 66); Ammanati, however, had the three-sided three-storey cortile of the Pitti Palace adorned with nothing but rusticated "Orders" (1558–77: Fig. 67).

Cosimo's participation in all building matters, e.g. Gaye, *Carteggio*, II, p. 498, and much other evidence and correspondence. His sense of correctitude, § 83. Even the Girandole renounced under him fantastic and frivolous forms and learned to represent in fireworks an octagonal classical Temple; Vasari, VI, p. 93, *V. di Tribolo.* Cf. § 195.

In general, rustication was regarded as the expression of the deepest solemnity. Attempts to give it a free and less reticent quality in details, in the court of the Archbishop's Palace in Milan, by Pellegrini (Fig. 68); more restrained at the Prigioni in Venice.

The beautiful new motive in columnar architecture created by alternating arches with straight entablatures, § 35.

Now also more common is the coupling (juxtaposition) of two columns, when strengthening (perhaps because of the width of the arch) is needed, but a pier is not wanted. Thus especially in the Genoese School: interior of S. Siro and the Madonna delle Vigne at Genoa (Fig. 69).

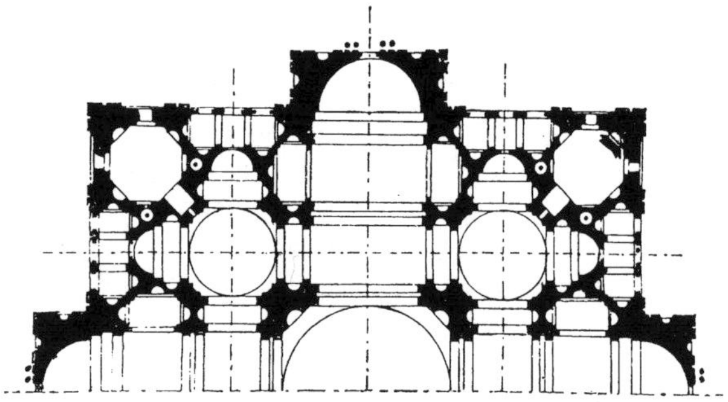

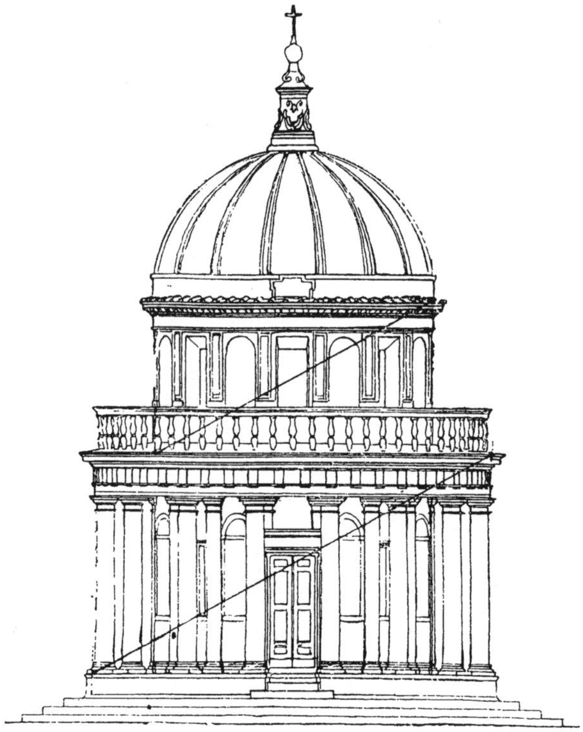

Fig. 70 *(above) Bramante's plan for St Peter's*

Fig. 71 *(right) Rome, S. Pietro in Montorio, the Tempietto*

§ 57 *Proportion*

By its use of the forms considered so far, together with the relevant ornamental forms, the Renaissance designed its buildings according to a particular law, that of proportion (§30, 33, 38).

Purely mathematical means will never lead to immutable principles, because apart from proportions a greater strength or weakness in the shaping of architectural form – even indeed variations in colour – contribute to the final effect, so that buildings of the same proportions may appear lighter or heavier.[1]

In recent times, however, a law of proportion has been discovered, which holds good under widely differing conditions. The author to whom we are indebted for the discovery of this law, August Thiersch,[2] has with the utmost kindness consented to allow his researches relating to the Renaissance to be reprinted here. The following explanations (as far as p. 75) are due to him.

A first step towards the discovery of the above-mentioned law was taken by A. Zeising (*Neue Lehre von den Proportionen des menschlichen Körpers* . . .), who refers to the Golden Section, that constant proportion taught by Euclid, in which the shorter section of a straight line is in the same ratio to the longer, as the longer is to the whole. Recording our welcome to it, we proceed a stage further.

There is as a rule a constant proportion and similarity among geometrical figures, as Euclid demonstrated in his *Elements*, Bk VI. By studying the most successful buildings of all periods we find that a basic form is repeated, and that the individual parts by their disposition and form always create figures similar to one another. There are infinitely multifarious figures which in themselves cannot be called either beautiful or ugly. The harmonious occurs only through the repetition of the principal figure of the work in its subdivisions.

This inner relationship of the individual members to the whole is particularly apparent in the buildings of Classical Antiquity, and upon it rests the unity and harmony of its appearance.

Just as that fundamental law of architectural proportions first made its appearance in Greek and Roman buildings, so it was to revive and rise to a new importance at the beginning of the Renaissance.

Whether architects followed it first in practice and then in theory, or the other way round, or indeed consciously at all, may remain undecided. That they observed it is certain, for it shines out from the finest monuments of the Italian Renaissance. The same splendid proportions as in Antiquity reappear by the attainment of harmony not merely in an approximate, but in a strictly geometrical, sense; indeed in its rich development the architecture of the Renaissance offers an even greater abundance of examples and proof than the re-

1 It is a pity that no single word exists [in German] which expressly embraces proportions [i.e. *Verhältnisse*] – by which is generally understood only height, width, and depth – and also plastic form.
2 *Handbuch der Architektur*, IV. Teil, 1. Halbband, pp. 38–77.

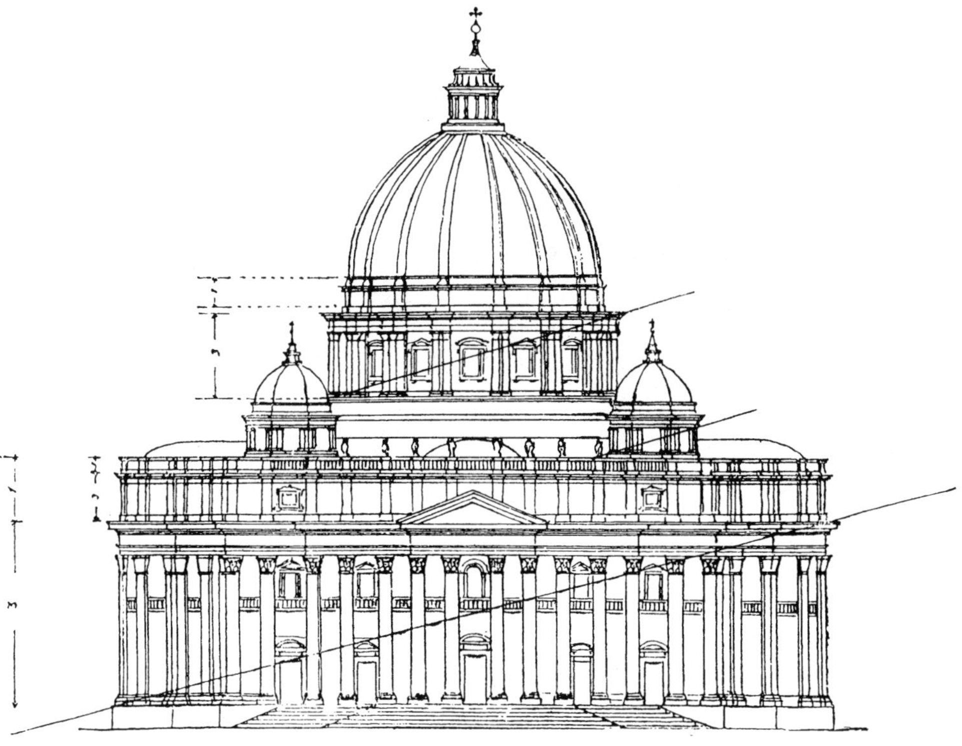

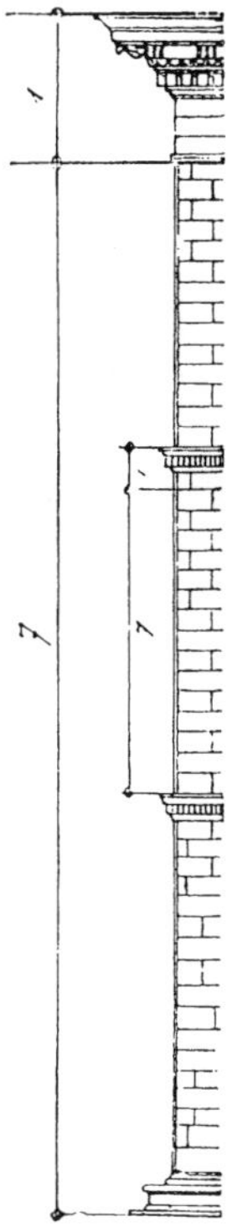

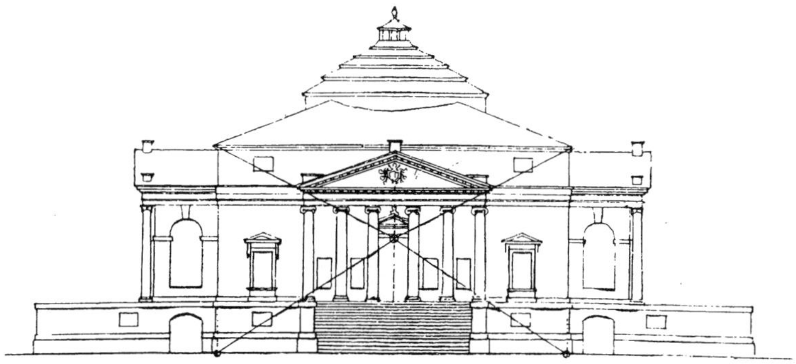

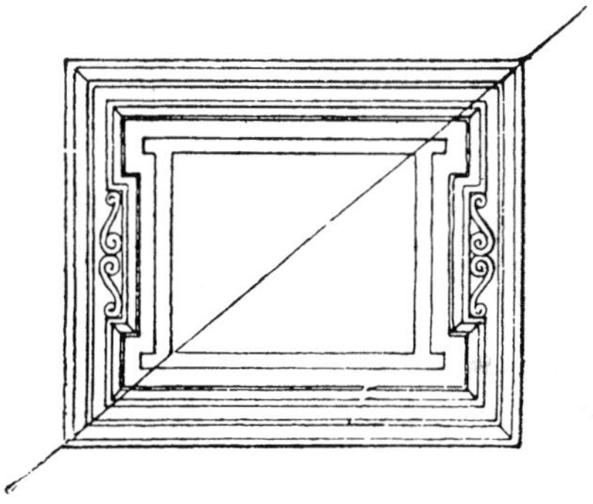

Fig. 72 *(above) Rome, St Peter's, based on Michelangelo's design*

Fig. 73 *(below) Vicenza, Villa Rotonda*

Fig. 74 *(above) Florence, Palazzo Strozzi, detail*

Fig. 75 *(below) Rome, Palazzo Massimi, detail*

mains of the Ancient world. Instances are presented at every step that we take in the company of a guide like Bühlmann (*Die Architektur d. klass. Altertums u. d. Renaiss.*).

In church-building Brunellesco introduced the same proportion of width to height for nave and aisles (S. Lorenzo and Sto Spirito in Florence); Florentine masters gave expression to this conformity in church façades in Rome and extended it to the doors. In aisleless churches, for which Alberti at Sant' Andrea in Mantua set the pattern, the chapels between the buttresses repeat the figures of the transept and relate to the latter as the smaller niches to the chapels themselves. This is still more decisively the case in the church of Sta Maria de' Monti in Rome (see Fig. 161 in § 76).

The organisation of Roman Triumphal Arches (the disposition of the side-parts analogous to the middle one) recurs on the monument to Doge Vendramin in Venice, as in the prelates' tombs in Sta Maria del Popolo in Rome (Fig. 292 in § 141). Simplest of all is the subordination of the side arches to the main arches in the transept of the church of S. Salvatore in Venice (Fig. 172 in § 77); it is repeated on the altars and wall-tombs of the church.

In churches of a centralised type the secondary domes conform in plan and elevation to the main dome (cf. Bramante's plan for S. Peter's in Rome, Fig. 70). Further, the drum beneath the dome develops into an upper storey and preserves externally the same ratio of width to height as the whole body of the church below. Examples are the Tempietto at S. Pietro in Montorio in Rome (Fig. 71), the Consolazione at Todi, and S. Peter in Rome in the form intended by Michelangelo (Fig. 72). It is not Michelangelo's least merit that he succeeded in preserving this harmony in the architecture of S. Peter's,

Fig. 76 *Florence, Palazzo Bartolini, detail*

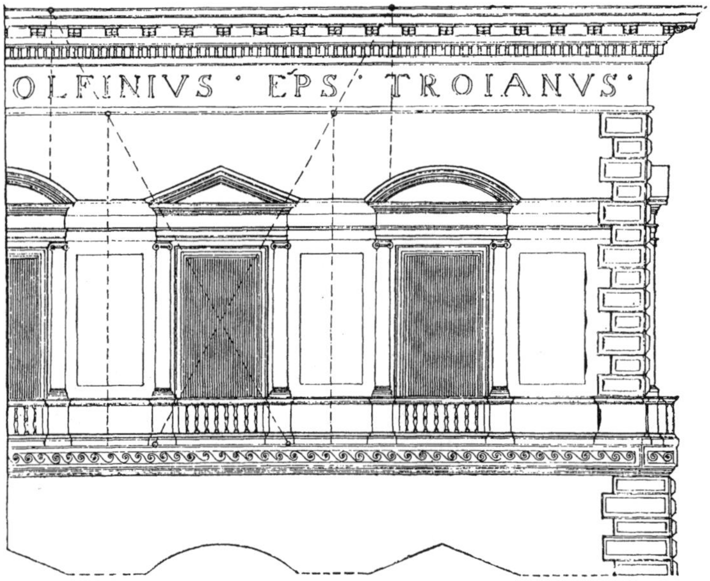

Fig. 77 *Florence, Palazzo Pandolfini, detail*

by providing the exterior of the church with a single large pilaster Order, repeating the proportions of this to the attic in the columnar Order of the drum. (Cf. the analogy of the disposition of the upper and lower storeys of Roman Triumphal Arches.)

If we turn to multiform private building, the same law confronts us in every component, major as well as minor.

An element added to the main structure or one placed in front of it has to accord with the latter in its proportions. The top storey of the Palazzo Pitti in Florence corresponds to the whole of the lower structure (being half as long, because half as high); the projecting porticoes of the Villa Rotonda (Fig. 73) repeat the figure of the house, etc.

For the articulation of the elevations the rule was first made in Florence: what the string-course is to the individual storey, the cornice is to the palace as a whole. At the Pal. Strozzi (Fig. 74) this axiom was exploited for the first time, with great success.

The overall height is divided into three almost equal parts. Each of the two lower storeys ends with a string-course, which, with the stone-course below it, constitutes an eighth part of the storey height. Corresponding to it, the cornice crowning all three storeys has been given three times the height of a string-course and, with its frieze, goes eight times into the overall height.

The same holds good for the Pal. Piccolomini at Siena. At the Pal. Gondi in Florence the ground floor forms a distinct base with heavier rustication, and the cornice therefore is only related in its proportions to the two upper storeys by assuming double the height of the string-course.

This is also the pattern of most Roman palaces. The moulding crowning the ground storey and distinguishing it as a base, relates to the latter as does the cornice to the rest of the façade (at Pal. Negroni the ratio is 1 : 12). These façades, however, lack the simplicity and strength characterising Florentine examples.

The Palazzo Farnese, however, gains effect in its turn because it follows the simple elevational system of the Pal. Strozzi and ends with a cornice and a frieze, which relate to the whole as do the string-courses with their friezes to the individual storeys. Here again the cornice is three times the height of the string-course, if we do not compare the perpendicular heights with one another, but the true intervals between the top and bottom edges – i.e. those dimensions which, regarded in perspective, foreshorten least.

For the window and door surrounds rules apply which go back to Antiquity. When a window-opening is appreciably higher than it is wide, a frame of equal width all round is somewhat unsatisfactory. This peculiarity is more noticeable with wide surrounds and slender openings than with narrow frames and constricted openings. The frame of vertical figures requires above or below, or in both places at once, an addition which makes the external outline similar to the inner one. With openings which form a horizontal rectangle, an enlargement of the surround is appropriate at the sides (Fig. 75). Just as the cella of a classical temple is so planned with columns and entablatures that the external line is similar to the internal, this is also the pattern with Renaissance windows and portals.

Where a simple window-frame is directly supported on a string-course, it takes the latter's proportion in the formation of the surround, and there is as a rule conformity between the inner and outer lines (windows of Pal. A. Massimi, Rome).

Generally the width and height of the surround are determined simply by the diagonals of the opening. This is also the case when, to a frame of constant size, pilasters

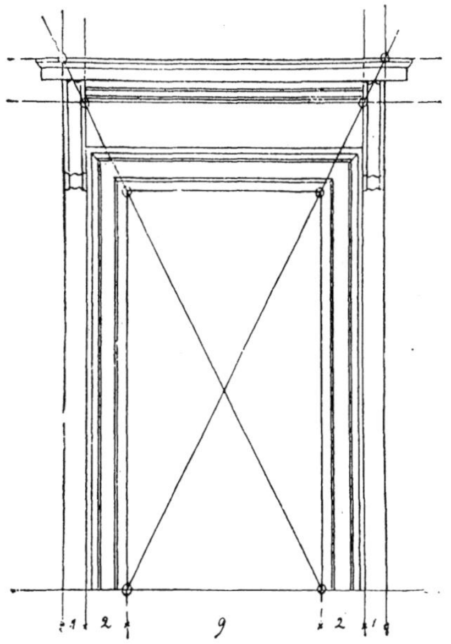

Fig. 78 *Diagram of door-frame*

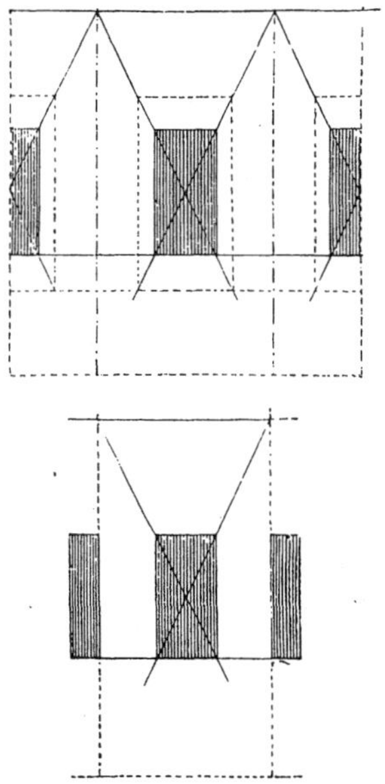

Figs. 79, 80 *Diagram of window proportions*

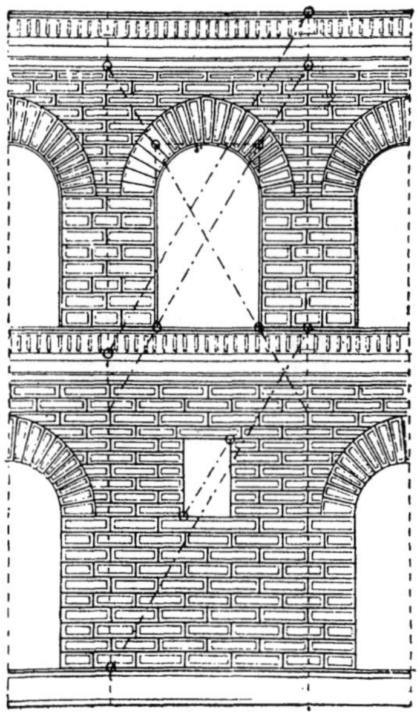

Fig. 81 *Florence, Palazzo Pitti, detail*

or engaged columns are added, as at the Palazzi Farnese, Bartolini (Fig. 76), Pandolfini (Fig. 77) etc., on the model of the aediculae of the Pantheon.

In these instances due regard is paid to the window-opening being partly masked by the parapet. (In this connection compare also the examples in Bühlmann's *Architektur des klass. Altertums u. d. Renaissance*, Pt II, 4th ed., Esslingen, 1919, pl. 41.)

Peruzzi and Vignola used diagonals principally for doorcases, although here no base-panel, as with windows, was feasible.

If, for example, the width of the doorcase goes three times into the width of the actual opening, the lintel with its crowning piece equals a third of the unobstructed door-height (Fig. 78). Or, if the door-opening is twice as high as wide, then the lintel has double the breadth of the jambs.

Especially important, moreover, are the proportions of wall-surfaces to window-openings. Florence once again leads with *exempla*. The proportions are most simply shown if one extends the round-arched window-openings to rectangles and then draws the diagonals. The result is then either that the diagonals of two adjoining windows converge below the upper bounding line of the wall-surface (Fig. 79), or that the lengthened diagonals of a lower opening coincide with the one above (Fig. 80). In the first case the wall-compartment is so divided by the central axes of the intervening wall-masses that it provides the window-opening with a surround of proportionately constant size; in the other case the whole wall-mass surrounds the opening at a proportionately constant width.

The Palazzo Pitti in Florence (Fig. 81) followed the first manner and so, more or less exactly, did most Roman palaces with their dominating wall surfaces; and especially the Pal. Bartolini and Pandolfini in Florence (Figs. 76 and 77). The second mode is adhered to in the Palazzi Riccardi, Strozzi, Gondi and Guadagni. If the width of the intervening wall is equal to that of the window, the height of the wall above is also equal to that of the window (topmost floor of the Pal. Strozzi in Fig. 82). When the intervening walls are narrower than the openings, as in the Pal. Guadagni (Fig. 83), the heights of the wall above the crown of the arches are proportionately lower than the windows. In this example the first type of harmony is also simultaneously attained.

The observation that the plain wall-surface between the windows and above them must have the same width can be traced back to the first case, and is based on the premiss that the window-height amounts to double its width (Palazzi Pitti, Bartolini, Pandolfini).

In elevations with pilaster Orders the same considerations are valid. The pilaster-frame stands in the closest relationship to the window-frame, which is surrounded by it. Either both form figures similar to one another, or the pilaster Order surrounds the window at the sides and above in accordance with the size of its diagonals at proportionately equal intervals, thus taking a share in the framing. Examples of the first type are offered by the lower storey of the Farnesina (Fig. 84), the Palazzi Stoppani and Ugoccioni, and also the Pal. Porto in Vicenza; examples of the other type by the upper storey of the Farnesina, the court façade of the Palazzo Massimi and the *piano nobile* of the Palazzo Ossoli, all by Peruzzi. The harmonising of window and pilaster-frame in the sense of geometrical similarity was also carried out by Michelangelo (Palazzo del Senatorio), Galeazzo Alessi, Sansovino and Palladio, wherever at all feasible, and in so doing they acted on the principle that the forms themselves should be as different as possible – profiled window-jambs confront plain pilasters; these contrast in turn with engaged columns, herms, or rusticated

Fig. 82 *(left) Florence, Palazzo Strozzi, detail*

Fig. 83 *(centre) Florence, Palazzo Guadagni, detail*

Fig. 84 *(right) Rome, Villa Farnesina, detail*

columns. Even the Venetian early Renaissance offers fine examples: Scuola di S. Marco.

The same proportions determine pilaster and column Orders associated with arches. Just as on the Theatre of Marcellus and Roman Triumphal Arches, the pair of columns or pilasters had to enclose the same figure as the two piers (arcading of Peruzzi, Palladio (Fig. 85) etc.). Palladio's Basilica is indebted for its harmonious appearance to this concordance in spite of the unpleasing width of the setting-out; the small columns have bases which act as counterparts to the pedestals of the large Order.

The division of the wall-surface also demands respect for the law that the parts should correspond to the figure of the whole. This applies especially to the main compartment of the wall-surface important by reason of its size or decoration. This harmonisation is often to be seen in Pompeian mural paintings and can be traced through the Renaissance, coming into universal use with the Rococo style. Examples are the Gran Salone of the Pal. Massimi (Fig. 87), the rooms in the Villa Farnese at Caprarola and the Sala del Gran Consiglio in the Doge's Palace at Venice. The arrangement is very common of placing the door of a large room close to the corner and thus relatively reducing the length of the wall by as much as the chandeliers reduce the height.

For elevations the same thing applies if the windows are grouped together or comprise units of varying width. At the Palazzo del Consiglio at Padua (Fig. 231 in §102) the central group of windows of the upper storey is similar both to the principal bay and to the whole façade, and in the Sapienza at Naples the Loggia to the whole. In the panels of door-leaves shapes were preferred which corresponded to the whole door, and which were surrounded by mouldings imitating the pattern of the door-frame (doors of the Vatican etc.). So also particularly in the Rococo period.

Finally, the design of details is also subject to the law of analogy. Window-surrounds with canopies take their form from the analogue of the house. The hood-mouldings of windows accord with the cornice; their projection and height are prescribed by it.

The mouldings themselves demonstrate the endeavour to bring the smaller parts into harmony with the large. The cornice-slab and the elements supporting it and lying under its shadow, as well as the plain frieze below, form a group, which is repeated in the mouldings of the architrave (in the upper part of the latter or in the whole). Peruzzi and Vignola followed this disposition by choice, and ordered the setting of the surround according to a steadily diminishing sequence (Fig. 88).

The concordance between the mouldings of capital and entablature followed in Classical Antiquity was also revived. The height and projection of the abaci are proportional to one another, the neck-ornament of the pilaster capital analogous to that of the frieze. Rosettes on the necking of the column correspond to the alternating triglyph frieze, or the foliage of the capital to its

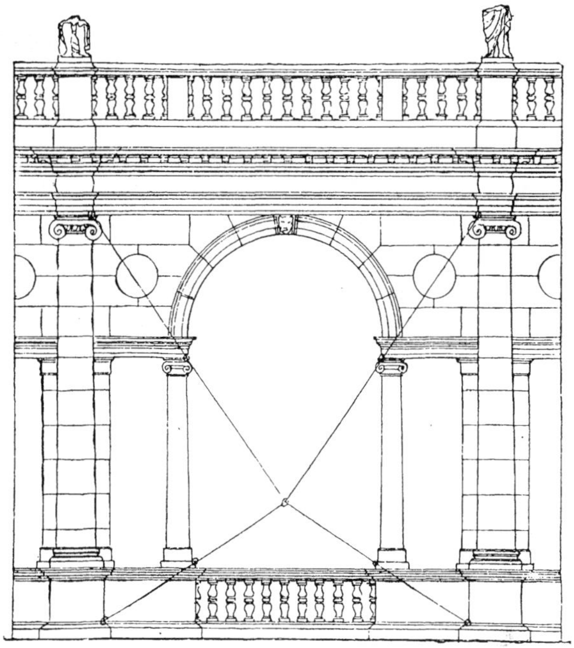

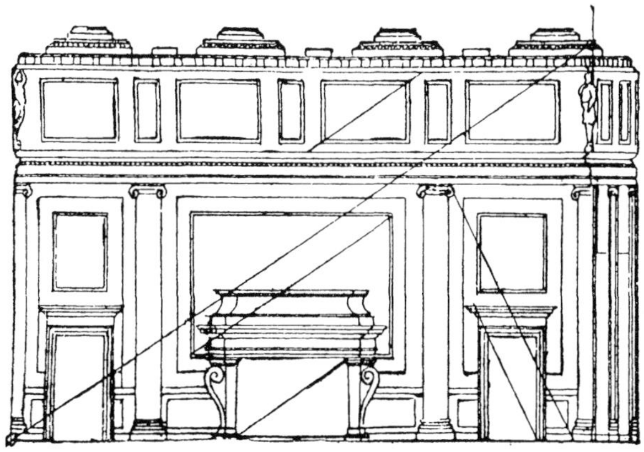

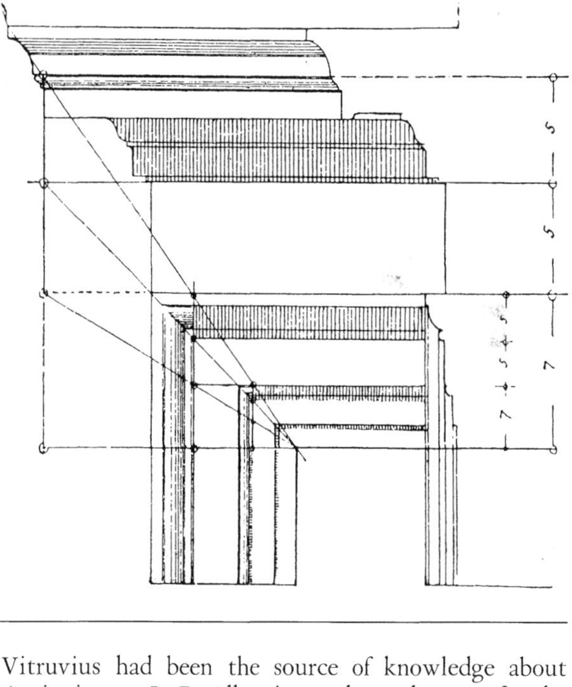

Fig. 85 *(above left) Diagram of arch, from Palladio*

Fig. 86 *(above right) Vicenza, the Basilica*

Fig. 87 *(above) Rome, Palazzo Massimi, detail of Salone*

Fig. 88 *(right) Diagram of mouldings*

foliated frieze. Beautiful examples are offered by the Venetian early Renaissance and the ordonnances of Alberti, Bramante etc.

The well-known law was extended to the composition of ornament. The acanthus leaf was divided into separate parts, and these in turn into similarly formed leaf-crenellations. The arabesque repeats the pervading motives in the delicate interwoven elements etc.

If we glance back once again over the whole of the Renaissance, the question recurs whether the architects of the period ever clearly enunciated in theory the law which they so loyally observed in practice. Just as Vitruvius had been the source of knowledge about Antiquity, so L. B. Alberti was the spokesman for the fifteenth century, expressing the guiding principles differently, but intelligibly enough.

A chapter on the *lineamenta* forms the introduction to his work *De re aedificatoria*. By their means the constituent parts of the work in its angles and lines had to correspond – *inter se conveniant totis angulis totisque lineis*. This was to be done by establishing angles and lines of a certain direction and with a certain connection – *adnotando et praefiniendo angulos et lineas certa directione et certa connexione*. In the IVth Book (c. 5) a description of a good composition is given, ending with the words: *Omnia ad certos angulos paribus lineis adaequanda* (cf. also the points made in §30 above; L. VI, c. 2; L. IX, c. 3 and 5).

The previously drawn lines and angles are thus aids to achieving proportionate figures.

Alberti, referring to his façade for S. Francesco at Rimini, used the words *tutta quella musica* for the mysterious harmony of the parts to the whole. (Lettera sulla cupola etc., *Opere volgari*, Tom. IV). "Musical proportions" (§26) also mentioned by Brunellesco's biographer, Antonio Manetti (ed. Holtzinger, p. 16).

Information on proportions is often given for individual cases, for example by Serlio, who does not, however, involve himself in a discussion of principle.

There was no lack of people at that time striving to deal with the matter in speculative ways. A monk, Francesco Giorgi, corrected the proportions of Jacopo Sansovino's church of S. Francesco della Vigna in Venice in 1534, using a Platonic theory of numbers, of which a small example is given in Vasari, VII, p. 504, n. 1, *V. di J. Sansovino*.

Proportions in their relationship to forms, and the latter to the former, remained the subject of the highest and subtlest artistic efforts. The problem lay in a style in which the real vitality was not in the design of individual forms (even if beautiful in themselves), but in their relationship to the whole. Those totally unable to accept this law must turn away from the Renaissance style and seek satisfaction elsewhere.

(NOTE: On Renaissance proportions see R. Wittkower, *Architectural Principles in the Age of Humanism*, 3rd ed., London, 1962: Francesco Giorgi's report is printed as an Appendix (see now also D. Howard and M. Longair in *Journal of the Society of Architectural Historians*, XLI, 1982, no. 2). On Alberti's *lineamenti* see S. Lang in Journal of the Warburg and Courtauld Institutes, XXVIII, 1965.) (PM).

CHAPTER EIGHT

The Architectural Model

§58 *Models of the Gothic Period*

While in the rest of Europe the architectural drawing (often a bold combination of geometrical and perspective projections) sufficed, in Italian architecture the model held the stage.

In Classical times complicated schemes, e.g. thermae, probably gave rise to models. The silver shrine of the Ephesian Diana? – *Acts*, xix, 24 ff. In the Middle Ages the left hand of the statue of a donor often held a sketch model of the church. The silver model of a whole town as a votive offering, no doubt with the principal buildings clearly represented: Parma, 1248 (Raumer, *Hohenstaufen*, IV, p. 182); Ferrara before 1441 (Diario Ferrarese in Murat., XXIV, col. 451).

The word *modello* often means "drawing", and we must interpret it as "model" only when the sense is unmistakable: on the other hand, *disegno* may equally signify a real model; e.g. Milanesi, II, p. 272 – *disegno de la cera* for a splendid altar, by which a wax model is almost certainly meant.

The Northern Gothic drawing on parchment gives the elevation, while the related ground-plan gives a shorthand version, showing the parts developing upwards from the core. The model of the Italians, however, demonstrates three-dimensionally how the rooms are to be shaped, partitioned, and disposed inside and out, as well as the overall appearance as it would be in the light of day.

It is an account which the artist renders, not to himself, but to the client, in order to stimulate the latter's imagination at a time when every major building implied a striving for originality, for the exceptional, and indeed for the colossal; indispensable especially for domes and for centralised buildings.

In Italy during the Gothic period a drawing was enough for simpler churches and palaces; Milanesi, I, pp. 227 f., 232, 246, and even for the new Cathedral of Siena only drawings on parchment are mentioned.

For the building of the dome of Florence Cathedral, on the other hand, it was only by means of a model that the necessary conviction and enthusiasm were forthcoming. Regarding Arnolfo's model and what remained of it, Vasari, I, p. 292, n. 2, *V. di Arnolfo*. After the model of Benci di Cione and Neri di Fioravante had been finally accepted in 1367, it was decided that all earlier models should be destroyed – *omne aliud designum factum et muratum et laboratum in dicta ecclesia*; isolated older models, however, turned up later (1379 and 1382); cf. Guasti, *Sta Maria del Fiore*, pp. 248, 265. The representation in fresco on the right-hand wall in the Capp. degli Spagnuoli in Sta Maria Novella, perhaps represents architectural projects of the middle of the fourteenth century, or Arnolfo's project.*

What happened in the case of S. Petronio, Bologna, about 1390, was exceptional because of the desire to be certain in advance of its feasibility and effect; in the palace of Giacomo Pepoli a model, one-twelfth actual size (i.e. fifty-three feet long), was built of stone and plaster, this being broken up in 1406; afterwards another, ten feet long, of wood and paper, was prepared, only to be destroyed as well; it was followed in 1514 by the one still surviving in the Opera (§23), by Arduino Ariguzzi (Fig. 89). Cf. (Bianconi), *Guida per la città di Bologna*, 1845, pp. 91, 104.

Quite late, at the beginning of the sixteenth century, there were models here and there in the north, e.g. in the Town Hall of Louvain one for the tower of S. Pierre.

§59 *Models of the Early Renaissance*

In the fifteenth century, contemporary with Brunellesco, the model became the general rule because the new style

* Now generally thought to represent a project of the 1360s. (PM).

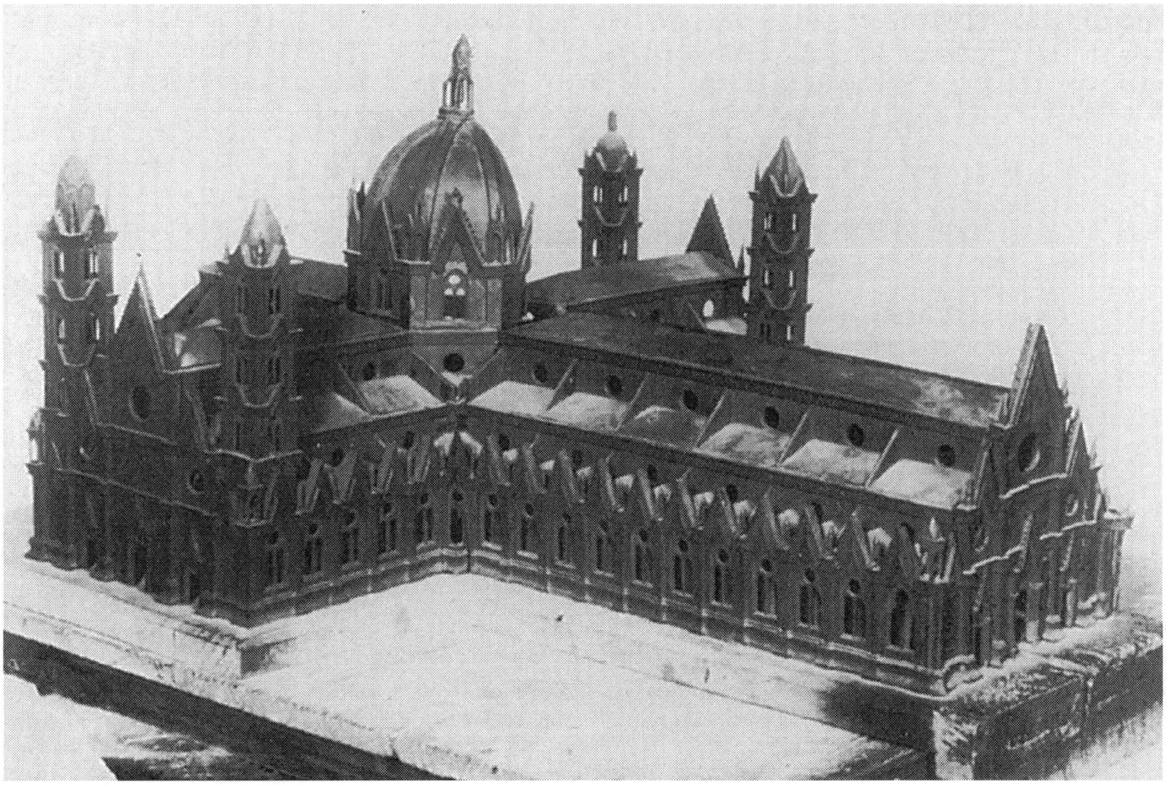

Fig. 89 *Model of S. Petronio, Bologna*

had to justify its unfamiliar appearance, and, by reason of its intrinsic laws, was pre-eminently suited to representation in this way. Moreover, many architects (§14) had begun as wood-workers and made models easily. For fortifications models had probably always been required.

Brunellesco constantly employed models, both small- and large-scale, and he also cut patterns for his masons of the complicated shapes of the blocks of stone used in the Cathedral dome, using turnips when necessary.

For the whole dome he made several models, from a small one which he could carry under his cloak to the largest, in brick; the remains of several are still preserved: Vasari, II, *Vita di Brun.*, passim; A. Manetti, *V. di Brun.*, p. 24 ff.; Guasti, *La Cupola di S. M. del Fiore*, passim.

For S. Lorenzo his supervision and his drawings sufficed, but he made models for the Capp. de' Pazzi, for Sto Spirito, for the polygon of the Angeli, and for the Palace of Cosimo de' Medici (which he himself broke in pieces when Cosimo, fearing the envy of his fellow-townsmen, rejected the project); finally, large schemes in clay and wood for fortifications. Manetti, *V. di Brunell.*, pp. 41, 46 ff., 57; Vasari, II, pp. 366 ff., 371, *V. di Brunell.* For the loggia of the Innocenti, according to Manetti, p. 42, he made no model, but only an exact drawing with a scale; the *modello* Vasari saw may have been the work of a successor.

His models gave all the essentials but not the ornamentation, "so that the unauthorised would not be able to steal from him" – more probably, however, in order not to corrupt the eye with that prettiness which can easily be given in such works.

Such at least was the view of Alberti (*Arte Edificatoria*, L. II, in *Opere Volgari*, IV, p. 261), who cautions everyone against models, which, adorned with painting, gilding and other decorations, are fit for vain and ambitious people to impose upon other ignorant people: only *modelli nudi e semplici* offer proof of the genius of the designer. Even with drawings he refuses to accept any painterly effects, even chiaroscuro, since the architect must express himself through his basic designs.

If unworthy artists ought thus to be dismissed, yet there were such decorators who became great – or at least respectable – architects and then were able to turn their skill in model-making to good use.

Giuliano da Sangallo's models for the Villa at Poggio a Cajano, for a palace for the Crown Prince of Naples, a palace for Ludovico Il Moro, an addition to S. Pietro in Vincoli in Rome, and a palace at Savona; this last, with elaborately worked decoration, he had to take in person to Charles VIII at Lyons, his client Cardinal Giuliano della Rovere (later Julius II) having presented it to Charles. He had also had to accompany the models already mentioned to Naples and Milan. Antonio da Sangallo the Elder's models for the church at Cortona (unrealised) and at Montepulciano: Vasari, IV, p. 288 f., *V. di Giuliano da Sangallo.*

When Filarete drew up plans for the rebuilding of the Cathedral of Bergamo in 1457 he had also to prepare a wooden model before he was commissioned to execute the work – v. Oettingen, *Antonio Averlino*, p. 34, with documents.

Vecchietta took a wooden model for the Loggia del Papa from Siena to Rome in 1460, but failed to get the job; Milanesi, II, p. 308.

Francione, *lignarius*, architect and teacher of Baccio Pontelli, submitted a model in the competition of 1491 for a new façade for Florence Cathedral (§70), when all the forty-five others only produced drawings; similarly for the dome of the sacristy of Sto Spirito in 1493; which collapsed, however, when the centering was removed; Gaye, *Carteggio*, I, p. 276; Vasari, IV, p. 447, n. 3, *V. di Cronaca*. A church model by Pontelli, Vasari, II, p. 653, *Vita di Paolo Romano*.

For the *tiburio* of Milan Cathedral (§23) many masters submitted models in 1490; Milanesi, II, p. 430, and even Francesco di Giorgio would scarcely have entered without one. He had already been successful in 1484 with his model for the church of the Madonna at Cortona; *Lettere sanesi*, III, p. 88.

In the Cathedral of Pavia the large, well-preserved and restored wooden model of the church, apparently by Cristoforo Rocchi, 1486 (Fig. 90).

For a wooden model by Bramante for the Canonica of S. Ambrogio in Milan, cf. v. Geymüller, *Die urspr. Entwürfe..*, p. 54.

§60 *Models of the High Renaissance*

In the sixteenth century model-making seems to have been mainly confined to large and complicated buildings, and important renovations and competitions, while drawings sufficed the Renaissance for ordinary works. Fortresses, as already noted, always had models made.

Julius II, according to legend, was so hemmed about by wood-workers with nothing to offer but models for S. Peter's which looked like barns that he commented laughingly: "We have nothing more than a church to build, for which a model is all we need; we have one already which is extremely good, so what are we to do with all these huts?" (taken from the old translation in Bernardini Ochini *Apologen*, Buch I, Apol. 23: the Italian original seems untraceable).

After the unfinished model for S. Peter's left by Bramante there followed those by Raphael, Peruzzi, Ant. da Sangallo the Younger and Michelangelo; Vasari, V, p. 467 ff., *V. di Ant. Sangallo*; VII, pp. 218, 249, *V. di Michelangelo*.

Bramante had also submitted a "wonderful" model for the main building of the Vatican; Vasari, IV, p. 158, *V. di Bramante*; Panvinio, op. cit. (§8), p. 365 f. Raphael's wooden model for the cortile with the Loggie; Vasari, IV, p. 362, *V. di Raffaello*.

Vitoni's wooden model for the Madonna dell' Umiltà, with which he charmed the Pistoians (1509); Vasari, IV, p. 165, *V. di Bramante*.

Under Leo X artists competed for the façades of the Cathedral and the church of S. Lorenzo in Florence with models and drawings; Vasari, VII, p. 188, *V. di Michelangelo*; VII, p. 495 f., *V. di Jacopo Sansovino*.

Michelangelo's continual model-making §50. The model of the richest of his five projects for S. Giovanni de' Fiorentini in Rome was made in ten days by Tiberio Calcagni under the eighty-five-year-old master's supervision; lost, together with the subsequent wooden model and the other schemes; Vasari, VII, p. 263, *V. di Michelangelo*. His model for the stairs of the Laurenziana (1559) came "in a little box" from Rome to Florence; Gaye, *Carteggio*, III, p. 12. Cf. Fig. 64. His design in fact needed this clarification.

Vasari had to take with him to Rome a wooden model of his alterations to the Palazzo della Signoria by command of the exacting Cosimo I, so that Michelangelo might judge them; Vasari, VII, p. 698, in his Autobiography; II, p. 439, *V. di Michelozzo*; VII, p. 260, *V. di Michelangelo*.

The fortress models by Sanmicheli; Vasari, VI, p. 361, *V. di Sanmicheli*.

The great cork model of the whole of Florence, perhaps the earliest of its kind; Varchi, *Stor. Fior.*, III, p. 56 ff., Vasari, VI, p. 62, *V. di Tribolo*.

Fig. 90 *Model of Pavia Cathedral*

CHAPTER NINE

The Design of Churches

§61 *The Lack of a Specific Church Architecture*

The Renaissance was unable to evolve its own organic or its own sacred style in the sense of the Greek temple style and the northern Gothic style. It applied to church architecture the forms and dispositions of Antiquity out of admiration, because it held them to be the best, and used them also and without hesitation in secular building.

The creation of an organic style depends to a high degree upon predisposition and chance, in particular upon a certain ingenuous simplicity and a lively affinity with nature; and there is reason for the fact that the phenomenon has occurred only twice in the history of art.

Barbarous and primitive peoples, however, have a purely religious architecture of their own, and it is irrational to suppose that such a style brings greater honour to a nation or a cultural era than a derivative style, which indeed may serve no less strong religious aspirations, and express in borrowed trappings independent and new ideas. Thus Early Christian architecture borrowed not merely isolated forms, but even actual bits of secular and religious Roman buildings, and with them created a great novelty.

Moreover, the derivative style has its own particular and great problems which an organic style would not be able to solve within the framework of its own laws.

It has first as a spatial style (§30, 32) a right to the forms of the organic etc. styles existing before it, and should use them according to the intrinsic needs by which its genius will guide it. It may perhaps hold some of these as specifically sacred, and at the beginning the Renaissance, too, regarded certain window- and door-forms in this light, until the architecture of palaces took away these forms from churches, and even (with Palladio) the pedimented portico. The character and purpose of the building are only expressed in the basic form; the details are common to the sacred and the secular.

It would be very dangerous to cite the less obvious piety of Italy at this time compared with the Gothic flowering in the North, as though the piety and orthodoxy of our northern master-builders of the thirteenth and fourteenth centuries could be precisely measured. On the other hand, the very pious Italians of the Renaissance built with no greater devotion than their contemporaries.

In the South the great and beautiful is holy in itself. It is for each one to decide whether this conception of holiness demeans holiness or exalts art. (Cf. Michelangelo's comment in the account of Francesco d' Olanda (1549), in Raczynski, *Les Arts en Portugal*, p. 14; "True painting is noble and pious of itself, for the striving for perfection raises the soul in devotion, bringing it closer to God and uniting it with Him" – in the sense intended by the speaker surely applicable to the arts in general.)

If then the religious uncertainty of our times proves anything at all, it is the uncommon susceptibility towards supposedly secular forms.

§62 *Character of the Centralised Building*

None the less, the Renaissance evolved to near-perfection the supreme architectural form for churches, one that had been largely ignored by Gothic: the centralised plan, and bequeathed it as a legacy to the piety of future generations.

The centralised building is the last in the realm of absolute architectural forms, as the Greek temple is the first. Its possibilities are still far from exhausted; although intervening periods may occur like the greater part of the nineteenth century, which was to repeat once again the lesson of the thirteenth, this great task will constantly recur and the experiments of the Renaissance will stand in their own right as indispensable preliminary stages.

In the North, late Romanesque imagination created

in the same years (soon after 1200) the decagon of S. Gereon at Cologne and the ideal image of the temple of the Grail, and soon followed the almost uniquely splendid Gothic experiment, the Liebfrauenkirche at Trier. A vast, perfect, octagon with stellar vault, the Karlshofer church in Prague; see Lübke, *Gesch. d. Architektur*, 6th ed., II, p. 141.

Significant for Italy is the fame and mythical status enjoyed by the Pantheon (see the various redactions of the *Mirabilia Romae*), and even more the high standing assigned to S. Lorenzo in Milan. Benzo of Alba in the eleventh century speaks (ad Heinr. IV, ap. Pertz, XIII, p. 680) of the original building, then in decay: *numquid est in toto mundo aula tam mirabilis*? Arnulf of Milan (Gesta Archiepp. Med., III, 24, ap. Pertz, X) with reference to the great fire: *templum cui nullum in mundo simile*. Fazio degli Uberti, about 1360 (*Dittamondo*, L. III, c. 4) believed himself "in the great and beautiful building" transported to Rome. Nor was the truest proof of admiration, imitation, lacking (§16). The impression rested upon the ingenious and imposing arrangement of an upper and a lower gallery embracing the space below the dome. (S. Lorenzo, extensively restored between 1573 and 1591, seems to us, despite the contrary view, engagingly if arbitrarily defended by Hübsch, in plan completely unecclesiastical, being originally a hall in a palace or thermae of the beginning, or perhaps the second half, of the fourth century; cf. especially the recent researches of Dehio and von Bezold, *Kirchliche Baukunst des Abendlandes*, pp. 49–57, and those of J. Kohte (Zeitschr. f. Bauwesen, 1890), who places the original building of the church after the middle of the sixth century, when, after the defeat of the Ostrogoths, Narses restored those towns, including Milan, that had been destroyed in the wars.)

The baptistries, sometimes with ambulatories, kept alive the central plan. Cf. the "Old Cathedral" of Brescia. With Gothic came a preference for the long type of building.

In the centralised building the central space dominates, wherever possible in the form of a high dome, essentially symmetrical, whether there are four equal transepts or a ring of chapels or galleries. Inside, the dome should hover in splendour above the open structure below, and outside tower impressively over it.

In respecting the arrangement of four identical transepts, which in time became predominant, all scruples were ignored in regard to the High Altar, which might be accommodated in a separate, specially consecrated, space of the highest honour in the eastern arm. It was never placed in the centre of a building, and a place inside a gallery, ambulatory, or the like was lacking in respect. In octagonal churches a special projection could be provided, sacrificing the unity of the plan, which could be rescued, however, by the Greek cross form.

The dome is fundamentally and inevitably linked to the central plan. All round and polygonal spaces require a termination on top which is similar to their groundplan. The often exceedingly complex centralised buildings sometimes incorporate every possible pure and mixed type of vaulting, of which the supreme manifestation is the main dome. The lofty, luminous cylinder and, externally, the drum were not attained until late.

This method of building in its perfection realises all the ideals of the Renaissance: absolute unity and symmetry, consummate distribution and articulation of space, harmonious development inside and out, coherent elevations, and brilliant exploitation of light.

We take into consideration also those structures which form the chancel of a long church, but are clearly designed in the sense of centralised plans and with this intention in mind. The latter were and remained the principal concern of this great architectural period, which applied all its efforts to them, whenever the opportunity arose. Its weak aspects start to appear where the lofty aim falters for external reasons.

§63 *The Earliest Centralised Buildings of the Renaissance*

The imagination of the fifteenth century was already fired by round and polygonal buildings, when Brunellesco introduced the centralised plan in an entirely new form, in two small churches.

Structures of this type depicted in backgrounds of altarpieces and reliefs: Vasari, II, p. 241, *V. di Ghiberti*; II, p. 676, *V. di Castagno*. Then especially in Perugian pictures and in intarsia-work on choir-stalls (§151) etc.

Often recurring, in particular, an octagonal domed structure, in part perhaps a mere reminiscence of the simpler baptistries of the Middle Ages, generally taking as model the image of the Dome of the Rock at Jerusalem (Kubbet-es-Sachra) as described by the Crusaders, which was regarded as a copy of the Herodian Temple; an idealised version of the often clumsy-looking form, e.g. by Perugino, is given by Raphael in his *Sposalizio*.

One such octagon actually realised in the fifteenth century: S. Giacomo in Vicovaro, above Tivoli, with the familiar elaborate, still predominantly Gothic, portal (*c* 1450, by Domenico da Capodistria: cf. Vasari, II, p. 385, n. 4 and 5, *Vita de Brunellesco*).

Then the new motives: Brunellesco's polygon (only begun) of the Angeli in Florence, 1434, §9. Manetti, *V. di Brunell.*, p. 46; Vasari, II, p. 372, *V. di Brunellesco*. A rapid sketch of the section in Giuliano da Sangallo's sketchbook in the Biblioteca Barberini in Rome;* Vasari possessed Brunellesco's original drawings. Regarding a drawing reproduced in distorted form by d'Agincourt, *Archit.*, pl. 50, formerly belonging to the monastery itself (and later to the Marchese G. Pucci), see Vasari, loc. cit., p. 372, n. 6, and for other sketches of the Renaissance period cf. Fabriczy, *Brunellesco*, p. 241, n. 1. It is an eight-sided domed space with the same number

* i.e. Cod. Barb. Lat. 4424 of the Vatican Library, published in facsimile by C. Huelsen, 1910. (PM).

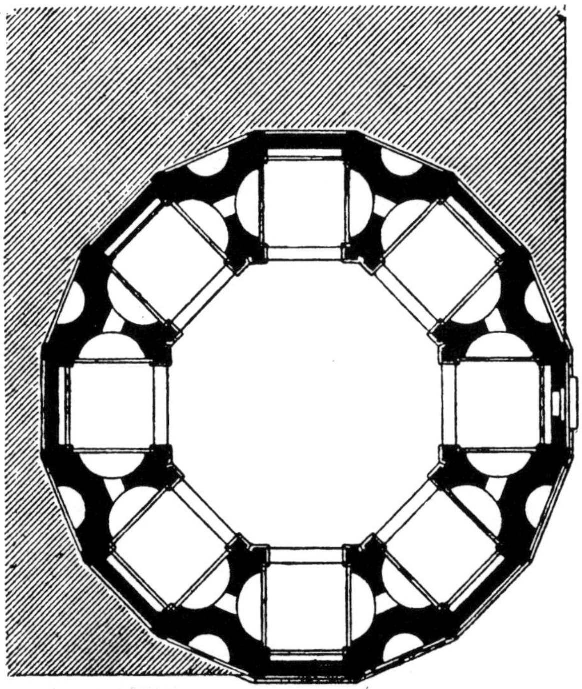

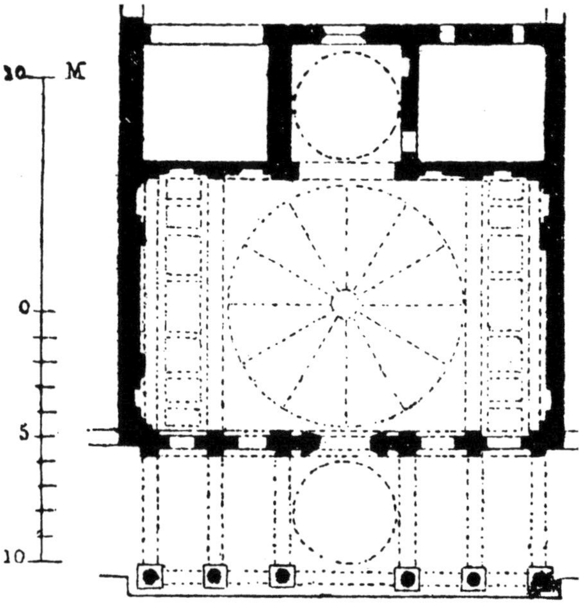

Fig. 91 *(left) Florence, Sta Maria degli Angeli, plan*

Fig. 92 *(above) Florence, Sta Croce, Pazzi Chapel, plan*

of high-openinged chapels, six of which were to be dedicated to the twelve Apostles; pure top-lighting through eight windows; in the thickness of the walls the first niches of modern architecture, not simply to economise on materials, but so that the principle of the dome construction could be carried through to the last detail (Fig. 91). In the sacristy of S. Lorenzo Brunellesco created for the first time segmental niches; later to be followed by – among others – Bramante, in Sta Maria presso S. Satiro in Milan, in the choir of Sta Maria del Popolo in Rome, and in several projects for S. Peter's: cf. v. Geymüller.

Actually executed: the Cappella de' Pazzi in the first cloister of Sta Croce (at the earliest 1429, probably not begun until after 1430), where a light, shallow dome rests upon two lateral arches (Figs. 92–94). The portico, cf. §35. Also the Old Sacristy of S. Lorenzo (the structure completed at latest 1429) may be cited here as the immediate precursor of the Capp. Pazzi (Fig. 178).

Alberti did not tackle the real problem of a dome poised above an open substructure; his two domes, designed essentially as monuments to a despot and a condottiere, were to rest in Roman fashion on massive masonry.

The one for S. Francesco at Rimini (1447), the monument of Sigismondo Malatesta (§6), is known only from a commemorative medal (in d'Agincourt, pl. 51) and from the *Lettera sulla cupola* (in *Opere volgari*, Tom. IV), but never realised. Alberti had to retain an earlier Gothic building with chapels, and redecorate it; over this was to be placed a dome of the proportions of the Pantheon or of the round rooms of thermae; in vain Alberti's clerk of the works, Manetti, proposed that a dome should be twice as high as wide.

The domed building of the Annunziata in Florence, endowed in 1451 by the commander-in-chief of the city-state, Lodovico Gonzaga of Mantua, who intended to install in it the booty, trophies and flags from his campaigns; a niche or chapel was probably to have contained his tomb (Fig. 95). It was perhaps influenced by the nymphaeum of the "Minerva Medica" in Rome, ringed above with windows, below with niches, opening into the church with a great arch; externally rough masonry, internally modernised. Vasari, II, p. 544, n., *V. di Alberti* and Gaye, *Carteggio*, I, p. 255 ff. The building, not devoid of singularities, begun in 1451 by Michelozzo, completed 1471–77 according to the plan, or with the collaboration of Alberti, aroused acute controversy at the time of its erection; cf. Braghirolli in Repertor. f. Kunstw., II, p. 59 ff. Among the effects of Manetti, who had also been in charge of the works here, was the model of a "round temple"; Gaye, op. cit., I, p. 171; no doubt of one of these two buildings. Also in his textbook *De re aedificatoria*, L. VII, c. 10, cf. 15, Alberti overlooks the true centralised building; he speaks at most of round basilicas, i.e. buildings like Sto Stefano Rotondo. He deliberately mixes Christian and pagan round buildings and gives the proportions of height to width according to his own measurements.

The Greek cross was also used by Alberti as a basic plan for a church: S. Sebastiano in Mantua, begun 1460, not completed. In a letter from Cardinal Francesco Gonzaga to his father, the Marchese Lodovico, of 1473, a curious avowal for the author and period: *attento che per essere fatto quello edifizio sul garbo antiquo non molto dissimile da quello viso fantastico de messer Baptista di Alberti, io per ancho non intendeva se l'haveva a reuscire in chiesa o moschea o synagoga.* Cf. Malaguzzi in Rassegna d' Arte, I, p. 13.

Fig. 93 *Florence, Sta Croce, Pazzi Chapel, transverse section*

Fig. 94 *Florence, Sta Croce, Pazzi Chapel, longitudinal section*

§64 *Later Centralised Buildings of the Fifteenth Century*

In the second half of the fifteenth century, experiments, new information, and ideal plans appeared, as well as important (and still existing) solutions to the problem.

In Poliphilus (§32) the section of a round, domed structure with an ambulatory, resting internally on a ring of piers with projecting columns; externally, piers with engaged columns and, rising from these towards the dome, elaborate flying buttresses: Fig. 13. A second description applies to a ruin of the type of the "Minerva Medica".

What became of the celebrated rotunda of Mantegna? – Vasari, III, p. 452, commentary on the *Vita di Mantegna*. In Mantegna's pictures there is often a round building with pilaster cladding and recessed upper storeys; thus in the Camera degli Sposi in the Castello di Corte at Mantua (as superstructure to a kind of Mausoleum) and in the *Triumph of Caesar*.

Francesco di Giorgio in his treatise (§31), *Lettere sanesi*, III, p. 117: "There are three principal forms of church, to which one can trace back the untold numbers that exist: the most perfect is the round one, the second is quadrangular or with separate façades, the third is a combination of the two." In any case, the centralised form is here regarded as supreme.

Highly unusual in the fifteenth century: Filarete's design for a centralised church with an octagonal, unequal-sided, central space, four oblong and four polygonal subordinate spaces diagonally ranged round the centre, and four slender towers accompanying the central space; cf. the ground-plan, reproduced by Dohme in the Jahrb. der preuss. Kunstsamml., III, p. 121.

The two elder Sangallo brothers came close to perfection in the form of the Greek cross on a smaller scale.

Madonna delle Carceri at Prato (Fig. 96), begun 1485, completed 1491, by Giuliano; over the short transepts with straight terminations there hovers above a shallow drum a light dome with twelve small round windows; a space of supreme charm with noble decoration.

Madonna di S. Biagio at Montepulciano (Figs. 97, 98), begun 1518 by Antonio the Elder, completed 1537, a similar ground-plan, but with strongly emphasised height and with the rugged sculptural quality of the sixteenth century. Cf. §79.

A beautiful centralised building on a Greek cross plan in Siena; Church of the Innocenti (S. Sebastiano), apparently 1507 (1490?), by Girolamo di Domenico Ponsi; the transepts extended as apses and covered by groined vaults, over the crossing a windowless encased dome.

Also the octagon form, copied from the baptistries, which had been so much preferred in the centralised buildings of Lombardy (cf. §65), now found a foothold, towards the end of the fifteenth century, in Tuscany. Examples: sacristy of Sto Spirito in Florence and Madonna dell' Umiltà in Pistoia.

If, as recently asserted without documentary support (Vasari-Milanesi, IV, p. 274, n.), Giuliano da Sangallo really designed in 1489 the model of the above-mentioned sacristy to the order of Lorenzo de' Medici, it would not have been impossible for him, in adopting the octagonal form uncommon in Florence until now for sacristies (cf. those of S. Lorenzo, S. Marco, Sta Felicita) and chapels (cf. Capp. Pazzi and Medici at Sta Croce, A. Pollajuolo's at S. Miniato, etc.), to have been inspired by the sight of Lombard octagonal buildings in process of construction (sacristy of S. Satiro in Milan, Incoronata at Lodi) in the

Fig. 96 *Prato, Madonna delle Carceri, section*

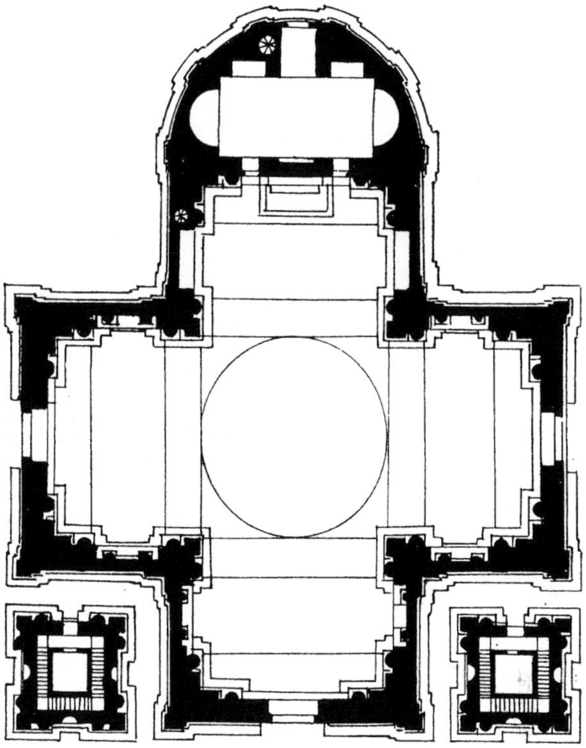

Fig. 97 *Montepulciano, Madonna di S. Biagio, plan*

event of his journey to Milan (where he delivered a model of a palazzo commissioned by Lorenzo de' Medici) having occurred in 1489 or earlier. On the other hand it would be easily understandable that the idea of an eight-sided basic shape came to him from the Florentine Baptistry, as indeed also the angles left exposed between pilasters, the dome with lunettes, and the linking of the little chapel with its cupola-lit vault point straight to Florentine prototypes (Baptistry, Brunellesco's Angeli and Capp. Pazzi etc.). For details of the building completed in 1496 by Cronaca cf. Mayreder and Holtzinger in the Allgem. Bauzeitung, 1885. Cf. Figs. 181, 182.

Under the influence of this sacristy, and not under Bramante's, there emerged Ventura Vitoni's Madonna dell' Umiltà at Pistoia (Figs. 99, 100). Vestibule and choir were under construction from 1494; the somewhat awkward central structure was begun in 1509, and the rather monotonous dome was completed later by Vasari. The vestibule, with its incomparable interior, recalls the portico of the Cappella Pazzi. In the octagon the handling of the angles commented upon above.

In every respect a failure: the octagon in Sta Maria della Pace in Rome, by an unknown master (Fig. 189).

Venice helped at least to keep alive the memory of the light-bringing drum and the shallow dome, until the great architectural movement firmly grasped this Byzantine element.

The many small churches of square plan with a dome over the four central piers are meant. The chief example of this arrangement: S. Giovanni Crisostomo (1497, by Mauro Coducci: Figs. 101, 102), but here the drum is lacking, which is present in later churches of this type. Regarding the structural problems of a large, high, central space there was nothing to be learned here, and not much about formal aspects, but the unique legacy of the Byzantine era to the Renaissance, which came via Venice, is highly significant in itself.

From one of the Venetian architects in question (Pietro Lombardo? Scarpagnino?) emanates the crazy splendour of Sta Maria de' Miracoli at Brescia (realised from 1488 by Giovanni da Verona) (Figs. 103–105), which might jestingly be called a centrifugal building, from the fact that the domes (two unequal large ones, and two smaller) shun in a formal sense the centre of the building.

In the spirit of Byzantine prototypes Baccio Pontelli created in 1492 the tetrastyle arrangement of Sta Maria Maggiore at Orciano, near Sinigaglia, cf. Laspeyres, *Die Kirchen d. Renaissance in Mittelitalien*, Figs. 172, 173, 177.

(NOTE: Ponsi's S. Sebastiano at Siena seems more likely to be *c* 1507 than earlier.

There is documentary support for Giuliano da Sangallo as the maker of the model of the sacristy of Sto Spirito: see W. and E. Paatz, *Kirchen von Florenz*, 1940–54, s.v. Sto Spirito.) (PM).

Fig. 95 *(opposite) Florence, SS. Annunziata, interior*

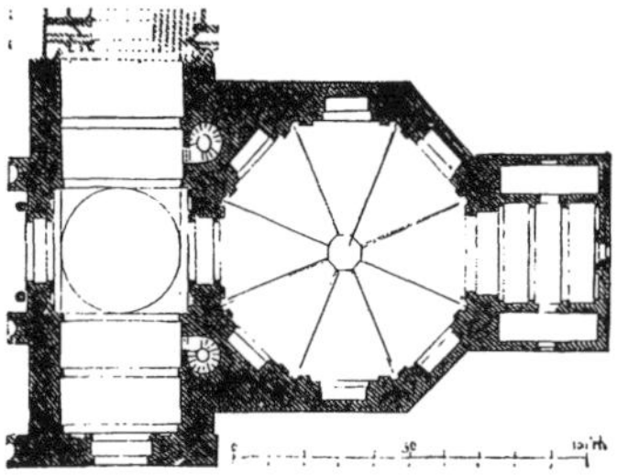

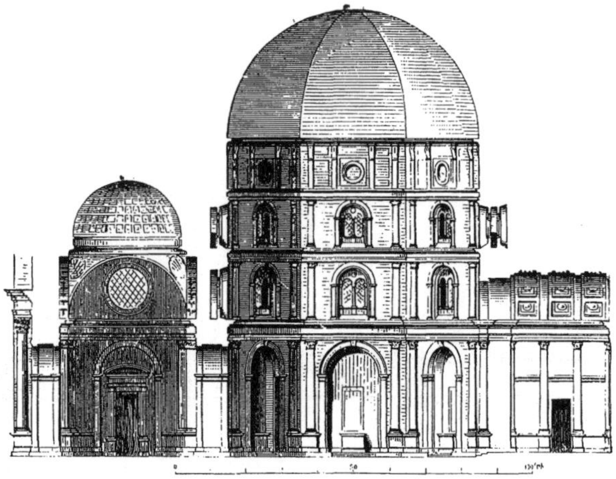

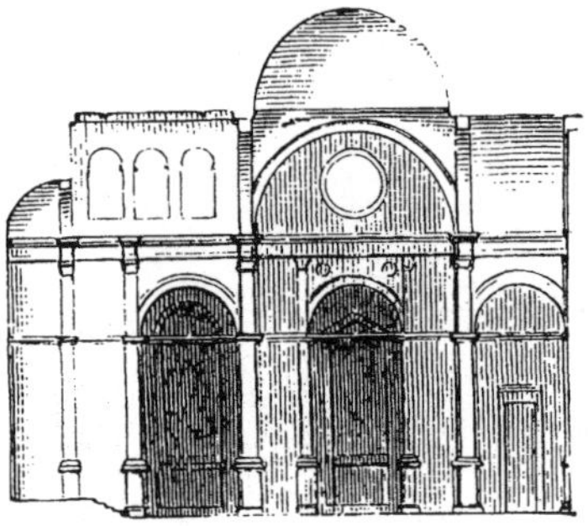

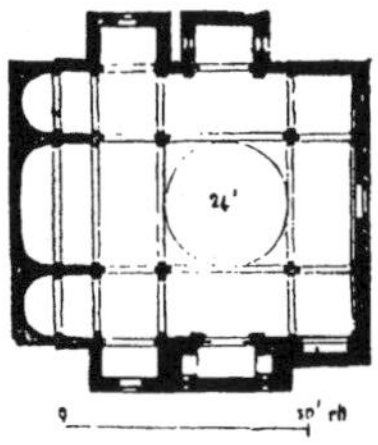

Fig. 98 (*above left*) *Montepulciano, Madonna di S. Biagio, elevation*

Figs. 99, 100 (*above*) *Pistoia, Madonna dell' Umiltà, section and plan*

Figs. 101, 102 (*left*) *Venice, S. Giovanni Crisostomo, section and plan*

Figs. 103–105 (*below*) *Brescia, Sta Maria de' Miracoli, plan and sections*

Figs. 106, 107 *Pavia, Sta Maria di Canepanova, plan and elevation detail*

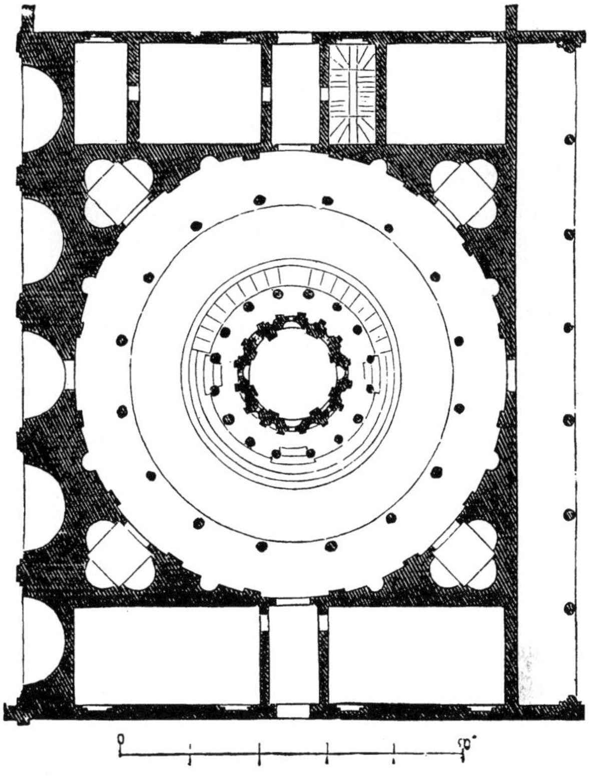

Fig. 108 *Rome, S. Pietro in Montorio, plan of the Tempietto*

§65 *Bramante and His First Centrally Planned Buildings*

For Bramante the centralised building had already become in his early period the fundamental task of his life. He had the great good fortune to realise the supreme architectural idea of his day, first in N. Italy in rich and exuberant forms, and later in more majestic and dignified ways.[1]

During his Milanese phase Bramante was only permitted a complete realisation of two centralised buildings, the sacristy of Sta Maria presso S. Satiro and the choir-tribune of Sta Maria della Grazie; to others, however, he lent, according to tradition (which made him into a generic term), his new ideas – Incoronata at Lodi, Canepanova at Pavia, Sta Maria at Busto Arsizio and others.[2]

The initial inspiration came to Bramante for the choir of Sta Maria delle Grazie, with its square chancel and apsidal-ended transepts (which, partly because of the street outside, had to be kept short), through buildings like S. Fedele in Como and its progeny, and for S. Satiro through the baptistries of the Middle Ages (Novara, Cremona etc.).

The chancel (*tribuna*) of Sta Maria delle Grazie on the outside is inventively handsome in its organisation and elaborate in its execution (unfortunately not entirely complete: §46); on the inside it is spatially enchanting. Only the lower part was executed under Bramante's direction in 1492–99; in the upper half he was let down by his successors, both in detail and in proportions.

The sacristy of S. Satiro and the other octagonal buildings of that period in the Milanese region: the substructure sometimes extended to make a square, with a number of common characteristics – the unfilled, often alternating semi-circular and rectangular niches; an upper gallery opening through arcading on to the interior (cf., among the medieval baptistries, e.g. S. Giovanni in Florence, Fig. 6); instead of this gallery sometimes a series of small niches to take statues; the polygonal dome (cloister-vault), later the hemisphere, externally plain as a rule, with a sloping roof – all reminiscent of older baptistries. The towers also reflect earlier times (S. Lorenzo in Milan, cf. 62): in fours of tabernacle form at Michelozzo's chapel in S. Eustorgio; then at Canepanova (cf. also §64, Filarete's design); or in pairs – Incoronata at Lodi.

Concerning S. Satiro, more details in §80.

1 Details of most of the buildings mentioned here in H. Strack, *Zentral- und Kuppelkirchen der Renaissance in Italien*, Berlin, 1882 (from the Zeitschr. f. Bauw. 1877–).
2 The small, unpretentious octagon of the Madonna del Riscatto outside Urbania (1464) cannot be shown to be the work of Bramante.

Fig. 109 *Rome, St Peter's, Bramante's first project*

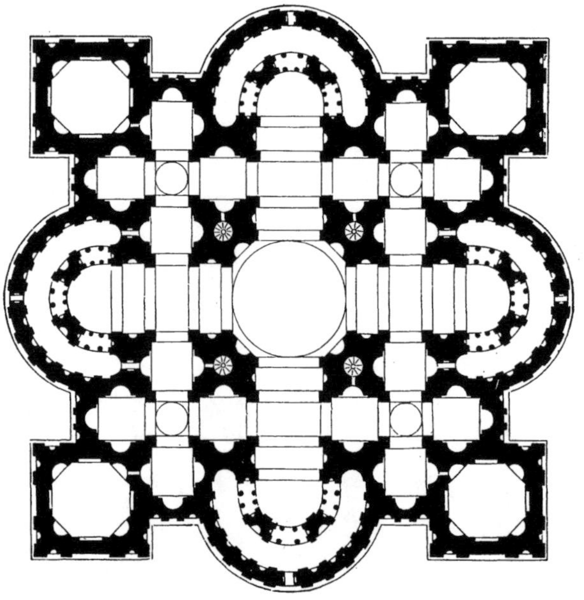

Fig. 110 *Rome, St Peter's, Peruzzi's plan*

Incoronata at Lodi, executed in 1488 supposedly to Bramante's plan by Giovanni Battagio (Batacchio), who had been engaged in 1487 on S. Satiro in Milan; continued by Dolcebuono; octagon with peculiar diagonally recessed niches and upper gallery, sumptuously decorated; choir and vestibule additions.

Sta Maria di Canepanova at Pavia (Figs. 106, 107), almost the same motive, refined and clarified; allegedly from 1492, to Bramante's design.

Sta Maria in Piazza at Busto Arsizio near Milan, octagon with dome, externally a square at ground level, while inside there are niches at the angles; built 1518–23 under Bramante's influence by Lonati to plans by Bellarati.

The same form, larger and more developed: S. Magno at Legnano, by Giacomo Lampugnano, 1504–29.

These buildings sometimes small and tucked away; where the elevations are developed: a sloping roof over an open polygonal colonnade, from which light enters the dome through round windows.

This polygonal colonnade combined with a sloping roof was also used with domes for long churches e.g. Sta Maria presso S. Celso, by Dolcebuono (§77), and for the church at Saronno, a building of worth in its older parts; partly of brick, begun in 1498 by Vincenzo dell' Orto.

For the dome of the Certosa at Pavia three stepped galleries, but no sign anywhere of a shallow dome.

Contemporary with Bramante (1489) the beginning of Sta Maria della Croce at Crema; inside octagonal, outside round with projections in very effective brick forms, by Giov. Batt. Battagio (Fig. 53).

Pretty octagonal chapel (dedicated to the Risen Christ) near the portal of S. Luca at Cremona, interior two-storeyed, exterior three-storeyed, the top row of windows corresponding to the vault. Almost entirely brick, in disciplined forms. Dated 1503.

The beautiful polygonal temple in Raphael's *Sposalizio* (1504) must be mentioned here at least (cf. §63).

§66 *Bramante and S. Peter's in Rome*

With the turn of the century Bramante revealed not only a change in his style (§27, 49), but took the decisive steps in the planning of churches the results of which were to extend into the distant artistic future. From the octagon he went over to the dome with drum above a Greek cross with apsidal ends.

In the octagon with niches and galleries the dome soon proved to be very wide, and thus impossible to place high in the air. Already the dome of the Grazie in Milan rested in practice in four arches.

The Tempietto at S. Pietro in Montorio in Rome (§53), together with the colonnaded cortile (unexecuted, but illustrated in Serlio, L. III: see Fig. 108), all in rounded forms; the wall-masonry enlivened throughout with niches, their incision in the thicker cylindrical wall surfaces presenting no problems to Bramante. For the elevation see Fig. 60.

The building of S. Peter's (§8). More recent literature: the large publication by H. von Geymüller: *Die ursprünglichen Entwürfe für St. Peter in Rom*, Vienna and Paris, 1875–80. C. A. Jovanovits, *Forschungen über den Bau der St Peterskirche zu Rom*, Vienna, 1877. Several articles by R. Redtenbacher. Letarouilly et Simil: *Le Vatican et St Pierre*. Regarding Michelangelo's contribution, among others, Garnier in the Jubilee issue of the Gazette des Beaux-Arts, 1874.

Owing to the impossibility of presenting here very

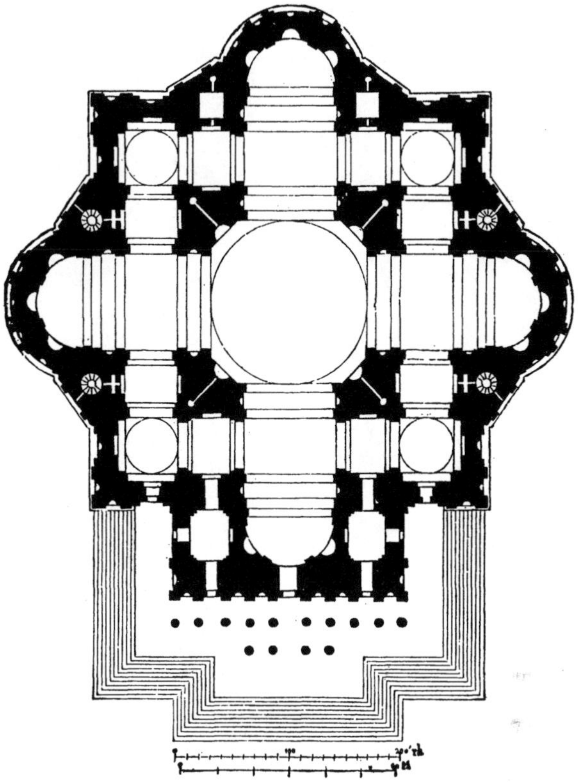

Fig. 111 *(left) Rome, St Peter's, Raphael's plan, from Serlio*

Fig. 112 *(above) Rome, St Peter's, Michelangelo's plan*

complicated and controversial researches in abbreviated form we must be content with the following:

Beyond all doubt Bramante wanted a centralised building,[1] and the magnificent plan (Fig. 109, or Geymüller, T. 4) is his work: the four arms of the Greek cross, internally ending in apses and externally with straight ends; the plan of the interior consisting entirely of rounded forms, everywhere enlivened with niches; the four corners filled with vast chapels and towers. A medal of Julius II certainly represents this scheme (with the inscription *Templi Petri Instauracio*, illustrated in Geymüller, T. 2, together with some versions); it may therefore have been regarded as definitive, at least for a time. There then appeared a revised plan, also by Bramante, which rounds off the four cross-arms and surrounds them with huge ambulatories, undoubtedly at both ground and upper levels (Geymüller, T. 12); perhaps a recollection of S. Lorenzo in Milan, perhaps also a recognition that the four large dome piers and their arches needed strengthening. For this design Bramante devised the form of dome which Serlio (L. III) illustrated: the drum externally ringed by a splendid peristyle. In the first design (Fig. 109) the shape of the dome piers excludes a peristyle round the drum (Geymüller, p. 167).

A revision of this project is offered by a plan provided by Serlio (Fig. 110; from his L. III), by the hand of Peruzzi, from 1505 a draughtsman in Bramante's office; the semi-circular terminations are cut short by ambulatories, as on the plan (Fig. 111) attributed to Raphael; cf. Geymüller, p. 229. Actually executed by Bramante himself were the four dome piers and the arches linking them, which still survive, little modified.[2]

That Michelangelo later called himself *esecutore* of Bramante's plan (Vasari, IV, p. 162, *V. di Bramante*) relates most fittingly to the centralised planning which was common to them both.

Raphael, who took over the supervision of the building in 1514, decided (was he influenced by the client?) to complete the scheme as a Latin cross, with a nave of

1 For a scheme in the form of a Latin cross, of 1503, see Geymüller, T. 25, fig. 2. To this probably refers the statement in Panvinio (§ 8) that Bramante also designed a nave, and Peruzzi *ejusdem exemplar decurtavit, ex oblongo quadratum fecit*. The latter assertion incorrect, cf. above regarding Peruzzi.

2 The choir begun under Nicholas V by Bernardo Rossellino was used by Bramante, partly for the rear wall of the transept, and partly for an apparently definitive choir which was removed in 1585.

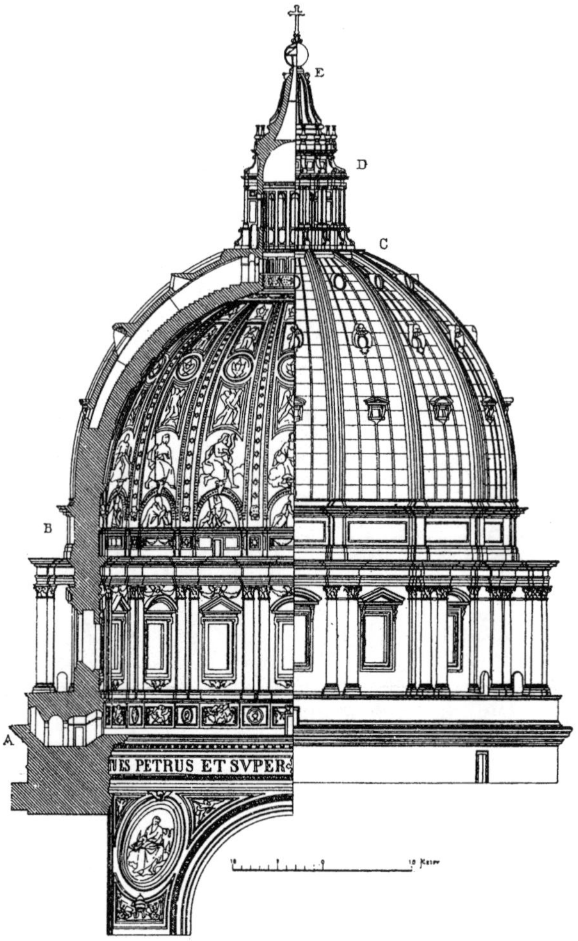

Fig. 113 *(above) Rome, St Peter's, drawing by Dupérac based on Michelangelo's design for the façade*

Fig. 114 *(right) Rome, St Peter's, elevation and section of the dome*

considerable length, with massive piers and deep side-chapels; all wall-surfaces with niches; and finally a portico with three rows of columns. Outwardly the plan of the whole appears much simplified; the solid flat walls with pilasters would have enclosed it (with the exception of the three apses). Leo X in his Brief appointing Raphael on 1 August 1514 (in Quatremère, ed. Longhena, p. 529; see also *Lettere Pittoriche*, VI, 2) appeals *alla propria stima e al vostro buon nome . . . e finalmente alla dignità e alla fama di questo tempio.* Cf. the Memorandum by Antonio da Sangallo, written at the end of 1514 or in 1515; commented upon in Geymüller, p. 293 ff.

Regarding the different possibilities of adjusting Raphael's ideas to the surviving plans by Giuliano da Sangallo, we refer to the comprehensive exposition in Geymüller, p. 318 ff.

The supposed plan of Fra Giocondo (Geymüller, T. 41), which once seemed to us an object of the younger Antonio da Sangallo's scorn, and a caricature of N. Italian peculiarities likely to cling to the Frate, had perhaps already been designed by 1505, in the way indicated by Geymüller (*Raffaello studiato come architetto*, p. 48), which would eliminate several difficulties.

After Raphael's death, Antonio da Sangallo[3] took charge of the building until 1546; his wish was to lengthen the church towards the front with an enormous show-piece. Almost half the space would have been squandered with completely separated front and side rooms, where, as Michelangelo (*Lettere Pittoriche*, VI, 9) jested, even coiners could establish themselves safely. The extant wooden model and a large engraved view of the façade show a taste for subdividing into many small parts, and, here and there, for dubious detailing. Little of Antonio's scheme was carried out.

Finally, Michelangelo took over in 1547, in his seventy-second year, because God had called him to it (*Lettere Pittoriche*, VI, 10), and out of the love of God and devotion to the Prince of the Apostles (Brief of Paul III) he persevered until his death in 1564, so that his retirement might bring no comfort to rogues and the building remain incomplete (*Lettere Pittoriche*, I, 6). Only his attainments and long-established fame made it possible for Paul III to give him absolute powers, and for the Popes who followed during Michelangelo's lifetime and

3 Peruzzi worked under him, at most as an assistant, and was not on an equal footing until the last years of his life.

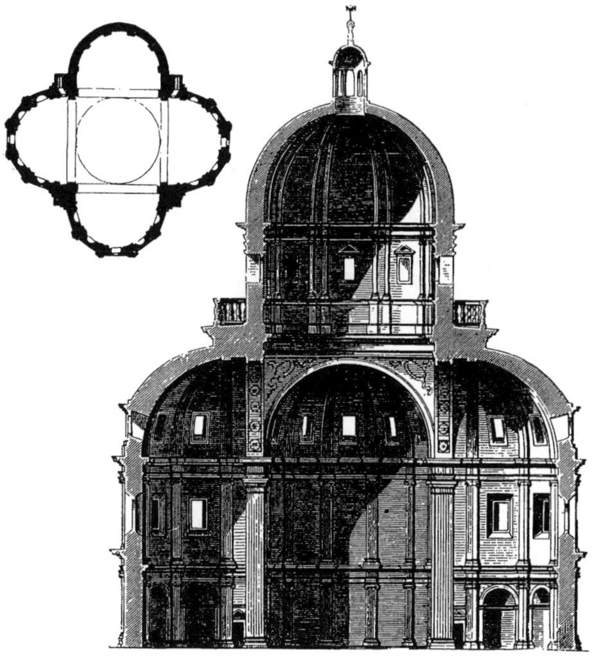

Figs. 115, 116 *(above)* *Todi, Sta Maria della Consolazione, plan and section*

Fig. 117 *(right)* *Piacenza, Madonna di Campagna*

after his death to retain, and continue with, his plan (Fig. 112), until Sixtus V was able to complete the dome in 1590. The plan of the whole shows an exquisite and most striking simplification of the centralised schemes of Bramante and Peruzzi; the façade with its splendid, free disposition of columns would have been entirely subordinated to the dome. (Illustrated, as it was intended to be, in engravings, among other records, of the Holy Year of 1600.) The external cladding of the rest of the church is not wholly happy, now also impaired by the failure to carry into effect (except in a few places) the balustrade so essential to it. Over all this soars the dome in its present form, entirely the master's work, in basic structural thinking – drum, double shell, lantern – harking back to Byzantine and Florentine precedents (cf. § 17, 47), incomparable in formal respects and, above all, in its wonderfully subtle outline (Fig. 114). Regarding the construction, cf. Durm in Zeitschr. für Bauwesen, 1887 (*Zwei Grosskonstrucktionen der Renaissance*).

The completion of the dome, "which had given cause for thought to a number of Popes", was effected under the resolute Sixtus V (1585–90) by Giacomo della Porta. (Baglione, *Vite de' Pittori*, p. 33, 76; the latter reference also for the saga of the construction.)

Michelangelo's place in history rests upon the vast variety of his activities; but his supremacy surely derives from satisfying the universal yearning of the Renaissance by building this grandest and most glorious of giant domes with its light-filled drum.

Thus by the genius and strength of purpose of the greatest master the church as a centralised structure was almost perfected, and to the western world appeared as such for forty years. It was not until 1606 that Paul V permitted the building of the present unfortunate nave.

(NOTE: For the dome of S. Peter's see R. Wittkower, *La cupola di S. Pietro*, Florence, 1964, and his *Idea and Image*, London, 1978.) (PM).

§ 67 *Other Centralised Buildings of the Sixteenth Century*

Meanwhile all over Italy predominantly centralised plans emerged for churches of the largest and smallest scale, some very accomplished of their type, others remarkable as evidence of a tremendous turmoil in the arts.

The Madonna della Consolazione at Todi (Figs. 115, 116), begun in 1508, relies in its design on Bramantesque ideas (even if Bramante did not perhaps himself submit a model); the architect in charge was Cola da Caprarola (with others); cf. the documents published by A. Rossi in the *Giornale di Erudiz. artist.*, I–III, and by Geymüller, *Entwürfe* . . ., p. 96 ff. Above the four main arches a substantial drum introducing light, as a true hemispherical dome with a lantern; the apses are still polygonal but vaulted with semi-domes; inside a magnificent effect obtained by height, spatial unity, and top-lighting; below rings of niches for altars. Such a church needs no façades. Cf. § 53.

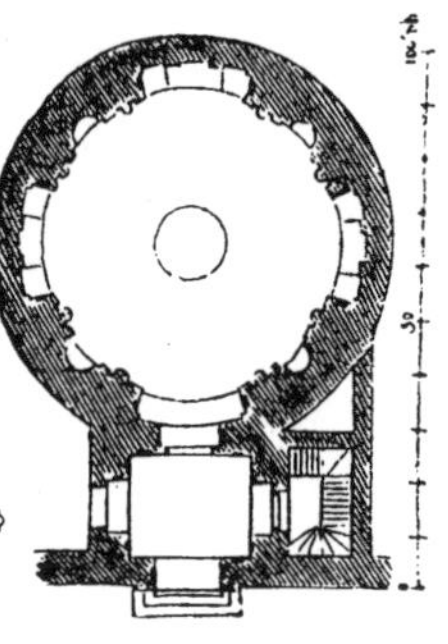

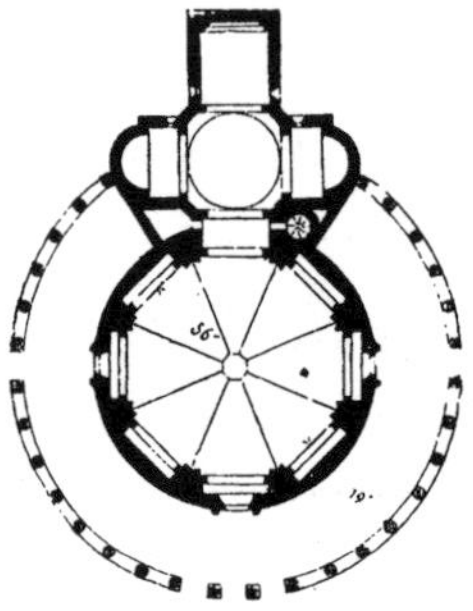

Figs. 118, 119 *Verona, S. Bernardino, Cappella Pellegrini, section and plan*

Figs. 120, 121 *Verona, Madonna di Campagna, plan and section detail*

The plan of the Madonna di Macereto, near Visso in the Marche, seems borrowed from Bramante; executed by Battista Lucano and others; cf. Laspeyres, *Die Kirchen der Renaissance in Mittelitalien*, Figs. 168 ff.; Geymüller, *Entwürfe* . . ., p. 98.

Raphael, who trained as an architect under Bramante from 1508, began in 1509, using an idea borrowed from one of the plans by his teacher for S. Peter's, S. Eligio degli Orefici in Rome, a Greek cross with short arms and a dome; cf. v. Geymüller, *Raffaello studiato come architetto*, pp. 19–24.

By Peruzzi a project with echoes of S. Vitale at Ravenna and another under the influence of S. Lorenzo in Milan; both in Redtenbacher, *Bald. Peruzzi und seine Werke*, pl. III, Figs. 1, 2. In the same book, an attempt by Peruzzi to outdo the Pantheon; a circular building almost six metres wider than the prototype (forty-two m.); as well as the open eye (*opaion*), windows in the drum above the niches; outside, a ring of columns.

Peruzzi's imagination was also occupied by an octagon (now lost) next to the Lateran Baptistry, which was drawn by other masters as well, e.g. Giuliano da Sangallo and Jacopo Sansovino.

Antonio da Sangallo the Elder's Madonna di S. Biagio at Montepulciano, see §64.

The younger Antonio da Sangallo cultivated the central plan in many of his churches: Sta Maria di Loreto in Rome (begun 1506), in the shape of an octagon, the lower structure externally a square; the two *tempietti* on the Lake of Bolsena (only one survives: octagon with niches), two projects for S. Giacomo degli Incurabili in Rome, churches at Foligno and Montefiascone, a design for S. Giovanni de' Fiorentini in Rome, a round building with sixteen chapels, each with a dome etc.; Vasari, V, pp. 450, 455 f., 484, 491, 506, 507, *Vita di Ant. da Sangallo*, with commentary; also Redtenbacher's article in the *Allg. Bauzeitung*, 1883, with reproductions of preparatory studies.

Jacopo Sansovino, who made sixty projects for churches, was only able to build one oval and one square church (the latter S. Martino in Venice) with centralised plans; Vasari, VII, p. 507, *V. di J. Sansovino*; Francesco Sansovino, *Venezia*, fol. 97. His plan for S. Giovanni dei Fiorentini in Rome, with a large central dome and four semi- (or whole?) domes over the arms of a Greek cross, was expressly preferred by Leo X to the plans of competitors for the sake of this form, but not executed: Vasari, loc. cit. p. 498. His built churches were otherwise all of the long-nave type. (Of the five plans, which Michelangelo prepared for S. Giovanni dei Fiorentini (cf.

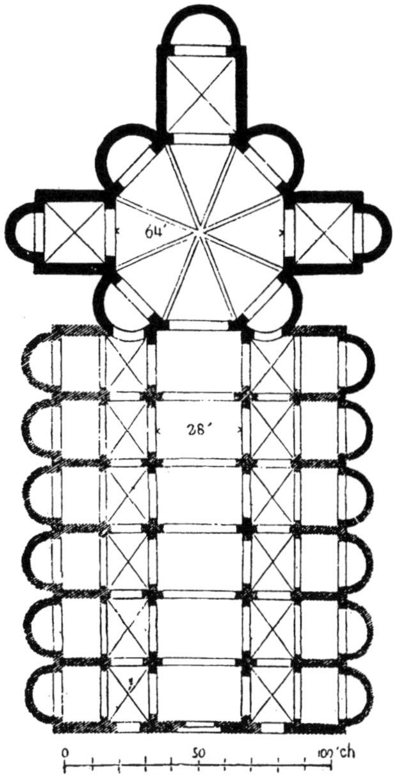

Fig. 122 *Milan, Sta Maria della Passione, plan*

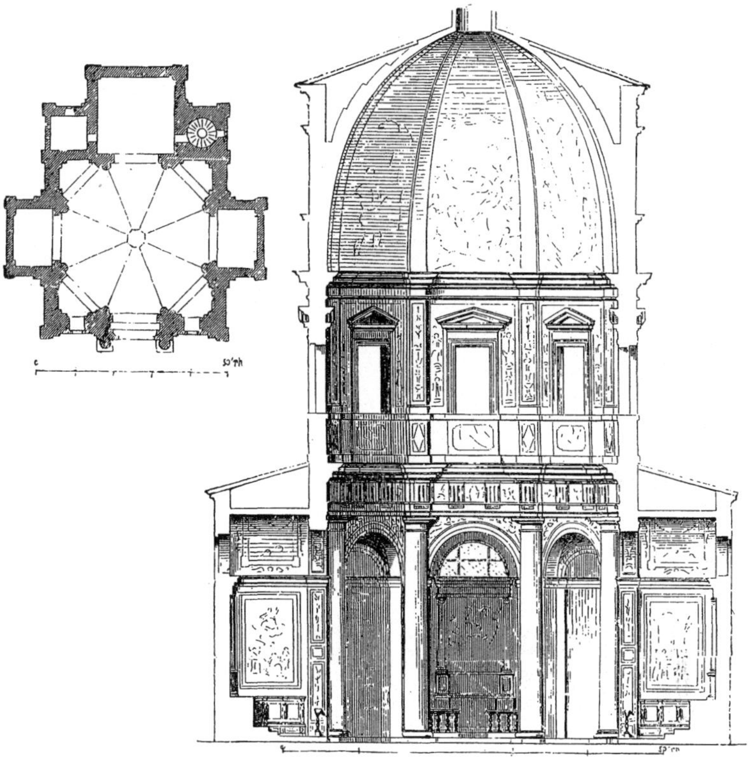

Figs. 123, 124 *Riva, Sta Croce, plan and section*

§60), Letarouilly thought – *Édifices de Rome moderne*, text p. 541 – he had discovered one, a large domical structure.)

Bernardino Zaccagni 1521: La Steccata in Parma, Greek cross with round ends, dome and small corner-chapels, splendidly effective in massing.

Rocco da Vicenza, 1524 onwards: Madonna at Mongiovino, tetrastyle plan with dome above the central square, short arms with barrel vaults, small cupolas over the squares at the angles; the choir projects.

About 1525, by A. Taramelli: Madonna di Campagna at Piacenza (Fig. 117), with octagonal dome over a Greek cross, smaller octagonal domes over the four angle-spaces.

Sanmichele: the round Cappella Pellegrini in S. Bernardino at Verona (Figs. 118, 119); internally the antique forms are executed with perception and splendour, including the coffers of the hemi-spherical dome.

Madonna di Campagna, near Verona (Figs. 120, 121), not realised until after Sanmichele's death (1559) and then inexactly, a large round church of singular layout; Vasari, VI, p. 354 f., *V. di Sanmicheli*; cf. p. 357, note 1, the octagonal domestic chapel of a villa.

Cristoforo Solari, known as Il Gobbo: Sta Maria della Passione in Milan, 1530, massive octagon with projecting substructures and a sloping roof (*tiburio*) fifty metres high, until 1692 a pure central plan (Fig. 122); the lower parts so noble and simple that they might belong to an earlier foundation of 1483.

By the same Solari (or according to others by Pellegrini or Tibaldi), the graceful high octagon near Riva (Ticino), unfinished externally (Figs. 123, 124), and in plan related to the Canepanova at Pavia (see Fig. 106), just as the Inviolata near Riva on Lake Garda goes back to the Incoronata at Lodi; supposedly 1601–18, cf. Strack, *Zentral- und Kuppelkirchen*, pl. 30, Fig. 16.

In the simpler form which can be traced back to the baptistries (see p. 83): Chiesa della Manna d' Oro at Spoleto, outside square, inside octagonal, in the angles niches, apparently begun 1527, altered (according to an inscription) 1681; Strack, loc. cit., pl. 29.[1]

Galeazzo Alessi: Sta Maria di Carignano in Genoa (1552), the interior of great beauty; the motive of S. Peter's applied in a completely free and novel fashion (Figs. 125, 126).

A simplification of the same motive, designed as a

1 Girolamo Genga's building, highly rated by Vasari, S. Gio. Battista at Pesaro (begun in 1543 according to an inscription), belongs, like its prototype S. Bernardino at Urbino (after the middle of the fifteenth century, related in some details to the cortile of the palace at Urbino), to the series of single-nave long churches, but deserves mention here because of the original plan of its choir (octagon with – formerly – three apses and groined vault: in Urbino square with hemi-spherical dome in addition to the apses).

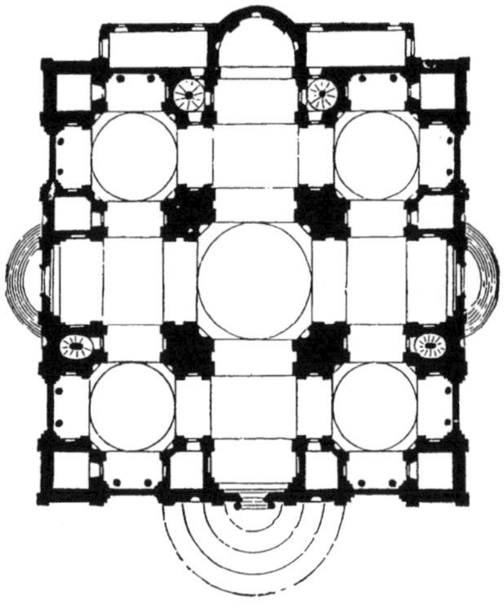

Figs. 125, 126 *Genoa, Madonna di Carignano, plan and section*

Greek cross, chapels in the angles, over the crossing a projected dome: Sta Maria di Loreto, near Spoleto, said to date from 1572.

In Serlio, Book V, thirteen ideal plans of churches, eleven of them centralised, mostly fanciful productions of his pen and compasses, secular and curious, e.g. a pentagon and two ovals.[2] The drum small or entirely omitted, but almost invariably top-lighting, Serlio being well aware of its value (L. III, fol. 50); the height of the dome barely equal to half the diameter, as was nearly universal before the wonderful, more parabolic, dome of S. Peter's.[3] Serlio's lament for the ungodly times, about 1540 (§10); he himself was devout – Gaye, *Carteggio*, II, p. 170.

Campanella, towards the end of the century, describes in his Città del Sole a magnificent round temple supported on columns; the single altar, with terrestrial and celestial globes, stands in the middle.

The Baroque style kept alive not only the Greek cross, often with corner chapels, but also the round church with niches; unfortunately too, surviving in fairly frequent use, the oval church, and from the last centralised buildings of the Baroque it would still be possible to learn, if one wished, a great deal.

The Baroque style was in this field the first to gain acceptance for generalised features, in which only greater or lesser building resources decided the individual character. (External and internal facing of the drum with pilasters, columns etc.; height increased by an attic; preference for the round form over the polygon, the hemispherical dome over the sloping roof (*tiburio*); sophisticated handling of the lower main supports, especially in the design of diagonally placed piers with pilasters or salient columns; the whole, wherever feasible, high in relation to the comparatively small area occupied by the building, with top-lighting only from the dome, transepts and windows in the choir vault. A number of bold variations on the centralised plan in the seventeenth century by the priest Guarini.)

2 Already by Peruzzi a project for an oval church for the hospital of the Incurabili in Rome; in Redtenbacher, *B. P. u. seine Werke*, pl. VIII, fig. 1.

3 Serlio's ovals are not more or less rectangular barrel-vaults with semi-circular ends, but genuine ellipses.

Fig. 127 *Rimini, S. Francesco ('Tempio Malatestiano')*

§68 *Triumph of the Long-Nave Type in the Interests of Façades*

Force of habit since the Middle Ages and the desire not to be hampered in adding chapels and other subordinate rooms ensured, despite the desire for true architecture, the ascendancy of the long over the centralised building, the latter being inordinately sensitive externally to any irregularity. The central plan continued in use for choir and dome, but the façade was liberated from any subservience to the whole.

The loss was greater than appears at first sight. In the realisation that harmony would be impossible between a choir building of this type and the façade, the architectural development of the exterior of the nave was generally abandoned; art and resources were concentrated upon two fundamentally disparate elements, dome and façade. The centralised building had either to do without façades (by having apsidal ends), or, by virtue of the dome, so dominating all the elevations that a façade-like development became unrealisable and they remained free from formal pomposity and isolated splendour.

§69 *L. B. Alberti's Façades*

As in the Gothic era, the façades of the most important churches also remained in the fifteenth century, to all intents and purposes, in a rough and provisional state.

With the exception of Venetian façades (§43), which are not typical, there are no significant completed façades by Brunellesco, Michelozzo, Rossellino, the two elder Sangallos, Cronaca etc. It is self-evident that the façade was now in essence merely a reinterpretation of its medieval counterpart, so little did it correspond to the true profile of the nave, but soared capriciously above the roof-line.

The type was fixed in general by L. B. Alberti; one or two Orders, of engaged columns or pilasters, with doors and windows in between; sometimes a pediment on the model of an Antique temple. The reconciliation of the narrow upper storey to the lower by means of large volutes at the sides, instead of the simple pitch of the lean-to roof of the aisles.

In principle Alberti conceived the façade (§57) with reference to S. Francesco (1447) as a splendid mask (Fig. 127); anyone wanting him to change his scheme would spoil *tutta quella musica*. In this instance the façade was

Fig. 128 *Mantua, Sant' Andrea*

Fig. 129 *Florence, Sta Maria Novella*

Fig. 130 *Pienza, Cathedral, elevation*

realised only to a level slightly above the ground storey, which includes a fine Order of Corinthian engaged columns, copied from the nearby Arch of Augustus. The medallions in the spandrels are also borrowed from this Arch.

S. Andrea at Mantua (Fig. 128), the first instance of a deliberately simulated temple frontispiece; four pilasters frame a huge opening and, at the sides, round-arched windows and smaller niches; above these a pediment. (On the proportions of such a pediment: *De re aedificatoria*, L. VII, c. 11.) The façade, including the vestibule, lower than the main building which, with a large loggia containing the great round window, towers above it.

At Sta Maria Novella in Florence (Fig. 129) Alberti encrusted the upper part of the façade above the medieval ground storey and offered the first example of side volutes, perhaps only permissible in the style of incrustation.[1] Below, the beautiful surround of the main door by him (cf. §48).

A precept which Alberti himself never heeded: *De re aedif.*, L. VII, c. 4, in which he advocated a portico extending in front of the whole façade with a larger, and in some way distinctive, central interval (cf. §70).

(NOTE: S. Sebastiano, rather than S. Andrea, was the first temple-front church façade: see R. Wittkower, *Architectural Principles*, London, 1962.) (PM).

§70 *Other Façades of the Early Renaissance*

The overall treatment of these fifteenth-century façades was, as a rule, somewhat hesitant and immature, since reliance was still placed on the supposed absolute value of individual Antique forms, which were not yet effectively handled and combined to make a whole. The smallest façades are in general the best.

On occasion the material and the fine detailing helped. In Rome the austere travertine always had dignity; Sta Maria del Popolo, the façade of 1477 (the volutes later), by an unknown master; S. Agostino, 1479–83, by Giacomo da Pietrasanta, notorious for the hideous volutes, which also disfigure Meo del Caprino's Turin Cathedral (1492–98).

The façade of the Cathedral of Pienza, *c* 1460, by the Florentine Bernardo (almost certainly Rossellino), corresponding to the nave and aisles of the same height, is powerfully developed in massive forms; here for the first time two pilasters rise through the pediment, extensions of those on the wall below (Fig. 130).

Handed down from the Middle Ages in many examples, especially in central and lower Italy: a square screen, two or three storeys high, mostly with a horizontal top, but also with a shallow pediment; portals, rose-windows, string-courses, and other decoration dis-

1 The extent of the participation of Giovanni Bettini, who was in charge of the works, must remain undecided.

Fig. 131 *Bologna, Madonna di Galliera, elevation*

Fig. 132 *Rome, Sta Maria dell' Anima*

tributed over the surface with a rich individuality of expression.

Transformed in the Early Renaissance: Madonna di Galliera in Bologna (Fig. 131). The façade of the Madonna della Quercia at Viterbo completely rusticated; on the pediment decorative sculpture.

From the sixteenth century: façade of Sta Maria dell' Anima in Rome (1514); the author debatable; with sensitive and refined detailing of the doors and three pilaster Orders, but a little meagre in total effect (Fig. 132).

With fuller relief in the forms, realised in ashlar masonry, with Doric, Ionic and Corinthian half-columns and niches: the front of S. Bernardino at Aquila, perhaps the grandest example of the type, 1527, by Cola dell' Amatrice. (In the same place several more square façades from the Middle Ages.)

Setting the pattern in many ways for single-nave churches in the fifteenth century, the nobly simple façade of the Madonna del Calcinaio at Cortona, by Francesco di Giorgio (begun 1485); see Fig. 155. Cf. among others, S. Pietro in Montorio in Rome (1472 onwards), a plain travertine screen with pediment, string-courses and angle pilasters, plus a door and a round window. Similar (1494, by Francesco da Lugano) Sta Maria de' Miracoli at Castel Rigone; portal and round window of 1512 by Domenico Bertini da Settignano.

In Venice incrustation and ornamental friezes and pilasters give a *festiva et hilaris facies*; cf. Sabellicus, *De Situ Ven. Urbis*, fol. 84, 87; even in the case of a leper-hospital, fol. 92; *usus tristis, sed frons loci laetissima.*

In the brick districts (§44 f.), there was soon a more original and free interpretation of classical forms (S. Pietro at Modena, Madonna di Galliera in Bologna (Fig. 131), 1470, with Lombard treatment of the angles and of the portal by Donato da Cernobbio, 1510–18), at others a felicitous and substantial transformation of these (façade of S. Satiro in Milan, §46).

Small façades quickly became grand entrances: the original Misericordia at Arezzo (the lower half still Gothic, 1375, the upper by Bernardo Rossellino); the Confraternità di S. Bernardino at Perugia, according to an inscription of 1461, by Agostino di Duccio (Fig. 58); Sto Spirito in Bologna.

Unpretentiously pleasing: two small façades in Siena; S. Caterina, 1465–74, by Francesco del Guasta and Corso di Bastiano, the portal by Mariano di Tingo; and Sta Maria delle Nevi, of 1471 (Figs. 133, 134).

In Perugia, Madonna della Luce, according to an inscription, 1519; and in Lombardy the church at Conigo near Binasca, 1505 (Paravicini, pl. 24).

Larger façades always appear rather barren and inadequate, e.g. of the churches of the time in Naples, Ferrara etc.; even of Sta Maria dell' Anima in Rome (1514), although there the brick surfaces, stone pilasters and other features, and the fine central entrance harmonise well (Fig. 132).

Fig. 133 *Siena, Sta Caterina, elevation*

Fig. 134 *Siena, Sta Maria delle Nevi, elevation*

Of the competition (1491) for a new façade for Florence Cathedral (§59) only the record has survived: Vasari, IV, p. 299 ff., in the commentary on the *Vita di G. da Sangallo*. Florence cared deeply about this building and its design; in the fourteenth century Arnolfo's project had to yield place to Giotto's because of its extreme plainness; now, at the end of the fifteenth century, the latter was called "irregular" – *sine aliqua ratione aut iure architecturae*, but what had been completed was not yet demolished: this occurred in 1586 in a similar competition.

In part the precedent of Early Christian basilicas, in part no doubt their own ignorance, in part Alberti's precept (§69) may have induced certain architects to place porticoes in front of churches. These detracted from the ecclesiastical character of the building, especially when they had an upper storey.

In Rome: S. Marco (Fig. 135), the lower portico after 1455, the upper one after 1466, by the native Roman Magister Petrus Paulus Antonisi; comparable with it is the three-storey Benediction Loggia at the Vatican, destroyed under Julius II, but built in 1463 by Giacomo da Pietrasanta (ill. from an old drawing in Müntz, *Les arts à la cour des Papes*, III). S. Pietro in Vincoli and SS. Apostoli, both of the last quarter of the fifteenth century, by unknown masters; for SS. Apostoli, Janitschek (Repert. für Kunstw., 1881, p. 214) suggests the authorship of Giacomo da Pietrasanta.

In Bologna: S. Bartolommeo a Porta Ravegnana, by Formigine (1516–30).

At the small Carmelite church of Sta Maria, Arezzo, the portico, a beautiful structure by Benedetto da Majano (?), projects on both sides two bays beyond the façade (Fig. 14); similarly at the Chiesa del Crocifisso at Marciano, near Monte Sansovino.

By doubling the colonnade the façade easily becomes a secular loggia, which the Middle Ages (at S. Ambrogio in Milan) and, indeed, later the Baroque style (at Sta Maria Maggiore and Sta Maria in Via Lata in Rome) knew very well how to avoid, while the double colonnade of the transverse building of the Lateran facing the obelisk, in other respects a fine building of the early Baroque period, under Sixtus V, by Domenico Fontana (1586), has a rather secular look about it.

In general, older churches were now also given new porticoes: the Cathedral of Narni (1497); the Cathedral of Spoleto – noble and splendid, built from 1491 by Ambrogio d' Antonio da Milano and Pippo d' Antonio da Firenze (Fig. 136); and, rather later, Sta Maria in Navicella in Rome (Fig. 137) – beautifully simple, attributed to Raphael without documentary evidence, simply because of its harmony.

The façade of Sta Maria at Abbiategrasso near Milan, begun according to the inscription in 1477 (1497?)* and with little doubt erected by Bramante, is thoroughly

* The date is now universally read as 1497. (PM).

Fig. 135 *Rome, S. Marco (Palazzo Venezia)*

Fig. 136 *Spoleto, Cathedral loggia, plan and elevation*

original; the main feature is a round-arched shallow niche of the height of the nave, on each of the antae of the side walls two coupled columns super-posed. The whole a kind of first step towards the grandiose terminating niche of the Giardino della Pigna of the Vatican.

§71 *The Façade of the Certosa at Pavia*

In a class by itself stands the façade of the Certosa of Pavia (Fig. 138), world-famous for its over-exuberant ornamentation (§51 and 136), and apart from this perhaps the most highly considered front of the fifteenth century. Its motive, independent of the Antique Orders, is that of the Lombard Romanesque tiered church façade with projecting piers and transverse galleries; within these well-established forms it accommodates every imaginable opulence in subtle nuances of expression.

According to an earlier commonly accepted view the building was designed by the painter Ambrogio Borgognone in 1473, but it was not actually begun until 1492 by Giovanni Antonio Omodeo, then continued in accordance with his (and Dolcebuono's?) model; middle gallery, 1500–1507 by Benedetto dei Brioschi among others, and finished in the following decades. The piers are partitioned, as in Lombard Gothic – e.g. Como Cathedral – into a succession of niches with statues (§51). The decoration is apportioned as follows: on the ground floor, nearest to the eye, sculpture and carved decoration in white marble; on the middle storey, now the top, wall-surfaces and borders incrusted with marbles of various colours, entirely appropriate here; an ornamental structure above was to have contained a large mosaic picture. One old drawing at least shows as a crowning feature a richly worked wall-surface terminating in a semicircle, which could only have been conceived as an element to be painted: a later design (*Palazzi diversi nell' alma città di Roma*, ed. Gio. Batt. de' Rossi, 1665) actually shows a painting here, but in a coarse, pedimented setting.

With a similar sense of splendour, but much more modest in means and scale: the square (cf. §70) marble façade of the Cathedral of Lugano (Fig. 139), probably by Tommaso Rodari, from 1517.

§72 *Façades of the High Renaissance*

In the sixteenth century the church front is a principal subject for a strengthened and now effectively handled architectural vocabulary (§49). The best abilities, however, were at first expended on projects which remained unrealised, or only applied to ceremonial decorations for festival occasions (§50).

Competition of 1514 by order of Leo X for the façade of S. Lorenzo in Florence; among the entries of Raphael, of one of the Sangallo, of the two Sansovinos and of Michelangelo, that of the last must surely have been regarded for some time as outstanding; the earliest façade with salient columns, at least on the ground floor (§37, cf. 43); and with unprecedentedly vigorous treatment of reliefs and statues (according to the incomplete sketch in the Casa Buonarotti). Cf. Vasari, VII, p. 188, note 1, *V. di Michelangelo*; VII, p. 495 f., *V. di Jac. Sansovino*. Both features, salient columns and the presence of sculpture, long foreshadowed in the architecture

Fig. 137 *Rome, Sta Maria in Navicella (in Domnica), elevation*

in Paduan and Ferrarese paintings and in ceremonial structures, especially Triumphal Arches.

Six important designs by the elderly Giuliano da Sangallo published by Redtenbacher (Allgemeine Bauzeitung, 1879), the last and finest of which compares with Michelangelo's in the contribution made by sculpture and would probably have excelled his in the general effect.

A comparable and still greater splendour must have prevailed in the façade decoration of the Cathedral, on the occasion of Leo X's visit in 1514, a gigantic Triumphal Arch with a wealth of imitation reliefs and statues.

As the finest work of this period Vasari elsewhere indicates the unrealised project of Girol. Genga for Mantua Cathedral (VI, p. 321, *V. di Genga*; cf. above, § 5, 67).

Regarding the façades projected by various masters for S. Peter's in Rome, the work of v. Geymüller should be consulted.

Serlio's contemporary theory of the Orders on façades (L. IV): Doric for churches of heroic and warrior Saints, Corinthian for churches of the Madonna and virgin saints, Ionic for saints *fra il robusto et il tenero*, e.g. for saintly matrons.

Serlio liked articulations in sharp relief, e.g. as the elevation in L. VII, p. 110, with three-quarter columns and projecting entablatures.

The obelisks, candelabra, statues etc., which crown the angles and centre of façades and, as it were, allow the residue of their strength to dissipate into the air, were used with particular profusion at this time; e.g. the obelisk-laden façade of Sta Maria dell' Orto in Rome (Giulio Romano?, renovated in 1792 by Martino Lunghi the Younger), and the project of the younger Sangallo for S. Peter's in which a Gothic element was certainly detectable in the many *aguglie*; Vasari, V, p. 467, *V. di Ant. Sangallo*. In point of fact, the Early Renaissance had already used on occasion this sort of ornament, partly as a legacy from the Gothic (§ 19).

(NOTE: The dome of Sta Maria dell' Orto may be by Giulio Romano, but the façade is by Vignola or one of his followers. Seventeen ninety-two is an impossible date for a renovation by Martino Lunghi the Younger (*d* 1657). (PM).

§ 73 *Façades of the Later Flowering*

In the period 1540–80 (cf. § 56) there became established, chiefly in Rome, a standard type of façade, which was

Fig. 138 *Pavia, Certosa*

then carried all over the world on the wings of the Counter-Reformation. In all its various expressions it strove always for a conventional harmony, which for that period had an absolute value.

The true mission of the Renaissance lay in the centralised building, which – as must be repeated once more – was able either to dispense with façades or subordinate them to the whole, especially to the dome. The unilateral development of the façade away from this concept was a misfortune. But it created, as Alberti had significantly observed in 1447, *una musica*, and some day lessons will again be learned from it, when certain misconceptions deriving from the architecture of our own century have disappeared.

The single-order façade, which Palladio in particular loved, is one step further away from architectural truth than the two-order façade, because it disregards the difference in width between the upper part (the nave only) and the lower part (nave plus aisles/side-chapels); in addition it is subject to serious disharmonies in details. Palladio admittedly performed wonders with it: façade of S. Giorgio Maggiore and especially Il Redentore in Venice (Figs. 140, 141).

The actual elements of the two-order façade, as they were then established and maintained well into the Baroque period, are the following: The Orders, below mostly Corinthian or Doric, above Composite, are preferably represented by pilasters, more rarely by half- or three-quarter columns, or free-standing columns with pilaster responds; – their grouping gave coherence to the façade; – friezes and architraves undecorated; – slight projection of the central part of the façade, and consequently also of the pediment; – vigorous handling of the main doorway, perhaps with salient columns, if the wall-orders otherwise consist only of pilasters; – niches; – square sunk panels, which may serve to suggest relief; – strong modelling of the principal window; – decoration of foliage and cartouches, perhaps continuing from capital to capital; – here and there the roof-edge adorned with balustrades, statues and acroteria; – the volutes solidly fashioned; – all these harmonised in their proportions both in relation to the size and to the greater or lesser plastic emphasis of the whole armoury of constituent parts.

Especially influential: the façade of Sto Spirito* in Rome by Mascherini; S. Caterina de' Funari and Sta

* The façade of Sto Spirito is mainly due to Antonio da Sangallo the Younger. (PM).

Fig. 139 *Lugano, Cathedral*

Fig. 140 *Venice, S. Giorgio Maggiore*

Maria de' Monti (Fig. 142, by Giacomo della Porta, who was under Michelangelo's influence); Sta Maria Traspontina (by Sallustio Peruzzi, Baldassare's son); a wealth of medium-sized and even small churches, all the more suitable as models.

Often, especially with smaller churches, the upper storey of the façade has the full width of the lower, so that a large part of it stands in the air. This was now the new form of the square screen (§70). The pattern was probably set by Michelangelo's project for S. Lorenzo in Florence (§72); one of the best-known façades of this type – S. Luigi de' Francesi in Rome.

The seventeenth century multiplied the components, emphasised them more strongly, and finally began to break and curve them.

§74 *Internal Arrangement of Long-Nave Churches: Basilicas*

Among buildings of longitudinal plan at the beginning of the Renaissance the basilica or flat-ceilinged colonnaded church seemed inclined to assume first place. But it was soon to take a backward step because it could not easily be accommodated to the most favoured form, a choir with a dome.

Italy still possessed at this time the great basilicas of the Early Christian period, Old S. Peter's and S. Paul's in Rome, the Cathedral of Ravenna etc. The merit of this way of building was well recognised. The Venetian Ambassadors of 1523 (§42) called Sta Maria Maggiore in Rome the finest of the seven Patriarchal Basilicas; *chiesa molto allegra*. Julius II, who as Cardinal restored SS. Apostoli in Rome, took pride in rebuilding the tribuna on a vast scale; *Vitae Papar.* in Murat., III, II, col. 1064.

Old basilicas sometimes still received superb coffered ceilings – e.g. S. Marco, Rome (by Marco de' Dolci, 1467–71), Sta Maria Maggiore (1493–98, by an unknown master). Cf. §158.

The Florentine basilicas of the Proto-Renaissance (§17) must have made a great impression on Brunellesco (Vasari, I, p. 332, *Vita di Andrea Tafi*). He obviously considered the basilica the most appropriate type of long-nave church.

Fig. 141 *Venice, Il Redentore*

Fig. 142 *Rome, Sta Maria de' Monti, elevation*

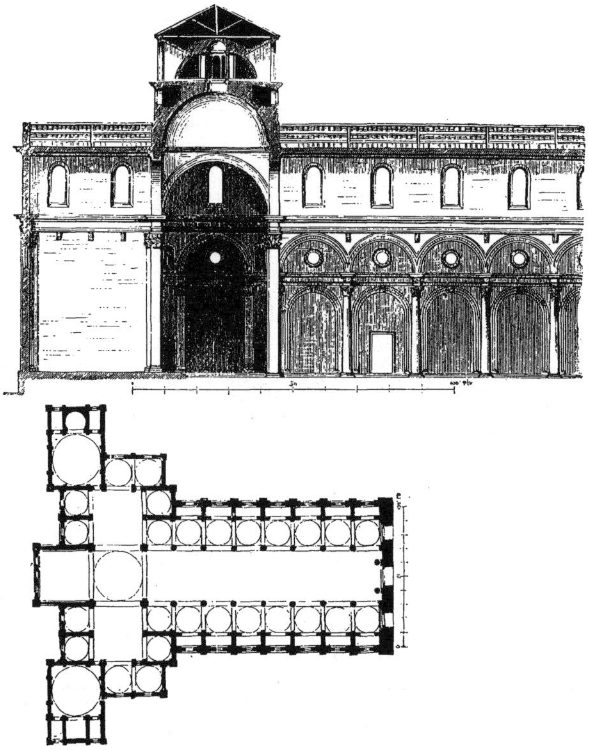

Figs. 143, 144 *Florence, S. Lorenzo, section and plan*

The surprising Cistercian type of choir formation in S. Lorenzo (Figs. 143–45), which the churches of the Mendicant Orders had particularly adopted, had been in course of construction since 1419 (before Brunellesco took charge of the building) to a plan by a Canon Dolphini and was probably not, as Manetti (*V. di Brunellesco*, ed. Holtzinger, p. 47) implies, pulled down, but retained by Brunellesco in view of the limited resources available at the time (cf. Fabriczy, *Brunellesco*, p. 159). The latter designed the nave originally without chapels, but these were decided upon after consultation with Giovanni de' Medici before the building was begun. In carrying out the work the architect in charge, A. Manetti Ciaccheri, made a mess of the chapel scheme and the dome over the crossing.

In Sto Spirito (after Brunellesco's model of 1435, by 1445 construction fairly far advanced, completed later with certain deviations) the colonnaded aisles extend round the transepts and choir, with splendid vistas, but secular-looking bipartite terminations; the whole wall-surface is punctuated by semi-circular niches, which were not closed on the outside until later to form a straight outline. The placing of the (in its present form later) High Altar in the middle of the crossing mitigates the impression made by the two parts of the transept ends and, in association with the dome erected to Brunellesco's model over the crossing, tends to merge the long structure of the nave with the centralised layout of the chancel (Fig. 146). Brunellesco immensely developed at S. Lorenzo the whole majesty and consequence of his arcuated columnar architecture (§35) and a full and mature sense of space. (The interval between columns = that from the column to the wall-pier = half the nave width.) Externally, S. Lorenzo had a Roman entablature with consoles above a plain wall (Fig. 187); otherwise the two churches are very simple, the façades of rough masonry only.

In Tuscany also of the fifteenth century: only the Cathedral of Cortona with (false or real?) barrel vault, said to be by Antonio da Sangallo the Elder.

Alberti (L. VII), who here also mingles the pagan and Christian, extols the basilica however for its better acoustics (in comparison with vaulting), and, against his earlier prejudice, permits arches over columns, speaks of basilicas with an upper storey and large windows in the wall above, prescribing for the latter metal grilles, and describing the profiles and decoration of ceiling coffers and their beneficial alternation with roundels. Yet he prefers the vault because of its greater *dignitas* and security against fire.

In N. Italy there is a significant number of columnar churches with barrel vaults which are interrupted by shallow domes, or begin and end with them.

Cf. for this Lübke, *Gesch. der Architektur*, 6th ed., vol. II, p. 299 ff. S. Francesco at Ferrara, 1494, by Biagio Rossetti; S. Benedetto (also at Ferrara), begun 1496 by Girolamo da Brescia, completed *c* 1550 by Battista and Alberto Tristani; S. Sisto at Piacenza, 1499–1511, by A. Taramelli (cf. §80).

The aisles, roofed simply with cupolas, open into

Fig. 145 *Florence, S. Lorenzo, interior*

rows of deep chapels; opulent rounded ends to choir and transepts, sumptuous decoration, but an almost total absence of top-lighting.

Simpler basilicas with barrel vaults: Sta Maria in Organo in Verona, 1481, and S. Bartolommeo a Porta Ravegnana in Bologna.

Finally, an important offshoot of the Florentine School: the Cathedral of Faenza by Giuliano da Majano, begun 1474, three-aisled basilica with rows of chapels, transept and medieval chancel (square choir with polygon); with the exception of the domed crossing, all spaces have top-lit vaults, in which – to support the latter along the nave – every second column is replaced by a pier; over the arcades a continuous entablature; in the arches above large round windows. (Cf. the publication by Graus in v. Lützow's Zeitschrift f. bildende Kunst, 1889, p. 64 ff.)

Flat-roofed basilicas: Sta Maria in Vado at Ferrara, 1495, by Biagio Rossetti and Bart. Tristani after a design by Ercole Grandi; S. Michele in Venice, 1469, by Mauro Coducci (§41, 43); SS. Piero e Paolo at Murano, 1509.

S. Zaccaria in Venice, 1456, by Martino Lombardo (or Ant. di Marco?) (Fig. 147), still half-Gothic, with wide spans, to which two cross-vaults and a dome correspond; the choir with ambulatory on two storeys.

Servi (or Concezione) in Siena (Figs. 148, 149), a columnar church with cross-vaults, the aisles still with pointed arches (not by Peruzzi), the transepts with polygonal ends by a Northern Italian, Domenico di Pietro (cf. Milanesi in Pantanelli, *Fr. di Giorgio e l'arte in Siena*, p. 74). On the details of the nave cf. Fig. 19.

Later (in Genoa and Naples) the dawning Baroque style re-adopted the basilica. The Annunziata at Genoa, magnificent of its type, by Giacomo della Porta; S. Filippo in Naples etc.

§75 *Flat-Ceilinged Single-Nave Churches*

The flat-ceilinged single-vessel church with rows of chapels on either side appeared much more frequently. This became the basic form for the churches of the monastic orders, which had from time immemorial had a single nave with added chapels, originally placed as occasion demanded, but subsequently in a symmetrical manner.

Thus S. Francesco and S. Domenico at Siena etc. Now the walls were regularly opened into a succession of chapels, the intervening piers strengthened into sideways-extending walls which carried the roof-trusses

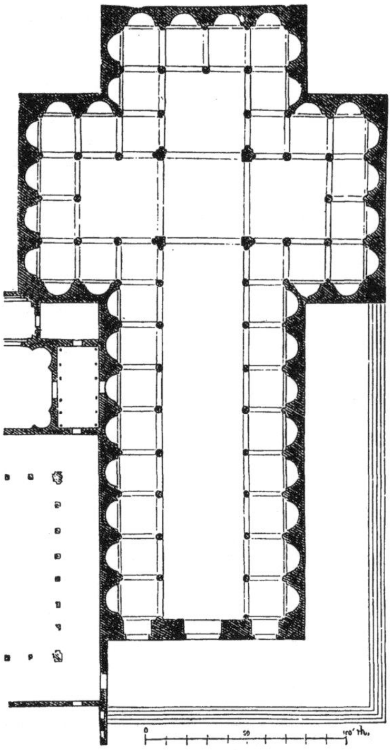

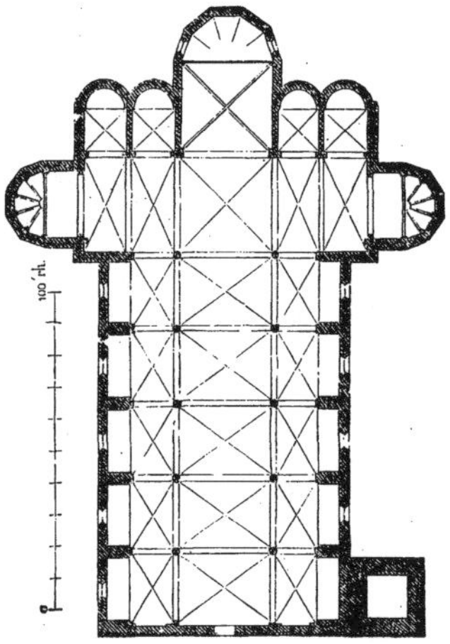

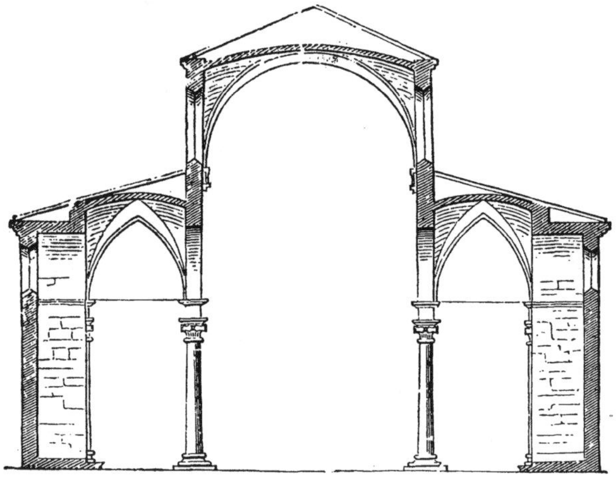

Fig. 146 *(above left) Florence, Sto Spirito, plan*

Fig. 147 *(above right) Venice, S. Zaccaria, interior*

Figs. 148, 149 *(above) Siena, Sta Maria de' Servi, plan and section*

securely. A principal aim of the Renaissance was thereby attained – a wide, unobstructed nave, and the eye became so accustomed to it that it demanded the same thing in vaulted churches.

The architectural problem lay essentially in the relationship of the width of the nave to its height and length, and in the design of the chapel entrances. (Alberti's assumptions in *De re aedif.*, L. VII, c. 4, that the chapels should be uneven in number or of this or that fixed width of opening, are gratuitous.) Chapel openings vary from the simplest pilaster Orders to the grandeur of Triumphal Arches. The chapels themselves might be smaller and more numerous, or larger and fewer, with greater or slighter depth. The altar could stand against the east wall of the chapel, thus enjoying direct light from a side window, or occupy the centre of the chapel, against the flat back wall or in a semi-circular niche, in which case it had either no light of its own or the light

Fig. 150 *Florence, S. Francesco al Monte, interior*

from two side windows. The chapels were sometimes treasuries of painting and sculpture, while architecture was confined to bare essentials, when no special extensions – chapels with their own domes and the like – were specified.

The upper walls were given a second pilaster Order or decorative paintings. The entrance to the choir was preferably made through a large arch. This arrangement is more favourable than the basilica to façades, because of the width of the nave.

A few great architects have conferred immortal distinction upon this modest building type: G. da Sangallo (?), Sta Maria Maddalena de' Pazzi in Florence (built in 1479 under the direction of the abbot, Ant. Brilli). Cronaca, *c* 1487 onwards, S. Francesco al Monte (also called S. Salvatore del Monte), Florence, *la bella villanella* (Fig. 150).

In the long-nave system the Cathedral of Città di Castello is very similar – begun 1482, finished 1540; architect (or architect in charge?) Elia di Bartolommeo Lombardo.

Jacopo Sansovino: S. Marcello in Rome (1519), and later, perhaps under the influence of a doctrinaire theorist (§57), S. Francesco della Vigna in Venice, 1534.

Antonio da Sangallo the Younger: Sto Spirito in Rome (§73).

In Naples this was the dominant church form of the good period: church of Monteoliveto etc. In Sta Maria delle Grazie (1517–24), Triumphal Arch type chapel entrances. In Naples the coffers of the ceiling often replaced by larger panels with paintings on canvas.

§76 *Single-Nave Vaulted Churches*

Single-nave vaulted churches with side chapels hardly attained satisfactory development in the fifteenth century, but, about the middle of the sixteenth century, in a felicitous metamorphosis became the predominant, and soon in the whole Catholic world the operative, type.

Everything depended upon the development of the vault. The pure barrel vault, which is really effective only when it acts as a dark corridor between two light spaces (as in Raphael's hall in the *School of Athens*), is either too dark or is impaired by light from below. Brunellesco's Badia at Fiesole, with barrel vaulting over transepts and nave and a top-lit crossing, offers, as a building of the greatest simplicity, no criterion; even the chapels open separately into the nave, without a framing Order. Cf. §81.

Alberti's nave of S. Andrea at Mantua (Figs. 151, 152) with coffered barrel vault 53 feet wide and 95 high, over chapels in threes separated by massive walls, and framed by rich pilasters; the painted coffering of the vault, the cornice and mouldings of the side chapels belong to the original decorative scheme. The whole immensely powerful and of evident influence on the motive of the transepts of S. Peter's in Rome. The nave lit only from below by the lunettes of the chapels and small round windows over them: all the greater the impact of the light coming from the (later) dome.

Basically related is Francesco di Giorgio's Madonna del Calcinaio at Cortona, begun 1485, the dome (1509–13) by Pietro di Domenico di Nozzo (Figs. 153–55).

S. Giorgio in Verona, entirely or partly by Sanmicheli. The undecorated barrel vault over four chapels on each side grouped in pairs; the light-providing dome space without transepts. The forms elegantly simple.

Cross-vaults, which permitted windows above (§48), in S. Pietro in Montorio in Rome, where in each bay of the latter two round niches are hollowed out below. In the nave of Sta Maria della Pace only one.

The very ingenious building of the Monastero Maggiore at Milan (Fig. 156) by Dolcebuono, 1503–19 (§23, 48), built purely for frescoes and decoration and yet beautiful without regard for these. Above the niches of the ground floor runs a gallery, which is bounded on the outside by the window-wall, on the inside by a graceful disposition of columns; over it a lightly articulated oblong painted (§23) cross-vault. Similar cross-vault with rich arabesque decoration, attributed to Borgognone, in the sacristy of Sta Maria della Passione in Milan; in the lunettes half-length figures of Saints.

The rebuilding of S. Giacomo Maggiore at Bologna 1493–1509; between the wall-piers, projecting inwards, ornamental chapel-niches were placed in threes and the nave roofed with a series of top-lit vaults.

Two of Peruzzi's schemes for S. Domenico in Siena; the nave and transept in one, in the other only the nave with three domes; the piers drawn inward and, like the walls, provided with niches; see Redtenbacher, *B. Peruzzi und seine Werke*, pls. 9, 10.

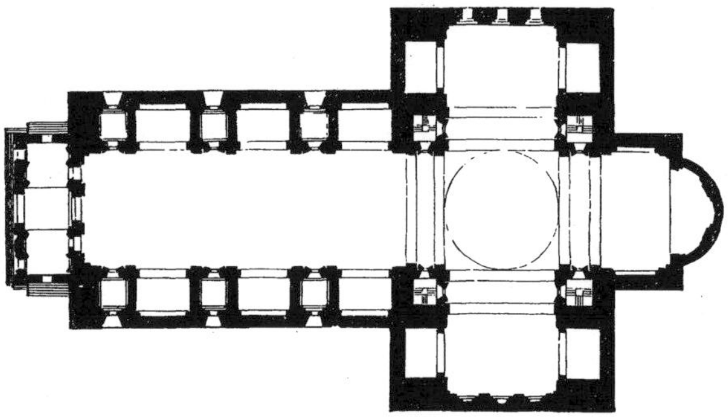

Figs. 151, 152 *Mantua, Sant' Andrea, interior and plan*

The fundamental step to a standard form was that the barrel vault was again preferred, but pierced with windows, and the resultant irrational forms brought into harmony by rich stucco-work.

Still of the fifteenth century: the Carmine at Padua, barrel vault with succession of lunettes and spandrels (Figs. 157, 158).

By the beginning of the Counter-Reformation that most influential building type was perfected, with a fairly short, but wide and high nave lit by windows in the barrel vault and lined by large, but not deep, chapels in the closest association with the domed plan described above (§67) as the centralised building of the Baroque period. The transepts project on plan little or not at all beyond the chapels of the nave.

The decisive building and model for larger churches: il Gesù in Rome, by Vignola (Fig. 159).

For smaller churches: Sta Maria de' Monti (Figs. 160, 161), by Giac. della Porta, with particularly fine stuccoed barrel vault.

The incisions of the windows form spandrels on the cylindrical surface of the vault. For the semi-dome of the choir windows were now also favoured. Vaults as a whole were still only rarely constructed and coffered homogeneously, relying more on a freer construction and decoration.

Palladio: Il Redentore in Venice, with vaulting left smooth and white; in its planning, spatial proportions and disposition (with half-columns and pilasters) one of the supreme masterpieces of the late Renaissance; the façade (§73) perhaps the pre-eminent single-order example.

Enduring too in individual single-nave churches the rows of top-lit vaults; S. Fedele in Milan, by Pellegrini, and its close copy, the nave of S. Gaudenzio at Novara.

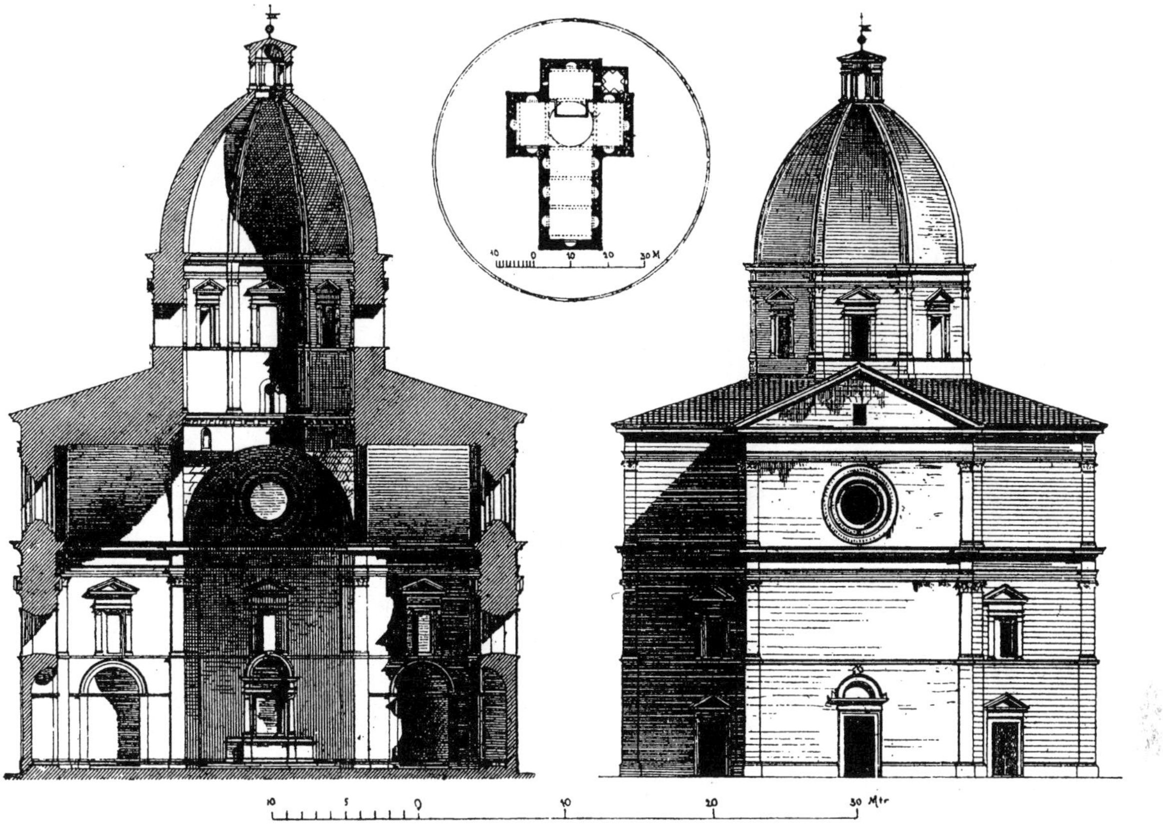

Figs. 153, 154, 155 *Cortona, Sta Maria del Calcinaio, section, plan and elevation*

§77 *Three-Aisled Vaulted Churches*

Three-aisled (or, rather, nave-and-two-aisled) vaulted churches display every conceivable form, ornamentation, and method of illumination. The finest of them are those comprising relatively few elements and approximating to the forms of the central plan.

The rebuilding of S. Peter's as Nicholas V wanted it (*c* 1450), would have been a gigantic three-, or, with the rows of chapels, five-aisled church, with cross-vaults and round windows in the upper walls: *Vitae Papar.*, in Murat., III, II, col. 933 ff.

Under the certainly not very happy influence of this project Giacomo da Pietrasanta seems to have designed (1479) S. Agostino in Rome, and another master (1472) Sta Maria del Popolo; cross-vaults; lighting from above; piers with engaged columns. Cf. §48. Also the influence of the Basilica of Constantine? Of Serlio's projects in his Vth Book the eleventh belongs here, the twelfth to the previous paragraph.

The most impressive building of this type, the Cathedral of Pavia (Figs. 162, 163), designed in 1486 by Cristoforo Rocchi, probably with the help of Bramante (cf. Milanesi, II, 435 and v. Geymüller, *Ursprüngliche Entwürfe*, p. 36); three-aisled with cross-vaults and an octagonal domed space of the same diameter as the nave and both aisles. It remained a fragment and the complete form is known only from the surviving model (§59, Fig. 90).

S. Giovanni in Parma (Figs. 164–66), three-aisled with cross-vaults, by Bernardino Zaccagni (1510), with polygonal chapels along the nave; richly painted architectural elements.

Pius II gave a nave and two aisles of equal height with cross-vaults to his church at Pienza, because he had seen this arrangement in an Austrian church and found it more handsome and the lighting better; Pii II, *Comment.*, L. IX, p. 430. Cf. §8, 22, 83.

(Was the Gothic Cathedral at Perugia still being built at that time?)

Sta Maria dell' Anima in Rome (1500), the interior by a Northern architect; here, too, equal aisle-heights, cross-vaults – and lofty, misshapen wall-niches.

Equal aisle-heights as well in the cross-vaulted Fontegiusta at Siena (1484, by Francesco Fedeli da Como) and Sta Maria Annunziata at Camerino, where allegedly in 1494 Corinthian columns with entablatures and cross-vaults were installed in a Romanesque construction.

Among churches with barrel vaults the Annunziata at Arezzo by Antonio da Sangallo the Elder is very fine; he ventured to insert a wall with windows between the range of piers and the vault. In addition the ingeniously contrived vestibule, the graceful shallow dome, the elegance and judicious economy of decoration (Figs. 167, 168).

On the other hand, every barrel vault that receives its light solely from the lateral aisles loses the sense of

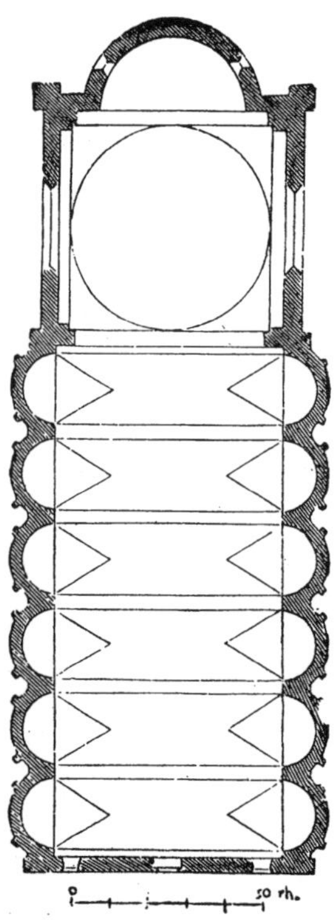

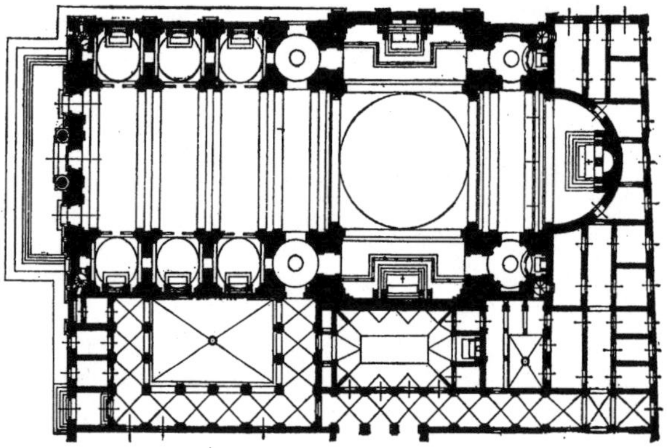

Fig. 156 *(above left) Milan, S. Maurizio (Monastero Maggiore), arcade*

Figs. 157, 158 *(above) Padua, Il Carmine, detail and plan*

Fig. 159 *(left) Rome, Il Gesù, plan*

religious solemnity, however noble the architecture: Sta Maria presso S. Celso in Milan, by Dolcebuono, begun in 1493 (cf. documents in Calvi, *Notizie*, II, 180); the façade by Galeazzo Alessi, the forecourt of 1514–26 by Bernardino Zenale. Even Raphael with his barrel vault over the nave of S. Peter's (§66) would not have evaded this disadvantage; the younger Antonio da Sangallo criticised this nave as long, narrow, high, and extremely dark; Vasari, V, p. 477, in the commentary on the *V. di A. da Sangallo*. Also Raphael's piers, as supports for such a high barrel vault, would have formed rather deep *coulisses* – i.e. they would scarcely have permitted a sidelong view into the aisles.

Successful solutions began when the longitudinal movement of the vault (the function of Gothic) was abandoned in principle and the nave was split up into separate domed-type spaces.

Unique instance: the church of S. Lorenzo in Damaso (Fig. 169) enclosed within the Cancelleria in Rome; a longish central space, covered at both ends with barrel vaults, with a round, shallow, dome in the middle, into which is fitted on the left side a single source of light (a large semi-circular window); below on three sides colonnades; the end an apse. (Since the most recent restoration the central space has a flat roof.)

S. Giustina in Padua, begun 1521 by Alessandro Leopardi, completed 1532 by Andrea Moroni (Figs. 170, 171); Vasari, II, p. 609, *V. di Vellano*. The nave: the side-aisles lined with rows of chapels carry transverse barrel vaults supporting the three shallow domes of the nave. Transepts and choir: a most lavish composition, with rounded ends to all the spaces and four high domes. The grandest spatial and light effects. (The capitals, §53.) Regarding the similarity with Fra Giocondo's scheme of 1505 for S. Peter's, see the author's *Cicerone*, 10th ed., II, 1, p. 304.

S. Salvatore at Venice by Giorgio Spavento, designed 1506, completed 1534 (Figs. 172, 173), extraordinarily fine, without any such pompous appurtenances to the choir; the motive the same as at S. Marco, the domes – here three in succession – each resting on four wide arches, the angle-spaces forming free passages on slender pillars; the domes independently lit by lanterns.

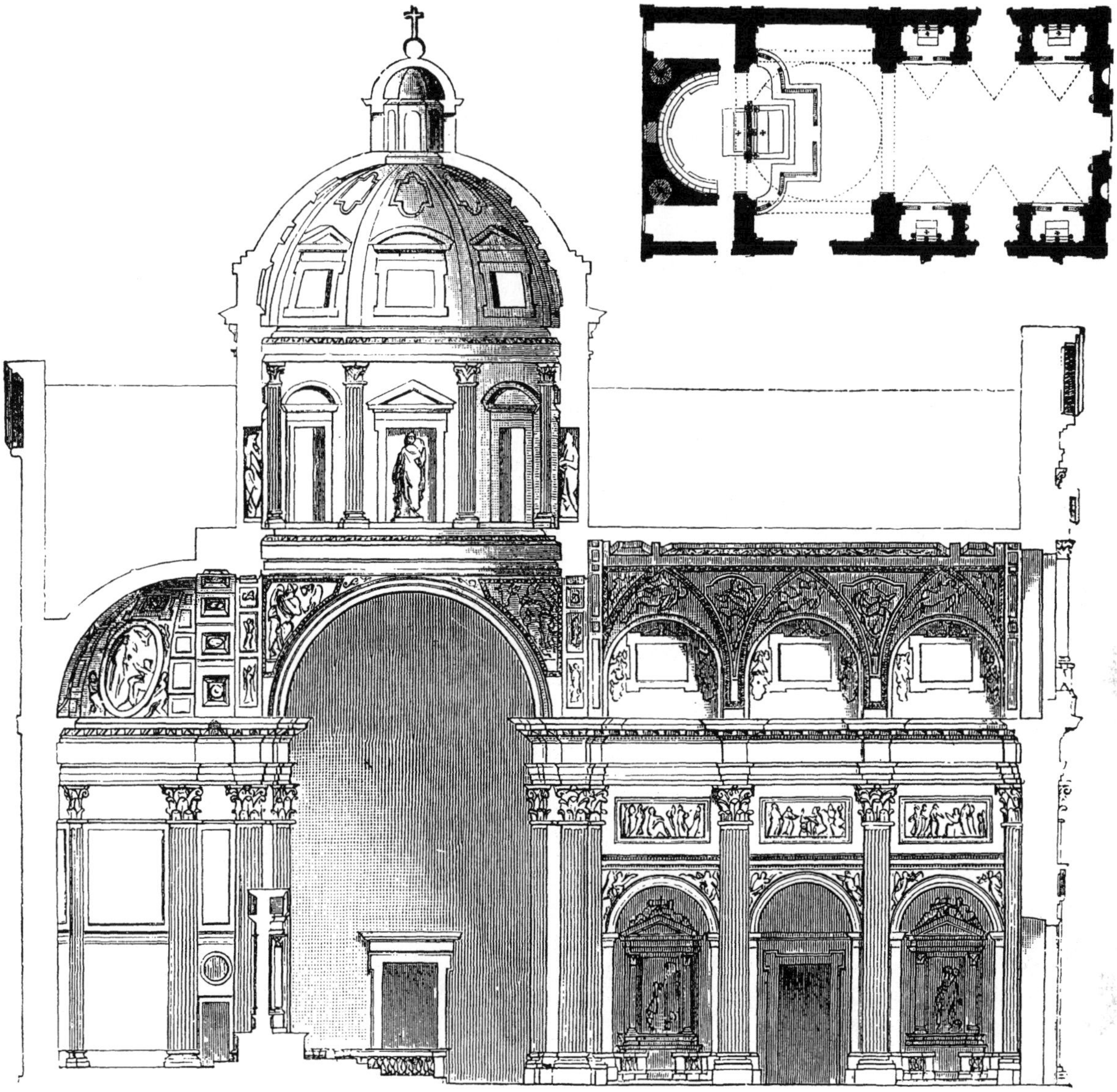

Figs. 160, 161 *Rome, Sta Maria de' Monti, section and plan*

(The same basic motive, but with three cross-vaults instead of domes, already (1507) applied at S. Fantino, Venice.)

(Similarly at S. Sepolcro, Piacenza, by Alessio Tarameli, completed 1534.)

The interior of Mantua Cathedral by Giulio Romano, an original and excellent work, created under inhibiting conditions of various kinds (Fig. 174).

Padua Cathedral, 1551–77, by Righetto and della Valle, relies on the inspiration of these buildings, of the N. Italian columnar churches mentioned in §74, and of Michelangelo.

(Three-aisled Benedictine churches of differing plan, of this period and a little later: S. Benedetto at Mantua; S. Giorgio Maggiore at Venice, by Palladio (Fig. 175); the Badia de' Cassinensi at Arezzo, by Vasari, original but secular arrangement.)

(An enormous pilgrimage-cathedral for a world turning again to Catholicism: Madonna degli Angeli at Assisi, three-aisled with barrel vault and a vast cupola over the *Portiuncula* of S. Francis; by Galeazzo Alessi (with Vignola's collaboration?). The huge dark barrel vault is succeeded by a flood of light from the dome.)

§78 *The Campanile in the Early Renaissance*

The campanile, in the Middle Ages generally separate from the church, but sometimes treated as a majestic showpiece, was for the Renaissance mostly only a necessary evil.

Giotto's campanile in Florence and the tower of Pisa enjoyed lasting admiration. The Torrazzo of Cremona, begun in legendary times, the highest tower in Italy; on

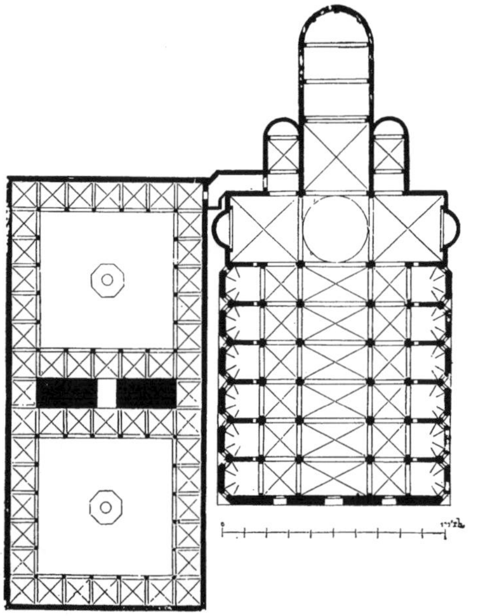

Figs. 162, 163 *(above left and centre) Pavia, Cathedral, plan and octagon*

Fig. 164 *(above right) Parma, S. Giovanni, plan*

Fig. 165 *(below left) Parma, S. Giovanni, transverse section*

Fig. 166 *(below right) Parma, S. Giovanni, longitudinal section*

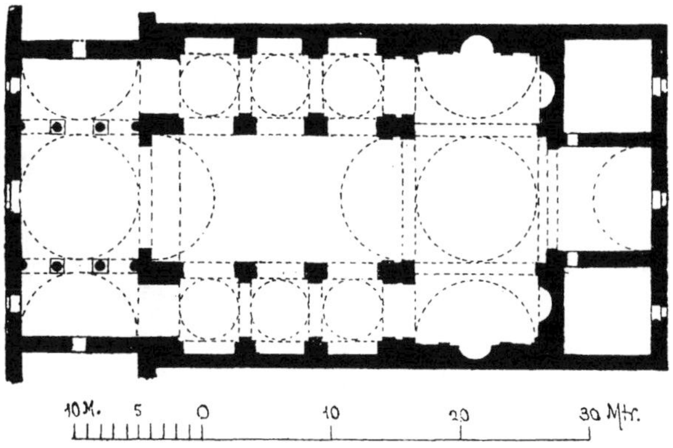

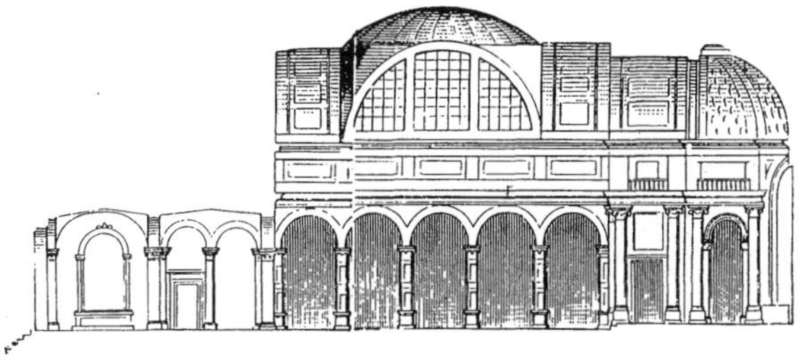

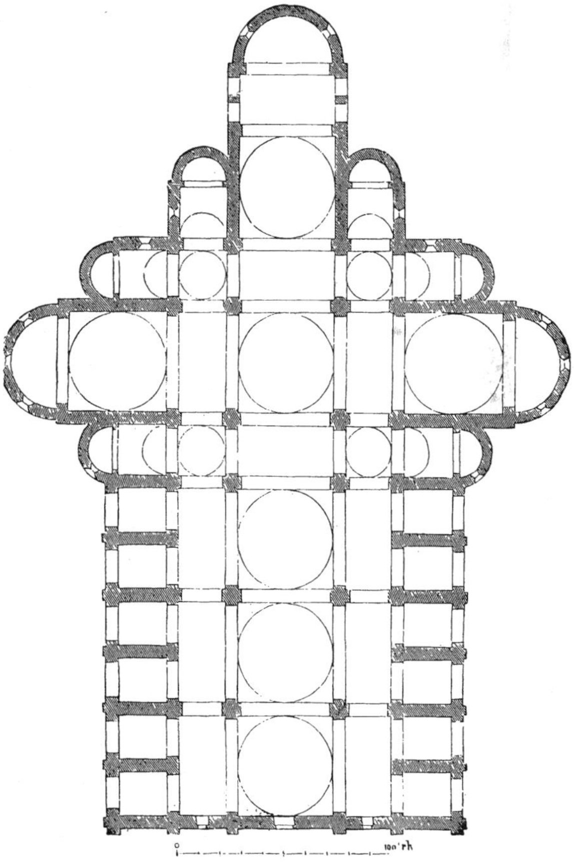

Fig. 167 *(top left) Arezzo, SS. Annunziata, plan*

Fig. 168 *(above centre) Arezzo, SS. Annunziata, interior*

Fig. 169 *(below) Rome, S. Lorenzo in Damaso, section*

Fig. 170 *(above right) Padua, Sta Giustina, section*

Fig. 171 *(below right) Padua, Sta Giustina, plan*

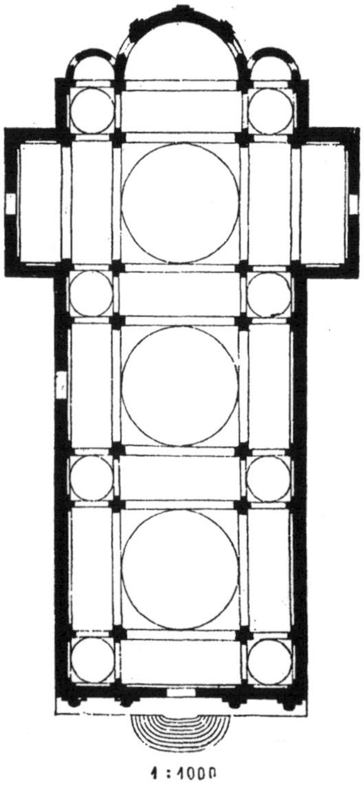

Figs. 172, 173
Venice, S. Salvatore, section and plan

an upper gallery lines were drawn in the sixteenth century, pointing to every place in the district (Anonimo Morelliano).

The campanile of S. Mark's in Venice, rebuilt after its collapse in 1902, almost formless in 1498, had already cost more than 50,000 ducats (Malipiero in Arch. stor. VII, II). Its gilded top shone out to the home-coming Venetian many miles away across the sea *velut saluberrimum sidus*; Sabellicus, *De situ Ven. urbis*, fol. 89.

There were also cases in which the church tower, acting also as the town-tower, required a nobler form, and in any case it could not stand in conspicuous disharmony with the church. The Renaissance even tried to clothe it with the Orders of Antiquity, and, indeed, with several of them superimposed, but exhibited great confusion, especially with regard to the top.

Northern Gothic, where the tower has an organic life and is the model for the entire formal vocabulary, appears here to incomparable advantage. The Antique Orders, skilfully graduated and effectively alternated with pilasters, attached and free-standing columns, were certainly capable of helping to produce a relatively fine tower, although one always feels that tower architecture does not come about in this way. But even this modest goal was rarely attained.

Alberti's theory of towers, *De re aedif.*, L. VIII, c. 5, is an uninspired product of his imagination; rectangular towers should be six diameters in height, round ones four; or the former at least four and the latter three; the finest tower – *turris decentissima* – however, should be a mixture of both types, with three round storeys above a square plinth and ground storey, then a square of four open arches and finally a round monopteros with a hemispherical cupola; proportions and details are given in each case.

Naturally, nobody heeded him. The round or polygonal forms are likely to be found at the top, as on two secular towers in Bologna; Bursellis, *Annal. Bonon.*, in Murat., XXIII, col. 909, 911; the account of how in 1455 a church tower was moved back eight yards in col. 888.

Fig. 174 (*opposite above*) *Mantua, Cathedral, interior*　Fig. 175 (*opposite below*) *Venice, S. Giorgio Maggiore, interior*

Fig. 176 *Ferrara, Cathedral campanile*

Fig. 177 *Rome, Sto Spirito, campanile*

Fantastic forms of towers in the splendid buildings in the frescoes by Benozzo Gozzoli (Campo Santo, Pisa) and others.

The best-furnished fifteenth-century tower (engaged columns with arches, strong angle-pilasters, all in marble in courses of various colours) is that of Ferrara Cathedral (1451–93: Fig. 176).

Those towers which have only slender angle-pilasters to frame the storeys are quite lamentable. (One of the better of these is the one at the Madonna della Quercia in Viterbo.)

The best results occurred when either the pilasters were omitted altogether and wall-strips applied which have no fixed system of proportion, e.g. on a number of towers in Venice (whose verticality Sabellico, op. cit., L. II, fol. 86 perhaps extolled too soon), or when the pilasters were freely handled, so that for example they ran through two storeys, creating a more impressive feature.

Thus, on the brick tower of Sto Spirito in Rome, which in its rugged simplicity is perhaps the noblest campanile of the Early Renaissance (Fig. 177).

Fig. 178 *Florence, S. Lorenzo, Old Sacristy, section*

Fig. 179 *Milan, S. Eustorgio, chapel elevation*

§79 *The Campanile in the Sixteenth Century*

The sixteenth century gave its more robust formal idiom to campanili, incorporating them, sometimes in twos or fours, into the design of churches, and harmonising them more closely with the Orders used on the churches themselves.

Individual towers admired at that time: Vasari, V, p. 353, n. 1, *V. di Baccio d' Agnolo*; VI, p. 356, n. 1, *V. di Sanmicheli.*

On occasion a certain fear of towers in the design appears, as if of uninvited guests. At the church of Montepulciano (§64), where they stand at the front of the Greek cross and fully correspond to the Orders of the main building, they remain separated from the latter by narrow spaces. (Only one was executed, see Figs. 97, 98.)

In Geymüller, pl. 42, the project for a façade of S. Peter's (now in the Albertina, Vienna), perhaps by Raphael, but more likely by Perino del Vaga; the towers would have been among the most accomplished of the Renaissance.

In contrast, the design of the younger Antonio da Sangallo (§66) for S. Peter's (in the *Speculum Romanae Magnificentiae*) with towers, on which columns, half-columns and obelisks are heaped in the silliest manner.

Among Serlio's church plans the eleventh and twelfth in the Vth Book belong here (cf. §67).

The top of the campanile at times belongs to a completely anarchic world of the imagination beggaring all description. If the top storey was quadrangular, however, there was as a rule a four-sided, rather flat roof, as on the campanili of Roman basilicas; thus, too, at Sto Spirito (§78); or a pyramid of stone, or of timber with a lead covering. Daniele Barbaro, who had the campanile of S. Mark's before his eyes, required that the height of such pyramids should be one-and-a-half times the base (ad *Vitruv.*, L. IV, c. 8).

As on the façade, so on the tower the Baroque style knew how to exploit strengths and weaknesses much more effectively. Huge windows, rustication at the angles, with massive consoles beneath the stages, vigorously modelled ornament (festoons, lions' heads etc.), broken and decorated pediments, alternation of stone and brick etc.

Fig. 180 *Venice, Sta Maria de' Miracoli, interior*

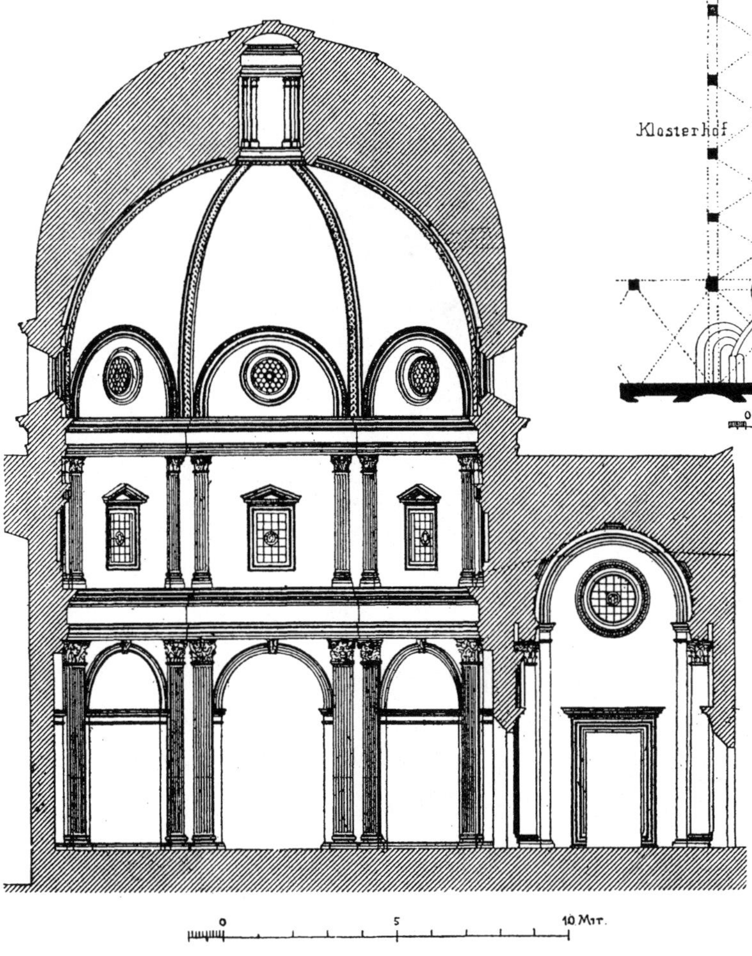

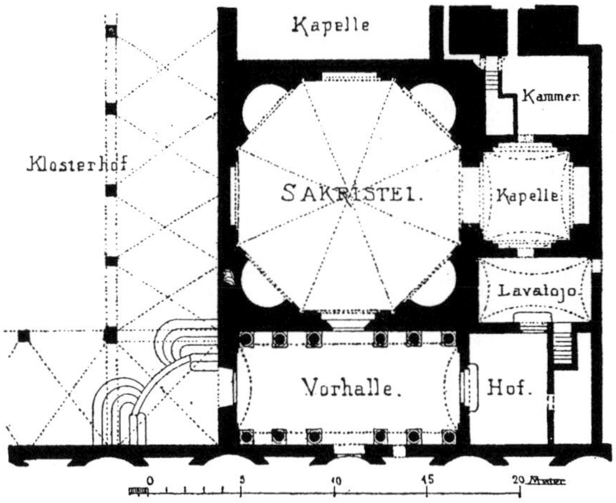

Figs. 181, 182
Florence, Sto Spirito, Sacristy, section and plan

The unfinished simple and solid campanile next to S. Chiara in Naples, once ranking as a fourteenth-century work – and thus vindicating the priority of Naples in the Renaissance – is now acknowledged to be later than 1600 (D'Agincourt, pl. 54).

§80 *Individual Chapels and Sacristies*

Individual chapels and sacristies added to churches are sometimes among the best achievements of the Renaissance, if only because it is working here in its true element, in that they are for the most part centrally planned. In the fifteenth century a type emanating from Florence was especially dominant: a large rectangle with a dome, and beyond it a smaller room with a cupola. The octagon also came to the fore.

In practice the sacristy also serves as a chapel, on account of its altar.

Of the more celebrated chapels, that of S. Antony in the Santo at Padua is the only longitudinal structure, in this instance open down one of the long sides.

The Florentine type at its simplest in Michelozzo's Sacristy of S. Marco (1437), where the main space has a simple cross-vault, and in his Cappella Medici del Noviziato at S. Croce. Richer and more splendid, with its own light-disseminating dome, Brunellesco's Old Sacristy of S. Lorenzo (Fig. 178), on plan (Fig. 144) at top left, the corresponding room on the right being Michelangelo's work (§80) containing the Medici Tombs; Brunellesco's Cappella de' Pazzi at S. Croce (§63); Michelozzo's end chapel behind S. Eustorgio in Milan (according to an inscription begun 1462: cf. §65), in which the smaller extension with a cupola contains the splendid sarcophagus of S. Peter Martyr; the exterior a noteworthy brick building (Fig. 179).

Gradations of otherwise very common forms: quadrangular chapel with wall-niches set back and top-lit vault (like that of the Cardinal of Portugal at S. Miniato, Florence, 1461–66, built by Antonio Rossellino, ornamented by the della Robbia and Ant. Pollajuolo); similarly, the sacristy of S. Felicita, 1470, elegant pilasters and mouldings; two chapels of this kind at S. Pietro de' Cassinensi at Perugia with rich articulation of the walls, probably by the Florentine Francesco di Guido, *c* 1500 (Laspeyres, Figs. 214, 215): or with a shallow dome; or the same space with an extension providing light and carrying a cupola (e.g. several chapels in Bolognese

Fig. 183 *Milan, S. Satiro, Sacristy, detail*

Fig. 184 *Florence, S. Lorenzo, Medici Chapel, section*

churches); or there was a tendency to give the main space semi-circular windows – lunettes – or the dome a ring of small round windows; or even a drum with windows (as the Cappella di S. Biagio in SS. Nazaro e Celso at Verona); or, by setting back the walls, there arises a Greek cross; thus in the graceful chapel of S. Giovanni in Genoa Cathedral the drum rests on three barrel vaults and an entrance, like a Triumphal Arch and still half-Gothic.

The most decorative in Venice: the choir of Sta Maria de' Miracoli, 1480–89, by Pietro Lombardo (Fig. 180) – the little chapel of Guglielmo Bergamasco, as well as the quadrangular one at SS. Apostoli with angle-columns and cupola; and the hexagonal one adjoining S. Michele, 1527–34, a sacred pavilion.

The Colleoni Chapel at Bergamo (§5), with lavish external incrustation, the inside greatly altered.

In the two entrance-chapels at S. Sisto, Piacenza (§74), a large central composition is squeezed into a space which ought to be three times as big.

Octagons: Cronaca's sacristy (§64, Figs. 181, 182), and Bramante's at S. Satiro in Milan (Fig. 183), in a confined space, enclosed all round, with niches below, a lovely frieze in the middle, a charming upper gallery and very beautiful skylight – *E perchè veniva ad essere oscura, come quella che era triplicata, escogitò luminarla d' alto* (Anon. Morelliano) (§136).

In the sixteenth century the Greek cross, or at any rate a system of four arches with a high dome, became the favourite form for a sumptuous chapel. Raphael brought it to a high degree of perfection in the Capp. Chigi (Fig. 185) of Sta Maria del Popolo in Rome (the obliquely placed piers with their niches and trapezoidal pendentives make it a S. Peter's in miniature). The Baroque syle also revealed its keenest sense of beauty in such buildings: chapels of Sixtus V and Paul V at Sta Maria Maggiore, Capp. Corsini at the Lateran.

Michelangelo's Sagrestia Nuova (Medici Chapel) at S. Lorenzo in Florence (Fig. 184), on the other hand, is again related in plan to the motive of Brunellesco and Michelozzo, but attains in its cubic proportions and in general effect (despite the great wilfulness of the details) a supreme beauty. Architecture and sculpture are so synthesised that the master might have modelled sar-

Fig. 185 *Rome, Sta Maria del Popolo, Chigi Chapel*

Fig. 186 *Siena, Cathedral, Cappella di S. Giovanni*

cophagi, statues, pilasters, mouldings, niches, doors and windows from the same clay. The greatest unity in the handling of space, light, and form. (But quite a number of niches intended for statues were left empty: Vasari, VII, p. 203, n. 2, *V. di Michelangelo*, and the Madonna and the two saints were originally intended for a different placing. Even for the sarcophagi a different form and arrangement was (according to H. Grimm) probably made originally; though Michelangelo might well have prescribed the existing plan, or at least approved it.)

In addition, a few chapels are also to be found from the beginning of the sixteenth century: Capp. S. Giovanni in the Cathedral of Siena (Fig. 186), Capp. Caraccioli in S. Giovanni a Carbonara, Naples (1516: very pretty); then Sanmicheli's chapel already mentioned in S. Bernardino, Verona, the masterpiece of this type, cf. §67, Figs. 118, 119.

§81 *The Exterior of Long-Nave Churches*

The external treatment of long churches, apart from the façade, choir, and dome, which took their cue from the central plan, remained on the whole somewhat neglected.

As well as the reason mentioned in §68, we must take into consideration the frequent breaking-up of the long sides by the addition of chapels; unfinished façades also had an adverse effect on the long sides.

Brunellesco gave the basilica of S. Lorenzo (Fig. 187) a beautifully simple cladding of pilasters (on the rows of chapels), string-courses and consoles, the latter perhaps inspired by S. Frediano at Lucca; similar ones on the Badia at Fiesole.

Otherwise cladding with pilasters of the side-aisle walls and the upper structure was very rarely provided in the fifteenth century: S. Severino in Naples (by Mormandi, 1490), the Pontano chapel also in Naples (1492), a few North Italian brick churches etc. Even in Venice only Sta Maria de' Miracoli has the full incrustation treatment with pilasters on the sides.

Of high, indeed unique, value: the white marble Cathedral of Como. The exemplary and explicit inscription on the exterior of the chancel: *Cum hoc templum vetustate confectum esset, a populo Comensi renovari coeptum est MCCCLXXXXVI. Huius vero posterioris partis iacta sunt*

Fig. 187 *Florence, S. Lorenzo, detail of side elevation*

fundamenta MDXIII, XXII. Decembris, frontis et laterum iam opere perfecto. Thomas de Rodariis faciebat. Begun as Gothic and slowly extended from the façade, the nave remains Gothic inside, but so built that the bays, narrow to start with, become wider and more splendidly spacious; outside re-cast as a magnificent Renaissance structure, partly on Bramante's advice (south portal, dated 1491, three adjacent windows and string-courses), cf. v. Geymüller, *Entwürfe*, p. 39 ff. The projecting supports are given pedestals and cornices in a freely Antique fashion, above them instead of pinnacles candelabrum-like ornament of much more beautiful design than any similar French translations from the Gothic; the wall-surfaces enframed with mouldings. Transepts and choir, Rodari's building (from 1513), with polygonal terminations, one of the finest buildings of Italy, outside with the forms of the nave refined and ennobled (the dome modern). Cf. v. Bezold, Deutsche Bauzeitung, 1885.

In the course of the sixteenth century the pilaster cladding of the long sides became the rule, but usually in a cold and perfunctory form. After Michelangelo's Corinthian Order and attic on the outside of S. Peter's (a feature of questionable value) the Baroque style had a model for a pilaster Order, just as after S. Fedele in Milan (by Pellegrini) there was a precedent for two half-column or pilaster Orders superimposed.

Often now in place of pilasters slightly salient buttresses, on to which volutes like those of the façade (§69, 70) rolled down from the upper part of the nave.

Individual especially opulent schemes had a continuous balustrade along the edge of the roof. At S. Peter's such a motive was intended by Michelangelo, and the few places where it was actually carried out show how much depended upon its effect (§66).

§82 *General View of Church Architecture*

The Renaissance relied in church building upon bringing about a true feeling of all that was highest by the sublimity and beauty of the architectonic impression. It needed no sacred style (§61, 62); its supreme and particular work, the centralised building, would have been a holy place in itself without regard to purpose and even without consecration.

Alberti, *De re aedificatoria*, L. VII, c. 3, 5, 10, 12, 13, 15, gives this feeling a more strongly pagan flavour than others. In the temple the divine presence (*superi*) stoops down to receive our offerings and prayers. But even if the divinity is not concerned about the fallible buildings of mankind, yet piety may be much enhanced if the temple has something about it which rejoices the heart and compels admiration. Anyone entering should be so captivated with wonder and awe that he would cry out: "This place is worthy of God!" The effect should be such that one remains in doubt whether art or the sense of eternity is the greater. The site he requires should be isolated, in the middle of a piazza or a broad street, and the building should stand on a high base. Inside, he advocates only one altar, since the sacrament derives from the Early Christians' *agape* and only later periods "stuffed everything with altars". His eulogy of dim lighting is also perhaps an Early Christian recollection, although he speaks at the same time of the Ancients, who "kindled in the bowls of their candelabra great sweet-smelling flames".

Extremely significant for the dominance of architectural form is his polemic against frescoes, which belong, if anywhere, in the entrance vestibule; instead of them he demanded altarpieces, or preferably, statues for the interior. He twice recommends incrustation, if only perhaps to avoid frescoes (cf. §265).*

The windows he required to be of middling size and at a height that only permitted a view of the sky. Indeed the awe engendered by a measure of darkness stimulated devotion. (Cf. Thom. Morus, *Utopia*, Basle, 1563, p. 146.)

At this time, *c* 1450, M. Savonarola also speaks of a relationship between dark street-arcades and a mood of reverence, with reference to Padua; in Murat., XXIV, col. 1179. On the other hand, Pius II, *Comment.*, L. IX, p. 431, praises the lightness of his church at Pienza.

§ 83 *The Symmetry of the View*

Not to impair the symmetry of the view (§ 30), at least in the interior, was the impression intended above all others. The fifteenth and sixteenth centuries made very considerable sacrifices to this end, both in existing churches and in new buildings. The sister-arts were indeed to find themselves subordinated to the overall architectural effect.

Earlier churches were full of built-in features, e.g. obtrusive tombs and altars; these were purged, and strict regulations laid down for new work.

As early as 1391 the erection of a grand altar in Florence Cathedral by the second pier on the right was permitted only if the altar were no wider than the pier and no coats of arms placed near it: Gaye, *Carteggio*, I, p. 534.

In the fifteenth century the Popes were particularly strict. Nicholas V (1447–55) decreed in advance for his new scheme for S. Peter's that no tombs, even of Popes or prelates, should pollute this temple; *Vitae Papar.*, in Murat., III, II, col. 935.

Pius II (1458–64) allowed the old building to stand, but demolished the very irregular chapels and rebuilt them regularly, so that the view of the interior became *augustior et patientior*. When he added a large chapel to contain the skull of S. Andrew everything near it had to be moved, including tombs of Popes and Cardinals, which had "arbitrarily monopolised" the space in the church; Platina, *De vitis Pontiff.*, p. 312; *Vitae Papar.*, op. cit., col. 985.

In the church of his new town, Pienza (§ 8), we are supposed to glance (as we enter) over the entire three-aisled church (§ 77), with all its chapels and altars clearly illuminated and exquisitely furnished; everything, with the exception of the many-coloured vault, was either stone-colour or was a very light tone; here, too, frescoes were excluded (cf. § 82) and painting confined to the altarpieces, the work of Sienese masters, while the rather large windows were glazed with plain glass only. In Pienza on 14 September, 1462, Pius issued a Bull: no one should be buried here, except the members of the Chapter in their vault; nobody impair the light colour of the walls and piers, put up paintings, affix plaques, add chapels, or erect more altars etc. Cf. the sources quoted above and Pii II, *Comment.*, L. IX, p. 430 ff.

Sixtus IV (1471–84) once again "cleansed" S. Peter's and the Lateran, and made S. Peter's lighter by renovating the windows with thin marble sheets and glass; *Vitae Papar.*, op. cit., col. 1064.

This spirit of conformity was detrimental, notably in Tuscany at the time of Duke Cosimo I (and sometimes owing to him), to many old works of art (§ 56).

The Cathedral of Pisa, until 1540 full of ancient altarpieces of varied origin and size, was now given nothing but altars of a uniform marble pattern, into which paintings (by generally inferior people) were inserted, representing the same saints as those in the earlier pictures; Vasari, V, p. 127, *V. di Sogliani.*

On Cosimo's orders the new altars in Sta Maria Novella in Florence had to correspond to the intervals between piers. He had the Cathedral whitewashed. Vasari, VII, p. 417, Vasari's *Autobiography*; VI, p. 141, *V. di Bandinelli.*

The spirit of the Counter-Reformation was also very favourable to the "purification" of churches. Carlo Borromeo met with many over-filled churches in his archbishopric of Milan; pompous monuments towered above the very altars or hovered over the heads of worshippers (on consoles or propped-up columns); added to these the mass of suspended weapons and flags: all such was removed, so that the churches were used only for the service of God. Ripamonti, in Graevius, *Thesaurus Ital.*, II, II, col. 892.

In this connection consideration must be given to the early emergent practice of achieving a seeming enlargement of space by the use of perspective to give an impression of depth into the wall. Bramante used this device on two occasions, in the false choir behind the altar of S. Satiro in Milan, and in the niches of the Incoronata at Lodi, when he was participating in Battagio's scheme (§ 65).

* No §265 appeared in this book as published. Burckhardt's scheme for further sections on painting and sculpture were never carried out (see Introduction, p. xvi); 265 would have been on fresco-decoration. (PM).

CHAPTER TEN

Monasteries and Buildings of Religious Orders

§ 84 *Monasteries in the North and South*

In the planning of monasteries the Middle Ages had already attained a considerable degree of perfection. Even in the North they often showed a greater monumental development than anywhere in Italy before the Renaissance.

The usual complex of rooms: chapter house, dormitory, refectory, scriptorium, abbot's or prior's lodging, cloisters, store-rooms, infirmary, hospice, stables etc.; in the plan of the monastery at S. Gall of 820 they were dispersed over a great square.

The most considerable Italian monasteries had perhaps by the tenth century a more self-contained layout deriving from Roman villas; notably Farfa and Nonantula: *Historia Farfens.* in Pertz, *Monum.*, XIII, pp. 530, 533, 546.

In the twelfth century, however, the North was ahead in the scale of the layout, and also in its monumental development. Cf. Caumont, *Abécédaire*, and the publications of the Comité historique des arts et monuments. A Belgian abbey had, for example, the same roof-heights for the entire main block; *Gesta abbatum Trudonens.*, in Pertz, Monum., XII, regarding the reconstruction after 1160.

In Italy hardly one monastery building of the twelfth to the fourteenth centuries was to be found of the rank of the richer northern abbeys. A Cato-like voice in favour of simplicity in monasteries and even in their churches; Matteo Villani, L. VIII, c. 10.

But the Italian monastery building possessed an element which in time greatly simplified free communication. This was the portico, instead of the closed cloister, which was open to the outside only by means of doors and windows.

Also in the case of closed walks with parapet-walls, as for example the cloisters of the Lateran and S. Paolo (§ 16), and even of solid walls with windows, e.g. the Campo Santo at Pisa, the amount of light and air coming in was appreciably more than in the North. By far the commonest since Roman times, however, were open arcaded galleries – with antique columns, e.g. the splendid atria of the Cathedrals of Capua and Salerno (eleventh century), which may be cited here. In the cloisters of Rome Antique columns were used now and then, as at the Aracoeli.

The character of the open gallery, of columns or piers, often of two, even three, storeys, lies essentially in the fact that it was understood, like the cortile of a secular building, as a living form of monastic building, while the Northern cloister – always on only one level, or with only a modest, closed upper storey – formed a separate, enclosed space.

In addition, the open gallery permitted, for a smaller outlay, very much greater freedom in planning, especially of bays, and the contents of the gallery (frescoes, monuments) were also visible from the cortile.

Moreover, while the northern monastery had only one cloister, in Italy the colonnaded gallery extended round all courts and served as the architectural expression of any kind of passage anywhere in the monastery. Main examples of the Gothic period: the cortili of the Santo at Padua; the courts and external galleries etc. of S. Francesco, Assisi. At the Madonna della Quercia, Viterbo, above a Gothic ground-floor a fine upper Ionic gallery by Danese di Cecco da Viterbo (*c* 1500).

§ 85 *A Summary View of Monastic Architecture*

The Renaissance succeeded in building in Italy much larger and finer monasteries than did the North in the fifteenth century. The splendidly logical layout and the beauty and variety of the colonnaded architecture gave it high significance. Individual instances of the main interior rooms achieved occasionally a standard of development which was already recognised as classic at the time.

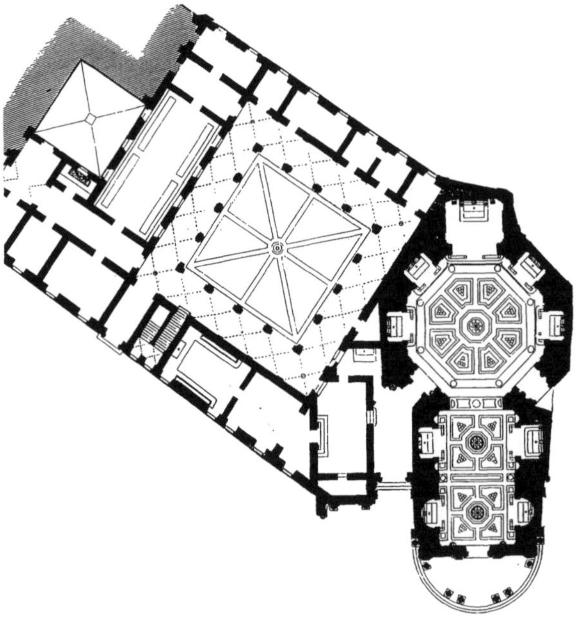

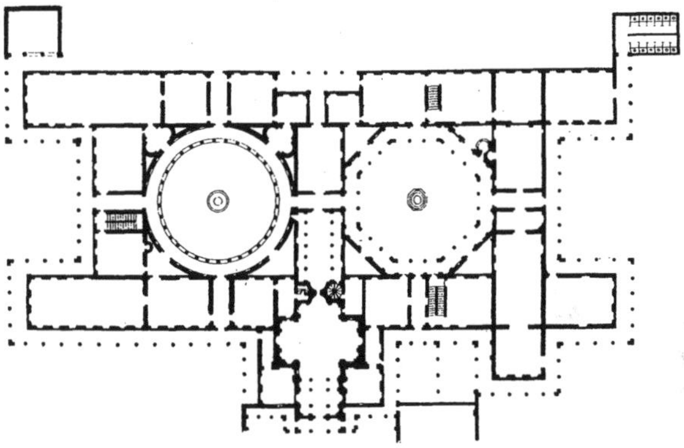

Fig. 188 *(top) Rome, Sta Maria della Pace, section and elevation of cloister*

Fig. 189 *(left) Rome, Sta Maria della Pace, plan of church and cloister*

Fig. 190 *(above) B. Peruzzi, design for a cloister*

The disintegration of the Benedictine Order in the North at this period is well known. In Italy apart from the great Certose, Camaldulensian and Cassinese monasteries, Vallombrosa and La Verna, for their artistic associations, ought probably to be considered, but the author is not familiar with them.

The colonnaded building, on columns or piers, creates out of the contrast between the storeys – whether the upper one has a wall with windows or an open colonnade – out of the proportions of the length and breadth to the height, out of wide or narrow bays, out of the handling of arches, mouldings and medallions in spandrels, with an ever fresh enthusiasm, one noble and graceful work after another. Many monastic cortili are listed individually in the author's *Cicerone*. A low parapet-wall was often retained, perhaps to prevent the penetration of damp from the court or garden.

Special features: §35 (Giul. da Sangallo); §46 (Certosa, Pavia). For convents of canons regular Brunellesco's Badia at Fiesole was an incomparable model; for Domini-

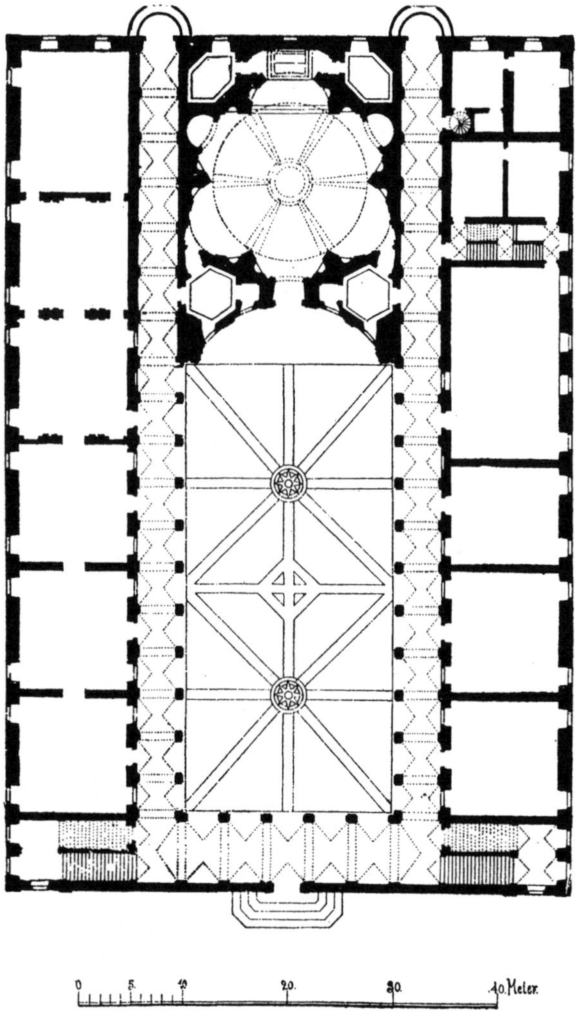

Fig. 191 *(left) Rome, Sant' Ivo della Sapienza, court*

Fig. 192 *(above) Rome, Sant' Ivo della Sapienza, plan*

can friaries that of S. Marco in Florence; built 1437–52 by Michelozzo: Vasari, II, p. 439 ff., *Vita di Michelozzo* ("the best-designed, finest and most commodious monastery in Italy": the eulogy is relative, to be understood of buildings of the Mendicant Orders, for the older Orders built more grandly).

Among Brunellesco's cortili the finest is the second at Sta Croce.

Cortili with piers: of unrivalled beauty, and at the same time simple: the atrium of Sta Maria presso S. Celso in Milan (§46), by Bernardino Zenale, perhaps after Crist. Solari, 1514–26; – also Bramante's court in the Canonica adjoining Sta Maria della Pace in Rome (Figs. 188, 189); between each pair of the much lower piers of the upper floor stands a column – i.e. above the centre of the lower arch (as in some Palazzi at Bologna, §46). Pedants condemned this delightful motive, and Serlio, L. IV, fol. 176, advanced only lame excuses for it. Perhaps by an immediate predecessor of Bramante the former monastery of the Umiliati at Cremona, now a presbytery: almost the same fine plan, but as a colonnaded cortile, predominantly in brick. In his earlier colonnaded cortili, at any rate in two at S. Ambrogio in Milan (now a military Hospital),* Bramante had given the upper, enclosed storey a pilaster Order, where also two bays correspond to one in the lower arcade.

* Now the Università Cattolica del Sacro Cuore. (PM).

Fig. 193 *Milan, Palazzo di Brera, court*

Among octagonal colonnaded cortili (Fig. 190) actually executed is that of S. Michele in Bosco, Bologna, dating from the good period of the sixteenth century; at the angles, and broken to conform to them, are piers with Corinthian pilasters; in the intervals each pair of columns carries an arch in the centre and a straight entablature at the sides. (Around, half-obliterated frescoes of the Carracci School.)

Fine wells and cisterns: the *pozzo* of S. Pietro in Vincoli in Rome, 1512; formerly, too, the one of the Gesuati in Florence.

Celebrated libraries: that at S. Giorgio Maggiore in Venice, endowed by Cosimo de' Medici in exile, 1433, and the vaulted three-aisled library of S. Marco in Florence, 1437–52, both by Michelozzo (the latter survives unaltered[1]).

Cf. the view into the Vatican Library, and in particular the building executed under Sixtus IV, used as a background for the well-known fresco by Melozzo da Forlì in the Vatican, in which Platina is represented kneeling before the Pope.

A famous refectory: the one endowed by Eugenius IV in 1442 at S. Salvatore, Venice, with richly sculptured cloister; Sansovino, *Venezia*, fol. 48. (Now lost?)

Monasteries of the higher rank, especially in the country or on spacious sites in towns, were sometimes provided with an extensive range of buildings bordering large gardens. S. Giustina in Padua, with its five cortili, once had – with its gardens, pastures and fishpools – the circumference of a mile; entirely surrounded with walls and water, and better described as *castrum* than *claustrum*: M. Savonarola in Murat., XXIV, col. 1143.

Exceedingly big: S. Severino, Naples; S. Ambrogio in Milan; Monte Cassino (with imposing atrium) etc.

Very complete: the Certose of Pavia and Florence; the latter, with the exception of the church, almost entirely Renaissance; the ground-plan in Grandjean and Famin, *Archit. Toscane*, arbitrarily altered. The Baths of Diocletian in Rome (Sta Maria degli Angeli), converted into a Certosa by Michelangelo, with its court of a hundred columns, now turned into a museum.

Of the monasteries near Florence destroyed in 1529,

1 This remarkable building, a large three-aisled hall, the central one with a barrel vault, the (wider) sides cross-vaulted, was soon to find itself almost exactly reproduced (1452), but with a different arrangement of columns, in the library at Cesena, the foundation of a Malatesta of Rimini. The plan might have been typical of libraries and perhaps found again elsewhere?

enthusiastic descriptions in Vasari, III, p. 570 ff., *V. di Perugino* (the monastery of the art-loving Gesuati, with a vista through all the colonnades into the gardens), and in Varchi, *Stor. Fiorent.*, III, p. 86 (monastery of S. Gallo).

Libraries, refectories, and grand staircases were often rebuilt in the seventeenth century in the grandiose Baroque taste.

Among Peruzzi's drawings in the Uffizi three fine projects for large monasteries, which were to contain *inter alia*: church, sacristy, confessionals, oratory, chapter-house, parlatorium, refectories, cloisters with fountains, hospital, hospice, library, steward's lodging, kitchens, larders, bakery, granary and oil-store, wash-house etc., as well as large gardens and galleries for summer and winter living; cf. Fig. 190, after the drawing reproduced in Redtenbacher, *B. Peruzzi u. seine Werke*, pl. 13.

(NOTE: The second cloister of Sta Croce is by an unknown follower of Brunelleschi, *c* 1452.

For monastic libraries see now J. O'Gorman, *The Architecture of the Monastic Library in Italy, 1300–1600*, New York, 1972.

Fragments of the refectory of S. Salvatore are said to be preserved in what is now the Direzione dei Telefoni, next to the church. (PM).

§86 *Bishops' Palaces and Universities*

Of episcopal residences, which may well come close in some respects to monastic premises, little has been preserved from the fifteenth century, though there are some excellent examples from the sixteenth.

That of Padua, built by Bishop Pietro Donato in 1445, excelled even contemporary Papal lodgings; it contained two very large saloni, two chapels, a host of rich rooms, large store-rooms, stabling for fifty horses, and a magnificent garden; Savonarola in Murat., col. 1171.

The Bishop's Palace at Pienza perhaps set the standard for the time? (Cf. the plan, Fig. 200, and also the publication by Mayreder and Bender, with text by H. Holtzinger, in the Allg. Bauzeitung, 1882.)

In the Archbishop's Palace at Pisa the colonnaded cortile in the manner of Brunellesco's cloisters, but larger in its proportions, and of white marble. (End of the fifteenth century.) In the Vescovado at Vicenza, in the cortile an elegant colonnade of 1494.

Of the first half of the sixteenth century, the simple and good Vescovado at Pavia.

Of the period 1540–80, the Arcivescovadi in Milan (Fig. 68) and Bologna, by Pellegrini, and in Florence, by Giov. Ant. Dosio; the first sombre, imposing (§56), in the last an unassuming court, with only seven columns and a couple of piers, but sophisticated and charming (cf. Proverbs, IX, 1).

These buildings are distinguishable from secular palaces by a slight, recognisable, nuance, difficult to define. The offices round the cortile sometimes give them the character of administrative buildings.

In a similar way the buildings of schools and universities approximate to monasteries, while seminaries, as complexes of lecture-rooms, were best disposed about a colonnaded cortile.

From the fifteenth century, the cortile of the University of Pisa reflects Brunellesco's type. A confusing description of the Collegio del Cardinale at Padua in Savonarola, in Murat., *cit.*, col. 1182. Spain and England have much finer examples.

From the sixteenth century Sansovino's beautiful (present) court of the University of Padua (1552), double colonnade with straight entablatures; and the majestic cortile of the Sapienza in Rome (Figs. 191, 192), perhaps after a design by Michelangelo; on the street side the building is characterised by the blind wall of the ground floor.

In the Jesuit colleges, even the earliest, the courts are genuine school quadrangles, and their lofty colonnades lead clearly into classrooms and not into monks' cells.

Fig. 194 *(opposite above) Genoa, the University, court*

Fig. 195 *(opposite below) Siena, Sta Caterina, court*

Fig. 196 *(above) Venice, Scuola di S. Rocco, elevation*

Fig. 197 *(right) Venice, Scuola di S. Rocco, plan*

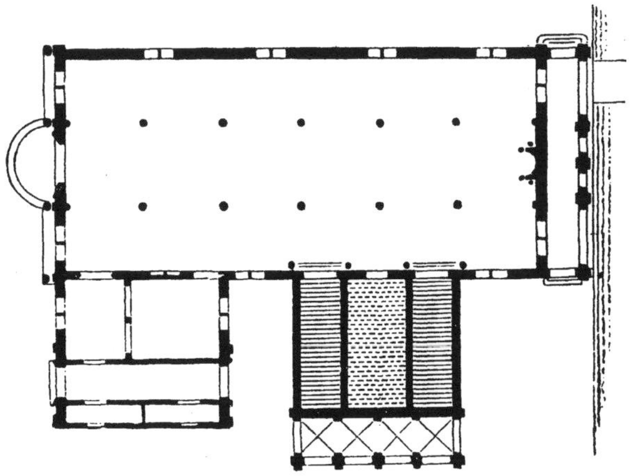

The earliest big one: the Collegio Romano, by Ammanati; the finest of the seventeenth century that of the Brera in Milan and the University of Genoa (Fig. 194), both former Jesuit colleges.

§87 *Buildings of Religious Confraternities*

The confraternities, or Scuole, endowed as corporate bodies, to protect the interests of fellow-countrymen in a foreign town, for common humanitarian activities, or for purposes of devotion, and often very rich (thanks to regular contributions and bequests), manifested themselves not only in magnificent processions, but in the monumental design of their buildings.

A large principal space of some sort was needed – whether enclosed or in the form of a courtyard – for assembly, councils, mounting of processions etc., – an altar in this space or in an adjoining chapel – a wardrobe for robes and banners (*gonfaloni*) – for wealthier brotherhoods also offices, counting-houses etc. Among the architectural features for these requirements must be mentioned: a simple chapel, serving also as an assembly-room; surplus resources expended, for example, on a sumptuous façade, at the Misericordia at Arezzo, and the Confraternità di S. Bernardino at Perugia (§70), cf. §51 and Fig. 58.

Two oratories superimposed, richly furnished; thus, S. Bernardino and S. Caterina at Siena; besides small or medium-sized courts; thus, Peruzzi's beautifully simple little cortile at S. Caterina (Fig. 195).

Typical form for Central Italy: an oratory and a colonnaded cortile; very fine at S. Giovanni Decollato in Rome, and in several confraternities in Florence, particularly Lo Scalzo, where besides Andrea del Sarto's frescoes the felicitous arrangement of the little colonnaded cortile merits attention; or the society built its chapel on to an already existing cloister, e.g. the Capp. de' Pittori in the monastery of the Annunziata.

In Venice earlier, only large simple rooms, filled with panel-paintings of the old Venetian School; Sabellicus, *De situ venetae urbis*, L. I, fol. 84; L. II, fol. 87. Later, the building became a self-contained palazzo which, apart from secondary rooms and staircase, consisted of a large lower hall and an equally big upper room with an altar: Scuola di S. Marco (1485), below, a colonnaded hall with a timber ceiling; Scuola di S. Rocco (from 1517) (Figs. 196, 197), below, as above, a vast room; decoration of the greatest splendour, with a wealth of paintings on canvas, even on the ceilings; in S. Giovanni Evangelista an elegant forecourt of 1481; the other Scuole almost all date from the Baroque period. In the Scuola di S. Rocco a very fine staircase.

The corporate institution and significance of the Venetian Scuole: Sansovino, *Venezia*, fol. 99 ff., a principal source which we should not neglect. Cf. fol. 57, the Confraternity of the Lucchesi, who had arranged their premises to the best advantage in the sixteenth century.

In addition, the Scuole often donated works of art of all kinds to the churches of the city, just as the Guilds did; perhaps a Holy Sepulchre in the cathedral of the town concerned (*Diario Ferrarese*, in Murat., XXIV, col. 390, for the year 1500); or a painting or relief, on which the often numerous officers of the Confraternity kneel beneath the cloak of the Madonna of Mercy, held aloft by angels (Vasari, I, p. 682, *V. di Spinello*; V, p. 165, *V. di Rosso*), or before an Enthroned Madonna with patron saints, or on either side of the suffering Christ (fresco by Luini in the Ambrosiana in Milan).

CHAPTER ELEVEN

The Architectural Character of the Palazzo

§88 *A Retrospective Glance at Earlier Italian Palace Architecture*

The domestic architecture of the Renaissance, which until now has practically dominated that of all civilised peoples, possessed as its most important characteristic a regular plan, a legacy of the Italian Gothic period (§21).

Nowadays, symmetrically built houses and palaces with Northern Gothic details represent sheer ingratitude to Italian architecture, without which there would be no symmetrical plan.

But in transplanting Venetian Gothic, which is certainly in harmony with symmetry, one does not remain nationalistically German any more than when one adopts the maturer forms of the same motivation, the Renaissance.

To build asymmetrically in Northern Gothic forms we need luck, money, and the appropriate mood, as well as total freedom from English Gothic detail, for on the Continent a more pleasing and polished expression of similar ideas is to be found distributed over many Late Gothic civil buildings.

The Italian Gothic palazzo had from its origin nothing in common with the mountain castle and its almost inevitably irregular plan, since from the eleventh century the principal dwellings of the nobility had always been in the towns.

In particular, such a palace had the façade drawn straight and not capriciously irregular; it had the same level for all the rooms on any one storey, so that one was not obliged to go from one room to another by neck-breaking steps; it had regular corridors giving access to rooms and did not rely on narrow, twisting passages, or on perpetual recourse to spiral stairs. Already the unity of ground-plan and elevation set the pattern for all other unities and architectural logic.

For polite private architecture a certain measure of superior design and finish was considered indispensable, although in the fourteenth century the word "palace" was used only for princely and public buildings.

(An established terminology recognised throughout Italy still existed in the fifteenth century and not later, though probably in individual towns. In the *Diario Ferrarese*, in Murat., XXIV, esp. col. 220, 337, and 390, there is throughout a sharp distinction between *palazzi*, *palazzotti* and *case*. In Venice everything was officially called, with the exception of the Doge's Palace, a *casa*, but in practice very many private houses were described as *palazzi*: Sansovino, *Venezia*, fol. 139.)

§89 *Emergence of Rules for Three-Dimensional Proportions*

The theorist Alberti gives, instead of aesthetic rules for the palace as a building, only a programme for its contents. In addition, however, he lays down the first principles according to his own observations for the three-dimensional proportions of individual rooms.

That the palace precincts formed part of the community was an understood fact since the fourteenth century, and would not have seemed to him worth stating. He himself built at least the Pal. Rucellai. Cf. §30, 40.

The principal sources: *De re aedific.*, L. V, c. 2, 3, 18; L. IX, c. 2, 3, 4. It appears to be more a patron than an architect who is speaking (cf. *Kultur der Renaiss.*, pp. 135, 140, 398 and note). He asks for many things, both in respect of function and propriety, but offers no solutions, and would have liked best to build everything at ground level, since stairs only disturb buildings, *scalas esse aedificiorum perturbatrices*. Given Florentine custom and the necessity to build high this naturally remained no more than a wish.

He discusses the rules of three-dimensional space not in relation to the palace, but to the suburban villa (IX, 3),

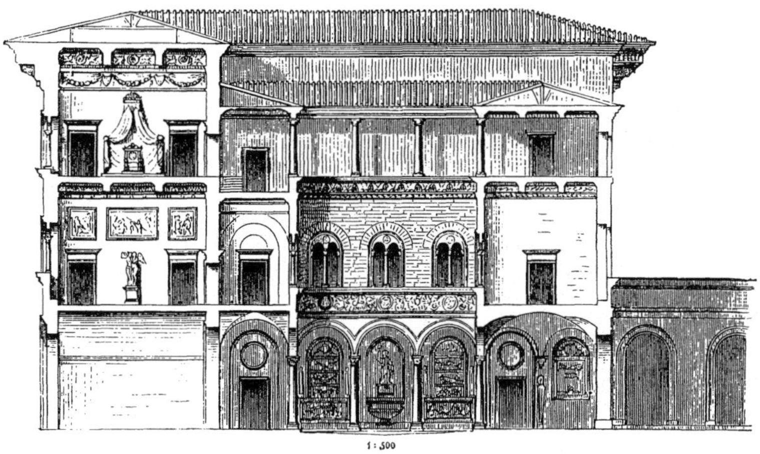

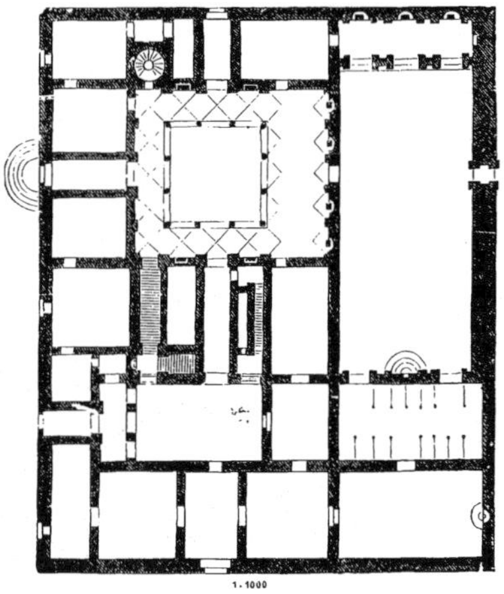

Figs. 198, 199 *Florence, Palazzo Medici-Riccardi, section and plan*

which makes no difference to our considerations. If he and others were scarcely at one as to whether they should be treated as mandatory or as a theoretical ideal, the Renaissance was becoming, nevertheless, clearly aware of itself, for the first time, as the architecture of space and mass. From a plethora of data let us take a few examples. Alberti gives the proportions adjusted according to whether the rooms are round or square, flat-roofed or vaulted. Larger rectangular rooms should have a width 5/4 the height if vaulted; 7/5 if flat-roofed – in both cases presupposing that the breadth to length is 1:2, for with 1:3 proportions different rules apply. With large dimensions the proportions are not the same as with small, because the angle of vision is different. Cortili should at most be twice as long as wide. Bedrooms are best 1/3 narrower than their length. Colonnades (*porticus*) have proportions of 3 or 4:1, and here a ratio of 6:1 should not be exceeded. For the narrow side of a room there should be a single window, which must be decisively higher than wide or wider than high. (In practice the equilateral window was banished from the principal storeys and was used only as a lucarne in the frieze or as a barred-window in a deliberately austere rusticated ground storey.) If the window is higher than wide, its opening should be $1\frac{1}{2}$ times as high as it is wide, and not amount to more than 1/3, or less than 1/4, of the total internal wall-area; it should start at between 2/9 and 4/9 of the height of the room above the floor. If the window is wider than high, and thus supported on two colonettes, its opening must be between 1/2 and 2/3 of the width of the wall. In the long wall there should be, where possible, an uneven number of windows, perhaps three – as with the Ancients – the wall being divided into five or seven parts with windows in three of them which in height should be 7:4 or 9:5 of the width, and so on.

Compared with the scanty similar information in Vitruvius, L. VI, c. 4–6, which take into account neither vault nor windows, an uncommonly big step forward is apparent here.

§90 *Nature and Beginnings of the Renaissance Palace*

The general ideal of civil architecture was less clearly expressed in residences and public buildings, which had their own particular and multifarious purposes to fulfil, than in private palaces, which displayed their unity of purpose and function on their façades and by their general similarity of character were able to form definite stylistic groups.

The palazzo in this particular sense is a monumental structure, in which each, or at any rate the principal, elevation expresses only one idea, and that with great emphasis, while the ground-plan is defined in a regular geometrical pattern.

The individual functions which had to be performed under one roof conformed to this unity at least as well as to a scattered layout; there was also the fact that the similarity of purpose made it easier to adapt the favourable aspects of the internal arrangements to a more functional and more beautiful form, which would be a public benefit.

An organism in the stricter sense cannot be expected of the palazzo, since the many and various things which it embraces may not be expressed collectively, but are subject to the inventive resource of the artist.

Soon after the beginning of the fifteenth century, independently of the formal principles of the Renaissance, there began a movement in palace design which led to a fundamental advance in function and convenience. Cf. in Milanesi, II, p. 144, the important letter (1428) from Jacopo della Quercia living in Bologna to the authorities in his native Siena, who inquired about the significant buildings associated with one particular master: the man in question, Giovanni da Siena, was employed by the Marchese (Nicolò) d' Este in Ferrara at three hundred ducats a year and free board and lodging for eight persons in building a large and strong castle in the town, "not a master with a trowel in his hand, but a *chonponitore e giengiero*" (i.e. engineer); in Bologna itself was the ex-

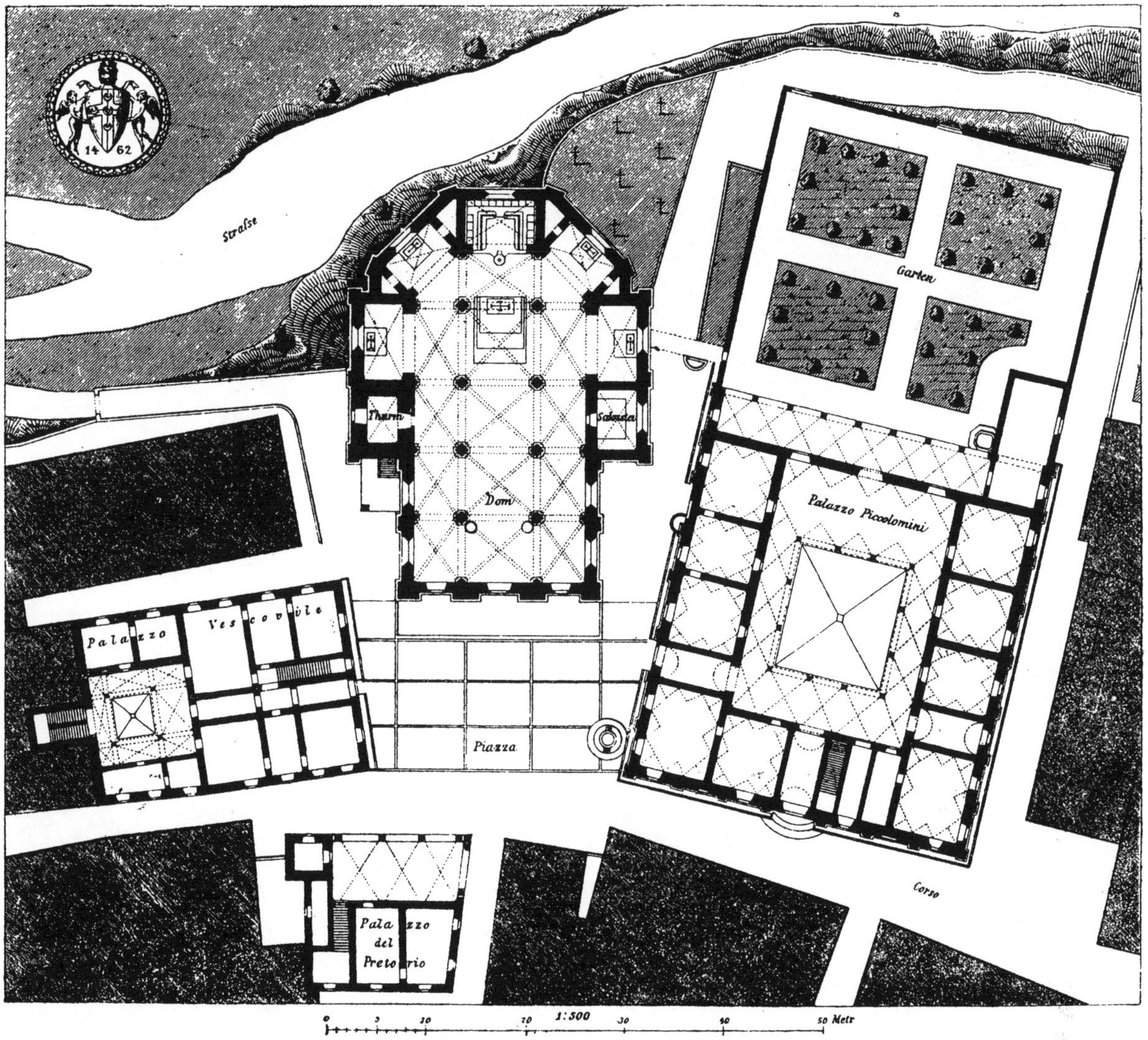

Fig. 200 *Pienza, plan of Cathedral and palaces in centre*

cellent Fioravante, who had built the elegant palace of the Papal Legate, and in Perugia the castle of Braccio da Montone; in form he inclined more than the other towards the *pelegrino* – i.e. to what was then foreign and new, the Renaissance (as also used by Manetti, *Vita di Brunellesco*, ed. Holtzinger, p. 43); he, too, did not handle a trowel or any other tool.

Notable palaces of this period: that of the Colonna in Gennazzano; cf. Pii II *Comment.* L. VI, p. 308; and especially that of the Patriarch Vitelleschi (*d* 1440) at Corneto (now Pal. Soderini), erected as a lodging for great lords, and even Popes, with thickly shaded and well-watered gardens; Paul. Jovii *Elogia* (sub Jo. Vitellio); Jac. Volaterran., in Murat., XXIII, col. 152.

It is very relevant to the history of the early Renaissance that the palaces of the Aragonese kings have disappeared, while those of the Popes and Sforzas have been rebuilt and all the other remains of the princely buildings of the time, except for Urbino and Mantua, have not yet been systematically investigated.

§91 *The Tuscan Type*

Among the positively evolved palace types the Florentine-Sienese, the earliest, occupied first place for a long time and set for the whole of Italy the basic and authoritative standard, together with the new formal vocabulary emanating from Florence.

The development of the façades cf. §39, 40, where the principal buildings are enumerated.

The key building was the palace of Cosimo de' Medici (later Pal. Riccardi, now Prefecture) in the Via Larga (now Cavour), Florence, by Michelozzo (Figs. 198, 199), which was begun only in 1444, after the Pal. Pitti had been started; later considerably rebuilt inside and also enlarged, but the well laid out stairs next to the cortile still survive.

Francesco Sforza had presented Cosimo with a palace in Milan; the latter sent Michelozzo there and had a new building erected, comprising ground and upper floors only, which was rated a marvel in the skilful succession

Fig. 201 *Florence, Palazzo Gondi, court*

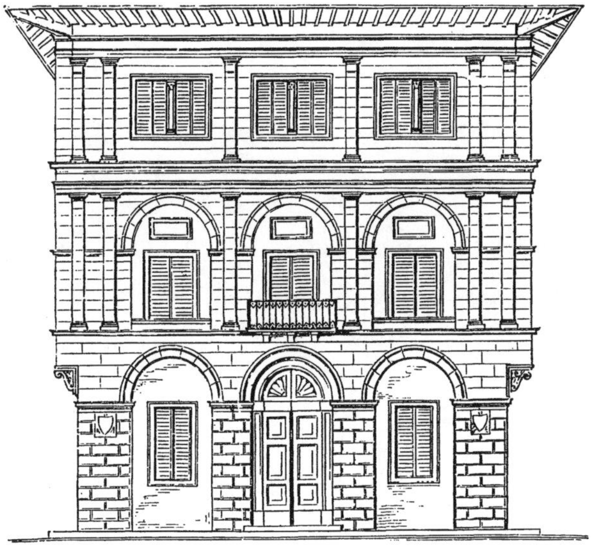

Fig. 202 *Florence, Palazzo Serristori, elevation*

of rooms, the correctness of their planning and their decoration. A detailed, but far from explicit, description is given in Book XXI by Filarete (§31) and printed in the supplements to the *Anonimo Morelliano*. Now Casa Vismara in Via de' Bossi; only the portal is preserved, the side figures later (now in the Museo Archeologico in the Castello Sforzesco) and the lower colonnade of the first cortile, round arches and octagonal piers.

The vital principle of the Tuscan façade is the total symmetry of treatment, the rejection of any special feature in the centre or at the corners of the composition.

Proof of the lofty attitude of Florentine art, which in an age addicted to ornament renounced everything which could in any way divert the attention, even magnificent doorways, and applied its resources even-handedly to a single whole.

Even when perhaps the windows are designed with greater splendour, e.g. in the palace of Pius II at Pienza, they are all equally so.

Of the planning of the interior and the dominant intentions behind it, Pius gives a most important account in relation to his palazzo at Pienza (Fig. 200). Pii II, *Comment.*, L. IX, p. 425 ff. Other references to Pienza, II, p. 78; IV, p. 200; VIII, p. 377, 394; IX, p. 396. Cf. §8, 11, 40; also the publication by Mayreder, Bender and Holtzinger in the Allgem. Bauzeitung, 1882.

Rooms of every description, including dining-rooms for three different seasons, lie conveniently about the cortile, sometimes on the vaulted ground storey, sometimes above it. To the right, and adjoining the colonnade (as in the Pal. Medici) the gently rising main staircase; twenty broad steps, each a single stone nine feet long, lead to a landing with a window, and twenty thence in the reverse direction to the upper corridor; the same thing applies to the second-storey stairs. (Spiral staircases, then a principal item of luxury in Northern royal castles, were regarded by the Tuscans as permissible only in the service quarters, as indicated in the account of Casa Vismara, or as secret emergency stairs.) The first floor no longer had an open gallery on the court side, but an enclosed passage with quadrangular windows and a flat coffered ceiling; from it doors open to the right into a large room, to which two small rooms and a closet are linked; left into the summer dining-room, connecting with the chapel. At the back, which is open to the air on all three storeys to exploit the fine view,[1] there is a large room with several (in this case, six) symmetrical doors which ever since then has usually served in Italian palaces as a waiting room or ceremonial room, festively decorated with tapestries. The doors on the shorter sides lead into two small state rooms. The top floor has the same plan as the middle one, but is less richly decorated. The building full of light and convenience (a special extension for the kitchen at the rear); everywhere the same level and nowhere a step to climb. The main axial view passes through the vestibule, cortile, the back of the building and outer colonnade to the end of the garden. (Cf. §97.)

In cortili the Tuscan school remained on the whole loyal to the column until well into the Baroque period; a particularly elegant prototype, the cortile of the Pal. Gondi in Florence (by Giul. da Sangallo). The character of the stone, *pietra serena*, perfectly fitted the graceful simplicity of all the elements of courts of this type (Fig. 201).

Probably unique of its kind is a project by Giuliano da Sangallo of *c* 1480 for a Medici palace in the Via Laura in Florence (drawing in the Uffizi, reproduced by Redtenbacher in the Allgem. Bauzeitung, 1879, p. 2),* a building half urban palazzo, half villa, free-standing amid gardens, embracing on three sides a cortile with amphitheatrical rows of seats, and strongly articulated by salients and wings; in every respect symmetrical. A preliminary study for it seems to be the plan dated 1488 in Giuliano's sketchbook in the Bib. Barberini (now in the Vatican). Was the plan, known at least in its principal features from Serlio's very cursory sketch, for the palace of Poggio Reale at Naples, which Lorenzo de' Medici is said to have roughed out for Giuliano da Majano (§118), based on this new idea of Sangallo?

1 This opening of a palace on the garden side occurs quite often in Italy up to recent times, but here and there the opened part has since been walled up to form new rooms. In the Pal. Farnese in Rome all three storeys of the garden elevation incorporated large open galleries, that of the middle storey being walled in when the Galleria of Annibale Carracci was made there. Another very fine example: the garden front of the Pal. di Firenze, in Rome, by Vignola.

* G. Marchini, *G. da Sangallo*, Florence, 1942, dates this *c* 1498. (PM).

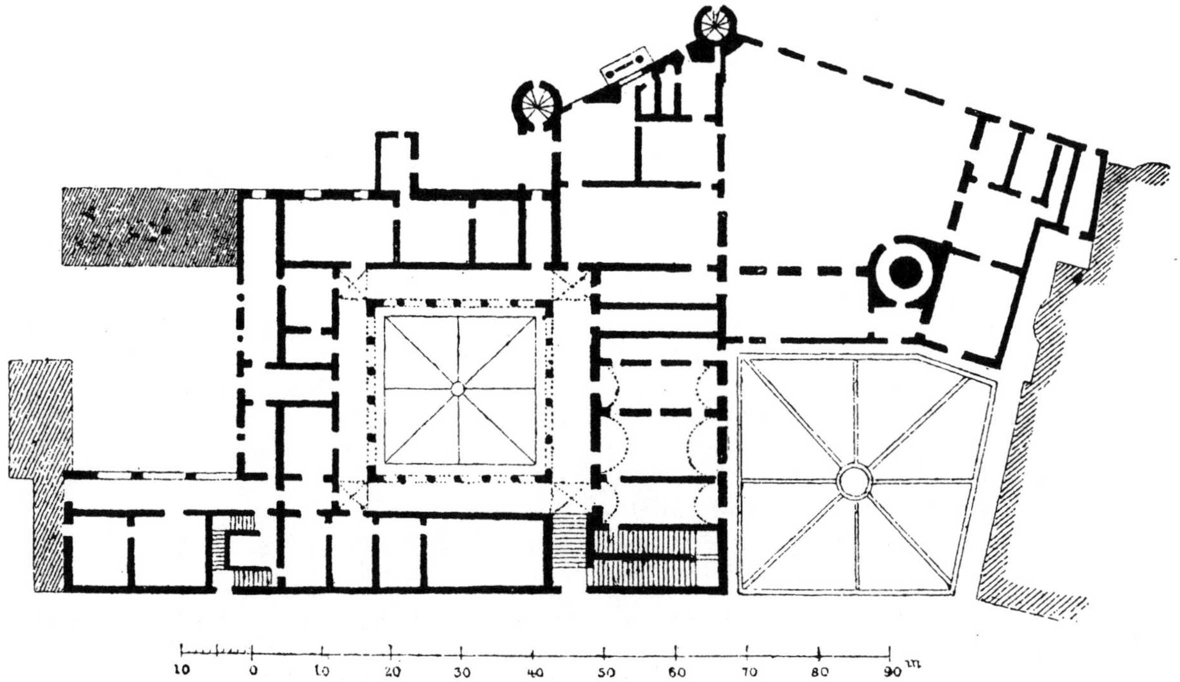

Fig. 203 *(above) Urbino, Palazzo Ducale, court*

Fig. 204 *(below) Urbino, Palazzo Ducale, plan*

§92 *The Influence of Tuscan Palace Architecture*

There grew up a widespread prejudice in favour of Tuscan palace architects. Towards the end of the fifteenth century the Florentine house acquired through Baccio d' Agnolo the formal solemnity which allows one to forget palatial size and splendour.

The ubiquity of Tuscan masters and rustication in Italy: §15 and 40. The dissatisfaction of Federigo of Urbino and Lorenzo il Magnifico §11. Giuliano da Sangallo's many-sided activities, §59. Clearly the Tuscan façade was less in demand than the excellently contrived interior.

Whoever expects enlightenment concerning the architectural form of the house from Franc. Maria Grapaldus, *De partibus aedium*, is doomed to disappointment.

Regarding Baccio d' Agnolo (1460–1543), the father of two not unworthy sons, see Vasari, V, pp. 351, 354 and §152. About his houses (promoted since then to palazzi): Bartolini (Fig. 59), Serristori (Cocchi, 1469–74, not by Baccio) (Fig. 202), Levi (Ginori), Rosselli etc., cf. the author's *Cicerone*, 10th ed., II, I, p. 301 f. A particularly noble house façade in Siena: Pal. della Ciaja (now Constantini), op. cit., II, p. 134. As a general rule the omission of rustication (§9, 39) is characteristic of the house in contrast to the palazzo, but by no means always. Mass and form and the restraints that these may imply were and remained in each individual case matters of finer artistic sensibility.

§93 *The Palace of Urbino and the Buildings of the Romagna*

Next to the Palazzo Medici, the Palace of Urbino in particular ranked in the fifteenth century as a classic example of its type; later the massive brick palace of the Bentivogli in Bologna became the third to join the company.

Regarding the Palace of Urbino, see Vasari, II, p. 661, in the commentary on the *V. di Baccio Pontelli*, and III, p. 70, n. 4, *V. di Francesco di Giorgio*; also Antonio di Francesco Mercatello (1480), in Cod. Vat. Urb. lat. 785, excerpted in Schmarsow, *Melozzo da Forlì*, p. 353 ff., and also the further literature cited there and the analysis of the building, as well as the splendid work by Arnold, *Der herzogl. Palast von Urbino*, 1857, and Th. Hoffmann, *Die Bauten des Herzogs Federigo von Montefeltro*, 1905. Cf. also the rhymed Chronicle by Giovanni Santi, *Federigo da Montefeltro*, ed. by H. Holtzinger, 1893, Bk XIV, cap. 59, 60. The great Federigo da Montefeltro was engaged in building and decorating the palace from 1447; from 1467 Luciano da Laurana's involvement in the work is known; a Patent of Federigo of 1468 confirms him officially as master of the works, which he continued to direct in all essential respects until the end (Fig. 204); by him, not by Baccio Pontelli, according to Mercatello the marvellous cortile (Fig. 203), as also the library, studiolo and state rooms. In the internal adornment (but not before 1479; cf. Vasari, II, p. 669 ff.; Müntz, *Les arts à la cour des Papes*, III, p. 75) there took part as *lignaiolo* Baccio Pontelli who, in 1481, also sent to Lorenzo il Magnifico in response to a request brought to him by Giuliano da Majano, an exact drawing of the palace: Gaye, *Carteggio*, I, p. 274. In general the palace, although sited on rugged, sloping ground, and therefore externally irregular, enjoyed the highest reputation for its completely functional layout and princely splendour. The main stairs, according to Vasari the most excellent that ever were till then, are none the less (in a manner which still clearly indicates the modesty of the fifteenth century in matters of staircases) kept out of sight. Probably also by Laurana the fine colonnaded cortile in the small Ducal Palace at Gubbio (1474–80), "one of the finest which one can see", in the opinion of the Venetian ambassadors mentioned in §42. (Cf. the publication of Laspeyres in the *Zeitschrift für Bauwesen*, 1881, and the work by Th. Hoffmann mentioned above; the latter believes that the hand of Francesco di Giorgio is identifiable here.)

Besides the palace at Urbino and the Pal. di Venezia in Rome, Filippo de Lignamine (writing in 1474, printed in Eccard, *Scriptores*, I, col. 1312) extols especially the palaces of Count Tagliacozzo in Bracciano and Gio. Orsini, Archbishop of Trani, in Vicovaro, which rival each other in splendour, garden and water architecture, colonnades and size of rooms.

The palace of the Bentivogli at Bologna, destroyed in 1506, not a precursor but perhaps the supreme flowering of the brick architecture of the Romagna; Paul. Jovii, *Elogia* (sub Jo. Bentivolo), cf. *Kultur der Renaiss.*, p. 509. Several members of this semi-princely house still had their own private palaces.

Regarding Bologna and the Romagna in general, §6, 45. The Bolognese façades do not form lengthways a self-contained composition, since their ground storeys incorporate the continuous street-arcades. In the absence of an identifiable centre, the doors, standing in the shadow of the colonnade and hence not a fit object for ornament, could be placed wherever convenient. Cortili and staircases, apart from the often great beauty of their forms, were generally arranged in quite small spaces, a convention continuing until late in the Baroque period. (The cortili, cf. §46, Figs. 205, 206, 207.)

In Ferrara the incomplete and half-ruinous Pal. Scrofa, by Biagio Rossetti, 1502, with magnificent cortile, which has on the garden side a colonnaded loggia and a square room painted with excellent frescoes (Fig. 208; cf. Fig. 51).

§94 *The Venetian Type*

Venice, in relation to the design of palaces, was heir to an accomplished Gothic tradition and was the home of the idea of grouped elements – in this sense the opposite to and complement of Florence.

For the following: Sansovino, *Venezia*, fol. 139 ff., and

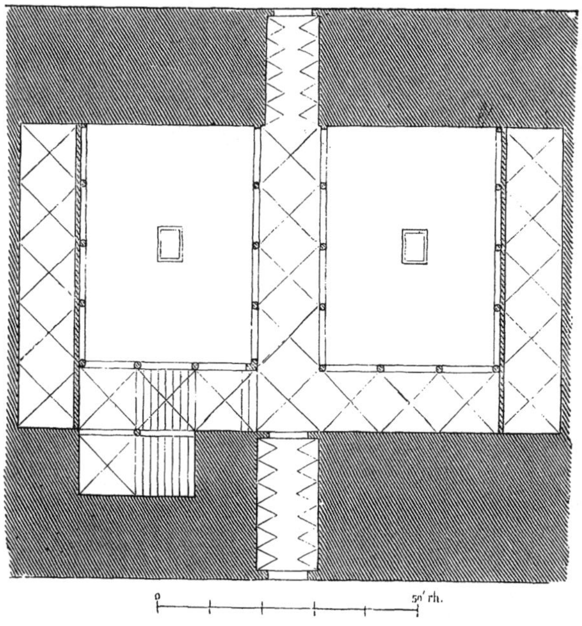

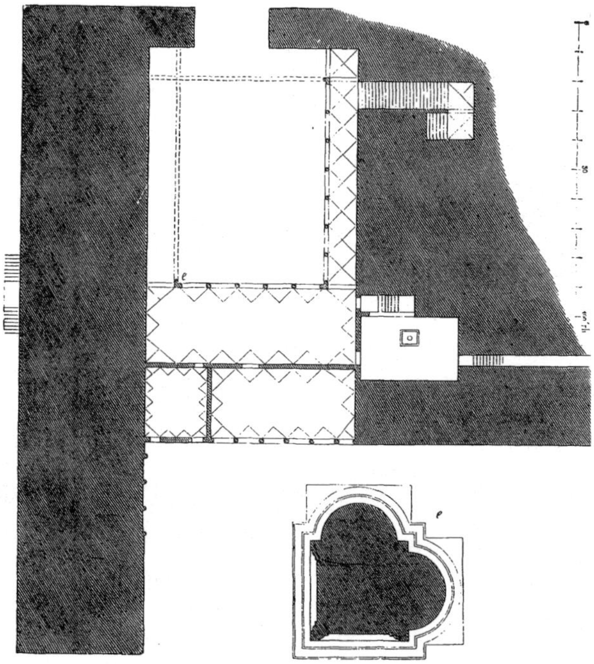

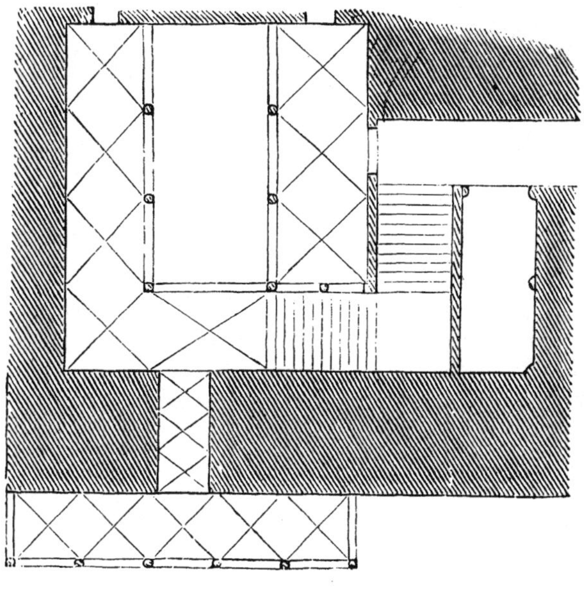

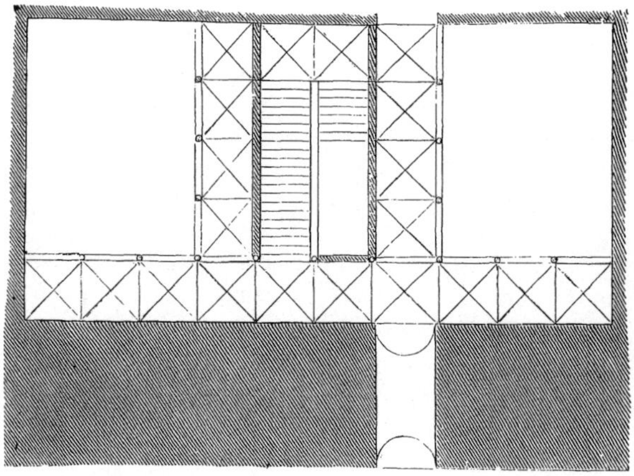

Fig. 205 *(above left) Bologna, Palazzo Pizzardi, plan*

Fig. 206 *(left) Bologna, plan of house near Palazzo Pepoli*

Fig. 207 *(below left) Bologna, Palazzo Fantuzzi, plan*

Fig. 208 *(above right) Ferrara, Palazzo Scrofa, plan*

Serlio, L. III, fol. 79; also L. IV, passim. Sabellico is rewarding only for decoration, not for the structural plan. Regarding the Gothic palaces, § 21; the incrustation of façades, and its consequences, § 42, 43.

A large room with two rows of lesser rooms on either side extends right through the customary three storeys and opens in much the same manner at each end, on to a canal and a side-street or piazza. On the ground floor a door or water-gate and smaller windows, the secondary rooms often serving as cellars. On the two upper floors the principal room (*Salone*) occupies the whole depth with large loggie or windows grouped in threes at both ends, and on either side symmetrically placed doors; along both its sides small rooms, each with two windows.

The windows usually have balconies. (The more strictly interpreted architecture repudiated balconies supported on consoles, cf. § 102, and Serlio for the same reason shows in his Book IV a fine Venetian façade, on which the balconies, by retracting the upper part of the wall, rest securely on the wall of the ground floor. (As on the Pal. del Podestà, Bologna, 1492 onwards.))

The stairs, generally in the ancillary rooms, are of little significance here; all the more to be admired are some not found in private palaces: those in the Scuola di S. Marco and the felicitously planned and worthily ornamented staircase in the Scuola di S. Rocco (§ 87), as also the Scala d'Oro in the Doge's Palace.

Fig. 209 *Verona, Palazzo Bevilacqua*

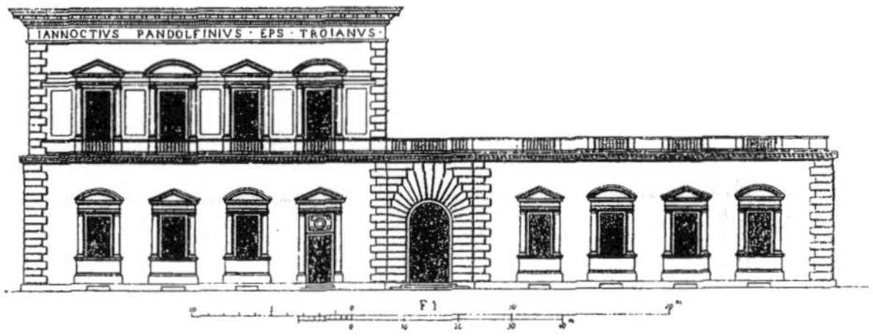

Fig. 210 *(above) Verona, Palazzo Pompei, elevation*

Fig. 211 *(below) Florence, Palazzo Pandolfini, elevation*

Cortili, where they existed, for long enjoyed no special importance of their own, other than to provide a measure of light for the building and for the cisterns, whose water was considered wholesome only when exposed to air and light.

At the beginning of the sixteenth century, following the marked growth of architectural display (§42), costly accommodation became the rule, and Sansovino and Sanmicheli were permitted to arrange their cortili with pillared arcades, and on the exterior apply classical forms on a very large scale to particular features of the design.

Such cortili were described as built *alla romana*. Jacopo Sansovino built "according to the rules of Vitruvius" the Pal. Delfino, Pal. Cornaro etc.

Sanmicheli, with even greater freedom, opened the upper storey of the Palazzo Grimani with giant windows like triumphal arches. In his Pal. Bevilacqua at Verona (Fig. 209) he gave to the upper floor, above a rusticated ground storey, a highly festive character; to the Pal. Pompei, also in Verona, an air of austere splendour (Fig. 210).

Milan, however, among a wealth of excellent buildings had no special palace-type, while Genoa did not acquire one until later. Naples is strikingly devoid of palaces of the good period.

The Milanese brick cortili etc. §46. Regarding Genoa, §105. In Naples a preference for grand entrances was already noticeable in the fifteenth century; the only truly classical building, the Palazzo Gravina (now Post Office), by Gabriele d' Agnolo, has been so much altered that it would be better not to have survived.

§95 *Rome and Roman Patrons*

Rome, which attracted to itself the energies of all Italy, not only because of the varied background of the artists, but also because of the differing aims of the patrons, had at first no dominant palace-type. In the years 1500–1540 it was the city of constant novelty and diversity, the great centre for exchanging architectural ideas.

Letrouilly, *Edifices de Rome moderne*, 3 vols.

The patrons: the prominent families, who earlier had been satisfied with the buildings of the landed nobility; their standards rose from 1470, as, for example, an Orsini who was building a palace at Bracciano: *non tam ad frugalitatem romani proceris* (i.e. Baron) *quam ad romanor. pontificum dignitatem*; Jac. Volaterran., in Murat., XXIII, col. 147.

The richer cardinals and their increasing architectural luxury since Pius II, cf. §8. Under Sixtus IV, whose spendthrift nephew Cardinal Pietro Riario introduced the earliest known ventilating system at a princely

Fig. 212 *Rome, Palazzo Farnese, elevation detail*

Fig. 213 *Rome, Palazzo Sciarra, elevation detail*

reception in his palace – admittedly, a merely temporary device with bellows (1473); cf. Corio, *Storia di Milano*, fol. 417 ff. (cf. below, §188).

Palazzo della Cancelleria, 1486–89, built for Cardinal Raffaello Riario – Pal. Giraud-Torlonia (for Cardinal Adriano di Corneto) – Pal. Farnese (for Paul III when cardinal) and others.

Several of the most important palaces and houses were built by prelates of all ranks, secretaries of the Papal Curia, etc. Partly no doubt because there was no safer haven for capital and also because such men had no direct heirs. Added to this, architectural ambition and the desire to perpetuate one's name, which could easily be repeated in the inscriptions on friezes.

The architectural rivalry of secular families sought to express equality of status; that of clerical princes was turned towards originality.

Anyone who let off his ground floor as shops still wanted to have a palace, and the rents helped to cover the greater costs of building. This was the case with Bramante's Pal. Caprini (later the House of Raphael), the Pal. Vidoni-Caffarelli and the house of Branconio d' Aquila (Raphael, see below), the Pal. Maccarani and Cicciaporci (Giulio Romano), Pal. Niccolini (Jacopo Sansovino); mostly prelates' buildings.

The important Papal palaces also naturally influenced in many ways the style of private palazzi.

Fig. 214 *Rome, Palazzo Caprini (House of Raphael), elevation detail*

§96 *Roman Types of Façade*

Rome possessed above all the noblest rusticated façades with pilasters.

Pal. Giraud-Torlonia and the Cancelleria, §40, 56, 95; Figs. 34, 35. Pre-Bramantesque façades, §41.

The direct opposite, however, was created by a number of façades with strict separation of stone detail and wall-treatment, so that plinth, windows, doors, mouldings and quoins, entirely of stone, stand out as emphatically defined sculptural features (§54) from a stucco wall-surface, but Orders of engaged columns and pilasters are omitted.

If we want to talk of a Roman palace-type, this was the main one.

The earliest example of large stucco surfaces, from which only mouldings, windows and portals are excepted (still without rustication at the corners): the east and north fronts of the main building of the Pal. di Venezia (under Paul II, 1464–71), still crowned by battlements carried on consoles (Fig. 30).

The consummate development of the type: Pal. di Sora, wrongly attributed to Bramante.

The finest example is not in Rome, but in Florence: Pal. Pandolfini, 1516–20, built to Raphael's plans by Francesco and Aristotile da Sangallo (Fig. 211), with exquisite resource in detail and noble proportions.

The largest and most influential instance: Pal. Farnese in Rome, by the younger Antonio da Sangallo, begun before 1534 (Fig. 212).

Later: Pal. Sciarra (Fig. 213); Pal. Ruspoli and others.

When windows were given vigorously modelled surrounds and even free-standing columns (§51), the eye could very well do without pilaster Orders.

Next to this type, which was long to remain dominant, yet another celebrated group of buildings emerge, their principal characteristics lying, although with marked differences, in a very strong contrast between ground floor and *piano nobile*. Ever since Bramante had championed a boldly modelled mode of expression, he liked to add half-columns, even coupled ones, while his disciple, Raphael, added niches as well; the ground storey mostly heavily rusticated (sometimes simply stucco over a rubble core); the remaining surfaces often of ashlar masonry panels.

The key buildings were Bramante's Pal. di S. Biagio in the Via Giulia (the law-courts projected by Julius II) and Pal. Caprini (later Pal. de' Convertendi, now destroyed). The first palace – only the ground floor was executed – was designed with a façade ninety-seven metres long; towers being intended above the centre and at the four corners. Pal. Caprini, acquired in 1517 by Raphael, completely altered externally *c* 1580; cf. Lafreri's engraving (Fig. 214), and also Gnoli in the Archiv. stor. dell' arte, II, p. 145 ff.

By Raphael: Pal. Vidoni-Caffarelli in Rome, later partly altered and extended (Fig. 215).[1] Without rusticated ground storey and engaged columns, but also strikingly imposing in the form of windows, quoins, mouldings, etc. – Pal. Pandolfini in Florence, 1516–20, built to Raphael's plans by Fr. da Sangallo (see above).

A quintessence of every form, which Raphael contrived to concentrate according to the laws of beauty in one façade: the house of the Papal Camerlengo, Branconio d' Aquila, usually wrongly called Raphael's own house (Fig. 216), known only from an engraving, and a drawing by Parmigianino (in the Uffizi), destroyed in 1667; Vasari IV, p. 364, n. 2, *V. di Raffaello.* Below, under

1 Pal. Uguccioni in Florence, with its two upper storeys (Fig. 62), earlier attributed to Raphael, was built *c* 1550 by Mariotto di Zanobi Folfi.

Fig. 215 *Rome, Palazzo Vidoni-Caffarelli, elevation*

five great arches with Doric half-columns, shops, with the windows of a small mezzanine above them; in the *piano nobile* five windows with strong pediments and half-columns, with niches for statues in between; above the pediments splendid stucco swags, and between these the lucarnes of a second mezzanine; finally, the five windows of the top storey, with alternating oblong, framed, wall-panels.

For this building and Raphael's other palaces cf. Geymüller, *Raffaello Sanzio studiato come architetto*, the relevant section pp. 51–59.

The front elevation of the Pal. Spada (Vasari, VII, p. 70, *V. di Dan. da Volterra*), by Mazzoni (Fig. 217), is despite its effectiveness only a misconceived imitation of the Palazzo d' Aquila; but the façade to the cortile is considerably better.

In contrast to all these, the façades mentioned in §95 by Giulio and Sansovino achieve a strong and pleasing impression by the simplest means; at the top mostly panels of masonry.

The greatest possible unity of the crowning cornice (§38) was maintained on façades of the utmost variety in Rome.

The great three-arched loggia by Giacomo della Porta occupies the centre of the rear elevation of the Pal. Farnese, flush with the rest of the frontage; it is given a special, lighter cornice, the top of which nevertheless continues in line with that of the whole palace (by Michelangelo, §50).

It was not until the middle of the seventeenth century that the Baroque style broke with this custom.

§97 *Cortili of Roman Palazzi*

The cortili of Roman palaces embrace every conceivable combination within this style, the sublimest pillared architecture with engaged columns, the finest colonnades, the most ingenious inventions which give the illusion of grand features in a small compass, and finally the most brilliant expedients for creating a monumental impression with few materials and little space. Sometimes they are triumphs of perfect proportion and visual beauty.

Arcades with half-columns: the most important example from the fifteenth century – the arcade, realised only in part, of the larger court of the Pal. di Venezia (§37); from the sixteenth century and supremely accomplished, the cortile of the Pal. Farnese (Fig. 218) by Antonio da Sangallo the Younger, probably not uninfluenced by the Bramante design for the law-courts in Via Giulia (§96); the two lower storeys of the Pal. Farnese closely related to the Theatre of Marcellus, the top one – by Michelangelo – enclosed, with windows.

The cortile of the Cancelleria (Fig. 219), excellently proportioned in length to width and height, with two arcades on Doric columns all round; above them an enclosed upper storey with Corinthian pilasters; the columns probably came from the adjoining church of S. Lorenzo in Damaso, which was recast and given piers in place of them (§77).

The octagonal pier, which was more frequent about the middle of the fifteenth century (Fig. 220), had quite gone out of use since Bramante's time.

Other good cortili of the Golden Age: in the Pal. della Valle, Pal. Lante etc.: of the late Renaissance, Pal. Lancelotti.

In several cortili, sometimes by little-known architects, the arcade was actually open only on one or two sides and simulated on the others, filled in with a wall which contained windows (occasionally blind); the upper storey was also continued right round in the same way; only by this most beautiful and legitimate of all decep-

Fig. 216 *Rome, former Palazzo Branconio d'Aquila (after Geymüller)*

tions was a strict harmony achieved for the whole scheme. Perhaps the earliest example: Pal. Linotte (Regis) in Rome (Fig. 221), probably by A. da Sangallo the Younger, built between 1517–24 for a French prelate.

In quite small dimensions a grander impression was created by the judicious exploitation of a vista and the play of light, with the aid of a few columns, a fountain, or a garden entrance. (How much of all this will be preserved in the present rebuilding of Rome is uncertain.)

A grand perspective, deliberately contrived: according to Michelangelo the *Farnese Bull*, as a fountain feature, was intended to be visible through the entrance vestibule with its Doric columns, the cortile and the colonnade behind; on the same axis a bridge over the Tiber was to lead into the gardens of the Farnesina; Vasari, VII, p. 224 f. *V. di Michelangelo*. Cf. §91, the palace in Pienza.

Incomparable were the two main cortili of the Vatican: Cortile di S. Damaso by Bramante and Raphael (the Loggie, cf. §60), and the huge Cortile di Belvedere (§35, begun 1503), unhappily never realised completely; a lower cortile and an upper ornamental garden – Giardino della Pigna – linked to each other by vast ramp-staircases (§117, 126; Fig. 222), now replaced by Biblioteca, Braccio Nuovo etc.; a colossal apse, crowned by a semicircular gallery, forms the terminating feature of the colonnaded architecture embracing the Giardino della Pigna.

§98 *Irregular Ground-Plans: Mezzanines*

Rome is also the city where architects learned to erect noble, monumental buildings on cramped, irregular sites.

Fig. 217 *Rome, Palazzo Spada*

Florence, from time immemorial, had had too many straight streets to be forced to fit good buildings into hopelessly distorted and mis-shapen sites. In Rome under Julius II and Leo X everything was concentrated on the Campus Martius, Via Giulia, the vicinity of the Pantheon, the Piazza Navona etc.; in a word, the tangle of streets of constricted medieval Rome.

Baldassare Peruzzi applied the resources of his mature scholarship to the Pal. Massimi alle Colonne (from 1535), located in a winding and (until 1888) narrow street, sacrificing the façade as a whole, but raising its curvature to a motive of the greatest charm in the ground floor portico and distributing corridors, stairs,

Fig. 218 *(left) Rome, Palazzo Farnese, detail of court elevation*

Fig. 219 *(above) Rome, Palazzo della Cancelleria, court detail*

saloni and a small, though uniquely beautiful, cortile (§35) in the most admirable fashion over an irregular ground plan (Fig. 223). Every one of the individual forms is among the best of the Golden Age.

In the Pal. Linotte (cf. Fig. 221) Ant. da Sangallo the Younger (?) erected on a tiny, though not irregular, plot a supremely notable building with the most elegantly disposed little cortile and staircase (§97).

In Serlio, L. VII, f. 128, the earliest directions for dealing with irregular plans, probably based on examples from Rome.

About this period mezzanines came into wider use in Rome, although the better architects did not give them the external character of a real storey.

Smaller storeys at the top for servants, with small windows, which were often at that time worked into the crowning cornice, and long existed everywhere.

The Roman innovation lay in the fact that the owners also wanted smaller rooms in the centre of the house, if only for easier heating in winter, as Serlio expressly states.

Moreover, if any storey contained large and small rooms next to one another, a false ceiling had to be introduced into the latter, often well below the real one, an empty space (a so-called *vano*) being thus formed, which was frequently abandoned to the mice and to darkness, but has also been gladly used as living accommodation. Serlio, L. VII, p. 28: *Tutti li luoghi mediocri et piccoli si ammezzaranno per più commodità*, i.e. whenever a room was too small in relation to the normal height of the storey it was halved.

For a time, however, the windows concerned were installed with no particular method or regard for external effect; in a frieze, or in the base of the Order immediately above, or in the same compartment of the wall as the main window below – thus in the top storey of the Cancelleria (Fig. 34) and of the Pal. Giraud (Fig. 35) – or within the curve of an arch. From 1540 the

Fig. 220 *(above) Rome, former small Palazzo di Venezia, court detail*

Fig. 221 *(right) Rome, Palazzo Linotte*

mezzanine was shown externally as a storey in its own right, not to the advantage of the composition, which in the good period liked as few and as large divisions as possible.

(On Sanmicheli's palaces in Venice and Verona, §94, very daring partitioning occurs; but only on one occasion, in the cortile of the Pal. Canossa in Verona, did he treat the mezzanine as a separate intermediate storey.)

§99 *Roman Staircases*

Staircases also (cf. §91) owe to Rome an important advance in the convenient and the imposing, as could hardly be otherwise in the city of ceremonial.

All stairs of the fifteenth century seem steep to the sixteenth; e.g. those of Cronaca in the Pal. Strozzi and in the Pal. della Signoria in Florence; Vasari, IV, p. 447, 451, *V. di Cronaca.*

Bramante in various (now mostly altered) rooms of his Vatican building knew how to deal with stairs of every type: Vasari, IV, p. 148, *V. di Bramante*; on the other hand, the staircases of the Cancelleria are still relatively steep, as are also those of the Farnesina by Peruzzi (or Raphael?).

The first entirely commodious staircase, wide and with pilaster-cladding throughout, is that of the Pal. Farnese, by the younger Ant. da Sangallo.

From that time no more inferior staircases were built, so long as the necessary resources were available.

Also spiral staircases intended for service and transport etc., sometimes without steps (i.e. with ramps), suitable for mules, were now given a monumental treatment; thus Bramante's in the Vatican (d'Agincourt, pl. 57), with changing Orders on the inner spiral. Other famous spiral staircases: Giulio's in the palace at Mantua, Genga's in the Monte Imperiale at Pesaro; Vasari, V, p. 544, *V. di Giulio*; VI, p. 319, *V. di Genga*; not much later, Vignola's at Caprarola.

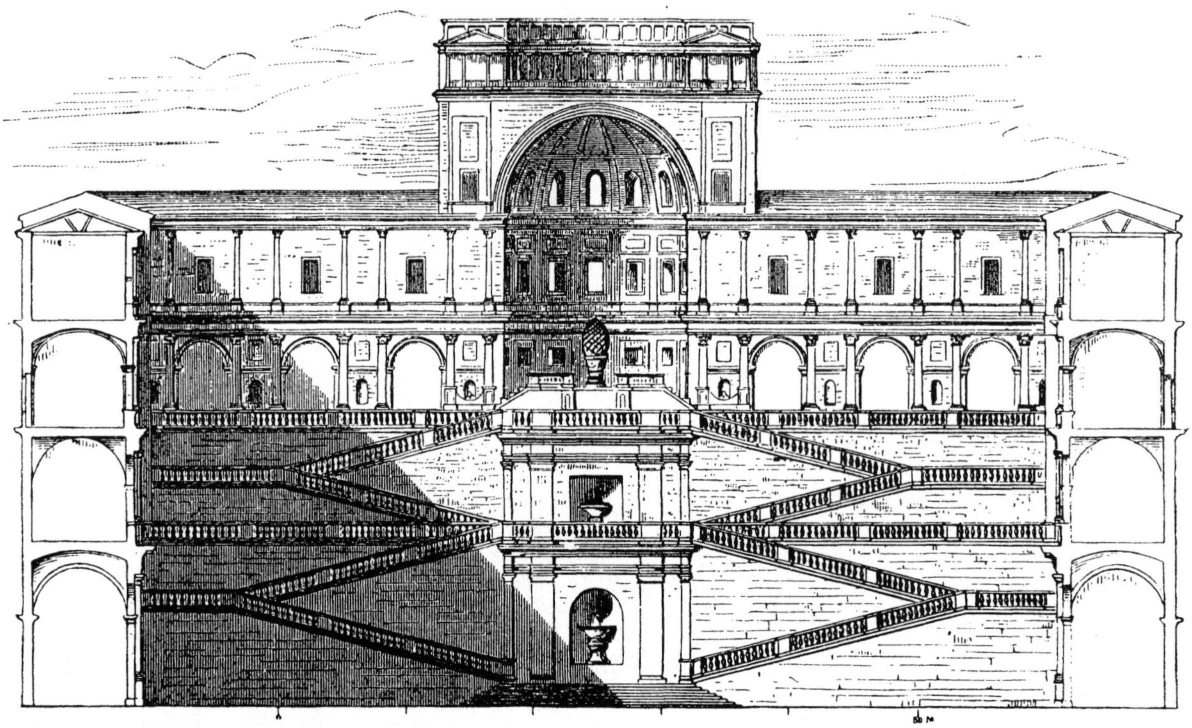

Fig. 222 *Rome, Vatican, transverse section of the great court of the Belvedere in its original state*

In Peruzzi's design for the Villa Belcaro at Siena there is a *scala equitabilis* with broad steps; similarly in three sketches for the Pal. Ricci in Montepulciano; cf. Redtenbacher, *B. Peruzzi und seine Werke*, pls. 15, 17–19.

Michelangelo's staircase, designed in Rome, for the vestibule of the Biblioteca Laurenziana in Florence, which caused such a sensation, is, like the vestibule itself (§56), an incomprehensible jest on the part of the great master (Fig. 64). Further details in Vasari, VI, p. 92, *V. di Tribolo*; VII, p. 236, *V. di Michelangelo*; Gaye, *Carteggio*, III, p. 12; *Lettere Pittoriche*, I, 5; see above §60.

§100 *Palaces in Serlio*

Besides the executed buildings consideration must be given to Serlio's comprehensive work (§31), which contains not only a wide-ranging appraisal of all contemporary palace architecture, but numerous drawings of great value, partly his own and partly provided by Baldassare Peruzzi.

Mainly at the end of the Third Book, and also in the Fourth and Seventh. The influence of this publication, §12, 31. We quote from the quarto edition [Venice, 1566].*

Serlio was already exploiting the more striking elements of architectural expression, which had come into use since Raphael: §51, 54, 96. He makes abundant use of mezzanines, but without always acknowledging them externally as storeys in their own right.

Some of the ideal façades of Book VII (p. 120 ff.) were to teach, in particular, the difference between *un' architettura soda, semplice, schietta, dolce e morbida* and *una debole, gracile, delicata, affettata, cruda, anzi oscura e confusa.*

Very fine and to some extent truly definitive solutions: the arcaded elevations somewhat in the Bolognese manner (Fig. 224) or for embracing large piazze (L. IV); columns with straight entablatures (Fig. 225); every two columns with straight entablature, carrying arches (Fig. 226); simple piers with arches; arches with engaged columns fronting the load-bearing piers (Fig. 227); massive piers each with two engaged columns and a niche between; even buildings which are expressly designed for already existing much-too-short or much-too-slender columns. For all such he composed an invariably new upper structure, sometimes as a real or simulated gallery, sometimes enclosed and with or without Orders. (Also in the VIIth Book a few gallery façades.)

There are also some excellent façades among those of the Venetian type (L. IV).

In the VIIth Book further exercises on irregular ground-plans (p. 128); palace building on sloping sites (p. 160), more or less on the Genoese principle: the palace in front, on the street; the cortile against the slope, which assumes the form of a masonry retaining-wall, and above it the water-tank. On p. 168 ff. he

* Burckhardt says only the "quarto edition", but this is the one printed in Venice in 1566: the 1619 Venetian edition, also quarto, has a clear enough description of *sala, salotto, saletta.* (PM).

Fig. 223 *Rome, Palazzo Massimi, court*

teaches how uneven window-intervals can lose their disturbing effect by symmetrical repetition like the *discordis concordante* of a part-song. Unfortunately in his description of the interior his definition of *sala*, *salotto* and *saletta* (p. 148) has been irretrievably distorted by misprints.*

In honour of his French patrons he talks of large and splendid chimneys and roof-windows, of the kind which the French Renaissance, i.e. Gothic clad in Renaissance forms, had taken over from the Middle Ages. In Italy there were in any case the lightly ornamented Venetian chimneys or those in the guise of painted, battlemented little turrets, as for example on the palace at Pienza, but without any importance being attached to them. An appearance like Chambord, where the most telling and characteristic architectural forms are located on the roof, would only have aroused merriment in Italy.

(Alberti, *De re aedificatoria*, L. VI, c. 11; L. IX, c. 4, accepted the validity of obelisks, foliated acroteria, and statues as the only desirable roof decoration, but in the fifteenth century they were almost never used on secular buildings, and in the sixteenth century only rarely, partly out of reverence for the sovereignty of the cornice.)

§101 *Public Palaces: the Great Halls*

Palaces for public purposes were especially characterised by large halls and an arcade-like opening on the outside. The Middle Ages with their vigorous political life had already largely established the forms of such buildings (§21).

* See previous note.

Fig. 224 *Design for a façade (I), from Serlio*

Fig. 225 *Design for a façade (II), from Serlio*

From the various terms and definitions we abstract: Palazzo del Comune – della Ragione – del Consiglio – de' Tribunali – del Podestà – del Prefetto: moreover, the terms often changed.

Of the great halls, scarcely one has been preserved in the form given to it by the golden age; even the Sala del Gran Consiglio in the Doge's Palace and the upper Sala of the Scuolo di S. Rocco in Venice are dominated by late Venetian paintings; the great Sala in the Palazzo della Signoria in Florence – as it has appeared right up to our own time – is effectively the work of Vasari, who succeeded in giving it a splendid termination at the far end. Of the one in the Pal. Comunale at Brescia, as also of that in the inner part of the Pal. del Podestà in Bologna (170 × 74 ft), once used for the conclave which elected John XXIII, later as a theatre, and latterly for ball-games, the author is unable to provide information concerning the interior. The ceilings, coffered or painted, are suspended from the roof-frames.

None of these buildings came up to the Salone in Padua in sheet magnitude. The proportion of size to height, and the illumination are hardly satisfactory in any, so that such rooms have to yield pride of place to the great halls in the grander private palaces (§91), and to the great monastic refectories and chapter-houses with top-lighting, especially those which are vaulted.

The most beautiful great hall of the Renaissance, admittedly when the style was already waning, is, in my opinion, the Sala Regia of the Vatican with its magnificently stuccoed barrel vault (§177) by Perino del Vaga and Daniele da Volterra (after Ant. da Sangallo), its five doors, and its single vast window placed high up.

Vasari enumerates the great halls with reference to that in Florence, which he himself altered: IV, p. 451, *V. di Cronaca*; one in the Pal. di Venezia in Rome (?); one built in the Vatican by Pius II and Innocent VIII, rebuilt; one in the Castello (Nuovo) in Naples (?); then those of the Palace in Milan (rebuilt in any case), the Palace at Urbino (in which there is no specially big room), and the familiar ones in Venice and Padua.

§ 102 *Colonnaded Architecture of Public Buildings*

The open colonnade is an expressive indication that the building in question is public property. Not only was the ground floor often largely or almost entirely given over to it, but the upper storey also assumed at least its outward forms.

Even to already existing official buildings a colonnade might well be added; *Annales Placentini* in Murat., XX, col. 958, 960, *sub anno* 1479.

Already in the Middle Ages the ground floor underneath the Sala in Palazzi Pubblici, Pal. della Ragione (i.e. law-courts), Broletti etc., in N. Italy formed in practice a public concourse. An ideal picture of such a palace in the frescoes of the *Story of Joseph*, by Benozzo Gozzoli in the Campo Santo, Pisa. The Pal. del Podestà, earlier enclosed at ground-floor level (Florence, Pistoia), was

Fig. 226 *Design for a façade (III), from Serlio*

Fig. 227 *Design for a façade (IV), from Serlio*

now on occasion given an open colonnade; its general requirements in M. Savonarola, in Murat., XXIV, col. 1174: Saloni, chapel, office, rooms of all types, officials' lodgings, stables etc. The more important buildings are as follows:

Pal. Comunale at Brescia (Fig. 229), built 1492–1508 by Formentone, later altered by others, with massive lower arcade, inside on columns and on piers outside; with richly decorated exterior. (The attic later.)

The pretty Pal. del Consiglio at Verona (Fig. 230), built from 1476 by Fra Giocondo, below (at least in front) completely open, with a balustrade and two small flights of steps.

The still more handsomely designed Loggia del Consiglio at Padua (Fig. 231), begun in 1501 by Annibale Maggi da Bassano; on the ground floor seven bays between columns, the three middle ones opening on to an impressive flight of steps.

The Pal. del Podestà at Bologna, rebuilt 1492–94, probably by Giovanni di Pietro da Brensa and Francesco Fossi da Dozza; the ground floor a vast pillared arcade with florid rustication (§21) and half-column Order; the upper floor, slightly recessed, with pilaster Order and very big windows or doors, which together give almost the impression of an open gallery. (For the Sala, cf. §101.)

The Pal. Prefettizio at Pesaro, begun before 1465 by Luciano da Laurana; a pillared arcade of six arches below, and an upper storey with five large windows above.

Pal. del Pretorio at Lucca, with enclosed upper storey (Fig. 232).

Pal. del Pretorio at Pienza, *c* 1460 (Fig. 233), also enclosed above, with distinctive pinnacled tower.

Setting back the upper storeys of a number of these buildings was for the good reason that there was a certain reluctance to rely on balconies supported on brackets when the authorities were obliged to show themselves on festive occasions. Cf. §94. (The upper storey is noticeably set back for no such reason on Raphael's Pal. Pandolfini (Fig. 211, §96); the same on the Pal. Uguccioni (Fig. 62); Giorgio Vasari the Younger remarks on this architectural peculiarity with reference to a sketch of this palace (Uffizi): *fa bellissimo vedere et un grandissimo comodo.*)

The whole exterior and the general layout of the Doge's Palace in Venice belong to the Gothic period, but the cortile, so far as it was completed, was carried out in the richest forms of the Renaissance and in white marble (by Bregno, Scarpagnino, Guglielmo Bergamasco) and not particularly designed to have the character of a public building of such status; its value lying more in the brilliant features (grand staircase, arcades, groups of windows; in the interior the Scala d' Oro, and a few rooms which have preserved their appointments of the fifteenth and early sixteenth centuries).

The Procuratie Vecchie in Venice, designed as offices and official lodgings, the ground floor for shops, on the Piazza side a continuous open arcade (piers below, columns on the two upper storeys), probably because the

Fig. 228 *Rome, Vatican, Sala Regia*

festive significance of the Piazza S. Marco would not have tolerated enclosed façades. (The Procuratie Nuove repeat the motive of the Biblioteca, §103, with the addition of an upper storey. Cf. §114.)

Also the Exchanges, the Loggie de' Mercanti, together with the halls of the Guilds, followed, if on a smaller scale, the motive of civic buildings by prescribing a lower arcade with stairs and minor rooms, and an upper Sala for meetings. Cf. the project in Serlio, L. VII, p. 116, and from the Gothic period the Loggia de' Mercanti at Bologna. Occasionally a chapel was provided, in which Mass was said every morning *ad devotionem et commodum mercatorum*. Thus in the Palazzo della Mercanzia at Siena, which with its chapel (document of 1416 in Milanesi, II, p. 82; cf. p. 93) looks on to the Piazza; at the back, towards a street at a higher level, the Loggia (now the Casino degli Uniti, previously de' Nobili) was built (cf. §104, Fig. 236).

§103 *Sansovino and Palladio: Arcades*

In some of the palaces already mentioned the proportion of the length to the number of bays in the arcades is arbitrary, and in two quite exceptional buildings, Jacopo Sansovino's Library in Venice and Andrea Palladio's Basilica in Vicenza, a completely dominant role is allotted to the double arcades as such, developed indeed to a supremely monumental degree.

The Library §53, Fig. 61. The criticism made when the building was projected, that it would be too low for its length, was unjust, since as an arcaded structure it would have no fixed length. The architect, however, in justifying his action, offered excuses instead of the real reason – assuming that his son's version (Franc. Sansovino, *Venezia*, fol. 115) accurately reproduces his father's submission. The latter, for example, freely admits that his building was designed to be low in comparison with the Doge's Palace, but without accommodating itself to it, because the Palace represented the majesty of the Republic, demanding such consideration in all events, and of course a subordinate role for the Library. That the meagre height is excused by the meagre depth is also an evasion; the meagre depth would not have excluded a massively composed high building, and the narrow side towards the Riva could have been masked. Venice wanted a masterpiece, not of design, but of execution.

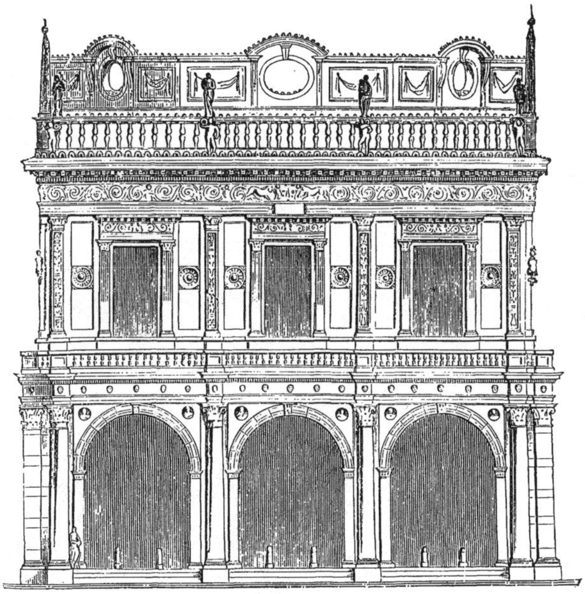

Fig. 229 *(left) Brescia, Palazzo Comunale, elevation*

Fig. 231 *(above) Padua, Loggia del Consiglio, elevation*

Fig. 230 *(below) Verona, Loggia del Consiglio, elevation*

Fig. 232 *(above) Lucca, Palazzo del Pretorio*

Fig. 233 *(right) Pienza, Palazzo del Pretorio*

Fig. 234 *(opposite above) Vicenza, the Basilica*

Fig. 235 *(opposite below) Florence, Loggia de' Lanzi*

While it was being built, Serlio published in 1544 (L. IV, fol. 154 or 155), supposedly for a space-saving Venetian house with shops in the lower arcade, a design which very finely interprets Sansovino's ideas in its simplicity, slenderness and patrician character (cf. Fig. 227).

Palladio had been rebuilding since 1549 the old Palazzo della Ragione of his home-town Vicenza, a not quite regular oblong, surrounded by a lower Doric and an upper Ionic colonnade (Fig. 17); at both levels, between the engaged columns of the principal Order, an arch is introduced on free-standing smaller columns of the same Order. This was the origin of the "Basilica", the public building, such as was desired all over Italy, entirely ringed by arcades, as with the marble Tower of Pisa. At the corners the irregularities are concealed with consummate skill (Fig. 234).

§ 104 *The Family Loggie*

Ultimately the fifteenth century was obliged to satisfy an idiosyncratic custom, the building of triple-arched open loggie, in which corporations or private families gathered or received visits on festive occasions.

M. Savonarola in Murat., XXIV, col. 1179 cites, *c* 1450, the splendid decorated "Lodia" supported on four marble columns "which is the seat of the Rectors and patricians".

By the sixteenth century the custom had obviously gone out; Vasari, VI, p. 556, *V. di Giovanni da Udine*: "The Medici loggia was built for convenience and for citizens' assemblies, as was the custom at that time of the noblest families." According to the *Lettere Sanesi*, III, p. 75, Pope Pius built his own, so that the Piccolomini could meet there *per esercizi pubblici di lettere di affari*. In Latin it was originally called *theatrum*: Milanesi, II, p. 323. According to the *Vitae Papar.*, Murat., III, II, col. 985, another palace was to have been built there.

In 1478 Florence had twenty-one such family loggie, plus another half-dozen that may have been forgotten: Varchi, III, p. 107 ff.

The imposing Loggia de' Lanzi in Florence must have served as the architectural prototype, in which the chief ceremonial acts of the Republic were performed; built

Fig. 236 *Siena, Loggia degli Uniti*

Fig. 237 *Piacenza, Palazzo Farnese, elevation detail*

1376–82, and perhaps designed by Benci di Cione and Simone di Francesco Talenti, after it had been said (in 1356) that a loggia was fit for a tyrant and not for a free state: Matteo Villani, L. VII, c. 41 (Fig. 235).

But the family loggie of the fifteenth century, mostly facing the palace of the family concerned, had to be content with the character of an agreeable architectural embellishment.

Preserved: the loggia of the Rucellai in Florence, opposite their palazzo, built in 1468 by Guidotti, probably not to a design by Alberti.

In Siena: the Loggia de' Nobili (now degli Uniti) at the back of the Pal. della Mercanzia (§ 102), on four piers (1417, the upper part later), simple and elegant (Fig. 236); also the above-mentioned Loggia del Papa, built in 1460 by Antonio Federighi, with slender, wide-span arches on columns, with the inscription: Pius II, to the fellow-members of his family, the Piccolomini.

Many a colonnade fragment in Italian towns may have been such a loggia, which has lost its distinctive character.

§ 105 *Palace Architecture of the Aftermath: Exteriors*

Palace architecture experienced its definitive development through the masters of the period 1540–80, at a time of political calm, the Counter-Reformation, and increasing refinement under Spanish influence.

The masters: Giulio Romano; Giacomo Barozzi, called Vignola; Giorgio Vasari; Bartolommeo Ammanati; Galeazzo Alessi; Pellegrino Tibaldi, known as Pellegrini; Andrea Palladio and others.

Florence under Cosimo I, Genoa since Andrea Doria skilfully kept at peace and were essentially subservient

Fig. 238 *Vicenza, Palazzo Valmarana*

Fig. 239 *Vicenza, Palazzo Porto-Barbaran*

to the politics of Spain; Venice entirely directed to the shrewd retention of possessions already gained.

Cosimo I systematically encouraged the idleness of the rich, and it was also in sympathy with the spirit of the Counter-Reformation that the classes which had been active hitherto should devote themselves to the refinements of retirement. In Rome this way of life culminated in rivalry between the older families and those of the constantly emerging Papal Nipoti.

The immediate architectural result of refinement was the increasing width and height of buildings, with still greater simplification, as well as coarseness of detail, now often to the point of mere rough-and-readiness.

Galeazzo Alessi held fast to a rich and dignified individuality of execution longer than others.

Of the façade-types the Roman in the narrower sense (§96), deriving essentially from the Pal. Farnese, now enjoyed very widespread use.

To this type belongs the majority of later Roman palaces; perhaps from Ammanati's Pal. Ruspoli onwards.

This very free form was to be the favourite for the Baroque style, which was able to transform, fantastically and capriciously, windows, doors, quoins, and mouldings. It was and remained very sensitive, however, to proportions. (Vignola's vast Farnese Palace at Piacenza, from 1558, almost without ornament, depending simply on its proportions (Fig. 237).)

The square windows of the mezzanines were boldly placed and rather large, above those of the relevant principal storey, so that the mezzanine has the formal effect of an intervening storey.

The type is easy to develop so that it conforms to an austere, self-contained *grandezza*.

Also the motive of one or two engaged-column Orders (more rarely pilasters), above a rusticated ground

Fig. 240 *Vicenza, Palazzo Chiericati*

or basement storey, often appears, but seldom executed with real care or distinction.

From Bramante (§96) this type spread to Raphael and Giulio Romano and then to Palladio, who, however, had to content themselves as a rule with stuccoed brick for their engaged columns and columns. (Pal. del Te at Mantua, §119.)

A wholly dignified and elaborate realisation in dressed stone has to be sought for in the works of Galeazzo Alessi and his Milanese disciples (Pal. Marino in Milan, now Municipio, with herms on the upper storey, a not uncommon form of the time; cf. the so-called *Omenoni* or Giants, on the house of the sculptor Leoni in Milan).

For the influence which Bramante's façade of the Pal. Caprini (§96; Fig. 214) exercised on Palladio (see his sketch at Chiswick*) cf. von Geymüller, *Raffaello studiato come architetto*, p. 99. Palladio used this motive of a rusticated ground-floor and engaged-column Order (more often pilasters in his case) on the upper storey of the Pal. Marcantonio Thiene (one of his earliest buildings, begun 1556), on the Pal. Trissini dal Vello d'Oro, Pal. Orazio Porto and Pal. Schio-Franceschini. On other palaces he also gave the ground storey an engaged-column Order, thus on the Pal. Porto-Barbaran (Fig. 239) and Adriano Thiene. Finally, he placed a single Giant Order on high bases on the Pal. Valmarana (Fig. 238), Giulio Porto and del Capitano. A mezzanine-type storey was popular as an attic. With the austerity of these basic motives there is at times an odd contrast in the lavish ornamental sculpture of the wall-surfaces (Pal. del Capitano and Porto-Barbaran).

A few of the more opulent palaces in Venice still maintain the opening of the façade, now in the form of magnificent colonnades.

Pal. Contarini, by Scamozzi; also, from the seventeenth century, Longhena's show-buildings, Pal. Pesaro and Pal. Rezzonico.

Palladio's masterpiece of domestic architecture, the Pal. Chiericati (cf. §35) in Vicenza (Fig. 240), is faced, both below and above, almost entirely with open colonnaded galleries with straight entablatures.

On the constricted sites of Genoa the proportions of façades were generally sacrificed and given over to some form of agreeable decoration. This varies from rustication (fantastically applied) to painting all over. Several of Alessi's façades, however, by no means neglected the beauty of proportions.

In Bologna the local colonnaded architecture conformed also to the forms of the Florentine-Roman school; for example on the Pal. Malvezzi-Medici by Bart. Triachini, of admirable effect and excellent proportions (Fig. 241). With strong leanings to the Baroque, the Pal. Fantuzzi by Formigine (Fig. 242).

Public buildings with ground-floor colonnades are also sometimes among the grandest of the period.

Palladio's Basilica, 1549, §103; highly effective with simple means – Vasari's Uffizi, §35; grand and noble, the Collegio de' Nobili and other buildings round the Piazza

* This drawing, now in London, Royal Institute of British Architects (Burlington-Devonshire Collection), is no longer generally accepted as by Palladio. (PM).

Fig. 241 *Bologna, Palazzo Malvezzi-Medici, elevation detail*

Fig. 242 *Bologna, Palazzo Fantuzzi, elevation detail*

de' Mercanti in Milan, by Vinc. Seregno, after the manner of Alessi's cortili, §35, 106.

(NOTE: The Palazzo Marino, Milan, damaged by bombs in 1943, has since been extensively restored.) (PM).

§106 *Palace Architecture of the Aftermath: Interiors*

In the interior the vestibule in particular now acquired a wider importance for the numerous servants attending visitors.

The doorway already offered a large and wide entrance. To the Florentines, and even to Bramante, the vestibule was seldom more than a barrel-vaulted passage. It now becomes a large and high vaulted room, generally pierced by lunettes. The entrance of the Palazzo Farnese, with its barrel vault over Doric columns, was admittedly not achieved again.

The vestibule grew into one of the most important parts of a commission, while the stairs (§99), hitherto merely dignified and convenient, henceforth are consciously presented to the eye and the imagination as an aesthetic feature, and related directly to the vestibule.

Chief novelty: the doubling of the stairs for the sake of symmetry, as had been the custom in gardens and cortili since Bramante (§126, cf. Fig. 222). Either one began at the bottom with two different stairs, or one flight of stairs might be divided into two parts from the first stair-head; landings, banisters, the placing of columns, the arches of vaults etc., were now given for the first time their own aesthetic rules; in addition the poetry of light and of the vista, which found its consummation only in the exploitation of every resource.

Fig. 243 *Vicenza, Palazzo Thiene-Bonin-Longara, court*

An impassioned and certainly influential programme for the enrichment of staircase architecture: Vasari, I, p. 147, *Introduction*. Palladio, *I quattro Libri dell' Archit.*, I, cap. 28: Great care is to be used in the positioning of stairs, for it is emphatically not easy to find a fitting place for them without incommoding the rest of the building; a separate area is above all proper to them; they need three openings: an entrance door as conspicuous as possible as one sets foot in the house, large window in the middle, and exit at the top. Good stairs should be well lit, at least four feet wide and easy to climb, so that they invite one, so to speak, to go up. The steps ought not to be more than half a foot high (lower with high staircases), but not less than four inches. The tread should extend at least a foot, at most one-and-a-half. After eleven or thirteen steps (the number must be odd, so that one begins and ends on the right foot), a rest (*requie*) should be introduced. Straight stairs are to be planned in two or four flights; in the latter case a square intervening space serves as a light-well; spiral stairs are sometimes circular on plan, sometimes oval, occasionally with a column in the middle.

The greatest merit, however, lay with that steep city of stairs, Genoa, where they have had to contend from time immemorial with putting a good (and handsome) face on the countless steps; the stairs in the Genoese Doge's Palace (after 1550), and in all succeeding palaces.

The cortili no longer have the refined elegance of the best of the earlier work, but instead sometimes an austere grandeur or an ingeniously contrived splendour.

The austerity of the pillared and colonnaded galleries of Ammanati and Palladio. The latter alternated, as on his façades, with one and two Orders, which he, following the model of Antique colonnaded (Corinthian) atria, extended all round or applied only to the front and back elevations. To the second type belongs the cortile of the Pal. Valmarana;* here the continuity of the upper loggia, supported on columns, is effected by prolonging it on the columnless sides as a deep cornice. In the Pal. Marcantonio Thiene the cortile, in harmony with the façade, has rusticated arcades on the ground storey and pillared arcades with pilasters on the *piano nobile*. Pillared arcades with engaged columns on the Roman model (§97) are exemplified by the incomplete second cortile in the convent of the Carità (now Accademia) in Venice, where for the front cortile on two sides a giant two-storey colonnade was projected; one such realised at the Pal. Orazio Porto in Vicenza.

The original and magnificent cortile in Alessi's Pal. Marino (Municipio) in Milan (Fig. 244); his most beautiful cortile, the one formerly in the Pal. Sauli in Genoa (Fig. 245); the motive, §35.

Ingeniously disposed colonnaded cortili in particular also in Bologna (§93; from this later period, among others, the Pal. Zucchini), in Florence (Pal. Non-Finito, by Cigoli); in Genoa, most of the palazzi of the end of the sixteenth century, predominantly with coupled columns in cortili and on staircases (cf. §56, end).

There is much less good to be said about the pillared cortili of palaces; the colossal cortile of the Pal. Pitti in Florence with its rusticated colonnading on three storeys, by Ammanati (Fig. 67), does not equal Pellegrini's Archiepiscopal Palace in Milan (Fig. 68) as a work of art.

In time, however, the cortili were handled less interestingly and expenditure directed far more to large dimensions than to finer artistic execution.

The corridors, now high, wide, and vaulted throughout, preserved their mostly simple pilaster Orders. Inside, the earlier dispositions remained essentially dominant, but adjusted to the bigger scale.

The high and wide architecture of the vestibule brought with it some changes. Of the new rooms perhaps only the *Galleria* must be mentioned, a long and comparatively narrow room, according to Scamozzi's statement a northern importation.

* Burckhardt says Valmarana, but he must have had the Pal. Thiene-Bonin in mind (Fig. 243). (PM).

Fig. 244 *(opposite above) Milan, Palazzo Marino, court* Fig. 245 *(opposite below) Genoa, Palazzo Sauli, former court*

CHAPTER TWELVE

Hospitals, Fortresses and Bridges

§ 107 *Hospitals, Inns and Pleasure Buildings*

Hospitals and other charitable buildings, whatever their interior appointments might be, opened out into a great colonnade, as a symbol of welcome and as a waiting place, with an enclosed structure above.

Alberti, *De re aedific.*, L. V, c. 8, gives only the essential requirements, but not the architectural form of hospitals.

Brunellesco's beautiful Loggia degli Innocenti at Florence, which also masks the church of the Foundling Hospital (Fig. 246).

(The hospital loggia in the Piazza Sta Maria Novella was not built until 1489–96.)

Ospedale del Ceppo at Pistoia, with a frieze of coloured reliefs above the loggia (Fig. 247).

Ospedale Vecchio at Foligno; the front, with upper and lower colonnade, is preserved; in the former, two bays to each one of the latter; between the two a low mezzanine with small canopied windows; fifteenth century.

Portico of the Putte di Baracano at Bologna.

At the medicinal baths of Viterbo Nicholas V (1447–55) had several buildings erected, of "princely" commodiousness and beauty. *Vitae Papar.*, in Murat., III, II, col. 929. No information given about the form.

Very important and still largely preserved: the Hospital of Sto Spirito in Rome, the main building from the period of Sixtus IV (begun 1471, completed 1482); with hitherto open (but recently closed) loggia; dome in the middle of the two long principal rooms, two of the four cortili original.

The Ospedale Maggiore in Milan has an enclosed, north-west-facing show façade, but was projected by Filarete with open lower loggie, § 44. Inside only the minor cortili old; the celebrated main cortile by Richini. Regarding the scheme for the interior, cf. Filarete's Treatise, Book XI.

For S. Giacomo degli Incurabili in Rome Peruzzi did two designs (partially preserved); in one a pillared cortile, garden loggia etc.; other projects by Ant. da Sangallo the Younger (apparently under Peruzzi's influence), reproduced by Redtenbacher, *Peruzzi*, pl. 8, and Allgem. Bauzeitung, 1883, p. 52 f.

Individual inns and hostelries were fine enough to occasion individual mention. The Ox Inn at Padua (*c* 1450), with cortile, public rooms, innumerable bedrooms and stabling for two hundred horses, was completely "lordly": Savonarola in Murat., XXIV, col. 1175.

The finest and largest *osterie* were outside the Porta S. Gallo in Florence, for the tradespeople's fairs; destroyed 1529. Varchi, ed. Milanesi, III, p. 86.

A peculiar series of paintings, developed in and on such buildings, sometimes of a droll and frivolous type, sometimes arms of princes: Lomazzo, *Trattato dell' arte*, p. 349.

Buildings for purposes of public entertainment probably had, as yet, no distinctive architectural form, or were merely temporary buildings, or, if handsome, have in any case perished.

Regarding the whole architectural and decorative character of the Renaissance theatre, see below § 192 ff.

Duke Galeazzo Maria Sforza of Milan (1466–76) had built for ball-games "spacious, large rooms . . . and also for music": Corio, *Storia di Milano*, fol. 426.

Falconetto (cf. § 26) built in Padua a rotunda for musical performances "small but pretty". Milizia, *Memorie degli Architetti*, I, p. 269, thought he recognised a copy of this no longer surviving building in Palladio's Rotonda (properly, Villa Capra, Vicenza).

In the house of the music-loving Luigi Cornaro at Padua (now Pal. Giustiniani), who had Falconetto in his household for many years, the elegant annex contains in the cortile on the right an octagon with niches, which must have served for such a purpose. Arbitrarily altered, Serlio, L. VII, pp. 218, 223. Cf. § 119.

Fig. 246 *(above) Florence, Loggia degli Innocenti and Piazza di SS. Annunziata*

Fig. 247 *(below) Pistoia, Ospedale del Ceppo*

Fig. 248 *(above) Naples, Porta Capuana, after removal of upper additions* Fig. 249 *(below) Perugia, Porta S. Pietro*

Fig. 250 *Naples, triumphal arch of Alfonso of Aragon*

§ 108 *Fortified Buildings*

At a time when even war was often subject to art and elegance, the fortress also had, so far as possible, to be drawn into the circle of aesthetics. Thus it happened that individual princes and entire dynasties, obliged to reside in fortified castles for long periods, expected them to be comfortable and beautiful. The battlements of the Middle Ages disappeared; severe mouldings, occasionally supported on consoles, rustication on wall-surfaces, or at least at the angles, became the universal mode of expression both for the walls of bastions and ramparts as well as for towers and free-standing structures, so far as resources permitted.

The Italian battlement, crenellated on top, supplies for the last time the continuous crowning feature to the splendidly picturesque fortified buildings of Bellinzona, the work of the last Visconti (1412–47).

Instead of the "high" fortifications Federigo of Urbino (§6, 11) introduced the "lower" kind, less easily damaged by artillery: Vespasiano Fiorent., p. 121.

Rustication in pointed (diamond-shaped) form on the two giant frontal towers of the Castello of Milan; with carved balls (the Medici emblem) on the Fortezza da Basso in Florence.

Large fortified buildings of the good period, calculated – in addition to their warlike purpose – to create a great impression on the imagination: the stronghold of Civita Castellana, by Antonio da Sangallo the Elder (1494); the harbour-fort of Civita Vecchia, begun by Bramante in 1508, completed by Michelangelo.

Francesco Sforza was not allowed to attempt the reconstruction of the destroyed Castello of the Visconti in Milan until he promised to provide the city (by doing so) not only with security against an enemy, but also an architectural ornament; cf. Beltrami, *Il castello di Milano*, and v. Oettingen, *Ant. Filarete*, p. 17.

The Castello of Palo (not, as was earlier thought, by Bramante). Fine individual sections of fortifications in Nepi (1499), by Antonio da Sangallo the Elder, and Grottaferrata (after 1484).

Almost all noteworthy architects were also fortress-builders and engineers, and as such often found more favour with the great than by their artistry in the narrower sense (see the biographies of the three Sangallos, Sanmicheli, and others in Vasari, and regarding Franc. di Giorgio, both in Vasari and Milanesi, II, p. 416–end, as well as C. Promis and A. Pantanelli, in the writings mentioned in §31). The famous letter with which Leonardo da Vinci introduced himself to Lodovico il Moro shows this clearly. *Lettere Pittoriche*, I, Appendix I; Facsimile and detailed commentary in Müller-Walde, *Leonardo da Vinci*, p. 158 ff. But Girolamo Genga (1476–1551) did not conceal that fortress architecture, in which he was a master, seemed to him "rather valueless and unworthy". Vasari, VI, p. 319, *V. di Genga*.

The fortified buildings of the fifteenth century Popes: *Vitae Paparum*, in Murat., III, II, col. 929 (Nicholas V); 985 (Pius II); 1018 (Paul II); etc. Müntz, *Les arts à la cour des Papes*, I–III.

On the Castello of Ostia, 1483–86, by Baccio Pontelli, cf. the author's *Cicerone*, II, 1, p. 143.

§ 109 *Renaissance Gateways*

The showpiece of the fortified building was the gateway, both externally and internally. The fifteenth century had on occasion allowed the whole wealth of the Corinthian and Composite Orders to appear in the pilasters

Fig. 251 *(above) Verona, Porta S. Zeno, elevation*

Fig. 252 *(right) Rome, Porta Pia*

and other elements of this feature. The obvious prototype, the Roman Triumphal Arch, was however never scrupulously copied.

Porta Capuana in Naples, from 1485, by the Florentine Giuliano da Majano; between two towers an arch bordered with Composite pilasters, with deep frieze; the attic later, the superstructure modern (Fig. 248).

Outstandingly fine: Porta S. Pietro at Perugia, already begun by 1448, but in 1475 contracted out to Agostino di Duccio of Florence, interrupted in 1481 (§38), and hence without a crowning cornice: Mariotti, *Lettere Pittoriche Perugine*, p. 98; Graziani, Cronaca di Perugia in Archiv. stor., XVI, I, p. 605, and Matarazzo, ibid., XVI, II, p. 8, n. At the side of the gateway, projecting wings with niches; all angles with Corinthian pilasters (Fig. 249).

A building of unique type is the splendid marble Triumphal Arch of Alfonso, a high white structure between two dark towers of the Castello Nuovo in Naples (Fig. 250), 1453–70, by the Milanese Pietro di Martino, the design latterly attributed sometimes to Alberti, sometimes to Laurana. It is almost the only Renaissance building to display the Antique Orders in their full formal panoply. Of the two towers one has recently been restored. Cf. Miniero Riccio, *Gli artisti ed artefici che lavorarono in Castelnuovo a tempo di Alfonso I e Ferrante I*, Napoli, 1876.

In the sixteenth century a more severe, even sombre, air was given to the gateway and the Doric and Tuscan Orders applied to it in association with rustication, as indicated above (§52). Sanmicheli (1484–1559) perfected the conventional architectural vocabulary of the fortified building. The medieval gate-tower disappeared completely.

The gates of Padua (1515) mark the transition from the more ornamental to the austerer type; the Porta Portello, attributed to Guglielmo Bergamasco (1518); by Falconetto the Porta S. Giovanni (1528), on the principle of a single-arch Triumphal Arch, externally with engaged columns, inside with pilasters left rough; and the Porta Savonarola (1530).

Sanmicheli, as master-builder of fortresses to the Venetian Republic, erected there the fort of S. Andrea di Lido with its fine water-gate (cf. §4), and in Verona the Porta Nuova, Porta S. Zeno (Fig. 251) and Porta Stuppa or del Palio. The design in each case individual, the mode of expression exploited with great energy. The engaged columns and pilasters sometimes correct in form, but mostly rusticated in accordance with wrongly interpreted prototypes from unfinished Roman buildings, while capital and base together with the entablature are correctly composed. Mingling of robust sculptural elements, masks, lions' heads etc., especially on keystones; strong modelling of voussoirs of arches; occasionally flat-arched lintels. It is this style of monumental fortified building which subsequently influenced more or less the entire West and came to be regarded as classical.

Typical unorthodox forms in the Fourth Book of Serlio, e.g. columns, on which smooth elements alternate with rusticated. (Later, his Book on Portals, §54.)

Alessi's gate on the Molo Vecchio at Genoa on the town side with massive pilasters, on the outer side extremely coarse. The later harbour-gates completely and exaggeratedly rusticated.

Occasionally ornamentation is added to a gateway, which has nothing in common with such fortified architecture.

Fig.253 *Florence, Ponte Sta Trinità*

Porta Sto Spirito in Rome, segmental in plan (the earliest instance of this attractive device, later so much used), with four prominent engaged columns, by the younger Ant. da Sangallo, unfinished; Porta del Popolo, supposedly by Vignola, of Triumphal Arch type; Porta Pia, by Michelangelo, who *c* 1559 prepared schemes for many other gates of Rome (Vasari, vii, p. 260–61); designed with the intention of making the opening, executed with the greatest sculptural effect, to appear as imposing as possible by surrounding it with small windows and mock crenellations, etc. The architectural forms entirely arbitrary in themselves and subordinated solely to this purpose (Fig. 252).

(NOTE: For the Triumphal Arch at Naples see now G. Hersey, *The Aragonese Arch at Naples*, Yale and London, 1973.) (PM).

§110 *Bridges*

The period 1540–80 was the first to create bridges with an artistic significance of their own.

From the fifteenth century: Ponte Sisto in Rome, already adopting the form of Antique bridges.

Palladio's magnificent schemes for a three-arched Rialto bridge in Venice. Ammanati's Ponte Trinità in Florence; the forms of the three arches adjusted with the freedom of genius to the rise towards the centre (Fig. 253).

Covered bridges were at any rate advocated by Alberti in the fifteenth century (*De re aedif.*, L. VIII, c. 6), who was in fact said to have built a roof over the Ponte Sant' Angelo in Rome, on instructions from Nicholas V: Vasari, II, p. 546, *V. di Alberti.* The bridge over the Ticino at Pavia still has a fine and rather early roof.

CHAPTER THIRTEEN

Improvements and Town Planning

§111 *Levelling and Paving*

The Renaissance is the time of urban improvements in the widest sense, if only because its abiding principle lay in regularity, while its monumental architecture demanded a certain measure of open space and a unifying harmony with the built environment.

Northern Gothic in towns, where the lack of space increased their defensive qualities, placed churches of the highest quality upon constricted irrational sites, their organic perfection seemingly untouched by their surroundings. The Italian theory (e.g. Serlio, L. VII et passim) required, on the other hand, in front of each façade wherever feasible a piazza, its four sides corresponding to the latter's length.

As each symmetrically disposed front presupposed a flat area in front of it, and as in Italy in the fourteenth century not only palaces, but even houses adopted a regular form, the finer streets had to be levelled. The maintenance of the level, however, was only attainable by paving, which accorded not only with the sense of cleanliness of contemporary Italians, but where possible in materials and execution their artistic sense also.

Numerous accounts in all city and princely histories. *Selciare* or *salegare*, pave with cobbles; *ammattonare*, with bricks on end; *lastricare*, with stone slabs. Florence was the earliest to be paved throughout with bricks on end, and, in the busiest places, with slabs. Its paving indeed had a legendary origin: Gio. Villani, I, 38. Slab paving before 1250 in streets, where bricks were previously used; Vasari, I, p. 249, *V. di Arnolfo*, a rather exaggerated claim. The piazza by the Baptistry with bricks, Via Nuova with slabs (1289); Gaye, *Carteggio*, I, p. 418 f. The monks of Sto Spirito were given a present of a paved way alongside their church in 1297, p. 434. Paved ways ordered round all public buildings and through gates (1333), p. 478. The piazza by the Baptistry (1339) paved with slabs (Della Tosa, *Annali*, in Guasti, *Sta Maria del Fiore*, p. 53). The Piazza della Signoria, however, first completely paved in 1351, and then only with bricks; Gaye, *Carteggio*, I, p. 502, with documentary references to the purpose: beauty, prevention of mud and dust. The monks of SS. Annunziata in 1421 requested a contribution towards the paving of the piazza in front of the church, to increase visits to the church, p. 549; in 1437 paving of the streets from Sta Maria Novella as far as the Cathedral, p. 553; in 1449 paving of the Lungarno from the Ponte Sta Trinità to the Ponte Carraja, in 1460 the same thing for the Piazza S. Apollinare, ibid., p. 558 f., 564 etc. In Siena the semi-circular brick-paved Piazza was given in 1513 concentrically converging lines of travertine slabs, *Lettere sanesi*, III, p. 12. In Piacenza the Piazza was paved in 1469 with marble and brick to a design of rectangles, *Annal. Placent.*, in Murat., XX, col. 927. The paving of Rome began under Eugenius IV (1431–47) on the Campus Martius; Flaminio Vacca in Fea, *Miscellanea*, I, p. 70; extended under Nicholas V, Platina, *Vitae Pontiff.* p. 298; systematically continued, with bricks, under Sixtus IV, Infessura in Eccard, *Scriptores*, II, col. 1897; Corio, fol. 416; Julius II had many streets brick-paved; Albertini, L. III, fol. 95 (ed. Schmarsow, p. 42 ff.). In Venice brick paving first came to the Piazza San Marco in 1382 or 1394; the present marble surface in any case not before the end of the sixteenth century; Sansovino, *Venezia*, fol. 105; the streets were long unpaved and very dirty, fol. 172. Milan acquired its paving from 1412, Decembrio in Murat., XX, col. 998, and again from 1469, Corio, *Historia di Milano*, fol. 414. Lodovico il Moro had the whole of Vigevano paved, Cagnola in Archiv. stor., III, p. 188. The Cremonesi commissioned Filarete in 1454 to take charge of the paving of their Piazza del Duomo, Corio in Politecnico, XXI, and W. von Oettingen, *Filarete*, p. 20. In Ferrara they started (1417) with the piazza, which, as later on the streets, was given a gravel paving; *Diario Ferrarese* in Murat., XXIV, col. 183, 202, 245 f. Also Bologna in the great improvements of 1470, when only favoured places got paving, Bursellis in Murat., XXIII, col. 897. In Perugia brick paving was laid from 1425, Graziani, *Cronaca*, in Archiv. stor., XVI, I, p. 318. At Assisi the main road was paved as far as Sta Maria degli Angeli on the orders of Cosimo de' Medici, Vasari, II, p. 444, *V. di Michelozzo.* In Naples the Viceroy Pietro di Toledo was the first to provide paving (from 1532), using bricks; cf. his *Life* in Arch. stor., IX, p. 22.

§ 112 *Street Improvements*

Before the coming of the Renaissance, and still more subsequently, big street improvements were carried out, often at great sacrifice, partly from expedience, partly as concessionary measures in the interests of townscape, with emphasis on straight lines as their precondition.

A very striking exception: L. B. Alberti, *De re aedificatoria*, L. IV, c. 5; L. VIII, c. 6, where admittedly the straight line was advocated for main streets with houses of even height and with similar porticoes, but elsewhere for practical as well as aesthetic reasons the excellence of serpentine winding was acknowledged. (The town will appear larger, the houses be presented to the eye gradually and variously, shade will never be entirely lacking, the wind thwarted, and defence against an enemy simplified.)

In Florence in 1339 it was decided at the instigation of the Cathedral authorities to make certain streets by the Duomo and the Baptistry lower, to enhance the view of these buildings (documents in Guasti, *Sta Maria del Fiore*, p. 51), and in 1349 S. Romolo was demolished to create an open piazza, for which straight frontages were stipulated; Gaye, *Carteggio*, I, p. 499. In 1319 costly houses were being bought for demolition to make way for the enlargement of the Pal. della Signoria, ib. p. 456.

In the fifteenth century especially, the more important cities competed in making their narrow and crooked streets broad and straight. Obstructing projections, balconies, and wooden constructions for the popular habit of working in the open air were almost completely abolished.

In Siena an amenities authority, the Ufficiali dell' Ornato, advised on improvements and expropriations; Milanesi, II, p. 337 ff., 345, cf. 353.

In Bologna in 1428 the enlargement and embellishment of the Piazza; in 1470 the removal of wooden projections; in 1496 a main street, that of the "Rome Pilgrims" (there were similar ones in other towns, e.g. Piacenza), was straightened after large demolitions; in 1497 another also, Bursellis, *Ann. Bonon.* in Murat., XXII, for the years mentioned. The Ode by Codrus Urceus, *de renovatione Bononiae* (*Opera*, p. 303).

In Ferrara *c* 1480–90 straight streets were opened up from the Palazzo to the old Castello etc.; Tito Strozza, *Aeolosticha*, p. 188, 199. In the new quarters a series of straight streets was laid out, one with poplars on both sides, 1457; *Diario Ferrarese* in Murat., XXIV, col. 202.

Removal of all projections in Perugia (1426); in Milan and Pavia under Lodovico il Moro (*c* 1490, cf. § 163).

For the cities ruled by despots this was represented by Alberti as inevitable, *De re aedific.*, L. V, c. 1, because from balconies and the like resistance to soldiers would be too easy. Hippias of the Pisistratidae admittedly took away all projecting structures from the Athenians, but only to sell them back again at a high price.

The rebuilding of whole quarters in Mantua (1526–46) under the direction of Giulio Romano armed with supreme powers; Vasari, VI, p. 548, *V. di Giulio.*

Incidentally, an early Florentine state prohibition of thatched roofs in a small country town (1367); Gaye, *Carteggio*, I, p. 518.

§ 113 *The Fate of Street Arcades*

To the despots, who at times had to fight in the streets, or at least frequently order their soldiers to march through them, street colonnades, like obstructions of every type, were especially repugnant. In earlier times these must have been a predominant feature in a number of towns where they no longer exist. Rome and Naples for political reasons had no such colonnaded buildings.

When King Ferrante of Naples visited Sixtus IV in 1475, he gave the Pope to understand that he could never truly feel himself master of Rome, so long as the narrow streets, balconies, and porticoes survived. In fact, the Pope had shortly before, on New Year's Day, 1475, issued on his own initiative a Bull relating to the *instauratio* of the city. The demolition of the Maeniana and of other prominent buildings began in 1480, not, as Infessura (in Eccard, *Scriptores*, II, col. 1897, 1900) infers, under the pretext of street-paving, but according to the Bull (in Müntz, *Les arts* . . ., III, p. 182 ff.) on the basis that such constructions were a hindrance to traffic, especially in Jubilee years. The satisfaction expressed by the Romans over such works is shown in an epigram by Bandolini, in Müntz, III, p. 189; in the same place also, songs of praise for particular street improvements.

Sixtus devoted the utmost personal zeal to the matter and did not hesitate to act despotically. Jac. Volaterran. in Murat., XXIV, col. 166, 185. Senarega, in Murat., XXIV.

General account: Albertini, fol. 82: Sixtus IV first destroyed the dark porticoes, widened the streets and piazze of the city and had them brick-paved; many derelict churches were rebuilt by him from the ground up, according to their original design. In this subsequent Popes were to follow him. List of relevant streets and piazze from Sixtus to Julius II, fol. 94.

Earlier improvements to Rome under Nicholas V, who, among other things, created by demolition the piazza at the Ponte Sant' Angelo, after hundreds of people had been crushed on the bridge at the Jubilee of 1450. Sixtus IV built the Ponte Sisto in order to divert the returning stream of pilgrims in that direction during Jubilees; *Vitae Paparum*, in Murat., III, II, col. 924, 1064; Müntz, op. cit. Pius II exploited in 1462 the occasion of his Corpus Christi celebrations at Viterbo (§ 187), by destroying all projections and balconies in the main street, "to restore to public possession what had been taken from it".

In 1499 Alexander VI, anticipating the pilgrimages in the coming Jubilee year, laid out parallel to the Borgo (Vecchio) the via Alessandrina (Borgo Nuovo), in which the houses were not to have a height of less than seven *canne* (i.e. about 52½ feet); D. Gnoli in Nuova Antologia, 1887.

Later, Clement VII "improved" Rome very recklessly and without compensating injured parties; Varchi, *Stor. Fiorent.*, I, p. 45; Paul Jovii. *Vita Pomp. Columnae.*

In Naples many porticoes survived Ferrante, among them antique, cavernous examples in which robbers and assassins lurked. All such, including those which had survived and those which made policing difficult, were destroyed by the Viceroy Toledo from 1532; see his *Life* in Archiv. Stor., IX, p. 18. By way of compensation the Neapolitan philosopher Campanella piled colonnade on colonnade in his *Città del Sole.*

Country towns liked to retain their porticoes, while great houses shed them. And Bologna with its arcades is even today in some ways the most beautiful city in Italy.

§114 *The Piazza as a Monumental Concept*

Of the grander new schemes and alterations the piazze must now be considered. They had perhaps taken the place of the Forum of classical Antiquity in the towns concerned, and with their colonnades and adjoining church (or Cathedral) recalled its porticoes and Temples. Even for piazze of the second rank and for market-places, imposing and well-proportioned arrangements were at least attempted. The letting of premises behind the arcades was not considered unworthy of the state, if it was the landlord.

In Venice the Piazza S. Marco had, *c* 1490, opposite the Procuratie Vecchie, a similar arcaded building, and the ground-floors of both were let as shops. On the Piazzetta opposite the Doge's Palace there was also an arcade, which formed a ground-floor of shops and hostelries. More difficult to excuse was the assignment even of the upper arcade of the Doge's Palace to commerce; Sabellicus, *De situ venetae urbis*, fol. 89 f. Even round the two columns stalls and worse were accommodated; not until 1529 was all this removed and an unobstructed view obtained towards the water: Vasari, VII, p. 501, *V. di Jac. Sansovino*; Sansovino, *Venezia*, fol. 116.

The project for a magnificent colonnaded piazza as the centre of the large, systematically replanned commercial quarter at the Rialto; Vasari, V, p. 269 ff., *V. di Fra Giocondo*; in place of his plan the simpler buildings of Scarpagnino and Sansovino came later.

How much the piazza was conceived as a place of commerce is shown by Savonarola in Murat., XXIV, col. 1179, who classifies the piazze of Padua according to the number of their shops.

In Florence the Piazza della SS. Annunziata only achieved symmetry in the course of time, when – to Brunellesco's loggia of the Innocenti – a counterpart was built by Antonio da Sangallo the Elder; the entrance-portico of the church itself, which forms the main frontage of the piazza, was not added until 1601. The width of the roads leading into it necessitated the erection of entirely separate colonnades (Fig. 246).

Michelangelo may have thought differently when he advised Cosimo I to extend the giant motive of the Loggia de' Lanzi round the entire Piazza della Signoria: Vasari, I, p. 603, n. 1, *V. di Orcagna.* In this case all the street-openings would have been vaulted over.

That a piazza should be laid out with regard to the view of a building was an ideal pursued, in Florence at any rate, in early times; Vasari, II, p. 381, *V. di Brunellesco*, who wanted to make a piazza between the choir of Sto Spirito and the Arno. (Similarly, cf. Milanesi, II, p. 225; a chapel in Siena, 1444.)

The Florentine Alberti took (L. VIII, c. 6) the recipe for his Forum from Vitruvius, and stipulated Triumphal Arches for its entrances.

The piazza of Fabriano splendidly reconstructed in 1451 for Nicholas V, by Bernardo Rossellino, *Vitae Papar.*, in Murat., III, II, col. 929. The piazza of Pienza (Fig. 200). Here, as later in Michelangelo's design for the piazza of the Capitol, and similarly Bernini's piazza in front of S. Peter's, the piazze widen towards the cathedral, a device by the architect to give the small piazza the appearance of adequate depth; at the same time, a view of the enchanting landscape is disclosed at the side of the Cathedral.

The piazza of Parma, where during civil commotions the man who held it was regarded as the victor, was for this reason refurbished with walls, gates, and guard-houses in 1478 by the Milanese Governor: *Diarium Parmense* in Murat., XXII, col. 282, 296.

In Siena in 1508 there was a scheme to provide the semi-circular piazza with an arcade running all round; Gaye, *Carteggio*, II, p. 482; Milanesi, III, p. 307.

Among the buildings of Lodovico il Moro the *bella et ornata piazza* at Vigevano became celebrated; Cagnola, in Archiv. Stor., III, p. 188. Even today the huge piazza has its complete range of colonnades with shops, and on one side the façade of the Cathedral.

Remarkable and, of their type, fine attempts to introduce a symmetrical colonnaded structure with largely enclosed upper storey for shops, business and administrative offices along a piazza, at any rate on one side: in Bologna the portico of the Fioraje (by Vignola) near S. Petronio; in Brescia a building of this kind in the Piazza Vecchia; at Faenza, the Loggia del Commune. In Vignola's building at Bologna a small mezzanine is even inserted above the pillared arcade.

§115 *New Towns and Quarters*

New plans for towns certainly appeared rarely, but the most famous theorists worked on them to illustrate their ideas.

Alberti, especially *De re aedific.*, L. IV, c. 5 ff., L. VIII, c. 6 ff.; Francesco di Giorgio, *Trattato*, ed. Promis, and in

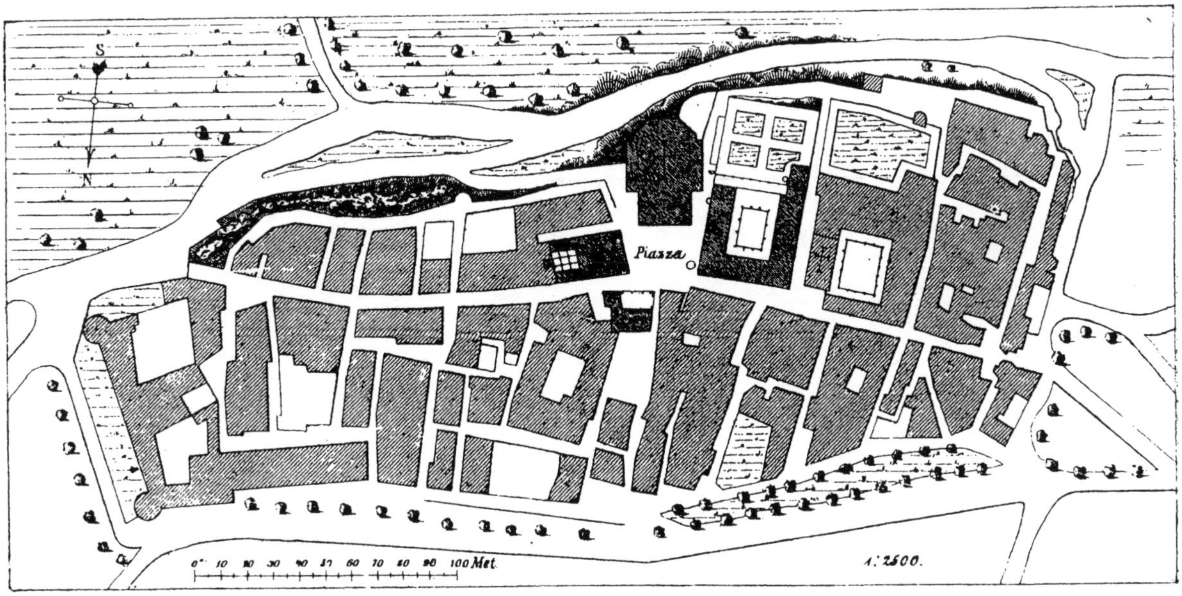

Fig. 254 *Plan of Pienza*

an extract in Della Valle, *Lettere Sanesi*, III, p. 112; ideal picture of a newly founded town – Sforzinda – in Ant. Filarete, *Trattato*; cf. in v. Oettingen, *Filarete*, p. 41 ff. The very exaggerated imaginary picture of a town – frescoes by Benozzo Gozzoli in the Campo Santo at Pisa, *The Tower of Babel*.

Corsignano rebuilt, 1458–62, as the city of Pienza (Fig. 254) by Pius II shows as a very substantial achievement of this short spring-time the Piazza bordered by palazzi and the Cathedral; other palaces near-by on the Corso; the town, narrow and set on the saddle of a hill, extending about 350 metres and covering an area of barely 17 acres; cf. Mayreder, Bender and Holtzinger in Allg. Bauzeitung, 1882.

The rebuilding of Ostia by Cardinal d'Estouteville under Sixtus IV, "with new streets and houses for ornament and profit"; *Vitae Papar.*, in Murat., III, II, col. 1064.

In the very important new quarters of Ferrara (§ 112), which took shape under Duke Ercole I (*d* 1505), rectilinear architecture was the rule, wherever possible with intersections at right angles. In 1497 it was noted that building did not keep pace with the increase of population, and that there were no more houses to let.

The most significant general plan of architectural merit of the sixteenth century was Castro,* which Paul III's son, Pierluigi Farnese, had carried out by Antonio da Sangallo the Younger (*d* 1546). When the place was demolished in 1649 everything was destroyed, but Sangallo's drawings are still in the Uffizi, Florence. Details: Vasari, V, p. 500 ff., *V. di Sangallo* (Commentary); a ducal *osteria*, dwellings and palaces for suite and officers, most apparently with colonnades; a church with monastery; a mint etc. Has the complete plan of the contemporary fortifications been preserved anywhere in identifiable form? Palmanova, an entirely symmetrical octagon, dates only from 1593.

Of the great plan of Nicholas V, who wanted to rebuild the whole Roman Borgo (§ 7) from the Ponte Sant' Angelo up to, and including, S. Peter's and the Vatican, only a contemporary description has survived: *Vitae Papar.*, in Murat., III, II, col. 931 ff. (*Life of Nicholas* by Giannozzo Manetti), of which Vasari, III, p. 100 ff. is merely a summary. The new Borgo, as the home of all those having any connection with the Curia, was to comprise three parallel colonnaded streets, all opening into the great piazza in front of S. Peter's; the middle one opposite the main door of the church, that on the left in the area of the obelisk (then standing to one side), and the one on the right towards the Porta Palatina of the Vatican. The latter, as also the front elevations of S. Peter's disclosing an increasing splendour, of which no account is possible here. For an architect with imagination a rewarding theme for restoration (or, rather, reconstruction). (*Theatrum* means here a loggia or open colonnade, *coenaculum* generally a large room. According to another opinion, the obelisk was already to have been transferred to the main axis of S. Peter's.)

(NOTE: For Manetti's *Life of Nicholas V* see now T. Magnuson, *Studies in Roman Quattrocento Architecture*, Stockholm, 1958.) (PM).

* Lago d' Iseo.

CHAPTER FOURTEEN

Villas

§ 116 *Types of Villas*

Villas in Italy had an earlier and always greater significance than in the rest of Europe, and Florence again led the way for the whole country.

Cf. *Kultur der Renaiss.*, p. 399: Gio. Villani, XI, c. 93, for the year 1338; anyone with the means to do so built villas in the country richer and finer even than their town-houses, so that strangers believed themselves to be already in Florence when they were still three miles off. Big spenders of this kind were taken at the time for "silly people". Towards the end of the fifteenth century the Perugians also had villas finer than their town dwellings; Matarazzo in Arch. Stor., XVI, II, p. 8.

From early times there was a distinction between the country house proper, for lengthy stays and as an economic unit, and the *villa suburbana* for recreation, close to the town or in the outskirts, for briefer visits, but generally adapted to overnight stays. Theories were propounded about both. But if their requirements were different, in architectural features they inevitably agreed in many respects.

Leon Battista Alberti, perhaps the real author of the treatise on domestic matters which, under Pandolfini's name, sets such store by country life, gives in his *De re aedific.*, L. V, c. 15–17, a description of a Villa, and (L. IX, c. 2–4) that of a Villa Suburbana. For the first, however, it sticks simply to the programme, to the enumeration of the rooms, which should be grouped around a common *sinus* or central space. As in the country there is no reason to build high, everything is thought of as at ground level. The detail partly according to Vitruvius and the *scriptores rei rusticae*.

The suburban pleasure-house, its intrinsic value dependent on its artistic form, should, in Alberti's view, be of bright and inviting design and sited on a gentle slope; transparent, full of light and air; *arrideant omnia*; alternating square and round rooms with angular ones, and mingling curved and straight lines; an inner, linking hall – *sinus interior* – around which everything is theoretically grouped, everything on one level, ground-storey only; *conclavia*= small rooms, *coenacula*= saloni. As painted wall-decoration landscapes and bucolic or genre subjects are recommended.

The alternation of rooms also in Sannazaro (*Senazar. eleg.*, L. III, 3, *de exstruenda domo*, 1496–1501): *Jungantur longis quadrata, obliqua rotundis*. The central *sinus* is conceived as oval or round:

Aedibus in mediis parvi sinus amphitheatri
Visendas regum praebeat historias[1]

The villa projects in the Seventh Book of Serlio, so far as they are to be understood as *villae suburbanae*, show simply self-contained individual rooms, which are connected only by the central *sinus* or salone; the latter round, oval, octagonal or quadrangular, already with a *lanternina* in the centre. If the salone is oblong, buffet and chimneypiece are placed opposite one another in the middle of the two long sides. All service functions in the basement; storage perhaps in a concealed upper floor with lucarnes; the single-storey appearance always strictly adhered to, the smaller rooms often halved in practice. The individual elements sometimes deliberately isolated from one another and only linked by passages etc. to the main salone.

Palladio and Scamozzi (*Architettura*, L. III) held fast to the large central room, sometimes featuring it externally by a dome; and increasing the size by having two storeys and also steps. On the other hand, Roman architects of the best as well as the declining period designed the building without the central room, perhaps with two

1 The villa which Sannazaro actually built at Posilippo was destroyed by the Spaniards under Philibert of Orange in the subsequent wars. Sannazaro, gravely ill as a result, had the pleasure of learning in 1530 that Philibert had perished, and declared that he was now happy to die, since the barbarian enemy of the Muses had got his reward: Paul. Jovii, *Elogia*, sub Sannazario.

Fig. 255 *Rome, Vatican gardens, Casino di Pio IV*

principal saloni or colonnades running parallel, with secondary rooms on each flank and an upper storey, which corresponded to the ground-floor entirely, or only partly in a lighter type of building.

§117 *Further Theories of Villa Architecture*

In general, the *villa suburbana* was to adopt, as an architecture of pure fantasy, the most varied forms. Its rooms had the sole object of creating a pleasing or noble impression; inevitably, among both clients and architects whimsy and extravagance, as well as originality, would be found.

In Book VII of Serlio, p. 28, the notorious plan of a villa like the sails of a windmill; p. 42, the admission that novel devices were needed to escape from common usage; round, even oval cortili with arcades in villas, pp. 27, 250* (cf. §120, the Villa at Caprarola). Other follies, p. 38, etc. The belief that in the country things were permissible which would not be allowed *in luogo civile e nobile*, p. 16.

The external aspect was principally characterised, in contrast to the town house, by openness to the outside in the form of loggie, as a visible symbol of love of the open air, welcome and airiness – in the sharpest contrast to the country houses of the North.

Serlio, VII, p. 46: "in the country arcades are much handsomer to look at than (enclosed) façades; there is more delight – *più diletto* – in allowing the eye to penetrate the darkness between the arches than to admire a wall where the gaze can go no further".

There is no doubt that architecture achieves a supreme sense of invitation in a motive borrowed from the Thermae: the large, deeply recessed, semi-circular niche. Only Bramante used it, and then not in a villa, but as the concluding feature of the huge cortile and garden in the Vatican (Giardino della Pigna). But Pietro da Cortona exploited it with studied purpose a century and a half later for the façade of his Villa Sacchetti, called il Pigneto.

Of its own accord the unity of treatment which was the absolute law for the town palazzi, at least of the old Tuscan School, now disappeared. Even symmetry was at times abandoned.

The villa had no true main façade, as it was felt to be standing in the open; on each of its sides, or on any one of them, a loggia would occupy either the middle between two salient wings, or be grouped with various elements at the expense of symmetry. Very early the tower, a relic of castellated architecture and its functions, was to become an established feature of the villa; it remained an irrational element, if it were not doubled or quadrupled.

* There is no p. 250 in Serlio's Book VII, but p. 31 has a villa design with an oval court. (PM).

Fig. 256 *Rome, Villa Madama, section through the Villa and court*

The Renaissance, however, never flirted with asymmetry in the guise of the picturesque; it only conceded what was unavoidable.

For this reason the effect was always valid. Theory was not the supreme arbiter here, being entirely silent on such matters. The deciding factor was a monument of the utmost elegance like the Villa Pia (by Pirro Ligorio, in the Vatican gardens). To this otherwise strictly symmetrical building a tower was added in the left background (Fig. 255), as if it needed one final note to create the impression of a happy accident. To the right, a special addition for the staircase, almost out of sight.

Sometimes the special conditions of the site also resulted in asymmetry. Cf. the obscure, but very engaging, description of Giovio's villa (now, to the best of our knowledge, disappeared) built out into Lake Como: Paul. Jov. *Elogia literaria, Musei descriptio.* The principal room, with top-lighting on all sides, contained his celebrated collection of portraits.

§118 *Villas of the Early Renaissance*

Chronologically, as well as stylistically, the Florentines outstripped all other builders of villas.

The deliberate demolitions of 1529, when Florence was besieged by the Spaniards, destroyed the best over a wide area. Perhaps the architectural backgrounds of the frescoes by Benozzo Gozzoli (Campo Santo at Pisa), and here and there also the intarsie on choir-stalls, which contained so many views of imaginary buildings, give some idea of what they were like.

The few still surviving from the fifteenth century are more or less reconstructed: Villa Michelozzi (or Bellosguardo) still has the lower colonnade and tower; regarding other buildings by Michelozzo, Villa Mozzi, Villa Ricasoli at Fiesole, as also the Medici villas at Caffaggiuoli (still castle-like), Trebbio and Careggi, cf. Vasari, II, p. 442, *V. di Michelozzo*, and VI, p. 281, *V. di Pontormo*, and the author's *Cicerone*, 10th ed., II, 1, pp. 124, 126. The Villa Mozzi, on a steeply sloping site, contained service rooms below, and the saloni, living accommodation, and special rooms for books and music above.

(In a grander and freer style, for Lorenzo il Magnifico; Poggio a Cajano, by Giuliano da Sangallo, with a large salone, its barrel vault being permitted only after the architect had built one like it in his own house in Florence: Vasari, IV, p. 270, *V. di G. da Sangallo.*)

The fine and simple country house of Poggio Reale, built for Alfonso, Crown Prince of Naples in 1487 by Giuliano da Majano,[1] which was above all famous for the trick fountain in the cortile, has now vanished and is known only from the rough illustration in Serlio, L. III, p. 121, based on information from Marcantonio Michiel, in which plan, section, and elevation do not quite correspond, and the external colonnades have been tacked on. The building comprised two ranges of arcades round a square cortile, and twenty-four small rooms, to which were added at the angles three above and three below; the whole open, transparent, relying on shade and airiness.

Of the villas not by Florentine masters of the fifteenth and early sixteenth centuries most have gone or been seriously mutilated.

The Magliana near Rome, already existing under Sixtus IV, reconstructed and embellished by Inno-

1 Vasari, II, p. 470, and IX, p. 256; also Luca Pacioli (*Divina Proporzione*, ed. C. Winterberg, p. 148) speaks of a model which Lorenzo il Magnifico roughed out for Giuliano da Majano for the *degno palazzo detto dogliuolo* (probably a corruption of *poggio reale*) *alla città di Napoli* (cf. §11). Cf. also §91. The claim originating with Baldi (*c* 1585), that the villa was by Luciano Laurana, is merely hypothesis; Baldi's lack of judgement in architectural matters is typified by his suggestion that Brunellesco collaborated on the palace at Urbino!

Fig. 257 *Rome, Villa Madama, section through the garden (Villa at left)*

cent VIII: Infessura, in Eccard, *Scriptores*, II, col. 1948, 2007, 2010. It was the usual objective of Innocent's excursions into the country. The latter had the Belvedere at the Vatican built as a place for recreation, at a cost of 60,000 ducats (ibid., col. 2007); Müntz, *Les arts . . .*, III, p. 74 (where Giacomo da Pietrasanta is suggested as architect). The villa was later much altered, including the present Galleria delle Statue (formerly containing frescoes by Mantegna and Pinturicchio), the eastern rooms, and especially the cortile, which was originally four-sided and surrounded by simple high walls. Julius II had trees planted and the angles adorned with niches which accommodated the principal treasures of the newly founded Vatican Museum. Clement XIV gave the cortile an octagonal loggia, the angles being converted in 1805 into enclosed rooms. Cf. A. Michaelis in Jahrbuch des kaiserl. deutsch. archäolog. Instituts, V, 1890, pp. 5–72.

In Ferrara Duke Borso (1450–71) seems to have built a number of small country houses, of which illustrations may perhaps be seen in the frescoes of the Pal. Schifanoia. Alfonso I (1505–34) built, on an island in the Po, Belvedere, with densely wooded park and a wild animal reserve, and, on the other side of the town, surrounded by trees and ramparts, Montana, with paintings and fountains; both *mediocria aedificia*, which were liable to be sacrificed in a war.

The Palazzina della Viola in Bologna, with loggie, built by Giovanni II Bentivoglio *c* 1497, later decorated by Innocenzo da Imola with mythological frescoes. (It is now the School of Agriculture.)

§119 *Villas of the High Renaissance*

In the sixteenth century the villa suburbana was pre-eminently the object of the greatest and noblest artistic endeavours; a number of monuments reflect the most agreeable fantasy without being fantastic.

For the cardinal's vigne of *c* 1500 (and there were certainly buildings in this field which set the architectural standards) we have little more than the superficial account in Albertini (*De mirabilibus urbis Romae*, L. III, fol. 89), where they are thrown in with the palazzi.

The Farnesina (built in 1509 for Agostino Chigi), *non murato, ma veramente nato*; Vasari, IV, p. 593, *V. di Peruzzi*. Extolled, even without Raphael's frescoes, in a publication of January, 1512: *Suburbanum Agustini Chisii per Blosium Palladium*, quoted in *Anecdota Literaria*, II, p. 172. The simplest of schemes, at ground level mainly colonnades of differing character, and saloni above; the exterior intended to have grisaille decoration, but complete even without it. (That Raphael rather than Peruzzi designed the building, is suggested as probable by v. Geymüller, *R. Sanzio studiato come architetto*, pp. 24–42.)

The Villa Madama, at the foot of Monte Mario outside Rome, really the vigna de' Medici (Figs. 256, 257), designed in his last years by Raphael for Cardinal Giulio de' Medici, later Pope Clement VII; parts of it executed by Giulio Romano; the authentic façade and plan in Serlio, L. III, fol. 120, cf. fol. 131; infinitely superior to the executed building (below, besides the three-arched colonnade only a niche on each side still surviving; an upper storey of three windows and two niches;

the pilasters below Ionic, those above Corinthian). In the building as it now exists the interior of the loggia, quite apart from the decorations, is of wonderfully rich appearance with large niches and different types of vaulting; at the rear, initial indications of a peculiar round cortile; restoration of the whole dubious.

The entire rich pre-history of the present building as well as the intended garden schemes in v. Geymüller, *Raffaello* . . ., p. 59 ff.; 91 ff., where, from Raphael's draughtsmen's plans the supposed elevations and sections have been evolved; a fertile variety of conclusions. Cf. Th. Hofmann, *Raffael als Architekt*, I, Die Villa Madama.

Closely related to the authentic plan for the façade of this villa: Falconetto's garden loggia with salone above, in the cortile of the Pal. Giustiniani at Padua, built for Luigi Cornaro (dated 1524) and standing at right angles to the building mentioned in § 107. Below, five open arches; above, five windows; the exterior and the rich decoration of the interior (§ 176) noble throughout.

In Florence, via Valfonda 59, the Stiozzi-Ridolfi (now Giuntini) house, according to Vasari by Baccio d' Agnolo, master of a superior domestic architecture (§ 92), deliberately irregular, with colonnaded cortile, secondary court, garden, garden colonnade, and tower.

This irregular layout and, with it, great picturesque charm was also characteristic of the small vigne and farmhouses round Florence (Figs. 258, 259, 260). A south-facing loggia for drying the fruit, a tower serving as dovecote, from which the work in the fields could also be supervised, linked with a few modest living-rooms, were often the constituents of such buildings, rendered attractive by the enchantment of the site and the intuitive exploitation of the landscape.

Villa Lante in Rome, on a spur of the Janiculum, by Giulio Romano before 1524, at present inaccessible and only inadequately known from illustrations: Vasari, V, p. 534, *V. di Giulio*.

Pal. del Te at Mantua, also by Giulio, begun before 1527 for Duke Federigo Gonzaga, who at first wanted no more than occasional accommodation near his famous stud-farm; only a ground floor and mezzanine with a

Fig. 258 *(opposite top) Villa near Florence (I)*

Fig. 259 *(opposite left) Villa near Florence (II)*

Fig. 260 *(opposite right)* Castello, *Villa Cavacchia, near Florence*

Fig. 261 *(above) Mantua, Palazzo del Te, loggia*

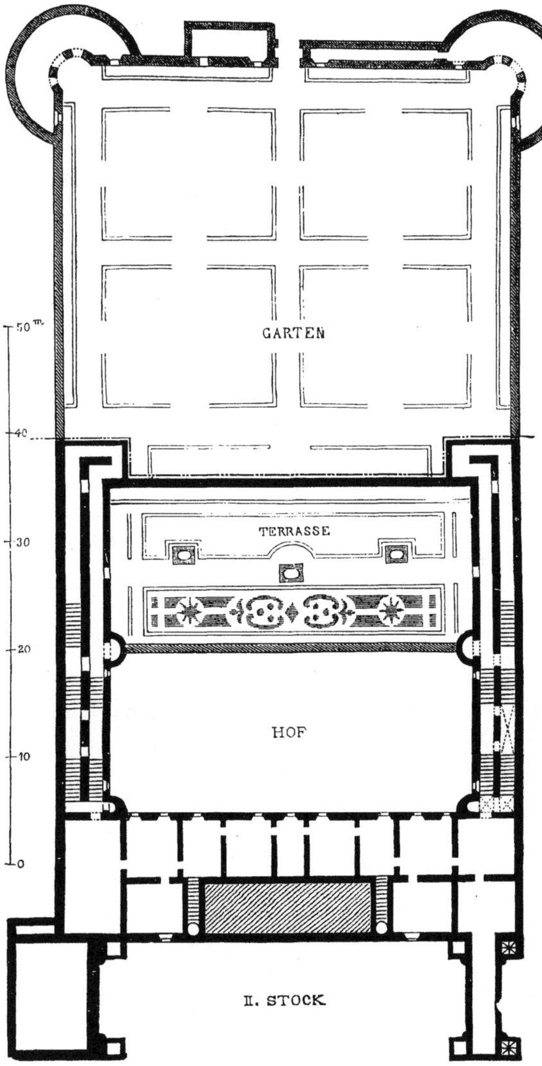

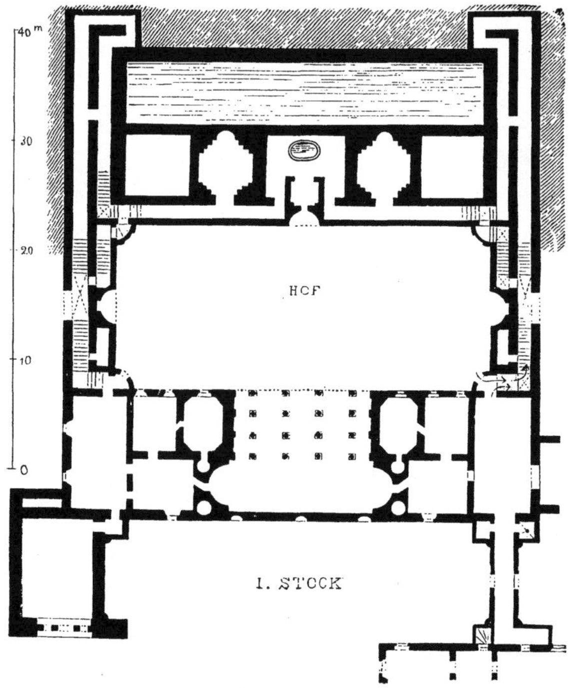

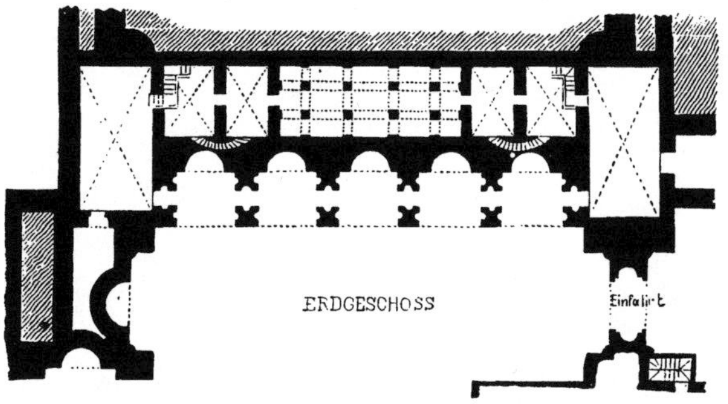

Figs. 262, 263 *(above) Pesaro, Villa Imperiale, plans*

Figs. 264, 265 *(opposite) Pesaro, Villa Imperiale, elevation and section*

Doric Order and heavy rustication (§54), which was no doubt intended to symbolise the association with farming purposes; for the rest, for lack of stone, all in brick with rough-cast facing. Subsequently the Duke was induced to have the building extended round the four sides of a cortile; facing the cortile an open loggia with coupled columns, among the finest of the entire Renaissance (Fig. 261); the remaining rooms, of the most varied sizes and character, richly adorned with frescoes and stucco work (§176). Significant as the first monumental building in substitute materials, when plain brick could have been freely used, and as an example of the use of rustication as a plausible expression of rusticity.

Marmirolo, which Giulio also built, after a plan had already been submitted in 1523 by Michelangelo (Vasari, VII, p. 364, in the commentary on the *V. di Michelangelo*; and Gaye, *Carteggio*, II, p. 154), has completely disappeared. The many rooms to house great princely retinues were famous, as were the waterworks, the splendid gardens and the luxuriant clusters of grapes on the pillars. Leandro Alberti, *Descrizione di tutta l' Italia*, 1577 ed., fol. 396.

So also the Villa Soranza by Sanmicheli, not far from Castelfranco, which at the time was considered far and wide as the perfect villa: Vasari, V, p. 291, *V. di Sanmicheli*.

In the Uffizi the design for the villa of the Cardinal of Sta Croce on Monte Amiata, designed as a bathing-establishment by Antonio da Sangallo the Younger, reproduced by Redtenbacher in Allg. Bauzeitung, 1883, p. 58.

Villa Monte Imperiale near Pesaro (Figs. 262–65), built by Girol. Genga (probably 1529 or 1530) for Duke Francesco Maria della Rovere of Urbino. Never finished,

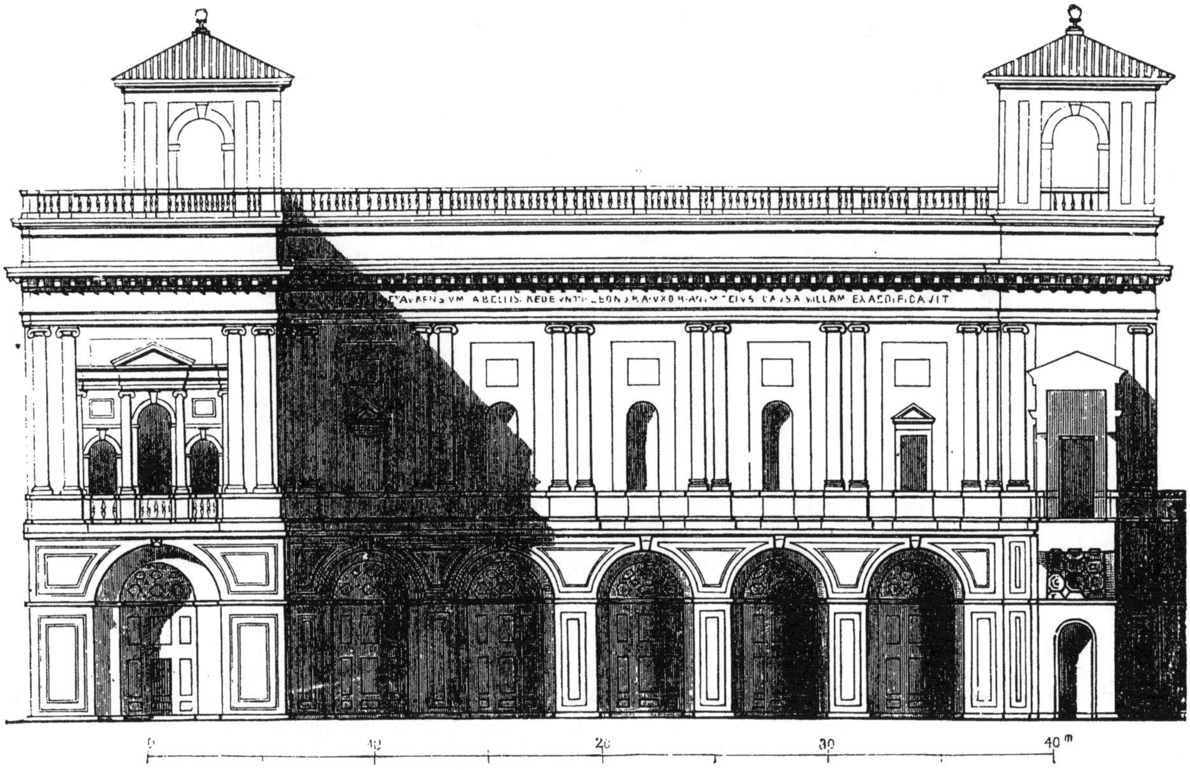

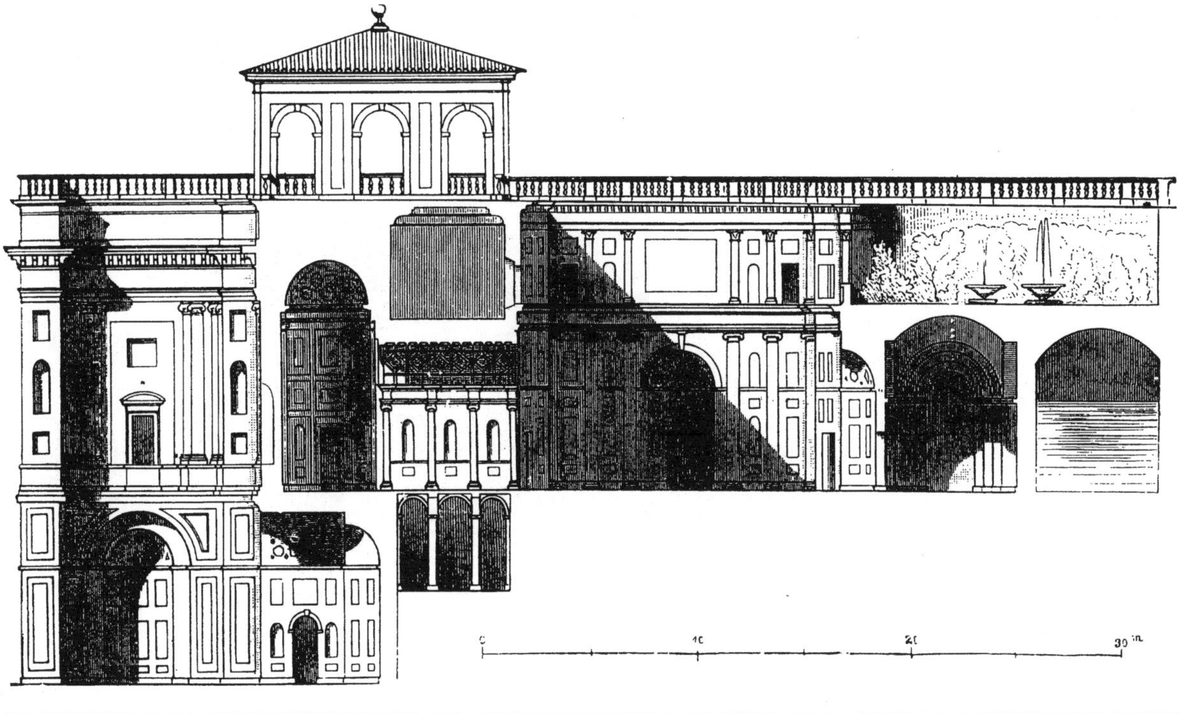

but even in its present ruinous state of imposing effect; the building follows the steep slope in three stages; below, an impressive arcaded storey with an enclosed pilaster-clad façade above. *Piena di camere, di colonnati e di cortili, di loggie, di fontane e di amenissimi giardini*, once visited by all travelling princes: Vasari, VI, p. 319, *V. di Genga.*

At Cricoli near Vicenza the villa of the Trissino family, after the plan of the founder Giov. Giorgio Trissino (§12); a façade once again (like Cornaro's garden loggia at Padua) very like the authentic one of the Villa Madama, but enclosed between two salient (? older) towers. (*Il Forestiere istruito . . . di Vicenza*, pl. 33.)

In *Pauli Jovii Elogia literaria* as an introduction, the

Fig. 266 *(opposite above) Caprarola, near Viterbo, Villa Farnese, plan and section*

Fig. 267 *(opposite below) Rome, Villa Giulia*

Fig. 268 *(above) Rome, Villa Giulia, garden*

Fig. 269 *Tivoli, Villa d' Este*

Latin description of the villa (now lost) built out into the lake near Como by Giovio himself, extraordinarily attractive, but too vague to permit of a hypothetical reconstruction.

The aesthetic law of villa architecture of the Golden Age will only become fully comprehensible when the relevant remains have been fully investigated all over Italy and comprehensively studied. A record, for example, of the villas scattered round Siena, which originated entirely or in part with Peruzzi, is still wanting. The beautiful garden elevation of the Villa Colomba (in Schütz, fol. 103) is hardly by Peruzzi. A plan of the Villa Belcaro in Peruzzi's hand in the Uffizi (rep. by Redtenbacher, *Peruzzi u. seine Werke*, pl. 15).

(NOTE: For the Farnesina see C. Frommel, *Die Farnesina und Peruzzis Architektonisches Frühwerk*, Berlin, 1961. See also D. Coffin, *The Villa in the Life of Renaissance Rome*, Princeton, 1979; E. Verheyen, *The Palazzo del Te in Mantua*, Baltimore and London, 1977; A. Pinelli, O. Rossi, *Genga Architetto*, Rome, 1971 (the Villa Imperiale at Pesaro has been restored); for the Villa Trissino, see R. Wittkower, *Architectural Principles*, cit.) (PM).

§120 *Villas of the Aftermath*

Among the villas of the period 1540–80 the most noteworthy were true country seats, designed for hosts of servants. Already there were signs here and there of a monotonous vastness, and even of the style of the urban palazzo replacing less rigid rural charm. A few of the smaller casini, however, rank with the best.

The huge pentagonal Caprarola, the Farnese stronghold, a few hours north of Rome, by Vignola, who here provided one of the patterns of modern fortification. Massive ramps, earthworks, five bastions, and above all this the main building, of two Orders with a great open arcaded loggia on one side. Within, a large round cortile with pillared arcades, one of the most imposing creations of all secular architecture: Vasari, VII, p. 107, *V. di T. Zucchero* (Fig. 266). (An older project by Peruzzi, for Ser Silvestro da Caprarola, with pentagonal pillared cortile, see Redtenbacher, op. cit., pl. 16.)

Well preserved: Villa Lante alla Bagnaja near Viterbo, by Vignola, most beautifully terraced with modest means, the main axis splendidly featured with fountains and stairs.

To Vignola also is attributed the most important surviving villa suburbana, the Vigna di Papa Giulio III near Rome (now a museum), *c* 1550. (Varying shares by Vasari, Michelangelo, Ammanati, and the Pope himself.) Of the palace, the front portion valueless; the semicircular loggia (Fig. 267) of dubious effect; the second loggia beyond the cortile and the sunken court terminating the whole with its still deeper grotto, are of elegant, picturesque appearance, but already with a conscious variety of motives. (Fig. 268: the furthest part not completely finished.)

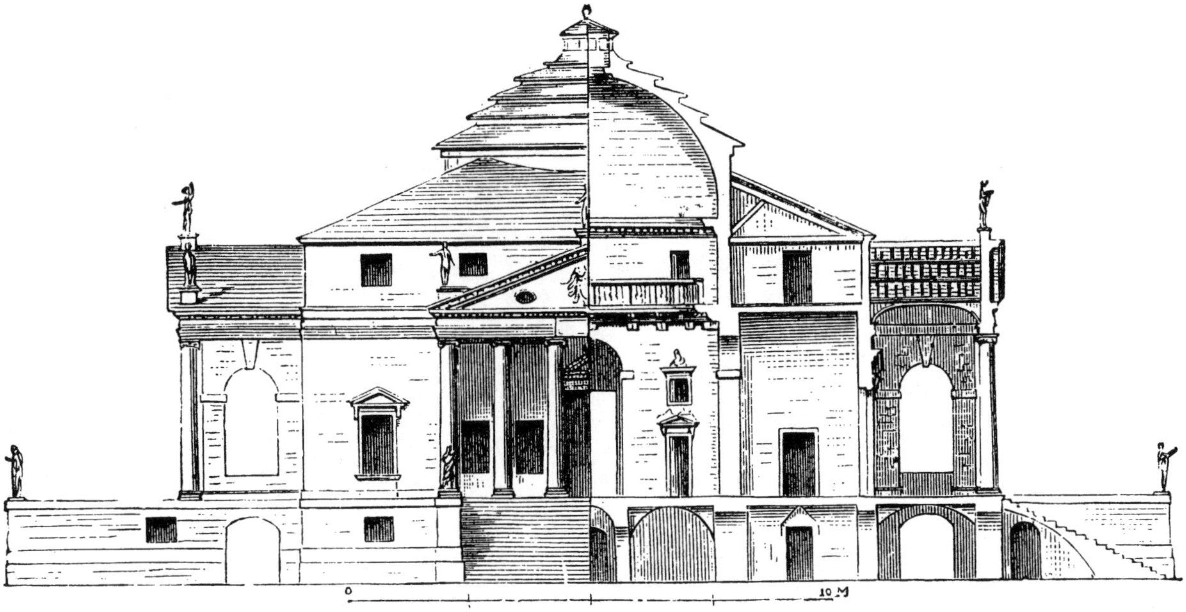

Fig. 270 *Vicenza, Villa Rotonda, elevation and section*

At the Villa d' Este, Tivoli (1549), the palace large, but unimportant and later (Fig. 269).

Of the villas of Duke Cosimo I Medici that of Castello near Florence (by Tribolo) still generally regarded as significant; Pratolino in the Apennines was chiefly famous for its gardens and water.

In and around Genoa are, or were, the best works by Alessi (1512–72); the now demolished Pal. Sauli (Fig. 245) was a kind of suburban villa with a very fine colonnaded cortile in front (in this respect recalling the French type *entre cour et jardin*); the other villas (all still lived in and not easily accessible) are rectangular palaces (with upper and lower Orders of pilasters and engaged columns), their rustic character none the less expressed in the colonnade opening of the ground or upper storey and in their formal character among the best of the period: Villa Pallavicini delle Peschiere; Villa Cambiaso (with its very impressive ground-floor colonnade); Villa Scassi (now swallowed up by the freight-yard of Sampierdarena); by a later architect: Villa Podenas, called Il Paradiso, in which a large, continuous, colonnaded gallery occupies the front of the entire middle storey, and several more. Other villas of the period have been ruined or rebuilt. By Alessi also the castle of Castiglione in the lake of Perugia.

Of Palladio's villas, the celebrated Villa Rotonda, or Capra, near Vicenza (cf. §116, Fig. 270) is a villa suburbana; most of the rest are large, symmetrical country seats, dominating their farm buildings and often exquisitely laid out, always with a large central salone; in this respect alone Palladio misinterpreted the true architectural form of the villa, by not always opening the façade as a loggia, but permitting a Temple portico, with pediment, to stand in front of a closed wall; and even when the façade is open, there occurs, instead of an authentic loggia-form, generally with engaged columns, a Temple colonnade – two-storeyed even – with a pediment.

Of the casini of this period the Palazzina at Ferrara (1599) retains a glimmer of its former grace, while the Villa Pia (§117, Fig. 255), in the Vatican gardens, by Pirro Ligorio *c* 1560, has been completely preserved; an oval terrace with the building itself at the back, a pavilion in front with substructure, at the two rounded ends small entrance colonnades; the whole intended for stucco-work, fountains, and a special garden setting, which is now the only shortcoming.

(NOTE: For the Casino di Pio IV see G. Smith, *The Casino of Pius IV*, Princeton, 1977.) (PM).

§121 *Villas of the Baroque Period*

In the Baroque period from 1580 onwards Rome and its environs became the most important location for the further development both of the country villa and the villa suburbana. The former approximated in details to the austere forms of the contemporary town palazzo, while preserving the loggia as the principal feature (Fig. 269). The latter, on plan now frequently outstandingly handsome and with airy colonnades and convenient stairs perfectly adapted to leisured living, nevertheless never again reached genuine purity of architectural expression. Rustication and flat framing-effects of all types contrast with insertions of Antique reliefs, an extravagance exclusive to Rome. Separate small casini correspond to the larger villas, on a different level but on the same axis.

Influential country villas: Villa Aldobrandini and Villa Mondragone, near Frascati. Ville suburbane: Villa Montalto Negroni (from the time of Sixtus V) with

Fig. 271 *Rome, Villa Medici*

main building and casino, the latter by Domenichino; V. Borghese, V. Mattei etc.; perhaps the most effective, the garden side of the Villa Medici on Monte Pincio (Fig. 271).

§122 *Baths*

In the villas the bath-installations occasionally attained the status of architecture.

Among these surely belongs the stufa in the Villa Lante in Rome; Vasari, V, p. 534, *V. di Giulio Romano*, with frescoes of the *Loves of the Gods*. The younger Sangallo designed for Cardinal Marcello Cervini, later Pope Marcellus II (§29), a plan for a bath on the Antique pattern with *frigidarium*, *tepidarium*, *calidarium*, which was to be erected at a villa in Vivo: Vasari, V, p. 518, in the commentary on the *V. di Ant. Sangallo*.

At the Villa Grimaldi at Bissagno near Genoa, Alessi built a round bathroom with a dome, its baths receiving hot water through the jaws of sea-monsters, and cold from the mouths of frogs; around it a passage-way with eight niches, four of them occupied by individual baths, four by windows and doors; between them herms supporting a cornice; from the vault there hung an ingenious candelabrum, with a great bowl representing the firmament; the ante-rooms and adjacent accommodation also finished in the most elegant manner: Vasari, VIII, p. 544, *V. di Leoni*.

Regarding the "stufetta" of Cardinal Bibiena (the so-called Bath of Julius II) in the Vatican, there is a reference in Bembo's letter of 1516 (*Lettere Pittoriche*, V, 57, 58), from which we learn only that Raphael was given the subjects for the murals by Bibiena, but did not know where to put the small marble statue of Venus.*

* The text more easily available in V. Golzio, *Raffaello nei Documenti*, Vatican City, 1936. (PM).

CHAPTER FIFTEEN

Gardens

§ 123 *Gardens Principally of Botanic Interest*

The gardens of palaces and especially of villas were no doubt arranged in early times in regular lines, perhaps in strict conformity with the building concerned. If, to begin with, the artistic side was somewhat neglected, the causes lay in the interests of botany and utility.

Cf. *Kultur d. Renaiss.*, p. 287. The garden of the Medici villa at Careggi in the time of Lorenzo il Magnifico was described as a collection of countless individual species of trees and shrubs.

The magnificent garden of Poggio Reale near Naples, laid out by the Crown Prince Alfonso (§ 118), who in 1495 as a fugitive King paid homage to botany by taking with him to his asylum – Sicily – *toutes sortes de graines pour faire jardins*; Comines, L. VII, c. 11, or *Charles VIII*, c. 17. The principal account, from the Vergier d'Honneur, verbatim in Roscoe, *Leone X*, ed. Bossi, Tom. IV, p. 226, and in Müntz, *La Renaissance.*, p. 435. Besides the palace, a number of ornamental buildings, small lawns, fountains, streams, antique statues; an enclosed park with all the fruit-trees which the climate permitted; bay trees, flowers, and endless rose-gardens; then a special game reserve, stables, dairies, vineyards with grapes of every kind, and huge vaulted cellars. Obviously the domestic needs of the great house, the demand for flowers on festive occasions, and botanical predilections far outweighed artistic ideals.

In the garden at the front of the Vatican Palace, as Nicholas V wanted it to be *c* 1450, *herbae et fructus* of all varieties as well as waterworks would have found their place; *Vitae Papar.* in Murat., III, II, col. 932.

In the palace garden at Ferrara, which Ercole I (*d* 1505) probably had laid out hurriedly in the 1480s, among the box-hedges, the vine-leaves on marble columns, the painted and gilded pavilions, and the fountain with seven outlets, no ornamental or fruit-bearing tree was lacking, so that even here the practical side of gardening had its recognisable place. Titi Strozzae, *Aeolostichon*, L. II, p. 209.

Another pleasure garden in the city, with rooms for lodging (1497), contained, among other things, a fish-pond with bridges over it: *Diario Ferrarese*, in Murat., XXIV, col. 346. Regarding Belvedere and Montana, see § 118.

A park for exotic animals, which were a whim of the period (*Kultur der Renaiss.*, p. 288), laid out by Duke Ercole in 1471 directly in front of the city involving costly expropriations, *Diario*, cit., col. 236. Poggio Reale also contained a menagerie. In Palermo, Otto de S. Blasio mentions (in 1194): *hortum regalem amplissimum . . . omni bestiarum genere delectabiliter refertum.*

§ 124 *Infiltration of Architectonic Elements*

Meanwhile the attainment of ever more fanciful effects was early to become an accepted aim, as was implied by the enthusiasm with which gardens were generally discussed. This impression might rest as much upon the architectonic discipline of the layout as on especially fine details. Water displays, however, were to play a relatively small part until well into the sixteenth century, since the great Roman water-extravaganzas, precursors of the European, did not begin until Sixtus V.

Vague early mentions of outstanding gardens from time to time, e.g. Matteo Villani, IV, c. 44, a *famoso giardino* in the Pal. Gambacorti at Pisa, where the Emperor Charles IV, a great amateur of gardens, stayed in 1354.

Imaginary pictures, sometimes of inspiring beauty in Aeneas Sylvius (*Epistola* 108, p. 612, the Garden of Fortuna) and in Poliphilus (*Hypnerotomachia*, cf. § 32: an extract in Temanza, p. 28, the Island of Cythera). Other examples in the frescoes of Bennozzo Gozzoli (Camposanto at Pisa) and in fifteenth-century panel-paintings.

Influence of descriptions of gardens in Pliny's *Letters*, or, when these were not yet familiar, in other writings of Antiquity: the Hippodromus in the gardens of the Castello of Milan before 1447, *Vita Phil. Mariae Vicecomitis, auct. Decembrio*, in Murat., XX, col. 1008. Cf. Pliny, L. V, *Ep.* 6.

Leon Battista Alberti (1450) was the first to define some of the features which were subsequently to become characteristic of the grand Italian garden; *De re aedificatoria*, L. IX, c. 4: grottoes of tufa, which were early imitated from Antiquity, in which impatient owners replaced the mossy greenery with green wax; a fountain grotto encrusted with shells; a garden portico, offering sunshine or shade according to the season or time of day; an open space (*area*); jeux d'eau; evergreen box-lined paths; myrtle and laurels; ivy-clad cypresses; individual parts of the garden round or semi-circular, and in general in those shapes which are beautiful in an architectural plan: (? *cycli et hemicycli, et quae descriptiones in areis aedificiorum probentur*), and bounded by thick hedges. From Antiquity were also taken: Corinthian columns to support the vine-clusters; inscriptions traced in box borders; trees planted in quincunx shapes; for hedges, roses were especially recommended; oaks, it was said, were more fitting in farmsteads than gardens. At about this time humorous genre statues were already appearing in gardens; Alberti permitted them, provided they were not obscene.

Scarcely one of the older fountains survives. The whole art-form of the fountain, and the disposition of the sculpture, remains for the fifteenth and even for the early sixteenth century, despite numerous accounts, no more than hypothetical. However good the craftsmanship, stone, cement, and metal joints succumb eventually to damp; moreover these earlier works were adapted to a much more sparing use of water, and would have seemed worthless when the water-extravaganzas were introduced.

Villa d' Este at Tivoli, laid out under the direction of Pirro Ligorio, with the waters of the Teverone freely available, built up in terraces, and with regard for the surrounding landscape (Fig. 269). Accurate description and aesthetic appraisal by E. Paulus, Allg. Bauzeitung, 1863, with illustrations by E. Gnauth.

§ 125 *Antique Sculptures and Ruins*

The Italian garden early concluded a double pact with the antiquities of Rome: fragments of sculpture and inscriptions, which could not be used as decoration for the interiors of buildings, made an impressive and, as was no doubt soon appreciated, elegiac effect amid the vegetation on a garden wall; also on the garden front of villas Roman reliefs were often generously applied. Thus genuine architectural remains provided not only their poetic beauty, but were imitated in gardens. Undoubtedly Roman gardens laid out in real ruins provided the stimulus.

Poggio in the *Dialogus de Nobilitate*, which he produced before 1440 (*Poggii Opèra*, ed. Argentin., fol. 25), mockingly comments that he adorned his own little garden (at Terranuova near Florence) with fragments of marble remains, so that posterity would accord him some fame for the novelty of the thing. The small garden of the Pal. Medici-Riccardi, at that time entirely filled with antiquities, was the scene of Michelangelo's studies; Vasari, IV, p. 256, *V. di Torrigiano.*

Use on a large scale: on the garden side of the Palazzo della Valle in Rome, an entire façade filled with reliefs and a mixture of sculptural fragments, as well as statues in niches: Vasari, IV, p. 579, *V. di Lorenzetto*, at the time of Raphael. Exactly contemporary in Rome, the giardinetto of the Archbishop of Cyprus "with fine statues among other antiquities", including a *Bacchus*; Vasari, V, p. 597, *V. di Perino*, who painted bacchanalian scenes on the walls, cf. § 128. Giulio Romano preferred to bring his antiques into the house itself; Vasari, V, p. 549, *V. di Giulio.*

Statues were also placed in special pergolas, which were given the form of temples etc. As the ingenious inventor of the wooden lattice specially adapted to climbing plants, Girolamo da Carpi was famous *c* 1550, and it was he who provided such devices for the Quirinal garden of Cardinal d' Este (founder also of the Villa d' Este at Tivoli): Vasari, VI, p. 477, *V. di Garofalo.*

Regarding the sentimental attitude towards ruins cf. *Kultur der Renaissance*, 4th ed., p. 211. The first idealised view of ruins, with a description, in Poliphilus (an unillustrated excerpt in Temanza, p. 12);* remains of an imposing vault and colonnades penetrated by old plane trees, laurels and cypresses, and surrounded by undergrowth. Cf. the ruined palaces in fifteenth-century paintings of the *Adoration.* Landscapes with ruins alone, Vasari, VI, p. 551, *V. di Gio. da Udine.*

The first significant artificial ruins in the park (*barchetto*) near the Palace at Pesaro: a house which was a very fine representation of a ruin, with an excellent spiral staircase in it like Bramante's in the Vatican: Vasari, VI, p. 319, *V. di Genga* (*c* 1530).

Architectural expression varied between the ruinous, the grotto-like, and the rusticated, a mode evolved long before, in other circumstances.

An impression of this confusion in a letter by Annibale Caro of 1538, *Lettere Pittoriche*, V, 91, in which what are probably the Farnese gardens on the Palatine are mentioned, before Vignola gave them their later form. At the end of a long, leafy walk there was a wall of dark, porous tufa in deliberately random blocks, with irregular bosses and hollows, the latter intended to hold plants; the whole setting off *un pezzo d' anticaglia rosa e scantonata*; in the middle, a door, with rough-hewn stones at the sides and overhanging solid stone above, like the entrance to a cave; right and left, springs rising from heavy rustication and falling into troughs made out of sarcophagi, with recumbent statues of water-gods above them; the arbour covered with ivy and jasmine on

* See now any of the facsimile editions of the *Hypnerotomachia*. (PM).

the side-walls and with vine-leaves over the pillars; the overall character – *ritirato, venerando.*

Artificial ruins were, properly speaking, quite rare; on the whole, the preference was either for the architecture to be complete (e.g. in the individual triumphal arches, fountain façades etc. of the Villa d' Este, in fairly rich forms, or elsewhere a pseudo-rustic rustication), or for simple tufa construction without pretensions, sometimes encrusted with shells in the Antique taste. Alberti, op. cit., already mentions this.

§ 126 *Complete Dominance of Architecture*

In the fifteenth century the dominance of architecture over gardening became not merely a matter of fact, by surrender to architects, but also an expression of principle. Bandinelli to Guidi (1551); *Lettere Pittoriche*, I, 38: *le cose che si murano, debonno essere guida e superiori a quelle che si piantano.*

Serlio's plans of garden plots, end of Book IV, "which could also serve *per altre cose*", are actually laid out like regular decorative panels of architectural ornament.

With changes of level, as soon as stepped layouts came into vogue strictly symmetrical schemes of terraces, balustrades and stairs gained the upper hand.

Notably effective the magnificent ramp-stairs which led in Bramante's great Vatican building (§97, 117 and Fig. 222) from the lower cortile to the upper garden (Giardino della Pigna), which is terminated by that huge hemicycle with its colonnaded gallery above. The upper garden undoubtedly contained those *pratelli e fontane*, which Bandinelli (ibid) presents as a model.[1] That the ramps were actually executed is proved by old illustrations in the *Speculum Romanae Magnificentiae.* In their place there later appeared the armoury, library and Braccio Nuovo, so that the majestic long perspective of the cortile and garden was lost. Bandinelli mentions further schemes, which Raphael carried out for Leo X and Clement VII; at that time Raphael laid out the gardens at the Villa Madama for Cardinal Giulio de' Medici, later Pope Clement VII; besides the one existing, alternative schemes for something much bigger, § 119.

The stairs, which soon for the sake of appearance were designed in palazzi as double flights (§ 106), had even earlier been duplicated in the grander gardens. The central landings, wherever possible placed in the main axis of the villa, now demanded special decorative treatment, principally with grottoes and fountains.

Two double ramps, one above the other, with a kind of grotto, in Bramante's cortile, mentioned above.

Earlier symmetrical staircase with marble balustrades, and even colonnades, in the lower garden of the Pal. Doria at Genoa, by Montorsoli from 1529 onwards.

A principal example in this context: Villa d' Este at Tivoli (§ 120, 124), where the double staircases and their central niches, etc. can hardly all belong to the first scheme of 1549.

Alessi's villas: V. Pallavicini, parts of the design old, but restored.

The smaller, more ornamental elements, like flowerbeds, orange-groves, statues, small decorative fountains earlier scattered throughout the whole garden, were, towards the middle of the sixteenth century, relegated to a so-called "show-garden" (or *giardinetto*), i.e. to a separate symmetrical parterre close to the actual palazzo or villa. The site was, where possible, below the main level, sheltered from the wind and facing south, the paths paved with stone slabs. The style was closely related – indeed almost identical – to the gardens in palace cortili.

Already existing in the large garden behind the Vatican, obviously as a sunny place for walking in the colder seasons: later, a normal feature of the larger villas. (May this outer Vatican garden, which contains among other things the Villa Pia, § 117, 120, have been a scheme by the younger Ant. da Sangallo? A plan *per la vignia del Papa* by him survives: Vasari, V, p. 482, commentary on the *V. di Sangallo.*) The inner Vatican garden – Bramante's – mentioned above, was probably the prototype.

(NOTE: For the Belvedere see now J. Ackerman, *The Cortile del Belvedere*, Vatican City, 1954.) (PM).

§ 127 *The Part Played by Large Trees*

How early larger trees had been included in the design, as effective masses, cannot be ascertained; individually and in avenues and in smaller clumps they had always been used; but their serious and large-scale exploitation with terraces, stairs etc. can only have begun when the gardens were really large and the architectural principles of their layout fully developed.

Unfortunately, the schemes significant in this respect were either never entirely carried out or have been destroyed; Giulio's (or Raphael's) garden at the Villa Madama (Vasari, V, p. 526, *V. di Giulio*), Vigna di Papa Giulio III, and the Orti Farnesiani by Vignola; Michelangelo's project for Marmirolo (§ 119), actually "both for the garden and for the dwelling in it" (1553), had probably to be shelved, because the Mantuan treasury had been strained by an elaborate theatrical spectacle.

1 It is not clear whether the Venetian Ambassadors of 1523 were speaking of this garden or merely of the cortile of the Belvedere (in Tommaso Gar, *Relazione della Corte di Roma*, p. 114 f). At the time one half of the garden (the present Giardino della Pigna?) was planted with roses, laurels, mulberries and cypresses, the other (the cortile of the Belvedere) paved with tiles, among which, arranged regularly, rose the finest orange trees; in the middle, opposite one another, *Tiber* and *Nile*, linked by fountains; in niches stood the *Apollo Belvedere* and the *Laocöon*, and close to the latter the *Vatican Venus*; in a colonnade a fountain watering the plants of the garden. Cf. A. Michaelis, *Der Statuenhof im vatikanischen Belvedere*, in Jahrb. d. archäolog. Instituts, 1890, p. 5 ff. Under Julius and Leo all this was accessible; Hadrian VI resolved, while still in Spain, to close everything; *Lettere di Principi*, I, p. 87.

On Sangallo's plan for the rear Vatican garden a note reads "place for firs and chestnuts". At Castello near Florence a dense screen of pines was placed at the end of the orchard, masking the dwellings of workers and gardeners, but in the middle of the main garden a "thicket" (*salvatico*) of tall cypresses, pines, laurels and shrubs, with a maze and fountain at the centre, and elsewhere another thicket of cypresses, pines, laurels and oaks, with a pool in the middle: Vasari, VI, p. 73 ff., *V. di Tribolo*. (At the Villa Madama a special gate led into a similar *salvatico*; it was flanked by Bandinelli's two *Giants*; Vasari, VI, p. 144, *V. di Bandinelli*.) The great massed oaks, however, had to wait for some time. Castello, loc. cit., described not so much as it was and is, but as Tribolo designed it (from 1540?). Besides the waterworks (see below) pranks in the garden plan itself, e.g. several mazes. One was also laid out at Careggi in a circular cortile; Vasari, VI, p. 680, *V. di Pontormo*. The idea was certainly very old, and familiar from time immemorial in castle and monastery gardens.

§ 128 *Gardens of Venice*

In Venice, where confined space and salt winds forbade the planning of large plantations, fountains were only possible with pumps, and stairs – because of the uniform level – had no place; but compensation was found in decoration and the addition of painting and sculpture. The inclinations of merchant-venturers also remained faithful longer there to the collecting of botanical specimens.

Sansovino, *Venezia*, fol. 137, in which all the more important gardens are enumerated, including some with fountains. Titian's garden, extolled in general terms in a letter of Priscianese, in Ticozzi, *Vite de' Pittori Vecellii*, p. 80.

No doubt this Venetian garden-style influenced many a *giardinetto* in the rest of Italy. Where a small cortile inside a palace was formed as a garden, the vegetation might sometimes play a smaller part in relation to the other decoration. As very little of the type has been preserved, we must turn to a copy, the little Hofgarten in the Residenz at Munich.

Regarding the artistic development of the wooden framework of arbours, which became particularly prominent in smaller gardens, cf. § 125.

Regarding the paintings on the walls, loggie, fountain-niches etc., of these small gardens, some later information in Armenini, *De' veri Precetti della Pittura*, p. 197 ff. He stipulates especially landscapes rich in incident and restrained in colour, naming among the garden-paintings preserved from that time, those in the garden of Casa Pozzo at Piacenza, by Pordenone, and those already referred to in § 125 by Perino del Vaga in the Archbishop of Cyprus's garden in Rome, where the frescoes (of Bacchanalian themes) were based on the statues there. Monochromatic mythological paintings; Vasari, VI, p. 237, *V. di Gherardi*. For the rest, L-B. Alberti speaks, *De re aedific.*, L. IX, c. 4, of garden-paintings also: *amoenitates regionum, et portus, et piscationes, et venationes, et natationes, et agrestium ludos, et florida et frondosa.*

§ 129 *Gardens of the Baroque Period*

It was not until the earliest villas of the Baroque period (§ 120, 121) that the Italian garden style reached fruition, and not without the determining influence of Castello and other Medici villas, as well as of the Villa d' Este.

Total exclusion of the botanical element: fruit trees and espaliers in separate concealed sections; the kitchen garden as a rule, and as far as possible, out of sight, but far from neglected; behind the dense screens of laurel and cypress of the walks, vegetable plots and the like let out to rent; development of water-devices on a grand scale, with practical jokes increasingly eliminated; imposing, strictly architectonic composition; all changes in level treated architecturally; the trees, especially oaks, in mass effects; steps and balustrades handled as essential elements; the "show" garden in contrast to the rest; a predilection for vistas of fountains, grottoes, groups, etc.

BOOK TWO

Decoration

CHAPTER ONE

The Nature of Renaissance Decoration

§ 130 *Relationship to Antiquity and to Gothic Decoration*

The Renaissance was not much less attracted by the decorative work of Roman Antiquity than by its buildings. Upon that decoration rests the world of ornamental forms, which it began to develop partly in monumental furniture and buildings, partly in separate and movable objects.

With the high and lively sense inspiring the new art, it did little harm that at the beginning not much distinction was made between the good and the debased Roman periods. The principal models, to start with, were a limited number of splendid door-surrounds, then altars, tripods, candelabra, vases, sarcophagi etc. The stucco-work and paintings of the Baths of Titus did not come until later.

Architecture, more than once threatened by the dominance of a decorative style, held to the course of its high destiny thanks to the activities of the great Florentines (cf. § 34). In the fifteenth century sculpture could protest with more reason that decoration was taking over part of its purpose.

Pompon. Gauricus, *De sculptura liber* (before 1505), in Jac. Gronov., *Thesaur. graecar. antiquitatum*, Vol. IX, col. 738 (Brockhaus ed., p. 118): the sculptor's object is man; *ut hominem ponat, quo tanquam ad scopum tota eius et mens et manus dirigenda, quanquam satyriscis, hydris, chimaeris, monstris denique, quae nusquam unquam viderint, fingendis* (the figurative elements of arabesques and such are in general meant) *ita praeoccupantur, ut nihil praeterea reliquum esse videatur. Dii Deaeque omnes! neminem unum esse qui, quo sibi proficiscendum sit, videat! qui ad finem respiciat!* . . .

Apart from a tendency to exaggeration, the enclosing and framing element reached a level of development and exploitation as in no other period of art, and yet not so that one would have wished it otherwise; the relationship of the frame to the objects enclosed, whether in sculpture or painting, was logical and inherently harmonious.

In no other field of art and culture does the Renaissance show itself so wholly attuned intellectually to Roman Antiquity as here. It improves upon the tradition freely and naturally, as if it were its own property, with ever fresh combinations, and achieving in places a supreme beauty.

The Cosmati (§ 16) were already in their decorative work true precursors of the Renaissance.

Gothic detail was to prove for fourteenth-century Italians even more disastrous in decoration than in architecture; to no purpose they had tempered it with Roman horizontals and mouldings, classical foliated work etc., making it still more irrational. Their hankering for something different must have risen to a peak a hundred years before, in the North, Gothic gave birth to its last gloriously vital offspring, the decorative style of the declining fifteenth century. While in Italian architecture Gothic still maintained its place beside the Renaissance (§ 23), in decoration it was instantly extinguished almost completely, when the first works of the new style took shape. (The very few exceptions in Venice, see *Cicerone*, II, p. 181 and in Genoa, p. 159, prove the rule.)

The utmost scope was immediately accorded to the new decoration, from an intellectual as well as a material standpoint.

§ 131 *The Architectonic Element and Surface Ornament*

Renaissance decoration, however, was prevented by imperceptibly effective precedents from developing a style entirely divorced from architecture and self-sufficient, as Antiquity had been able to do.

The most important tasks, tombs and altars, which had been treated as architectural subjects since the Middle Ages, largely remained so. At the same time the architectonic formation of the entablature and base was retained instead of the ornamented wave-scroll mouldings of the Roman decorative style; and the pilaster with its capital. Also in forms like, for example, candelabra and holy-water basins, the freedom and flowing quality of Antiquity was not completely attained; missing are the foliated facings of the top edges, the variety of the vegetable mouldings and of the *cavetti*. Certainly, with such calculated richness, the target might well have been missed without a strong architectonic element.

It was otherwise in Northern Gothic, where the decorative style is plainly an exceedingly simplified and animated architecture.

In relation to Antiquity it was perhaps essentially new that Renaissance decoration was capable of covering successfully surfaces of every type with ornamental forms.

Classical Antiquity adorned surfaces or panels with figurative representations (reliefs or single figures in relief on altars, on the sides of candelabra, funerary urns etc., and mural paintings) or it surrendered them, on walls, to incrustation, i.e. it allowed the material to speak. Only tapestries had neutral decorative forms in their design, i.e. repetitive motives.

In addition roofing elements had always had to try to express lightness by their decoration. In this respect the Romans undoubtedly went further, as we can detect from surviving remains (soffits between temple columns, coffering on flat ceilings and vaults); their *lacunaria*, which have become proverbial, were often overloaded with splendour. But nothing like enough was preserved or known for it to have been useful for surface decoration in the Renaissance.

In the Middle Ages the Romanesque, as well as the Gothic, styles were content with painted decorative motives, where surfaces were not given over to figures.

Gothic, besides, cut up its surfaces with the forms of its tracery and rib-work borrowed from windows.

The decoration of Islam, painted, glazed, or in mosaic, is simply an extension of carpet-themes without regard to the peculiarities and limitations of a given surface. The shortcomings of the principle are particularly apparent on vases. The same applies, more or less, to Byzantine surface-decoration.

The only precedents for what the Renaissance was preparing to do were late Roman pilasters, chiefly of the period of Diocletian, which incorporated arabesques surrounded by a frame-moulding. (Pilasters on the Arco de' Leoni and other gates at Verona; on the Arch of the Goldsmiths in Rome the pilasters have only a decoration of military trophies.) Other preserved soffits, i.e. ornamented rectangular panels on the underside of architraves (Rome, Temple of Castor and Pollux).

The Renaissance above all respected and honoured a particular surface as such. The distribution or extension of the ornamental motive within the space, its relationship to the surrounding frame or border, the depth of its relief or colour, and the correct handling of every material often combined to reach perfection in its way. Vasari's view, however, was that, on the whole, Antiquity was not equalled: VI, p. 297, *V. di Mosca*.

§ 132 *Summary of Modes of Expression*

The formal vocabulary of Renaissance decoration is extraordinarily rich and speaks simultaneously in different voices in almost every individual work. The principal element is a plant-concept, representing every nuance from the almost true-to-life to the fantastically imaginative and, on the other hand, to a rigid, stony quality. Then come figurative representations, for which the decoration serves only as a frame; next figurative ornamentation within the decoration itself, with men and animals as still-life objects; finally, metamorphoses from the vegetable to the human and animal. All this may be represented in the lowest or the highest relief, even in linear patterns, monochrome or many-coloured, with idealised or almost realistic painting; indeed in certain stucco-works nearly every conceivable mode of expression may be employed.

The flowering for more than a century of this great and complex art form is essentially due to the circumstance that the greatest architects, sculptors and painters continued to employ it and often devoted a large part of their lives to it. Cf. § 14. The sculptors for long treated the decorative and the figurative as of equal value in a formal sense (§ 130), while the painters were inevitably involved in decoration in relation to the painting of ceilings; the great architects, however, almost all loved ornamental work, and, if none the less they designed their buildings to be simple and grand, for them this factor, especially from Brunellesco onwards, has to be taken all the more deeply into consideration.

A confluence of almost all decorative modes of expression occurs in Raphael's Loggie. The inspiration given by the Baths of Titus and other painted and stuccoed interiors of Antiquity was here in every way greatly surpassed.

CHAPTER TWO

Decorative Sculpture in Stone

§ 133 *Importance of White Marble*

Although every material has its own proper qualities, which cannot be replaced by surrogate materials, it is important to note that in Tuscany, the centre of progress, white marble was (and remained) the principal material.

This was already the case with the entire Pisan school of sculpture. Only white marble invited continuous refinement of forms and was capable of competing with the marble artefacts of Antiquity.

Other types of stone, terra-cotta (whether plain or glazed), stucco, bronze, precious metals, wood, and even decorative painting, all benefited from the leadership of this incomparable material.

In sharp contrast, the Late Gothic style of decoration in the North was based on wood-carving, even when executed in stone and with forms originally derived from stone.

§ 134 *Arabesques*

Even if every type of decoration has its own rules and every individual work of importance demands a special standard of judgement, an appreciation of the history of ornament must be specially directed to stone-carving, particularly marble, and within this category above all to the arabesque.

Rabeschi in the stricter sense are only the vertical infill of pilasters, as is clear from the context in Lomazzo, *Trattato dell' arte*, p. 421 (cf. § 137), in which they are distinguished from friezes (*fregi*). But the Italians were already using the term to describe any kind of consistent ornamental infilling and surface adornment.

The task lay in fashioning idealised and realistic plants, both in relation to the leaves and to the entwining shoots and branches, mingling them cleverly with living as well as still-life objects; or, if the basic motive, instead of a plant, was a trophy, to compose this with attractively inter-related objects.

The plants, the idealised generally approximating (Fig. 272) to the acanthus and the vine-leaf, the realistic imitating every conceivable leaf and fruit, customarily began at the bottom with a candelabrum-foot or bowl, sometimes indeed the candelabrum itself forms, with intervening shells and other elaborate stages, the actual stem around which the leaves twine. In church portals the bowl provided an idealised imitation of a water-pail, in which branches of trees were stood on festivals, leaning against the jambs. Nesting and pecking birds enlivened the whole. (Benv. Cellini I, p. 31, noted that in Lombard decoration ivy and bryony predominated, in Tuscan and Roman bear's breech – i.e. acanthus.)

The more trophy-like arabesques sometimes consist of weapons, which are fastened to a staff (so prominent on the door-posts of the Palace at Urbino), but generally of an original mixture of every possible object living or dead. Even in the holiest places, in the arabesques of marble altars, profane details were entirely admissible; certainly there were sacred elements, cherubim and the like, but most were secular and irrelevant. Once more, the carrier of the whole is transformed into a magnificent structure composed of candelabrum-like members, on which are animals, fabulous beasts, the heads of animals, human forms, with small groups used as supporters, draperies, borders, escutcheons, arms, bands, garlands with medallions, cornucopias and other decorative conceits. Antiquity, from its practice in its friezes of trophies, had at one time no doubt turned to an increasing use of trophy-decoration, e.g. on two pillars in the Uffizi galleries, which are not very successful; it had also adopted (§ 131) military insignia on its pilasters; but of the variety of riches, and certainty in handling them, which the growth of vertical ornamentation now achieved, hardly the first traces are detectable in Classical times. Essentially associated with this, the Renaissance scorned (§ 35) fluting from the beginning.

In the fifteenth century the arabesque was generally symmetrical, i.e. the animals and objects are either in

Fig. 272 *Lugano Cathedral, marble decoration*

Fig. 273 *Rome, Sta Maria del Popolo, marble frieze*

pairs or are represented facing straight forwards; in the sixteenth century we find them picturesquely disarranged, viewed obliquely, and often restless in effect.

Marble sculpture also attained the highest standards in friezes, in light and animated terminals and crowning pieces, in infilling of every kind, in which the forms of sarcophagi, urns and other ornamental objects still appear.

Beside, and mingled with, this light fantastical ornament, characteristic of the arabesque, one was introduced, closer to nature and more robustly modelled, in the form of festoons of fruit (Fig. 273), volutes, masks, beasts, the feet and heads of animals, shells etc., together with human forms in higher relief or free-standing.

§ 135 *Siena and Florence*

Florence and Siena were from the outset the most important workshops, whence the new style of marble decoration spread throughout Italy. Rome, which possessed the greatest number of outstanding works, was in this respect wholly dependent upon Tuscany.

Siena had the priority with Jacopo della Quercia, who made the Tomb of Ilaria del Carretto in Lucca Cathedral in 1406, the earliest work of the genuine Renaissance, with genii and festoons; Vasari, II, p. 112, n. 1, *V. di Quercia* (Fig. 274).

The high significance which Siena bestowed upon marble works, by no means exclusively commissioned from fellow-townsmen such as Vecchietta (1412–80), is apparent from the detailed contracts with the Florentine Bernardo Rossellino for a door in the Pal. Pubblico (1446) (Milanesi, II, p. 235), and with Urbano da Cortona for a grand altar in the Cathedral (ibid., p. 271) etc. The Milanese Andrea Bregno worked 1481–85 on the great wall-altar of Cardinal Piccolomini in the Cathedral (ibid., p. 376, cf. § 144; Michelangelo later did some figures for it, from 1501); Benedetto da Majano carved the glorious marble ciborium for the high altar in S. Domenico. And towards the end of the century Siena possessed in Lorenzo di Mariano, called Il Marinna, one of the greatest masters of this craft, and a major sculptor. He made the marble cladding for the entrance to the Libreria in the Cathedral (*c* 1497); and the high altar of Fontegiusta (1509–19), perhaps the finest of all the works of this type, both in the figurative and decorative sense (Fig. 294); Vasari, III, p. 517, *V. di Pinturicchio*; Milanesi, III, p. 76 f. Antonio Federighi created (1464) one of the beautiful marble seats (right) in the Loggia de' Nobili, the second (left) being by Urbano da Cortona (Fig. 275).

The uninterrupted practice of this branch of art was maintained only in Florence, where, in 1478, fifty-four workshops were to be found "for works in marble, sandstone, in relief, bas-relief, and leaf-carving"; Fabroni, *Laurent. Med. Magnif. vita*, Adnot 200. Undoubtedly much was exported.

Beautiful and very restrained ornamental work in the Badia at Fiesole; the lectern in the refectory by Piero di Cecco; the lavabo in the anteroom to it by Francesco di Simone Ferrucci; both members of the School of Desiderio da Settignano (*c* 1460). The sacristy lavabo in S. Lorenzo, a simple and inventive work of genius, by Verrocchio (earlier attributed to Ant. Rossellino, or even Donatello: Vasari, II, p. 414, *V. di Donatello*). The works of Donatello, not devoid of eccentricities, had little influence on the type as such; rather more those of Michelozzo, who is known (Gaye, I, p. 117) as Donatello's *compagno* in the *arte dell' intaglio*, especially the decoration of the chapel

Fig. 274 *Lucca Cathedral, tomb of Ilaria del Carretto*

in the Pal. Medici, and his altar-tabernacles in S. Miniato and the Annunziata etc.; cf. § 34; less, on the other hand, those of Bern. Rossellino. (Tomb of Lionardo [Bruni] Aretino in Sta Croce.)

For consummate richness and taste in composition and scale: Desiderio da Settignano (Tomb of Carlo Marsuppini in Sta Croce (Fig. 276); wall-tabernacle in the transept of S. Lorenzo). His pupil, Mino da Fiesole, of great importance as a decorator; above all else the one who brought to Rome the perfected style of decoration in marble; Vasari, III, p. 116, *V. di Mino*, with an unjust polemic against him; his best-preserved works the Tombs in the Badia in Florence; in Rome, besides a few original works, the influence of Mino apparent in many altars, prelates' tombs, ciboria etc., especially in Sta Maria del Popolo.

A masterpiece of exquisite harmony: the pulpit in S. Croce in Florence, by Benedetto da Majano (Fig. 277). The culminating point was reached in the choir of Sta Maria del Popolo in Rome by the two prelates' monuments, by the Florentine Andrea Sansovino (§ 141).

Much Roman work is anonymous: the influence of the enduring activity of Mino da Fiesole and other 'foreigners' was decisive here. The Anonimo Morelliano extols a certain Cristoforo da Roma because of his delicate foliage, with reference to S. Vincenzo in Cremona. (Cf. § 136.) In 1506 *i primi scultori di Roma* were considered to be (*Lettere Pittoriche*, III, 196) Giovan-Angelo Romano and Michel Cristofano da Firenze.

The last Florentines to be both celebrated decorators and sculptors were Andrea da Fiesole (Vasari, IV, p. 475 ff., *V. di A. da Fiesole*) and Benedetto da Rovezzano (ibid., p. 529 ff., *V. di Rovezzano*); the latter worked on chimney-pieces, hand-basins, escutcheons with strap-work, tombs, gates, and a Saint's tomb, fragments of which are now exhibited in the Uffizi;* his arabesques are coarser than those of his predecessors. Cf. also his wall-tabernacle in the Pinacoteca at Spoleto.

Of the pupils of Andrea da Fiesole, Maso Boscoli and Silvio Cosino (both from Fiesole), the latter became in due course an assistant to Michelangelo, and then worked on stucchi in Genoa with Perino del Vaga.

* Now in the Bargello; other fragments are said to be in S. Salvi. (PM).

Fig. 275 *(top) Siena, Casino de' Nobili, balustrade*

Fig. 276 *(above) Florence, Sta Croce, detail of Marsuppini Tomb*

Fig. 277 *(above right) Florence, Sta Croce, pulpit*

Fig. 278 *Florence, Bargello, relief by the Della Robbia School*

In the glazed terracottas of the Della Robbia School, the arabesque, because of the inferior material, is simpler than in marble; but the robust composition of the whole, the splendid garlands of fruit, and the judicious alternation of the purely plastic, painted plastic and purely painted give these objects a very high value. (Altars, niches for statues; the lavabo in Sta Maria Novella, Florence, etc.) Their colours – yellow, green, blue, violet and white. (Fig. 278.)

(NOTE Much of the decorative sculpture mentioned by Burckhardt can be found in the photographs in *Courtauld Institute Archives*, 2, *15th and 16th Century Sculpture in Italy*, 1976. Rome forms Parts 1–3 and 6.) (PM).

§ 136 *The Rest of Italy*

The decoration of the Palace at Urbino appears divided between Tuscan and North Italian influences. Naples and Genoa possess little of superior worth which is indigenous. North Italy remained a region on its own.

In the Palace of Urbino magnificent door-cases (§ 134), chimney-pieces (Fig. 279), mouldings etc., sometimes recalling the Bolognese style. Some painted in gold and blue.

Naples in the fifteenth century depended on Florence (tombs by Rossellino, Donatello etc.) and only late in the sixteenth century acquired an independent school of sculptor-decorators – Giovanni da Nola, Girolamo Santacroce, Domenico di Auria – when in the rest of Italy the two types of work had already diverged. (Monumental tombs in many churches, the Auria fountain near S. Lucia.)

Genoa in the fifteenth century was essentially an adherent of the North Italian style; the best examples a number of door-cases, among them a splendid one on a house in the Piazza Fossatello, originally from a church. One of the finest Genoese doorways now in the Victoria and Albert Museum in London.* In the sixteenth century the works of Montorsoli; and, more classical, the tabernacle in the chapel of S. John in the Cathedral (§ 80), by Giac. della Porta, 1532.

* There are three such doorways (Nos. 410, 411 and 416) in the V. & A., and it is impossible to tell which Burckhardt had in mind. (PM).

Fig. 279 *Urbino, Ducal Palace, chimneypiece*

Fig. 280 *Genoa, Palazzo Pallavicino, doorway (1503) by Michele and Antonio Carleone, now in the Victoria and Albert Museum, London*

In Venice incrustation (§ 42, 43) was a rival of decoration; the latter is essentially confined to the most lavish possible infilling of pilasters, friezes, window-surrounds (Sta Maria de' Miracoli, inside and out; Scuola di S. Marco; back of the Doge's Palace), while altars and monuments made only modest use of it, and from the beginning of the sixteenth century abandoned it almost entirely, in order to turn to purely figurative and architectonic forms. On the whole, the architecture here was more decorative, and decoration more architectonic, than elsewhere. But apart from a few fantastically rich chimney-pieces in the Doge's Palace (see below) the works of Alessandro Leopardo were real marvels of a conception of beauty unaffected by the prevailing mode: the base of the equestrian statue of Colleoni (1495), the Tomb of the Doge Vendramin in SS. Giovanni e Paolo etc. (see below, § 141). In the Venetian arabesque the intricately intertwining ornamental work is a much better creation than the vertically growing plant motive, and certainly than the trophy-like feature.

In the rest of North Italy there were separate styles for marble and for brick, stucco and other less precious materials. The latter's principal home was Bologna, where the best work of this type was by Formigine and Properzia de' Rossi; by the former the entire plan and decoration of the first chapel on the right in S. Martino. (The nearby marble objects, monuments etc. are less typical and derive directly from Florence; but a marble-craftsman, Jacopo Duca, became particularly famous for his leaf-carving; Vasari, III, p. 146, *V. di Ercole Ferrarese.*) With great originality the splendid stucco monument to Card. Gozzadini (*d* 1536) in the Servite church, by Gio. Zacchi, extends round the inner side of a doorway as a triumphal arch with niches and statues. The most important terracotta decoration is probably that on the façade of the Ospedale Maggiore in Milan (§ 44, 107; Fig. 281) and the arcades of the cortile of the Certosa of Pavia (§ 46). On the whole, the decoration in this inferior material, for all its wealth and profusion, is less sensitively handled, and, especially in stucco, in the course of time became somewhat pompous.

At Cremona the lavish terracotta cortile of the present Monte di Pietà, the colonnade of the ground floor (formerly) open, the upper floor closed with an arrangement of arches above engaged columns in the form of candelabra, and with elegant windows; rich narrative friezes on a smaller scale.

Fig. 281 *Milan, Ospedale Maggiore, detail of façade*

Fig. 282 *Pavia, the Certosa, window*

The marble style had its most important manifestation on the façade of the Certosa at Pavia (§ 71), where leading masters undertook decoration as well as sculpture: Gio. Ant. Amadeo, Benedetto da Briosco, Cristoforo da Roma (§ 135), Andrea Bregno (§ 135), Cristoforo Solari, called Il Gobbo (§ 67), Agostino Busti, known as Lo Zarabaja (Zarabaglia, not Bambaia,* cf. Vasari, IV, p. 542, n. 2), and others. Of unique splendour and beauty are especially the mullions in the form of candelabra and the decoration of the windows in general (by Amadeo: Fig. 282).

Added to this, much interior decoration; together with a number of altars and monuments in Milanese churches (Sta Maria delle Grazie etc.), works inside and on the Cathedral of Como, on the façade of Lugano, the Colleoni Chapel at Bergamo, altar-surrounds in churches in Vicenza and in Verona; formerly at Cremona (now in the Louvre) the extravagant portal of the Palazzo Sansecondo, with candelabrum-type engaged columns; at Piacenza the portal of the former Palazzo Landi, now Tribunali, 1484, by Gio. Battagio, equally laden with exuberant decoration; the upper part with twin volutes forming a pediment and three statues (the cortile with some pleasing terracotta remains); Verona; finally, in the Santo at Padua the decoration of the pillared loggia, which forms the entrance to the chapel of S. Antony, the left angle-pilaster by Girol. Pironi, for which Matteo and Tommaso Allio from Milan later provided a pendant on the right, freely modelled on it. (For Pironi and Giovanni da Vicenza, who did much work in their home district, Vasari, VII, p. 526, *V. di Jac. Sansovino.*)

The common factor in this Northern Italian marble

* Nevertheless, always now called Bambaia. (PM).

Fig. 283 *(above left) Como Cathedral, portal*

Fig. 284 *(left) Brescia, Palazzo Comunale, a capital*

Fig. 285 *(above) Milan, S. Satiro, detail of pilaster*

style, by comparison with the Florentine, is its profuse richness, freely mingled with a transmutation of Gothic forms. The pyramids of Como Cathedral (§ 81); the salient portal columns (§ 37, 51), now in some instances transformed into splendid candelabra richly adorned with figures, e.g. at the side portal of Como Cathedral (the so-called Porta delle Sirene, Fig. 283), the one from Cremona (in the Louvre), and on the door in the Piazza Fossatello, Genoa, mentioned above. The relief in ornamental forms is deeper, the plane of the relief more filled-up, indeed over-filled (cf. Fig. 284). The detailing of the style in the best works is as noble, refined and imaginative as the best in Florence.

The baser materials prove at a disadvantage precisely by participating in this very richness; their beauty is more readily to be found in a certain discipline, especially in a temperate use of inanimate objects, as the wonderful interlacing ornament of the pilasters in the Sacristy of S. Satiro in Milan (Figs. 285, 286) clearly shows. (Probably part of the building by Bramante, cf. § 80.) Here one does not miss the white marble – as little, indeed, as with the Della Robbia (§ 135).

For the beginnings of the entire North Italian style of decoration the "book of grotesques" by Troso da Monza, a painter of *c* 1450, rich in content and still quoted by Lomazzo (*Trattato dell' Arte*, p. 423), must have been important.

§ 137 *The Decorative Spirit of the Sixteenth Century*

Almost from the beginning of the sixteenth century the sculpture on tombs and altars, grown to life-size and the near-gigantic, absorbed resources and attention. The architectonic framework shed more and more its arabesques and other adornments and once more became simply architecture. Decoration was soon to apply most of its energies to vaulting.

Michelangelo's enmity towards the arabesque in sculpture: *gli intagli . . . se bene arrichiscono l' opere, confondono le figure*; Vasari, VI, p. 308, *V. di Mosca*. (Of his mortar and salt-cellar for the Duke of Urbino all traces are unhappily lost; Vasari, VII, p. 282, n. 2, p. 383, Comment., *V. di Michelangelo*. Cf. § 177.) Mosca's works, despite all their skill, are aesthetically far behind the earlier, better things, and cast by deep under-cutting a marked shadow which is contrary to the true spirit of the arabesque. (Cladding of a chapel in Sta Maria della Pace in Rome, etc.) The same holds good for the work by Stagi in Pisa Cathedral. The outstanding works of this period are for the most part in those features where a more realistic treatment is called for, e.g. in garlands, the parts of animals, bucrania (the motive of a base by Bandinelli in S. Lorenzo, Florence), and also in coats-of-arms (§ 168).

The changed attitude of the time is reflected very clearly on the Santa Casa in the church at Loreto, its architectural framework (by Bramante, who designed the model in 1510)* revealing a number of elements made more architectonic, which a few decades earlier would have been entirely devoted to decoration. (Incrustation of stylobates, fluting of columns, stricter adherence to all the tenets of Classical Antiquity.) The very beautiful festoons here are by Mosca.

Even the octagonal so-called Coro beneath the dome in the Cathedral of Florence, fashioned under Bandinelli's direction supposedly on the model of a wooden one made by Brunellesco, would certainly have been more richly ornamented in the fifteenth century: Vasari, VI, p. 176, *V. di Bandinelli*.

But the urge towards richer forms broke through again, and in an unfortunate way. Wherever the true Renaissance applied its own forms of ornament, the Baroque style used architectural forms, but absurdly reduced, bunched or broken. The theoretical expression of this in Armenini's description of a free-standing high altar (*De' Veri Precetti della Pittura*, Ravenna, 1587, p. 164): the latter must be round or octagonal, to ensure an equally advantageous view from all sides, with *tribune, mensole, partimenti, nicchie, risalti, rompimenti di cornice, con diversi ordini variati, cosi finestre, figurine et maschere di rilievo, festoni, balaustri, piramidi* etc., all where feasible inlaid with variegated stones and edged with gold: a modest example of such a materially lavish high altar in Sto Spirito, Florence by Giovanni Caccini (1600–1604).

The leading decorators of the period around 1525–50 are recorded by Lomazzo, unfortunately without in any way distinguishing their types of work, or looking far beyond Lombardy; *Trattato dell' Arte*, p. 421: for the friezes of chapel vaults (i.e. stucco and painting) and façades (stone), with putti and masks, are to be noted for our period, in particular Ferrari (undoubtedly Gaudenzio), Perino (del Vaga), Rosso, (Giulio) Romano, Il Fattore (Penni), Parmigiano, Correggio, (Giovanni da) Udine, Pordenone. For special masks and foliage: Soncino; for foliage alone: Niccolò Picinino and Vincenzo da Brescia (these latter probably stuccatori); and the man who best (the Ancients apart) carved leaf-ornament was Marco Antonio (?). (The foregoing refers entirely to friezes and horizontal elements.) In relation to arabesques much was to be said; if Stefano Scotto was undoubtedly the most distinguished, Gaudenzio, who was his first pupil and also Lovino's (Ber. Luini), excelled him in this field. (Lomazzo now returns to friezes, in that they comprised narratives painted in the debased manner of the time, bordered by stuccoed or painted cartouches, putti, shields, masks, festoons of fruit, inscriptions etc.) In these fields the most inventive, apart from the actual makers of grotesques, were Gio. Batt. Bergamo and Evangelista Lovini, brother of Aurelio, who (the last-named?) was excellent in this and other matters, also Lazaro and Pantaleo Calvi, Ottavio Semino, brother of

* The model was paid for in June, 1509: see A. Bruschi, *Bramante architetto*, Bari, 1969. (PM).

Fig. 286 *Milan, S. Satiro, sacristy (now baptistry)*

Andrea, Vincenzo Moietta, and in Antiquity (from Pliny, *H. N.*, XXXV, 37) Serapion. Later, Silvio Cosini gets an incidental mention.

The section on lamps, candelabra, fountains etc., p. 426, deals only with the late period, in which Lomazzo wrote; Ambrogio Maggiore, famous for his vases, vessels, utensils and carriages, for example, belongs to the time of the book itself (1585).

§ 138 *The Tomb and the Cult of Fame*

The monumental tomb of the Renaissance, incomparably the most important task of decorative art combined with sculpture, originated essentially under the influence of the cult of fame. The desire of the individual for an imperishable name, and the zeal of a city or corporation for the honour of its celebrated members both needed the support of the arts.

The saint's tomb, in the thirteenth and fourteenth centuries a special category of sculpture, assumed in the fifteenth century merely a subordinate role. To judge by the account, only the grave of S. Savinus in the Cathedral of Faenza, by Benedetto da Majano (1468), was a work of high quality; Vasari, III, p. 337, *V. di Ben. da Majano.* An engaging work is the Arca di Sant' Apollonia in Brescia Cathedral, a sarcophagus with three reliefs rich in figures, with a tabernacle above it with figures, and a *Madonna* in the lunette. In the crypt of the Cathedral (formerly S. Tommaso) at Cremona is the tomb of SS. Pietro and Marcellino, said to be by Ben. Briosco, 1507. And in S. Lorenzo, in the same city, that of S. Mauro (more correctly, SS. Mario and Marta), 1482, by the famous Gio. Ant. Amadeo (§ 136), both praised by Anonimo Morelliano. (The reliefs from the latter tomb transferred in recent times to the two pulpits of the Cathedral.) The common feature of all these works is the narrative relief, in which the fifteenth century abounds, taken over from medieval saints' tombs; they are distinguished also from others by the absence of recumbent statues, the saint being represented standing or enthroned above the sarcophagus. On the Arca di S. Domenico in his church at Bologna the upper structure is really only a version of a Gothic motive. Dating from the beginning of the sixteenth century (1506) the tomb of S. Giovanni Gualberto, by Rovezzano, was intended to be a very large scheme; of what was actually completed only a few reliefs are preserved in the Bargello; Vasari, IV, p. 532, *V. di Rovezzano.* The tomb of Gamaliel in Pisa Cathedral, insignificant. The medieval feature of having the sarcophagus carried by statues, no longer occurs anywhere with saints' tombs.

In place of saintliness other ideals of life emerged entailing veneration. Theological and practical scruples regarding burial in churches had no effect.

In the fourteenth century the tomb had served for the glorification of political power and spiritual repute. Apart from the Angevin tombs in Naples: the monument to Bishop Guido Tarlati in Arezzo Cathedral, a work with a political purpose; Vasari, I, p. 395, *V. di Giotto*; I, p. 434, *V. di Agostino e Agnolo*; then the well-known group of free-standing Gothic tabernacles with the tombs of the ruling family della Scala at Verona. Giangaleazzo Visconti (*d* 1402) wanted to be represented enthroned at the top of seven steps in the Certosa of Pavia, with, on the right, the tomb of his first wife with her children, and on the left that of his second wife with hers; Corio, fol. 286. The type of tomb of famous lawyers, doctors, and astrologers in the fourteenth century in Florence was called *monumento rilevato, sepultura rilevata*, in Filippo Villani, *Vite*, pp. 19, 26, 45; a sarcophagus carried on supporting columns or wall-brackets was implied. The cities brought about a veritable cult of tombs for celebrated fellow-citizens and even foreigners (*Kult. d. Renaiss.*, 3rd ed., p. 173 ff.), and Florence, where the state was in the habit of at least decreeing great monuments, led the field. In 1396 the decision to erect in the Cathedral "lofty and magnificent sepulchral monuments adorned with marble sculptures and other ornaments" for Accorso, Dante, Petrarch, Boccaccio and Zanobi della Strada, and indeed – if their bones were unobtainable – as cenotaphs. But the matter was not pursued; in 1430 the intention was revived for Dante and Petrarch and shelved again; Gaye, *Carteggio*, I, p. 123.

There was a kind of anticipation in having a monumental tomb painted in monochrome on the wall of the Cathedral, e.g. those still visible of the theologian Marsili and of Cardinal Corsini (after 1405), already in the Renaissance style; Vasari, II, p. 56, *V. di Bicci.*

The condottieri were treated in a singular manner. For the terrible John Hawkwood in 1393, when he was still alive, a monumental tomb in marble was stipulated, in which he was to be buried *quando morietur*; Gaye, *Carteggio*, I, 536; but later it was agreed to have him painted in chiaroscuro on the wall of the Cathedral, life-size on horseback, by Paolo Uccello, together with another condottiere, Piero Farnese; Vasari, II, p. 211 and n., *V. di Uccello.** Presumably this Farnese had to yield place in 1455 to the large painted equestrian figure of Nic. da Tolentino (*d* 1434), which now provides the pendant to Hawkwood's; by so doing, the state showed a rather lukewarm pride in its usual custom towards deserving mercenary leaders: *aliquid* [sic] *ad eorum honorem et gloriam retribuere*; Gaye, op. cit., p. 562. According to Fabroni, *Magni Cosmi vita*, Adnot. 52, a simple marble tomb underneath, which is missing, should have been associated with the fresco in the church. An example of an equestrian monument, painted only, at Siena, Vasari, II, p. 110, n. 2, *V. di Quercia*; the same in the Piazza at Lucca, Paul. Jov. *Elogia*, with reference to Picinino; King Mathias Corvinus of Hungary was painted in Rome in the form of an equestrian figure in fresco on the Campo de' Fiori, ibid., with reference to Corvinus.

It was an enduring custom in Florence to have celebrities buried in the Cathedral, as, for example,

* This mistake is not due to Vasari. It seems to have been Baldinucci's, incorporated into a note by Milanesi. (PM).

Fig. 287 *Rome, Sta Maria del Popolo, tomb of Cardinal de Castro*

Fig. 288 *Florence, S. Miniato al Monte, tomb of the Cardinal of Portugal*

Brunellesco, although his family vault was in S. Marco; Vasari, II, p. 383. But his and several other monuments are very modest.

Far more splendid: the tombs of the two State Secretaries in Sta Croce (§ 135), Lionardo Aretino and Carlo Marsuppini (Fig. 276).

In Venice the state had definite categories of monument-raising and took really seriously the equestrian effigy for its condottieri. The altar and tomb of the Zeno chapel in S. Marco represent the thanks of the state for the large legacy of Cardinal Gio. Batt. Zeno; Sansovino, *Venezia*, fol. 32. His entire estate, according to Malipiero, amounted to two hundred thousand ducats.

In Italy the monument always remained tangible evidence of fame of any kind; numerous tombs of poets, scholars, high officials and lawyers, great soldiers etc. (Even the splendid tomb of a celebrated courtesan; Vasari, V, p. 622, *V. di Perino.*)

Fruitless prohibition of tombs in churches, cf. § 83. On moral and theological grounds a Spanish bishop inveighs against it; Vespasiano Fiorentino, p. 307; on hygienic grounds, Alberti, *De re aedific.*, L. VIII, c. 1, where, indeed, he advocates cremation.

§ 139 *Tombs of the Rich and Prominent*

Very early wealth and rank asserted their claims on the arts, to gain an equal status with the famous on consecrated ground. In the second half of the fifteenth century especially, the growing sense of splendour led to a proliferation of lavish sepulchral monuments.

Already in 1350 Petrarch complained that wealth supplanted fame; *De remediis utriusque fortunae*, p. 39: *fuere aliquando statuae insignia virtutum, nunc sunt illecebrae oculorum; ponebantur his quae magna gessissent, aut mortem pro republica obiissent . . . ponebantur ingeniosis ac doctis viris . . . nunc ponuntur divitibus, magno pretio marmora peregrina mercantibus.*

In Padua and Bologna the Gothic tombs of the professors in the universities there, which might also have been derided, appear as a rule to have been paid for by the testamentary provisions of the individual concerned, and hardly ever by order of the state. Accounts in M. Savonarola, in Murat., XXIV, col. 1151 ff., especially col. 1165, the imposing tomb of a doctor, in which his ancestors – a whole family of Asclepiades – were immortalised with him; and in Bursellis, *Annal. Bonon.*, in

Fig. 289 *Rome, Sta Maria della Pace, Ponzetti Tomb*

Murat., XXIII, passim. The latter says it repeatedly (e.g. col. 877) and explicitly about fifteenth-century tombs. Those of the nobility were self-evidently a matter for the family, but the tomb of the celebrated jurist Mariano Socino (the bronze statue from it, by Vecchietta, now in the Bargello, Florence) was probably paid for by his native Siena; Vasari, III, p. 79, n., *V. di Franc. di Giorgio*.

In the course of time it became a matter of status, and on the part of heirs, or the corporation concerned, a matter of duty, loyalty and courtesy to put up splendid monuments; many saw to it in their wills, and those wanting to be doubly certain had the tomb prepared (and even installed) during their lifetime, like the Roman prelate, on whose grave one reads:

Certa dies nulli est, mors certa; incerta sequentum
cura; locet tumulum, qui sapit, ante sibi.

For Roman prelates the monumental tomb, like the building of a palace (§ 8), was a means of preserving a part of their inheritance from confiscation. In Naples from *c* 1500 onwards, an elaborate tomb was a matter of status; Jovian. Pontan. *Charon*: "People took more trouble over their tombs than their homes." Sannazaro, *Epigrammata, De Vetustino* ridicules one such man, who led the most wretched life, but saved up for his mortuary chapel, early in the morning dragging architects and marble-workers to all the antique ruins and not releasing them until the afternoon, dead tired; grumbling over cornices, friezes, columns etc., and constantly changing his mind: "Leave people therefore to eat in peace; and if you want to devote all your efforts to your burial, then have yourself interred on the *Gemoniae scalae*".*

A soldier of fortune, Ramazzotto, who (*c* 1526) had his tomb erected by Alfonso Lombardi in S. Michele in Bosco, near Bologna, but died much later elsewhere, poor and forgotten; Vasari, V, p. 85 and n. 1, *V. di Lombardi*. Cf. § 256 (above the sarcophagus the figure in armour, reclining and asleep; behind, a pillar with a *Madonna* on a smaller scale) †.

§ 140 *The Most Important Types of Tomb*

The tomb-types of the thirteenth and fourteenth cenuries were for the most part relinquished, and those remaining were beautifully converted to conform to Renaissance ideals. Often with great beauty of execution they generally had conspicuous defects. The sarcophagus mounted on wall-brackets (the *sepolcro in aria*; Sansovino, *Venezia*, fol. 5, 6, etc.; also *sepultura rilevata*) had indeed the merit of not obstructing circulation, but the recumbent statue on top remained either invisible or, slanting forwards, inevitably created an odd effect.

Varieties: the Bolognese, with statuettes beside and over the portrait-statue, probably also at the corners of the sarcophagus itself, which is decorated with reliefs. The Paduan/Veronese, with a pointed arch projecting from the wall and resting on consoles, poised over the sarcophagus, and with paintings as well.

(The Christian humility of the Hierarchy required that the body should be lain in earth, so the sarcophagus displayed above was empty; Benedict XI, who died in 1304 in Perugia, was buried in S. Domenico *sub terra, sicut ipse mandavit dum adhuc viveret, ne in alto poneretur, sed sub terra, ex magna humilitate quam habebat. Brevis hist. ord. praedic.*, in Martène, *Coll. Ampliss.*, VI, col. 373.)

In Naples the type of saint's tomb, especially the sarcophagus carried by three or four statues, had also become customary for great and princely personages; above it was a niche with baldacchino, and curtains drawn aside by angels. These types were also not extinct in the Renaissance; even the last-mentioned occurs.

The front rank was henceforth occupied by the type in which the sarcophagus with a reclining figure stands at a reasonable height, in a more or less decorated shallow niche; very beautiful early examples in two tombs of the School of the Cosmati, *c* 1300 (Consalvo

* These steps in Rome were where the bodies of criminals were exposed. (PM).

† This section was never published, see Introduction, p. xvi. (PM).

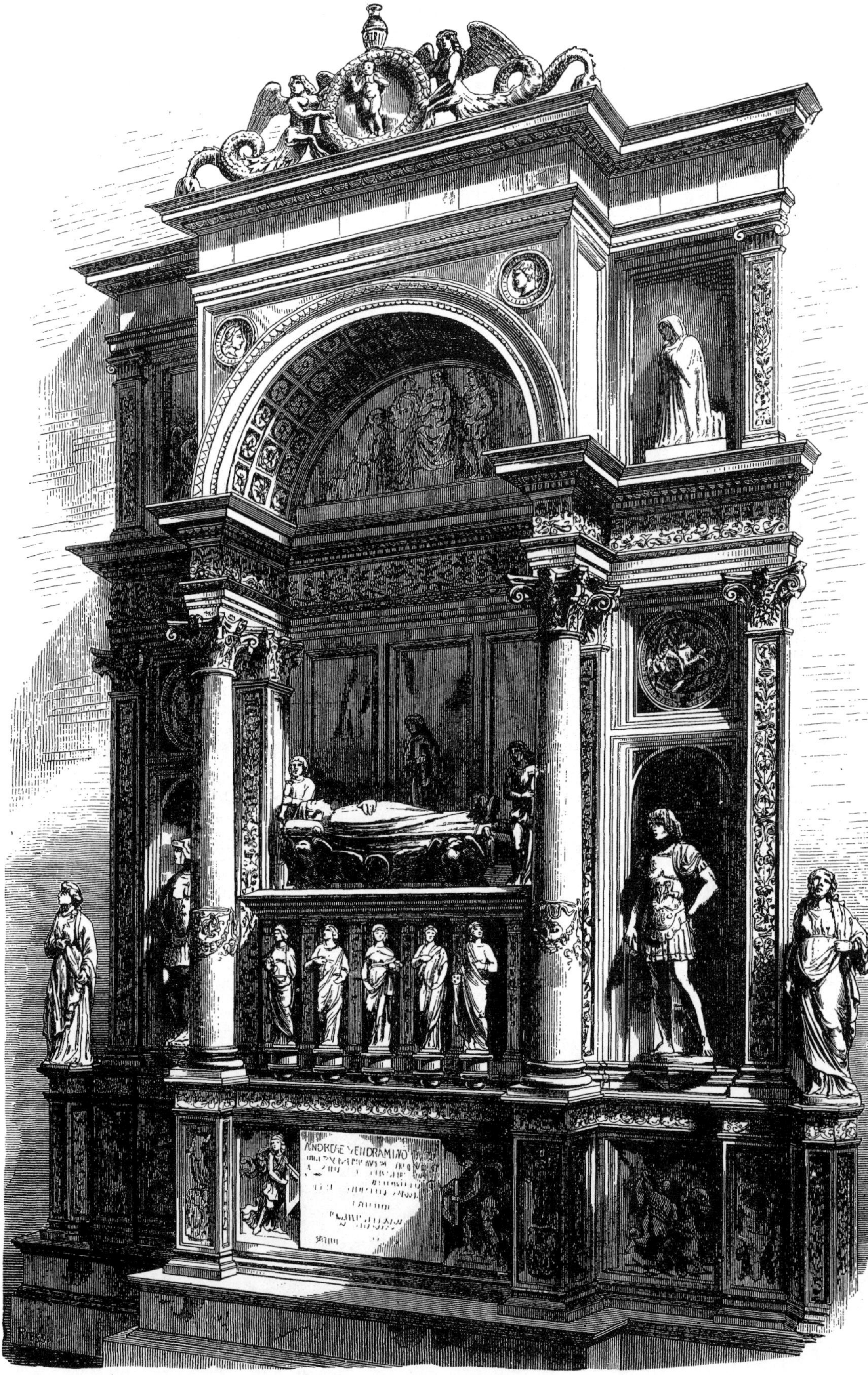
ANDREAE VENDRAMINO

Fig. 290 *(opposite) Venice, SS. Giovanni e Paolo, tomb of Doge A. Vendramin*

Fig. 291 *(above) Venice, SS. Giovanni e Paolo, Mocenigo Tomb*

Tomb in Sta Maria Maggiore; Durantis Tomb in Sta Maria sopra Minerva), in which angels hold the shroud at the head and the feet of the dead man; the niche filled with mosaics.

The Renaissance above all gave the sarcophagus an air of freer movement, often full of grace and splendour, with exquisite plant decoration; it raised it off the ground on lions' claws, placing over it a distinctive bier, on which the dead man lay. In the portal-like niches above, either a round or a lunette relief with a half-length Madonna, sometimes accompanied by patron saints and angels; until well into the fifteenth century the curtain was retained, which the angel (now a nude putto) seated or standing on the sarcophagus held or pulled aside; the jambs of the niches in some instances contained statuettes of the Virtues or of saints; sometimes the niche over the sarcophagus was left free and the relief of the Madonna is placed in an upper structure crowned with candelabra or figures.

This was the form of tomb which perhaps contributed most to the long duration of a style combining decoration and sculpture. To harmonise forms free-standing and in half-relief of widely differing scales, with an exquisite niche and the superbly detailed forms of arabesques, was an end worthy of the highest endeavour. No earlier style had so worthy an aim.

This was the predominant type of Roman monumental tomb from the end of the fifteenth century, in particular of those in Sta Maria del Popolo (Fig. 287). For us they have to take the place of those which perished with Old S. Peter's (Panvinio, cf. § 8).

Famous prototypes: the tomb of the Cardinal of Portugal, by Antonio Rossellino, in S. Miniato, Florence (Fig. 288); (a repetition ordered at the same time for Naples: Vasari, III, p. 95, *V. di Ant. Rossellino*); exceptionally, the sarcophagus in both instances is not a Renaissance design but a copy of an austere porphyry sarcophagus in the Piazza della Rotonda in Rome.

The tombs of Lionardo Aretino and Carlo Marsuppini (the latter by Desiderio da Settignano) in Sta Croce, § 135 (cf. Fig. 276); the works of Mino da Fiesole in the Badia, Florence.

§ 141 *Secondary Types of Tomb*

Simpler sepulchral monuments also often contained splendid features, while grandiose works sometimes only repeated Gothic ideas. Free-standing tombs, by their nature exceptional, did not form a type on their own.

To the simpler types belongs the one perhaps originated by Simone (di Giovanni Ghini?), in which the niche is shaped not as a portal, but as a semi-circular wall-recess edged with foliage, accommodating the sarcophagus; tombs of Giannozzo Pandolfino (*d* 1457) in the Badia, Florence, and in S. Trinita, Florence (by Giul. da Sangallo?), etc.

Very often there also appear commemorative slabs with reliefs and inscriptions, and many of this kind, e.g. the Ponzetti monuments (1505 and 1509) in Sta Maria della Pace in Rome (Fig. 289), and some in Milan, are among the best of the period.

In Venice several elements of the medieval tomb were retained in the forms of the new style; the sarcophagus remained a rectangular oblong with statuettes at the corners or at the front (Vendramin Tomb in SS. Giovanni e Paolo, Fig. 290, Zeno Tomb in S. Marco); it rested on statues of heroes (tombs of the Doge Mocenigo, 1476, in SS. Giovanni e Paolo, by the Lombardi, with rich ornamentation, Fig. 291, and other examples); in view of its generally lofty position a standing, rather than recumbent, statue was more often placed upon it, attended by

Fig. 292 *Rome, Sta Maria del Popolo, tomb of Cardinal Ascanio Sforza*

warrior pages or Virtues. Cf. A. G. Meyer in the Jahrbuch der preussischen Kunstsammlungen, 1889.

The sarcophagus carried on consoles was retained here also, as it was for the most part in N. Italy generally. (Milan: fine examples in Sta Maria delle Grazie, the Brivio Tomb in S. Eustorgio, etc.)

Above such sarcophagi in Venice frequently wooden equestrian statues of condottieri.

In Naples the tomb of Cardinal Brancacci (in S. Angelo a Nilo) by Michelozzo and Donatello is another almost complete translation of the local Gothic type (§ 140) into the new style. Otherwise there are to be found the most varied combinations on the tombs of warriors, statesmen and nobles, which here predominate over those of prelates.

The supreme accomplishment of the marriage of decoration and sculpture is still the two tombs in the choir of Sta Maria del Popolo in Rome (Fig. 292), by Andrea Sansovino, begun in 1505; the niche interpreted as triumphal arch architecture with most beautiful friezes and arabesques, and with incomparable funerary statues and associated sculpture.

The free-standing tomb occurs in Italy only in individual instances; that of Martin V in the Lateran with Simone's (di Giovanni Ghini?) bronze figure of the Pope in low relief; Cardinal Zeno's in S. Marco, Venice, also bronze, with statuettes on the sarcophagus; lastly, the magnificent bronze monument of Sixtus IV in S. Peter's by Pollaiuolo, evolved from the concept of lying in state.

The Turriani Tomb in S. Fermo at Verona exists only in fragments (bronze sphinxes, which carried the sarcophagus, by Andrea Riccio).

A last great work in the spirit of the early Renaissance, although of the sixteenth century; the tomb of the French general Gaston de Foix, who fell in 1512. Of various fantastically elaborate earlier projects only drawings have survived; the tomb was executed according to a reduced plan by Agostino Busti, called Bambaia, and his assistants in S. Marta in Milan. Its dispersed remains are to be found, partly in Milan (Museo Archeologico in the Castello, Ambrosiana, and elsewhere), partly in Turin, and in the V. and A. Museum, London; among them, in the most delicate marble-work, deeply undercut trophies and histories.*

§ 142 *Sepulchral Monuments of the Sixteenth Century*

Soon after the beginning of the sixteenth century the process started, although only gradually, by which sepulchral monuments also absorbed the decoration, indicated above (§ 137).

Michelangelo's attitude to decoration § 137. Of his doubtless idiosyncratic ideas for monuments to Dante (1519) and the prodigy Cecchino Bracci (1544) nothing has been preserved; the tomb of Gian Giacomo de' Medici, Marchese di Marignano, in Milan Cathedral, his last composition of this type (1560), is indifferent architecture with good sculptures by Leone Leoni. (Vasari, VII, pp. 257, 361, 388, 398, *V. di Michelangelo*, with commentary.)

Beyond any classification stands the great imaginative assignment, which was to have been his life work, the Tomb of Julius II. Cf. for this Schmarsow in the Jahrb. der preuss. Kunstsammlungen, V, pp. 63–77. Regarding the Tombs of the Medici in S. Lorenzo, Florence, see above § 80.

These Medici tombs soon served as models, both in relation to the very free allegorical interpretation of the figures and to their reclining posture on the volutes of the sarcophagi.

Independent of this: Prospero Clementi, who used to place two mourning figures seated at the sides of a sarcophagus or monument. (Prato monument in the crypt of Parma Cathedral, and especially the influential sepulchral monument to Andreasi (*d* 1549) in S. Andrea at Mantua; here the two allegorical figures are seated beside an altar, which bears an urn (later so popular) and the bust of the dead man in high relief, with a bronze swan at the base.)

The pyramidal form of monumental tomb, inaugurated in Raphael's *maravigliosa sepultura* of Agostino Chigi in Sta Maria del Popolo in Rome (Fig. 185), owes its origin solely to the antiquarian interests of the time. Evidence that the design of this tomb goes back to Raphael, and the execution, minus a few changes under Alexander VII, to Lorenzetto, has recently been convincingly presented by D. Gnoli in Archivio stor. dell' arte, II, p. 317 ff. There too allusion is made to the contemporary predilection for the pyramid, which appears in the backgrounds of paintings as well as in the reconstructions of the Tombs of Mausolus, Porsena etc. by Antonio da Sangallo and Peruzzi, among others. L. B. Alberti had already included the pyramid among his tomb-forms, drawn exclusively from Antiquity: *De re aedific.*, L. VIII, c. 3.

On the tombs, at times enormous, of Jac. Sansovino and his school in Venice and Padua the architecture has less decorative detail than, for example, even on his Library. No doubt he shared Michelangelo's view.

Under the influence of Northern princely tombs with symmetrically kneeling figures on top, the artistically insignificant and ostentatious tomb of Pietro di Toledo was fashioned by Giovanni da Nola in S. Giacomo degli Spagnuoli in Naples.

The largest types of the period 1540–80, and to some extent also of the ensuing Baroque period; the sarcophagus with large statues seated, leaning, or standing on, against, or beside, in a now deep (and, where possible, semicircular) niche; the wall-architecture encrusted with reliefs, with a seated or standing portrait-statue in the middle.

* J. Pope-Hennessy, *Catalogue of Italian Sculpture in the V. & A. Museum*, London, 1964, s. v. Bambaia, suspends judgement on the provenance of these fragments from the Tomb of Gaston de Foix. (PM).

For sepulchral monuments also not only drawings were required, but (as for buildings) models, generally of wood or wax.

In this regard numerous statements: a competition of models, Vasari, III, p. 369, n. 1, *V. di Verrocchio*; other mentions: VI, p. 60, *V. di Tribolo*; ibid., p. 125, *V. di Pierino*; ibid., pp. 144, 164, 165, *V. di Bandinelli*.

Among secular monuments statues of princes, and equestrian statues of generals are found on public piazze.

In relation to decoration already mentioned are: Leopardo's base (§ 136) and Bandinelli's (§ 137), the latter intended for a statue of Giovanni, father of Duke Cosimo I. In the French invasion of 1797 the statues of the princes of the house of Este at Ferrara and those of the Doria at Genoa were lost.

Characteristic of the spirit of the Renaissance was the fact that the Bolognese in 1471 marked their newly adjusted frontier with the Ferrarese, not in the medieval manner with a cross or a small chapel, but with a pyramid bearing their arms: Bursellis, *Ann. Bonon.*, in Murat., XXIII, col. 899.

(NOTE: The Medici Tomb in Milan Cathedral is not now thought to have any connection with Michelangelo. For the Chigi Chapel in Sta Maria del Popolo, see now J. Shearman and M. Hirst in Journal of the Warburg and Courtauld Institutes, XXIV, 1961.) (PM).

§ 143 *The Free-Standing Altar and the Aedicule Against a Wall*

Of the richer altar-forms of the Middle Ages the Renaissance repeatedly reproduced delightfully the insulated or attached aedicule on columns, but in the instances which have been preserved, rarely on an elaborate scale.

Prototypes from the earlier period: in the older Basilicas; from the Gothic period: in S. Paolo and in the Lateran in Rome.

Michelozzo's aedicule in the Annunziata, Florence, for the miraculous image by the door, of uncertain richness (executed by Pagno di Lapo, 1448–52); the one over the nave altar in S. Miniato is simpler and finer, its covering a barrel vault open at the front, with glazed coffering inside.

The manifestly very sumptuous altars of this type (1460–1500) in Old S. Peter's, which Panvinius (§ 8) enumerates, are all lost. Similarly those recorded in Albertini (*De mirabilibus urbis R.*, L. III, fol. 86). Cf. certain drawings in Grimaldi's Codex in the Biblioteca Barberini in Rome.* The former high altar of Sta Maria Maggiore (1483), hypothetically restored in Letarouilly, III, pl. 311.

The high altar in Spello Cathedral, a simple and good design, graceful and elegant in execution, by Rocco da Vicenza, 1515.

The bronze aedicule to cover a bronze group: Zeno chapel in S. Marco, Venice (Fig. 293).

Of the sense of splendour, of which the Renaissance was capable and which must have been displayed especially in the additions to the structure, hardly a single surviving monument conveys any idea, not even the Tempietto of the Volto Santo in Lucca Cathedral. The free-standing Baroque altar, § 137.

§ 144 *The Wall-Altar*

With altars set against the wall, painting, so far as Italy was concerned, already had a dominant role and maintained it, but the wall-altar made of marble or other sculptural materials became one of the supreme tasks of sculpture and decoration combined. The setting of both painted and sculptured altars tended to follow, in the richer examples, the model of Antique formal gateways and triumphal arches, but with an inspired freedom.

The North, as is generally known, long remained faithful to the shrine with carved figures, and assigned painting to the side-wings only, while in Italy it was allowed to be the principal feature.

That in Italy, besides the painted altar-panels, a separate category of carved altars was able to come into being, may be attributed to an aesthetic conviction of the high value of sculpture following the achievements of the Pisan School.

The first significant sculptured wall-altars of the Renaissance are probably the glazed terracotta reliefs of Luca della Robbia and his School, in the Cathedral at Arezzo and in several Florentine churches (S. Croce, SS. Apostoli, etc.); generally with an unassuming decorative surround.

Thereafter sometimes large wall-tabernacles were attempted, painted, or in stucco or terracotta, e.g. the one in S. Domenico at Perugia (1459) by the Florentine Agostino di Duccio. At Padua, in the Eremitani† church, two such, admittedly without altar-tables, but certainly intended for them, 1511. In view of the enthusiasm of this period for polychrome sculpture and stucco-work in vaulting, a more frequent use of this mode of decoration could well be expected on altars.

The marble wall-altar, often with magnificent decorative arabesques, assumed the most varied forms, from the plain unframed relief to the triumphal arch type, in which the central compartment might be allotted to an especially venerated sacred object (tabernacle, image of the Madonna), or a figure in relief, or a statue. An upper lunette occasionally contained a fine relief.

Altars by Mino da Fiesole and his School, in the Badia, Florence; in S. Ambrogio there; in Sta Maria del Popolo in Rome, etc.

In the fifteenth century sculpture, above all of the side-figures, was as a rule in high relief; but, for example, also free-standing sculpture on the S. Regulus altar in Lucca Cathedral, by Civitale, 1484.

* Now published – see Bibliography. (PM).

† The Eremitani was destroyed in the Second World War. (PM).

Fig. 293 *Venice, S. Marco, the Zeno Altar*

Fig. 294 *Siena, Fontegiusta, the High Altar*

The masterpiece of Lorenzo di Mariano, known as Marinna, in Fontegiusta at Siena (Fig. 294), § 135. In Siena Cathedral, the Piccolomini Altar (1485) by Andrea Bregno of Milan; a large niche with sculptures all round, and inside it the altar itself with a particularly splendid superstructure.

Here and there the ineptitude of a smaller sacellum within a larger; *uno scatolino in un altro scatolino*, perhaps on the model of Roman buildings of the period of decline, like the Porta de' Borsari in Verona (window of the upper part). Even in Italian Gothic one finds the insertion of one framing-element into a similar, larger one, e.g. on several fine tombs of the Angevin period in the churches of Naples, or in S. Domenico in Perugia on the tomb of Benedict XI (*d* 1304), wrongly attributed to Giovanni Pisano.

Particularly noble and with exquisite angels in the spandrels beside the central arch: the altar of Cardinal Borgia, later Alexander VI, in the sacristy of Sta Maria del Popolo in Rome.

In Como Cathedral Rodari's marble altar (1492) and a magnificent large carved wooden altar, coloured and gilded.

A number of richly decorated marble altars in Naples, especially in Monteoliveto; here among others, famed for their sculpture, as well as for their beautiful, restrained, decorative setting; excellent altars by the Florentines Antonio Rossellino and Benedetto da Majano; also later ones by Giovanni da Nola and others. Other splendid altars and tombs in the church, rich in marble, of S. Giovanni a Carbonara. Cf. Vasari, V, p. 93, *V. di Michelangelo da Siena*, in which it is said of Naples: *quella città, dove molto si costuma fare le cappelle e le tavole di marmo . . .*

In Palermo the works of the Luganesi Antonello and Domenico Gagini, importations of the very decorative Lombard style in the spirit of the Certosa of Pavia; a rich altar in S. Zita; a niche with a Madonna statue in the Museo; an extraordinarily rich holy-water basin in the Cathedral etc.

Marble frames round pictures, especially in Venice, sometimes rich and fine; calculated perspectively as a continuation of the architecture in the painting.

§ 145 *The Sixteenth-Century Altar*

In the sixteenth century the decoration of altars was reduced to a simple architectural surrounding, whether for a life-size, or even a colossal, statue, or for an altarpiece, often of imposing size. It was only now that

the six sacella (altar-niches) in the Pantheon began to serve as prototypes.

In Venice life-size statues, singly or in groups on rather frigid architecture, held the field with Jacopo Sansovino and his School, alongside the most celebrated paintings of Titian.

Perhaps the last very richly ornamented altars: Mosca's two in Orvieto Cathedral.

The altars in New S. Peter's in Rome, according to Panvinius (§ 8), p. 374: *altarium tympana maximis columnis et capitulis corinthiis pulcherrimis fulciuntur*; they were the first big, entirely architectural, frames for paintings.

To Vasari (VI, pp. 345, 363, *V. di Sanmicheli*) an altar like that of S. Giorgio in Verona, in which mouldings and pediment curve with the wall, still appears something extraordinary (it is the one with the painting by Paolo Veronese); in the Baroque style curved ground plans later become a commonplace.

Instead of these columnar settings others attempted Baroque and elaborate, even polychrome, surrounds of stucco, with herms and the like; Vasari, VII, p. 52, *V. di Daniele da Volterra* (who thus surrounded his *Descent from the Cross*); VII, p. 418, *Opere di Primaticcio*, referring to the frames by Pellegrino Tibaldi.

The first really enormous altar-monstrosity, and that the brain-child of Pius V in 1567; Vasari, VII, p. 705 f.; Vasari's *Autobiography*. Pius commissioned from him, for the monastery of his native Bosco, "not an ordinary picture, but a vast *macchina*, like a triumphal arch, with two large pictures, one in front and one at the back, and some thirty narrative paintings, with many figures, in the smaller compartments". Soon the prodigious Jesuit altars followed with several pictures one above the other.

Groups of free sculpture on altars, with no other framing: Vasari, VI, pp. 178–88, *V. di Bandinelli*, whose groups are in the Cathedral, S. Croce, and the Annunziata in Florence; Andrea Sansovino's (in S. Agostino, Rome) and Michelangelo's (in S. Peter's) no longer have their original surroundings.

The mensa of the altar in the good period was either simply ornamented or given over to sculpture; bronzes by Donatello in the Santo at Padua, Ghiberti's Arca di S. Zenobio in Florence Cathedral in the form of an altar-table, marble mensa in S. Gregorio in Rome, all with narrative reliefs.

§ 146 *Screens, Pulpits, Holy Water Basins, Chimney-pieces etc.*

Besides tombs and altars, altar-rails, screens, lecterns, pulpits, sacristy-fountains, holy water basins; and, in secular buildings, chimney-pieces, were treated wherever possible as decorative works in white marble. In many of these works the finest possible expression of the subject appears to have been attained.

The superb choir-gallery in the Sistine Chapel of the Vatican (Fig. 295); several chapel-enclosures (Fig. 296) in S. Petronio in Bologna; one of the stone benches of the Loggia de' Nobili in Siena, § 135.

Fig. 295 *(opposite) Rome, Vatican, Sistine Chapel, gallery*

Fig. 296 *(above) Bologna, S. Petronio, chapel screen*

Fig. 297 *(right) Perugia Cathedral, pulpit*

The pulpits, by now as a rule no longer resting on several columns but on a single support; or hung from a pier or a wall of the church, sometimes reached the highest level of magnificence. Simple and beautiful the pulpit in the refectory of the Badia at Fiesole, by Piero di Cecco, *c* 1460; the grandest the pulpit in S. Croce in Florence, by Benedetto da Majano, with the celebrated reliefs (§ 135, Fig. 277); appreciably less grand the one in Sta Maria Novella, by Lazzaro d' Andrea – still very beautiful the one in Lucca Cathedral by Matteo Civitali, 1498. (Donatello's bronze pulpits in S. Lorenzo exist principally on account of the reliefs.)

Outside pulpits, facing the piazza in front of a church: on Prato Cathedral, with vigorous ornament and Donatello's reliefs: the two at Spoleto Cathedral by Ambrogio da Milano and Pippo d' Antonio da Firenze (Fig. 136, § 70); the one on Perugia Cathedral (1439), from which S. Bernardino preached in 1441; Graziani, Archiv. Stor., XVI, I, p. 442 (Fig. 297). The sermons, for which these pulpits principally existed, see *Kult. d. Renaiss.*, p. 467 ff. These pulpits had canopies or roofs, which those inside the church did not have. The external pulpits facing large piazze served not only for sermons, but also for the exposition of important relics, the one in Prato, for example, for exhibiting the Girdle of the Madonna: Vasari, *Vita di Donatello.* Hence, no doubt, the rejoicing putti in the reliefs.

The fountains of sacristies and refectories, in which the water did not well up from a spring, but flowed by turning a tap, mostly took the form of ornamented niches; Verrocchio's in S. Lorenzo; della Robbia's masterpiece in Sta Maria Novella (§ 135); others in the Certosa of Florence, in the Badia at Fiesole by Francesco di Simone Ferucci (*c* 1460), in the Palace of Urbino, and elsewhere.

Finally, the holy water basins, an exercise in unconstrained fantasy in decoration, and conceived as such early and with originality in those in Siena (by Antonio Federighi, 1462) and (a few years earlier) Orvieto, § 135 (Figs. 298, 299), in which the chief motive of all Antique decoration, the tripod, is delightfully and individualistically revived; others with round or polygonal supports, often of high quality, especially in Tuscan churches, Pisa Cathedral etc.

The marble candelabrum, which Alberti (*De re aedific.*, L. VII, c. 13) derived in theory (wrongly) from vases, appears simply in the form of decoration; additionally at least once (Fig. 282) with exuberant fancy as mullions; and also (§ 136) as a magnificent form of salient column on church portals. Only the Gothic period fashioned the Easter candlestick in marble; now they were made of bronze.

With chimney-pieces, which were the monumental feature of every respectable living-room, the accent sometimes lay upon the imaginative interplay of the whole design (the older apartments of the Doge's Palace in Venice; Fig. 300), sometimes on a felicitous accord between the carving of the frieze and its supports (several in the palace of Urbino (Fig. 279); then Palazzo Gondi in Florence, chimney-piece by Giul. da Sangallo;

Fig. 298 *Siena Cathedral, Holy Water basin*

Fig. 299 *Orvieto Cathedral, Holy Water basin*

Palazzo Roselli, chimney-piece by Rovezzano; Palazzo Massimi in Rome, chimney-piece by ? Peruzzi). Splendid large chimney-pieces in the Pal. Doria in Genoa. Serlio's chimney-pieces (L. IV) were already somewhat Baroque and subject to French influence.

Overmantels, in the French Renaissance and then in the Baroque phase in Italy very intricate (with busts, statues and architectural forms), did not exist in the good period, or were confined to a simple fresco painting. Cf. § 169. Busts on chimney-pieces, to begin with probably placed there as the safest and best position in the room, Vasari, III, p. 373, *V. di Verrocchio.*

§ 146a *Decoration of Fountains*

The combination of running water with the forms of architecture and sculpture, undoubtedly early achieved by the peoples of Antiquity, and highly prized as one of the most rewarding of art-forms, has, comparatively speaking, left us with few tangible monuments or records.

All fountain-decoration is perishable, because even with the greatest care in the execution damp will break up stone-work in the course of time, and because the supply of water is subject to variation; changes in religious attitudes and also in taste could be destructive to figurative decoration.

The peace of the Roman Empire at one time accorded the capital a lavish water supply on a scale probably never experienced elsewhere, and even provincial towns were able to use their resources abundantly for this purpose. The Renaissance had before its eyes an inspiring reminder of this in the form of the ruins of aqueducts and baths. To what extent it may also have been familiar with the fountains of the Byzantine world and of Islamic palaces and mosques is difficult to judge.

A lasting survival of the Christian Roman Empire, the *cantharus*, i.e. the flowing or spouting spring in the forecourt or entrance of a church, sometimes with a roof supported on columns (the most notable instances in

Holtzinger, *Die altchristliche Architektur in systematischer Darstellung*, p. 14 ff). Presumably monasteries throughout the Western world profited early from this feature by interchange of information, both in relation to current practice in hydraulics and to possible decoration. Besides the main source in the principal court there was also one for hand-washing near the refectory. (In the monastery of Lobbes, on the Sambre, the ante-room of the refectory was provided towards the end of the tenth century with underground piping with a fountain, which spouted upwards and over an upper bowl, and then through four openings in it flowed down into another bowl below; Pertz, *Monumenta, Scriptores*, Tome VI, *Gesta abbatum Lobiensium*, c. 29.) Elsewhere for the same purpose a simple ewer with several outlets had to suffice, each having its closable tap or *obex*. (Similarly at Gorze monastery, near Metz; Pertz, op. cit., *Vita Johannis Gorziensis*, c. 63; also tenth century.)

The fonts of baptistries, filled not from a spring, but by pouring water into them, could become examples of ornamental or figured decoration.

Simplest form of basins: the stone *pozzo* or well, still today in many Italian towns the all-purpose domestic source, and in Venice the only one. Its richer art-form in the later Middle Ages that of a large capital of Corinthian character, probably also with figured decoration. Its upper part, carrying the pulley for the bucket-chain, of wrought iron. (Elaborate example of the latter type – according to a photograph – in the Palazzo Saracco at Ferrara.)

The most important larger type of fountain of the late Middle Ages in Italy was the town fountain, its water generally acquired at great sacrifice, and then only if the town owned the land where the source was. Towns of some standing, even up to the present day, have only one of this kind, which is frequented day and night as the only good drinking-water; artistically, most of them are only modestly appointed.

In the North the Gothic drinking-fountain with pipes, naturally relying on the forms and decorative symbolism of a church finial; later often culminating in a fairly large statue of a saint. Exception: the fountain, cast in pewter in 1408, of the Town Hall of Brunswick; three super-imposed basins, with multifarious water effects.

In Italy Viterbo (praised by Aeneas Sylvius for its wealth of fountains) still possesses two drinking-fountains of the Gothic period: Fontana Pianoscarana and Fontana Grande, the latter with two upper bowls which have special sprays; the figured ornament confined to lions' heads.

Siena has large sunken basins, of which only the Fonte Gaia will be mentioned because of its sculptural decoration. (Regarding the Sienese water system, especially: Milanesi, *Documenti*, I, p. 247; II, pp. 44–52, 76–80, 96–101, 374, 447; III, pp. 278, 306. The city was very proud of it and was far from pleased when the fountains ran short of water when distinguished foreigners were present.) Of the medieval fountains of Florence precise information is lacking. (The principal source of supply, Monte Murello, is not plentifully supplied with water.)

In Perugia the well-known Fontana Grande (1274–80) with three basins; the ornamental sculpture by Pisan and Florentine masters, apart from its artistic worth important as eloquent evidence of what at that time imagination, learning and religion sought to combine in a town fountain.

With the coming of the Renaissance the more lavish applications of the fountain system shifted to the dwellings and gardens of princes and the powerful. Florentines figured prominently as protagonists of the now advanced science of hydraulics and of its artistic treatment. The discovery of Antique basins, sometimes richly fashioned in marble, and the early and splendid use of the new style in the holy-water basins mentioned above (§ 146) may well have considerably influenced the forms of decoration. Water-gods and other water creatures from Antiquity, now absorbed into the whole new vocabulary of decoration, were particularly suited to the symbolism of fountains, as was the livelier animal creation.

The very freely interpreted so-called dolphin became a symbol of all water-life, and from that of men was added the *putto*, newly created by the Renaissance, the naked child.

Hardly one fountain of the fifteenth century, however, has been preserved in its complete context and the evidence of illustrations from devotional pictures, frescoes and miniatures leaves much to be desired.

On hydraulics copious data and directions in the tenth Book of L. B. Alberti, *De re aedific.* He stipulates without preamble, as he had already done in the ninth Book for gardens, extensive ornamental waters "at many places and unexpectedly little springs of water, *praerumpant aqulae*" (by which is probably meant the practical joke springs, which unexpectedly spurted on visitors). As architectural consultant to Pope Nicholas V, in addition to Bernardo (presumably B. Rossellino) for the proposed great rebuilding of the Vatican (§ 115) he may also have been responsible for the lavish water programme for a garden and two cortili, "for use and for show", in a manner which the surrounding "heights" (*vertex montis*) would scarcely have provided.

The first fountain (1409–19) decorated in the fifteenth-century spirit was the Fonte Gaia at Siena, still a town well, laid out as early as 1343 as a sunken basin; it preserves today a marble wall-surround with religious and allegorical reliefs on the inside; on the parapet in free-standing sculpture two (formerly four?) mothers each with two children, also lions and she-wolves, the symbol of the city, spouting water and ridden by *putti*; an important work by Jacopo della Quercia; Vasari, II, p. 116, *V. di Quercia*. The remains are in the museum; modern reproductions, of the reliefs only, *in situ*.

For Cosimo de' Medici, Michelozzo carried pipe-runs to his country villas at Cafaggiuolo and Careggi, and in Assisi from the high ground to Sta Maria degli Angeli, where a "fine and rich" well-house was erected: Vasari, II, p. 443, *V. di Michelozzo*. In such surroundings the

Fig. 300 *Venice, Doge's Palace, chimneypiece*

figurative decoration took shape which impressed the rest of Italy. The masterly, freely handled marble basin of the sacristy in S. Lorenzo in Florence is probably by Donatello; for the Medici he fashioned a much admired granite vessel with a jet of water, and another of the same type for the garden of the Pazzi, which is said still to exist. Moreover, in more recent times (thanks to Bode) his bronze group of *Judith and Holofernes* (Loggia de' Lanzi) has been identified as the fountain-group of the Pal. Medici; the water gushed from the corners of the wine-skin and from the masks on the three-sided base, the reliefs of playing putti parodying drink and drunkenness. (Probably soon after 1440.)

No longer existing: the marble fountain by Antonio Rossellino famed as a fine work in the second cortile of the Pal. Medici, with putti (obviously in the round) who held the jaws of dolphins open to discharge the water: Vasari, III, 93, *V. di A. Rossellino.*

Also Florentine and among the best work: in the V. and A. Museum in London the exquisite terracotta group of two putti with a dolphin, a model for a fountain group.

Commissioned from Verrocchio by Lorenzo il Magnifico a fountain at Careggi, later placed in the cortile of the Palazzo della Signoria in Florence; the jumping putto with a spouting dolphin, in bronze; Vasari, III, *V. di Verrocchio.*

Florentine fountains elsewhere: Giuliano da Majano (according to a not very lucid account in Vasari) built in Naples the royal pleasure house of Poggio Reale "with splendid fountains and conduits to be found in the cortile. And for the town and the houses of the nobility and for the piazze he submitted drawings for many fountains, with beautiful and original [*capricciose*] inventions."

To the order of King Matthias of Hungary (*d* 1490) a fountain made in Florence; according to Poliziano:

Tusca manus, Tuscum marmor, Rex Ungarus auctor,
Aureus hoc Ister surgere fonte velit.

At Ferrara in the Palace garden of Duke Ercole I a fountain (of Florentine work?); above, a hydra with seven heads dispensing an abundance of water, below, a richly carved marble bowl. On the Piazza there, a marble fountain, for which the pipe-runs at any rate entailed much expenditure and many alterations (1481–92).

A relative standstill in all the architectural activities of the Medici after the first expulsion of the family (1494) until the secure period of government with the rise of Duke Cosimo I in 1537. But in 1515 Giovanni Francesco Rustici was working on a small bronze *Mercury*, once more as a fountain-figure for a court in the Pal. Medici, poised over an orb and probably closely resembling the celebrated later one by Giovanni Bologna; the piping, which passed upward through the figure, culminated in a turning movement, either of the figure itself or of an implement in its hand. (On this point Vasari, VI, 602, *V. di Rustici*, is unclear. Presumably also the bronze *Grazia* mentioned by Vasari as pressing her breast was also a fountain-figure.)

In Rome a greatly increased exploitation of water began with Sixtus IV (1472–84), with improvements to the supply and with the cleansing of the ancient Aqua Virgo, after Nicholas V (through the Florentines Alberti and Bernardo?) had made a start and had erected on the Piazza di Trevi a marble fountain with the massive embellishment of the Papal and City arms.

In front of S. Peter's there rose, under Innocent VIII at the latest, a large spouting fountain with two basins and carving (*lapidibus marmoreis figuratis* – Infessura, in Eccard, *Scriptores*, II, col. 1993), improved or completed under Alexander VI ("a fountain such as cannot be found in the whole of the rest of Italy"); it was built in the atrium behind the *cantharus*, familiar from drawings, with the great bronze pine-cone.

Under Alexander VI, and due to Cardinal Lopez, there was also a famous fountain near Sta Maria in Trastevere, with Bramante's participation.

Anyone with influence in the Curia at that time seems to have obtained water for gardens or vines. When the supply of the Acqua di Trevi was reinforced, one of the members of the Curia, Dossi, built a marble fountain in his nearby garden, with ancient proverbs carved on it. A later general verdict in Doni, *Disegno* (ed. Venice, 1549, fol. 12), after mentioning fountains with human and animal figures, water-systems etc.; *et chi vuol vedere fontane mirabili, guardi ne' palazzi delle vigne* [sic] *de' prelati in Roma.*

For landowners of this kind the various ways of effectively maintaining an adequate supply may be imagined, and it is the subject of letters by Annibale Caro (1538) and Claudio Tolomei (1543); *Lettere Pittoriche*, V, p. 29 and p. 91, cf. § 125. The water had to gush, trickle, and drip into concealed earthenware containers, now rising, now falling; one and the same water had to plunge, ripple, and spurt from pipes, fall as rain and well up in the middle of the basin; another supply glistened and, from it, trick jets would spring up; in time the effects of condensation, dew, and bubbling noises were effectively imitated; in addition, partly the result of invention and partly based on ancient ruins and records, on and inside grottoes: rusticated tufa, stalactites, antique remains, shells, corals, snails, and a fitting vegetation everywhere. For the beginnings of the Baroque period in such matters, cf. Vasari, I, *Introduzione*.

Julius II (1503–13) augmented once again (1509) the Aqua Virgo and ran the water to the new buildings of the Vatican from two miles away, ostensibly for a fountain in the Belvedere, but chiefly for the new building, and probably for the large garden behind. Regarding the connection between running water and the celebrated Vatican antiquities, cf. § 126 and note. Bramante planned that all the water used in the Belvedere and in the upper part of the great new cortile (the subsequent Giardino della Pigna) should be accumulated again in the lower part for a very fine fountain: Vasari, *V. di Bramante*; the present one much later.

Michelangelo's intentions with regard to the group of the *Farnese Bull*, cf. § 97. Use of Antique water-gods leaning on urns; *Nile* and *Tiber* at the Capitol, on the external double stair, designed by Michelangelo, of the Palazzo del Senatore; there was soon a modern copy – Vasari, *V. di Pierino da Vinci*, and then copies everywhere.

For the decoration of fountains of the Raphael period the garden designs of the large villa for Cardinal Giulio de' Medici (§ 119), known afterwards as the Villa Madama, must have been especially resourceful, though admittedly less in what was executed than in the frequently and markedly varied schemes described in v. Geymüller, *Raffaello . . . come architetto*. For the contribution of Giovanni da Udine (§ 175), cf. Vasari, *V. di Udine*; it is thought that he imitated – and surpassed – a room surviving from Antiquity with a mass of maritime symbols and motives, which had been discovered in Rome shortly before, and which was thought to be a shrine of Neptune; there was also talk of an elephant's head spouting water, also of a thicket of trees and rocks with water flowing out of stalactites etc., the whole crowned by a gigantic lion's head, covered with maidenhair ferns and other appropriate plants.

Towards the middle of the sixteenth century decorative architecture and sculpture, already for the most part looking to the dawn of Mannerism, were moving towards large fountain-structures both on public piazze and in gardens, even though the availability of water was hardly on a commensurate scale. Of the modern conventional watery world of mythological, allegorical and heraldic content, representations are here for the first time identifiable in their entirety: godlike, human, and animal creatures, often ending in fishtails. The use of urns linked with spouting animals provides lively motives, and the more decorative execution avoids those exactingly delicate details which were not always felicitous in contemporary art. The plan and form of the whole, the sequence, ornament and size of the upper bowls and lower basin, sometimes provided with supporting figures, were more often treated with a genuine sense of beauty: the water-spout now received a multitude of inventions of the most varied character. Among simpler examples: the wall-fountain and niche; in palaces and gardens, grottoes with stalactites, stucco-work and sculptures of all kinds preserved to this day.

The favourite master, Giov. Agnolo Montorsoli (born near Florence after 1500, died 1563: Vasari, VI, p. 629 ff.), in style, like all the following, dependent upon Michelangelo; his principal works the two large city fountains in Messina, on the Marina and near the Cathedral; the latter a three-bowl structure with four river-gods, eight sea-monsters, dolphins, masks, reliefs, the statue of Orion on top, all in Carrara marble.

Bandinelli indeed undertook (letter to Duke Cosimo in 1550, *Lettere Pittoriche*, I, 37) to create a fountain, which would surpass not only these, but all that the earth could show and the Romans and Greeks create.

In Genoa Montorsoli was employed by the house of Doria as architect (including fountains). A sea-monster, fashioned for this family, soon went to Spain for Cardinal Granvella. (The Neptune with chariot and sea-horses in a basin surrounded by eagles, in the large garden directly behind the palace, is not thought to be his, but by Taddeo Carlone.)

The Villa d' Este (§ 124) at Tivoli, laid out by Pirro Ligorio *c* 1550, with its unrestricted use of the waters of the Teverone a model for all water-splendours; the whole present setting and sculpture of fountains and grottoes not created or refurbished until the Baroque period; the many Antique statues, which stood in the villa (also probably connected with the waters), were transferred in the eighteenth century to the Vatican.

In the Vigna di Papa Giulio III (1550–55), beyond the Porta del Popolo in Rome, principally by Vignola, the water-works never completely realised; even in the sunken cortile at the back, a haven of refreshing coolness, only the nymphaeum in the middle completed (Fig. 268).

In addition, basically stemming from Vignola: the fountains and terraces of the Villa Lante alla Bagnaja near Viterbo; the waters of Caprarola; and in Rome the former ascent to the Orti Farnesiani from the gate by the Forum, with flights of steps and grottoes in terraces.

In a different sense influential at this time were the fountain-sculptures of the ducal Villa Castello near Florence (so named after an ancient water *castellum*), which were made from 1546 by Nic. Pericoli, known as Tribolo, and his assistants; here one saw (and still sees in part) figures of children, among them one copied from the Antique *Boy with a Goose*; female figures wringing the water out of their hair, sea-rams and other wonders of the deep, Antaeus crushed by Hercules as a figure spouting water, giant mountain-gods with dripping beards, and the already familiar river-gods with urns, water-jokes of all kinds, dripping grottoes and also the merest frivolities. Vasari, VI, 72 ff., 91, *V. di Tribolo.* Ibid., *V. di Pierino da Vinci.* Ibid., *V. di Montorsoli.* (Of stalactites (*tarteri*) Antonio da Sangallo produced for the Duke a pack-load by way of experiment; his accompanying letter (Gaye, *Carteggio*, II, p. 344) shows that stalactites were already much in use in Rome, and that certain Antique ruins were spoken of in this context as patterns. In relation to the general designs which have been mentioned above, we find here an emphasis on individual ideas and even pure chance: how far this would have been true of the water-decoration of Cosimo's other villas, and those of his immediate successors, we cannot say with precision.)

For basins people sought enormous monoliths; one in granite from Elba, twelve braccia wide, for the Boboli Gardens: Vasari, *V. di Tribolo.*

Subsequently the great master of post-Michelangelo sculpture – who, it should not be forgotten, was a Fleming, Giovanni Bologna, from Douai (1529–1608) – also made his name with masterpieces of fountain sculpture. His celebrated winged *Mercury* (Florence, Mus. Nazionale) once stood above a bubbling pool in the middle of the ground-floor colonnade of the Villa Medici in Rome; at Bologna the Neptune fountain on the Piazza (1564) combines first-rate execution with delightful and resourceful choice of motives in a flexible composition; in the Giardino Boboli in Florence there towers above the fountain on the island (1576) a pillar with three large river-gods, dominated by a statue of Oceanus, majestically simple beyond any other in Italy or the entire West.

On the Piazza della Signoria, very extravagant in bronze and marble, but of only minor consequence, the *Neptune Fountain* by Ammanati. In Rome, in the contemporary Florentine manner, the extremely graceful Fontana delle Tartarughe, by Taddeo Landini (1585).

With the coming of the real Baroque (*c* 1580) there coincided another impressive increase in Rome in the exploitation of water. Sixtus V (1585–90) carried the Acqua Marcia, now called after him the Acqua Felice, into the city; under Paul V (1605–21) followed, partly fed by the Lago di Bracciano, the Acqua Paola. Rome now first consummated its new architectural type, and Baroque, spreading from there throughout the world, became to a great extent a combination of all that was noble in architecture with the animation of water.

(NOTE: For the Fonte Gaia see now A. C. Hanson, *J. della Quercia's Fonte Gaia*, Oxford, 1965.

The terracotta group of two putti with a dolphin might be V. & A. 468 (After Tribolo) or 471 (Pierino da Vinci).

On the Rustici fountain figure, with a turning movement, Vasari seems in fact quite clear: *fra le mani un instrumento che è fatto, dall' acqua che egli versa in alto, girare. Imperochè, essendo bucata una gamba, passa la canna per quella e per il torso; onde, giunta l' acqua alla bocca della figura, percuote in quello strumento bilicato con quattro piastre sottili soldate a uso di farfalla, e lo fa girare.*

The Neptune Fountain by Montorsoli was seriously damaged in the Messina earthquake of 1908.) (PM).

CHAPTER THREE

Decoration in Bronze

§ 147 *The Technique and Largest Castings*

Bronze ornament was almost entirely independent of Antique precedents, and was more a free expression of the sense of beauty and genuine luxury of the Renaissance, sometimes also an inspired translation of forms currently used in marble.

Bronze objects from Antiquity must have been very rare at that time and were hardly ever copied. Apart from bronze doors, like those of the Pantheon, the only relevant evidence known to me: Verrocchio finished in 1469 a bronze candlestick *a similitudine di certo vaso* (Gaye, *Carteggio*, I, p. 569), by which may be understood, if only by surmise, an Antique bronze vessel.

The technique of casting was one long since perfected, a tradition uninterrupted because of the founding of bells and cannon; the general extravagance of the fifteenth century, especially in the prosperous towns of N. Italy, did the rest. In the Cappella Zeno in S. Marco in Venice, altar and tomb of bronze; bronze reliefs and entire wall-tombs of bronze at Padua; by Donatello, Vellano, Riccio: cf. also § 141. Undoubtedly the most important bronze altar in Italy, the great High Altar of the Santo in Padua, a work of Donatello and his assistants, was later dismantled and latterly, but probably incorrectly, reassembled. The description of a large and magnificent bronze altar, gilded and with silver figures, 1521–26, in Sta Maria della Misericordia at Bergamo, in the Anonimo Morelliano (it has now disappeared: according to Vasari, IV, p. 151 n. 1, *V. di Bramante*, the lustrous metal was chosen because the chapel was dark). In Rome some Papal tombs are of bronze: Martin V's by Simone (di Giovanni Ghini?), Sixtus IV's and Innocent VIII's by Antonio Pollaiuolo (§ 141).

Works of this type, because the bronze has to conform essentially to the idiom of marble decoration, did not play a determining part in ornament as a whole. On the tomb of Sixtus IV, the downward-flowing volutes of the catafalque make a splendid effect.

(NOTE: This section is surprisingly brief and contains noticeable omissions. The *Marcus Aurelius*, for example, was one of the best-known surviving pieces from Antiquity and was certainly copied. The technique of casting on a large scale was not perfected until well into the sixteenth century – cf. Cellini's constant troubles. The Venetians were certainly the most skilled casters, as is seen in the history of all three bronze doors for the Baptistry at Florence.) (PM).

§ 148 *Doors, Screens and Altar-Rails*

Ceremonial doors and screens were originally peculiar to bronze. With regard to the first the Renaissance was simply following a custom to which the whole of the Middle Ages had adhered.

On the two celebrated doors by Ghiberti (S. Giovanni, Florence), the sculpture predominates throughout, so far as the door-leaves are concerned. On the other hand the fronts of the jambs and lintels of both, and of the third door (with leaves by Andrea Pisano, which he was supposed to replace with new ones), are highly important as perhaps the earliest instances of the more naturalistic arabesque, the festoon (§ 134). This was indeed specifically an idealised representation of stakes standing in pots, about which foliage, flowers and fruit were entwined, disposed round the doorways on church festivals (Fig. 301). On the third door naturalism almost goes beyond permissible limits.

The doors of S. Peter's, cast in 1433–45 by Filarete, are in their decorative elements still rather stiff; the frames round the reliefs filled out with scrolls in spirals with numerous figurines. Donatello's small doors in the sacristy of S. Lorenzo in Florence are noteworthy only for their extremely animated figures of saints.

Also on the bronze doors by Jacopo Sansovino in the choir of S. Marco in Venice and by Guglielmo Monaco of Alfonso's Triumphal Arch in the Castello Nuovo at Naples relief predominates over decoration throughout. The beginning of the Baroque style on the doors of Pisa Cathedral by Gio. da Bologna. Older, but not significant,

Fig. 301 *Florence, Baptistry, detail from Ghiberti's second door*

Fig. 302 *Florence, Palazzo Strozzi, lantern*

bronze doors in the crypt of Naples Cathedral, by Tommaso Malvito between 1497 and 1507.

The strikingly small number of such doors is explained, among other reasons, by the rarity of completed façades, § 69. Donatello projected a door for the Baptistry of Siena to no purpose: Vasari, II, p. 414, *V. di Donatello*; Milanesi, II, p. 297. We omit very simple bronze doors. According to Malipiero (Archiv. Stor., VII, I, p. 339) Charles VIII in 1495 took away the bronze doors from the Castello of Naples and sent them to France as a token of victory. The very fine bronze screen in Prato Cathedral (Cappella della Cintola), by the Florentine Bruno di Ser Lapo, 1444, with graceful interpretation of Gothic motives; delicate interlacing and figurines; as crowning elements palmettes and candelabra (1461, by Pasquino di Matteo da Montepulciano). Regarding the intertwined ropes of bronze above the Medici sarcophagus in S. Lorenzo in Florence, an instance of truly wonderful naturalism, in Vasari, III, p. 362, *V. di Verrocchio*. Regarding the bronze screens by the Sienese

Fig. 303 *Florence, Palazzo Strozzi, torch-holder*

Fig. 304 *Venice, Sta Maria della Salute, Easter candlestick*

Fig. 305 *Venice, Piazza S. Marco, socket for banners*

Antonio Ormanni at the entrance to the Libreria, and where one looks through into the undercroft of the Cathedral of Siena; and also in S. Agostino; Milanesi, II, p. 458; Vasari, II, p. 518, in the Comm. on the *V. di Pinturicchio*, and III, p. 688, n. 1, *V. di Signorelli*. Regarding the rail and candelabra of Sansovino's altar in S. Spirito, Florence; Vasari, IV, p. 512, *V. di Andrea Sansovino*. The screens for the chapel of S. Antony in the Santo at Padua, designed by the excellent decorator Tiziano Mino, remained unexecuted owing to his death in 1552; Scardeonius, in Graev. *Thesaur.*, VI, III, col. 428. The stucco-work in the chapel, see § 177.

An aesthetic law of uniform validity was not detectable in such works, some being more rigidly architectonic, others more gaily decorative. Bronze screens, altar-rails etc., have survived in large numbers only from the Baroque period.

Wrought-iron screens, in Gothic days sometimes perfect of their kind (the best perhaps in the sacristy of S. Croce in Florence; another famous one in Orvieto Cathedral (1337) cf. Della Valle, *Storia del Duomo di Orvieto*, p. 111 and Doc. 35; others mentioned in Milanesi, I, p. 309; II, p. 13, 14, 163), differ from the formal vocabulary of the Renaissance and harmonise less sympathetically. In the first half of the sixteenth century a certain Gio. Batt. Cerabalia was famous for ornamental ironwork (Lomazzo, p. 423), but whether in particular for screens is not stated.

At the end of the fifteenth century in Florence Niccolò Grosso, called Caparra, was a specialist in wrought-iron banner and torch holders for the ground floors of palaces; by him are the well-known lanterns on the Pal. Strozzi (Figs. 302, 303). Lorenzo il Magnifico indeed wanted to send Grosso's works abroad as presents: Vasari, IV, p. 445 ff., *V. di Cronaca*. These vigorous, noble, and at the same time rugged, ornamental pieces belong of course only to the Florentine rusticated palazzo.

§ 149 *Candlesticks and Miscellaneous Objects*

The upright bronze candlestick of the Renaissance has no connection with Antique or medieval prototypes; its nature is rather that of an Antique marble candelabrum translated into the formal language of bronze.

Since bronze candlesticks have survived in large numbers, especially from Pompeii, there can be no doubt about this. They invariably lack the vase-like bulge and tapering – in a word the weightiness, which an altar-candlestick needed as the bearer of a heavy candle (not just a lamp).

Fig. 306 *Padua, bronze voting-urn*

Fig. 307 *Siena Cathedral, ciborium*

The marble candelabrum (§ 146) as a model is also indicated by the occasional luxuriant foliage and the infilling of those elements, which in the Antique bronze candelabrum were left open, e.g. the space between the strongly modelled claw feet.

The finest candlesticks both for altar-candles and for larger ones: several in the Certosa of Pavia, also in some Venetian churches, e.g. the Salute. Then the large Easter candlestick by Andrea Riccio in the Santo at Padua, 1507–16, of extraordinary richness in reliefs, corner-figures and ornaments of every type, and of exquisite taste in all details; but the whole has too many parts in proportion to the size, which also applies to Bresciano's Easter candlestick in the Salute in Venice (Fig. 304). Ornamental candlesticks, lamp-stands, mortars, vessels etc. in the V. and A. Museum, London. Others, see below in relation to the goldsmith's art.

The widespread monumental sense of splendour led to the making of objects in bronze which otherwise would have been made of stone or iron and in inferior forms.

The richly ornamented bronze base of an Antique

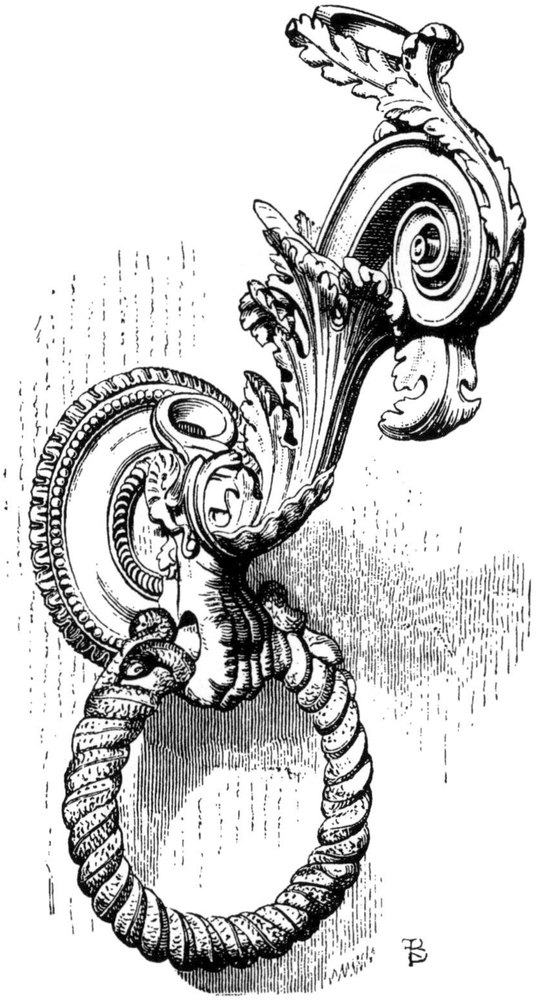

Fig. 308 *Siena, Palazzo del Magnifico, bronze ring for torches or banners*

Fig. 309 *Bologna, door-knocker*

bronze statue in the Uffizi, probably by Desiderio da Settignano (§ 135).

The supports for the flag-staffs on the Piazza S. Marco in Venice, by Alessandro Leopardo (§ 136), perhaps the finest conceivable solution to this particular problem (Fig. 305).

A bronze ballot-urn at Padua (Fig. 306).

The splendid and original altar-tabernacles in Siena Cathedral (1465–72) by Vecchietta (Fig. 307), and in the church of Fontegiusta by Lorenzo Marinna.

Regarding the somewhat earlier works of Giovanni di Turini at Siena (*d c* 1454), the small door of a balustrade, a holy water basin, a tabernacle etc.: Vasari, III, p. 305, in the Comment. on *V. di Pollaiuolo*. Cf. § 181.

Michelangelo's ciborium for Sta Maria degli Angeli in Rome, in Vasari's day already largely cast, seems not to exist any longer.

Regarding the candlesticks and tabernacle by Girol. Lombardo we must turn to Vasari, VI, p. 480, n. 3, *V. di Garofalo.*

The bronze door-rings and hooks at the Palazzo del Magnifico, Siena (Fig. 308), by Giacomo Cozzarelli (*c* 1500), who also cast beautiful consoles for figures of angels in the Cathedral; Milanesi, III, p. 28. Somewhat later Carlo d' Andrea and his son Giovanni, ibid., p. 68, worked there on similar objects. Small bronze holy water basin in Fontegiusta, by Giovanni delle Bombarde, 1480, and in the Cathedral sacristy by Gio. da Turino, the latter enamelled and supported by angel. The door-knockers in Bologna are almost all of later origin (Fig. 309).

Of the bronze (in Paul II's case, silver) wine-coolers, coal-scuttles and similar furniture, of which Benvenuto Cellini in particular speaks, nothing of any consequence has been preserved. Where the most finely ornamented bells and cannon are to be found, the author does not know.

Bronze furnishings with inlay *all' azimina*, in Venetian houses; Sansovino, *Venezia*, fol. 142.

Of the two bronze cistern-outlets in the cortile of the Doge's Palace (1556 and 1559), the one with lavish figure-decoration, in particular, may give an approximate idea of Benvenuto's vanished works.

CHAPTER FOUR

Works in Wood

§ 150 *Decline of Decorative Painting*

In the Middle Ages the decoration of the wooden surface of walls, seats, and fittings, generally consisted of painting and gilding. A superior decorative style could not emerge until woodwork came to rely entirely upon plastic form, and also on the inlay of graphic designs with woods of various colours (intarsia).

Given that even the marble sculpture of the Pisan school was still sometimes polychromatic, and in the North the carved wooden shrine glittered in rich colours until late, it can cause no surprise that e.g. in Siena, in 1370 a wooden candlestick, in 1375 a ballot-box, in 1380 a reliquary, and in 1412 a sacristy cupboard, as well as very large choir-stalls (see below), were painted; Milanesi, I, pp. 29, 31, 46. Giotto* had of course adorned the sacristy cupboards of Sta Croce in Florence with his celebrated panels (*Life of Christ* and *S. Francis*). The archive-chest also, for which the Florentines paid twenty-two gold florins in 1354, was probably a magnificent painted work: Gaye, *Carteggio*, I, p. 507.

The purely plastic development of the framing parts could only be accomplished when the surfaces were no longer given over to painting, but to the subdued language of intarsia, with which the carved parts now had to compose a harmonious whole.

The last workshop from which painted woodwork of every type was turned out in quantity, that of Neri di Bicci; cf. Vasari, II, p. 85, Comment. on the *V. di Lor. Bicci.*

Intarsia is a younger sister of mosaic and stained glass. It presupposed, as with every deliberate renunciation of richer means of representation, a marked refinement in artistic skill. An early home of intarsia was Orvieto, where the mosaic façade perhaps also recalls wood-mosaic. The earliest known craftsmen, however, who in 1331 provided the choir-stalls with inlay-work of ebony, box, walnut and poplar, were almost exclusively Sienese, as was the Cathedral architect of the time, Giovanni Ammanati, who prepared the designs; Della Valle, *Storia del Duomo di Orvieto*, p. 109 and Doc. 31; cf. Milanesi, p. 199. In the meantime, none the less, painted work reappeared, even in Siena, where the already famous stalls of 1259 in the Cathedral choir (Milanesi, p. 139) were to give place to work which has since also disappeared (1363–97: Milanesi, p. 328 ff.). This was richly figured and for the most part either painted or gilded; no mention is made of intarsia. This may have been the last Gothic stall-work of high quality. On the threshold of the new style stood the present stalls of Orvieto Cathedral, by the Sienese Pietro di Minella (working before 1433), with intarsia handled in a most accomplished manner, both for figures and ornament (Fig. 310).

About the time of the beginning of the Renaissance were to be found in a single Sienese master, Domenico di Niccolò, the three related arts combined: intarsia, stained-glass painting (or at least glazing) and figured floor-mosaic; Milanesi, II, p. 238 f.

§ 151 *Status of Intarsia*

In the fifteenth century intarsia, especially applied to choir-stalls, was recognised as the most important element of decoration in wood and determined the craftsman's reputation. Besides sacred figures and narratives the Renaissance entrusted to it two of its most important tasks: the inlays sometimes represented supremely beautiful free ornament, sometimes views of imaginary buildings, which must be regarded as the unfulfilled ambitions of contemporary architectural taste (§ 63). A trade actually never profitable, despite high prices, this art-form passed in time largely into the hands of the religious Orders.

Regarding intarsia in general and the colour-staining

* These are the panels, now attributed to Taddeo Gaddi, most of which are in the Accademia, Florence. (PM).

Fig. 310 *Orvieto Cathedral, choir-stall*

Fig. 311 *Verona, Sta Maria in Organo, choir-stall*

Fig. 312 *Parma, S. Giovanni, choir-stall*

of woods in particular, Vasari, I, p. 202, *Introduzione*, where, however, it is spoken of rather disparagingly.

The best-known masters in the fifteenth century: Domenico di Niccolò of Siena, Giuliano and Benedetto da Majano, Francione, Giuliano da Sangallo and others. In 1478 Florence had no less than eighty-four workshops of intarsiatori and other wood-decorators: Fabroni, cf. § 135.

About 1500 and later: Gio. and Ant. Barile, Baccio d' Agnolo, the Florentine Tasso family; in N. Italy the Lendinara, properly Canozzi (cf. Caffi, *Dei Canozzi o Genesini Lendinaresi*, in Politecnico, XIX); Fra Giovanni da Verona (cf. Franco, *Di Fra Giov. da Ver. e delle sue Opere*, Verona, 1863); Fra Damiano da Bergamo, pupil of a Slav monk in Venice; Fra Vincenzo da Verona; Fra Raffaelle da Brescia.

In the early phase of decline: Baccio d' Agnolo's sons Giuliano and Domenico; Bartol. Negroni, called Riccio (details in Vasari, VI, p. 414, in the Comment. on the *V. di Sodoma*).

From 1421 the already mentioned Domenico di Niccolò gave lessons in this art in Siena to apprentices on the instructions and with the support of the state; Milanesi, II, p. 103; but in 1446 he complained that it did not pay and hardly anybody wanted to persevere with it, ibid., p. 237 (and Gaye, I, p. 155); two other masters were lamenting in 1453 that they had grown old and impoverished from it, Mil., II, p. 287. (Petition of another old and poor wood-decorator, from 1521, ibid., III, p. 75.)

In point of fact, intarsia could best be practised by monks with a completely secure existence, and they were principally Olivetans.

In Florence two town-pipers applied their considerable leisure to this art; Vasari, III, p. 344, *V. di Ben. da Majano.*

As it was essentially a matter of the degree of delicacy in execution, clients requested samples from the masters; thus in 1444 the Orvietani: Della Valle, *Duomo di Orv.*, Doc. 67.

For figurative representations the intarsiatori often followed the compositions of others; thus Fra Damiano, a great artist in his way, used the designs of Bernardo Zenale, of Troso of Monza, and of Bramantino among others for the choir-stalls of S. Domenico at Bergamo (Anonimo Morelliano) (now in S. Bartolommeo); also for his famous stalls in S. Domenico at Bologna with

Fig. 313 *Pisa Cathedral, choir-stall*

Fig. 314 *Bergamo, Sta Maria Maggiore, choir-stall*

their infinite wealth of incident the same may be assumed. He worked also from drawings by Salviati (Vasari, VII, p. 16, *V. di Salviati*) and of Vignola (ibid., pp. 105, 131 f., *V. di T. Zuccaro*). Two of his pupils reproduced on the stalls of Sta Maria Maggiore at Bergamo compositions of Lorenzo Lotto (Anon. Morelliano). For S. Agostino in Perugia Perugino is said to have sketched out the stall-work for Baccio d' Agnolo; Vasari, III, p. 605, Comm. on the *V. di Perugino.*

§ 152 *Intarsie According to Subject*

The intarsie on choir-stalls and sacristy cupboards which present architectural views, are regarded as the earliest, although with only limited justification.

Vasari, I, p. 202, *Introduzione*. He refers to perspectives of buildings as having been the earliest, because their predominant rectilinearity was easiest to represent in wood. But art does not always begin with what is technically easiest, and the stalls of Orvieto with their very finely executed half-length figures refute him. It is true, however, that in the fifteenth century intarsia without figures was on the whole predominant, and the grand and richly figured schemes were not initiated until *c* 1500.

Brunellesco, the originator of perspective, is supposed to have turned the attention of the intarsiatori especially to architectural views; Vasari, II, p. 333, *V. di Brunellesco*, and above § 32a. The fat carpenter – *il grosso legnaiuolo* – who, in the famous *novella*, became his victim, was called Manetto Ammanatini.

The most important surviving works entirely or largely of perspective type are the inlays of choir-stalls in Siena Cathedral (1503, by Fra Giovanni da Verona); the doors of Raphael's Stanze in the Vatican (by Fra Giovanni, the carved parts by Gian Barile); in the sacristy of S. Marco in Venice (1520 onwards, by Antonio and Paolo da Mantova, Fra Vincenzo da Verona and others, where the miracles of S. Mark serve essentially as accessories to large townscapes); in the Capp. di S. Prosdocimo in S. Giustina in Padua; in Sta Maria in Organo in Verona (1499, by Fra Giovanni: Fig. 311);

Fig. 315 *Palermo, S. Martino, choir-stall*

Fig. 316 *Siena, Sta Maria della Scala, organ loft*

and most especially in S. Giovanni at Parma (by Zucchi and Testa); also in a chapel of S. Petronio at Bologna, from S. Michele in Bosco, exquisite examples (by Fra Raffaelle da Brescia, 1521); also in S. Giovanni in Monte there (1517–21, by Paolo Sacca).

By Giuliano and Antonio da Sangallo (see their *Lives*, Vasari, IV, p. 268 and n., with Comment., p. 295 ff.); probably no intarsie have been preserved. The Camera della Segnatura originally had panelling with intarsia perspectives all round, below the frescoes, by Fra Giovanni, like the doors: Vasari, IV, p. 337 f., *V. di Raffaello*; V, p. 622 f., *V. di Perino*. For this master see Vasari, V, p. 130 ff., *V. di Fra Giocondo*. Also lost: the entire rich furnishing of S. Elena in Venice, the sacristy cupboards and choir-stalls, their intarsie, by Fra Sebastiano da Rovigno *c* 1480, containing no less than thirty-four views of famous towns: Sansovino, *Venezia*, fol. 76. Also lost are the celebrated stalls in the choir of the Santo in Padua, by the brothers Lendinara, concerning which some publications appeared as early as the fifteenth century; cf. Selvatico's note in Vasari, III, p. 404, *V. di Mantegna*.

Most closely associated with these are the inner sides of cupboard doors with still-life subjects, liturgical vessels, books, musical instruments etc.

They occur not only on doors, but also in choir-stalls, especially the lower parts of the backs, and are perhaps the first instances of still-life in modern art, often with an inclination towards illusion, yet displaying a certain stylistic idealism.

Sometimes the principal panels are decorated with exquisite arabesque work patterned in the most agreeable fashion.

The best in Florence: the panelling of the sacristy of S. Croce, in this case not the central compartments, but the framing elements; then the choir-stalls in Sta Maria Novella in their upper parts, an early and outstanding work by Baccio d' Agnolo (§ 92); in Venice, the panelling of the choir of S. Marco; at Verona the lower parts of the stall-backs of Sta Maria in Organo (cf. Fig. 311); in Milan, the choir-stalls in Sta Maria delle Grazie, 1470 (cf. Arch. stor. dell' arte, VI, p. 236).

Finally, figured intarsie, sometimes large narrative

Fig. 317 *Rome, Sta Maria sopra Minerva, organ*

sequences and friezes extending round the whole choir, enjoyed the widest repute (§ 51).

In figured work Domenico di Niccolò was at first outstanding among the Renaissance masters, with his intarsie in the upper chapel of the Pal. Pubblico in Siena. Then the Florentines Giuliano and Benedetto da Majano; Giuliano's priests' stall (i.e. the former, not the present, one on the High Altar of Pisa Cathedral); his audience-room door in the Pal. Vecchio in Florence, on which his brother Benedetto and Francione helped him (§ 59), with portraits of Petrarch and Dante. Benedetto made chests with intarsie for King Matthias Corvinus of Hungary, which, like most of his other works in wood, have now disappeared: Vasari, II, p. 468 f., *V. di G. da Majano*; III, p. 334 ff., *V. di Ben. da M.* Several intarsiatori were then carrying on their business in Hungary. Figured intarsie in the choir-stalls of the church at Pienza, praised by Pius II (*Comment.*, L. IX, p. 431). Antonio Barile of Siena, who decorated the now vanished stalls of the Certosa of Maggiano, partly with perspectives, partly with figures, was allowed to make an intarsia self-portrait somewhere among them, and to add his name and the words: *caelo, non penicillo excussi 1502*, since his work looked as if it were painted. His nephew Giovanni Barile, who helped him at Maggiano, is on the other hand better known for the carved parts; Milanesi, II, p. 398; III, pp. 52, 74; and Vasari, IV, p. 415, in the Addenda to the *V. di Raffaello*, in which the works of both Barile are recorded.

The most famous works in N. Italy: Fra Damiano's stalls in S. Domenico at Bologna (1528–50), with countless narratives and an intarsia frieze, the inscription (§ 161) entwined with figures of children; the stalls at Sta Maria Maggiore, Bergamo (cf. § 151; the histories not shown in Fig. 314). Of less importance: the figured elements of the intarsie in the sacristy of S. Marco in Venice, those in Genoa Cathedral, etc. The Bishop's throne in Pisa Cathedral has charming histories by Giovanni Battista Cervellesi (or del Cervelliera), 1536.

§ 153 *Carved Wooden Choir-Stalls*

The carved framing elements of choir-stalls offered in their own fashion an ideal architecture, like the settings of marble altars and tombs. The material permitted the most sumptuous openwork between the supporting members, and superstructures of the most varied outline (Figs. 312, 313).

The decorative or figured ornament above the top edge, which so lightly and charmingly terminated the animated decoration of the whole was of a fragile nature, and in the course of restoration, especially if taste had changed, might often be sacrificed.

Very beautiful carving on the stalls in Genoa Cathedral and in Sta Maria Maggiore at Bergamo (Fig. 314). Later in date, and still most excellent: the Bishop's throne, together with the adjoining rows of stalls in Siena Cathedral, 1569, by Bartol. Negroni, known as Riccio; in sculptural quality (putti, sea-monsters, etc.) uncommonly noble and rich, the whole most splendid in effect. Other, and also very rich, choir-stalls of this later period in S. Martino, Palermo (Fig. 315), and in S. Severino, Naples.

Of seats for secular authorities the finest of all in the Cambio at Perugia; also the so-called Scanno in the Pal. del Comune in Pistoia, first-rate. In the museum at Siena pilasters from a wall-facing by Ant. Barile, rich and very pleasing.

The finest seat-backs carved in relief are those of the celebrated stalls in S. Pietro at Perugia, by Stefano da Bergamo, *c* 1535, under the influence of the decoration of Raphael's loggie. Narrative scenes carved in relief did not appear until the period of decline.

For free-standing polygonal central lecterns, the lower part of which might also serve as a bookcase, the one given by Paul II to the Aracoeli in Rome (*Vitae Papar.*, in Murat., III, II, col. 1009) may provide a model; of those preserved, the best in the Badia at Florence and in Sta Maria in Organo, Verona, where the carved parts of the stalls are also of particular elegance; in the same church the large wooden standard candelabrum by Fra Giovanni. At the moment of the style's decline the choir-lectern in S. Pietro at Perugia.

Of wooden lofts, especially for organs, the best are to be found at Siena: that of Ant. and Gio. Barile (1511) in the Cathedral above the sacristy door, and the splendidly forceful example in the Chiesa della Scala, attributed, perhaps incorrectly, to Bald. Peruzzi (actually by Gio. di Pietro Castelnuovo?) (Fig. 316). A rich and elegantly handled organ gallery, entirely gilded, in the Minerva in

Rome (Fig. 317). Regarding screens and stalls in the vanished monastery of the Gesuati at Florence (§ 85), Vasari, III, p. 571, *V. di Perugino*. Screens and lofts are often still painted and gilded; Milanesi, III, p. 187 f.

On the earliest stalls of the Renaissance, e.g. Milanesi, II, 240, 286, *c* 1440 *gorgolle* (i.e. gargoyles, cf. §18) still appear – a motive which, as is well known, was transferred from Gothic architecture to decoration. But they were probably already transformed into sea-monsters, dolphins, etc., and no longer designed to project.

§ 154 *Wooden Doors and Wall-Panelling*

The wooden doors of the fifteenth century generally have a simple framework and richly ornamented panels, with intarsie (§ 152) if in sheltered positions, or with carved decoration on the exterior. Later the panels were more often unadorned or were given coats of arms, while the framework displayed fine profiling, carved foliage and the like.

For church doors in the fifteenth century, general directions in Alberti, *De re aedif.*, L. VII, c. 15; they were to be fashioned more solidly than ornamentally from cypress or cedar-wood with gilded knobs, while their ornament was to be in modest relief, not intarsia.

Good work of the fifteenth century: in S. Croce in Florence in the sacristy and Capp. de' Pazzi; in Lucca Cathedral; several palaces and churches in Naples; Parma Cathedral etc., as also the door mentioned in §152 in the Pal. Vecchio in Florence.

The very fine combination of carving (Gio. Barile) and intarsia (Fra Giovanni) on the communicating doors between the Stanze of Raphael in the Vatican, 1514–21, cf. § 152. An excellent carved door with the arms of Julius II, formerly in the Pal. Apostolico at Bologna (now in the Museo Civico?).

Perhaps supreme in this category the carved doors of the Vatican loggie, with the arms of Clement VII and great lion-heads in roundels in the centre.

A simpler door of quality in the Uffizi in Florence.

Serlio in Book IV gives only the contemporarily accepted disposition of the panels, not the decoration of individual examples.

Wholly decorated wall-panelling of the period has hardly been preserved anywhere except in monastic refectories and sacristies, where the walls required a cladding of wood to continue in harmony with the wall-cupboards. In secular buildings *boiseries* of merit are no longer to be found.

Of the *boiseries* which have been preserved the author is not at present able to indicate the best examples. It may well be that none of the Florentine interior panelling has survived; it was destroyed, partly because the fashion changed, e.g. when tapestries were preferred, partly also to enable decorative and valuable paintings, often quite miniature-like, to be removed: Vasari, II, p. 148 f., *V. di Dello*.

These paintings, which might constitute a kind of frieze in the panelling, were of no little importance in the development of narrative composition in a broad format, and for mythological, allegorical and secular history painting in general. Sandro Botticelli painted for just such a purpose, for example, four scenes from a tale of Boccaccio; Vasari, III, p. 313, *V. di Sandro*; also the four little pictures of the Trionfi of Petrarch (mentioned in the Comm., p. 328) could well have had a similar purpose. Vasari, IV, p. 139, *V. di Piero di Cosimo*, whose *storie di favole* were on panelling, also p. 141, *storie baccanarie*. Also the four pictures with small figures, which Vasari, V, p. 196, *V. di Franciabigio*, mentions, had perhaps such an object. The contractors for woodwork sometimes exploited their own likes and dislikes in the choice of a painter; Vasari, V, p. 56, *V. di A. del Sarto*. In the grand salone of the Borgherini during the Siege of 1529 the intention was to remove Andrea's little paintings in order to sell them in France; they remained only because it would have been necessary to destroy the panelling (ibid., p. 26).

Regarding the whole of this question cf. in Kinkel, *Mosaik zur Kunstgeschichte*, the important section: "Anfänge weltlicher Malerei in Italien auf Möbeln".

Otherwise the door would most likely be decorated with a painting. The Anonimo Morelliano mentions in Venice two such doors by Palma Vecchio, with a *Ceres* and a *Nymph*; other doors, which were painted by a pupil of Titian, Stefano, in a room in the Casa Odoni; chests and bedsteads were also painted by the same hand.

Titian's *Tribute Money* (Dresden) was once on a closet door in the Palace at Ferrara, apparently in the very *camerino* which contained the celebrated mythologies by Dosso, Bellini and Titian himself; Vasari, VII, p. 434 f., *V. di Tiziano*.

§ 155 *Altarpieces and Frames*

The altarpiece (*ancona*) of the fourteenth century consisted of a system of large and small panels, held together by a Gothic *sacellum* of gilded wood. The fifteenth century, which gradually adopted a unified altarpiece, now required an architectonic setting for it, the splendour of which had to correspond with the richness, and even the colour, of the altarpiece. Some of the finest decorative ideas of the Renaissance are found in these frames, which sometimes entailed great expense.

The polyptych form was retained by Fra Angelico da Fiesole until about the middle of the century, and even longer by the Venetians; at times it was translated into the style of the Renaissance, chiefly in North Italy, where *ancone* lasted into the sixteenth century. Cristoforo Ferrarese (1446) is known as a maker of the splendid Gothic frames of Muranese altars: Sansovino, *Venezia*, fol. 91.

Of the altar-frames of the Renaissance the few in white marble were mentioned in § 144. There was, however, a marked lack of colour; those in wood generally blue and gold, but also natural wood with very little gold. In rare, early, instances intarsia was used: Milanesi, II, p. 257.

Fig. 318 *Giovanni Bellini, altarpiece in Sta Maria dei Frari, Venice*

The altar-step (*predella*) often with small paintings, but also in the form of an ornamental base. At the sides, forming a frame, two pilasters with arabesques; the pilasters carrying an entablature with a rich frieze and, occasionally, above it a carved openwork crowning piece.

The altars in Sta Maria Maddalena de' Pazzi and in the choir and transept of Sto Spirito in Florence, where the altarpieces generally approximate to a square in shape, offer the widest selection; Filippino Lippi, from whom perhaps several of the altarpieces originate, was in the habit of designing the frames; Vasari, III, p. 474, *V. di Filippo Lippi*; at other times Antonio da Sangallo the Elder and Baccio d' Agnolo acted for him; the high prices received by Baccio for his frames; Vasari: V, p. 351, n. 2, *V. di Baccio.*

In Perugia in 1495 the Augustinians contracted with Mattia di Tommaso da Reggio for a frame for their high altar (painted by Perugino) *con colonne, archi, serafini, rosoni, e diverse fantasie* both at the front and at the back, for 110 florins (*c* 40 Bolognini); Mariotti, *Lettere pittoriche perugine*, p. 165 (no longer extant). For another frame an agreement was made with Perugino himself for 60 gold ducats; Vasari, III, p. 588, n. 2, *V. di Perugino.* A late and celebrated frame-maker, Eusebio Battoni, *c* 1553; ibid., p. 624, in the Commentary.

Fra Bartolommeo avoided showy frames and preferred to paint an architectural setting for his figures; Vasari, IV, p. 188, *V. di Fra Bartolommeo.* As a rule the painters probably decided upon the main forms and designed the frame even when the scheme involved polyptychs with salient columns; Vasari, IV, p. 245, *V. di Raff. del Garbo*, Comment.; an altarpiece by him with a framework of richly gilded salient columns, ibid., p. 236. It was a most lavish creation and one quite common at the time, but most painters did not like it, because of the strong cast shadows.

By far the greatest reputation in this field was enjoyed by the two Barile: Antonio, who put his name on his frames, even those of *Madonnas* intended for private devotion; and Giovanni, who made the original frame for Raphael's *Transfiguration* (long since vanished); Vasari, IV, p. 412, in the Comm. on the *V. di Raffaello.*

In Venice after 1470 a certain Moranzone was well known; Sansovino, *Venezia*, fol. 57, cf. 59. The finest surviving frame there is that of Bellini's altarpiece of

1488 in the sacristy of the Frari (Fig. 318), blue and gold, with sirens and candelabra on top. The finest in Padua is the one for Romanino's altarpiece in the Capp. di S. Prosdocimo in Sta Giustina (now in the Museo Civico).

Venetian portraits also famous for their frames: one with gilt foliage in the Vendramin Collection (Anon. Morelliano); Serlio's for Titian's portrait of Francis I (Aretino's satire on Francis, 1539; *L'ha cinto d' ornamento singolare quel serio Sebastiano architettore*).

In these frame-settings the approach of the Baroque style is early and perceptibly announced. Mannerism and Naturalism exempt painters from all constraints in decoration.

§ 156 *Furniture*

With reference to the wooden furnishings of palaces and grand houses descriptions have been preserved which lead us to suppose that these accorded with the rest of the decoration to create for us a predominantly dignified impression.

In Venice, where the complete ship's captain required his cabin to be *intagliata, soffittata e dorata*, i.e. carved, gilded and richly ceilinged (Malipiero, *Ann. Venet.* in Archiv. Stor., VII, II, p. 714, anno 1498; for the State vessels, Comines, VII, 15), luxury was indeed developed uniformly and extended generally throughout all the classes of society.

Sabellico (§ 42) was already saying, *c* 1490: *nulla ferme est recens domus quae non aurata habeat cubicula* (fol. 90).

In Francesco Sansovino's time, *c* 1580 (*Venezia*, fol. 142), the situation was this: countless buildings had, in the bedrooms and other rooms, timber ceilings with gilding and paintings; almost everywhere the walls were covered with tapestries, silk materials, gilded leather and rich panelling . . . In the living quarters elegant bedsteads and chests with gilding and painting, especially with gilded mouldings . . . The sideboards with countless vessels of silver, porcelain, pewter and bronze with inlaid work . . . In the saloni of the great, clusters of weapons with the shields and banners of ancestors who had commanded on land or at sea . . . The same held good for the middle and lower classes; . . . even with very modest chests and beds of walnut, green covers, carpets, pewter and copper-ware, gold necklaces, silver forks and rings.

Elsewhere this situation was less common. Bandello, Part I, Novella 3, the description of a bedroom: the bed with four cotton mattresses, covered with fine silk and gold-embroidered linen sheets; the bedspread of carmine satin, embroidered with gold threads and the edges fringed with a mixture of gold thread and carmine silk; four pillows splendidly worked; bed-curtains all round of *tocca* striped with gold and carmine (here the text is obscure); on the walls, instead of woven tapestry, nothing but carmine velvet with exquisite embroidery; in the middle of the room a table with an Alexandrian silk cloth; around the walls eight richly carved chests and four chairs covered with carmine velvet; a few pictures by famous hands . . .

Part III, Nov. 42, the dwelling, which a rich lover of the celebrated Roman courtesan Imperia had built for her; among other things a *sala*, a *camera* and a *camerino* with lavish velvet and brocade and the finest carpets; in the *camerino*, where she received only the most distinguished people, the walls were covered with gold brocade (patterned or embroidered); on an ornate *etagère* (*cornice*) of ultramarine and gilt, magnificent vessels were to be found, of alabaster, porphyry, serpentine and many other costly materials. Round about stood many richly carved chests (*coffani e forzieri*), all of great value. In the middle was a small table, the most beautiful imaginable, covered with green velvet; on top lay a lute or a cithern or the like, beside music-books and a few richly ornamented small volumes, which contained Latin and Italian poems.

Part IV, Nov. 25, yet another charming account of this kind.

Giovanni della Casa, while he was away in 1544, handed over his beautiful Roman home to Cardinal Bembo: *con un bellissimo camerino acconcio de' suoi panni molto ricchi e molto belli, e con un letto di velluto, e alquante statue antiche e altre belle pitture*, among them a portrait by Titian.

The genuineness of all materials, the apparent symmetry of arrangement, the respect for general convenience, must have given a dignified character to such rooms (compared with our century of substitutes).

Leather wall-hangings with stamped gold patterns, generally floral arabesques, which were already so very widespread in Venice in the sixteenth century, were in 1462 still regarded as a foreign decoration, and indeed their source was Andalusia: Pii II, *Comment.*, L. VIII, p. 384 (approx.). Their effect, too, is one of dignity. Carpets and tapestries were specially intended to conceal walls and floors completely from view: Ariosto, *Orl. Fur.*, XII, 10.

In contrast to this, painted wooden panelling may have remained in fashion in Florence for longer? Cf. § 154.

§ 157 *The State Bed and the Chest* (Cassone)

Of all furniture the state bed was the most monumentally designed; it occupied, not a corner, but the middle of a wall; next came *cassoni*, the chests on which the arts sometimes lavished their highest skills.

When the Venetian ambassadors (§ 42) waited on the Duchesses of Urbino at Pesaro; *e la camera era nuova, fatta a volta, la maggior parte di essa profilata d' oro e arazzata dall' alto in basso, con una lettiera in mezzo, sotto un padiglione, coperta di seta*. Beds like this, of the best period, have hardly survived anywhere. Even the most precise description (Milanesi, III, p. 245) dates only from the beginning of the Baroque (1574): the feet with harpies, festoons etc., the four posts of the Composite Order, wreathed with foliage; the frieze with figures of children

Fig. 319 *Berlin, Kunstgewerbemuseum, a chest (the feet modern)*

and animals, with foliage in parts; the head-end with four herms and three panels between; above these (obviously under the canopy) a pediment with several sculptured figures.

Of the *cassoni* only a few still exist, but enough to give us an idea of the animation, splendour, and richness of forms attained in this field. Of those by Baccio d' Agnolo, with figures of children in relief; Vasari, V, p. 352, says, some forty years later, that they would no longer be so well made in his own day. (A particularly fine chest in the Kunstgewerbemuseum in Berlin, Fig. 319; several in the V. and A. Museum, London.)

Besides pure carving there continued for a long time a mixed category of carved work and elaborate, almost miniature-like, painting, associated with paintings set into the wall-panelling; cf. § 154 and the extract there quoted from Kinkel, *Mosaik z. Kunstgeschichte*.

Paintings on bedsteads, whether on the four sides or on the canopy, are not often found: Vasari, II, p. 213, *V. di Uccello*, who himself used his perspective views for this purpose; V, p. 286, *V. di Fra Giocondo*; Carotto's *Choice of Hercules*, painted as a bed-head (*testiera*); ibid., p. 342, *V. di Granacci*, stories of Joseph in Egypt, *sopra un lettuccio*, in the state bedroom of the Borgherini, § 154, where also the cassone-paintings by Pontormo, ibid., VI, p. 261, *V. di Pontormo*, present the same theme.* It more often occurs that not only bed and chests, but also parts of the panelling and at any rate the door, were painted by the same hand; Anonimo Morelliano, ed. Frizzoni, p. 160 – by Stefano, a pupil of Titian, in Andrea Odoni's house in Venice.

Cassone paintings: principal source, Vasari, II, p. 148 f., *V. di Dello*; the subjects were from Ovid's *Metamorphoses*, from Roman and Greek history, or hunting, tournaments and scenes from *novelle*. "The most excellent painters were not ashamed of such work, as many nowadays would be": ibid., II, p. 556, *V. di Lazzaro Vasari*; ibid., III, p. 36, *V. di Pesello*, tournament-pictures; ibid., VI, p. 455, *V. di Aristotile*, the works of Bacchiacca; Milanesi, II, p. 355, contracts of 1475 and later. In time, *cassoni* tended to become entirely sculptural in character.

Paintings on cupboards, round wooden panels (*?rotelle*) and other furnishings, entirely mythological in content, by Giorgione; Vasari, IV, p. 104, in the Comment. on the *V. di Giorgione*.

We ought here at least to mention categories which have entirely disappeared: paintings on the harness of horses, with figures of animals or with a burning forest, from which animals rush headlong: Vasari, II, p. 555, *V. di L. Vasari*; III, p. 547, *V. di Francia*; IV, p. 498, *V. di San Gimignano*; VI, p. 316, *V. di Genga*. Next, the painted carriages at the annual Florentine festa – Vasari, V, p. 221, *V. di A. del Sarto*; VI, p. 256, *V. di Pontormo*: mere carnival floats are not considered. In Ferrara in 1506 a painted and gilded State coach (of Lucrezia Borgia), and in 1508 a gilded cradle are mentioned: Arch. Stor. dell' Arte, 1894, pp. 301, 306.

Paintings on musical instruments: supremely fine the inside of the lid of a clavichord, with the story of Apollo and Marysas; said to be by Correggio, but more likely by Bacchiacca, formerly in the Pal. Litta, Milan. According to Vasari, VI, p. 276, *V. di Pontormo*, Bronzino

* Some of these paintings are in the National Gallery, London; others are in Florence and Rome. (PM).

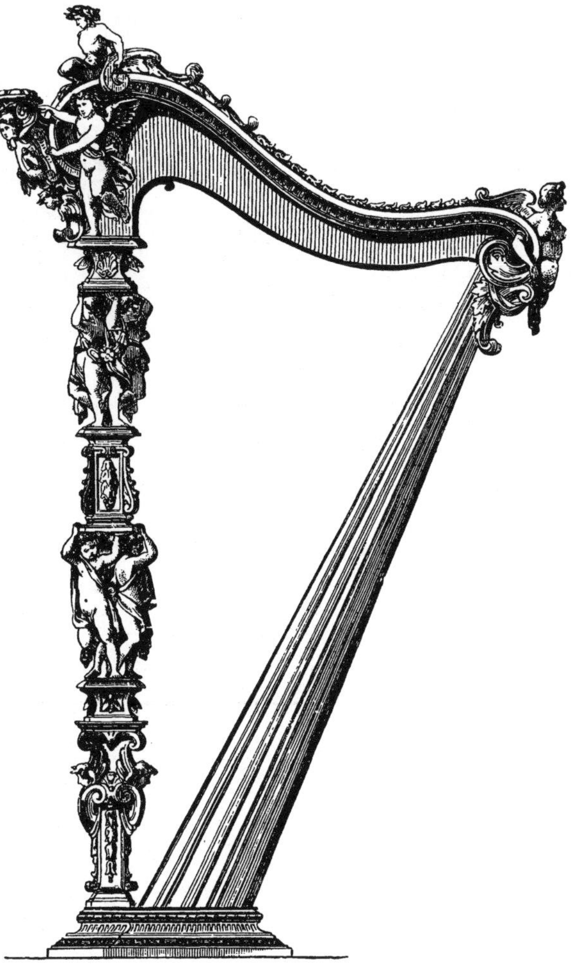

Fig. 320 *Florence, Uffizi, design for a harp*

painted a clavichord for the Duke of Urbino. Lomazzo proposed (*Trattato*, p. 347) putting the portraits of the greatest virtuosi on these instruments, three to each. A magnificent harp in a drawing in the Uffizi (Fig. 320).

§ 158 *The Carved Flat Ceiling*

The flat wooden ceilings (*palchi*) in churches and palaces in the fifteenth century have as a rule a simple configuration, but brilliant painting and gilding. Towards 1500 the nobler and finer forms of Antique coffering were combined with them; in the sixteenth century some of the loveliest ceilings were almost or completely colourless and became a major field for wood-carving; but the filling of ceiling panels with actual paintings was already beginning. The effect was everywhere worked out according to the colour of the walls, or in palazzi to the tapestry hangings.

Palchi of the fifteenth century increasingly with symmetrical coffers: in S. Marco in Rome, gold, white and blue, by Marco de' Dolci (1467–71); then in the Pal. Vecchio in Florence the ceilings of the Sala dell' Udienza and Sala de' Gigli, the latter with hexagonal coffers, both masters of the Tasso family; Vasari, III, p. 342, note, *V. di Ben. da Majano*; cf. p. 343. (Of Michelozzo's, Vasari, II, p. 437, nothing seems to have survived; similarly the certainly important ceiling of the Sala del Gran Consiglio of 1497; Vasari, V, p. 351, n. 1, *V. di Baccio d' Agnolo*, must have given place later to Vasari's own. The high costs of the ceilings in this palace; Gaye, *Carteggio*, I, p. 252.) In Venice on some of the magnificent ceilings of the fifteenth century in the Doge's Palace and in the Accademia the coffer gives place to the rosette, the container to the contained; the latter a flower, and escutcheon or the like, of wood or stucco, mostly gold and blue; also one entirely gold with cherubim. The ceilings in the richer private house in Venice, according to Comines, VII, 15, gilded as a rule in at least two rooms, cf. § 156: Armenini (*De' veri precetti . . .* p. 158) later derides the excessive fiery red which one noticed on them in addition to gilding, and which pleased the 'Magnifici' – i.e. the nobles of Venice – beyond measure. In Milan, formerly in the Pal. Vismara (§ 91), the ceilings generally blue and gold, with the arms of the Sforza and Visconti. A richly coffered ceiling in gold and colours in the Palace at Urbino.

Ceilings *c* 1500, architecturally nobler and more discriminatingly ornamented: in Sta Maria Maggiore in Rome (1493–98), white and gold, by an unknown master, with the arms of Alexander VI; in S. Bernardino at Siena, contracted (1496) to Ventura di Ser Giuliano, predominantly blue and gold, the cherubim of the individual coffers are no longer carved, but perhaps moulded in *carta pesta*: Milanesi, II, p. 456; those by Ant. Barile in the Chigi house in Siena, certainly excellent, but scarcely surviving? Cf. Milanesi, III, p. 30. A contract of 1526, also Sienese, p. 85. Austere, yet extremely beautiful; all the flat ceilings in the Pal. Massimi in Rome (Fig. 321). A considerable number of Florentine *palchi*, probably more painted than carved, were the work of Andrea Feltrini; Vasari, V, p. 208, *V. di Morto da Feltre*.

Uncoloured ceilings, in which the wealth and splendour of the carving specifically reject colour. The principal example: the Biblioteca Laurenziana in Florence (after 1529?) beautifully and freely designed by Michelangelo, executed by Carota and Tasso; the motive repeated in the tiled floor (Fig. 325), realised by Tribolo; Vasari, VII, p. 203, *V. di Michelangelo* (cf. § 160). The large front sala at the corner of the Pal. Farnese in Rome; and many ceilings of the early Baroque style, which, with such patterns to follow, often achieved excellence.

Serlio's theory at the end of his Book IV: on the whole, colour belongs to the vaulted, monochrome to the flat ceiling; for expensive carving, illusionistic painting in chiaroscuro may be substituted; the lower the room, the smaller the compartments of the ceiling; gilding may be added to rosettes, and so on. More important than all this is the magnificent design he reproduces for the ceiling of a large room, giving the characteristic profiling of the mouldings and the structural framework, as well as the designs of the infilling;

Fig. 321 *Rome, Palazzo Massimi, ceiling*

the following small designs are also among the best and most pleasing (Figs. 322, 323).

The deterioration of the carved ceiling began in the second half of the sixteenth century, with a studied disrespect for logical timber-work. A central large compartment with a round or oval framing (for arms or figured decoration) had long been accepted, but now the beams of the entire ceiling were beginning to run in irrationally curved and jagged lines, which negated any sense of load-bearing function. Domenichino in 1617 made the ceiling-motive of the nave of Sta Maria in Trastevere extend to a number of zig-zag points, because the patron, Cardinal Aldobrandini, bore stars in his coat of arms: Passeri, *Vite de' Pittori*, p. 22.

§ 159 *The Painted Flat Ceiling*

Early in the sixteenth century there began the infilling of individual compartments of a ceiling with paintings, the figures being seen from below, with more or less accuracy in the perspective effect. In addition there appeared a form of false perspective, which gave the impression of an upward continuation of the room.

Paintings naturally presupposed larger and freer compartments or panels than simple decoration. Also, to avoid cast shadows, the idea of beams was abandoned and a free, often splendidly profiled and ornamented, frame was preferred. It began principally in Venice; but, remarkably, generally by non-Venetians; the (former) ceiling of the Sala de' Pregadi in the Doge's Palace, with twelve *Virtues* in *sotto in sù* perspective; Vasari, V, p. 116, n. 5; *V. di Pordenone*; ceilings in the palace of the Patriarch Grimani; Vasari, VI, p. 323, *V. di Genga*, and VII, p. 18, *V. di Salviati*; in a palace of the Cornaro family, VI, p. 358, *V. di Sanmicheli* (Vasari's own ceiling paintings); in a refectory and a sala of the Doge's Palace, VII, p. 46, *V. di Salviati* (paintings by G. Porta).

Not until Paolo Veronese (Vasari, VI, p. 369 f., *V. di Sanmicheli*) and Tintoretto did the Venetians themselves accept ceiling paintings more eagerly; Titian's (now in the sacristy of the Salute) are said to have been painted, according to Sansovino, fol. 83, "in the first flower of his youth", but actually belong to his middle years (*c* 1543–

Fig. 322 *Ceiling design (I), from Serlio*

Fig. 323 *Ceiling design (II), from Serlio*

44). Another soffitto by him, ibid., fol. 100. After the 1570s the soffitti of the principal rooms of the Doge's Palace, especially the Sala del Gran Consiglio, by Tintoretto and Paolo Veronese and others; large paintings of varying shapes, set in exceedingly rich and varied gold frames, important as prototypical of dawning Baroque. In Paolo's compositions the perspective is not strictly from below, but rather obliquely.

Vasari's ponderous narrative ceiling-pictures in the great Salone of the Pal. Vecchio in Florence, to the orders of Cosimo I; Vasari, VII, p. 700 f., in his Autobiography. The flat ceilings of all the churches in Naples decorated with paintings.

Of the painted flat ceiling in Sta Maria dell' Orto in Venice, which was perhaps the earliest with a simulated – and indeed very deceptive – colonnade, apparently with coupled spiral columns, only the rapturous description in Sansovino, *Venezia*, fol. 59, and in Vasari, VI, p. 509, *V. di Garofalo*, has survived. The same masters, Cristoforo and Stefano da Brescia, painted several more of this type. Naturally, vaulted ceilings offered this branch of art scope of a very different kind. Cf. Bramante's illusionistic choir, § 83. As a substitute for, and after-effect of, the ceiling of Sta Maria dell' Orto perhaps that of S. Pantaleone, by Fumiani (*d* 1710); acts and glory of the Saint in a large and splendid colonnade, painted on canvas and nailed in position.

(NOTE: On Venetian ceilings see now J. Schulz, *Venetian Painted Ceilings of the Renaissance*, Berkeley, Calif., 1968.) (PM).

CHAPTER FIVE

Pavements, Calligraphy

§ 160 *Pavements of Hard Stones, Marble and Tiles*

The monumental treatment of floors, especially in churches, exploited the techniques of Antiquity and of the Middle Ages in new and original ways.

In circles close to the Popes and in certain particularly splendid chapels a purely linear mosaic of hard stones continued in use; especially of white marble, porphyry and serpentine, which had been handed down from the Early Christian period to the Cosmati. Martin V's mosaic (after 1419) in the nave of the Lateran, one of the first works of a Papacy liberated from the Schism; *Vitae Papar.* in Murat., III, II, col. 858; Nicholas V (from 1447) wanted the same for his rebuilding of S. Peter's; ibid., col. 935. Floors of the Sistine Chapel, the Stanze of the Vatican, the memorial chapel of the Cardinal of Portugal in S. Miniato, Florence, and the chapel in the Pal. Medici, Florence.

Alberti, *De re aedific.*, L. VII, c. 10, requires in the *pavimentum*, first and foremost, "lines and figures, which relate to music and geometry".

Figured, and indeed narrative, mosaics in marble of various shades are almost unique to the Cathedral of Siena, but are on a grand scale and dating from two centuries – from 1369 up to *c* 1550 (Fig. 324). Regarding this unique instance, cf. Milanesi, I, p. 176 f.; II, p. 111 f., 377, 437, etc. Vasari, I, p. 199 f., *Introduzione*; V, p. 645 ff., *V. di Beccafumi.*

The aesthetic question as to how a marble floor of simple configuration may be composed of slabs of two or three colours in harmony with a large building was answered in particular by that of Florence Cathedral; Vasari, IV, p. 458 ff., Comment. on the *V. di Cronaca*, who from 1499 began mainly with the choir chapels, admittedly with a richer and more dynamic theme; V, p. 354, *V. di Baccio d'Agnolo*, who seems subsequently to have done the main work. The crucial point was that from now on there was complete emancipation from carpet-like motives, still discernible in the earlier Roman mosaics; it was now a matter of lines, which correctly guided the eye, and of masses, which corresponded correctly to the individual parts of the interior.

That the floor-design, when there was a richly decorated flat ceiling, had to correspond to the design of the ceiling or vault, was accepted since the Laurenziana (§ 158) as self-evident, e.g. in Armenini, *De' veri precetti...*, p. 159. According to Vasari, VI, p. 92, *V. di Tribolo*, it might appear as if the idea belonged to the latter, but if Michelangelo designed the ceiling, he was probably also responsible for the floor.

The latter consists of a design in white and red tiles, which then and later often appeared in secular buildings and made a fine effect. Vasari I, p. 200, *Introduzione.*

In coloured and glazed ceramic flooring tiles the Middle Ages had already explored the possibilities. The few surviving instances known to the author from the Renaissance are at Bologna, in S. Giacomo Maggiore (Capp. Bentivoglio, before 1458) and S. Petronio (1487: fifth chapel on left); in addition (according to Molinier, *La céramique italienne au XVe siècle*) in S. Giovanni a Carbonara in Naples, in the monastery of S. Paolo at Parma, Sta Maria del Popolo in Rome (third chapel on right); also (according to Archiv. Stor. dell' Arte, II, p. 162) in S. Elisabetta at Viterbo, in the Vescovado at Padua (1491, by Gio. Antonio and Francesco d' Urbino) etc. – see the author's *Cicerone*, 10th ed., II, p. 222.

In the fifteenth century the pattern was generally in slight relief; thus, in the (no longer extant) sacristy of S. Elena in Venice (1479), where the oblong hexagonal, white and blue tiles alternately included a black eagle and labels inscribed with the donor's name, Giustiniani; certainly a most elegant complement to the magnificent intarsie of the wall-cupboards; Sansovino, *Venezia*, fol. 76. A contract for such tiles at Siena (1488), Vasari, III, p. 688, n. 1, *V. di Signorelli.* Those, now completely worn down, in the Vatican loggie, which Raphael commissioned from the Della Robbia in Florence, Vasari, IV, p. 363, *V.*

Fig. 324 *(above) Siena Cathedral, detail of floor*

Fig. 325 *(below) Florence, Laurenziana Library, floor*

di Raffaello, were smooth. Those in the inaccessible top storey of the loggie, from the time of Pius IV, have not been preserved. The *pavimento* of the Capp. Lando in S. Sebastiano at Venice, 1510, the family coat of arms encircled with flowers, leaves, weapons, and beasts; perhaps work from Faenza; cf. Archiv. Stor. dell' Arte, II, p. 389.

§ 161 *Inscriptions and Calligraphers*

Inscriptions, as an integral part of works of art, at this time were modelled upon Roman inscriptions of the best period. As letters were held to be beautiful in themselves they were sometimes used in giant sizes, as a separate art-form.

The inscription on the façade of Sta Maria Novella in Florence, by L. B. Alberti, incrusted in porphyry; Vasari, I, p. 110, *Introduzione*.

The enormous inscription on the east side of the Vatican Palace, to the specific instructions of Julius II, who made fun of Bramante because of his desire for hieroglyphs or rebuses; Vasari, IV, p. 158, *V. di Bramante*.

About the middle of the sixteenth century there lived in Padua a priest, Francesco Pociviano, called Mauro, who in painting and writing excelled all calligraphers, and in the carving of letters all sculptors, and who may well have carved Bembo's epitaph in the Santo. He was also in demand for inscriptions in fresco; Scardeonius, in Graev. *Thesaur.*, IV, III, col. 429, where another local calligrapher, Fortebraccio, is mentioned.

Regarding the connection with epigraphy as a branch of literature, see *Kultur der Renaissance*, 3rd ed., p. 310. An entire transept, that of Sta Maria sopra Minerva in Rome, adorned under Paul II *pulcherrimis epigrammatibus historiisque*; *Vitae Papar.*, in Murat., III, II, col. 1034. Inscriptions in bedrooms; Ang. Politiani *Carmina*.

The very large inscription on the upper frieze of the Pal. Pandolfini in Florence. Mottoes or names often repeated many times in window-heads, ever since the Pal. di Venezia in Rome.

As festal decorations the familiar inscribed hanging banners, still in use in Italy today for theatre publicity; e.g. at the Possesso of Alexander VI, 1492; *una tavola al modo antico pendente*; Corio, *Storia di Milano*, fol. 451 ff., in which also huge ciphers in elaborate scrolled settings on the awnings over streets are praised.

A happy contrast to the austerity of the large Roman uncials* is sometimes found in the figures of children playing round them. Perhaps the earliest example of this was a frieze-painting by Pordenone on a private house in Mantua, Vasari, V, p. 113, *V. di Pordenone*, and Armenini, op. cit., p. 205. Then on the frieze of the choir-stalls by Fra Damiano in S. Domenico at Bologna, § 152.

Calligraphy, in the Italian script of the fifteenth century aimed at the utmost simplicity and beauty, and outlived for quite a time the introduction of book-printing, despite the outstanding elegance of the latter.

The desire for miniatures helped keep it alive. The calligrapher of the miniaturist Clovio, Monterchi, is mentioned in Vasari, VII, p. 560, *V. di Clovio*. Calligraphers usually gave their names in their works.

Regarding the attempts, perhaps going back to Leonardo, to reform lettering, evidenced by, among others, Luca Pacioli, *Divina proportione*, ed. Winterberg; cf. Dehio in Repertorium für Kunstwissenschaft, IV, p. 269 ff.

* Burckhardt uses the word *uncial*, but he clearly means Roman majuscule letters (PM)

CHAPTER SIX

Painting of Façades

§ 162 *Origin and Extent*

A principal branch of painted decoration, the painting of façades, is represented by relatively few remains which are insufficient to provide a complete picture, although it once helped significantly to determine the aspect of whole cities.

Its origin is to be sought in the Madonnas and other sacred representations, with which walls in the south of Europe had been adorned since time immemorial. (Very old examples in Assisi, Perugia etc.; one or two from the fourteenth century, e.g. a Madonna with Saints and angels bringing flowers by Stefano da Zevio, in Verona.) The rest of the façade was perhaps decorated with a carpet-like repeating pattern.

In the fifteenth century, besides a growing proficiency in fresco painting and in perspective, there came a delight in the decorative forms of the new style of building and a desire to have these exactly realised in all their richness, in paint, on the façades, when financial resources did not run to rustication or incrustation, or to more lavish treatment of architectural forms; and also if one was in no position to determine symmetry of proportions. It was now possible for the humblest of walls to be given artistic merit. Then there was the attitude of the patrons, who were no more shy of polychrome façades than of gaily coloured clothes; realising their transitory nature, that vigorous artistic era undoubtedly relied on its descendants to provide paintings of equal excellence, judging that one should enjoy whatever the genius of the age offered.

But the artists, among them some of the greatest, were not reluctant to seize the occasion of being able to paint monumentally, with great freedom in the choice and interpretation of subjects, for the daily inspection of a whole population. What in the way of excellence they achieved was present fame, and nothing else. This branch of art rose to serious competition with architecture proper, after initially being regarded as only an economical substitute. In Venice the position *c* 1500 was *molto più dilettano (a) gli occhî altrui le facciate delle case et de' palagî dipinte per mano di buon maestro che con la incrostatura di bianchi marmi, di porfidi et di serpentini fregiati d' oro* (§ 42): Lod. Dolce, *Dialogo della Pittura*, p. 146 (Florentine ed.).

Of the splendid aspect, which such façades often afforded in narrow streets, no town today offers more than a remote impression. *Cicerone*, II, I, p. 263 ff. lists the most significant of the few surviving.

In the sixteenth century the following were rated particularly rich in painted façades: Venice, Genoa, Pesaro and Mantua; Armenini, *De' veri precetti* . . . , p. 205.

§ 163 *The Patrons*

Examples occurred in which, either at the instigation of princes or by voluntary agreement, whole rows of buildings or streets were given a continuous painted embellishment.

A similar continuous painted treatment, at least of a decorative kind, is to be assumed in Ferrara in 1472 under Ercole I; *Diario Ferrarese* in Murat., XXIV, col. 243; in December a start was made on building a loggia for the money-changers in front of the Rigobello tower, and on painting the palaces of the Signori and the shops of the leather-merchants (*le banche de li calgari*?). Afterwards, col. 247, it was called the Palace of the Leather Shops with Paladins, i.e. probably Charlemagne's Paladins.

Lodovico il Moro had projecting structures (§ 112) in the streets of Milan and Pavia removed and the façades painted, ornamented and embellished; Cagnola in Arch. Stor., III, p. 188.

In Brescia on the Corso del Teatro (Contrada del Gambero) an extensive series of mythological paintings by Lattanzio Gambara is still preserved.

Much more common, however, in the nature of things, are the façade paintings commissioned by individual property-owners to their own taste.

Figs. 326, 327 *(above, opposite)* *Florence*, sgraffiti *on façades*

The point of departure in the devotional image (§ 162) is already clear; they were certainly often the pride of their owner, and a recognisable symbol of his house at a time when people wanted to be different and did not shun the limelight.

Also on some public buildings, very early façade-paintings, as an expression of some common idea or recollection; thus in Venice in the fourteenth century the Pal. del Comune (1324) was covered on all sides with paintings, no doubt of a political content; at the most frequented spot in the city – the portico of the Rialto – a victory at sea over King Pepin (Charlemagne's son), and a map of the world were painted; Sansovino, *Venezia*, fol. 133, 134. Similar paintings on some of the buildings of contemporary despots, e.g. on the palace tower of the Carrarese residence in Padua; M. Savonarola, in Murat., XXIV, col. 1174; it was said, *c* 1500, of the Palazzo of Braccio Baglione in Perugia: *e era tutta quella casa penta* (i.e. *dipinta*) *dentro e de fora, de la cima insino a terra*, together with both towers. Even the big, tendentious, allegorical pictures, with which Cola de' Rienzi excited the Romans at his first appearance in 1347, may have been painted on the walls.

Fig. 328 *Rome,* sgraffito *on a façade in via Sta Lucia*

§ 164 *Methods of Façade Painting*

Mural painting mostly presented a more or less elaborate, decoratively interpreted, simulated architecture, enlivened by figurative ornaments of every conceivable kind. Beyond question, it exerted a mutual influence on festal decoration.

Published accounts, especially in Vasari, are one-sided in that they mention almost exclusively the figurative element and scarcely suggest the large decorative contribution.

A single category, it seems, remained peculiar to Hans Holbein the Younger: the illusionistic representation of a real building seen from below in perspective, with human figures at the windows, galleries etc., in the costume of the time. (Drawings for his lost façade-paintings are in the Basle Gallery.) Pompeii has similar paintings, but without the striving after illusion.

A major difference lies in the methods of presentation, in which full or partial polychromy, monochrome and *sgraffito*, sometimes singly, sometimes in combination (or exquisite contrast) are applied, depending upon whether one wanted to retain more or less of the semblance of architecture or of decorative sculpture. Later, stucco in relief also came in.

All simplifications in colour have the advantage that ageing and fading are visible less quickly and that restoration is easier than with complete polychromy.

Sgraffito is produced without actual painting, the wall being first coated black, then white, and the design revealed by partly scraping away the upper layer (Figs. 326–28). The chief drawback is that dust gets ingrained in the pattern. Cf. Vasari, I, p. 192, *Introduzione*; V, p. 206, *V. di Morto da Feltre* (in which the discovery is attributed to Andrea Feltrini, but is certainly much older).

From the beginning complete polychromy seems to have been popular for the façades of N. Italy, especially Venice; Verona possesses to this day, besides several other façades, perhaps the most important work of this type; the Casa Borella, formerly attributed to Mantegna, gold-painted pilasters with arabesques and, framed by these, narrative representations on a blue ground; frieze with festoons and putti, etc.

In addition, a great wealth of colour gradations and often really enchantingly effective combinations: polychromy of individual figures and historical scenes, or of the latter alone; also decoration in two shades of stone-colour; so that, for instance, the simulated architecture is shown reddish, the mock-sculpture white; or the first light grey, the second (especially statues, vases and trophies) gold or bronze; extremely bold treatment of festoons, sometimes more idealised and stone-coloured, sometimes realistic and natural-coloured for the foliage and fruit. Two very good painted façades on two small houses on the Piazza delle Erbe in Verona.

Also, alternating polychrome and stone-coloured parts according to the storeys or the importance of the respective wall-surfaces.

Finally, monochrome painting, chiaroscuro, *pitture di terretta*, in any one colour such as grey, green, red, violet, gold-brown etc., sometimes changing according to the storey or particular parts of it. Last of all, *sgraffito*, see above.

Raphael and his School, above all the great façade-

Fig. 329 *Rome, painted façade in via Giulia*

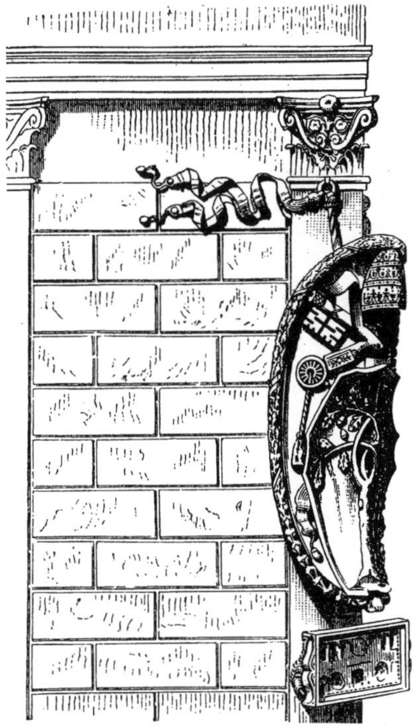

Fig. 330 *Rome, Palazzo della Cancelleria, Papal arms*

decorators Polidoro da Caravaggio and Maturino, preferred monochrome, and perfected that style of figured representation which showed a painted sculpture, but without submitting servilely to the stricter conditions of sculpture (Fig. 329). Victories, Abundance etc. on the Tiber side of the Farnesina, grey on grey, to Raphael's invention; frieze with the story of Niobe on the Pal. Lancelotti (via della Maschera d' Oro 7) in Rome, by Polidoro, grey on grey except for the gold-brown picture of the gods in the middle.

§ 165 *The Testimony of the Writers*

In subject-matter façade-painting remained throughout the good period free from all doctrinaire limitations, creating a grand decorative impression, wide in its range, and without having to give expression to philosophical and poetical theories. These came soon enough with the arrival of the decline, when Vasari wondered greatly at the lack of significance in Giorgione, who had been allowed to paint on walls things which nobody could explicate, but which were merely beautiful and lively. Vasari thought it better to understand, and crammed the whole of human life into a single façade: VI, p. 230, *V. di Gherardi*, in a mass of allegories.

The significant passages in Vasari are: III, p. 221, *V. di Don Bartolommeo*; p. 221, *V. di Verrocchio*;* pp. 392, 395, 406, 407, *V. di Mantegna*; p. 510, *V. di Pinturicchio*.

IV, p. 95 ff., *V. di Giorgione*; p. 420, *V. di Marcilla*; p. 490, *V. di S. Gimignano*; pp. 592–611, *V. di Peruzzi*.

V, pp. 34, 39, *V. di A. del Sarto*; p. 98, *V. di Alf. Lombardi*; pp. 111–17, *V. di Pordenone*; p. 135 f., *V. di Girol. da Treviso*; pp. 141–54, *V. di Polidoro e Maturino*; p. 179 f., *V. di Bagnacavallo*; p. 206, *V. di Morto da Feltre*; pp. 292, 297, 308, 314, 315, 319, 320, *V. di Fra Giocondo*; p. 453, *V. di A. da Sangallo the Younger*; p. 596 ff., *V. di Perino*; p. 634 f., *V. di Beccafumi*.

VI, p. 18, *V. di Soggi*; pp. 230–37, *V. di Gherardi*; p. 256, *V. di Pontormo*; p. 366 ff., *V. di Sanmicheli*; p. 384 f., *V. di Sodoma*; p. 450 ff., *V. di Aristotile*; pp. 466, 475, 507, 513, 520, *V. di Garofalo*; p. 542, *V. di Rid. Ghirlandaio*.

VII, p. 45, *V. di Salviati*; pp. 76–88, *V. di T. Zucchero*; p. 417, *V. di Primaticcio*; pp. 428–33, 462, *V. di Tiziano*.

In addition, scattered references in Gaye, *Carteggio*, I, p. 334 (regarding the Mantuan façade-painters Polidoro and Guerzo, 1495), and II, p. 137, Giorgione's frescoes; in the Anon. Morelliano (with reference to the Casa Cornaro at Padua and the Pal. del Podestà at Bergamo, as well as the Porta Pinta there); Lomazzo, *Trattato dell' Arte*, pp. 227, 264, 271, pertinent passages on Lombard façade-painters; p. 413 – on Dosso Dossi; Milanesi, III, p. 65 f., Sodoma's façade, paid for with a horse.

Sansovino, *Venezia*, gives little more than what was known from other sources – fol. 143, a façade by Battista Moro; fol. 135 on the Fondaco de' Tedeschi. Titian's frescoes on this Fondaco are described briefly by Ridolfi

* The page reference is clearly wrong but there seems to be no significant mention of façade-painting in the *Vita di Verrocchio*. Several of the other references to Vasari are, at best, marginal. (PM).

(quoted in Ticozzi, *Vite de' Pittori Vecelli*, p. 22) without any attempt at an interpretation, which, indeed, would hardly be possible.

Serlio, *Architettura*, Book IV, fol. 192, an important passage, mainly in praise of chiaroscuro.

A façade, painted by Albrecht Dürer in Venice, was counted among the sights of Italy: *Lettere Pittoriche*, III, 166, in a letter from Doni to Carnesecchi.

Armenini, p. 202 ff., repeats Vasari. We cannot investigate here in any kind of circumstantial detail an almost completely vanished branch of art, the more so since the sources, as noted, hardly mention the purely decorative side. A rapid survey must suffice.

§ 166 *Themes Used in Façade-Painting*

At first, many individual figures performed no iconographic function, acting essentially as a beautiful and symmetrical infill, closely associated with the illusionistic architecture.

Nudes of every type and colour, and every pose, sometimes as load-bearers – i.e. herms – sometimes as genii, especially children (putti) in large numbers; sirens, trains of tritons and nereids as friezes; also tritons and nereids in pairs, holding medallions, individually and apparently often in niches; heroes and philosophers, unnamed and in no particular context.

A religious theme entailed sometimes only a principal picture of a traditional type, sometimes the entire façade.

Principal pictures: Crucifixion with Saints, Madonna with Saints; Paradise or the Fall of Man; all compatible with genre scenes of an earthy type, as a façade in Verona proves.

When the whole façade was alloted to a cycle of Christian images, other Biblical stories appeared: full-length Prophets, Christian Virtues; as friezes: the nations bringing tribute to Roma-Fides, victories over the Turks, Deeds of Samson, etc.

In the good period few allegories appeared and these were obviously chosen for the beauty of the motives.

Thus on the Fondaco de' Tedeschi at Venice (from 1504, with the superb frescoes all round by Giorgione, Titian and others, of which hardly a trace remains visible), the famous figure by Titian, sometimes considered to be Judith, sometimes Germania; elsewhere Venezia riding on a lion. Then the Roma mentioned above, with the attributes of Fides.

Ceremonies and processions are chiefly found on friezes; poetry and painting had long been accustomed to triumphal progresses of every sort.

Regarding Triumphs, cf. *Kultur der Renaissance*, p. 415 ff.; 4th ed., p. 144 ff. There were processions of warriors, prisoners, senators, porters carrying booty, chiefly costly vessels and also the tribute of vanquished peoples; also ancient games, chariot-racing, and – as light-hearted parodies – triumphs of putti, parades of armed children; finally, processions of pilgrims.

The secular-narrative theme began with mythological scenes, sometimes without any precisely defined association; then followed the early history of the relevant city and, finally, Roman and also contemporary history, probably idealised.

Labours of Hercules, Fall of the Giants, story of Niobe (Polidoro), incidents from the Odyssey, Vulcan's Forge (Raphael), Mars and Venus, and, as a showpiece of foreshortening, the winged Mercury.

Myths of Ancient Rome (on façades of Polidoro's time), of Cortona and elsewhere; stories of Alexander the Great, Caesar, etc.; as an instance of foreshortening, the Leap of M. Curtius (also by Holbein).

Of contemporary events: Charles V's taking of Goletta.

Genre is represented partly by classical, partly by completely naturalistic scenes, which blend innocuously with sacred subjects.

Wrestling and other games of the ancient world, and, especially, representations of sacrifices.

A peasant wedding, a dance of hunchbacks, an excursion by water and similar motives. By Amico Aspertini (Vasari, V, p. 179 f., *V. di Bagnacavallo*) jests and grotesques on house façades and even on ecclesiastical buildings; *in somma non è chiesa ne strada in Bologna, che non abbia qualche imbratto di mano di costui* (of which, however, nothing has survived).

Animals and inanimate objects were sometimes represented on façades with supreme mastery. Stone-coloured medallion-heads appeared in quantity.

Friezes with fighting animals; trophies and vases as loot (very fine examples, to judge from engravings, by Polidoro); festoons of every type, masks, etc.

Medallions with the heads of the first twelve Emperors; cardinals' heads etc.

Frescoes on garden walls, § 128.

§ 167 *The Passing of Façade-Painting*

Well before the middle of the sixteenth century façade-painting fell prey to slick and unscrupulous methods, but the use of motives from the good period gave significance to later versions when the originals no longer existed. Armenini, op. cit., p. 205; after the deaths of Polidoro and Maturino the decline first manifested itself in the revival of complete polychromy (never abandoned in North Italy).

In the period from 1530 by far the greater part of this type is in Genoa (perhaps older, an excellent small façade in Piazza dell' Agnello); on average, of slight importance, especially in the decorative elements; in Florence some good work from a much later period; in Verona, where monochrome now first really gained acceptance, much first-rate work of the Venetian School. Lombard country houses of this period, sometimes painted overall, e.g. a villa at Bissuccio, not far from Varese.

Façades of mixed painting and stucco still surviving are almost entirely from the Baroque period and on small churches rather than houses; of Genoese façades of this type: Pal. Pessagno, Salita S. Caterina, already richly Baroque.

(Purely stuccoed façades, cf. § 96.)

Even on the lesser works of this later time striking resources are revealed, indicating how great must have been the efforts devoted during the best period to this branch of art.

The whole subject of façade-painting, today a misunderstood ruin and little regarded by travellers or artists, should be properly recorded and photographed as a government responsibility.

More closely related to façade-painting than might be supposed: the decorative settings for illuminated Mss and the woodcut ornament of many title-pages in printed books. The latter certainly, often presented nothing but what people were accustomed to see painted round doors and windows, and indeed this was particularly characteristic of books *c* 1480–1550, depending upon the respective decade.

§ 168 *Coats of Arms: Painted and Carved*

Coats of arms, completely free from the strict rules of Northern heraldry and treated as a matter of uninhibited splendour, form a not insignificant element of façade-painting and of decorative sculpture.

Italy had as little share in the true system of heraldry as in genuine chivalry, and constantly mixed up emblems and proper heraldic devices. Regarding this confusion (not to be pursued further here) there is an instructive reference in Decembrius, *Vita Phil. Mariae Vice-comitis*, in Murat., XX, col. 996. Also, what Serlio proposes at the end of his Fourth Book shows that he knew nothing about the subject. Artistically decisive was the fact that one was neither tied to any particular tradition in the form of the escutcheon, nor in the crest, and followed entirely the laws of beauty in the design of supporters.

Coats of arms carved across the angles of rusticated palazzi of the fifteenth and sixteenth centuries (Fig. 330); then, in 1537, the enormous arms of Charles V and Duke Alessandro de' Medici on the Fortezza da Basso in Florence, the first with two life-size nude Victories, the second with two other figures; Vasari, IV, p. 544, *V. di Baccio e Raff. da Montelupo*; arms of Clement VII, now perished; VI, p. 301, *V. di Mosca*; alteration to a carved papal coat of arms under a new Pope, ibid., p. 303; huge coats of arms of Paul III at Perugia, in which for the first time the markedly prominent tiara and crossed keys stand out, in association with festoons and masks, ibid., p. 306. The arms over the main window of the Pal. Farnese in Rome, Vasari, VII, p. 223, *V. di Michelangelo*.

Far commoner were painted arms, of which very splendid examples must have appeared early, provided with all kinds of appropriate trimmings, e.g. those of Giangaleazzo Visconti, which the city of Siena had painted in 1393 on the Porta Comollia at a cost of twenty gold florins; Milanesi, I, p. 33. A particularly opulent group of arms was the one painted on the occasion of the arrival of Lucrezia Borgia in 1502 at the Palace of Ferrara: "the arms of the Pope, the King of France, and of the illustrious House of Este, with angels, hydras and other handsome embellishments"; *Diario Ferrarese*, in Murat., XXIV, col. 401. In Via de' Banchi in Rome there was a frescoed coat of arms of Leo X by Baldassare Peruzzi, with three putti, *che di tenerissima carne e vivi parevano*, Vasari, IV, p. 596, *V. di Peruzzi*. Beccafumi's façade with the arms of Julius II in the Borgo in Rome, Vasari, V, p. 634. Rosso Fiorentino began his career with similar works; Vasari, V, p. 156, *V. di Rosso*. But the greatest master of this technique must have been Jacopo Pontormo, and indeed from early in his career: Vasari, VI, pp. 247, 250, 258 f., 261, *V. di Pontormo*. His reputation was already established by 1514, when Leo X came to Florence and all his adherents had Medici coats of arms *in pietre, in marmi, in tele ed in fresco*; Pontormo's setting for one of these at the Annunziata, consisting of Virtues, putti etc., drew even from Michelangelo an exclamation of delight; other arms by him in the Castello, on the Casa Lanfredini, in the Casa Spina, Florence; all probably long vanished, but undoubtedly reflected in all the better armorial paintings of the sixteenth century; and perhaps in the arms of Paul III, also lost, by Francesco Salviati in a palazzo in Rome, "with a few large nude figures, which won the greatest approval"; Vasari, VII, p. 15, *V. di Salviati*.

In a part of the Vatican later rebuilt there seems to have been a coat of arms of Julius II, supported by genii, by Raphael or under his direction. According to Dehio's illuminating suggestion (Jahrbuch d. königl. preuss. Kunstsammlungen, I) the well-known *Putto al fresco* in the Accademia di S. Luca may well have been sawn out of this painting. A pupil of Raphael, perhaps Giulio, would in that case have painted the *Isaiah* in S. Agostino, attributed to Raphael, and borrowed for his accompanying figures the two putti of the coat of arms; one of these therefore would have been a replica of the one in the Accademia, with which it agrees.*

Of the coat of arms, which all authorities had painted in every township under their jurisdiction (Milanesi, II, p. 397, for the year 1482), and of the princely arms and devices, with which landlords adorned their inns (Lomazzo, p. 349, with comic indignation about such misuse), it is not necessary to speak here. Also of the arms, which newly appointed officials had painted or carved in the buildings concerned (Pal. de' Tribunali, at Pistoia; Pal. del Podestà in Florence) no series has survived worth mentioning in an artistic context.

* This view is now universally rejected: cf. L. Dussler, *Raphael, A Critical Catalogue*, London, 1971. (PM).

CHAPTER SEVEN

Interior Painting and Stucco-Work

§ 169 *Friezes and Wall-Decorations*

Of the decorative painting of interiors mention must be made first of the frieze, which was generally executed in polychromy as an intermediate element between the coffered and painting ceiling, and the tapestry-hung or otherwise decorated walls.

Has anything significant of this type been preserved from the fifteenth, or from the best period of the following century? The frieze might be a continuous painting or interrupted by real or painted supporting figures; the subjects were genre, mythological or historical; in the Baroque age, mainly battles and other scenes from Roman history, more rarely landscapes and views of buildings (the latter in the top-most gallery of the Vatican loggie).

Among leading masters are recorded: Gio. da Udine, frieze of children, lions, arms etc. above a mural painting of simulated incrustation, now lost; Vasari, VI, p. 544 ff., *V. di Udine*; Pordenone's frieze of children with a boat, in the Pal. Doria (at Genoa?); Battista del Moro, friezes with battles in the Pal. Canossa, Verona; Vasari, V, p. 297, *V. di Fra Giocondo*; Perino del Vaga, frieze with female figures, in Gianettino Doria's house in Genoa, ibid., V, p. 616, *V. di Perino*; Dan. da Volterra's friezes in the Pal. Farnese in Rome, ibid., VII, p. 56, *V. di Ricciarelli*. Such friezes were to become mass-produced by Taddeo Zucchero, ibid., VII, pp. 76, 82 f., 90, *V. di T. Zucchero*.

The theory of these friezes did not appear until later (1587), in Armenini, *De' veri precetti . . .* , p. 185: their height should amount to between 1/5 and 1/6 of the room's, including architrave and cornice; their content pedantically prescribed. The wall under the friezes, actually intended for tapestry, was, however, given (except in Genoa, where it remained white down to the marbled socle) a kind of decoration, e.g. in Lombardy simply a roughly executed fake-architecture of columns, incrustation and green festoons: ibid., p. 197, for friezes in garden rooms.

Sometimes the walls were painted with imitation tapestry – *a damaschi* – as in the Sistine Chapel, and as Julius II (Gaye, II, p. 488) threatened, if his painters did not satisfy his requirements in the Vatican apartments. Into such painted tapestries histories were also sometimes inserted; Lomazzo, op. cit., p. 317.

Sculptured friezes, e.g. the one comprising weapons and trophies in the Palace of Urbino (no longer in its proper place, but exhibited separately), naturally remained a rare exception; Vasari, III, p. 72, n. 1, *V. di Franc. di Giorgio*: another example; in the Pal. del Te at Mantua a stucco frieze with scenes of Roman soldiers after Trajan's Column; Armenini, p. 185.

Frescoes above chimney-pieces (§ 146) more often had a kind of natural association with fire, e.g. Vulcan's furnace with Venus; Vasari, V, p. 586, *V. di Giulio Romano*; the Goddess of Peace setting fire to weapons, ibid., p. 598, *V. di Perino*; *cose ignee* as Armenini, op. cit., p. 201, puts it. Oil paintings, irrespective of subject, which were to be accorded a place of honour also finished up over the chimney-piece; Vasari, VI, p. 467, *V. di Garofalo*. Chimney-piece frescoes in France, ibid., VII, p. 34, *V. di Salviati*.

As well as cursorily painted architecture, of which Lomazzo speaks, from the beginning of the sixteenth century there were better examples, by masters who were able to create a certain illusion in their rich architectural forms (perspective painting, cf. § 32a). Whatever still survives of painting in this manner by Peruzzi I am not in a position to say.

An upper room in the Farnesina should still have on the walls, even if modernised, his painted perspectives of columns, which make the room seem bigger on account of the view they seem to offer, as Vasari says.*

In the dining-room of Giovio's villa (Paul. Jov. *Musei*

* This reference is, of course, to the Sala delle Prospettive, which must have been inaccessible in Burckhardt's day. (PM).

descriptio) there was a fictive colonnade, very deceptively painted. For the period around the middle of the sixteenth century, Vasari, VII, p. 108, *V. di Zucchero.* How Bramante exploited a genuine recess in order to create the effect of a colonnade, see § 83.

Finally, as goes without saying, many walls were devoted to large historical frescoes, with which we would not be concerned here, if they had not sometimes revealed an elaborate decorative treatment of figures and histories. The narrative part is distinguished in scale and tone, the rest is monochrome socle, a larger wall-painting, a metallic-coloured medallion; Virtues or other allegorical figures leaning in pairs above the socle paintings, seated over the door-lintels, and all in a larger symmetrical relationship (the Gran Salone of the Castel Sant' Angelo, by Perino del Vaga).

§ 170 *Decorative Painting of Architectural Elements*

Painted pilasters, tympana and friezes, which often appeared as frames for fifteenth-century frescoes, received an infill of decorative forms, derived basically from those used in marble decoration.

Among the significant casualties to art and its traditions may well be the decorative paintings of all kinds, which were undoubtedly present in the many Roman churches of the last quarter of the fifteenth century, but later had to yield to the alterations and new decorative ideas of the Baroque period, having had, perhaps, great influence both in and beyond Rome. Cf. in Albertini (fol. 83–85) the long list of churches built or established in the time of Sixtus to Julius by Popes, titular cardinals and foreign nations.

For a list of such framing-paintings, especially of the School of Perugia, see *Cicerone*, p. 277 ff.; 10th ed., II, p. 247 ff. Among the Florentines, Andrea di Cosimo and especially Filippino Lippi are said to have done the best work; Vasari, III, p. 189, *V. di Cosimo Rosselli*; ibid., pp. 461, 473, *V. di Filippino Lippi.* Among the Paduans, who were already representing in their pictures so much richly ornamented architecture, Squarcione with his collection (§ 25) may have provided the principal impetus, but *c* 1453 a certain Donatello was painting admirable decorations in the Bishop's Palace at Treviso (*Memorie Trevigiane*, I, pp. 97, 111), and he might well have been the famous Florentine; regarding his stay in N.E. Italy at this time, Vasari, II, p. 411, n., *V. di Donato.*

Stone-colour, occasionally with gold, was already revealing its close relationship with carved decoration. Very fine in the settings of Mantegna's frescoes (Eremitani, Padua) the contrast of the stone-coloured work with the polychrome festoons, over which putti clamber.

More important is the decoration of real pilasters, friezes, etc., above all in N. Italian churches, where the brick construction could find no better substitute for the lack of a fine material than painting, often richly figured and polychromatic. Attachment to any particular association of subjects was (cf. § 134), only superficial or non-existent; putti to be found by the thousand, often full of childish mischief; a train of nereids as a frieze in a small cupola of the chapel painted by Falconetto (§ 26) in SS. Nazzaro e Celso at Verona. Good, purely ornamental, arabesques on a dark background on the piers of this church, as in the Incoronata at Lodi (Battagio; cf. § 83); predominantly ornamental instances, perhaps by Alessandro Araldi (*d* 1528), on the older section of the pilasters in S. Giovanni, Parma. Similarly in S. Sisto at Piacenza. Noble and rich pilaster-paintings in the Monastero Maggiore in Milan (Fig. 331), the back half being an almost completely preserved example of Lombard decoration. Finally, and of relevance here, the wall-piers consisting of three pilaster-faces, polychromed, in the Libreria at Siena Cathedral.

Among largely figured decorations, generally putti playing, in some cases of Correggio's School, should be named: the frieze in S. Giovanni at Parma, and the one (with nothing but genii) in S. Benedetto at Ferrara. Later, and more pompous, the work in the Steccata at Parma, in S. Francesco at Ferrara (by Girolamo da Carpi), and others.

The extensive paintings, which Luca Signorelli made on the walls below his celebrated frescoes of the End of the World in Orvieto Cathedral, are unique; painted in grisaille in imitation of sculpture of the kind he liked to represent in his pictures, and including elaborate arabesques as well as figurative work, the latter with a number of allusions to the main frescoes; in the middle of the panels, polychrome and framed – some round, some rectangular – half-length figures of those poets who wrote about the next world.

§ 171 *The Painting of Vaulted Ceilings in the Early Renaissance*

Painting on vaulted ceilings, established throughout the Middle Ages in Italian churches, had here and there something of the decorative character it had once had with the Romans.

By this is particularly implied the decoration by Cimabue in the Upper Church of S. Francesco at Assisi (third bay of the nave, counting from the door): medallions with half-length portraits, festoons spreading out of vases carried on the heads of genii, etc. Obviously, a late echo of Early Christian vault-paintings.

Otherwise, however, especially in the School of Giotto, where sacred figures and even histories (Incoronata at Naples) on a blue background were the rule, and the Renaissance itself often accepted such features. The semi-domes of apses were given large fresco representations of the glory of Heaven, the Ascension, the Coronation of the Virgin (Filippo Lippi, Borgognone, Melozzo); also vault-painting properly speaking, of which more below, to a high standard.

A richer flowering of decorative vault-painting took place in the fifteenth century simultaneously with a growing liberation from the cross-vault – which did not allow of a picture in the middle – and from ribbed and

Fig. 331 *(left) Milan, Monastero Maggiore, detail of pilaster*

Fig. 332 *(above) Rome, Vatican, Stanza della Segnatura*

groined construction (§ 48). This ability to fill a given surface in the loveliest conceivable manner, which was manifested in marble (§ 131, 134) and in wood-decoration (§ 159 ff.), was now expressed in colour, with uninhibited abundance and freedom, both in secular buildings and in churches. The authors were at the same time great history painters.

Among the earliest, perhaps still half-Gothic, works may well be the golden beasts on a blue ground on the vaulted ceilings in the Castello of Pavia, which formed a complement to the well-known wall frescoes (Anon. Morelliano). The blue background had already occurred in the exquisite decorative mosaics of the fifth century.

The latest painted Gothic tracery, gold on blue, § 23.

First the Renaissance had to decorate existing Gothic vaults; glorious paintings on the shell of the choir of Mantegna's chapel in the Eremitani in Padua, green festoons with white ribbons on a blue ground, with figures and medallions between; also those by Girol. Mazzola on the oblong cross-vaults in the nave of Parma Cathedral, polychrome medallions with half-length portraits, putti, festoons etc.; the ribs painted in two colours. Finally, one of the older rooms in the Appartamento Borgia in the Vatican, with frescoes apparently by Pinturicchio, contains on its still almost Gothic cross-vault magnificent arabesques with polychrome figures and golden architectural motives on a dark blue ground, partly in stucco relief (between 1492 and 1494; perhaps with the help of Torrigiano, Vasari, IV, p. 260, *V. di Torrigiano*).

In keeping with the freer forms of the vault of the Early Renaissance and by the complete elimination of ribs, a number of splendid decorations were now composed in Upper Italy: those in the transept of the Certosa of Pavia and the portico of the cortile there, the latter extremely graceful and original in its arrangement, perhaps by Bernardino Luini.

In the house of the condottiere Colleoni in the Città Alta at Bergamo a room with the *volta à specchio* preserved, in which both the central compartment and the lunettes and coving are decorated exclusively with roundels (half-length figures of Saints, portraits, coats of arms, etc.). Well disposed, by masters of the Milanese School, after 1475. The roundels of the coving are carried by stone-coloured figures of children.

Falconetto's chapel (§ 170) at Verona; the decoration chiefly stone-colour, the figures polychrome; clearly a determined effort to get closer to the decorative forms of Antiquity.

By his collaborator, Francesco Morone, the more freely and simply composed vault of the sacristy at Sta Maria in Organo, Verona.

On the vault of a room beside Correggio's pavilion in the convent of S. Paolo, Parma, outstandingly fine, discreetly figured arabesques on a dark blue background, by Aless. Araldi.

Also the splendid vault mosaic of the sacristy of S. Marco in Venice, free-floating scrollwork with medallions, should at least be mentioned here.

Lastly, we must not forget the few surviving small vaults with elegant glazed terracotta coffering from the Della Robbia workshop: over the tabernacle of the nave-altar in S. Miniato, Florence; in the portico of the Capp. Pazzi, Sta Croce, Florence; in the portico of Pistoia Cathedral etc. The principal work, i.e. the vault in the little stateroom of Cosimo the Elder, with rich figurative ornament, has disappeared; Vasari, II, p. 174, *V. di Della Robbia.*

§ 172 *Vaulted-Ceiling Paintings of the School of Perugino*

The School of Perugino, in their numerous vault-paintings, interpreted their task rather stiffly, as if the decorative element had to be regarded as a stone framework.

After the real ribs had been abandoned, a system of painted ribs was introduced, which made almost no use of the transformation of angles into strings of fruit which had already appeared in Mantegna's work.

Infilling of individual compartments by polychrome designs or roundels and secondary subjects, sometimes coloured and sometimes stone-coloured, imitations of reliefs and the like.

(An earlier Perugian painter, Benedetto Bonfigli, painted, according to Mariotti, *Lettere pitt. perugine*, p. 225, n., for Innocent VIII in Rome "handsome and elegant grotesques", but he was not of Pietro Perugino's School, with which we are concerned here.)

Among the best examples are the vaulted ceilings by Pietro's pupils in the Cambio at Perugia; and the one by Perugino himself in the Stanza dell' Incendio of the Vatican, which Raphael preserved as a work of his master, although by comparison with his own grand and free compositions it seems timid.

(In the Stanza della Segnatura Raphael indeed retained the plan and several small individual works by Sodoma, but repainted the principal compartments of the vaults. As these Vatican Stanze are roofed with cross-vaults, rather carelessly and imprecisely executed, the decorations cannot really be considered as a norm for the Renaissance, Fig. 332.)

Pinturicchio (§ 171) in the design of the vault of the choir of Sta Maria del Popolo in Rome is particularly harsh and severe, although the details are very fine in parts, and the whole (with the Coronation of the Virgin, the Fathers of the Church, Evangelists and Sybils) has a solemn effect.

The chapel by him in the Aracoeli, and the sacristy of Sta Cecilia (by his pupils) are at least worth mentioning for their vault-decoration.

A good sketch in pen and ink, attributed to Pinturicchio, in Paul Rouaix, *Les styles*, p. 104, for a square vaulted ceiling with twelve intersecting spandrels.

A great step forward in the appreciation of the effect of colour, in freedom of composition, and in the abundance and choice of decorative forms is apparent in his vault (a *volta a specchio*: § 55) in the Libreria of Siena Cathedral. The very liberal section of the contract concluded with

Fig. 333 *Rome, Vatican, Sistine Chapel, diagram of decoration*

him in 1502 (§ 174) insisting only on the utmost beauty, in Vasari, III, p. 519, Comm. on the *V. di Pinturicchio*; and in Milanesi, III, p. 9. The influence of Antique painting of the type of the Baths of Titus is shown by the alternation of colour surfaces. (Pinturicchio's paintings in the Castel S. Angelo have disappeared.)

Garofalo's paintings on the vaults of two rooms in the Archiepiscopal Seminary at Ferrara (1519) lean rather towards the austere tradition of the School of Perugino, but tempered by a certain liveliness in detail, and vindicated by the discipline of a scheme of only two colours in the decorative parts. Solemn and splendid: the entire vault decoration in S. Benedetto at Ferrara (§ 170).

In the Farnesina in Rome the effect of complete illusion in the painted stone framework on the vaulted ceiling of the Sala di Galatea was early admired: Vasari, IV, p. 593, *V. di Peruzzi*.

Michelangelo, too, chose as a setting for his deeply serious paintings on the vault of the Sistine Chapel a strict stone framework, but he enlivened it throughout with enchanting subsidiary figures of every type and function, as well as in a variety of colours, apart from the principal figures and narratives (Fig. 333).

§ 173 *The Beginnings of Stucco-Work*

By the side of, and soon also in association with, painting relief decoration in plaster or stucco had appeared, about the middle of the fifteenth century, on vaulted ceilings, at first probably to represent coffers, later to give a sharper emphasis to forms of every type.

L. B. Alberti, who took particular pride (§ 48) in the design and execution of stucco coffering for all kinds of vaults, mentions in *De re aedificatoria*, L. VI, c. 9 (*c* 1450): *signa* and *sigilla* (i.e. probably decorated squares and individual figures) of plaster poured into moulds, and varnished (*unguentum*) to approximate the appearance of marble. They were normally of two types: in relief (*prominens*) or in depth (*castigatum et retunsum*), the first being more suitable for walls and the second for ceilings, since parts suspended in relief easily fall off.

In fact Donatello's reliefs and ornaments on the vault of the Old Sacristy of S. Lorenzo in Florence are made of plain stucco. This was the first total emancipation from medieval vault-decoration, probably already founded on studies of Roman vaults (then better preserved than now). Regarding these and other stucco matters; Vasari, II, pp. 396, 407, 415, *V. di Donatello*.

From then onwards several fifteenth-century painters, in their frescoes and even in panel-pictures (Carlo Crivelli) added certain parts, especially weapons, attributes and architectural details in stucco relief, e.g. in the frescoes of the legend of S. Catherine in the Appartamento Borgia (perhaps by Pinturicchio), in which the splendid buildings, triumphal arches, etc. stand out in gilded relief; the same thing is done with the gilded stucco ornament in the ceiling decoration of one of these rooms, § 171. Besides colour an element of stronger impact was wanted, at least for certain individual parts of the decoration.

Moreover, people in the fifteenth century were used to plaster and other materials which could be poured or moulded, from the temporary festal decorations, on which they were used in large quantities.

But vault-decoration remained (as distinct from painting proper) throughout the century essentially an extremely agreeable infilling of individual parts of vaulted ceilings with scroll-work, putti, festoons etc., all of it painted only.

§ 174 *Influence of Antique Grotesques*

A general change took place in the whole decoration of walls and especially of vaults after the discovery (or closer examination) of the so-called grottoes, i.e. ornamented rooms in thermae or palaces of Antiquity. The relationship between stucco and colour, the forms, arrangements and subjects found in them made the strongest impression on the dawning High Renaissance. They were sometimes directly copied, sometimes merged with prevailing methods of decoration. The consequences extended to all other branches of decoration.

The word 'grotesque', which, through the later decadence of the art acquired a false meaning, indicated at that time the decoration derived from the 'grottoes' of Antiquity. Its first authoritative use occurred in the contract of 1502 with Pinturicchio (§ 172), requiring him to decorate the vaulted roof of the Libreria with those colours, fantasies and patterns which he held to be the most elegant, beautiful and visually effective (*vistosa*), in good, fine and durable colours, according to the type (*forgia*: read *foggia*?) and design, which is now called *grottesche*, with an alternating decoration of individual compartments (*con li campi variati*) as handsome and graceful as possible.

The beginning of the study of 'grottoes' is supposed to have occurred through a certain Morto da Feltre, of whom only Vasari (V, p. 210 ff., *V. di Morto*) knows anything. Morto came to Rome as a young man at the time when Pinturicchio was painting in the Appartamento Borgia and the Castel S. Angelo for Alexander VI, (i.e. 1492–98). He drew not merely whatever he could find "underground" in Rome (undoubtedly, in effect, the Baths of Titus), but also whatever survived in the Villa Adriana at Tivoli, at Pozzuoli, and in Baiae and the neighbourhood. After this and a short stay in Rome he is said to have gone to Florence and later to Venice. Of his decorative work in these two cities nothing has survived, and also nothing of the work of his Florentine pupil Andrea Feltrini, a very versatile decorator of façades, ceilings, ceremonial banners, foliage for expensive and elaborate fabrics, etc. Cf. also, regarding the beginning of grotesques, Schmarsow in the Jahrb. d. preuss. Kunstsammlungen, III.

First, a more durable stucco, which would not fall off

in fragments (§ 173), had to be rediscovered. Vasari's recipe: I, p. 139, *Introd.*, c. 4; principal reference, VI, p. 552, *V. di Udine*; instead of marble dust also pulverised flint, VI, p. 219, *V. di Gherardi.* Now for the first time large, richly coffered vaults could be produced with ease.

The chief significance of stucco, however, was that it helped to raise the vaulted ceiling to a level of uninhibited splendour (§ 55), that it gave strength and lightness to the parts of the composition, and in the presentation of forms of every type alternated and vied with painting, sharing a legitimate place with it. It could easily also turn into real sculpture, and could conjure up – in colour, white, or gold – every conceivable decorative motive at any level of fantasy or reality.

A further consideration is that, at the same time, decorative painting reached its zenith, sometimes in association with stucco and sometimes without it, and that all this decorative art existed sometimes for its own sake and sometimes to provide a setting for the great frescoes of the time; that the greatest masters adopted it; and that every School and every town interpreted the problems differently, resulting in a vast wealth of motives, which infinitely surpassed those bequeathed by Classical Antiquity. It was, however, thanks to Antiquity that it received the decisive inspiration without which this great movement would have been inconceivable.

§ 175 *Raphael and Giovanni da Udine*

The decisive factor in this new and flourishing branch of art was that Raphael took an active part in it, raising it by his own works to its full stature, and thus winning to its cause his own best pupils.

The first important work, which shows the influence of "grottoes", Pinturicchio's ceiling in the Libreria in the Cathedral of Siena (§ 172), must already have been known to Raphael, if he (as Vasari thought) supplied Pinturicchio with compositions for the frescoes there, or only, as is more probable, shared in the execution.

In Rome, not yet under Julius II, but probably under Leo X, his great decorative activities began, clearly dependent upon his studies of Antiquity, and chiefly with the help of Giovanni da Udine, who had come to him from the School of Giorgione and was also employed on accessories from time to time in Raphael's paintings: Vasari, VI, p. 549 ff., *V. di Udine.* Besides the Baths of Titus, the remains (still preserved at that time) of the Baths of Diocletian and of the Colosseum served as models. (Facsimile of Udine's studies of the latter in Basan's book.)

Loggie of the cortile of S Damaso in the Vatican: in the lower gallery the ceiling by Udine, probably painted to Raphael's general directions only, with simulated coffering or vine-leaves, interwoven with other foliage and enlivened by all kinds of animals; independent of Antique models – a work showing Udine's mastery of such subjects.

The world-famous gallery (Fig. 334), an arcade of fourteen bays with square vaults *a specchio*, built by Raphael and no doubt designed specifically for the decoration; the latter he is said to have sketched out himself: Vasari, IV, p. 362, *V. di Raffaello*; the execution by Udine and his assistants, partly also by Perino del Vaga: Vasari, V, p. 593, *V. di Perino*; the Biblical compositions, four in each vault, were executed by other pupils. The decoration, alternating with the utmost freedom between stucco and painting, follows Antique patterns only in individual motives of the vaults, on the jambs of the arches, and in those parts of the piers comprising separate framed paintings; by far the greatest part is of Raphael's own invention, particularly the rising infills of the main pilasters, each time in fresh combinations of figures, ornament and foliage of every kind. Beautiful, clearly co-ordinated and differentiated decoration; abundance of artistic ideas of all kinds. The windows, which give into the interior of the palace from the loggia, stand out against a sky-blue background and are hung round with strings of polychrome fruit, which are among Udine's best works. The innumerable small individual pictures, painted and stuccoed (sometimes as cameos) as well as all the figurative decoration having for the most part (deliberately) no connection with the Biblical themes, sometimes directly borrowed from Antiquity (Fig. 335).

As early as *c* 1550 the loggie were copied in their entirety for a commercial associate of Fugger in Antwerp and again for Spain, including even the glazed flooring-tiles (§ 160) as an essential part of the effect: Armenini, p. 180.

Closely related to the principal pilasters already mentioned: the three surviving side-borders of Raphael's tapestries, splendidly spatial, the best that of the *Three Fates*. Nothing remains of those designed by Udine, which were purely decorative.

Originating with Udine alone are said to be the stuccoes and paintings in the ground-floor hall of the Villa Madama, Rome; intended by the alternation of vaulting forms for a multifarious wealth of decoration, and by its niches to accommodate statues, the loggia still provides in its present ruinous state* an incomparable complement to the Vatican loggie: Vasari, V, p. 526, *V. di Giulio.*

The third main work, the painted vault of the large front sala of the Appartamento Borgia in the Vatican, with little paintings of the planetary deities and a central painting of four hovering Victories around the Papal coat of arms, perhaps as a whole largely Antique; the forms and colours and their distribution in relation to the proportions of the large and not very high sala perfect. (By Udine and Perino del Vaga, not until after Raphael's death; designed for frescoes on the walls.)

* The Villa Madama has been extensively restored since Burckhardt wrote. (PM).

Fig. 334 *Rome, Vatican, the Loggie*

In the Farnesina, among other things the fine strings of fruit, by Udine, with which the cove of the vaults in the front loggia are painted (with Raphael's *History of Psyche*: Fig. 336).

Much of what Vasari cites has disappeared; in Venice there is still a magnificent ceiling in the Pal. Grimani (dense foliage enlivened with birds) and in Udine a ceiling in the Archiepiscopal Palace. That the decorative glass-paintings in the third cortile of the Certosa of Florence are by Udine is hardly likely, but the windows of the Biblioteca Laurenziana are probably his: in each case the Medici arms, surrounded by arabesques and ornamental figures felicitously disposed; colours used sparingly, so as not to diminish the light.

(NOTE: Burckhardt underestimates the importance of the discovery of "grotesques" in the Golden House of Nero and their exploitation by members of the Raphael circle – see now N. Dacos, *La découverte de la Domus Aurea et la formation des grotesques*..., London, 1970. For the side-borders of Raphael's tapestries, see L. Dussler, *Raphael, A Critical Catalogue*, London, 1971.) (PM).

§ 176 *Giulio Romano and Perino del Vaga*

Of Raphael's pupils Giulio Romano was the most deeply versed in the study of Antiquity (§ 27) and in the scholarship of its rich forms of decoration, and for this reason during his later career in Mantua was particularly occupied on the adornment of the Palazzo del Te. Perino del Vaga, in the service of Andrea Doria at Genoa, decorated (from 1529) the ceilings and vaults in his palace with exquisite motives of the most varied kinds.

Giulio's proficiency in stucco especially, and his preference for it was also shown in his own house at Mantua, both inside and out: Vasari, V, p. 548, *V. di Giulio*. Still extant in Rome some vaulted ceilings by him in the Villa Lante.

The Palazzo del Te outside Mantua, by Giulio Romano (§ 54, 119), the most complete group surviving intact of many decorated rooms of differing size, height, architectural design and purpose, the decoration largely as an accompaniment to cycles of pictures; these presented in very varied forms and arrangements, in oil as well as fresco. Colour and decorative motives determined according to the scale and function of the room; alternation of painting and white or polychrome stucco. Apart from the palace the annex of the Casino della Grotta, with elegant small rooms about a little garden. Not everything happily thought out, but much of it very good.

In the city of Mantua: Palazzo Ducale or Pal. di Corte, the old ducal residence; abundant choice of decorated Sale and other rooms of various periods, from the Camerino of Isabella Gonzaga to the seventeenth century, and a few modern rooms. By Giulio Romano here the fine, ingeniously planned, Sala de' Marmi (formerly containing Antique statues belonging to the House of Gonzaga), the Sala di Giove and others.

Perino's works in the Pal. Doria in Genoa: the lower colonnade with characteristically detailed and decorated soffitto (Histories) and extending all round the spandrels of the vault, on which seated divinities are very happily installed; the Galleria with wall frescoes of the heroes of the House of Doria and with a vaulted ceiling of supreme splendour, which combines in itself every possible manner of presentation, whether flat or raised, monochrome or polychrome, in a relatively small space; a sala with a ceiling painting of the Battle of the Giants, of which the frame or vault-springing, which runs all round, is both handsome and splendid (see Fig. 337, from Gauthier, *Edifices de Gênes*, unhappily only a detail, and inaccurate); several rooms with central paintings on the ceiling and every type of figured and decorative embellishment on the spandrels, intersections and lunettes of the vault. (A few rooms, mostly stuccoed white, are in a somewhat later style.) Cf. Vasari, V, p. 613 ff., *V. di Perino*. His other extremely numerous works in these and related fields, perhaps with the exception of those in the Castel S. Angelo (ibid., p. 628), have largely disappeared; and also the chapels in Roman churches, which he seems to have been the first to decorate with "grotesques" in this newer sense (ibid., pp. 621, 626). But much may be preserved which does not bear his name, as in his later Roman days he supplied designs for every possible decorative purpose and snatched up commissions at modest prices.

Fig. 335 *Rome, Vatican, the Loggie, detail*

A close, although not precisely definable, relationship with the School of Raphael is disclosed by the uncommonly fine vaulted ceiling in the back summer-house of the Pal. Giustiniani, sometime house of Luigi Cornaro (§ 119), at Padua. The passage regarding this house in the Anonimo Morelliano, in which Raphael is mentioned, does not, however, refer to this secondary building. Fabriczy (*Zeitschrift f. bild. Kunst*, XXIII,

Fig. 336 *Rome, Villa Farnesina, loggia*

p. 118 ff.) conjectures that the builder, Falconetto, who was in Rome in 1524, was also the creator of the decorations.

§ 177 *White Stucco*

Besides polychrome stucco a distinct practice developed of using white, with at most a discreet gilding, for rooms and vaulted ceilings, to which one wanted to give a solemn, monumental character, and also for any such exposed to the weather.

Incomparably handsome and entirely independent of "grottoes", the white and gold vault decoration of the chapel of S. Anthony in the Santo at Padua, executed by Tiziano Minio, designed by Jacopo Sansovino: Vasari, V, p. 325, n. 1, *V. di Fra Giocondo*. Falconetto's son-in-law, Bartol. Ridolfi of Verona, was rated thereafter as the outstanding stucco decorator of those parts. The passage from Lomazzo regarding other N. Italian decorators, § 137.

The vast coffered barrel vault of the Sala Regia of the Vatican (§ 101) with coats of arms and genii almost in the round; a work of Perino and Daniele da Volterra considered very fine in this context and in a period already declining artistically (regarding the latter's other decorative works cf. Vasari, VII, pp. 50–58, and the author's *Cicerone*, 10th ed., II, 1, p. 260). Clearly closely related: the last chapel in the left transept of Sta Maria del Popolo.

For Cardinal Trivulzio's villa at Casale Salone on the Via Tiburtina near Rome (nr Lunghezza) Falconetto created in association with Daniele da Volterra in 1521 and 1524 an elaborate decoration of grotesques.

Regarding individual, very handsome motives in plain stucco by Baldassare Peruzzi the author is unable to provide more detailed information. (Title page of Gruner's *Decorations* . . .)

Conspicuously fine, although not entirely pure in style, the white *stuccature* in the lower hall at the back, and the staircase in the Pal. de' Conservatori on the Capitol. They supposedly originated under the supervision of Michelangelo, who must also have supplied the main feature of the gilded vault-coffering of S. Peter's, though he did not care for the detail of decorative forms (§ 137) and avoided them on the ceiling of the Sistine Chapel.

An excellent ensemble in the chapel of the Cancelleria in Rome; on the lower part of the walls inferior paintings in beautifully ordered frames; then, higher up, a rich cornice on consoles and large semicircular paintings in ornamental surrounds; finally, the elegant, elaborately compartmented, vaulted ceiling with white stucco figures on a gold ground, and in between four small pictures, coats of arms, and emblems, with sparing use of a few colours (Figs. 338, 339).

Fig. 337 *Genoa, Palazzo Doria, detail*

§ 178 *Later Decorative Painting and Works in Stucco*

As a task of the utmost delicacy and of a peculiarly happy fantasy this method of decoration was to suffer noticeably, as soon as it became the mere subject of luxury and the concern of artists no longer able to devise what was fitting to the location and form of the building, who worked hurriedly and catered for the taste of clients in search of pomp.

In the Doge's Palace in Venice the Scala d' Oro, chiefly by Battista Franco under Jacopo Sansovino's direction (1538), laboriously grand and completely lacking in the rhythm and freedom of the Raphael manner, with a manifest incongruity between the painted elements and the coarse *stuccatura*; by Franco also a chapel in S. Francesco della Vigna, with painted coffers delicately "alla romana", as Fr. Sansovino (*Venezia*, fol. 14) expresses it. Cf. Vasari, VI, pp. 579, 584, 585 f., *V. di Batt. Franco.*

In the Pal. Pubblico at Siena, Sala del Concistoro, the vaulted ceiling richly painted with decorations and Roman histories by Beccafumi (1535), who had previously worked with Perino at Genoa; very circumstantial account in Vasari, V, p. 640, *V. di Beccafumi.*

About Pastorino's decoration completed in 1552 in the Loggia degli Ufficiali (or Uniti, also Casino de' Nobili) I must refer to Vasari, IV, p. 436, Commentary on the *V. di Marcilla.*

Particularly instructive is Vasari, VI, p. 213 ff., the life of Cristofano Gherardi; the decoration in stucco and colours already (*c* 1540) infected by hasty improvisation, in uneasy complicity with festal decorations (which must have accustomed the eye to a general crudeness of effect and deception) and an all too close kinship with mass-produced façade painting. Surviving by Gherardi: among others a vaulted and a flat ceiling in the Palazzo Vitelli (a Porta S. Egidio) at Città di Castello; on the latter the coffers are entirely decoration, while the mythological narrative pictures are oddly distributed over the beams. Later the prolific and superficial Federigo Zuccaro (1543–1609), who among other things provided all the principal rooms of Caprarola and a large front room of the Vigna di Papa Giulio III, etc., etc., with narrative and mythological paintings, decorations, and even *stuccatura*; here and there highly effective, when he reproduced traditional motives, beautifully detailed and handled.

Regarding the vaulted ceiling of a chapel in the

Fig. 338 *Rome, Palazzo della Cancelleria, chapel detail*

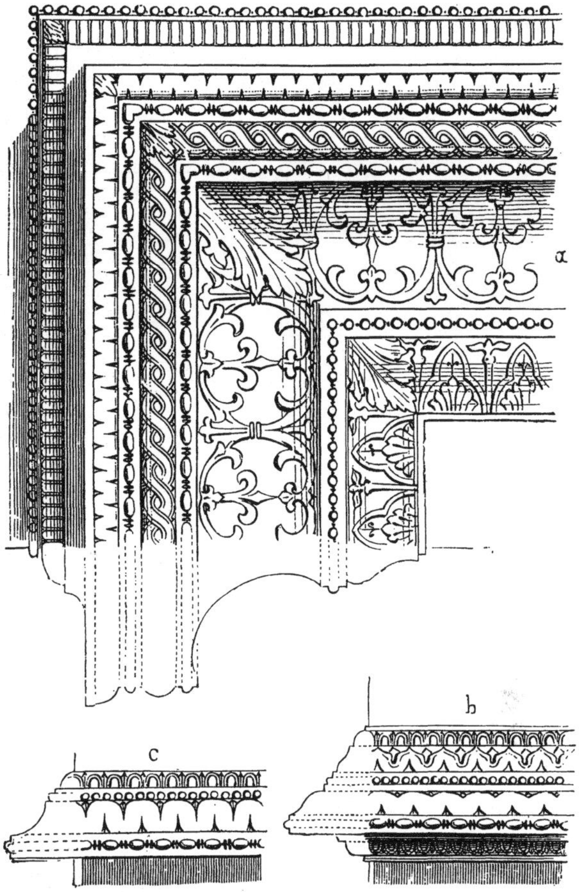

Fig. 339 *Rome, Palazzo della Cancelleria, chapel, mouldings*

church at Loreto, by Franc. Menzocchi, reference must be made to Vasari, VI, p. 324, *V. di Genga*; and for the works of Forbicini to VI, p. 368, *V. di Sanmicheli*; for Vasari's principal *stuccatore*, the highly resolute (*terribile*) Marco da Faenza, to VII, p. 422, *V. di Primaticcio*; for Pellegrino Tibaldi's works, ibid., p. 417; these are vaulted ceiling *stuccature* and altar-settings of his earlier style, after 1550; parts of the façade of Milan Cathedral stemming from him clearly reveal even in marble the audacious hand of the *stuccatore*. Wholly painted by Tibaldi, the vaulted ceiling of the Loggia de' Mercanti at Ancona, in a charming arrangement; the best, the figures seen from below, seated on the cornices – which are also excellent in the lower sala painted by Tibaldi at the University of Bologna.

Of the School of Dosso Dossi the graceful painted arabesques (1559) on the ceilings of the Palazzina at Ferrara.

Vasari believed he was the first to introduce decorative stucchi into Naples, when he modernised the Gothic refectory of a monastery (§ 22) and was able to please himself with "rectangular, oval and octagonal" patterns: Vasari, VII, p. 674, *Autobiography*.

§ 179 *Decadence of the Type*

In the second half of the sixteenth century the impetus engendered by the thermae and palace rooms of Antiquity was gradually extinguished; the dawning Counter-Reformation thrust upon ceiling and mural decoration a host of narrative tasks and associated allusions, which could not be so freely resolved, aesthetically, as the figurative representations once had been in the Loggie; in addition, the naturalistic conception intruded, making it impossible for such scenes to be a handsome sympathetic presence in a decorative space and to harmonise with it. On the other hand, stucco was now for the first time exploited in its full splendour, freedom, and vitality as a bordering, flexibly extending, and supporting element in vaults. Also the most capricious form of setting, the *cartoccio* or cartouche (§ 50), was used on a large scale.

The painted ceiling arabesques in the first gallery of the Uffizi in Florence, 1581, by Poccetti; those in the Vatican Library and in the Sala Ducale of the Vatican, cheerful and rich, but already in poor taste; those of the Galleria Geografica there, overladen with scenes from ecclesiastical history, by Ant. Tempesta.

Poccetti's other works, always among the best of the

period; the middle bay of the portico of the Innocenti in Florence; and, for mixed stucco and painting, the vault of the chapel of S. Anthony* in S. Marco and the small colonnade (left) of the cortile in the Pal. Pitti. Also relatively good: one of the chapel vaults painted by the two Alberti in Sta Maria sopra Minerva in Rome, and parts of the *cupolette* of the right aisle in Sta Maria presso S. Celso, Milan, by Cerano (Crespi), Campi etc.

Of the predominantly stuccoed vaults, among which the simple monochrome, perhaps with gold, was preferred, probably that of Sta Maria ai Monti in Rome (by Giac. della Porta?) became the most influential and may well have been the finest of this late period. Next to it, although dating from the beginning of the seventeenth century, the vault of the portico of S. Peter's, by Carlo Maderna.

Many individually showy chapels, chiefly in Rome, from *c* 1560; the vaulted ceilings becoming coarser and more garish as the style of the altarpieces and murals appeared more naturalistic, and their prevailing tonality darker.

About 1587, it was possible to argue as Armenini did: the Ancients had arrived at the idea of grotesques through seeing accidental faults in walls, hence this type of art was without any rules and compounded of every liberty (*De' veri precetti* . . . , p. 193); certainly (p. 195) after a short flowering they now quickly degenerated, because of a desire to please the ignorant; *perciochè le si dipingono crude, confuse, et piene di sciocche invenzioni, per li molti campi troppo carichi di bei colori che sono fuor di misura* . . . (How were proportion and beauty to be achieved, if one conceded only an accidental origin and had no inkling that Antique decorations derived from embellished architectural forms? Something different could have been learned from Vitruvius, VII, 5.)

In the meantime, in Venice and Naples flat ceilings with large compartments for paintings (§ 159) triumphed completely.

* Burckhardt presumably meant S. Antoninus, but the frescoes are actually in the Cappella del Sacramento. (PM).

CHAPTER EIGHT

Goldsmiths' Work, Ceramics and Related Crafts

§ 180 *General Status of this Art*

It is not possible for us to present with adequate completeness the art of the Renaissance goldsmith from the many written accounts and the few and inaccessible surviving examples. The tasks remained largely the same as in the Gothic period, but in the available descriptions the great stylistic change is hardly suggested.

Does Italy offer inventories and illustrated records of secular and ecclesiastical treasures like those in the North of the sacred collections of Wittenberg and Halle? Or like those of individual princely so-called *Kunstkammern*? Among the latter is an inventory like that of the Elector Maximilian I of Bavaria, of the period after 1625 (in v. Reber, *Kurfürst Max. I v. B. als Gemäldesammler* (Festrede), 1892), because in it is set out what the goldsmith's art of the fifteenth century had accumulated.

What has been lost to the world by subsequent theft and melting down (cf. e.g. Varchi, *Stor. fior.*, IV, 89) can only be surmised, when one considers that Brunellesco, Ghiberti, L. della Robbia, Masolino, Pollajuolo, Verrocchio, Finiguerra, Domenico Ghirlandaio, Sandro Botticelli, Francesco Francia, Andrea del Sarto, among others, started partly, and sometimes remained, goldsmiths. In the more important centres of art the craft of the goldsmith had high status. The Statutes of the Goldsmiths in Siena (1361) in Milanesi, I, p. 57, and in Gaye, *Carteggio*, I, p. 1, show this clearly. Florence, indeed, had about the year 1478 only 44 *botteghe d'orefici, argentieri, gioiellieri* (Fabroni, *Laurent. Magn.*, Adnot. 200), but they included several of the most reputable artists of the city. In Franco Sacchetti (Novella 215), the boast of a Florentine goldsmith that the sweepings from his shop were worth 800 florins a year.

The fourteenth century had achieved so much in this art and used enamels and precious stones with such refinement that further technical progress was scarcely possible. The only thing which the later period contributed in this connection may have been a more facile working of semi-precious stones into handsome vessels for display, and the enrichment of enamels with some new colours.

Antique gold objects were as good as non-existent, so that the masters of the Early Renaissance had to develop from their common new style one that would be applicable to the goldsmith's craft. The sculpture of the new period, resourceful and versatile as it was, came to their aid in an essentially different way than had happened in earlier centuries.

Just as they planned surfaces, treated relief, shaped foliage, animals' heads, claws, masks etc., arranged gold and silver and enamels in contrasted settings, and inlaid precious stones and gems, so imagination had to find, as best it could, a way to express itself in every individual job. In the fifteenth century a nobler sense of splendour as well as a desire for the ultimate pomp and polish had risen to importance, and a rapid glance over the more significant accounts, arranged according to subject, will show the scope open to this branch of art.

§ 181 *Ecclesiastical Works of the Early Renaissance*

While statues entirely of silver were still made, sometimes of a considerable size, the production of silver altar-shrines ceased, work being at most confined to the additional adornment and completion of what had been begun earlier.

Regarding silver figures of saints Vasari has little to say; probably most of them, when he was writing, were already melted down. Saints, Angels etc., about a *braccia* high,* partly enamelled, also a silver group of the

* Burckhardt uses the word *ell*, but in English this is a measure of about 45 inches; the *braccia*, used by Vasari and other Italian writers, is only about half that length (PM)

Assumption with angels, on a dado with enamelled narrative scenes, works of Gio. Turini (§ 149) from the years 1414–44, in the commentary on the *V. di Pollajuolo*, Vasari, III, p. 304 ff. Siena, with which we are concerned here, especially the sacristy of the Cathedral, was rich in such works; Milanesi, II, pp. 184, 220 f., 278, 291 ff., 328, 350 f., where the works of Turini are mentioned to some extent. A silver *Christ* a *braccia* high, of 1474, in Sansovino, *Venezia*, fol. 97.

Heads of silver plate or gilded bronze to contain the skulls of saints appear to have gone out of use at about this time, but the Sienese as late as 1466 had the skull of their patroness, S. Catherine, mounted in this way; Milanesi, II, p. 332.

By reason of its weight and size an exception may well have been provided by the silver statue, which the impious Cardinal Pietro Riario donated shortly before his end (1473) to the Santo in Padua; *Vitae Papar.* in Murat., III, II, col. 1060. Also the silver *Apostles* of the Papal chapel, some by Verrocchio (Vasari, III, p. 359, *V. di Verrocchio*) may have been particularly big.

For silver and golden altar-shrines Venice, in particular, possessed several prototypes in the form of Byzantine *pale*; Sansovino, *Venezia*, fol. 63, 74, etc.; Sabellicus, *De situ Ven. urbis*, fol. 85, 90. But this category now died out completely; at most something was occasionally fashioned for the celebrated silver shrines of the Baptistry of Florence and the Cathedral of Pistoia (Vasari, I, p. 442, 443 and n.; *V. di Agostino e Agnolo*; and III, p. 287 f., *V. di Pollajuolo*). The *Coronation of the Virgin, with Angels*, 150 pounds of silver, which Julius II donated to Sta Maria del Popolo (Albertini, *De mirabilibus urbis Romae*, L. III, fol. 86) may well have been a free-standing group. The magnificence of marble altars (§ 144) left silver ones completely forgotten. A bronze altar § 147. The Florentines in 1498 were to have the *pala* of their Cathedral and all the silver in the Annunziata melted down because of the financial crisis; Malipiero in Arch. Stor., VII, p. 526.

Also, there is little talk of monstrances; somewhat more often of silver candlesticks and reliquaries.

Has a single important monstrance of the Early Renaissance, indeed of the whole Italian Renaissance, survived at all? The decorative powers of the time would inevitably have been revealed in decisive fashion here. A contract for a monstrance (1449). Milanesi, II, p. 259.*

Of the hanging lamps in the Annunziata in Florence (Vasari, III, p. 254, *V. di Ghirlandaio*) and of the certainly beautiful candlesticks three *braccia* high, by Ant. Pollajuolo (ibid., p. 288, *V. di Pollajuolo*) nothing remains. On the other hand an elegantly ornamented hanging lamp (Fig. 340) in S. Marco, Venice. A contract for a splendid silver candelabrum in Siena (1440) in Milanesi, II, 193. Two candlesticks of jasper, belonging with the silver *Christ* mentioned above, with the arms of the Doge Marcello (1474).

On the so-called paxes of Tommaso Finiguerra the niello designs are especially important, but the framing is also decorative: Vasari, III, p. 287 and note, *V. di Pollajuolo.*

Silver and even gold votive objects were inevitably melted down in the course of time, and indeed even by the church authorities.

Reliquaries of gold and silver were still created, and sometimes in forms artistically superb; one recalls that a Filippo Maria Visconti, that the State of Venice, and that the Popes collected relics; and at least some bronze reliquaries were of supreme artistry (Ghiberti, Cassa di S. Giacinto, Bargello). Very little, however, has survived from the fifteenth century; e.g. the silver *cassetta* for the habit of S. Bernardino by Francesco d' Antonio (1460), which is still preserved in the Osservanza at Siena; Vasari, III, p. 306, in the Comment. on the *V. di Pollajuolo*; Milanesi, II, p. 314. (Incidentally an interesting motive from the previous century, silver figures of saints, bearing in their hands caskets with their own relics; Milanesi, I, p. 289, of the year 1381, may be mentioned.)

Regarding the various Papal tiaras, *Vitae Papar.*, in Murat., III, II, cols. 887 and 1009: Paul II's famous one, by the Roman goldsmith Paolo Giordano; Jac. Volaterran. in Murat., XXIII, col. 195; Sixtus IV's, conspicuous by its jewels. Vasari, III, p. 358, *V. di Verrocchio*: his (no longer extant) morses for episcopal vestments. The treasures of the Papal sacristy under Julius II enriched by a new series of silver-gilt *Apostles*, perfunctorily recorded in Albertini, *De mirabilibus . . . Romae*, L. III, fol. 86. Cf. some documents in Müntz, *Les arts à la cour des Papes*, I–III, passim.

(NOTE: The obvious omission here is the Silver Altar of the Baptistry in Florence, with surviving panels by Michelozzo, Antonio Pollaiuolo and Verrocchio; see L. Ettlinger, *A. and P. Pollaiuolo*, London, 1978.) (PM).

§ 182 *Secular Works of the Early Renaissance*

Among the secular tasks of the fifteenth-century goldsmith, single bowls and dishes for various forms of voting, and bowls for hand-washing in public palaces assumed great importance.

Pollajuolo's large silver basin for the Signoria of Florence (1473); details of the commission, Gaye, *Carteggio*, I, p. 571; a silver-gilt bell also there. The hand-basin for the Palazzo Pubblico at Siena (1437), with four enamelled coats of arms, details of the commission in Milanesi, II, p. 174; the (drinking?) bowl for the Mercanzia Guild (1475), with foliage and fluting, ibid., p. 355. Perhaps to be included here also the two fine large bowls by Verrocchio, one with animals and foliage, the other with dancing children; Vasari, III, p. 358 f., *V. di Verrocchio*. The fairly large silver-gilt vases,

* Cf the vast monstrance in the ceremonial procession of Charles V and Clement VII through Bologna, 1530, only cursorily portrayed in Hoghenberg (Hirth, *Kulturgeschichtliches Bilderbuch*, Nr 534)

which Paul II, among others, had made for "formal banquets", two of them (together?) weighing 118 pounds, must have been wine-coolers; *Vitae Papar.*, in Murat., III, II, col. 1009.

In Perugia there was for the ceremonial banquets of the town council a silver nef which can be imagined either as a table-centre or as a mobile wine-vessel. In 1449 a nef was commissioned and in 1489 one (perhaps the same) was presented to a nephew of Alexander VI, while in 1512 a new one was ordered from the goldsmith Mariotto Anastagi to Perugino's splendid design; with four wheels, two horses (? sea-horses) and 19 figures, among them a *Fortuna* holding the sail, a helmsman, the town's patron Saint, Ercolano, and many putti are mentioned. Archiv. Stor., XVI, p. 621, of which Appendice IX, p. 615 (with the Annali decemvirali); Mariotti, *Lettere pittor. perug.*, p. 171. (A silver ship of sixteenth-century Northern work illustrated in Rouaix, *Les styles* . . ., p. 124.)

Entire princely sideboards, on which stood vessels of silver and gold in their dozens, may well have been thought of merely as capital available for minting, but were nevertheless of fine design.

Just as for the North the inventories in De Laborde, *Les ducs de Bourgogne*, are noteworthy, for Milan, for example, it is the inventory of valuables which went with Valentine Visconti to France in 1389, as the dowry of the bride of the Duke of Orleans; in Corio, *Stor. di Mil.*, fol. 266; there were table-centrepieces, bowls and dishes, table candlesticks, services of cutlery in dozens, even silver night-light holders, mostly with enamel, altogether 1,667 mark-weight of silver.

The table-ware of the assassinated Galeazzo Maria Sforza (*Diarium Parmense*, in Murat., XXII, col. 359), which was sold to pay the senior officers, contained among other things a service entirely of gold, with 12 of everything. Lodovico il Moro owned at that time another collection of costly vessels, which he ceremoniously displayed in 1489 at a princely reception; Gaye, *Carteggio*, I, p. 411. Moro's medals, cf. Malipiero in Archiv. Stor., VII, I, p. 347.

The sideboard of Borso of Ferrara, a bare mention in *Diario Ferrar.*, in Murat., XXIV, col. 216.

On formal occasions two or more improvised statues of Wild Men stood guard by the sideboard; Phil. Beroaldi, *Orationes, nuptiae Bentivolorum.*

Jovian. Pontan., *De splendore*, advocated for the display-sideboard a variety of individual pieces, both in materials and shapes, even if they, e.g. drinking vessels, served one and the same purpose: *aliae atque aliae formae, calices, item crateres, gutti paterae, carchesia, scyphi* . . .

Besides the sideboard (*ornamenti da camera*) princes kept for their palace chapels *ornamenti della cappella*, candlesticks, chalices, patens etc.

In 1473 Cardinal Pietro Riario displayed the greatest luxury on the occasion when he offered hospitality to Leonora of Aragon, in his palazzo in the Piazza SS. Apostoli in Rome, on her journey as the bride of the Duke of Ferrara: four candlesticks from the Cappella, besides two golden figures of angels, a prie-dieu with lions' claw feet, entirely of silver and gilded; a complete set of fire-irons, but all of silver; a silver commode with a golden chamber-pot inside, etc. In the dining-room a grand sideboard of 12 stages, full of gold and silver vessels with precious stones; in addition, the table-service wholly of silver and changed after each dish.

Fig. 340 *Venice, S. Marco, hanging lamp*

As collectors of precious stones Alfonso the Great of Naples and Paul II are especially named: Jovian. Pontan., *De splendore*; Infessura in Eccard, *Scriptores*, II, col. 1894, 1945. Also Müntz, *Les arts* . . ., II.

Magnificent arms are often mentioned, but from the fifteenth century almost nothing noteworthy of this kind seems to have survived.

Silver helmets as a present from governments to condottieri; from Siena to Tartaglia, 1414; Florence to Federigo of Urbino, 1472, a work of Pollajuolo;

Vasari, III, p. 298, n., and p. 304, in the Comment. on the *V. di Pollajuolo.* The weapons and accoutrements of Charles VIII, looted in 1495 at the battle on the Taro (Malipiero, *Ann. Veneti* in Archiv. Stor., VII, I, p. 371), were undoubtedly Northern work: the gold, crowned, helmet with enamel, the sword, the seal-box, the gold triptych, allegedly handed down from Charlemagne.

§ 183 *The Art of the Goldsmith in the High Renaissance*

The art of the sixteenth-century goldsmith is distinguished from that of the Early Renaissance by a greater freedom and fluency in all decoration, thanks to heightened visual perception.

We are obliged to speak hypothetically, as an adequate conspectus of the works of the fifteenth century is entirely, and of those of the sixteenth century largely, lacking. French, German and other works which were created under strong Italian influence from the early sixteenth century were easily taken for Italian.

From a perhaps only superficial knowledge of N. Italy Hans Holbein the Younger achieved a free and vibrant beauty in his designs for goldsmiths' work which is astonishing (Basle Museum, British Museum, and Hollar's engravings).

A great wealth of information in the autobiography of the great Florentine Benvenuto Cellini (1500–71), especially in the first half; his works in every branch of this art: a goblet, morse for the Papal pallium, reliquaries, the cover for a Book of Hours, seals, drinking vessels, large wine-coolers, silver utensils of every sort, salt-cellars, including one very famous one still preserved (in Vienna), candlesticks (some of them presumably surviving in the Treasury of S. Peter's),* jewellery, women's finery, rings, buckles for girdles, gold damascening for steel blades etc., not to mention statues, reliefs, and medals. His two *Trattati* are particularly instructive regarding the latter types. (*Tratt.* I, c. 5; with regard to the small gold crucifixes fashionable among cardinals *c* 1530, mainly Caradosso's work.) In collections a great deal is attributed to Cellini, but almost nothing reliably, and as for the works mentioned in the Autobiography they remain for us pure speculation, except for a few very well-known ones.

In general seemingly characteristic of him, the fashioning of vessels and utensils, exuberant, full of vitality and finally wholly emancipated from architectural forms; resolved in lavish foliage, cartouches, masks and the like, intermingled with small fields of delicate relief.

Other famous names occur as originators of designs for metal-workers; Raphael supplied (1510) the drawing for a large bronze dish with embossed ornament, which a certain Cesarino executed for Agostino Chigi; Quatremère, *Vita di Raff.*, ed. Longhena, p. 327, n.; Michelangelo provided (1537) the drawing for a silver salt-cellar for the Duke of Urbino, with beasts, festoons, masks, and a figure on the cover; Vasari, VII, p. 383, in the Comm. on the *V. di Michelangelo.* Perugino's nef, 182. The famous designs of Girolamo Genga for drinking vessels got no further than a wax model; Vasari, VI, p. 320, *V. di Genga.*

Metal vessels, whether bowls, dishes, or vases, reproduce very clearly the aims and abilities of the Renaissance by the manner in which surfaces are filled as completely as possible and handsomely patterned with figurative decoration and the ornament of the new century.

The narrative often crowded with figures (on bowls on the circumference, on vases in the form of an encircling frieze) usually depicting scenes from Antiquity, especially the histories and loves of the water-gods (cf. Lomazzo, p. 345), in which the artist followed in the simplest way the fanciful form of each vessel and freely imposed its lines. When the narrative was divided into separate parts the oval shape came into favour and also very freely designed cartouches of every type. In addition, foliage, masks, putti, dolphins and such.

§ 184 *Vessels of Semi-Precious Stones and Crystal*

As an essentially new theme, vessels appeared of hard and precious stones † and engraved crystal, the feet, handles, rims, lid-fastenings etc. being given exceedingly ornamental and fanciful forms in gold, enamel and precious stones.

It would be difficult to say how early hard agates, jaspers and lapis lazuli etc. were generally cut into the forms desired by craftsmen; in this respect certainly the Middle Ages were far behind Antiquity, and in Italy the Early Renaissance behind the High Renaissance.

In place of the sideboards of princes and great personages the cabinet of the rich amateur now came into prominence, in which vases of hard stone with costly mountings assumed the place of honour.

The harmony of the vibrant forms and the colour of the stones with their settings is now one of the supreme objects of decorative art.

In the setting itself two ways of presentation alternate, smooth enamel on gold or silver, and decorative forms, in relief and enamelled, around precious stones. On feet and handles human and animal masks, dragons, sea-monsters, also human figures of various kinds.

In the combination of colours the diversity of the Middle Ages is now completely abandoned, all the decoration being carefully matched to the colour of the vessel. The command of contrast between enamel and relief, enamel and metal, polished and matt, is already an accomplished fact.

---

* Nothing is now (1980) attributable to Cellini in S Peter's (PM)

† Recently Brunn (Sitzungsberichte der Kgl. Akademie der Wissenschaften in München, 1875, Bd. I, Heft 3) has attributed on very strong evidence both the onyx vase in Brunswick and the Farnese onyx bowl in Naples to Renaissance artists.

On crystal vases with engraved ornament and narrative scenes the setting is strikingly delicate and elegant.

The most important collection is still considered to be the Tesoro in the Pal. Pitti, Florence (with authentic works by Cellini), which the author has never succeeded in seeing.* Another in the Uffizi, in which is to be found the celebrated casket of Clement VII, with Valerio (Belli) Vincentino's histories engraved in crystal. An onyx vase at Naples (Fig. 341).

In the sixteenth century Venetian private cabinets were rich in such objects. List in the Anonimo Morelliano, with references to the collections of Odoni, Antonio Foscarini, Franc. Zio, Mich. Contarini. A crystal bowl (of five pieces in silver-gilt mounts), with engraved stories from the Old Testament, was by Cristoforo Romano; a larger three-handled porphyry bowl by Piermaria da Pescia, who buried this work in 1494 when the French entered Rome; subsequently it was sold on several occasions as Antique. (This implies that fine work in porphyry was already being done in Rome under Alexander VI.) As well as vases of precious materials the same collectors possessed others of damascened bronze, porcelain, glass etc. On the other hand, no one then carved ivory vessels.

The nautilus shell with a supporting figure and ornament, already very handsome in the sixteenth century – but hard to date more precisely.

§ 185 *Adornment, Weapons and Seals*

Women's festive dress was sometimes very rich in adornment of all kinds with gems; the usual piece of finery in men's clothes was the medal on the cap.

This is not the place to discuss medals as a special branch of the arts. Gold and enamelled ones, with figures which stood out almost in the round, generally served to adorn head-gear; the principal master of this craft was Caradosso: Benv. Cellini, *Trattato*, I, c. 5.

At a Roman church festival in Raphael's time (1519; see Gaye, *Carteggio*, I, p. 408) a few women who were present on a dais, some probably prostitutes, are described: Lucia Bufolina, dress of silver brocade, girdle of spun gold with four enamelled heads of Emperors; Sofonisba Cavaliera, girdle with antique gold coins; Faustina degli Alterii, gold head-band with the 12 Signs of the Zodiac in enamel; Imperia Colonnese (perhaps the one mentioned in § 156), girdle of gold buttons (cf. Raphael's *Joanna of Aragon*) and an enamelled *palla* (?), on which the elements were shown; Sabina Mattuzza, girdle of ingeniously combined gold coins, cornelian and jasper.

This one account provides more clues than all the relics of this kind actually preserved.

Furthermore, the sixteenth century was the age of the most magnificent weapons; even if they rarely, if ever, were actually used. This was particularly true of the silver shields, which were certainly not really carried on those occasions when the most splendid helmets and harness appeared.

Fig. 341 *Naples, onyx vase*

Accoutrements and helmets of Italian workmanship of the first rank, now generally dispersed abroad (Madrid, Vienna, Paris, London, St Petersburg) have ornamental and figured designs damascened on the steel or incised

* The Museo degli Argenti is now open as part of the Pitti Palace. The casket of Clement VII, by Belli, is now there. (PM).

Fig. 342 *Naples, maiolica plate*

with gold and silver; Vasari, VII, p. 43, *V. di Salviati*, with reference to Franc. dal Prato. Occasionally the ornament is also in relief, e.g. on the helmet and shield of Francis I, in the Uffizi, said to be by Benvenuto. A shield in the Armeria in Turin is also attributed to him.

Magnificent dagger hilts and handles, with figures and foliage in original combinations are found here and there. The wide dispersal of such treasures does not help in assessing their art-historical significance.

Among the conventional paraphernalia of the eminent were seals, mostly of silver. It was Paul II who substituted a more handsome – *artificiosiori sculptura* – form for the uncouth, if time-honoured, seal for the Papal Bulls; *Vitae Papar.*, in Murat., III, II, col. 1011. Much finer, however, had always been many other seals. Apart from their impression, which, for example, was often very rich in the fifteenth century in the case of the mandorla-shaped seals of Cardinals, depicting the Saints of their titular churches, or events from their Legends, the handle was also sometimes extremely elegant. Ghiberti (*Comment.*, p. xxxiii) mounted an Antique engraved gem in the form of a seal, so that the gold handle represented a dragon set in ivy leaves, and Benvenuto himself liked to design the handles of seals as animals or figurines, e.g. the seated Hercules on the gold seal of Cardinal Ercole Gonzaga; Benv. Cellini, *Trattato*, I, c. 6.

Perhaps the most important, predominantly ornamental, work of the entire style which still survives in Italy – the Farnese Casket, by Gio. de' Bernardi, in the Naples Museum, of metal with corner figures, reliefs, and six cut-glass ovals; the lid with a figurine of a reclining Hercules between the halves of a broken pediment.

§ 186 *Majolica and Other Pottery*

The artistic treatment of ceramic ware and glass has never since Antiquity risen so high as in the Renaissance, or, indeed, subsequently. The majolicas took first place, with their glazes in a restricted number of colours.

A true porcelain in our sense, translucent or entirely white in texture, was not yet known, and the many "porcelains", chiefly in Venetian collections, must be understood as majolica – i.e. glazed earthenware.

Already in the Middle Ages this had often advanced to the frontiers of art by its rich uninhibited form and by colours and gilding; in the fifteenth century perfection in glazing was to be reached by the Della Robbia workshop; but only in the sixteenth century was the full freedom of decorative modelling and two-dimensional ornament applied. This is what gives it its value, more than the painstakingly painted historical scenes, even if Raphaelesque and other well-known motives are employed.

The chief evidence: Vasari, VI, p. 581 f., *V. di Batt. Franco*; cf. VII, p. 90, *V. di T. Zucchero*; Benv. Cellini, *Vita*, II, c. 8; Quatremère, *Vita di Raffaelle*, ed. Longhena, p. 290, n.

Fig. 343 *Naples, maiolica plate*

By 1526 there were indeed amateurs who stood to lose 600 ducats on their "porcelains" – e.g. Giberti, Clement VII's secretary, on the occasion of the first (Colonna) storming of Rome; *Lettere di Principi*, I, 106, Negri to Micheli. It is nevertheless accepted that at least the majolica workshops of Pesaro and Castel Durante would not have attained their peak until *c* 1530/40 when Duke Guidobaldo II of Urbino employed Battista Franco (§ 178) as designer; in addition the duke had acquired a large number of sketches by Raphael, Giulio Romano and their pupils as patterns. Somewhat later, for example, Taddeo Zucchero supplied the drawings for an entire service, which was fired at Castel Durante for Philip II.

On Faenza-ware (*faience*) figurative painting was sparingly used and occupied either the centre alone or the rim (if we understand Vasari correctly); cf. Malagola, *Memorie storiche sulle majoliche di Faenza*, and F. Argnani, *Le ceramiche e majoliche faentine dalla loro origine fino al principio del secolo XVI; appunti storici*, Faenza, 1889.

The few colours, generally only blue, violet, green, yellow, white and black, were sufficient not so much for reproducing large compositions agreeably, but rather for adorning typically and well all the forms and profiles of the vessel and the surfaces between. Sometimes animals, foliage and other motives were both treated in relief and painted.

The best are the large shallow dishes (Figs. 342, 343), sweetmeat plates, salt-cellars, ink-wells and the like; these mainly without painted figures, with graceful and sparingly applied arabesques, by which they were likely to indicate their manufacture in Faenza. The basic form of the vessel or utensil is as a rule excellent and designed specifically for its purpose, and not to recall the past. In Vasari's time this branch of art had spread throughout Italy.

Of copies of Greek vases (in red and black), which Vasari's grandfather Giorgio had attempted at Arezzo in the fifteenth century, nothing has come down to our day; Vasari, II, p. 557, *V. di Lazzaro Vasari*.

Also of the manufacture at Modena, the pottery of which in the fifteenth century is acclaimed by Codrus Urceus in a poem (his *Opera*, p. 384, ad Lucam Ripam), nothing else is known; he himself owned an extraordinarily fine pottery lamp.

For glass objects of all kinds the factories at Murano in Venice were long famous; they not only possessed all colours and copied every precious stone, but also as early as the fifteenth century made *millefiori*; Sabellicus, *De situ Ven. urbis*, L. III, fol. 92: *brevi pila includere florum omnia genera*.

(NOTE: It seems unlikely that Giberti's collection would have been worth 600 ducats if it were really only modern maiolica: Far Eastern porcelains were known, perhaps as early as the fifteenth century, and "alla porcellana" seems to have been maiolica made in imitation of porcelain. Giberti's collection is described as *porcellane* and was obviously rare and valuable.) (PM).

CHAPTER NINE

Temporary Decorations

§ 187 *Festivals and Festival Artists*

Temporary decorations, for religious and secular festivals and ceremonies, had in the fifteenth century the character of gaiety and splendour combined, in which the rich interplay of the forms of the architectural decoration of the time harmonised with every sort of colourful addition.

Regarding Feste in general, cf. *Kultur d. Renaiss.*, p. 401 ff.; 4th ed., II, p. 132 ff.

The most important accounts (the description of the Triumphal Entry of Alfonso the Great into Naples in 1443, printed as an appendix to the *Dicta et Facta Alphonsi*, by Ant. Panormita, is only revealing for the procession, not for the conjectural decorations): Pii II, *Comment.*, L. VIII, p. 382 ff., his celebration of the Feast of Corpus Christi at Viterbo in 1462; Corio, *Storia di Milano*, fol. 417 ff., the reception of Leonora of Aragon by Cardinal Pietro Riario in Rome (1473), cf. § 182; ibid., fol. 451 ff., Coronation and Possesso (i.e. procession from the Vatican to the Lateran) of Alexander VI (1492); Phil. Beroaldi, *Orationes*, fol. 27, Nuptiae Bentivolorum, i.e. the marriage of Annibale Bentivoglio and Lucrezia d' Este (*c* 1490).

The art of festal decoration stemmed like most things of the new cultural epoch from Florence; as early as the fourteenth century Florentine *festaiuoli* were travelling about Italy (Gio. Villani, VIII, 70), who certainly at that time, and also later, not only erected but also provided the appropriate decorations, in which indeed, at least in the presentation of architectural themes, Florentine art excelled the rest of Italy. Besides Florence, Pistoia in particular must have had some importance in this respect, since for the Corpus Christi festival (above) at Viterbo Cardinal Niccolò Fortiguerra, who was a native of Pistoia, had *ludorum artifices* sent from there as his – very handsome – contribution to the decorations.

As well as the great Feasts, religious and secular life offered constant opportunities for decorations; *Apparati* at weddings and funerals, for which *c* 1500 in Florence Andrea Feltrini had a special name; Vasari, V, p. 208 f., *V. di Morto da Feltro*; banners of all kinds, see below; catafalques (*cataletti*) for Confraternities, some of which were by great masters, e.g. Beccafumi and Sodoma; Milanesi, III, pp. 166, 167, 185; Baldassare Peruzzi supplied one such and also an "admirable" bier; Vasari, IV, p. 596 and n. 2, *V. di Peruzzi*. (The biers on marble tombs provided splendid models for this, § 140.) Even at the burning of Vanities piety required that these should be arranged on a *talamo*, i.e. a kind of stylised funeral pyre; Infessura in Eccard, *Scriptores*, II, col. 1874; cf. *Kultur der Ren.*, p. 481.

§ 188 *Festival Decorations of the Early Renaissance*

Characteristic of the Early Renaissance is the over-abundant use of greenery, chiefly in the form of garlands; the free, fantastical, conversion of the Triumphal Arch into a building of colourful splendour; panels suspended on ribbons; the use of live people decked out in robes and attributes as statues. The awning, often spread over long streets and wide piazzas, was wherever possible of brilliant design.

That every individual household kept tapestries ready to be hung from windows and, especially in a colonnaded town like Bologna, exploited the wonderful contrasts between garlands and arches, goes without saying; temporary gilding of certain architectural elements also occurred, § 42. The garlands, to judge from illustrations, were sometimes peculiarly bulky and elaborate creations.

Then the designs, still common today, of coats of arms, name-scrolls etc., entirely of greenery and flowers, on walls and pavements. Thus Ferrara, at the Entrance of Pius II (1459) was *semenato d' herbe*; *Diario Ferr.* in Murat., XXIV, col. 204, certainly very artistically, *e piantati mai* (i.e. green boughs) *per tutto*, no doubt to carry the garlands and cloth awnings already mentioned.

Pius II especially praised the effect of the coloured cloth, through which the sun glowed, in the magnificent tent from which his Corpus Christi procession started; on the way there was an awning with the design of a red cloud, the next sky-blue with gold stars, then blue and white, and the red-brown of English woollen cloth.

A *festa* like this, in which not only the most magnificent altars, but entire stages with inanimate groups and living, speaking, and singing decorative figures appeared, in which fountains gushed wine, in which each of 18 green arch-piers carried a singing boy-angel, and in which the Resurrection and the Assumption were represented dramatically, was naturally a rare exception.

The principal architectural feature in honour of ceremonial entries and processions was now of course the Roman Triumphal Arch, yet even if this was expressly *al rito romano* (e.g. in Corio, fol. 490, anno 1497) it was by no means a strict, but only a superficial, imitation. Thus, at the Possesso of Alexander VI in 1492 the largest arch was supposed to be a copy of "the Arch of Octavian by the Colosseum", but with a completely free and splendid cornice of cornucopias and festoons, adorned with gilded reliefs (?), polychrome painting and an inscription-tablet hung in the arch. A second Triumphal Arch had gilded coffering with a central feature in the form of a shell; in 12 niches stood living, singing, girls, representing Oriens, Occidens, Liberalitas, Roma, Justitia, Pudicitia, Florentia, Caritas, Aeternitas, Victoria, Europa and Religio. Simpler arches with trophies, sea-monsters etc., were mostly blue and gold. A blue awning with a golden-yellow, richly ornamented, inscription was especially famous.

On the occasion of one Entry of Julius II a genuine Roman Triumphal Arch – Domitian's on the Campus Martius – was adorned with statues and paintings: Albertini, *De mirabilibus urbis Romae*, L. II, fol. 78.

At one of Lodovico il Moro's *feste* Leonardo's model for the equestrian statue of Francesco Sforza seems to have been placed under a Triumphal Arch.

In this context we inevitably think of the colossal wooden horse by Donatello (now in the Salone at Padua),* which is supposed to have carried a figure of Jupiter, and at a tournament was pushed along on a base of rollers or wheels.

In the whole of the West, but especially in Italy, tapestries were used in the fifteenth century to add lustre to *feste*, and indeed with no particular regard to the relevance and subject represented.

For the Corpus Christi *festa* already mentioned the cardinals had their entire stock of tapestries, some of them celebrated, brought to Viterbo.

For Leonora's reception at Cardinal Riario's house (cf. § 95, 182) the sacristies were manifestly obliged to produce their most valuable treasures, e.g. the tapestry of Nicholas V, with the story of the Creation, *il più bello che sia tra' Cristiani*; and another particularly beautiful one of the Assumption. (Among various stupidities there also appeared a child, gilded all over, who stood on a column and spurted water all round from a fountain.)

At church festivals even today, when tapestries with religious subjects are inadequate, they are helped out with mythological and even hunting scenes. On the whole, tapestries and garlands were what counted in the fifteenth century.

§ 189 *Sixteenth-Century* Feste

In the sixteenth century an extraordinary increase in expenditure on festival decoration is noticeable. It was the time when architects, sculptors and painters were trying out large-scale effects in this type of work and making experiments for monumental art (§ 50, 60), though certainly also becoming accustomed to superficiality and garishness.

Leo X's Possesso in Rome (1513); Giac. Penni's account in Roscoe, *Leone X*, ed. Bossi, V, p. 205 ff. The main theme of the allegories had to be, since the new Pope was well known, the artistic patronage that could be expected from him; for the triumphal arch of Agostino Chigi it was related to the dissolute pontificate of Alexander VI and the warlike one of Julius II:

Olim habuit Cypris sua tempora, tempora Mavors
Olim habuit, sua nunc tempora Pallas habet

Leo X's Entry into Florence, 30 November, 1515; two accounts in Roscoe, op. cit., VI, p. 280 ff.; also Vasari, V, p. 24 f., *V. di A. del Sarto*; V, p. 341, *V. di Granacci*; VI, p. 141, *V. di Bandinelli*; VI, p. 255, *V. di Pontormo*. At this time the famous false façade of the Cathedral, § 190.

Charles V's reception in Rome (1536) after the first African campaign; Vasari, IV, p. 545 f., *V. di Montelupo*; V, p. 464 f., *V. di Ant. Sangallo*; VI, p. 571 f., *V. di Batt. Franco*; in Siena, ibid., V, p. 644 f., *V. di Beccafumi*; Gaye, *Carteggio*, II, p. 245; Milanesi, III, p. 167, 185; in Florence, *Lettere pittoriche*, III, 12; Vasari, VI, p. 67, *V. di Tribolo*; VI, p. 637, *V. di Montorsoli* (cf. also p. 26); in Bologna, ibid, VII, p. 652, in Vasari's Autobiography.

Cosimo I's marriage (1539); Vasari, IV, p. 86, *V. di Tribolo*; VI, p. 576, *V. di Batt. Franco*.

The principal constituents of the earlier decoration, greenery, tapestries, and living statues, were soon to take their leave for good. Classical-architectonic gained the upper hand over uninhibited fantasy.

The admittedly late, but for the sixteenth century decisive, judgement of Borghini (1565): *Lettere pittoriche*, I, 56; "The only truth lies in wood and painted canvas in the shape of arches, façades and other buildings; greenery and tapestries may, if need be, do for merry-makings or even church festivals; living figures as Virtues etc. are a *magra invenzione*; the most desirable aim should surely be to be able to have something permanent built of stone", i.e. the growing *grandezza* can no longer tolerate the jolly village-fair style.

* The horse, apparently made in 1466, is not by Donatello. (PM).

§ 190 *Triumphal Arches*

Triumphal arches, now almost exclusively in stone-colour, adopted, if not particular Roman models, at least the exact details of Ancient construction. An early consequence of this is the use of stone-colour on statues, and chiaroscuro in paintings, which now imitate relief systematically.

The salient columns with statues above, already mentioned at Alexander VI's Possesso, now become the rule. Silvered columns with gilded capitals still appeared, but stone-colour predominated. At Leo X's Possesso, in which the earlier and later styles mingled, living figures still appeared on certain arches, e.g. even in the middle of a coffered vault of one there emerged a child, who recited two distichs, from a globe that suddenly opened; otherwise all statues were of stucco, except that on one arch genuine Antique statues and busts were used.

The arches at Leo's reception in Florence undoubtedly all had strictly architectonic forms; on the Piazza della Signoria there was a four-sided one, perhaps applying the motive of the Arch of Janus, for everything possible was certainly attempted in the way of different combinations. One appeared as if made entirely of porphyry.

Arches on later occasions (one very splendid at a Florentine *festa* of 1525; Vasari, VI, p. 452, *V. di Aristotile*) were sometimes "so grand and well proportioned" – i.e. in Vasari's sense, so closely related to correct architecture, that they only needed to be executed in marble to be numbered among the wonders of the world. (Cagnola's Arco del Sempione in Milan is well-known as a marble copy of a festal arch which had given great pleasure.) Also Serlio's specification and prototype is strictly classical (L. IV, p. 180).

An utter misunderstanding of the problem, i.e. the complete abnegation of gaiety and freedom was shown (1556) in Venice, on the occasion of the Entry of a Dogaressa, on a Triumphal Arch of the Butchers' Guild, the columns and pilasters displaying nothing but rustication; Sansovino, *Venezia*, fol. 154. Later Rubens adopted such a motive for some of his decorations in Antwerp for the Entry of the Cardinal-Infante, but he got round it by a felicitous Baroque freedom.

That almost all paintings of arches now only imitated reliefs, i.e. were realised in chiaroscuro, applied in general to the whole of festal decoration, even where polychrome representations would have been appropriate; e.g. Vasari, VII, p. 87, *V. di T. Zucchero*. The custom of façade painting may have contributed to this.

As well as arches there was much fake architecture, splendid façades, decorations of unfinished church fronts, and free-standing ornamental buildings.

At Julius II's Entry, § 188, after 1506, wooden colonnades with gilded arches on silvered columns extended along entire streets; Albertini, fol. 78.

The display of a large number of Antique statues on the house of Evangelista Rossi on the occasion of Leo X's Possesso must inevitably make one think of a large decorated wall of niches.

The false façade of the Cathedral, with simulated weathering, by Jacopo Sansovino and A. del Sarto, was rated a marvel of beauty at the Entry of Leo into Florence.

Several Roman monuments had also been copied at that time in Florence: Trajan's Column, an obelisk, the Meta Sudans etc. A dummy door at the Badia, because the real one did not lie exactly on axis with the street; a round temple with semi-circular entrance hall, etc.

Candelabra, ostensibly of marble and probably enormous, appeared at all events at Leo's Possesso, perhaps for the first time.

§ 191 *Festival Sculpture*

Sculpture, too, now applied all the force of its modelling to the decoration of *feste*, and often realised in colossal statues ideas which would never, or hardly ever, be feasible in permanent materials.

At Leo's Possesso, apart from the statues on Triumphal Arches, it was more a matter of small, ornamental, figures for fountains: a *Venus*, from whose breasts, and a *Spinario*, from whose wound, water gushed.

The Pope was received by his countrymen in Florence (1515), on the other hand, with sculptures, sometimes colossal, which alternated with decorations; a *Hercules* by Bandinelli, $9\frac{1}{2}$ *braccie* high (but a failure); a *Horse-Tamer* of the Quirinal type; a gilded equestrian effigy like *Marcus Aurelius*.

For the reception of Charles V there was mass-production modelling; Raffaello da Montelupo travelled post-haste to Florence before the Emperor, leaving 14 scarcely completed statues for the Ponte Sant' Angelo, to produce two river-gods in five days; in addition, on display were Montorsoli's *Hilaritas* and *Jason*, Tribolo's *Goddess of Peace*, *Hercules*, and the gilded equestrian statue of Charles himself; three other river-gods by the two last-named sculptors; a *Victory* by a certain Cesare, and *Prudentia* and *Justitia* by Franc. Sangallo, all of them colossal and several "extraordinarily big".

In Siena Beccafumi fashioned out of papier-mâché, over an iron skeleton, a vast equestrian statue of the Emperor in "Antique" costume, leaping over three figures representing conquered provinces; after Leonardo one of the first rearing horses in modern art. (According to others, instead of the provinces three river-gods, from whose urns water gushed.) Sodoma must also have worked on a horse at that time.

The rearing equestrian statue also appeared later at the wedding of Cosimo I, at which his father, Giovanni delle Bande Nere, was represented by Tribolo in this way, and of vast proportions.

At that time men vied with each other in the colossal; at Alfonso II of Ferrara's first Entry into Reggio (1558) there stood on the Piazza, 46 *palmi* high, the founder of the city, M. Lepidus, modelled in stucco by Clementi; *Lettere pittoriche*, I, Appendix 39; later colossi e.g. in

Vasari's description of the marriage of Francesco Medici (1565).

In all these activities speed was of the essence; e.g. Montorsoli modelled, life-size, within 24 hours a *Fides* and a *Caritas*, to adorn an improvised fountain, which played at the general chapter of the Servite Order; Vasari, VI, p. 636, *V. di Montorsoli.*

Artists engaged in such pressing work were caught up in a kind of frenzy, and when stimulated with good wine, ideas were generated which, at least during the festival, were accounted the most brilliant in the world; Vasari, VI, p. 573, *V. di Batt. Franco.* And if one of them sank, dead tired, on to a pile of leaves, he would be woken in the most flattering manner, as occurred with Vasari himself, *Lettere pittoriche*, III, 12.

With the people, great reputations were gained by transient works of this kind: Armenini, p. 71.

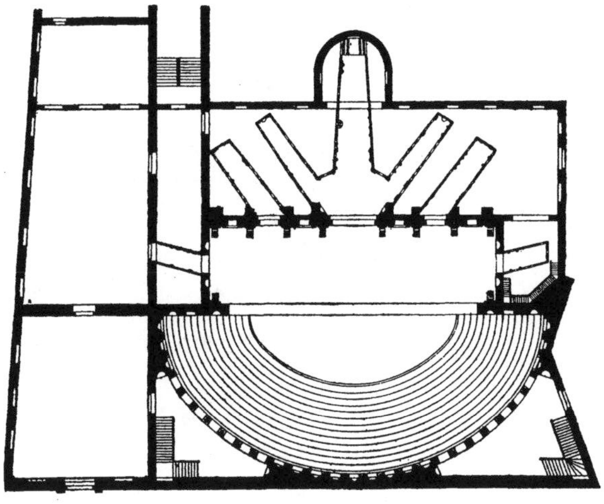

Fig. 344 *Vicenza, Teatro Olimpico, plan*

§ 192 *Theatre Architecture*

Dramatic performances, long customary only on festal occasions, took place in the cortili and sale of the great families and of prelates, and probably also in public piazze. Permanent theatres were not introduced until late and it was a long time before these attained any architectural form externally.

Regarding theatrical matters, cf. *Kultur der Renaiss.*, pp. 250, 277, 314, 401; 4th ed., I. pp. 285, 310 f.; II, pp. 34, 133.

Here too the Tuscans had long been rated as the experts, as in everything to do with *feste*. For the erection of a stage and its apparatus the Compagnia della Calza in Venice had to bring men from Tuscany in 1542. Cf. Crowe-Cavalcaselle, *Tizian*, II, p. 421.

Tragedy remained a loftier, infrequent, extravagance; the first theatres to be equipped as such were certainly for a considerable time for comedies only; Vasari, VI, p. 446 f., *V. di Aristotile* (in a sala of Cardinal Farnese in Rome); VI, p. 583 f., *V. di Batt. Franco* (in a building in the Via Giulia). Earlier, in 1515, the premises of Giuliano Medici, Leo X's brother, must have been fully organised for the purpose, at any rate for a time, as his nephew Lorenzo in the former's absence had a piece by Plautus presented; *Lettere di Principi*, I, 13. Palladio had already been building in Venice a semicircular theatre, which seems to have had Antique forms externally, "after the manner of the Colosseum", though only in wood; it was constructed for a single tragedy to be performed during a Carnival; Vasari, VII, p. 100, *V. di Tadd. Zucchero*; on the other hand, Palladio's existing Teatro Olimpico (Fig. 344) at Vicenza (1584) is formless on the outside; the auditorium transversely elliptical, with a colonnade above. While the latter is known to have served for both comedies and tragedies, the two permanent theatres in Venice, "very fine and built at great expense", one oval and one round, which Francesco Sansovino, *Venezia*, fol. 75 mentions (*c* 1580) were intended only for the performance of comedies at Carnival time. They accommodated very large audiences. The author does not say that they were the work of his father, Jacopo Sansovino.

A drawing in the Louvre, said to be by Sansovino, gives the longitudinal section of a theatre, which has, like the one in the Palazzo at Parma (1619, by Aleotti), superimposed above the auditorium, arcades of the type of Sansovino's Library; then, before the *scena* begins, a large entrance portal with windows above. But the niche-ornamentations etc. are too Baroque for Sansovino. (In the theatre at Parma, the *scena* is already deeply recessed, designed for scene-changes, with a curtain that can be drawn occupying the centre of an extremely splendid frontispiece with a rich Corinthian Order and statues in niches; next follow at the front the side doors to right and left, and then the auditorium with above it (wooden) double colonnades all round.) The arrangement of the rows of seats may at first have been left to chance. In time, however, their correct relationship to the stage and most convenient arrangement for seeing and hearing were established. What was the particular service in this context of Leonardo, who was called by Giovio *deliciarum theatralium mirificus inventor*, is no longer clear.

Aristotile da Sangallo at any rate tried to make the space for the audience as decorative as possible for a performance (1539) in the rear cortile of the Pal. Medici, Florence; an awning spanned the arena and on the walls were pictures of contemporary historical interest; Vasari, VI, p. 441, *V. di Aristotile*. The same treatment for the building erected in Venice by Vasari for the Compagnia della Calza, with niches between the murals; Vasari, VI, p. 223 ff., *V. di Gherardi*. Battista Franco introduced for cardinals and prelates, who did not want to show themselves in public, boxes (*stanze*) with *jalousies* (i.e. blinds); Vasari, VI, p. 583 f., *V. di Battista Franco*.

Serlio's directions for constructing the auditorium and the stage are to be seen in Figs. 345, 346. The stage, here enclosable, should rise towards the back by a ninth of its length; the front part of the stage at Vicenza was level to a depth of 12 feet and a width of 60, to accommo-

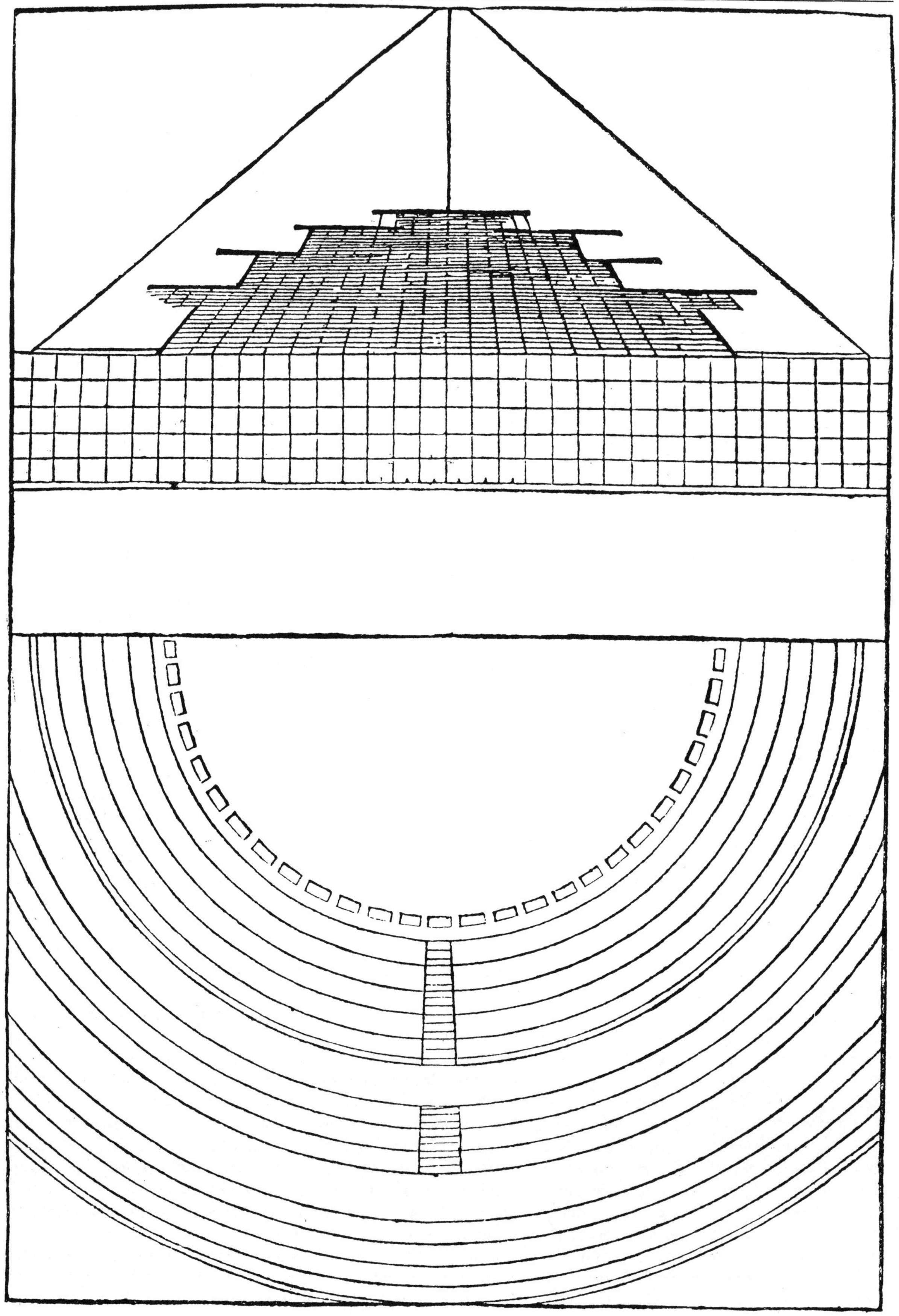

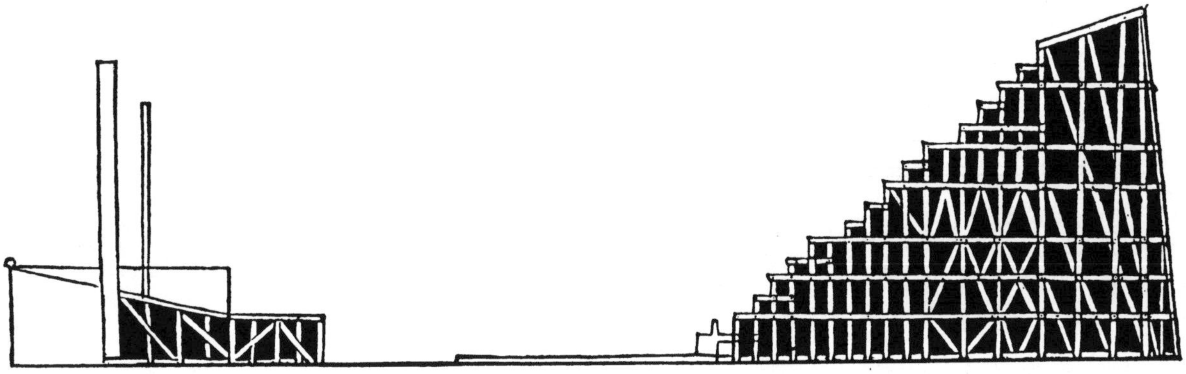

Fig. 345 *(opposite)* *Serlio, design for a theatre, plan and perspective*

Fig. 346 *(above)* *Serlio, design for a theatre, section*

date the ballets, in which even elephants had to appear. On this apron the buildings were not foreshortened in perspective.

Serlio did not locate the horizon, like others of the time, at the base of the back wall, but where the raked part of the stage met it (see "O" – at extreme left – in Fig. 346).

Palladio, contrary to the Antique and contemporary custom (cf. Serlio) gave the orchestra and *scena* the same level.

§ 193 *The* Scena

Earlier the *scena*, even for miracle-plays, had had only a setting of a generalised kind, but with the sixteenth century a definite indication of the place of the action, sometimes in a more idealised sense, sometimes more realistic, began to be used.

A theoretical and practical exposition of theatre organisation as a whole, *c* 1540, in Serlio, L. II, fol. 47 ff.

To begin with, the *scena* must often have represented a symmetrical ideal building with exits in the middle and at the sides; and with a number of pictures which together might constitute a frieze at the top; the whole space emphatically foreshortened; cornices, capitals etc. carved and projecting.

Thus the scenes in semi-religious presentations, Vasari, VI, p. 438 f., *V. di Aristotile*, "full of colonnades, niches, tabernacles, and statues, as were never seen before at such performances" (*c* 1532).

Thus, too, the "royal sala with two recesses, from which the narrators stepped out", in the first designs for scenery, mentioned in Vasari, V, p. 519, in the Commentary on the *V. di A. da Sangallo*.*

Also the play of *King Hyrcanus of Jerusalem* in Palladio's semicircle mentioned above, would have had such a *scena*. In its simplest elements, this type of scenery was often represented *c* 1500 in wide Florentine narrative paintings with many figures.

The other type of scene, and the one with which Serlio was concerned, comprised various buildings projecting as wings (as though there were a not very broad street in the central axis), "the smaller ones in front, the larger further back"; so that one saw the latter through the colonnades of the former; also a building closing the end; the whole sharply rising and diminishing at the same time. For comedies (Fig. 347) larger and smaller houses were chosen (tavern, bordello etc.) with upper loggie, balconies, and windows; for tragedies (Fig. 348) colonnades of princely splendour, with statues, also with a Triumphal Arch in the centre and so on; Serlio indeed also offers for a so-called "satyrical" drama (Fig. 350) a rustic scene with trees and cottages.

A Comic Scene of this more realistic type was done in 1515 by Baldassare Peruzzi, when the City of Rome celebrated the promotion of Giuliano de' Medici, brother of Leo X, to General of the Church; the rich and colourful invention of the houses, colonnades, windows etc. was admired; Vasari, IV, p. 595, *V. di Peruzzi*. Also the scenery for Bibbiena's comedy *Calandra*, which was given before Leo X, was full of different houses in *trompe l'oeil*, ibid., p. 600, cf. 610 n. If a still extant drawing by Peruzzi represents this *scena*, the background contained a number of buildings of Ancient Rome. (Serlio, end of Bk IV, praises Peruzzi's scenes, claiming that with all their beauty they would have cost less than anything of the kind before or after him.)

One may imagine similar scenes, where nothing specific has been recorded, for comedies in general and probably also for tragedies. Thus Vasari, III, p. 682, *V. di Indaco*; Vasari, V, p. 195, *V. di Franciabigio*; ibid., p. 341, *V. di Granacci*; ibid., p. 519, the second scenery designs mentioned in the Comm. on the *V. di Ant. da Sangallo*, in which the names are appended to the different houses; VI, p. 12, *V. di Lappoli*; ibid., pp. 316, 317, 330, *V. di Genga*; ibid., pp. 436–45, *V. di Aristotile*, apart from the exceptions mentioned above; ibid., p. 541, *V. di Rid. Ghirlandajo*; ibid., p. 583, *V. di Batt. Franco* (although one might imagine here a single idealised building, on account of the painted narratives and statues); VII, pp. 15, 27, *V. di Salviati*.

The *scena* of Palladio's Teatro Olimpico combined both:

* This is a reference to a drawing in the Uffizi, mentioned in the Commentary, but not referred to by Vasari himself. (PM).

Fig. 347 *Serlio, comic scene*

the splendid symmetrical building and (seen through five openings) the ascending streets with differing and asymmetrical buildings (Fig. 351).

That views of real buildings, even whole towns, appeared, is apparent from the passages on Peruzzi; in a decoration by Aristotile Pisa was recognisably represented. But so that one should not take such statements too literally, as the Prologue of Ariosto's *Negromante* warns us, the town represents Cremona –

So che alcuni diranno ch' ella è simile
E forse ancora ch' ella è la medesima
Che fu detta Ferrara, recitandosi
La Lena . . .

(another of the poet's comedies), but it was Carnival, when Cremona also might appear in the mask once worn by Ferrara.

§ 194 *Artistic Purpose of the* Scena

The ultimate aim sought by scene-designers was nevertheless in no instance illusion in our present sense, but an appearance of festive splendour, sufficiently captivating at the time for the poetry to be forgotten.

Serlio's directions include: how to make the moon rise; produce thunder and lightning; burn any desired object; set flying machines in motion; represent the sun by a crystal ball lit from behind (and make it move) . . .

Quite childish and directly opposed to our notion of illusion seem those so-called *pietre preziose*, with which the friezes of the buildings and the *scena* were ornamented; these were facetted cast vessels, either with coloured liquids or of polychrome glass, lit from behind; on the foreshortened surfaces of the buildings, it meant

Fig. 348 *Serlio, tragic scene*

that these also had to be shown in foreshortening, and also firmly fixed to prevent them being dislodged by the vibration of the ballets.

The windows as well, filled with coloured glass, paper, or cloth, were lighted like children's theatres today.

A rustic *scena*, installed by Genga for the Duke of Urbino, had all the leaves of trees and other greenery and flowers made of silk; on the banks of the water were a host of real sea-shells and corals, with which the splendid costumes of the shepherds and nymphs, the golden fishing-nets and sea-monsters composed of disguised human beings apparently harmonised excellently.

Very rightly, Serlio insisted on top-lighting by chandeliers for the stage, instead of the dubious effectiveness of the footlights in the modern theatre.

He cautions against characters being merely painted, but permits *intermezzi* by figures cut out of cardboard, whose lower extremities ran in a groove in the stage itself.

§ 195 *Fireworks and Table-Centres*

Fireworks were so developed in Italy towards the end of the fifteenth century that they were able to contribute a superior artistic character to festivities. (Also probably in Spain, cf. the firework display in Barcelona in 1501, in Hubert. Leodius, *De vita Friderici II Palatini*, L. II.)

Here, too, Florentines were indispensable. Phil. Beroaldus, op. cit. (§ 187): on the last evening of the *festa* there was a new and unfamiliar spectacle on the piazza in front of the palace (called by the people *Girandola* – i.e.

Fig. 349 *(above)* *Peruzzi, drawing for a stage scene, Florence, Uffizi*

Fig. 350 *(left)* *Serlio, satyric scene*

Fig. 351 *Vicenza, Teatro Olimpico*, scena

flame-circle), by a Florentine mechanic. (It seems to have misfired, but in spite of the cries of alarm and burnt clothing it gave pleasure because of its novelty.)

The theoretical work of Vanuccio Biringucci of Siena, *Pirotechnia*, 1st ed., Venice, 1540, was not available to me: regarding the author, cf. Milanesi, III, p. 124.

In Florence, what seems to have been an old custom had grown up for the Feast of S. John. The chief description of the Girandola in the first decades of the sixteenth century, rather obscure, in Vasari, VI, p. 92, *V. di Tribolo*, who, on the orders of Cosimo I (§ 56), removed the fantastic elements from fireworks and instead illuminated an octagonal Classical Temple. Cf. VI, p. 535, *V. di Rid. Ghirlandajo*, whose assistant Nunziata was famous in this speciality.

After fireworks, confectionery and table-decoration deserve notice, in so far as such things sometimes entailed great decorative and sculptural resource.

Occasionally indeed every dish was presented in fantastical form. An extreme example in Corio, *Stor. di Milano*, fol. 239 f., on the occasion of the marriage of a Visconti heiress to an English prince in 1368.

At the reception of Leonora by Cardinal Pietro Riario (§ 182, 187), Corio, fol. 417 ff., gilded delicacies, travestied dishes, e.g. a calf's head in the form of a unicorn, and one after another life-size mythological figures and groups, castles, all edible or stuffed with dainties; ships, wagons with oxen, even a mountain, from which a living man emerged to recite verses. There was more restraint at the Court of Ferrara at the celebrations in honour of the same Princess; *Diario Ferrar.*, in Murat., XXIV, col. 249; the confectionery modelled in every possible shape was handed over to the populace to be plundered.

Beroaldus, op. cit. (§ 187), leaves us with a rather extravagant impression of these pleasures; at the marriage described by him there were certainly plenty of frivolities, e.g. the animals still seemingly alive, deer gambolling about, porcupines with their quills still erect etc.; the real art was revealed, however, two days later at a dinner of a more intimate kind, with the most delicate figures and groups, probably made of gum tragacanth, which were then given to the guests as a present.

As a final vignette to conclude it may be worth mentioning a certain tastefully disposed trophy of game, with which an Abbot of Farfa received King Ferrante of Naples in 1476, on his journey to Rome: Jovian. Pontan., *De conviventia*.

Indices

There are two Indices, the first of names of architects and other artists and the second of places and buildings. In the case of major cities – Rome, Florence – sub-divisions have been introduced to help the reader to find any particular building quickly; the Cathedral comes first, followed by other churches, then secular buildings, with palaces and villas grouped together.

INDEX OF PERSONAL NAMES

Architects, Artists and Craftsmen

D'AGNOLO *see* BACCIO, DOMENICO, GABRIELE, and GIULIANO d'Agnolo
AGOSTINO di Duccio (da Firenze): 43, 98, 166, 210
ALBERTI, Giovanni and Alessandro: 258
ALBERTI, L. B.: 26, 27, 31, 32, 45, 54, 95, 102, 166
De re aedif.: 4, 31, 35–8, 39, 40, 46, 56, 57, 58, 78, 82, 106, 108, 116, 124–5, 133–5, 149, 162, 167, 169, 170, 172, 186–7, 188, 204, 209, 212, 215, 229, 236, 251
Della Pittura: 31, 75–6
S. Andrea, Mantua: 71, 97, 109
S. Francesco, Rimini: 76, 82
S. Maria Novella, Florence: 97, 238
S. Sebastiano, Mantua: 82
ALEOTTI: 269
ALESSI, Galeazzo: 38, 40, 73, 93, 112, 113, 156, 157, 158, 159, 160, 166, 183, 184, 187
ALLIO, Matteo and Tommaso: 199
AMADEO (Omodeo), G. A.: 25, 100, 199, 203
AMBROGIO d'Antonio da Milano: 99, 213
AMBROGIO Maggiore *see* MAGGIORE
AMBROGIO da Urbino: 49
AMMANATI, Bartolommeo: 67, 69, 132, 156, 157, 160, 167, 182, 218
AMMANATI, Giovanni: 224
ANASTAGI, Mariotto: 261
D'ANDREA *see* CARLO, GIOVANNI, and LAZZARO d'Andrea
ANDREA di Cosimo: 247
ANDREA da Fiesole: 195
ANGELICO, Fra: 229
D'ANTONIO *see* FRANCESCO and PIPPO d'Antonio
ANTONIO da Mantova: 226
ANTONIO di Marco: 107
ANTONIO, Marco: 201
ANTONISI, P.: 99
ARALDI, Alessandro: 247, 249
ARIGUZZI: 25, 77
ARNOLFO (di Cambio): 4, 20, 21, 77
ASPERTINI, Amico: 244
D'AURIA *see* DOMENICO d'Auria
AVERLINO *see* FILARETE

BACCHIACCA: 232
BACCIO d'Agnolo: 43, 60, 61, 139, 176, 225, 226, 227, 230, 232
BAMBAIA (Agostino Busti): 199, 209
BANCO, Nanni di, *see* NANNI
BANDINELLI, Baccio: 187, 188, 201, 210, 211, 217, 268
BARILE, Antonio: 225, 228, 230, 233
BARILE, Giovanni: 225, 226, 228, 229, 230
BAROZZI *see* VIGNOLA
BARTOLOMMEO, Fra: 230
BASTIANO, Corso di, *see* CORSO
BATTAGIO, G. B.: 54, 88, 125, 199, 247
BATTONI, Eusebio: 230
BECCAFUMI, Domenico: 236, 245, 256, 266, 268
BELLARATI: 88
BELLI, Valerio da Vicenza: 263
BELLINI, Giovanni: 229
BELTRAMO di Martino: 14
BENCI di Cione: 20, 57, 77, 156
BENEDETTO de' Benedetti: 39
BENEDETTO da Briosco: 100, 199, 203
BENEDETTO da Rovezzano *see* ROVEZZANO
BENOZZO Gozzoli *see* GOZZOLI
BERGAMASCO, Guglielmo: 151, 166
BERGAMO, Fra Damiano da, *see* DAMIANO
BERGAMO, Giovanni Batt.: 201
BERGAMO, Stefano da, *see* STEFANO
BERNARDI, Giovanni de': 264
BERNARDO di Lera: 46
BERNINI, Gianlorenzo: 170
BERTANO: 67
BERTINI, Domenico: 98
BETTINI, Giovanni: 97
BICCI, Neri di, *see* NERI
BOLOGNA, Giovanni da, *see* GIAMBOLOGNA
BOMBARDE, Giovanni delle: 223
BONFIGLI, Benedetto: 49, 249
BORGOGNONE, Ambrogio: 100, 109, 247
BOSCOLI, Marco: 195
BOTTICELLI: 229, 259
BRAMANTE: 25, 28, 29*n*, 35, 37, 40, 58, 59, 60, 64, 67, 79, 82, 87*ff*, 92, 99, 111, 122, 124, 125, 128, 142, 143, 144, 145, 147, 158, 159, 165, 173, 186, 187, 201, 216, 217, 235, 238, 247
S. Peter's: 8, 38, 71, 82, 88*f*, 91
Tempietto: 61, 63, 71, 88*f*
BRAMANTINO: 28, 225
BREGNO, Andrea: 151, 194, 199, 211
BRESCIA, Cristoforo, Girolamo, Raffaello, Stefano, and Vincenzo da, *see* CRISTOFORO, GIROLAMO, RAFFAELLO, STEFANO and VINCENZO da Brescia
BRESCIANO: 222
BRIOSCO, Benedetto, *see* BENEDETTO
BRONZINO: 232
BRUNELLESCO (Brunelleschi): 13, 26, 27, 33, 35, 36, 37, 39, 42, 43, 45, 54, 55, 56, 58, 64, 76, 78, 81–2, 104, 109, 121, 127, 128, 130, 162, 170, 192, 204, 226, 259
Florence Cathedral: 4, 21, 57, 78
S. Lorenzo, Florence: 71, 78, 82, 106, 121, 122, 123
S. Spirito, Florence: 4, 71, 78, 106
BRUNO di Lapo: 220
BRUOSCO (Bruoso) de' Benedetti: 39
BUGGIANO, Il (Lazzaro Cavalcanti): 37
BUON, Bartolommeo and Giovanni: 21
BUSTI, A., *see* BAMBAIA

CACCINI, Giovanni: 36, 201
CAGNOLA: 268
CALVI, Fabio: 29
CALVI, Lazzaro and Pantaleo: 201
CAMPI: 258
CANOZZI da Lendinara, family: 225, 227
CAPARRA, Niccolo Grosso da: 221
CAPRINO, Meo del: 97
CARADOSSO: 262, 263
CARAVAGGIO, Polidoro da, *see* POLIDORO
CARLO d'Andrea: 223
CARLONE, Taddeo: 217
CAROTA: 233
CAROTTO: 28, 232
CARPI, Girolamo da *see* GIROLAMO
CASTELNUOVO, Giovanni di Pietro: 228
CAVALCANTI, Lazzaro (Il Buggiano), *see* BUGGIANO
CECCO, Danese di, *see* DANESE
CECCO, Piero di, *see* PIERO
CELLINI, Benvenuto: 193, 223, 262, 263, 264
CERABALIA, Gio. Batt.: 221
CERANO *see* CRESPI
CERVELLESI, G. B.: 228
'CESARE': 268
'CESARINO': 262
CIACCHERI, A. Manetti, *see* MANETTI, A. C.
CIGOLI: 160
CIMABUE: 247
CIRIACO d'Ancona: 26, 28
CIVITALE, Matteo: 210, 213
CLEMENTI, P.: 209, 268
CLOVIO, Giulio: 238
CODUCCI (Codussi), Mauro: 46, 85, 107
COLA da Caprarola: 91
COLA dell' Amatrice: 98
CORREGGIO: 201, 232, 247, 249
CORSO di Bastiano: 98
CORTONA, Pietro da: 173
CORTONA, Urbano da: 194
COSIMO, Andrea di, *see* ANDREA
COSIMO, Piero di, *see* PIERO
COSINI, Silvio: 195, 203
COSMATI, The: 15, 191, 205, 236
COZZARELLI, Giacomo: 223
CRESPI (Cerano): 258
CRISTOFANO, Michel da Firenze: 195
CRISTOFORO da Brescia: 235
CRISTOFORO Ferrarese: 229
CRISTOFORO da Roma: 195, 199, 263
CRIVELLI, Carlo: 251

CRONACA, Il: 27, 42, 43, 55, 85, 109, 122, 147

DAMIANO da Bergamo, Fra: 225–6, 228, 238
DANESE di Cecco da Viterbo: 126
DANIELE da Volterra: 150, 246, 255–6
DESIDERIO da Settignano: 194, 195, 207, 223
DOLCEBUONO: 25, 38, 58, 88, 100, 109, 112
DOLCI, Giovanni de': 13
DOLCI, Marco de': 104, 233
DOMENICHINO: 184, 234
DOMENICO d'Agnolo: 225
DOMENICO di Auria: 197
DOMENICO da Capodistria: 81
DOMENICO di Niccolò: 224, 225, 228
DOMENICO di Pietro: 107
DONATELLO: 27, 194, 209, 212, 213, 216, 219, 220, 247, 251, 267
DONATO da Cernobbio: 98
DOSIO, G.-A.: 130
DOSSI, Dosso: 229, 243, 257
DUCA, Jacopo: 198
DUCCIO, Agostino di, *see* AGOSTINO
DUCCIO di Buoninsegna: 5
DÜRER, A.: 244

ELIA di Bartolommeo *see* LOMBARDO

FALCONETTO: 12, 28, 162, 166, 176, 247, 249, 255, 256
FEDELI, Francesco: 111
FEDERIGHI, Antonio: 43, 156, 194, 213
FELTRINI, Andrea: 233, 242, 251, 266
FERRARI, Gaudenzio: 201
FERRUCCI, Francesco di Simone: 194, 213
FIESOLE, Fra Angelico da, *see* ANGELICO
FIESOLE, Mino da, *see* MINO
FILARETE (A. Averlino): 11, 14, 23, 25, 26, 27, 32, 51, 55, 79, 83, 137, 162, 168, 171, 219
FINIGUERRA, Maso: 259, 260
FIORAVANTE, Neri di: 20
FIORAVANTE, Ridolfo: 135
FOLFI, M. di Zanobi: 64
FONTANA, Domenico: 67, 99
FORBICINI: 257
FORMENTONE: 151
FORMIGINE: 99, 158, 198
FORTEBRACCIO: 238
FOSSI, Francesco da Dozza: 151
FRANCESCO d'Antonio: 260
FRANCESCO di Giorgio (Martini): 25, 27, 29, 30, 32, 34, 79, 83, 98, 109, 139, 170
FRANCESCO del Guasta: 98
FRANCESCO del Guido: 121
FRANCESCO da Lugano: 98
FRANCESCO di Simone *see* FERRUCCI
FRANCESCO da Urbino: 236
FRANCIA, Francesco: 259
FRANCIABIGIO: 229
FRANCIONE: 79, 225, 228
FRANCO, Battista: 256, 265, 269
FULVIUS, Andreas (Fulvio): 29
FUMIANI: 235

GABRIELE d'Agnolo: 45, 141
GADDI, Taddeo: 55, 224*n*
GAGINI, A. and D.: 211
GAMBARA, Lattanzio: 239
GAROFALO: 251
GENGA, Girolamo: 29, 93*n*, 101, 147, 165, 178–9, 262, 273
GHERARDI, Cristofano: 256
GHIBERTI: 57, 212, 219, 259, 260, 264
GHINI, Simone di G.: 207, 209, 219
GHIRLANDAIO: 27, 28*n*, 259
GIACOMO da Pietrasanta: 40, 97, 99, 111, 175
GIAMBOLOGNA (Giovanni da Bologna): 216, 218, 219
GIOCONDA, Fra: 28, 30, 32, 55, 90, 112, 151
GIORDANO, Paolo: 260
GIORGIO, Francesco di, *see* FRANCESCO
GIORGIONE: 232, 243, 244
GIOTTO: 4, 113, 224, 247
GIOVANNI d'Andrea: 223
GIOVANNI Angelo Romano: 195
GIOVANNI de' Bernardi *see* BERNARDI
GIOVANNI da Nola: 197, 209, 211
GIOVANNI di Pietro da Brensa: 151
GIOVANNI da Siena: 134
GIOVANNI da Udine: 201, 217, 246, 252, 253
GIOVANNI da Verona, Fra: 85, 225, 226, 227, 228, 229
GIOVANNI da Vicenza: 199
GIROLAMO da Brescia: 106
GIROLAMO da Carpi: 186, 247
GIULIANO d'Agnolo: 225
GIULIO Romano: 13, 14, 25, 29, 39, 101, 113, 142, 144, 147, 156, 158, 169, 175, 176–8, 186, 187, 201, 245, 254, 265
GOBBO *see* SOLARI
GOZZOLI, Benozzo: 118, 150, 171, 174, 185
GRANACCI: 232
GRANDI, Ercole: 107
GROSSO *see* CAPARRA
GUARINI, Guarino: 94
GUERZO: 243
GUGLIELMO Bergamasco *see* BERGAMASCO
GUIDOTTI: 156

HOLBEIN, Hans the Younger: 242, 244, 262

INNOCENZO da Imola: 175

LAMPUGNANO, Giacomo: 88
LANDINI, Taddeo: 218
LAPO: 21
LAURANA, Luciano: 11, 139, 151, 166, 174*n*
LAZZARO d'Andrea: 213
LAZZARO de' Cavalcanti *see* CAVALCANTI
LENDINARA *see* CANOZZI
LEONARDO da Vinci: 32, 165, 238, 267, 268, 269
LEONI, L.: 14, 209
LEOPARDO, Alessandro: 112, 198, 210, 223
LIGORIO, Pirro: 174, 183, 186, 217
LIPPI, Filippino: 230, 247
LIPPI, Fra Filippo: 247
LOMBARDO (Lombardi) family: 207
LOMBARDO, Alfonso: 205
LOMBARDO, Elia di B.: 109
LOMBARDO, Girolamo: 223
LOMBARDO, Martino: 107
LOMBARDO, Pietro: 50, 122
LOMBARDO, Tullio: 49
LONATI: 88
LONGHENA, Baldassare: 158
LORENZETTO: 209
LOTTO, Lorenzo: 226
LOVINI, Aurelio and Evangelista: 201
LOVINO *see* LUINI
LUCANO, Battista: 92
LUGANO, Francesco da, *see* FRANCESCO
LUINI, B.: 201, 249
LUNGHI, Martino(?): 101

MADERNA (Maderno), Carlo: 258
MAGGI, Annibale: 151
MAGGIORE, Ambrogio: 203
MAJANO, Benedetto da: 36, 42, 43, 99, 194, 195, 203, 211, 213, 225, 228
MAJANO, Giuliano da: 24, 36, 43, 107, 139, 166, 174, 216, 225, 228
MALVITO, Tommaso: 220
MANETTI, Antonio Ciaccheri (Brunelleschi's assistant): 14, 82, 106
MANETTI, Antonio di Tuccio (Brunelleschi's biographer): 4, 13, 23, 27, 29, 76, 81, 106
MANGONE: 38
MANTEGNA: 14, 49, 55, 83, 242, 247, 249
MARCHISSI: 45
MARCO de' Dolci *see* DOLCI
MARCO da Faenza: 257
MARIANO di Tingo: 98
MARINNA, Il: 194, 211, 223
MARINO di Marco Cedrino: 24
MARTINO, Pietro di, *see* PIETRO
MASACCIO: 26
MASCHERINI (Mascherino), Ottavio: 102
MASO di Bartolommeo: 56
MASOLINO: 259
MATTIA di Tommaso da Reggio: 230
MATURINO: 243, 244
MAURO (F. Pociviano): 238
MAZZOLA, Girolamo: 249
MAZZONI: 144
MELOZZO da Forlì: 129, 247
MENZOCCHI, Francesco: 257
MEO del Caprino *see* CAPRINO
MICHEL Cristofano da Roma *see* CRISTOFANO
MICHELANGELO Buonarroti: 30, 38, 39, 79, 80, 92, 129, 130, 165, 167, 170, 182, 187, 194, 201, 209
  S. Peter's: 71, 79, 89, 90–91, 124, 212, 217, 223, 251, 256, 262
  Campidoglio (Capitol): 73, 256
  Pal. Farnese: 59, 144
  S. Lorenzo, Florence: 40, 60, 64, 100, 101, 104, 121, 122–3
  Laurenziana, Florence: 66, 79, 149, 233, 236
MICHELOZZO: 34, 39, 42, 82, 87, 121, 122, 128, 129, 135–7, 174, 194–5, 209, 210, 215, 260
MINO da Fiesole: 195, 207, 210
MINO (Minio), Tiziano: 221, 255
MINELLA, Pietro di, *see* PIETRO
MOIETTA: 203
MONACO, Guglielmo: 219
MONTELUPO, Raffaello da: 268
MONTERCHI (calligrapher): 238
MONTORSOLI: 187, 197, 217, 218*n*, 268, 269
MORANZONE (frame-maker): 230
MORMANDI (Mormandi): 123
MORO, Battista del: 243, 246
MORONE, Francesco: 249
MORONI, Andrea: 112
MORTO da Feltre: 251
MOSCA: 201, 212

NANNI di Banco: 57
NEGRONI, B. (Riccio): 225, 228
NERI di Bicci: 224
NERI di Fioravante: 57, 77
NICCOLÒ, Domenico di, *see* DOMENICO
NOLA, Giovanni da, *see* GIOVANNI
NUNZIATA: 275

OMODEO *see* AMADEO
ORMANNI, Antonio: 221
ORTO, Vincenzo dell', *see* VINCENZO

PACIOLI, Luca: 238
PAGNO di Lapo: 210
PALLADIO: 12, 13, 29, 38, 40, 66, 69, 73, 74, 80, 102, 110, 152, 154, 156, 158, 160, 162, 167, 172, 183, 269, 271
PALMA Vecchio: 229
PAOLO da Mantova: 226
PARMIGIANINO: 143, 201
PASQUINO di Matteo da Montepulciano: 220
PASTORINO: 256
PELLEGRINI, P. *see* TIBALDI
PENNI (Il Fattore): 201
PERINO del Vaga: 65, 121, 150, 188, 201, 246, 247, 252, 254–5, 256
PERUGINO: 49*n*, 81, 226, 230, 249, 251, 261, 262
PERUZZI, Baldassare: 5, 25, 28, 30, 33, 37, 46, 63, 69, 73, 74, 79, 89, 90*n*, 92, 94*n*, 109, 130, 132, 145, 147, 148, 162, 175, 182, 209, 214, 228, 245, 246, 256, 266, 271, 272
PERUZZI, Sallustio: 104
PESCIA, Piermaria da, *see* PIERMARIA
PETRUS de Capua: 58
PICININO, N.: 201
PIERINO da Vinci: 218*n*
PIERMARIA da Pescia: 263
PIERO di Cecco: 194, 212
PIERO di Cosimo: 229
PIERO della Francesca: 33
PIETRASANTA, Giacomo da, *see* GIACOMO
PIETRO da Cortona: 173
PIETRO di Domenico di Nozzo: 109
PIETRO di Martino: 166
PIETRO di Minella: 224
PINTURICCHIO: 249, 251, 252
PIPPO d'Antonio da Firenze: 99, 213
PIRONI, Girolamo: 199
PISANO, Andrea: 219
PISANO, Giovanni: 211
PISANO, Nicola: 19
POCETTI, B.: 257–8
POCIVIANO *see* MAURO
POLIDORO da Caravaggio: 243, 244
POLIPHILUS (Polifilo): 27, 32, 83, 185, 186
POLLAIUOLO: 83, 121, 209, 219, 259, 260, 261
PONSI: 83
PONTELLI, B.: 13, 85, 139, 165
PONTORMO: 232, 245
PORDENONE: 188, 201, 234, 238, 246
PORTA, Giacomo della: 91, 104, 107, 110, 144, 197, 258
PORTA, Giuseppe: 67, 234

QUERCIA, Jacopo della: 134, 194, 215

RAFFAELLE da Brescia, Fra: 225, 227
RAFFAELLINO del Garbo: 230
RAMO di Paganello: 4
RAPHAEL (Raffaello Sanzio): 27, 28–9, 30, 33, 38, 40, 60, 61, 63, 64, 65, 79, 81, 88, 89, 90, 92, 99, 100, 109, 112, 119, 122, 142, 143–4, 145, 147, 151, 158, 175, 184, 187, 192, 209, 217, 242, 243, 244, 245, 249, 252, 254, 262, 263, 265
RICCIO, Andrea: 209, 219, 222

RICHINI: 162
RIDOLFI, Bartolommeo: 255
RIGHETTO: 113
ROBBIA, Della (family): 121, 197, 201, 236, 249, 264
ROBBIA, Luca Della: 56, 210, 249, 264
ROCCHI, Cristoforo: 79, 111
ROCCO da Vicenza: 93, 210
RODARI, Tommaso: 100, 124, 211
ROMANINO: 231
ROMANO, Giovan-Angelo, *see* GIOVANNI
ROMANO, Giulio, *see* GIULIO
ROSSELLINO, Antonio: 121, 207, 211, 216
ROSSELLINO, Bernardo: 27, 43, 45, 54, 89*n*, 97, 98, 170, 194, 195, 215
ROSSETTI, Biagio: 45, 53, 55, 106, 107, 139
ROSSI, Properzia de': 198
ROSSO Fiorentino (Il Rosso): 201, 245
ROVEZZANO, Benedetto da: 195, 203, 214
ROVIGNO, Fra Sebastiano da, *see* SEBASTIANO
RUBENS: 268
RUSTICI, G. F.: 216, 218*n*

SACCA, Paolo: 227
SACCO, F. del: 13
SALVIATI, Francesco: 226, 234, 245
SANGALLO, Antonio da, the Elder: 36, 61, 63, 78, 83, 92, 106, 111, 165, 170, 227, 230
SANGALLO, Antonio da, the Younger: 29, 61, 79, 90, 92, 101, 102*n*, 109, 112, 119, 143, 144, 145, 146, 147, 150, 162, 167, 171, 184, 187, 209, 218
SANGALLO, Aristoyile da: 143, 269, 272
SANGALLO, Battista da: 30
SANGALLO, Francesco da: 143, 268
SANGALLO, Giuliano da: 24, 27, 28, 34, 37, 42, 55, 60, 63, 78, 81, 83–5, 90, 92, 100–101, 109, 127, 137, 139, 174, 207, 213, 225, 227
SANMICHELI, Michele: 6, 12, 79, 93, 109, 123, 141, 147, 166
SANSOVINO, Andrea: 14, 24, 34, 49, 100, 195, 209, 212, 221
SANSOVINO, Jacopo: 30, 50, 63, 64, 73, 76, 92, 100, 109, 130, 141, 142, 144, 152, 154, 170, 209, 212, 219, 255, 256, 268, 269
SANTACROCE, Girolamo: 197
SARTO, Andrea del: 132, 229, 259, 268
SCAMOZZI, Vincenzo: 66, 158, 160, 172
SCARPAGNINO: 151, 170
SCOTTO, Stefano: 201
SEBASTIANO da Rovigno, Fra: 227
SECCADINARI: 25
SEMINO, Andrea: 203
SEMINO, Ottavio: 201
SERAPION: 203
SEREGNO, Vincenzo: 159
SERLIO, Sebastiano: 12, 27, 29, 30, 32, 41, 46, 51, 59, 64, 65, 76, 94, 101, 111, 119, 128, 140, 146, 148–9, 152, 154, 162, 166, 168, 172–3, 174, 175, 187, 214, 231, 233, 244, 245, 268, 269–73
SETTIGNANO, Desiderio da, *see* DESIDERIO
SIGNORELLI, Luca: 247
SIMONE *see* TALENTI
SIMONE di G. Ghini *see* GHINI
SODOMA: 243, 249, 266, 268
SOLARI, Cristoforo (Il Gobbo): 93, 128
SONCINO: 201
SPAVENTO, Giorgio: 112
SQUARCIONE: 27, 247
STAGI: 201
STEFANO (Pupil of Titian): 229, 232
STEFANO da Bergamo: 228
STEFANO da Brescia: 235
STEFANO da Zevio: 239

TALENTI, Simone di Francesco: 156
TARAMELLI, A.: 93, 106, 113
TASSO family: 225, 233
TEMPESTA, Antonio: 257
TESTA: 227
TIBALDI (Pellegrini), Pellegrino: 25, 69, 93, 110, 124, 130, 156, 160, 212, 257
TINGO, Mariano di, *see* MARIANO
TINTORETTO: 234, 235
TITIAN: 188, 212, 229, 231, 234–5, 243, 244
TORRIGIANO: 249
TRIACHINI, Bartolommeo: 158
TRIBOLO: 13, 183, 188, 218, 233, 268
TRISSINO, G. G.: 179
TRISTANI, Alberto and Battista: 106
TRISTANI, Bartolommeo: 107
TROSO da Monza: 201, 225
TURINI, Giovanni da: 223, 260

UCCELLO: 203, 232
UDINE, Giovanni da, *see* GIOVANNI
URBANO da Cortona *see* CORTONA

VAGA, Perino del, *see* PERINO
VALERIO da Vicenza *see* BELLI
VALLE, della (Da Valle), Andrea: 113
VASARI, Giorgio the Elder: 265
VASARI, Giorgio: 14, 23, 24, 37, 65, 66, 69, 79, 85, 113, 150, 156, 182, 212, 234, 235, 257, 269
VASARI, Giorgio the Younger: 151
VECCHIETTA: 79, 194, 205, 223
VELLANO: 219
VENTURA di Ser Giuliano: 233
VERONESE, Paolo: 212, 234, 235
VERROCCHIO: 194, 213, 216, 219, 220, 259, 260
VIGNOLA, Giacomo Barozzi da: 30, 64, 66, 73, 74, 110, 113, 137*n*, 147, 156, 157, 167, 170, 182, 186, 187, 217, 226
VINCENZO da Brescia: 201
VINCENZO dell' Orto: 88
VINCENZO da Verona, Fra: 225, 226
VINCI, Leonardo da, *see* LEONARDO
VITO di Marco Tedesco: 23
VITONI, Ventura: 58, 79, 85
VITRUVIUS Pollio: 29, 30, 63, 65, 134, 172, 258
VOLTERRA, Daniele da, *see* DANIELE

ZACCAGNI, Bernardino: 93, 111
ZACCHI, Giovanni: 198
ZARABAJA *see* BAMBAIA
ZENALE, B.: 112, 128, 225
ZEVIO, Stefano da *see* STEFANO
ZUCCARO, Federigo: 256
ZUCCARO, Taddeo: 246, 265
ZUCCHI: 227

INDEX OF PLACE NAMES

ABBIATEGRASSO, Sta Maria: 99
ANCONA, Loggia de' Mercanti: 257
  Triumphal Arch: 59
AQUILA, S. Bernardino: 98
AREZZO, Cathedral: 4, 210
  Tarlati Monument: 203
  SS. Annunziata: 111
  Badia de' Cassinensi: 113
  Sta Maria delle Grazie: 36, 43, 99
  Misericordia: 60, 98, 132
  Pieve: 11
  Casa Montauti (di Vasari); 14
  Confraternità: 55
ASCOLI PICENO, S. Pietro: 39
ASSISI, S. Francesco: 19, 20, 126, 247
  Sta Maria degli Angeli: 113, 215
  Paving and streets: 169

BAALBEC: 40
BELLINZONA, fortifications: 165
BERGAMO, Cathedral: 79
  S. Bartolommeo, choirstalls: 225
  Colleoni Chapel: 6, 122, 199
  S. Domenico, choirstalls: 225
  Sta Maria Maggiore: 58, 226, 228
  Sta Maria della Misericordia: 219
  Colleoni's House: 249
BISSAGNO (Genoa), Villa Grimaldi: 184
BISSUCCIO (Varese), painted façade on Villa: 244
BOLOGNA (1 Churches, 2 Palaces, 3 Misc.)
  SS. Annunziata: 24
  S. Bartolommeo: 99, 107
  S. Domenico, Arca: 203
  – choirstalls: 225, 228, 238
  S. Giacomo Maggiore: 35, 53, 109, 236
  S. Giovanni in Monte: 24, 227
  Madonna di Galliera: 98
  S. Martino Maggiore: 53, 198
  S. Michele in Bosco: 129, 205, 227
  S. Petronio: 20, 25, 46, 212, 227, 236
  – model of church: 77
  Servi: 198
  Sto Spirito: 98
  Arcivescovado (Archbishop's Pal.): 130
  Pal. Apostolico: 229
  Pal. Bentivoglio: 139
  Pal. Bevilacqua: 35, 45, 53
  Pal. Fantuzzi: 158
  Pal. Fava: 53
  Pal. Malvezzi-Medici: 158
  Pal. of the Papal Legate: 135
  Pal. del Podestà: 45, 140, 150, 151
  Pal. della Viola: 175
  Pal. Zucchini: 160
  Doorknockers: 223
  Loggia de' Mercanti: 152
  Neptune Fountain: 218
  Portico delle Fioraie: 170
  Putte di Baracano: 162
  Street arcades, paving etc.: 168, 169, 170
  Torre Asinelli: 28
  University: 257
BOLSENA, Lake of, tempietti: 92
BRACCIANO, Pal. Orsini: 141
  Pal. Tagliacozzo: 139
BRESCIA, Old Cathedral: 81
  – Arca di Sta Apollonia: 203
  Sta Maria de' Miracoli: 85
  Pal. Comunale: 150, 151
  Piazza Vecchia: 170
BUSTO ARSIZIO (Milan), Sta Maria in Piazza: 87, 88

CAFFAGGIUOLO *see* FLORENCE, Villa Medici...
CAMERINO, SS. Annunziata: 36, 111
CAPRAROLA (Viterbo), Pal. Farnese: 74, 147, 182, 217, 256
CAPUA, Cathedral: 126
CAREGGI *see* FLORENCE, Villa Medici...
CARPI, Cathedral: 30
CASALE SALONE (nr Rome), Villa Trivulzio: 256
CASTELFRANCO, Villa Soranza: 178
CASTELLO (Florence), Villa Medici: 183, 188
CASTEL RIGONE (Perugia), Sta Maria de' Miracoli: 98
CASTIGLIONE DEL LAGO (Perugia), Castle: 183
CASTRO (Lago d' Iseo), demolished in 1649: 171
CESENA, Library: 129
CITTÀ DI CASTELLO, Cathedral: 109
  Sta Maria Maggiore: 24
  Pal. Vitelli: 256
CIVITA CASTELLANA, Cathedral: 15, 37
  Fortress: 165
CIVITA VECCHIA, Harbour fort: 165
COLOGNE, S. Gereon: 81
COMO, Cathedral: 100, 123–4, 199, 201, 211
  – Porta delle Sirene: 201
  S. Fedele: 15, 87
CONIGO (nr Binasca): 98
CONSTANTINOPLE, SS. Sergius and Bacchus: 58
CORA, Temple: 29
CORNETO (Tarquinia), Pal. Vitelleschi: 55, 135
CORSIGNANO *see* PIENZA
CORTONA, Cathedral: 36, 55, 106
  S. Domenico: 56
  Sta Maria del Calcinaio: 98, 109
  – model for: 79
  Model for church (A. da Sangallo): 78
CREMA, Sta Maria della Croce: 54, 88
CREMONA, Cathedral: 203
  Baptistry: 16, 87
  S. Lorenzo, Tomb of S. Mauro: 203
  S. Luca, Capp. del Cristo Risorto: 88
  S. Pietro, Doric cloister: 13
  Umiliati: 128
  S. Vincenzo: 195
  Monte di Pietà: 198
  Pal. Sansecondo: 199
  Pal. Trecchi: 46
  Paving and streets: 168, 201
  Torrazzo: 113
CRICOLI (Vicenza), Villa Trissino: 12, 179

DERUTA, Piazza and waterworks: 7

EMPOLI, Cathedral: 16

FABRIANO, Hospital: 23
  Piazza: 170
FAENZA, Cathedral: 36, 39, 107
  – Tomb of S. Savinus: 203
  Loggia del Comune: 170
FARFA, Monastery plan: 126
FERRARA: 171, 216
  Cathedral tower: 3, 118
  S. Benedetto: 106, 247, 251
  S. Cristoforo: 54
  S. Francesco: 106
  Sta Maria in Vado: 107
  House façades painted: 239
  Palazzina: 183, 257
  Pal. de' Diamanti: 45
  Pal. Roverella: 51
  Pal. Saracco: 215
  Pal. Schifanoia: 7, 175
  Pal. della Scrofa: 53, 139
  Model of city: 77
  Seminary: 251
  Streets and paving: 168, 169
  Villa Belvedere: 175
  Villa Montana: 175
FIESOLE, Cathedral: 34
  Badia: 4, 11, 16, 36, 39, 109, 123, 127, 194, 207, 213
  Villa Ricasoli: 174
FLORENCE (1 Cathedral and churches, 2 Public Buildings, 3 Palaces, 4 Villas, 5 Misc.)
  Cathedral: 3, 4, 55, 77, 79, 125, 201, 203, 212, 236
  – Arca di S. Zenobio: 212
  – Campanile: 113
  – Cupola: 20, 57, 58, 78
  – Façade: 11, 12, 99, 101, 267–8
  – Tomb of Brunellesco: 203–4
  S. Ambrogio: 210
  SS. Annunziata: 36, 82, 132, 195, 210, 212
  SS. Apostoli: 16, 17, 210
  Badia: 195, 207, 210, 228
  Baptistry (S. Giovanni): 16–17, 36, 54, 85, 87, 260
  – Bronze doors: 219
  Certosa: 9, 39, 129, 213, 253
  Sta Croce: 39, 56, 83, 121, 195, 204, 207, 210, 212, 213, 221, 227, 229
  – Second Court: 128
  – Pazzi Chapel: 35, 37, 54, 55, 56, 58, 64, 78, 82, 83, 85, 121, 229, 249
  Sta Felicita: 83, 121
  S. Francesco al Monte (S. Salvatore): 55, 109
  S. Gallo, monastery of: 130
  Gesuati, Convent of: 129, 130, 229
  S. Giovanni *see* Baptistry
  S. Jacopo sopr' Arno: 58
  S. Lorenzo: 35, 40, 55, 60, 64, 71, 78, 79, 100–101, 104, 106, 123, 194, 195, 201, 213
  – New Sacristy (Medici Chapel): 121, 122–3, 209
  – Old Sacristy: 58, 82, 83, 121, 216, 219, 220, 251
  S. Marco: 83, 121, 128, 258
  – Library: 129
  Sta Maria degli Angeli: 9, 78, 81, 85
  Sta Maria Maddalena de' Pazzi: 37, 39, 109, 230
  – Ionic capital: 34
  Sta Maria Novella: 58
  – Façade: 46, 55, 97, 238
  – Interior: 125, 213, 227
  – Lavabo: 197
  S. Michele *see* Or S. Michele
  S. Miniato al Monte: 16, 54, 83, 195, 210, 249
  – Chapel of Cardinal of Portugal: 121, 207, 236
  Or S. Michele: 4, 60
  S. Pancrazio: 37
  S. Pier Scheraggio: 17
  S. Salvatore *see* S. Francesco al Monte
  Lo Scalzo: 132
  Sto Spirito: 4, 35, 71, 78, 106, 201, 221, 230
  – Sacristy: 34, 55, 79, 83, 122
  SS. Trinità: 207
  – Cappella Strozzi: 35
  Archbishop's Pal. (Arcivescovado): 130
  Bargello *see* Pal. del Podestà
  Biblioteca Laurenziana: 66, 79, 233, 253
  – Floor: 233, 236
  – Stair: 148
  Fortezza da Basso: 165, 245
  Loggia degli Innocenti *see* Spedale...
  Loggia de' Lanzi: 36, 154, 216
  Pal. del Podestà (Bargello): 150, 195, 203
  Pal. della Signoria (Pal. Vecchio): 147, 150, 216, 228, 229, 233, 235
  – Capital by Michelozzo: 34
  Spedale degli Innocenti (Foundling Hospital): 78
  – Loggia: 14, 36, 78, 162, 258
  – Window: 55
  Spedale di Sta Maria Nuova: 162
  Uffizi: 37, 69, 158, 229, 257
  Pal. Antinori: 42, 43
  Pal. Bartolini: 43, 60, 61, 73, 139
  Pal. Gondi: 39, 42, 55, 73, 137, 213
  Pal. Guadagni: 43, 73
  Pal. Levi: 139
  Pal. Medici (Riccardi): 73, 135, 195
  – Chapel: 236
  – Court: 39
  – Façade: 42
  – Garden: 186, 216, 218
  – Model: 78
  Pal. Nonfinito: 160
  Pal. Pandolfini: 61, 73, 143, 151, 238
  Pal. di Parte Guelfa: 45, 55
  Pal. Pazzi-Quaratesi *see* Quaratesi
  Pal. Pitti: 9, 42, 54, 73, 135, 160
  – Court: 69, 258
  Pal. Quaratesi: 39, 43, 55
  Pal. Riccardi *see* Medici
  Pal. Roselli: 139, 214
  Pal. Rucellai: 45, 54, 61
  Pal. Serristori: 139
  Pal. Stiozzi-Ridolfi (Casa Stiozzi): 37, 176
  Pal. Strozzi: 42, 43, 54, 73, 147
  – Lantern and torch-holders: 221
  Pal. Uguccioni: 64, 73, 143*n*, 151
  Pal. Vecchio *see* Pal. della Signoria
  Villa Castello: 217–18
  Villa Medici at Caffaggiuolo: 174, 215
  Villa Medici at Careggi: 174, 185, 188, 215, 216

Villa Medici at Poggio a Caiano: 78, 174
Villa Medici at Trebbio: 174
Villa Michelozzi at Bellosguardo: 174
Villa Mozzi: 174
Boboli Gardens: 218
Loggia de' Medici: 154
Loggia Rucellai: 156
Model of city: 79
Piazza dell' Annunziata: 170
– della Signoria: 170, 218
Ponte Sta Trinita: 167
Streets and paving: 168, 169
FOLIGNO, Church: 92
Hospital: 162
FORLÌ, Palace: 6
FRASCATI, Villa Aldobrandini: 183
Villa Mondragone: 183

GENNAZZANO (nr Rome), Pal. Colonna: 135
GENOA, Cathedral, choirstalls: 228
– Capp. S. Giovanni: 122, 197
SS. Annunziata: 107
Madonna delle Vigne: 69
Sta Maria in Carignano: 63, 93
S. Siro: 69
Pal. Doria: 65, 187, 214, 254
– G. Doria: 246
Pal. Ducale (Doge's Pal.): 160
Pal. Pessagno: 244
Pal. Sauli: 160, 183
Villa Cambiaso: 183
Villa Pallavicini: 183, 187
Villa 'Paradiso' (Podenas): 183
Villa Scassi: 183
Gate on Molo Vecchio: 166
Piazza dell' Agnello: 244
– Fossatello: 197, 201
University: 132
GROSSETO, Cathedral: 5
GROTTAFERRATA, Fortress: 165
GUBBIO, Pal. Ducale: 139

IMOLA, Pal. Sforza: 45

JERUSALEM, Dome of the Rock: 81

LEGNANO (nr Milan), S. Magno: 88

LODI, Sta Maria Incoronata: 83, 87, 88, 93, 125, 247
LORETO, Cathedral: 24
Santa Casa: 201, 257
Pal. Apostolico: 63
LOUVAIN, S. Pierre, model: 77
LUCCA, Cathedral: 210, 213, 229
– Tomb of Ilaria del Carretto: 194
S. Frediano: 123
Pal. del Pretorio: 151
LUGANO, Cathedral: 100, 199

MAGGIANO, Certosa: 228
MALPAGA, Colleoni's House: 6
MANTUA, Cathedral: 6, 101, 113
S. Andrea: 39, 71, 97, 109, 209
S. Benedetto: 113
S. Sebastiano: 82, 97*n*
Pal. Ducale (Reggia, Castello di Corte): 147, 254
Pal. del Te: 6, 64, 158, 176–8, 246, 254
Villa Marmirolo: 178, 187
House of Giulio Romano: 14, 254
House of Mantegna: 14
Streets: 169
MARCIANO (nr Monte Sansovino), Chiesa del Crocifisso: 99
MARMIROLO *see* MANTUA
MESSINA, Fountains by Montorsoli: 217
MILAN, Cathedral: 3, 6, 23, 25, 79, 209, 257
S. Ambrogio, Atrium: 99
– Canonica: 35, 79, 128
– Court: 128
– Monastery: 129
Sta Babila: 58
S. Celso: 58
S. Eustorgio: 87, 121, 209
S. Fedele: 110, 124
S. Lorenzo: 15, 37, 81, 87, 89, 92
Sta Maria delle Grazie: 24, 53, 56, 87, 88, 199, 209, 227
Sta Maria Incoronata: 24
Sta Maria della Passione: 93, 109
Sta Maria presso S. Celso: 53, 55, 88, 112, 128, 258
Sta Maria presso S. Satiro *see* S. Satiro
Monastero Maggiore (S. Maurizio): 25, 38, 58, 109, 247
S. Satiro (Sta Maria presso S. Satiro): 82
– Choir by Bramante: 125
– Façades: 53, 98
– Sacristy: 83, 87, 122, 201
S. Sepolcro: 58
Pal. Marino: 158, 160
Pal. Marliani: 51
Pal. del Senato *see* Collegio Elvetico
Pal. Visconti (destroyed): 23
Pal. Vismara (Casa Vismara, Pal. Medici): 137, 233
Arcivescovado (Archbishop's Pal.): 69, 130, 160
Arco del Sempione: 268
Brera: 132
Broletto: 53
Casa Frigerio: 53
Casa Leoni (degli Omenoni): 14, 158
Casa Vismara *see* Pal. Vismara
Castello Sforzesco: 6, 53, 165, 186
Collegio Elvetico (Pal. del Senato): 38
Collegio de' Nobili: 158
Ospedale Maggiore: 6, 11, 162
– Court: 53
– Façade: 198
– Windows: 25, 51
Streets and paving: 168, 169
MODENA, S. Pietro: 54, 98
MONGIOVINO, Sta Maria: 93
MONTE AMIATA, Villa of Cardinal Sta Croce: 178, 184
MONTECASSINO, Monastery: 129
MONTEFIASCONE, Papal Palace: 23
Church: 92
MONTEPULCIANO, Madonna di S. Biagio: 63, 78, 83, 92, 119
Pal. Ricci: 148
MONTE SANSOVINO, Sansovino's House: 14
MONZA, Cathedral: 51
MURANO (Venice), SS. Piero e Paolo: 107

NAPLES, Cathedral: 220
S. Angelo a Nilo: 39, 209
Sta Chiara: 121
S. Filippo: 107
S. Giacomo degli Spagnuoli: 209
S. Giovanni a Carbonara: 123, 211, 236
Sta Maria delle Grazie: 109
Sta Maria Incoronata: 247
Monte Oliveto: 109, 211
Pontanus' Chapel: 123
S. Severino: 123, 129, 228
Pal. Colobrano: 45
Pal. Cuomo: 45
Pal. Gravina (Post Office): 45, 141
Pal. Poggio Reale *see* Villa Poggio …
Castel Nuovo: 150
– Triumphal Arch: 59, 166, 219
Fountain nr Sta Lucia: 197
La Sapienza: 74
Museum: 263, 264
Porta Capuana: 166
Streets and paving: 169, 170
Villa Poggio Reale, *modello*: 11, 78, 137, 174
– Garden: 185, 216
NARNI, Cathedral: 99
NEPI, Fortifications: 165
NÎMES, Amphitheatre: 40
NONANTULA (Modena), Monastery: 126
NOVARA, Baptistry: 88
S. Gaudenzio: 110

OLYMPIA, Philippeion: 50
ORCIANO (nr Sinigaglia), Sta Maria Maggiore: 85
ORVIETO, Cathedral: 20, 23, 212, 213, 221, 247
– Stalls: 224, 226
Palace: 21
OSTIA, Castello: 165
New city: 171

PADUA, Cathedral: 113
S. Antonio (Il Santo): 121, 126, 199, 212, 219, 221, 227, 255, 260
Carmine: 110
Eremitani: 210, 247, 249
Sta Giustina: 63, 112, 129, 226, 231
Capp. di S. Prosdocimo *see* Sta Giustina
Il Santo *see* S. Antonio
Palace of Ezzelino: 23
Pal. Giustiniani: 12, 162, 176, 254
Carrara Residence: 242
'Collegio del Cardinale': 130
Loggia del Consiglio: 55, 74, 151
'Ox' Inn: 162
Porta S. Giovanni: 166
– Portello: 166
– Savonarola: 166
The Salone: 150
University: 130
Vescovado (Bishop's Palace): 130, 236
Voting Urn: 223
PALERMO, Cathedral: 211
S. Martino: 228
Sta Zita: 211
Museo: 211
Garden: 185
PALMANOVA (Udine), Fortifications: 171
PALO, Castello: 165
PARMA, Cathedral: 209, 229, 249
S. Giovanni: 111, 227, 247
S. Paolo: 236, 249
La Steccata: 93, 247
Model of city: 77
Piazza: 170
Theatre in Pal. Farnese: 269
PAVIA, Cathedral: 111
– Model: 79
Certosa: 6, 35, 49, 53, 55, 56, 60, 88, 100, 127, 129, 198, 199, 203, 249
Sta Maria di Canepanova: 87, 88, 93
Bridge over Ticino: 167
Castello: 6, 21, 249
Palace opposite Carmine: 53
Streets and paving: 169
Vescovado (Bishop's Palace): 130
PERUGIA, Cathedral: 5, 213
S. Agostino: 226
S. Bernardino: 60
– Confraternity of: 98, 132
S. Domenico: 5, 210, 211
Madonna della Luce: 98
S. Pietro: 121, 228
Cambio: 228, 249
Castle of B. da Montone: 135
Fontana grande: 215
Pal. de' Tribunali: 54
Porta S. Pietro: 43, 166
Streets and paving: 168, 169
PESARO, S. Giovanni Battista: 93*n*
Palace: 186
Pal. Prefettizio: 151
Villa Imperiale: 147, 178–9
PESCIA, Madonna di Piazza: 37
PIACENZA, Sta Maria di Campagna: 5, 93
S. Sepolcro: 113
S. Sisto: 106, 122, 247
Casa Pozzo, garden: 188
Pal. Farnese: 157
Pal. Landi: 199
Pal. Tribunali *see* Pal. Landi
Streets and paving: 168, 169
PIENZA: 8, 11, 171
Cathedral: 36, 39, 55, 97, 111, 125, 228
Pal. Newton (Ammanati): 54
Pal. Piccolomini: 43, 45, 54, 61, 137, 145, 149, 154
Pal. del Pretorio: 151
Piazza and town plan: 170, 171
Vescovado (Bishop's Palace): 130
PISA, Cathedral: 125, 201, 203, 219, 228
– Holy water basin: 213
Baptistry: 3–4
Campanile (Leaning Tower): 15, 113, 154
Campo Santo: 126
Arcivescovado (Archbishop's Palace): 130
Pal. Gambacorti, garden: 185
University, Court: 130
PISTOIA, Cathedral: 249, 260
Baptistry: 11
Sta Maria dell' Umiltà: 58, 79, 83, 85
Ospedale del Ceppo: 162
Pal. del Comune: 228
Pal. del Podestà: 150
Pal. del Tribunali: 245
POGGIO a Caiano *see* FLORENCE, Villa Medici
POLA (Yugoslavia), Amphitheatre: 40, 42
PRAGUE, S. Charles: 81
PRATO, Cathedral, outside pulpit: 213
– Bronze screen: 220
Sta Maria delle Carceri: 55, 58, 83
PRATOLINO (nr Florence), Villa Medici: 183

RAVENNA, Cathedral: 104
S. Apollinare in Classe: 7
S. Severo: 7
S. Vitale: 92
Mausoleum of Galla Placidia: 7
RIMINI, S. Francesco ('Tempio Malatestiano'): 6–7, 39, 76, 82, 95
Arch of Augustus: 97
RIVA (Lago di Garda), Sta Maria Inviolata: 93
RIVA (Switzerland), Sta Croce: 93

ROME (1 Ancient, 2 Christian, i S. Peter's, ii Churches, iii The Vatican, iv Other palaces, v Villas, vi Misc.)
Amphitheatrum Castrense: 40–41, 50
Arch of the Goldsmiths: 192
Arch of Titus: 39
Basilica Aemilia: 61
– of Constantine: 111
Campagna, tombs in: 50
Castor and Pollux, Temple of: 192
Cecilia Metella, Tomb of: 42
Colosseum: 39, 40, 59, 252
Diocletian, Baths of (Sta Maria degli Angeli): 129, 252
Marcellus, Theatre of: 39, 61, 74
'Minerva Medica', Temple of: 82 83
Pantheon, The: 57, 59, 60, 61, 63, 73, 81, 92, 219
Porta Maggiore: 42
Septizonium: 38
Titus, Baths of: 192, 251, 252
S. Peter's
– Old S. Peter's: 104, 125, 207, 210, 216, 219, 236
– Benediction Loggia: 40, 99
– New S. Peter's: 38, 60, 64, 71, 79, 82, 88–91, 101, 111, 119, 124, 209, 212, 256, 258
S. Agostino: 40, 97, 111, 212
SS. Apostoli: 99, 104
Aracoeli *see* Sta Maria in Aracoeli
Sta Caterina de' Funari: 102
Sta Cecilia: 249
S. Crisogono: 15
S. Eligio degli Orefici: 38, 92
Il Gesù: 110
S. Giacomo degli Incurabili: 92, 94*n*, 162
S. Giovanni Decollato: 132
S. Giovanni de' Fiorentini: 30, 79, 92–3
S. Giovanni in Laterano (S. John Lateran): 67, 99, 122, 126, 209, 210, 236
– Scala Santa: 67
– Baptistry: 92
S. Gregorio Magno: 212
S. Lorenzo in Damaso: 64, 112, 144
S. Lorenzo fuori: 15
S. Luigi de' Francesi: 104
S. Marcello: 109
S. Marco: 8, 40, 56, 99, 104, 233
Sta Maria degli Angeli (Baths of Diocletian): 129, 223, 252
Sta Maria dell' Anima: 98, 111
Sta Maria in Aracoeli: 126, 249
Sta Maria di Loreto: 92
Sta Maria Maggiore: 99, 104, 122, 207, 210, 233
Sta Maria sopra Minerva: 207, 228, 238, 258
Sta Maria de' Monti: 71, 104, 110, 258
Sta Maria in Navicella (in Domenica): 99
Sta Maria dell' Orto: 101
Sta Maria della Pace: 85, 109, 128, 201, 207
Sta Maria del Popolo: 40, 64, 71, 82, 97, 111, 122, 195, 207, 209, 210, 211, 236, 249, 256, 260
Sta Maria Traspontina: 104
Sta Maria in Trastevere: 15, 234
Sta Maria in Via Lata: 99
S. Paolo fuori: 15, 58, 104, 126, 210
S. Pietro in Montorio: 55, 98, 109
– Tempietto: 60, 63, 71, 88
S. Pietro in Vincoli: 78, 99, 129
Sto Spirito (*see also* Spedale di Sto S.): 56, 102, 109, 118, 119, 162
Sto Stefano Rotondo: 82
Vatican: 7, 79, 217, 238
Appartamento Borgia: 58, 249, 251, 252
Biblioteca: 145, 257
Braccio Nuovo: 145, 187
Casino di Pio IV *see* Villa Pia
Cortile di Belvedere: 37, 63, 145, 217
– Villa Belvedere: 175, 187
– Stair: 147
Cortile di S. Damaso: 145, 252
Giardino della Pigna: 69, 100, 145, 173, 187, 217
Library *see* Biblioteca
The Loggie: 64, 252
Sala Ducale: 257
Sala Regia: 150, 255
Sistine Chapel: 64, 212, 236, 251, 256
Stanze: 226, 227, 229, 236, 249
– dell' Incendio: 249
– della Segnatura: 249
'Stufetta': 184
Villa Belvedere *see* Belvedere
Villa Pia (Casino di Pio IV): 174, 183, 197
Palaces
Pal. Branconio dell' Acquila: 61, 143, 144
Pal. della Cancelleria: 45, 60, 61, 63, 67, 142, 143, 144, 146, 147, 256
Pal. Capranica: 55
Pal. Caprini (House of Raphael): 64, 142, 143, 158
Pal. Cicciaporci: 142
Pal. de' Conservatori: 38, 256
Pal. Farnese: 59, 72, 73, 137, 142, 143, 144, 147, 157, 159, 233, 245, 246
– Court: 40, 144, 145
Pal. di Firenze: 137
Pal. Giraud-Torlonia: 45, 142, 143, 146
Pal. Lancelotti: 144, 243
Pal. Lante: 144
Pal. Linotte: 145, 146
Pal. Maccarani: 142
Pal. Massimi: 72, 74, 214, 233
– Façade: 145
– Court: 37, 146
Pal. Negroni: 72
Pal. Niccolini: 142
Pal. Ossoli: 73
Pal. Ruspoli: 143, 157
Pal. Sacchetti (Sangallo's House): 14
Pal. S. Biagio *see* Pal. dei Tribunali
Pal. Sciarra: 143
Pal. de' Senatori: 73, 217
Pal. Sora: 143
Pal. Spada: 144
Pal. Stoppani: 73
Pal. dei Tribunali: 8, 143, 144
Pal. della Valle: 144, 186
Pal. di Venezia: 8, 43, 45, 54, 139, 143, 150, 238
– Court: 39, 144
Pal. Vidoni-Caffarelli: 64, 142, 143
Villas
Villa Borghese: 184
Villa Farnesina: 63, 64, 73, 145, 147, 175, 243, 251, 252
– Sala delle Prospettive: 33, 246
Villa Giulia (Vigna di Papa Giulio III, now Etruscan Museum): 38, 182, 187, 217, 256
Villa Lante: 176, 184, 254
Villa Madama: 60, 175–6, 179, 187, 188, 217, 252
Villa Magliana: 174
Villa Mattei: 184
Villa Medici: 184
Villa Montalto-Negroni: 183
Villa Pia (Casino di Pio IV) *see* Vatican
Villa Sacchetti: 173
Misc.
Borgo: 7, 170, 171
Capitol: 170
Castel S. Angelo: 247, 251, 254
Collegio Romano: 67, 132
Fontana delle Tartarughe: 218
– di Trevi: 216
Lateran *see* S. Giovanni Laterano
Orti Farnesiani: 186, 187, 217
Ponte Sisto: 8, 167, 169
– S. Angelo: 167, 169
Porta Maggiore *see* Ancient Rome
– Pia: 167
– del Popolo: 167
– Sto Spirito: 167
La Sapienza (University): 130
Spedale di Sto Spirito (*see also* Sto Spirito): 56, 162
Streets and paving: 168
Vigna di Papa Giulio *see* Villa Giulia
SALERNO, Cathedral, atrium: 126
SARONNO, Church: 88
SAVONA, Pal. of Cardinal della Rovere: 78
'SFORZINDA' (Filarete's imaginary city): 14, 171
SIENA, Cathedral: 5, 123, 194, 213, 221, 223, 224, 226, 228, 236, 247, 249, 252, 260
– Piccolomini Altar: 211
S. Agostino: 221
S. Bernardino: 132, 233
Sta Caterina: 98, 132
S. Domenico: 107, 109, 194
Fontegiusta: 111, 194, 211, 223
S. Francesco: 107
Innocenti (S. Sebastiano): 83
Sta Maria delle Nevi: 98
Sta Maria della Scala: 228
Osservanza: 260
Servi: 36, 39, 107
Pal. Bandini-Piccolomini: 43
Pal. Chigi: 233
Pal. della Ciaia: 139
Pal. del Magnifico: 223
Pal. Marsigli: 11, 24
Pal. della Mercanzia: 152
Pal. Nerucci: 43
Pal. Piccolomini: 43, 54
Pal. Pubblico: 19, 194, 228, 256
Pal. Sansedoni: 11
Pal. Spannocchi: 43, 55
Fonte Gaia: 215
Fontegiusta *see* Churches
Loggia del Papa: 156
Loggia degli Uniti (de' Nobili): 152, 156, 194, 212, 256
Piazza: 170
Hospital: 23
Streets and paving: 168, 169
Villa Belcaro: 182
– Staircase: 148
Villa Colomba: 182
SPALATO: 37, 38
SPELLO, Cathedral: 210
SPOLETO, Cathedral: 99, 213
Manna d' Oro: 93
Sta Maria di Loreto: 94
Pinacoteca: 195
SULMONA, Pal. della Nunziata: 55
TERRANUOVA (nr Florence), Poggio's Garden: 186
TIVOLI, Hadrian's Villa (Villa Adriana): 251
Villa d' Este: 183, 186, 187, 188, 217
TODI, Sta Maria della Consolazione: 63, 71, 91
TREVISO, Vescovado (Bishop's Pal.): 247
TRIER, Liebfrauenkirche: 81
TURIN, Cathedral: 97

UDINE, Arcivescovado (Archbishop's Pal.): 253
URBANIA (Marche), Sta Maria di Riscatto: 87
URBINO, S. Bernardino: 93*n*
S. Domenico: 56
Pal. Ducale: 7, 139, 150, 193, 197, 213, 233, 246
– Court: 54

VALLOMBROSA, Monastery: 127
VATICAN *see* ROME, Vatican
VENICE (*see also* MURANO) (1 Churches, 2 Scuole, 3 Pal. Ducale (Doge's Palace), 4 Other palaces, 5 Misc.)
S. Andrea: 46
SS. Apostoli: 122
Sta Elena: 227, 236
S. Fantino: 113
S. Francesco della Vigna: 76, 109, 256
S. Giorgio Maggiore: 5, 102, 113
– Refectory: 129
S. Giovanni Cristomo: 3, 50, 85
SS. Giovanni e Paolo: 207
– Vendramin Monument: 71, 198, 207
S. Marco (S. Mark's): 112, 226, 227, 228, 249, 260
– Campanile: 116, 119
– Zeno Chapel: 204, 207, 209, 210, 219
Sta Maria de' Frari, Bellini Altarpiece: 230–31
Sta Maria de' Miracoli: 3, 50, 122, 123, 198
Sta Maria dell' Orto: 235
Sta Maria della Salute: 222
S. Martino: 92
S. Michele in Isola: 46, 49, 107, 122
S. Pantaleone: 235
Il Redentore: 102, 110
S. Salvatore: 71, 112, 129
S. Sebastiano: 238
S. Zaccaria: 24, 50, 107
Scuola di S. Giovanni Evangelista: 132
– di S. Marco: 50, 74, 132, 140, 198
– di S. Rocco: 50, 132, 140, 150
Doge's Palace (Pal. Ducale): 46, 50, 74, 133, 140, 150, 151, 152, 170, 198, 213, 223, 233, 234–5, 256
– Porta della Carta: 21
Pal. Contarini: 158
Pal. Corner (Cornaro): 141, 234
Pal. Corner-Spinelli: 46, 50
Pal. Dario: 50
Pal. Delfino: 141
Pal. Foscari: 9
Pal. Grimani: 12, 50, 141, 234, 253
Pal. Malipiero: 50
Pal. Manzoni-Angarani: 50
Pal. Pesaro: 158
Pal. Rezzonico: 158

Pal. Trevisan: 50
Pal. Vendramin-Calergi: 35, 45, 50
Pal. Zeno: 12
Accademia: 160, 233
Library (Biblioteca Sansoviniana): 30, 63, 152
Fondaco de' Tedeschi: 243–4
Fortress on Lido: 6, 166
Lazzaretto: 98
Piazza S. Marco: 170, 223
Piazzetta: 170
Prigioni: 69
Procuratie Nuove: 152
– Vecchie: 35, 151
Rialto: 167, 170, 242
Streets and paving: 168
Zecca (Mint): 64

VERONA, S. Bernardino, Capp. Pellegrini: 93, 123
S. Fermo, Turiani Tomb: 209
S. Giorgio: 109, 212
Madonna di Campagna: 93
Sta Maria in Organo: 107, 226, 227, 228, 249
SS. Nazzaro e Celso: 122, 247
Amphitheatre: 42
Arco de' Leoni: 192
Casa Borella, paintings: 242
Loggia del Consiglio: 55, 151
Pal. Bevilacqua: 141
Pal. Canossa: 147, 246
Pal. Pompei (Museo Civico): 141
Pal. Possoni: 55
Porta de' Borsari: 60, 211
– Nuova: 166
– Palio (Stuppa): 166
– S. Zeno: 166
Scaliger Tombs: 203

VICENZA, Basilica (Pal. della Ragione): 38, 74, 152, 154, 158
Pal. del Capitano: 158
Pal. Chiericati: 38, 158
Pal. G. Porto: 158
Pal. O. Porto: 73, 158, 160
Pal. Porto-Barbaran: 158
Pal. Schio-Franceschini: 158
Pal. A. Thiene: 158
Pal. M. A. Thiene: 158, 160
Pal. Trissino: 158
Pal. Valmarana: 158, 160
Teatro Olimpico: 269, 271–2
Vescovado (Bishop's Pal.): 130
Villa Rotonda (Villa Capra): 72, 162, 183

VICOVARO (nr Tivoli), S. Giacomo: 8
Pal. Orsini: 139

VIGEVANO: 6, 168, 170

VISSO (Marche), Madonna di Macereto: 92

VITERBO, Sta Elisabetta: 236
Madonna della Quercia: 98, 118, 126
Fontane: 215
Streets and paving: 169
Villa Lante alla Bagnaia: 182, 217

VIVO, Villa Cervini *see* MONTE AMIATA, Villa of Cardinal Sta Croce

Made in the USA
Columbia, SC
26 September 2022

67955613R00176